ON ARTHURIAN WOMEN

Essays in Memory of Maureen Fries

Scriptorium Press

On Arthurian Women

Essays in Memory of Maureen Fries

EDITED BY

Bonnie Wheeler and Fiona Tolhurst

Scriptorium Press
Dallas
2001

Scriptorium Press
Box 750432
Dallas, TX 75275–0432

Published 2001
Printed in the United States of America

Library of Congress Cataloging-in-Publication Data

On Arthurian women : essays in memory of Maureen Fries / Bonnie
Wheeler and Fiona Tolhurst, editors.

p.   cm.

Includes bibliographical references.
ISBN 0-9651877-1-3

1.   Literature, Medieval—History and criticism. 2. Women in
      literature. 3. Sex roles in literature.   4. Fries, Maureen. I.
      Wheeler, Bonnie, 1944- II. Tolhurst, Fiona.

PN682.W6 A77 2001

Printed on acid-free, 250-year-life paper
Manufactured in the United States of America

Cover design by Dean Corbitt
backcover photograph of Maureen Fries by Buzzell, 1955.

Acknowledgments

We extend our thanks to those who have made the publication of this book possible. First we would like to thank our contributors who have patiently endured our requests and swiftly responded to our queries. In addition, we are grateful to the Communities Foundation of Dallas which provided us with the staff support funding that made it possible for us complete this book in a timely fashion. The editors would also like to acknowledge Dean William M. Hall of Alfred University, whose generous support of Fiona Tolhurst made the early stages of editing this volume possible. Artist Dean Corbitt generously contributed the cover design, and to him we give our thanks. Finally, we thank Jeb Fries for his donation in honor of his mother.

Contents

PART II. ON WOMEN ARTHURIANS

photograph by Roger Siverson 1998

Maureen Fries
1931–1999

Maureen Fries,
Arthurienne Extraordinaire

BONNIE WHEELER and FIONA TOLHURST

On a snowy Sunday in January of 1999, scores of neighbors, friends, and colleagues came to a memorial service in Fredonia, New York, to bid farewell to Maureen Fries after her sudden death a few days earlier. In a short time, the chapel filled with people of all ages, appropriately well-dressed and speaking in the low voices that characterize such somber events. To this occasion, however, Maureen's son Howard brought large boxes filled with Maureen's ample collection of marvelous hats—the hats she was renowned for wearing. For this final event, every woman in the room chose or was given one of Maureen's hats to wear. Even a few men appropriated hats for their own. It was a chilly day, but the festive, loopy look of seventy-five women—and a few brave men—in Maureen's wildly diverse hats gave it a Mardi Gras gleam. Carnivalesque, poignant, ironic, triumphant: the event was infused with Maureen's characteristic verve. Maureen was a larger-than-life figure, a blood-sister to the Wife of Bath. She triumphed over her larger-than-life pains with a keen sense of joy and kindly generosity. She loved people and literature equally, and fused the two in her imagination. Her work as a scholar was never separate from her life as a woman: in all spheres, her life was a profound quest for excellence. Fries was addicted to narrative, to great and heroic stories about her real and fictional friends, especially her Arthurian friends. Not only did she tell good stories: good stories accumulated around her. The abundant Arthurian tales of adventure seem themselves often to have been carved from her ample life experience. Where Maureen went, wondrous adventures followed.

One such adventure began when, after rooming together at the International Arthurian Congress in Regensburg in the summer of 1979, Bonnie Wheeler and Maureen took a scholar's trip to medieval sites in southern Germany as they made their way to the Danube at Linz, where they would board a boat for Vienna. They arrived in Linz before the ship did and decided to have a light supper at the local hotel recommended by the boat personnel. They were seated in an walled garden at a corner booth with grapevines overhead. Only later did they learn that the place had once been a haunt of Adolf Hitler's. It retained some remarkable customs. Everything seemed normal enough as Maureen and Bonnie ordered their omelets. But as they waited for supper to arrive, the tranquil setting turned grotesque and vaudevillian: one by one, male customers came over to their booth, smiling and bowing in greeting. As they did so, the maitre d' instantly rushed over, screaming at these men to go away and leave the women alone. His words were matched by his actions as he jabbed the men with his fists and kicked them in the groin and backside. As one man left, another arrived, and altercations continued. The violence escalated, and Bonnie and Maureen decided that their omelets weren't worth the eggs broken to make them, but neither woman dared to attempt an escape. When their food arrived, the waiter ordered them to eat, fast. And they did, as table visitors kept arriving, and the maitre d' kept kicking. Finally, he screamed at an underling to open the ancient, creaking gates to the walled garden, and in lurched a taxi that screeched up to the edge of the booth to whisk the women away to their ship. 'What an excellent adventure!' said Maureen. Neither Bonnie nor Maureen ever understood the Custom of that Castle, but Bonnie did learn that, with Maureen, one entered the shadowland of medieval adventure.

Maureen Fries was graduated *magna cum laude* from D'Youville College in 1952, took her M.A. from Cornell University in 1953, and received her Ph.D. with highest distinction from the State University of New York at Buffalo in 1969. She began her teaching career at the State University of New York (SUNY) College at Fredonia where both she and her husband had been offered academic posts. She was the first female faculty member in the Department of English. She excelled as both a teacher and scholar, receiving the SUNY Chancellor's Award for Excellence in Teaching in 1977, being named the Kasling Lecturer at SUNY–Fredonia in 1985 (the highest faculty honor in recognition of scholarly achievement in the SUNY system), and achieving the rank of Distinguished Teaching Professor in 1990 (the highest rank granted for teaching in that system). As a middle-aged wife and mother, Fries began her full-time professional career at a time when women, especially middle-aged women, were rarely considered for academic posts. She also worked primarily on Arthurian literature, a field that was then considered a 'fringe' field or 'popular culture' interest rather than a legitimate subject worthy of scholarly attention. Maureen did much to enhance the image of her field—as well as to revivify the image of 'middle-aged' academic women. Maureen's son Jeb S. Fries describes her gift for teaching in this way: 'She was just a whiz in the classroom. She was able to interest lots of young people—especially those in Generation X—in literature that's a thousand years old.' One former student says that 'Many of her students became long-time friends' and describes her putting her students' needs first: 'She gave extraordinarily of herself to students, often taking on an overload in her teaching schedule in order to accommodate students wishing to take a course that wasn't being offered' (*Buffalo News*, 1/15/99).

Because she taught four courses each term for her entire career—a schedule that included courses in Chaucer, Arthurian Literature, First-Year Composition, Women's Studies, African-American Literature, and Native-American Literature—Maureen decided early that she would wait for the sustained respite of retirement to write monographs. Until then, she decided to live the life of a public scholar. She gave several conference papers each year and polished each of them for publication as an article. In fact, she liked to claim that she had published every conference paper she had ever given—a perfect 'batting average' preserved by the publication of her final conference paper from the 1998 meeting of the Southeastern Medieval Association (SEMA) in *Studies in Philology* (2002). Her avid conference-going enabled her to be very active in professional organizations such as the International Arthurian Society, the International Courtly Literature Society, the Modern Language Association, and the Medieval Institute at Kalamazoo. She was frequently the happy recipient of both internal and external research fellowships.

Maureen wrote close to fifty scholarly articles and book chapters on subjects ranging from Old Irish Sagas to Chaucer, Malory, Mary Stewart, and Arthurian films. Her work on female heroism is especially important in terms of its theoretical claims and its continuing importance to current scholarship: she was a foremother of Arthurian feminist scholarship. In addition, she was a generous (and exacting) scholarly colleague—she wrote over twenty–five book reviews, some for the *Times Literary Supplement* and scholarly journals, many for *Choice*. She also reviewed local theater productions, for which she won an honorary membership in the Alpha Psi Omega National Collegiate Fraternity for Honors Students in Theater Arts in 1983 'for excellence in reviewing student productions for the SUNY-Fredonia Theater Arts Department.' Her scholarship is assessed more fully by Don Hoffman in the closing essay in this volume.

Maureen's private life was extraordinarily difficult—an American tragedy on the days that it was not merely a compelling soap opera. Her story, troubles included, is one we share not only because it gives specific gravity to our account of Maureen, but also because we hope readers will see her life as triumphant. Hers was the life of an American academic woman who was part of the first wave of women to surge into the academy in the late 1960s and early 1970s. In the most turbulent period of her life, the mid-1970s, Maureen divorced. She also discovered that one of her children, Howard, was severely handicapped, and would require lifetime care—care she provided. Two other children lived close to (sometimes over) the edge and were sent to prison at various times. Maureen wrote and revised articles as she took long bus rides to the infamous Attica Penitentiary. She was deeply devoted to each of her children and all of them were equally bonded to Maureen. Of her four children, her charming eldest son Jeb is best-known to Arthurians, since in her later years she relied on his witty companionship when he accompanied her to conferences. Jeb expects at some point to publish his mother's pained and loving memoirs called 'An Attica Mother.' Maureen wanted readers to understand that, although college professors are not exempt from life's travails, intellectual life provides a rich reservoir from which one can draw at times of loss. Maureen's lovely, large Victorian home—full of light and life, books and paintings, located on a handsome street in a western New York town—is a glowing place that attracted a steady flow of family and friends and students.

It is often said that academe is the purest field of combat since there is so little at stake except ego, and Maureen, like many others, often felt that she lived in a professional minefield. Maureen's departmental history reads like an academic mystery in which all the bloodied bodies are doomed to return to life and meet again. Her department was cheerfully described to her friends as the 'Snake Pit,' a place where faculty members hissed at each other, harassment charges (as well as spouses) were flung back and forth, and departmental confidentiality was honored more in the breach than in the observance. From her perspective, every promotion and raise for which she was eligible was blocked until she fought for it. Maureen's phrase, famous among her friends and colleagues, for her various administrative and academic enemies was the 'Evil Empire.' At her retirement party in 1997, a former high administrative official at her institution (important enough to have a reserved parking space) told a bizarre story about how, in the dead of winter, Maureen once stole the bolted metal sign that marked his exclusive parking space and had it deposited on his desk. He gave her this sign as a special gift to mark her retirement. As he told this amazing tale, Maureen turned to her 'Arthurian Mafia' friends and said 'I never touched that sign. Why would I? I don't drive. I don't investigate parking lots. I don't even know how to use a hammer. I never even noticed it.' In this and other instances, Maureen felt herself the brunt of false accusation; at one time, she responded that 'X's accusation was the final fillip of a rich and malodorous concoction of slander and persecution.' On the other hand, at another point faculty member 'Y' pleaded with Maureen not to believe an uncorroborated report that he belonged to the Evil Empire, saying 'What is most important to me is that I not be included in the company of your persecutors: If you or an angel in heaven should allege that I have a membership in that infernal crew, I would declare that allegation a damned lie.' If the Evil Empire (with shifting membership) was as spritely as Maureen portrayed it (filled with such language as 'persecutors' and 'infernal crew'), it equalled anything found in her favorite blood-spewed novels about academic life. Like many academics in the late twentieth century, Maureen worked in complicated circumstances, but she also triumphed over those conditions. She acted with a generous spirit as, both officially and unofficially, she served as an omsbudsperson in her college to support other members of the faculty. In the end, of course, she was showered with honors by her university, as she well deserved.

Maureen Fries was always on a quest as serious as that of an Arthurian hero or heroine for wisdom and social justice. She was passionately involved in early 'second-wave' American feminism, pushing her institution and community to adopt and develop essential affirmative-action policies. In Chautauqua County, in 1982, her activism earned her the Callista Jones Award for Helping to Advance the Cause of Women, and her involvement in a community consciousness-raising group in the early 1970s led to her active participation in the local Women's Reading Group that was still meeting at the time of her death: she felt it was important that women scholars participate in discussion groups that keep feminist issues alive at a grassroots level. Maureen's commitment to public education was evident in her cooperative ventures with the Dunkirk, Fredonia, and Procton schools, and her commitment to public activism in her service as the chairwoman of the Affirmative Action Advisory Committee and Fredonia Faculty Senator within the SUNY system as well as her membership in the SUNY Statewide Task Force on Cooperative Recruitment and Talent Pool for Women.

The pressures of her personal life made learning for its own sake Maureen's real refuge and greatest joy. She said at her retirement party that, at the lowest point in her adult life, the study of Greek was her only source of pleasure. Her passion for learning something new, for gaining the exact and supple knowledge that can lead to wisdom, provided her a welcome refuge. Fries also had a special gift for intellectual friendships, all of which were marked by the give and take of ideas as well as intimate secrets. She loved the interweave of narrative: having the art of a great storyteller, she elicited stories from others, and she thought about her various friends as themselves works of art that required constant interpretation, redefinition, and critical commentary.

Not even the novelist David Lodge could imagine a conference-goer as inveterate or as productive as Maureen. Each conference was an important chance for her to hear and share ideas, to challenge her own prior theories and interpretations, and to foment change within her profession. She made new friends at each of the many conferences she attended from the early 1970s until late 1998. Her final 'new Arthurian friend' was Maud McInerney, who met Maureen for the first time on the bus ride they shared to the airport after SEMA 98, and Maureen immediately charmed Maud with her stories and questions; most of the contributors to this volume were Maureen's Arthurian pals or protégées. Bonnie Wheeler was among her earliest Arthurian pals. She met Maureen in the early 1970s during the annual medieval throng at Kalamazoo in its salad days. Maureen attended Bonnie's first conference paper (delivered in what was then a lounge next to the cafeteria), and they talked about Malory for hours afterwards. Somehow, in later years, it seemed normal enough that they had met at that venue, and even natural that Wheeler's podium on that day was a grand piano; later that night, Maureen added zest to the event by returning to that piano to sing and play her favorite ironic and sentimental Broadway tunes. Maureen, an instant friend, became a frequent visitor to Bonnie's home in Dallas (usually for New Year's, after the MLA convention), and there Bonnie for the first time learned all the words to Maureen's favorite song, 'Lydia, the Tattooed Lady.' Maureen was among those who encouraged Bonnie to take on the editorship of the journal that became *Arthuriana*, and Maureen provided crucial advice about its progress. She was working on a special issue of the journal when she so suddenly died.

In 1998, Bonnie organized a retirement session for Maureen at Kalamazoo; none of us who were there could imagine it would be her last appearance at that conference. The room was packed and few of us have heard such joyful laughter and felt such affectionate regard at any public occasion. Before her song, Maureen talked about Bonnie as her 'literary daughter,' and Fiona Tolhurst (who had been introduced to Maureen by Bonnie) as her 'literary granddaughter.' The remark was quintessential Maureen: for her, colleagues were family, not just friends, and there was no divide between her scholarly and familial worlds.

Maureen was always deeply concerned that her friends and colleagues find professional success. She was as generous to her male colleagues as to her female colleagues, but she was especially assiduous in promoting the confidence and work of junior women. Karen Cherewatuk of St. Olaf College has a lovely (and typical) remembrance of Maureen:

> When I was a graduate student at Cornell, I announced to my committee that I wanted to write on Malory. Bob Kaske and Art Gross (a Middle High German *Parzival* scholar) suggested we bring Maureen to campus for two days and "Why don't you arrange it, Karen?" So I called Maureen and invited her, including inviting her to stay at the house I was renting. Maureen showed up with a boyfriend, quietly explaining, 'I don't really like him that much, but I needed him to drive me.' She and I had a blast. She taught a seminar and taught it well. For the next year or so, as I dissertated, I'd receive occasional postcards from her: "Hi. How are you? Keep writing." It was an act of mothering I shall not forget.

Fiona Tolhurst first met Maureen at the 1997 International Congress on Lawman's *Brut* in New Brunswick, Canada. She had studied Fries's work as a graduate student, and then had the good luck to be placed on a panel with Maureen. Because Maureen was recovering from a foot injury and struggling against her ever-present asthma symptoms, Fiona, along with her husband Christophe (of whom Maureen was also very fond), offered Maureen supporting arms as they walked from the conference site to the hotel. That week a close friendship began; their physical proximity in western New York allowed their supportive friendship to flourish. Fiona visited Maureen in Fredonia every few months, and they helped each other edit their pieces for a Geoffrey of Monmouth special issue of *Arthuriana* that was published in the winter of 1998. The night before the issue was sent to Dallas for its final editing, Maureen called and said, 'I hate my last sentence. Might we fix it?' Thirty minutes later the entire final paragraph had been rewritten and much improved. This drive to find the perfect phrase every time typified Maureen's scholarship. At SEMA 1998, Maureen's last conference, she gave a paper based on an essay she had written many years earlier on Eve in medieval drama. In predictable Maureen fashion, she wore a perfectly coordinated suit-and-hat ensemble and read her paper with vigor and confidence. Also in typical Maureen fashion, she spent that evening chatting with friends in a pub. Several friends old and new enjoyed listening to Maureen share hilarious and moving tales from other conferences, and everyone could see how much she was enjoying her retirement. As Lorraine Stock remarked to Fiona, 'I have never seen Maureen so happy and relaxed. It is so good that she has made peace with all of the troubles in her life.' Maureen's circuit on that trip included a final visit with Bonnie in Dallas. There she gave a memorable lecture on Merlin, and spent pleasant hours discussing Malory, Old Irish, and (of course) friends and families.

It is a happy fact that, after a life filled with both personal and academic struggle, Maureen died in perfect peace. Having been honored at the special session at Kalamazoo 1998 and having made her epic journey to Alaska, Maureen died in her bed at home in Fredonia in January 1999. Though Howard thought she was sleeping, Fiona, who telephoned, suspected that something was wrong, so she called the Fredonia Police Department, and by happenstance reached an officer who was one of Maureen's former students. Even dead, Maureen starred in a drama involving, as usual, her family, former students, and her 'Arthurian Mafia.'

At his mother's memorial service, Howard said: 'She wouldn't wake up and she's gone to heaven now. We would go to the WalMart to get my pictures of our cats developed. Their hearts are broken because she's gone. I wish I had her living for good.' So do we all.

***

This volume, *On Arthurian Women: Essays in Memory of Maureen Fries*, honors Maureen by acknowledging both her ground-breaking analysis of female characters in Arthurian literature and her crucial role as a literary foremother to so many scholars, men and women alike. The first part of this book, *On Arthurian Women*, amplifies the tradition of studying Arthurian female figures that Maureen helped to establish. Here we present several new studies from several Arthurian texts of such characters as Guenevere, the various Elaine(s), the Lady of the Lake, Morgan le Fay and Morgause. Three essays consider Arthurian women who help us interrogate the notion of the lady: Olwen, Chrétien's Enide, and Wolfram's Belacane. In addition, expressing another of Maureen's interests, we provide a section of essays on oft-overlooked Arthurian 'bad girls,' studies of spunky women who do not conform to typical stereotypes of courtly ladies or virgins. Finally, we present a few essays on women in relation to modern adaptations of medieval Arthurian materials. Two of these essays (Hoffman, Kelly) consider the presentation of women in the novel, while Alan Lupack looks at women artists who have illustrated Arthurian texts; finally, Kevin J. Harty studies the figure of Isolde in film— Arthurian film studies is a field Maureen also helped to develop. A few of these essays, presented here in revised form, were first presented at the 1998 Kalamazoo session in Maureen's honor, and then published in *Arthuriana*

9.2 (Summer 1999), a special issue honoring Maureen that was guest-edited by Chauncey Wood.

The second section of this book, *On Women Arthurians*, binds life to literary study in ways particularly typical of Maureen Fries. It contains biographies and autobiographies of some of the women who have opened the field of literary study to Arthurian material, making major contributions in the field of Arthurian studies and enabling the field to gain recognition as an important and legitimate one. The list we present here is not exhaustive, for we have not been able to include the life stories of such luminaries as Helen Adolf, Rita Lejeune, Sister Amelia Klenke, and Mary Williams. But in the span of these few brief biographies and autobiographies we are able to document the lives and contributions of Lady Charlotte Guest, Jessie Laidlay Weston, Roger Sherman Loomis's trio of scholarly wives—Gertrude Schoepperle Loomis, Laura Hibbard Loomis, Dorothy Bethurum Loomis—Vida Dutton Scudder, Rachel Bromwich, Helaine Newstead, Elspeth Kennedy, Fanni Bogdanow, and Valerie Lagorio. Donald L. Hoffman's 'Maureen Fries: Teacher, Scholar, Friend' closes the volume with a loving and trenchant analysis of Maureen's contributions to Arthurian studies and an appreciation of Maureen as a person.

Maureen insisted that the academy and the world should celebrate vitality and variety: she was herself a one-woman spritzer. She demanded scholarly exactitude and loved a rotund Latinate sentence. If Arthurian literature captured the essence of her unflinching understanding of pain and loss, its utopian vision expressed her inexhaustible sense of hope and joy—and, of course, fun. Maureen ended her academic career with droll self-mockery by singing E.Y. Harburg's 'Lydia, the Tattooed Lady' both at her retirement dinner at Fredonia and at the Kalamazoo session in her honor. One stanza especially captures the essence of her personality and life:

> Lydia, oh Lydia, that 'En-cy-clo-ped-ia'
> Oh! Lydia, the champ of them all.
> For two bits she will do a Mazurka in Jazz,
> With a view of Niagara that no artist has,
> And on a clear day you can see Alcatraz...

Of course the last line is 'You can learn a lot from Lydia' and we did.

SOUTHERN METHODIST UNIVERSITY / ALFRED UNIVERSITY

PART ONE:

ON ARTHURIAN WOMEN

Guenevere's Tears
in the Alliterative *Morte Arthure*:
Doubly Wife, Doubly Mother, Doubly
Damned

REBECCA S. BEAL

Guenevere appears only twice in the Alliterative *Morte Arthure*, where her grieving responds to male violence. Her appearances bracket the other presentations of non-allegorical female figures in the poem and exemplify a continued connection between feminine loss and a patriarchal system based on 'wyrchipe.' (RB)

With minor exceptions, the Alliterative *Morte Arthure* restricts its presentation of female figures to a few key episodes:[1] Arthur's farewell to Guenevere; Arthur's colloquy with the Old Woman grieving at the grave of her raped nursling; the ladies of Metz pleading for their city; Arthur's dream-world encounter with Lady Fortune; and, finally, Guenevere's departure for the nunnery.[2] Of these episodes, all but the last involve Arthur's interaction with a speaking female, though only Lady Fortune—a projection of Arthur's own fears and aspirations—shares in cultural structures of power. The other episodes are repeatedly characterized by the attempts of a non-allegorical female character to avoid the inevitable grief that comes to her through male violence. Guenevere futilely weeps and rails against the loss of her lord, then swoons as he calls for his sword. The Old Woman begs Arthur not to fight the Giant; she doubts his eventual success, and, in any case, his defense comes too late for the Duchess of Brittany. Only the Duchess of Metz succeeds in obtaining peace for her battered city, and she does so at the cost of losing her husband. Guenevere weeps as she goes to take the veil, dressed as for death—facing the loss of her second husband and their children.

As my summary suggests, the two episodes in which the poem presents Guenevere—in the first weeping for the loss of her lord Arthur, in the second weeping as she departs for Caerleon, after hearing from Mordred of Arthur's return—are episodes which frame the other portrayals of feminine loss. Guenevere's appearances in the poem bracket the thematic repetitions of loss and serve as their primary exemplification.[3] In her grief for Arthur at the beginning of the poem, she anticipates the losses of the Duchess of Metz and other women made widows or separated from their husbands through the fortunes of war. In her last appearance, before Arthur meets and kills Mordred, and then, with his dying words, orders the secret execution of Mordred's offspring, Guenevere's mourning recalls the episodes in the poem focusing on the slaughter of children, particularly the conflict between Arthur and the Giant. In other words, Guenevere figures the types of feminine loss emphasized within the poem: first, the wife's losing her husband to war; second, the mother whose children are casualties in the power struggles of a patriarchal system. Further, she connects such losses to a system based on 'wyrchipe' [honor, worship].

The presentation of Guenevere's parting from Arthur begins with an emphasis on her tearful grief; indeed 'wepande' [weeping (697)] and 'teres' [tears (698)] are placed in exactly parallel positions—each the first alliterated word after the caesura—in the two lines opening the scene: 'Waynour waykly | wepande hym kyssiz, / Talkez to hym tenderly | with teres ynewe' [Guenevere, softly weeping, embraces him, / And speaks to him tenderly through tears beyond measure (697–98)].[4] In her following speech, the Queen explicitly connects her mourning at Arthur's departure with the upcoming war that will deprive her of her husband: '"I may wery the wye | thatt this werre mouede / That warnes me wyrchippe | of my wedde lorde. / All my lykynge of lyfe | owte of lande wendez, / And I in langour am left"' [I could curse the man who has caused this war, / That denies me the honor of my wedded lord; / All my life's joy is departing the land, / And I am left in desolation (699–702)]. If her words and tears convey her grief as connected to the war with Lucius, the following narrative recapitulates her emotion in gesture and reemphasizes the link between masculine war and feminine grief: 'And then cho swounes full swythe | whe[n] he hys swerde aschede, / Sweys in a swounyng, | swelte as cho walde' [And then suddenly she swoons, when he calls for his sword; / In a faint she falls, as if she would perish (715–16)]. Guenevere faints precisely as Arthur calls for his sword, the symbol of his next martial enterprise, the poem emphasizing her response by repeating it both before and after Arthur's mentioning the weapon.

Critics have suggested that, though derived from romance traditions, the scene suggests a positive marital relationship between king and queen.[5] But while Guenevere is clearly lamenting her husband's coming absence, she identifies that absence as adversely affecting her status or 'wyrchippe' [honor (700)]. In other words, the link between feminine loss and war comes at the very point where her husband would gain—in his enhanced honor acquired through conquest.[6] Arthur does seem to understand this aspect of Guenevere's mourning, to the point that Guenevere's 'wyrchipe' [majesty] becomes a key component of his charge to Mordred: "'I wyll þat Waynour my weife | in *wyrchipe* be holden'" [I bid that Guenevere, my wife, be maintained in *majesty* (652), emphasis mine]. But the king's care for a lady's welfare seems in the poem a function of his own 'wyrchipe,' not simply hers.

Just so will Arthur respond later in the poem, when he deprives the Duchess of Metz of her husband. Thus at the end of the siege of Metz, the poem presents the Duchess kneeling before Arthur, begging for mercy for her breached city. The price of peace is her husband's imprisonment. Thus, Arthur says to her: "'I gyf ȝow chartire of pes, | and ȝoure cheefe maydens…The duke es in dawngere, | dredis it boþþ lyttyll'" [I pledge peace to you and your peerless maids…But the Duke is in danger—doubt it but little (3058, 3061)].[7] The Duke's fate is underscored just five lines later: 'The duke to Douere es dyghte | and all his dere knyghtez, / To duelle in dawngere and dole | þe dayes of hys lyue' [The Duke is sent to Dover, with all his fine knights, / To dwell in bondage and dole all the days of his life (3066–67)]. How the Duchess responds is never recounted; rather the scene shifts to indicate Arthur's provision of regents and an endowment for her, both indicators of the King's magnanimity, a crucial element in defining his honor.[8]

But how effective is Arthur in providing for the Queen's 'wyrchipe'? By Mordred's own account, the regent-to-be lacks the honor acquired by the knights who go to war—when the others return, he could well be "'sette boþþ at lyttill'" [rated as nothing (686)]—and thus he begs Arthur to let him join the expedition. Mordred cannot constitute an adequate substitute for Arthur—a way of providing the honor Guenevere mourns as lacking—precisely because his honor is as derivative as Guenevere's own. Arthur's own provision for Guenevere's well-being, his appointing Mordred as regent, exacerbates the problem.

Guenevere, then, is implicated in the system of honor that drives Arthur to war and separates husbands from wives, as in the later example of the Duchess of Metz, whose husband goes to prison in Dover after Arthur conquers Metz. Indeed, the position of the Duchess with regard to her husband is akin to that of Guenevere at the beginning of the poem. Both women are married to men who are absent at war; both women are provided for by a magnanimous conqueror. They differ primarily in that one woman is married to the winner, one to the loser. Of course, at the end of the poem, when Arthur returns, that difference has been erased. Now Guenevere is married to the substitute Arthur, Mordred, as well as to Arthur, and both men are headed toward tragic ends. One difference remains between Guenevere and the Duchess of Metz: Arthur leaves the Duchess her children. Not so Guenevere.

In the Alliterative *Morte*, Guenevere, too, is a mother. Sir Cradok tells Arthur not only that Mordred has married Guenevere, but that she is pregnant, a detail that never appears in the poem's sources.[9] Cradok's news is amended when Guenevere appears at the end of the poem, the recipient of a letter from Mordred concerned in large measure for the safety of her (now plural) 'childire' [children (3907)].[10] How many children did she have with Mordred? The text is not clear on that score; rather it stresses her new husband's inability to provide for this family. Thus he tells her to escape: "'ferken oo ferre | and flee with hir childire, / Whills he myghte wile hym awaye | and wyn to hir speche, / Ayere into Irelande | into þas owte mowntes / And wonn thare in wildernesse | within þa wast landys'" [fly far off and flee with her children, / Till he could steal off and speak to her safely; / Make her way into Ireland, to those remote mountains, / And dwell there in the wilderness, out in those waste lands (3907–10)]. Mordred asks Guenevere to leave civilization and withdraw into the wilderness of Ireland, a clear diminishing of her earlier life in 'kydde castells' [great castles (654)].

Her response to this letter constitutes her last appearance:

> Than cho ȝermys and ȝee[ȝes] | at ȝork in hir chambre,
> Gronys full grysely | with gretand teres,
> Passes owte of þe palesse | with all hir pryce maydenys;
> Toward Chestyre in a charre | thay chese hir þe wayes,
> Dyghte hir ewyn for to dye | with dule at hir herte.
> Scho kayres to Karelyone | and kawghte hir a vaile,
> Askes thare þe habite | in pe honoure of Criste—
>
> [Then she wails and weeps there at York in her chamber,
> Crying great tears, she gruesomely groans,
> Goes from the palace with her peerless maids:
> Toward Chester in a chariot they lead her on her way,
> Dressed as for death, with dole in her heart.
> And she travelled to Caerleon and there took the veil,
> Requested the habit in the name of Christ…(3911–17)].

Again Guenevere weeps, then goes to Caerleon in garments signifying death or mourning, and the mention of Guenevere's children elides into their loss. And, though Guenevere does not speak in this second appearance, the text associates her loss this second time with male 'wyrchipe' [honor].

Arthur tells his annointed heir, Constantine, to dispose of Mordred's children—and Guenevere's: "'And sythen merke manly | to Mordrede children, / That they bee sleyghely slayne | and slongen in watyrs— / Latt no wykkyde wede waxe | ne wrythe one this erthe! / I warne fore thy *wirchipe*, | wirke alls I bydde"' [And then sternly mark that Mordred's children / Be secretly slain and slung into the seas: / Let no wicked weed in this world take root and thrive /—I warn you, by your worth, work as I bid (4320–22), emphasis mine]. The children are to die, and not by due process of law, but rather consumed as a threat to dynastic stability, which Arthur mentions precisely in terms of the 'wyrchipe' [honor] of his heir.

Given Guenevere's tears in her last appearance, and the close proximity of those tears to the mention of the children who are to be killed, she comes to resemble the figure of Helen's foster-mother, weeping over the grave of her murdered child, an episode that Lee Patterson has associated with the theme of 'the sacrifice of children.'[11] In this episode Arthur confronts a child-butchering monster, a Giant, but first he meets a mother figure mourning her child: 'there he fyndez / A wery wafull wedowe, | wryngande hire handez / And gretande on a graue | grysely teres' [there he finds / A worn, woeful old woman, wringing her hands, / And on a grave shedding shuddering tears (949–51)].[12] She identifies herself as the 'foster modyr' [foster mother (983)] of the young duchess in the grave, raped and murdered by the Giant. Helen's murder, explains the old woman, is part of a larger plan of aggression. For the monster has tortured Arthur's people precisely to provoke Arthur to submit (1009–12) or to fight. Both the raped young Duchess-fosterling of the grieving old woman and the cannibalized children the Giant murders, are counters in a vicious game of honor. If Arthur will send his beard in tribute, the depredations will stop; otherwise, they will continue until Arthur submits or fights, as he does, to defend his people and his own honor.[13] In the episode with the Giant, Arthur accuses the monster of murdering 'cresmede childyre' [christened children (1065)] and himself acts as a figure of law, rescuing his people and avenging the murder of children. At the end of his life, however, he takes another role, virtually replaying the role of the Giant he had earlier accused of consuming his people. Thus Arthur's order to kill 'christened children' in the later episode echoes the episode of the Giant of Mont Saint Michel, but with Arthur's position reversed. The poem ends with Arthur turning on his people, even as they turn on him. The most egregious instance is his ordering the deaths of Guenevere's children.

The Old Woman and Guenevere share particularly in their grief at the loss of children, although the one mourns a *fait accompli* and the other anticipates a loss—indeed, Ziolkowski believes that Guenevere may be pregnant when Arthur issues his order.[14] But if the king has scant comfort for the Old Woman, the poem has no sympathy whatever for Guenevere, at the end left without any honor at all. Thus, describing her about to take the veil, the poem condemns her: 'And all for falsede and frawde | and fere of hir louerde' [But all in falseness and fraud and fear of her lord (3918)].

The use of Guenevere as a key figure in the description of the feminine as a site of loss, of tears, should not be a surprise. This poem's portrayal of Guenevere at one level reflects a cultural context in which, as Marjorie Curry Woods points out, '[t]he emphasis in the schoolroom on the analysis and depiction of emotional states in rhetorically affective language encouraged students to focus on female characters' in a composition exercise asking them to represent a figure expressing strong emotion, often one of high status: Niobe, Andromache, or Dido.[15] These figures weep, but not like the Wife of Bath, who presents tears as a means of manipulation. Yet, for the boys growing up in the rhetorical tradition of the schools, and, presumably for the author of the Alliterative *Morte*, such tears were to be left behind as the young male reached maturity. The experience of women's tears was juvenile, 'so much smoke and wind,' as Augustine put it, recalling his own youthful rhetorical experiments in writing about feminine grief.[16]

By contrast, in the Alliterative *Morte*, the experience of the feminine migrates from the episodes of feminine loss I have examined in association with Guenevere to reappear in crucial scenes involving Arthur who, in the first part of the poem, is cast as Guenevere's opposite, precisely with regard to her tears. He thus says to her, when he takes his leave, '"I may noght wit of þis woo"' [I may not witness this woe], a phrase which could more literally be read, 'I may not have experience of this woe.'[17]

As the poem progresses, however, the knowledge he does not have earlier comes to him in full force, and indeed may be measured by the episodes of Guenevere's weeping that precede Arthur's own tears. Like hers, his tears are associated with his loss of 'wirchipe' or honor. The death of Gawain, whom he calls '"My wele and my wirchipe | of all þis werlde riche"' [My good and my glory throughout all this great world (3963)] leads to such grief that his own lords reprove him, again in terms of 'wirchipe' [honor]: '"It es no *wirchipe*, iwysse, | to wryng thyn hondes; / To wepe als a woman | it es no witt holden. / Be knyghtly of contenaunce, | als a kyng scholde"' [It is not worthy, in truth, to be wringing your hands; / To weep like a woman is not deemed wise. / Be manly of mien, as a king must (3977–79, emphasis mine)]. Later, when Arthur's Round Table is destroyed, his '"wytt and…wirchipe | away…for euer"' [greatness and…glory…all gone forever (4287)], he describes himself in feminizing terms which could easily be applied to Guenevere, after Mordred bids her go to Ireland: "'I may helples one hethe | house be myn one, / Alls a wafull wedowe | þat wanttes hir beryn; / I may werye and wepe | and wrynge myn handys'" [I can only make my home alone and hopeless on a heath, / Like a woeful widow in want of her man, / Waste away and weep and wring my hands (4284–86)].[18] Now Arthur knows the grief of the old woman at the grave of her nursling; now he weeps the same tears as Guenevere.

UNIVERSITY OF SCRANTON

Rebecca S. Beal (bealr1@uofs.edu) is Professor of English at the University of Scranton. There she devised a course in the Arthurian Legend which led to her work on the Alliterative *Morte Arthure*. She has also written on Dante's *Commedia*, and is currently engaged in a study of endings in late medieval literature.

NOTES

1   This article is dedicated to the memory of Maureen Fries, whose most important contribution to the study of the Alliterative *Morte Arthure*, including the figure of Guenevere, appeared as 'The Poem in the Tradition of Arthurian Literature,' in *The Alliterative* Morte Arthure: *A Reassessment of the Poem*, ed. Karl Heinz Göller (Cambridge: D.S. Brewer, 1981), pp. 30–43, 159–61. Maureen Fries also wrote about the Guenevere of the Alliterative *Morte Arthure* in the following articles: 'The Characterization of Women in the Alliterative Tradition,' in *The Alliterative Tradition in the Fourteenth Century*, ed. Bernard S. Levy and Paul E. Szarmach (Kent, OH: Kent State University Press, 1981), pp. 25–45; 'Female Heroes, Heroines and Counter-Heroes: Images of Women in Arthurian Tradition,' in *Popular Arthurian Traditions*, ed. Sally K. Slocum (Bowling Green, OH: Bowling Green State Univeristy Press, 1992), pp. 5–17; 'Women in Arthurian Literature,' in *Approaches to Teaching the Arthurian Tradition*, ed. Maureen Fries and Jeanie Watson (New York: The Modern Language Association of America, 1992), esp. p. 155.

2   While noting the poem's restriction of female figures from the chronicle tradition, Fries argues that the Alliterative *Morte Arthure* 'displays neither stereotyped antifeminism nor concomitant biased attitudes toward women' ('The Characterization of Women,' p. 32). Recent studies tend to disagree with this assessment. See thus Anne Clark Bartlett, 'Cracking the Penile Code: Reading Gender and Conquest in the Alliterative *Morte Arthure*,' *Arthuriana* 8.2 (1998): 56–76, and Jeff Westover, 'Arthur's End: The King's Emasculation in the Alliterative *Morte Arthure*,' *Chaucer Review* 32.3 (1998): 310–24.

3   Indeed Fries sees her as the only realistic female figure in the poem ('The Characterization of Women,' p. 31).

4   All citations of the Alliterative *Morte Arthure* are taken from *Morte Arthure: A Critical Edition*, ed. Mary Hamel (New York and London: Garland Publishing, 1984). Hamel indicates caesuras with a space; I have signalled them with a vertical

line [|]. English translations are from *The Alliterative Morte Arthure: A New Verse Translation*, trans. Valerie Krishna (Lanham, MD: University Press of America, 1983).

5 For the romance tradition see Fries, 'The Poem in the Tradition,' p. 36. Fries notes that the poet here adds to his sources the 'realistic and moving leave-taking between king and queen (695–716),' and that '[t]he initial impression is thus of a dignified, loving, and believable relationship' (p. 31). In 'The Alliterative *Morte Arthure* As a Witness to Epic,' in *Oral Poetics in Middle English Poetry*, ed. Mark C. Amodio (New York: Garland, 1994), p. 262 n37, Britton J. Harwood argues the scene contains the kind of moral found in oral epic poems, in this case that 'love is to be found only within marriage.'

6 For an analysis of Arthur's 'wyrchipe' as an element accruing to him from the oral-heroic tradition, see Donna Lynne Rondolone, '*Wyrchipe*: The Clash of Oral-Heroic and Literate-Ricardian Ideals in the Alliterative *Morte Arthure*,' in *Oral Poetics in Middle English Poetry*, pp. 207–39, esp. pp. 222–24, 228.

7 Hamel translates 3060–61, "'Do not doubt that the duke is in my power; (but) have no fear—he will endow you full well'" (*Morte Arthure*, n3060–61, p. 352). The difference between Hamel's and Krishna's versions hangs on different transcriptions of the Thornton manuscript's grapheme as 'u' rather than 'n'. Hamel also follows the Winchester manuscript's 'clarifying paraphrase.' As will be seen, the difference in interpretation does not affect my argument.

8 Elizabeth Porter, for instance, argues convincingly that according to laws of war, Arthur had the right to sack and pillage any city that he had taken by assault. 'In this case Arthur's *magnanimous* behavior in protecting the lives of the citizens, and even foregoing the humiliating ritual signifying unconditional surrender, which Edward III demanded at Calais, would be remarkable enough. However, if we look closely at the details of the surrender of Metz, it appears that the poet, who had a wide knowledge of the laws of war, intended to represent Arthur's behavior as a conqueror in an even more *magnanimous* light' ('Chaucer's Knight, the Alliterative *Morte Arthure*, and Medieval Laws of War: a Reconsideration,' *Nottingham Mediaeval Studies* 27 (1983): 70 [56–78], emphasis mine). For a different view of the siege of Metz, see Michael W. Twomey, 'Heroic Kingship and Unjust War in the Alliterative *Morte Arthure*,' *Kings and Kinship*, *Acta* 11 (1984): 133 [133–51].

9 Thus Fries: 'Geoffrey's famous passage at the end of his Book x on Mordred's incestuous relationship with Guenevere was followed by a refusal to comment upon it, at the beginning of Book xi; Wace used a courtly love affair to explain it; and Layamon's dream illustrated the results of the combined sin and treason. But in none of the chronicle or romance versions does Mordred get Guenevere with child; she is, in all other versions, barren' ('The Poem in the Tradition,' p. 38).

10 The subject of Guenevere's children has drawn attention, with Maureen Fries seeing Mordred's mention of them as indicating both 'concern for her and their children but also a desire to ensure succession' ('The Poem in the Tradition,' p.

135), and Michael W. Twomey reiterating the point from the perspective of medieval law: 'the true validation of a king was in the birth of an heir' ('Heroic Kingship,' 145). Fries also suggests that the opposite of having children, barrenness, implies an unhappy marriage ('The Poem in the Tradition,' p. 161 n25).

11 Lee W. Patterson, 'The Historiography of Romance and the Alliterative *Morte Arthure*,' *Journal of Medieval and Renaissance Studies* 13.1 (1983): 1–32, see esp. 24. Patterson notes that the theme first arises in the exaggerated world of the Giant of Mont Saint Michel, but that 'we are forced to recall it in less protected circumstances when at the end of the poem the dying Arthur, in another unique detail, commands that Mordred's children "'bee sleyghely slayne....'"' (24). See also Jan Ziolkowski, 'A Narrative Structure in the Alliterative *Morte Arthure* 1221 and 3150–4346,' *Chaucer Review* 22.3 (1988): 234–45; on Arthur's response to the children, see 245 n31.

12 In 'The Laments for the Dead,' from *The* Alliterative *Morte Arthure: A Reassessment of the Poem*, pp. 117–29, 176–77, Renate Haas reads the foster-mother as a 'conventional figure of mourning' (p. 119), but one whose gestures of grief are reduced in violence from earlier presentations (e.g., Wace and Geoffrey) . For Haas, the scene magnifies the evil of Arthur's antagonist, and so enhances the king's glory in victory.

13 Although Haas points out the way in which the Giant scene's description of Arthur's antagonist 'makes the hero's later victory appear all the more glorious' ('The Laments for the Dead,' p. 119), she also notes some anomalies, such as Arthur's apparent sense that the Old Woman does not need his comfort, a change from the tradition (p. 120).

14 'Narrative Structure,' p. 245 n31.

15 Marjorie Curry Woods, 'Weeping for Dido: Epilogue on a Premodern Rhetorical Exercise in the Postmodern Classroom,' forthcoming in *Latin Grammar and Rhetoric: Classical Theory and Medieval Practice*, ed. Carol Dana Lanham, p. 5. I am grateful to Professor Woods for allowing me to read this work in manuscript.

16 Cited in Woods, p. 4.

17 The translation is Hamel's (p. 279, n708).

18 On the feminizing of Arthur with reference to masculinity in the poem, see Jeff Westover, 'Arthur's End,' 319–20.

Malory's Guenevere:
A 'Trew Lover'

BEVERLY KENNEDY

The late medieval ideal of 'trew love' differed essentially from the ideal of 'fin amor' found in Malory's sources by making chastity a requirement. Lovers who were not free to marry were thus obliged to remain chaste until lawfully wed. Malory alters his French sources to make Guenevere exemplify, albeit imperfectly, this contemporary ideal of chaste love, and so assures his readers 'that whyle she lyved she was a trew lover, and therefor she had a good ende.' (BK)

In recent years, critics writing about Malory's Guenevere have tended to stress her positive qualities: courage in the face of danger, generosity in maintaining her knights and sound moral sense in judging the behavior of Arthur's knights. By so doing, these critics have deflected attention from the traditionally negative views of Arthur's Queen as seducer of Lancelot and cause of the fall of the Round Table, but they have not openly challenged this view.[1] Indeed, their positive assessments of the Queen's character rest upon the same unstated premise as the negative view, namely that Malory did not essentially alter the love story as related in the French Vulgate cycle. As I argue at length elsewhere, this premise is false.[2] Nevertheless, so long as critics continue to read Malory's *Le Morte Darthur* as though the premise were true, they will continue to overlook the many ways in which Malory altered his sources to create a Guenevere of whom he could say 'that while she lyved she was a trew lover, and therefor she had a good ende' (3:1120).[3]

'Trew' here means much more than just 'loyal'. In fact, Malory is referring to an ideal of 'trew love' which permeates late Anglo-Norman and Middle English literature. This ideal differs from the *fin amor* of earlier French romance, from which it derives, mainly in its emphasis upon chastity.[4] We see the first signs of this accomodation to Christian values in an early fourteenth-century *Art d'aimer*, whose Anglo-Norman author insists that 'bone amur ne qwert peché.' No matter how much the lover may desire his lady, he must not touch her, 'S'il ne soit de baiser, / Taunt que'il ad esposé.' Kissing is, of course, part of the greeting normally extended in courtly circles.

But any further physical contact, certainly the embrace 'ne du a nu,' than which there can be no 'grendrer joye' must await the sacrament of marriage, by which God blesses their union, body and soul, and sets them in His service.[5] In *Cleanness*, the Gawain-poet also expresses a positive attitude toward the pleasures of married love when he asserts that God devised the 'play of "paramorez" and wishes married lovers ("two true togeder…tyed") to enjoy "such merthe" that 'wel nyghe pure Paradys moght prove no better.'[6] Middle English romances typically conclude with the lovers' marriage after all obstacles to their union have been overcome, and both Anglo-Norman and English knightly heroes, married or unmarried, are admired for their chastity (e.g., Guy of Warwick and Gawain of *Sir Gawain and the Green Knight*).[7] In this 'moral economy,' to borrow David Burnley's phrase, it is no wonder, I think, that Malory should have chosen to alter his sources to represent Guenevere and Lancelot as 'trew,' that is to say, chaste lovers.[8]

***

Three earlier fifteenth-century texts consider the situation in which Guenevere and Lancelot find themselves, i.e., as true lovers not free to marry. Each deals with this delicate subject in a different way, but all three define true lovers as chaste lovers and all are texts Malory might have known. John Lydgate's *Temple of Glas* is a conventional dream vision in which the Dreamer witnesses the gathering of 'ful mani a þousand of louers,' who have come to 'complein / Vnto þe goddes, of hir wo and pein.' Some complain that they have been denied the freedom to marry for love. The heroine specifically complains that she is already 'bounde' to someone she does not love and now loves another with all her 'herte…in al honesti / …al be it secreli,' but she cannot see any way to be 'wiþ him.' She prays to Venus for help, and promises to obey her commandment. Subsequently, the lady's lover complains to Venus of his lady's refusal to return his love despite his long and loyal service. He asks Venus to help him by igniting his lady's heart to love him as he loves her. Venus answers both lovers' prayers. She promises the lady that she 'shal haue ful possession / Of him þat ʒe cherish nov so wel / In honest maner wiþoute offencioun, / Bicause I cnowe your entencioun / Is truly set…'. Venus promises the lover that his lady will love him truly; he must, however, accept that 'al hir cherisshing / Shal ben grovndid opon honeste' and so he must 'Lete reson bridel lust bi buxumnes / Withoute grucching or rebellioun.' The lady then accepts her lover 'fulli to [her] seruyse,' with the understanding that they must be patient until such 'time þat Venus list prouyde / To shape a wai for oure hertis ease.' They kneel before Venus, who admonishes them to be virtuous and patient, as their true love is tested by long delay, but she also gives them hope for the future:

> 'But tyme shal come þou shalt for þi sufferaunce
> Be wele apaide and take for þi mede
> Thi liues ioy and al þi suffisaunce...'

Meanwhile, until they may lawfully be wed, body and soul, Venus performs a type of marriage ceremony which binds the lovers' hearts together so 'that noȝt but deþ shal þy knot unbynd.'[9]

Lydgate's poem illustrates all the major characteristics of true love. First, such love is based upon admiration, not only for the beauty of the beloved but also for his or her virtues. This characteristic is evident in Lydgate's descriptions of the lovers.[10] Second, it must be freely given and one's mate freely chosen, a point also central to Chaucer's 'Franklin's Tale.' Third, true love is faithful until death, a point which, in the debate in Chaucer's *Parlement of Foules*, is made by the 'trewe' turtledove.[11] Fourth, if true love is passionate then it must also be chaste, for this is Venus's commandment.

Christine de Pizan's *Le livre du duc des vrais amans* also illustrates these cardinal points of 'trew love' but within the much more realistic setting of French aristocratic society. Indeed, it is possible that Christine's romance may be based on a real-life situation, the love affair of the Duke of Bourbon and the Duchess of Berry, wife of Philip of Artois. It is narrated from the Duke's point of view, but also includes letters and poems from the Duchess. As with the lovers in Lydgate's *Temple of Glas*, these noble lovers' love also is grounded in virtue, freely given, faithful, and both passionate and chaste. Their problem is how to express their true love without appearing to be guilty of sexual transgression. Their daytime meetings in the society of others provoke malicious gossip because they are not able to mask their feelings. The lovers then try meeting secretly at night in order to avoid such slander, but eventually they are forced to separate completely. Central to the romance is a long letter written to the Duchess by the Lady of the Tower, outlining the dangers true lovers face and advising her friend to give up her love. The wise Lady argues first that even if her friend is able to resist temptation and avoid the 'meffait de corps,' no one who knows that she is 'amoureuse' will believe in her innocence and 'les mauvaises langues jugeront.' Many an innocent woman has been ruined by such malicious gossip. Secondly, the Lady argues that no one, not even her most virtuous friend, can be sure that she will always be able to 'garder...mesure' in love, no matter how strong her resolution to remain chaste.[12] The Duke goes away from time to time, but the lovers' separation serves mainly to provoke sorrow and jealousy, especially on the part of the Duchess, and the romance concludes with what appears to be a final separation and the Duke's declaration of undying love.

In real life, the Duke of Bourbon and the Duchess of Berry eventually married. We will never know whether they actually exercised such heroic restraint as Christine's romance ascribes to her 'vrais amans.' Modern readers, operating with a very different set of assumptions regarding human sexual behavior, may find it hard to believe that two people passionately in love but unable to marry would even try to exercise such restraint, much less succeed in doing so. That Christine herself doubted young people's ability to remain chaste when passionately in love is evidenced by her inclusion of the Lady of the Tower's letter. Nevertheless she represented her true lovers as able to exercise sexual restraint and evidently expected her fifteenth-century readers to find that representation believable.

In his popular treatise, *The Fire of Love* (translated from the Latin into Middle English sometime after 1435), Richard Rolle takes a more pessimistic view of humankind's ability to exercise sexual restraint. His subject is those ardent friendships that may develop between men and women devoted to the religious life. He believes that it is possible to be a 'trew lufar,' that is, so 'steadfast' in the love of God that one is able to remain chaste, but he assumes that women will find this more difficult than men because of the greater frailty of their female nature. Consequently he warns religious men against the dangers of loving religious women, because even a man cannot hope to be 'so parfyte þat he in flesch may lyf & neuer syne.'[13]

It is, of course, impossible to prove that Malory knew any of these works; he clearly understood, however, the cardinal points of true love as defined by these works, for he illustrates all of them in his 'Tale of Sir Gareth,' for which no source has yet been found. First, true love is based upon admiration of the other's virtues as well as physical beauty. We note that Gareth is drawn by his lady's goodness, especially her courtesy and generosity, as well as her beauty; while Lyones admires Gareth's bravery and goodness, especially his prowess, justice, and courtesy. Second, true love is freely given; neither lover may *require* anything of the other, nor try to constrain his or her love. And we note that when Gareth expresses the opinion that he has 'bought [his lady's] love with parte of the beste bloode within [his] body,' Lyones quite rightly refuses to admit him to her castle and rather sends him away (1:327). At the same time she illustrates the third defining characteristic of true love by promising him lifetime fidelity. The main reason Lyones sends Gareth away is to create the opportunity to meet him in her brother's castle where she can test his love. Does he love the lady of the castle only as a beautiful object, the reward he deserves for his success in his quest to rescue her? Or, if he had a chance to know her, could he love her for herself? He not only could, he does—ardently. And this brings us to the last two defining characteristics of true love: when it is passionate it is also chaste. As soon as the two lovers are really 'hote in love,' they desire to be married. They pledge their troth and attempt to consummate a clandestine marriage immediately, in the Great Hall of her brother's castle.

Gareth and Lyones are fortunate in that, even though their attempts to consummate a clandestine marriage are frustrated by her sister, Lynet, both families eventually consent to their marriage. The presence of their romance in *Le Morte Darthur* reminds readers that marriage is the ideal consummation of true love; at the same time, it reminds them that arranged marriages, like that of Guenevere and Arthur, are more common in aristocratic society. Even as King Arthur allows his nephew Gareth to have 'his wyll and fre choyse' in marrying Dame Lyones (1:360), he also arranges that his nephews Gaharis and Aggravayne should marry Dame Lynet and Dame Lawrell, respectively (1:361).

***

Malory's version of the story of Guenevere's long and true love for Lancelot begins with her arranged marriage to King Arthur. Her father, King Leodegraunce of Camylarde, and her future husband are eager for the match. Leodegraunce will gain a powerful ally; Arthur, who thinks Guenevere is 'the most valyaunte and fayryst' damsel he has ever seen, expects the Round Table and one hundred knights as her dowry (1:97). We do not hear what Guenevere thinks of the match, only that when the time came, 'kynge Leodegreaunce delyverd hys doughtir Gwenyver unto Merlion, and the Table Rounde with the hondred knyghtes' (1:98). Arranged marriages were the norm among the aristocracy and gentry in Malory's day and there is evidence that many families, for reasons of patronage or profit, coerced their sons and especially their daughters into unwanted marriages.[14] However, Guenevere probably did not have to be coerced into marrying Arthur. He was a young king, renowned for his prowess and worship, and she might reasonably expect to grow to love him in time. Yet such an expectation seems never to have been realized. Malory alters his French sources for the first tale, 'The Tale of King Arthur,' to augment the signs that the young King is passionately fond of his queen.[15] But he offers no sign that she reciprocates his passion.

Malory also alters his French sources to make Merlin argue against the match, since he knows that Guenevere is destined to love Lancelot. In the

French romance, Merlin encourages the match and couches the prophecy regarding Guenevere's future love of Lancelot in language so obscure that Arthur cannot understand it. But Malory's Merlin tells Arthur plainly that Guenevere is not a suitable ('holsom') wife for him because 'Launcelot shulde love hir, and sche hym agayne' (1:97).[16] We can only speculate on Arthur's reasons for marrying Guenevere despite Merlin's prophecy. Perhaps he thought he could prevent its fulfillment by being the best of husbands. Or perhaps he was willing to risk its fulfillment for the sake of securing the Round Table and one hundred knights.

Finally, Malory is careful to alter his sources so that his readers will understand that Arthur was never Guenevere's 'trew lover.' By eliminating from his sources passages that suggest Arthur remains very fond of his wife in later years, Malory creates the impression that the King stopped loving Guenevere soon after they married.[17] This impression is confirmed when, after Lancelot has rescued Guenevere from the stake, Malory adds Arthur's declaration that he is 'much more…soryar' for the loss of his 'good knyghtes…than for the losse of [his] fayre quene; for quenys [he] myght have inow, but such a felyship of good knyghtes shall never be togydir in no company' (3:1184).

Malory is equally careful to make the first announcement of Guenevere's and Lancelot's love in such a way as to suggest that theirs will be a 'trew love.' First, he makes it clear that she initially loves him because of his knightly virtues:

> for in all turnements, justys and dedys of armys, both for lyff and deth, he [Lancelot] passed all other knyghtes…Wherefore quene Gwenyvere had hym in grete favour above all other knyghtis, and so he loved the quene agayne aboven all other ladys dayes of his lyff… (1:253).

If this passage underlines the major premise of true love, it also turns the major premise of *fin amor* on its head. Whereas in the French romance, young Lancelot believes that he owes all his prowess and virtue as a knight to Guenevere's love, in Malory's version, Guenevere initially loves him *because* of his peerless prowess and virtue as a knight. Lancelot, moreover, loves the queen not only because she holds him in greater favor than any other knight, but also because of her beauty and goodness. We learn this early in 'The Tale of Sir Tristram,' when Lancelot asserts in a passage original with Malory that Guenevere is 'the fayrest lady and most of bounté in the world' (2:487).[18]

Another fundamental characteristic of true love, lifetime fidelity, is found in this passage in the assertion that Lancelot will love Guenevere as long as he lives. Malory doesn't say as much for Guenevere at this time, so we may infer that her feelings for Lancelot still amount to no more than that 'love of friendship' which ideally characterized all feudal relationships. In fact, throughout this tale and the ensuing tales of 'Gareth' and 'Tristram,' Guenevere never has a private conversation with Lancelot. Their only social interaction occurs at major tournaments and she speaks to him only twice. Both cases of their reported speech are original with Malory and in neither case is she alone in speaking: first she and Arthur ask Lancelot to accept the prize at the Tournament of Maidens, but he refuses on the grounds that he does not deserve it (2:553); then at the Tournament of Surluse both she and King Bagdemagus request that Lancelot enter the lists disguised on the first day and he complies (2:653). Since Malory has systematically eliminated all evidence of a more intimate relationship to be found in his French sources, these two passages reinforce the idea that their love for one another continues to be a true 'love of friendship,' appropriate to their political relationship.

Finally, since chastity is the ultimate defining characteristic of 'trew love,' Malory affirms from the beginning that Lancelot and Guenevere's love is 'trew' in this sense by characterizing young Lancelot as a pious knight devoted to chastity 'for drede of god.' In Malory's version, the unmarried Lancelot's failure to love some eligible lady has given rise to a rumor that Queen Guenevere has 'enchaunte[d]' him. A young damsel tells Lancelot:

> For I cowde never here sey that ever ye loved ony of no maner of degré, and that is grete pyté. But hit is noysed that ye love quene Gwenyvere, and that she hath ordeyned by enchauntement that ye shall never love none other but hir, nother non other damesell ne lady shall rejoyce you; wherefore there be many in this londe, of hyghe astate and lowe, that make grete sorow' (1:270).

This rumor's strength stems from the fact that it not only explains Lancelot's extraordinary and lamentable failure to love any woman 'of no maner of degré' but also assuages the wounded pride and 'grete sorow' of the women who have presumably tried and failed to attract him. In responding to the damsel, Lancelot never denies that he loves the queen, but nevertheless exposes the falseness of the rumor by giving his own reasons for avoiding women. There are two.

First, he chooses not to marry because he is unwilling to give up the adventurous life of a knight in order to 'couche' with a wife. Second, he refuses to have anything to do with 'peramours…for drede of God' because he believes that lecherous knights will not be 'happy nother fortunate unto the werrys' (1:270). In other words, Lancelot believes that God will reward the virtuous knight with good fortune in his knightly endeavors and will punish the sinful with misfortune.[19] We have already seen Lancelot act according to these beliefs when he chose death in prison rather than take as 'peramour' any of the four queens who had captured him, and who claimed to 'know' that 'there can be no lady have thy love but one, and that is quene Gwenyvere' (1:257). On that occasion, too, Lancelot did not deny loving Queen Guenevere. He only denied loving her as the four queens would have had them love one of them, i.e., as 'peramour.' For, as he assures them, Guenevere is 'the treweste lady unto hir lorde lyvynge' and he is willing to stake his life on that in trial by battle (1:258).

Clearly, Guenevere's husband, King Arthur, also believes that she is a chaste wife, for when Morgan le Fay sets out to destroy Lancelot and the queen by convincing Arthur that his best knight and his wife are paramours, she fails utterly. Her first attempt, the so-called horn of chastity, is diverted by Lamorak to the court of King Mark, where ninety–six ladies of the court, including Queen Isode, are unable to drink cleanly from it. Mark would have had them all burnt at the stake, but his barons prevent him, on the grounds that the horn came "'frome the false sorseres and wycche moste that is now lyvyng,' who was 'allway in her dayes…an enemy to all trew lovers'" (1:430). Morgan's second attempt, the shield which she made Tristram carry to the tournament at La Roche Dure, also fails, though it makes Guenevere 'sore aferde' when she notices Arthur staring at it intently. The queen has good reason to be afraid, though she is innocent of any wrongdoing. As the Lady of the Tower reminded the heroine of Christine de Pisan's *Livre du duc des vrais amans*, a false accusation of adultery can be just as destructive as a true one, if the accused woman's husband believes it.[20] Fortunately for Guenevere, Arthur is rational as well as honorable. He chides Tristram for bearing a shield whose significance he does not understand, and so dismisses the matter. This appears to be sensible behavior, since in Malory's version there is no evidence of an adulterous relationship between Arthur's Queen and his best knight, and Arthur knows that Morgan is an enemy of his court. Later, he will dismiss the allegations made in King Mark's letter for the same reasons (2:617).

There are several possible reasons why Malory chose to retain these three suspect allegations from his French source, the prose *Tristan*.[21] For our purposes here, however, the most important reason is that, since he has carefully omitted from the *Tristan* all evidence of an adulterous relationship between Guenevere and Lancelot, he needed some way to keep the love story before his reader's mind. By choosing this way, he also manages to build up suspense regarding the progress of their love. Malory tells us nothing of Guenevere's feelings, but gives a strong indication that Lancelot's love for the queen has progressed beyond that 'love of friendship' appropriate to their political relationship. At the last great tournament in the 'Book of Sir Tristram,' the tournament at Lonezep, Lancelot allows Palomides to win the worship for love of Isode because, as he explains in a passage original with Malory, 'well I wote that love is a grete maystry. And yf my lady were here, as she is nat, wyte you well, sir Palomydes, ye shulde nat beare away the worshyp!' (2:740). This passage demonstrates that, like many other knights, Lancelot has now entered into the quest for worldly worship in hopes of making himself better beloved of his lady.

***

The begetting of Galahad and its aftermath constitute a major turning-point in the relationship between Guenevere and Lancelot in Malory's version of their love story. It marks the end of their distant and wholly public relationship as queen and loyal knight, and the beginning of a more intimate relationship. It also sharply increases the suspense regarding the progress of their love as, not once but twice, it appears that Lancelot is about to lie with the queen. The first time, a messenger comes to him at Castle Corbenic, shows him what appears to be Guenevere's ring and tells him that the queen bids him come to her that night at Castle Case. He dashes off on horseback in obedience to his lady's summons, but never sees his lady. Rather, he is drugged and put to bed with the daughter of King Pelles, Elaine, upon whom he begets Galahad. This incident eventually provokes the first conversation recorded between Guenevere and her knight in *Le Morte Darthur*. When the queen first hears the rumor that Lancelot has begotten a child upon Elaine, she is 'wrothe' and gives 'many rebukes to sir Lancelot and call[s] hym false knyght.' But when Lancelot tells 'the quene all, and how he was made to lye by her, "in the lyknes of you, my lady the quene,"' she holds him 'exkused' (2:802). Guenevere's forgiveness is original with Malory and is credible only because in Malory's version, Lancelot has never before lain with her. Therefore, she has no difficulty believing his explanation of mistaken identity. At the same time, such clear evidence of his desire to lie by her cannot help but affect her feelings for him.

That this is indeed the case may be inferred from the sexual jealousy Guenevere experiences when Elaine comes to court. To give her credit as a 'trew' lover, Guenevere does not doubt Lancelot until she notices his bashfulness in Elaine's presence. Most discourteously, he refuses to greet or speak to the mother of his child. The real reason for his behavior is that he is 'ashamed' of having drawn 'hys swerde to her on the morne aftir that he had layne by her.' But both Elaine and Guenevere misinterpret his behavior. Elaine, who loves Lancelot 'oute of mesure,' concludes that he cares nothing for her and in despair asks Dame Brusen to bring him to her bed that night. On the other hand, Guenevere concludes that he desires this younger and more beautiful woman and, in anger, bids Lancelot 'com to her chamber that nyght, "other ellys," seyde the quene, "I am sure that ye woll go to youre ladyes bedde, dame Elayne, by whome ye gate Galahad"' (2:803–4). Lancelot actually does think that Elayne is 'the fayrest woman that ever he sye in his lyeff dayes' (2:803), but his loyalty to Guenevere is unswerving. Once again he protests the unwitting nature of his begetting Galahad, but the queen is now convinced that Elaine is a rival for his love and so insists that he come to her chamber. Fidelity to her requires that Lancelot declare his willingness to 'be redy at [her] commaundement.'[22]

Guenevere's angrily stated intention is simply to prevent Lancelot from sleeping with Elaine, and Lancelot himself shows no enthusiasm for this first tryst. Indeed, the formality of his response to her echoes that of Guenevere when Arthur required her to accompany him to war (1:127) and suggests that he is aware of the danger they court, even if she is not. If they are able to avoid 'le meffait de corps,' no one will believe in their inocence should it become known that he was in her chamber that night. And if they are not able to avoid 'le meffait de corps,' they will be guilty of adultery, a mortal sin in the eyes of God and treason against their lord, King Arthur. Thanks to Dame Brusen's quick action, the reader never learns what might have happened that night if Lancelot had come to the queen's chamber. Before Guenevere's woman can reach Lancelot's chamber, Dame Brusen, disguised as Guenevere's woman, has led him away to Elaine's bed, in a 'chambir nygh by the quene' (2:804). This time Lancelot has all his wits about him and truly believes that he is 'lovynge and clyppynge' the queen. Some hours later, Guenevere, wide awake and extremely distraught, overhears Lancelot talking in his sleep and coughs loudly enough to wake him. He recognizes the sound of her 'hemmynge,' realizes that he has been tricked yet again, and leaps up like a 'wood man, in hys shurte.' Confronted by the infuriated queen, who calls him a 'false traytoure knyght' and banishes him for ever from her sight, he falls 'downe to the floure in a sowne' (2:804–05).

Guenevere and Lancelot are both doomed to suffer for many years because of her failure to trust him on this occasion. According to the anonymous *Art d'aimer*, one cannot be jealous unless one loves, but the real cause of jealousy is not love itself; it is a lack of trust ('tresoun' and/or 'mescreaunce').[23] Guenevere's trust in Lancelot could not withstand the certain knowledge that he had gone to Elaine's bed a second time. She accused him of betraying her ('treasoun'), but in fact, she betrayed him by assuming the worst. Had she been able to overcome her anger and sexual jealousy, both prompted by lack of trust, and allowed him to explain himself, she could have saved both of them years of separation and suffering. The truth is that Lancelot has been tricked a second time by Dame Brusen and that the trick succeeded only because he had no clear memory of his first experience of lying with Elaine, given his drugged state at the time, and no memory at all of lying with Guenevere. He was guided by someone who seemed to be Guenevere's woman, who assured him that his 'lady Quene Gwenyver lyeth and awaytyth uppon [him],' and was led to a chamber 'nygh by the quene,' into a bed where he was silently received with open arms. Malory tells us that Lancelot was 'glad' because 'he wende that he had had another in hys armys' (2:804), and in Malory's version Lancelot's mistake is understandable.[24] But that night Guenevere was in no mood to listen to another explanation, even if Lancelot had been capable of offering one. Later, when she learns that he has gone mad and disappeared into the forest, she begs his kinsmen to search for him, insisting that they 'spare nat for no goodys but that he be founden' (2:808). Later still, we learn that the search for him has cost her 20,000 pounds (2:831). Both observations, original with Malory, serve to remind us just how much wealth and power Guenevere wields as Arthur's queen. But that power and wealth are not enough to spare her the pain of Lancelot's absence from court for almost fifteen years, until just before the Feast of Pentecost at which his son Galahad will be knighted and the Grail will appear. During this long period of time, Hector assures Lancelot, everyone in Arthur's court, especially Guenevere, has been making 'suche dole and sorrow for you that hyt is mervayle to hyre and se' (2:831). And indeed, when Lancelot finally appears before the court, Guenevere is so overcome by emotion that she is incapable of speech and weeps uncontrollably, 'as she sholde have dyed,' while Hector and Percival tell what has befallen Lancelot since she so cruelly banished him.

Guenevere's next conversation with Lancelot tells us two things. First, their long and true love has survived her sexual jealousy and vindictive anger as well as their mutual suffering during years of separation. And second, no doubt partly because of all this, Guenevere is more passionately attached to Lancelot than she was before. When she realizes he is determined to set out upon the quest of the Sankgraal, her grief is such that she retires to her chamber so that 'no man should perceyve hir grete sorowys.' Lancelot notices that she is missing, and goes to her chamber to take his leave. She tearfully and angrily accuses him of having 'betrayde [her] and putte [her] to the deth, for to leve thus [her] lorde!' But Lancelot remains calm, asking her not to be 'displeased' and promising to come again as soon as he may 'with [his] worship.' His composure seems to help her regain her own, perhaps even to attempt a feeble joke, when she claims to regret that 'ever [she] syghe [him].' But there can be no doubt of her sincerity when she bids him farewell, praying that Jesus Christ will be 'unto [him] good conduyte and saufté, and all the hole felyshyp!' (2:872).

Lancelot returns to Camelot having achieved a high degree of moral and spiritual perfection and having been admonished by the hermit who heard his confession that he should 'no more com in that quenys felyship as much as [he] may forbere' (2:897). Lancelot so promised.[25] Soon after his return, however, Malory tells us that Lancelot 'began to resorte unto quene Gwenivere agayne and forgate the promyse and the perfeccion that he made in the queste' (2:1045). Malory also tells us that Guenevere and Lancelot now love 'togydirs more hotter than they dud toforehonde' (2:1045): in other words, they now love each other more passionately than they did before the Quest. Consequently, they are now in greater danger of committing what the Lady of the Tower calls 'le meffait de corps.' Indeed, Guenevere's situation is now precisely that of the heroine of Christine de Pizan's romance, and in Malory's version of the love story her initial behavior is also the same. She arranges to meet Lancelot by day in the garden or the long hall, where they have tête-à-tête conversations in full view of the court. Or, to quote Malory, she and Lancelot 'ha[ve] many such prevy draughtis togydir that many in the courte spake of hit' (2:1045).

Vinaver's conviction that the paragraph in which this sentence occurs agrees in substance with the fourth paragraph of the *Mort Artu* led the editors of the *Middle English Dictionary* to classify Malory's use of the idiom *hauen a draught* with the idiom *drawen a draught*. Thus we would take it to mean 'to play a trick, engage in a deceitful or sinful activity.' But the Middle English *hauen a draught* means simply 'to take a walk,' so what Malory is really telling us here is that Guenevere is frequently taking private strolls with Lancelot in full view of other courtiers.[26] How else would so 'many' in the court not only be aware of their behavior but also feel free to speak openly about it? The lovers' behavior is certainly indiscreet, but it is not illicit. As the Lady of the Tower observes in Christine de Pizan's *Livre du duc de vrais amans*, however, 'les mauvaises langues' will always leap to the conclusion that where there is love, there must also be sex.[27] Malory offers no indication that Guenevere and Lancelot are having an illicit affair. On the contrary, by telling us that Aggravayne, Mordred and others 'have [Guenevere and Lancelot] gretely in awayte' (2:1045), he suggests that they are not guilty—if only because their enemies still have nothing but suspicion to fuel their malicious gossip.

Before Guenevere thinks of resorting to secret, nocturnal meetings in an attempt to avoid slander, Lancelot decides to deal with it another way. He offers his services as champion in the lists and many ladies and damsels resort to him. As a consequence, he succeeds in avoiding the queen's company but this avoidance, in conjunction with his having to do with so many young and beautiful women, arouses her sexual jealousy again. She summons him to her chamber one day and accuses him of neglecting her. Lancelot defends himself eloquently, both on the grounds of his recent experience in the Grail Quest and the danger posed by their enemies. But Guenevere either doesn't believe him, or else hasn't really listened to him, for her angry response makes no reference to his arguments and concludes by banishing him from the court. Once again, her lack of trust in Lancelot must be accounted a fault, measured by the ideal of true love and this time she has less reason to mistrust him than she had when she suspected him of desiring Elaine of Corbenic. But Lancelot is still the most eligible bachelor in Arthur's service, and presumably in need of a wife and an heir to his kingdom of France. Indeed, in Malory's version, Elaine of Corbenic assured Guenevere that if it were not for her (Guenevere), she (Elaine) 'might have getyn the love' of Lancelot, her 'lorde,' and the father of her child, Galahad (2:806). It is, therefore, understandable that an aging Guenevere should fear Lancelot's being attracted once more to a younger, more beautiful, and marriageable woman.

This is exactly what appears to happen in the 'Fair Maid of Astolat' episode. Lancelot decides to disguise himself in the Winchester Tournament by wearing Elaine of Astolat's red sleeve. It is a perfect disguise because in Malory's text he has never done this much in his life for any woman, not even Guenevere. Elaine falls in love with Lancelot and, by her own admission, her love is so passionate, so 'oute of mesure,' that when he refuses to marry her, she begs him at least to take her as 'paramour.' In the end, she dies of her unrequited love and Guenevere, though initially furious with Lancelot for wearing Elaine's red sleeve, is so moved by the young maiden's death that she reproaches him for failing to do something to save her life. Lancelot explains that he could not give the Fair Maid what she required of him, and reminds the queen of a cardinal point of true love that she never should have forgotten: "'For, madame,' seyde sir Launcelot, 'I love nat to be constrayned to love, for love muste only aryse of the harte selff, and nat by none constraynte'" (2:1097).

One of the most important passages Malory adds to *Le Morte Darthur* to help his readers understand the relationship between Guenevere and Lancelot is the discussion of 'trew love' or 'vertuouse love' that prefaces the 'Knight of the Cart' episode, and concludes with the 'lytyll mencion' that 'whyle she lyved [Guenevere] was a trew lover and therefor she had a good ende.'[28] This passage not only reminds readers of what 'trew love' is (which the romance of Gareth and Lyones has already shown them), but also recapitulates the earlier history of Guenevere and Lancelot's true love. Malory's remarks about 'wyntre's rasure' and the danger it poses to 'trew love' refer to Guenevere's past fits of anger and jealousy, which their love has survived. His remarks about the need to reserve the 'first honoure to God' refer not only to Lancelot's sin, confessed during the Quest, of fighting for the queen rather than for God, but also to the promised reward of repenting and avoiding this sin in future: 'an worshyp in armys may never be foyled.' Malory then suggests why their love has endured so long. They are not like the lovers of nowadays, 'sone hote sone colde'; rather, as was customary 'in kynge Arthurs dayes,' they have loved for years without any 'lycoures lustis...betwixt them.'[29] But with his opening remarks on the power of 'the lusty moneth of May,' he prepares his readers for the possibility that in the episode which follows these true lovers will be 'constraynct[d]...to som manir of thynge' they have not done before (3:1119–20).[30]

Malory alters his source to make Lancelot's coming into the queen's chamber unpremeditated. Lancelot's stated intention is only to speak to the queen through a window barred with iron, and then return to his companion, Lavayne. As he and the queen are talking of 'diverce thyngis,' however, Lancelot expresses the wish 'that he might have comyn in to her.'

> 'Wyte you well, seyde the quene, 'I wolde as fayne as ye that ye myght com in to me.'
> 'Wolde ye so, madame,' seyde sir Launcelot, 'wyth youre harte that I were with you?'
> 'Ye, truly,' seyde the quene.
> 'Than shall I prove my myght,' seyde sir Launcelot, 'for youre love' (3:1131).

Lancelot seems surprised that his lady should be as 'fayne' as he; at least he feels he must ask again, to be sure. This suggests not only that he did not expect such a response, but also that the 'more hotter' love they have experienced since his return from the Quest has not yet resulted in their committing adultery. His subsequent pulling the iron bars 'clene oute of the stone wallys' becomes a rather impressive testimony to the strength of his present desire (3:1131).

Malory gives no evidence that Guenevere repents this sin.[31] But his handling of their next nocturnal meeting, when Aggravayne and Mordred have set a trap for them, suggests not only that she has repented it, but that she and Lancelot are not guilty of adultery on this occasion.[32] Malory explicitly refuses to tell his readers if the Queen and Lancelot were 'abedde' or not, and reminds them that 'love that tyme was nat as love ys nowadayes' (3:1165). This reminder, taken together with the actual words and behavior of the lovers once they realize that they have been trapped, strongly suggest that they are innocent. As Lancelot prepares to face his accusers unarmed, he kisses the queen and asks her to pray for his soul if he is slain. Her response is to assure him that if he is slain, she 'woll take [her] deth as mekely as ever ded marter take hys dethe for Jesu Crystes sake.' She also expresses the wish that their accusers would 'take [her] and sle [her] and suffir [Lancelot] to ascape.' Lancelot prays God to save him from such shame, and then opens the door, praying, 'Jesus Cryste, be Thou my shylde and myne armoure!' (3:1166–67). The queen knows that if Lancelot is slain, she will either be put to the sword immediately, there in her chamber, or taken prisoner to be burned at the stake later. That she should compare her willingness to die to that of a Christian martyr suggests that she has, indeed, repented her earlier sin and does not now fear death, knowing that she is innocent.

***

Aggravayne and Mordred's unsuccessful attempt to catch Guenevere and Lancelot 'with the dede,' and so prove their guilt, marks the last turning-point in the queen's relationship with Lancelot because it sets in motion the chain of events which leads to their final separation. After rescuing her from the stake and keeping her safe at Joyous Garde during the siege of Arthur and Gawain, Lancelot returns Guenevere to her rightful place beside her husband at Carlisle, at the same time assuring Arthur that she is 'trew and clene to you.' Malory gives Guenevere nothing to say in this most public venue. She does not even respond to Lancelot's speech taking leave of her, in which he beseeches her to pray for him, promises to pray for her and also advises her, should she ever be 'harde bestad by ony false tunges,' to send him word and he will save her (3:1202). The king and all of the courtiers present (except Gawain) are weeping. It is possible that the queen does not speak for fear of weeping too, and thus betraying her own sorrow at this final parting.

In the end, Malory's Guenevere decides to become a nun, not, as in his sources, to escape the vengeance of Arthur or Mordred but, after their deaths, to prepare herself for her own death by living a life of 'grete penaunce…prayers, and almes-

dedis' (3:1243). She evidently assumes that she will never see her banished
lover again, but it is clear that she continues to love him passionately, for
when he appears unexpectedly at Amesbury, she faints three times at the
mere sight of him. When she is finally capable of speech, she tells Lancelot
that he must henceforth forsake her company, return to his realm and there
take a wife 'and lyff with hir wyth joy and blys' (3:1252). Most uncharacteristically,
Lancelot refuses to obey his lady.[33] Rather, he reminds her that he, too, would
have chosen the religious life long ago, 'had not youre love bene' (3:1252–53).
Now, he continues, had he found her 'so disposed,' he would have wished to
take her back with him to France. But since she has decided to enter the
religious life, he wants nothing more than to do as she has done. We may
infer their mutual passion as much from his desire for a parting kiss as from
her refusal to grant it, and far more from their mutual 'lamentacyon as they
had be stungyn with sperys' and the 'many tymes they swouned' before
Guenevere's women finally carry her to her chamber (3:1253).

The suggestion that Guenevere might have married Lancelot after Arthur's
death is original with Malory, but perfectly in accordance with his depiction
of them as 'trew' lovers, given the romance convention that marriage was
the ideal consummation of true love. Of course, in so far as Malory was
writing a history of the reign of King Arthur, he could not alter the facts to
allow their marriage. Nevertheless, in his handling of the last years of their
lives, he shows them achieving a kind of spiritual marriage while she is a nun
and he a priest. On her deathbed six years after their final parting, Guenevere
prays that she 'may never have power to see syr Launcelot with [her] worldly
eyen' (3:1255). Richard Rolle would have approved such awareness of her
frailty as a woman and the pious desire to commit no further sins of the
flesh. Guenevere's dying words also suggest, however, that she is now and
perhaps has been for some time able to see Lancelot with her spiritual 'eyen'
and so to communicate with him in spirit.

The first sign of this spiritual communication is the 'vysyon' which comes
to Lancelot in his sleep, charging him to travel to Amesbury, where he will
find the queen's body, and then to take her body to be buried by Arthur's
side at Glastonbury. Lancelot acts upon the 'vysyon' immediately; it takes
him and his companions two days to travel the thirty miles to Amesbury,
and they arrive one half hour after Guenevere's death. Her companions tell
Lancelot that for two days her constant prayer had been that she not live to
see him with her 'worldly eyen.' They also tell him that before she died she
informed them that Lancelot had been a priest these last twelve months and
that he was even now on his way to 'fetch [her] cors.' How did she know

this? For that matter, who appeared to Lancelot in his 'vysyon' to tell him of her impending death and give him instructions regarding the disposition of her body? Malory does not answer these questions; it is, however, reasonable to infer from his narrative that the lovers have been communicating spiritually. Malory might say that God has given them a 'speciall grace,' such as He granted to Gawain so that he might appear to Arthur the night before the battle on Salisbury Plain (3:1234). Richard Rolle says that those 'trew lufars' whose souls have been warmed and illuminated by the 'fyer of þe holy gost' may love so well that they could almost believe there was 'bot on saule in þam both.'[34] Guenevere and Lancelot are separated by thirty miles, but their spiritual communication suggests that, despite this physical distance, and quite possibly through the 'fyer of þe holy gost,' they have consummated a spiritual marriage, a union of souls, as though there were, indeed, 'bot on saule in þam both.' This is, I think, a significant part of that 'good ende' which Malory predicted for Guenevere because 'whyle she lyved she was a trew lover.'

***

Malory's representation of Guenevere is embedded in late medieval English culture, and so adapted to appeal to an audience of prosperous English men and women proud of their nation and its history, including the reign of the great King Arthur.[35] His portrayal of Guenevere as Lancelot's 'trew lover' accords with the values and expectations of his audience, who would have found the lovers' repeated acts of treasonable adultery, as recounted in the French version of Arthur's reign, extremely offensive. Most potential readers of Malory's version would not have been intimately acquainted with the French version, as narrated in the massive Vulgate cycle of romances, though they would probably have been familiar with the notion that Lancelot was Guenevere's lover and they might even have heard of the 'Knight of the Cart' episode. By retaining this one possible instance of treasonable adultery, but placing it much later in the story, well after the Grail quest, Malory is able not only to show the long duration of Guenevere's and Lancelot's true love, but also to draw his readers' attention to it in his discussion of 'trew love' preceding their one, regrettable lapse from chastity. When they next meet by night in the queen's chamber, where they are trapped by the ambush of Mordred and Aggravayne, Malory strongly suggests that they are innocent, not only by explicitly refusing to tell his readers whether or not they are guilty, but also by reminding them of what he has said before about love in King Arthur's days (3:1165) and suggesting through the lovers' pious dialogue that they have both repented their former lapse. At the same time, by emphasizing the political ambition of the Queen's accusers Mordred and Aggravayne, Malory draws attention to an important fact of medieval political life: the political vulnerability of a king who lacks a legitimate successor because his queen is barren.[36]

Malory's representation of Guenevere is, however, most fully understood in terms of one aspect of late medieval English culture, the ideal of true love, explicated in treatises like the anonymous Anglo-Norman *Art d'aimer* and illustrated in romances like Chaucer's 'Franklin's Tale.' It is a common complaint of critics that readers gain an intimate view of Malory's Guenevere only when she is being angry and vindictive toward Lancelot. This is in large measure true, but also to be expected once Guenevere's love for Lancelot has become more passionate, since they cannot marry. Indeed, Guenevere's inability to trust Lancelot completely, and the jealousy and anger her distrust causes, illustrate the chief perils of true love. According to the *Art d'aimer*, mistrust and jealousy (Malory's 'wyntres razure') can potentially destroy true love and it is a tribute to the strength of the lovers' mutual devotion that their love survives these perils.[37] The problem is exacerbated when by the fact that their love becomes 'more hotter' when neither is young any more. Guenevere is married and middle-aged, but Lancelot is still an eligible bachelor. She fears that he will find younger women more attractive than herself, and her fears are fueled by his evident attractiveness to young and beautiful women, like the Fair Maid of Astolat. In these circumstances, even though Guenevere's mistrust, jealousy and anger must be regarded as faults according to the ideal of 'trew love,' I think Malory's late medieval English readers, especially the women, would have found them forgivable.

Guenevere's behavior as a 'trew lover' is more admirable when it comes to observing chastity. Richard Rolle believed that women would have more difficulty being 'trew,' i.e., chaste, 'lufars' because of the frailty of their nature. In Malory's version, however, Guenevere never seduces Lancelot.[38] On the contrary, she first commands him to come to her chamber because she thinks that he is sexually attracted to Elaine of Corbenic, and she wants to prevent him from going to Elaine's bed a second time. Later, when Guenevere's love for Lancelot is 'more hotter,' she does not immediately invite him to come to her chamber. Rather, she arranges that they should 'ha[ve]...prevy draughtis' (2:1045) together by day, in full view of the court. Still later, she resorts to secret nocturnal meetings to avoid the slander provoked by these private strolls, but Malory's handling of the first of these secret meetings, in the 'Knight of the Cart' episode, suggests that both the queen and Lancelot intended the meeting to be innocent. It is not, moreover, Guenevere who first expresses the wish that Lancelot might come in to her, but Lancelot. As a 'trew lover,' Guenevere should have refused him; her failure to do so is yet another fault, judged by the ideal of 'trew love.' But surely she may be forgiven for responding positively to this welcome assurance that Lancelot finds her desirable, even though she is no longer young. Certainly, Malory encourages his readers to forgive her, not only through his prefatory remarks on the power of the 'lusty moneth of May,' but also through his representation of her behavior during the next nocturnal meeting, when she and Lancelot are trapped by Mordred and Aggravayne.

It is arguable that Guenevere gives the greatest proof of her 'trew love' for Lancelot after Arthur's death when, by becoming a nun, she renounces the possibility of ever marrying Lancelot herself. She thereby frees him, if he so wishes, to marry a younger woman capable of giving him an heir to his kingdom. To be sure, this is not her only motive for entering the religious life, but it is certainly one of them, as we can infer from her unsuccessful attempt in their final interview to command Lancelot to return to France and there take a wife. The other motive is, of course, the desire to do penance for her sins and seek her soul's salvation. But even after she has taken up the religious life to these ends, she never stops loving Lancelot, nor does he stop loving her. Indeed, the spiritual marriage which they achieve in the religious life may be seen not only as part of the 'good ende' Malory predicted for her as 'a trew lover,' but also as an appropriate reward for her act of renunciation.

MONTRÉAL

Beverly Kennedy died in late December, 2000. She was Professor of English at Marianopolis College in Montréal, Canada. She wrote several articles on Sir Thomas Malory's *Le Morte Darthur*, and the book, *Knighthood in the 'Morte Darthur'* (1986; 2nd ed., 1992).

NOTES

1   Lindsay E. Holichek, 'Malory's Gwenevere: After Long Silence," *Annuale Mediaevale* 22 (1982): 112–26, was the first to attempt to redress the balance of criticism in Guenevere's favor; but see also Carol Hart, 'Newly Ancient: Reinventing Guenevere in Malory's *Morte Darthur*,' in *Sovereign Lady*, ed. Muriel Whitaker (New York: Garland Publishing, 1994), pp. 3–20, and Sarah J. Hill, 'Recovering Malory's Guinevere,' in *Lancelot and Guenevere: A Casebook*, ed. Lori J. Walters (New York: Garland Publishing, 1996), pp. 267–78. In her archetypal study of Arthurian women, Maureen Fries calls Guenevere a 'Heroine' supportive of patriarchal structures and at best 'only partially heroic' (Fries,

'Female Heroes, Heroines, and Counter-Heroes: Images of Women in Arthurian Tradition,' in *Arthurian Women: A Casebook*, ed. Thelma J. Fenster, Arthurian Characters and Themes [New York: Garland Publishing, 1996], pp. 59–76 at 66). Edward Donald Kennedy, 'Malory's Guenevere, "A Woman Who Had Grown a Soul,"' *Arthuriana* 9.2 (1992): 39–45, reprinted in this volume, argues that Guenevere establishes her moral and spiritual superiority to Lancelot by being the first to repent their sinful love and renounce the world, thus setting an example for him to follow. Hill, 'Recovering Malory's Guinevere,' p. 277, also thinks that Guenevere's example saves Lancelot. For a contrary interpretation of the lovers' relative spiritual awareness and readiness to repent, see Beverly Kennedy, 'Malory's Lancelot: "Trewest Lover, of a Synful Man,"' *Viator* 12 (1981): 409–56.

2   B. Kennedy, 'Malory's Lancelot,' 409–56.

3   Sir Thomas Malory, *The Works of Sir Thomas Malory*, ed. Eugène Vinaver, rev. P.J.C. Field, 3d edn., 3 vols. (Oxford: Clarendon Press, 1990). All page references to Malory's work are from this edition and will appear within parentheses in the text.

4   David Burnley, *Courtliness and Literature in Medieval England* (London: Longman, 1998), discusses the wide and complex semantic field covered by the French phrase *fin amor* and its English equivalent in his chapter on 'Courtly Love.' In his conclusion, at pp. 218–19, Burnley observes that in the context of late medieval popular poetry, this love came to mean 'true' love, 're-interpreted to correspond more closely with the requirements of religion' and with 'the demands of an urban, commercial society.'

5   'Un art d'aimer anglo-normand,' ed. O. Södergard, Romania 77 (1956) 289–330, respectively ll. 658, 1326, 659–60, 714–41, 676–83. Faithful marriage was traditionally regarded in the medieval period as a degree of chastity lesser than either virginity or celibacy, but nevertheless a form of chastity. Expressions such as these, extolling the sexual pleasures of marriage, were not common. In the late medieval period, however, there was a marked 'tendency among preachers and moralists…to exalt the order of marriage' (Gabriel Le Bras, 'Le doctrine du mariage chez les théologiens et les canonistes depuis l'an mille,' in *Dictionnaire du théologie catholique*, 16 vols. in 29 (Paris: Letouzey et Ané, 1905–72), 9: 2121–2317 at 2181.

6   *Cleanness*, ed. A.C. Cawley, J.J. Anderson in *Pearl, Cleanness, Pacience, Sir Gawaine and the Green Knight* (London: J.M. Dent, 1994), ll. 700–4.

7   Henry Ansgar Kelly, *Love and Marriage in the Age of Chaucer* (Ithaca, NY: Cornell University Press, 1975), pp. 312–13, 172–216, 225–42, argues that St. Bernard's sermons were instrumental in generating an ideal of married love in England that was 'both passionate and chaste,' and that most of the apparently illicit unions in Middle English romance would have been interpreted by their readers as clandestine marriages, including that of Troilus and Criseyde, to whose union there was no canonical impediment. Donnell van de Voort, *Love and Marriage in the English Metrical Romance* (Nashville, TN: Vanderbilt University Press,

1938), concludes that the presumption of clandestine marriage eliminates *all* illicit unions from the Middle English romances except for those found in Arthurian romance where one of the lovers is already married. On the late-medieval theory and practice of clandestine marriage, see Zacharias P. Thundy, 'Clandestine Marriages in the Late Middle Ages,' in *New Images of Medieval Women: Essays Toward a Cultural Anthropology*, ed. Edelgard E. DuBruck (Lewiston, NY: Edwin Mellen Press, 1989), pp. 303–20.

8   Burnley, *Courtliness and Literature*, p. 218. Critics have not sufficiently noted that Malory's *Le Morte Darthur* offers the *only* complete version of the Guenevere–Lancelot love story extant in Middle English. At least three other fifteenth-century authors avoided telling the whole story: the author of the alliterative *Morte Arthure* (ed. Edmund Brock, 2nd ed., EETS o.s. 8 [London: Oxford University Press, 1871, repr. 1967]), who clearly knew the French tradition but chose to ignore it, allowing Lancelot only a minor role and completely eliminating the love story; the author of the stanzaic *Morte Arthur* (ed. J.D. Bruce, EETS e.s. 88 [London: Oxford University Press, 1959]), who chose to translate only the tragic end of the love affair; and the fifteenth-century Scottish author of *Lancelot of the Laik* (ed. W.W. Skeat, EETS o.s. 6 [London: Oxford University Press, 1865, repr. 1965]), who broke off his translation of the French prose *Lancelot* just before the first meeting of Lancelot and Guenevere. In addition, there is Hardyng's *Chronicle*, ed. Henry Ellis (London: Rivington, 1812), whose brief account of Arthur's reign says nothing of the Queen's relationship to Lancelot, and has Lancelot marry Galahad's mother, Elaine.

9   John Lydgate, *The Temple of Glas*, in *Poems*, ed. John Norton-Smith (Oxford: Clarendon Press, 1966), pp. 67–112, respectively ll. 144, 144–46, 210–14, 335, 363–66, 834–47, 426–31, 869–79, 1074, 1082–83, the quoted passage at 1194–96, and 1269–70.

10 Lydgate, *Temple of Glas*, ll. 921–31, 970–75.

11 Geoffrey Chaucer, *The Parlement of Foules*, ed. Derek Brewer (London: Thomas Nelson and Sons, 1960; reissued 1967), ll. 582–88.

12 Christine de Pizan, *Le livre du duc des vrais amans, 1404*, in *Oevres poetiques*, ed. Maurice Roy, 3 vols. (Paris: SATF, 1886–96) 3.xv, 3.165, 3.167.

13 Richard Rolle, *The Fire of Love and the Mending of Life, translated from the Latin by Richard Misyn*, ed. Ralph Harvey, EETS o.s. 106 (London: Kegan Paul, Trench, Trübner, 1896; reissued Woodbridge: Boydell and Brewer, 1996), pp. 54, 84.

14 G.W. Owst, *Literature and Pulpit in Medieval England* (Cambridge: Cambridge University Press, 1933), pp. 381–82; Ann S. Haskell, 'Marriage in the Middle Ages: the Paston Women on Marriage in Fifteenth-Century England," *Viator* 4 (1973): 459–71.

15 Edward Donald Kennedy, 'The Arthur–Guenevere Relationship in Malory's "*Morte Darthur*,"' *Studies in the Literary Imagination* 4.2 (1971): 29–40, remarks that when the queen and the Round Table reach Arthur's court, Malory adds Arthur's expression of gladness that she has come, for he 'has loved hir longe' (1:98). Guenevere is silent. According to E.D. Kennedy, Malory also expands

the king's expression of his desire that the queen accompany him to war against the five kings. However, when Arthur tells her this, she responds with great formality and no apparent enthusiasm for the expedition: 'Sir, I am at youre commaundement, and shall be redy at all tymes' (1:127).

16 *Middle English Dictionary*, s.v. 'holsom' 2c; 'should,' 6 and 7.

17 E.D. Kennedy, 'The Arthur–Guenevere Relationship,' 30–36.

18 Later, in passages original with Malory, we learn of two other reasons why Lancelot might already love Guenevere for her generosity and compassion. When he was a young knight, she maintained him among the fellowship of 'Quenys knyghtes,' who bore white shields until they could be called 'renowned men of worshyp' (3:1121). And on the day Arthur knighted him, the Queen saved Lancelot from shame by bringing the sword he had lost in his 'hastynes' (2:1098).

19 For fuller discussion of Malory's representation of young Lancelot in the 'Tale of Lancelot' as comparable to his son, Galahad, and thus something of a prude, see Beverly Kennedy, *Knighthood in the Morte Darthur*, 2nd edn., Arthurian Studies 11 (Cambridge, UK: D.S. Brewer, 1992), pp. 111–16. For analysis of his belief system, shared with the Grail knights, see chapter 5 of B. Kennedy, *Knighthood*, 'Happy and Unhappy Knights.'

20 Christine de Pizan, *Livre du duc*, 3.165.

21 For fuller discussion of these reasons, see B. Kennedy, 'Malory's Lancelot,' 424–25, and 'Adultery in Malory's *Le Morte d'Arthur*,' *Arthuriana* 7.4 (1997): 63–91 at 73–74.

22 By contrast, in Malory's French source the queen shows no jealousy of Elaine, and Lancelot, who 'mout amoit sa dame,' joyfully accepts her invitation to her chamber that night ('Galahad and Perceval,' ed. H. Oskar Sommer, *Modern Philology* 5 (1907–08), 55–84, 181–200, 291–341, at 78.

23 *Art d'aimer*, ll. 890–97, 1012–92.

24 The author of Malory's French source observes that Lancelot enjoyed with Elaine 'autel soulas & autel joie comme il auoit coustume a faire a sa dame la roine, car il quidoit uraiement que che fust ele' (Sommer, 'Galahad and Perceval,' 79), leaving his readers to figure out for themselves how Lancelot could possibly be so mistaken.

25 Like the confession preceding it, this promise is original with Malory and suggests that Lancelot's sin was loving and serving the queen rather than God, not committing adultery with her. Indeed, had he been committing adultery with her, the hermit's admonition to avoid her company as much as possible in future would be morally absurd, tantamount to admonishing him to commit adultery less frequently in future. See B. Kennedy, *Knighthood*, pp. 260–62, and 'Malory's Lancelot,' 430–33.

26 *Middle English Dictionary*, s.v. 'draught,' respectively 3e, 3a. The woodcut Wynkyn de Worde placed at the head of Book XVIII of his 1520 edition of *Le Morte Darthur* (STC 803. Ann Arbor, MI: University Microfilms, n.d. Reel 16), shows the queen and Lancelot having one of these 'prevy draughtis.' On the right side of the woodcut, the queen is speaking privately to Lancelot, while two male

courtiers converse slightly behind them and to the left. For a reproduction and further discussion of this woodcut, see B. Kennedy, 'Adultery,' 758.

27 Christine de Pizan, *Livre du duc*, 3.165.

28 Malory may have been inspired to predict and provide a 'good ende' for Guenevere by Christine de Pizan's prayer that God grant 'bonne vie et puis a la parfin / Son paradis' to all 'les gentilz / Vrays fins loyaulx amans…' *Livre du Dit de Poissy* in *The Love Debate Poems*, ed. Barbara K. Altmann (Gainesville, FL: University Presses of Florida, 1998), ll. 2071–74.

29 Malory's description of love in King Arthur's days was possibly inspired by a fairly lengthy passage in *Reson and Sensuallyte*, a Middle English translation of *Les echecs amoureux*, made ca. 1412 and attributed to John Lydgate, which describes love in King Arthur's days as 'pure and fre, / Grounded on al honeste / Withoute engyn of fals werkyng, / Or any spot of evel menyng…' 'Vnleful lust was set a-syde' (John Lydgate, *Reson and Sensuallyte*, ed. E. Sieper, EETS e.s. 84 (London: Oxford University Press, 1901), ll. 3167–89.

30 I take the 'Knight of the Cart' to be the only actual incident of adultery between the queen and Lancelot in Malory's work. Robert Sturges plausibly argues, however, that Malory's language is sufficiently ambiguous to leave open the possibility that the lovers do *not* actually commit adultery that night and that Lancelot's 'plesaunce and hys lykynge' is to watch over his lady as she sleeps (Sturges, 'Epistemology of the Bedchamber: Textuality, Knowledge, and the Representation of Adultery in Malory and the *Prose Lancelot*,' *Arthuriana* 7.4 [1997]: 47–62 at 59.

31 In contrast, Malory offers strong evidence that Lancelot repents it, altering his source to show a Lancelot so overcome by the enormity of what he has done that he welcomes the hardship of imprisonment, and any other 'distress…that God sendys me,' and steadfastly refuses to lie by his gaoler's wife to be released, even though he knows that his lady may be 'brente in [his] defaute' (3:1135–36).

32 For arguments, based on contemporary law and legal practice, that Malory's text points to the lack of proof of adultery, see Robert L. Kelly, 'Malory and the Common Law: *Hasty jougement* in the "Tale of the Death of King Arthur,"' *Medievalia et Humanistica* n.s. 22 (1995): 111–40, and E. Kay Harris, 'Evidence against Lancelot and Guinevere in Malory's *Morte Darthur*: Treason by Imagination,' *Exemplaria* 7.1 (1995): 179–208.

33 Indeed, Malory's Lancelot has never been completely defined by Guenevere nor ever entirely in her power. Geraldine Heng seriously misreads Malory when she takes Lancelot's confession of his sins in the Quest as a generalizing 'profession' that all he is and ever does is for the queen (Heng, 'Enchanted Ground: The Feminine Subtext in Malory,' in *Courtly Literature: Culture and Context*, ed. Keith Busby and Karl Kooper [Amsterdam: Benjamin, 1990], pp. 283–300 at 288).

34 Rolle, *Fire of Love*, p. 41.

35 On the general fifteenth-century belief in King Arthur as an historical figure, see Lister M. Matheson, 'King Arthur and the Medieval English Chronicles,' in

King Arthur Through the Ages, ed. Valerie M. Lagorio and Mildred Leake Day (New York: Garland Publishing, 1990), 1:248–74.

36 Malory thus makes explicit what remained implicit in his thirteenth–century sources, where the association of a barren queen and the accusation of adultery had become something of a narrative convention 'which allowed oblique discussion of many of the issues regarding the evolution of queenship during this period' (Peggy McCracken, *The Romance of Adultery: Queenship and Sexual Transgression in Old French Literature* [Philadelphia: University of Pennsylvania Press, 1998], p. 11).

37 *Art d'aimer*, ll. 880–1092.

38 Rolle, *Fire of Love*, p. 54.

Malory's Guenevere:
'A Woman Who Had Grown a Soul'

EDWARD DONALD KENNEDY

At the end of *Le Morte Darthur* when Lancelot mentions to Guenevere his failure on the Grail Quest, his statement reminds the reader of another failure: Galahad, who had saved so many, had been ultimately unable to save his father. This role is ironically reserved for Guenevere: the woman who had been the reason for Lancelot's downfall finally leads him to salvation. (EDK)

In the final book of T.H. White's *The Once and Future King*, with its now familiar title *The Candle in the Wind*, the chapter that tells of Lancelot and Guenevere being found together by Mordred, Agravaine, and other knights begins with the following words: 'Guenevere waited for Lancelot in the candle-light of her splendid bedroom, brushing her grey hair. She looked singularly lovely, not like a film star, but like a woman who had grown a soul.'[1] My attention was drawn to this scene about thirty years ago by Derek Brewer's introduction to his edition of the final two tales of *Le Morte Darthur*. Brewer mentions it in order to show how different Malory's work is from that of a modern realist.[2] To be sure, White, in adapting *Le Morte Darthur* as a novel, probably added as much that was derived from twentieth-century psychology, politics, and pedagogical theory as from Malory's text. The description of Guenevere as a 'woman who had grown a soul,' however, was arguably suggested by Malory.

Thelma Fenster and Terence McCarthy rightly observe that throughout most of *Le Morte Darthur* the portrait of Guenevere is primarily a public one, with little emphasis on her character as wife and mistress.[3] Just as Lancelot in Malory is always 'Sir Lancelot,' she is always 'Queen Guenevere' or the queen. In most of Malory's book Guenevere is a conventional lady of romance—imperious, jealous, and demanding—with an occasional individualizing trait such as the sense of humor that she demonstrates when she sees Sir Dinadan entering a tournament dressed as a woman and laughs so hard she falls down.[4] Her character acquires depth, however, in the last book where she becomes, in Brewer's words, 'the most fascinating, exasperating, and human of all medieval heroines.'[5] She is, as Lancelot describes her, the 'moste nobelest Crysten quene' whom he 'never fayled...in ryght nor in wronge' (3:1166). With those words Lancelot expresses the complexity of their relationship, a relationship marked by both virtue and sin. When Lancelot and Guenevere are found together Guenevere says to Lancelot, 'Wyte thou well that I woll [never] lyve longe aftir thy dayes. But and ye be slayne I woll take my dethe as mekely as ever ded marter take hys dethe for Jesu Crystes sake' (3:1166). Although Lancelot is not slain and outlives Guenevere, the statement is nevertheless prophetic of Guenevere's own final days. She meets death 'as mekely as...[a] marter.' The suggestion for White's 'woman who had grown a soul' was undoubtedly derived from Malory's depiction of Guenevere in this last book.

The final meeting between Lancelot and Guenevere is one of the best known scenes in *Le Morte Darthur*. The queen has become a nun at Amesbury. When Lancelot visits her at the convent, she says to all those present: 'Thorow thys same man and me hath all thys warre be wrought, and the deth of the moste nobelest knyghtes of the worlde; for thorow oure love that we have loved togydir ys my moste noble lorde slayne' (3:1252). Thus she begins with a lament for the loss of Arthur and the Round Table, showing a concern for the group that, as Brewer observes, is so typical of Malory's work.[6] Guenevere also accepts responsibility for what she and Lancelot have done and is concerned with her own sinfulness and salvation:

> 'Therefore, sir Launcelot, wyte thou well I am sette in suche a plyght to gete my soule hele. And yet I truste, thorow Goddis grace and thorow Hys Passion of Hys woundis wyde, that aftir my deth I may have a syght of the blyss[ed] face of Cryste Jesu, and on Doomesday to sytte on Hys ryght syde; [fo]r as synfull as ever I was, now ar seyntes in hevyn' (3:1252).

She tells Lancelot that he must leave her for good:

> 'I requyre the and beseche the hartily, for all the lo[v]e that ever was betwyxt us, that thou never se me no more in the visayge....for thorow the and me ys the f[lou]re of kyngis and [knyghtes] destroyed. And therefore [go] thou to thy realme, [an]d there take ye a wyff, and lyff with [hir] wyth joy and blys. [A]nd I pray the hartely to pray for me [to] the Everlastynge Lorde [tha]t I may amende my mysselyvyng' (3:1252).

Lancelot rejects the advice that he marry, saying that he could never be 'so false unto you of that I have promysed'; instead he too will withdraw from the world to lead the life of a religious: 'But the same desteny that ye have takyn you to, I woll take me to, for to please Jesu, and ever for you I caste me specially to pray.' Guenevere, now using the formal 'ye' instead of the familiar 'thou' form of address, responds: 'A, sir Launcelot, if ye woll do so and holde thy promyse! But I may never beleve you…but that ye woll turne to the worlde agayne.' Lancelot, in denying that he will do this, recalls the Grail quest, when he would have forsaken the world had it not been for Guenevere's love. He concludes by telling her,

> sythen ye have taken you to perfeccion, I must nedys take me to perfection, of ryght. For I take recorde of God, in you I have had myn erthly joye, and yf I had founden you now so dysposed, I had caste me to have had you into mine own royame. But sythen I fynde you thus desposed…I wyl ever take me to penaunce and praye whyle my lyf lasteth, yf that I may fynde ony heremyte…that wyl receyve me' (3:1253).

But when he asks, 'Wherfore, madam, I praye you kysse me, and never no more,' the Queen's response is 'Nay,…that shal I never do, but absteyne you from suche werkes (3:1253).

This scene does not appear in most manuscripts of Malory's French source, the Vulgate *Mort Artu*. There Lancelot never sees Guenevere after he takes her back to Arthur and leaves Loegres in exile; when he returns at the end he learns that she has died.[7] In this work Lancelot's giving up Guenevere some time before the end of the romance is a step in what Jean Frappier describes as his *évolution*, his slow development into a true Christian after he fell back into sin when he returned to Arthur's court from the Grail quest.[8] Here Guenevere enters the convent not out of remorse but because she fears that either Mordred or Arthur will kill her, and she tells the abbess that her suffering and fear ('*l'angoisse et la poor*') made her wish to become a nun.[9]

A final farewell between Lancelot and Guenevere at the convent does, however, appear in one manuscript of the French *Mort Artu*, Palatinus Latinus 1967. Frappier argued that this scene is an interpolation that was not part of the original *Mort Artu*.[10] In this text Guenevere tells Lancelot that she has become a nun because she fears the vengeance of Mordred's sons. Although Lancelot assures her that he has killed the sons and that she can therefore leave the abbey, she refuses because she believes they should spend the rest of their lives doing penance. Lancelot says that he wants what she wants and he too will do penance. As he leaves the abbey, he asks her to forgive him for his misdeeds, and, unlike Malory's version, in which she refuses to kiss him, she chastely kisses him good-bye, an act that was undoubtedly intended to remind the reader of the first kiss between Lancelot and Guenevere in the earlier romance of the Vulgate Cycle, the *Lancelot en prose*. Guenevere spends the rest of her life praying for the souls of Arthur and Lancelot.[11]

Malory had probably not read this version, since his primary source for the final episodes of *Le Morte Darthur* was a late fourteenth-century English verse adaptation of the French romance known as the stanzaic *Morte Arthur*, which also has a final scene between Lancelot and Guenevere and which may have been conceived independently of the French Palatinus version.[12] In the stanzaic work, as in Malory's *Le Morte Darthur*, Guenevere enters the convent out of remorse for sin, not because of her fear of Mordred's sons, and the language of Malory's version closely follows the English verse romance: Guenevere accepts responsibility for 'thys sorowfull werre' and regrets that her lord 'that had no pere' is slain. As in Malory's version, she expresses concern for her sin: 'I-sette I am In suche A place,/ my sowle hele I wyll A-byde.' She hopes to atone for her sins so that after her death 'Throw mercy of hys woundys wyde' she will 'haue A syght of hys face/ At domys day on hys Ryght syde.' She tells Lancelot to leave her company, return to his kingdom and marry; and Lancelot, as in Malory's version, says that he could never be untrue to her and that he too will live a life of penance. As in Malory, he asks for one last kiss and she tells him to 'thynke on that no-more.'[13]

It is easy to see why Malory would have been attracted to this scene in the stanzaic romance, for in its presentation of Guenevere's acceptance of responsibility for the war and for the death of Arthur, it accords with Malory's vision of the fall of Arthur's kingdom in which each of the other major characters—Gawain, Arthur, and Lancelot—also accepts responsibility before dying. Both Gawain and Arthur regret that they had ever fought against Lancelot: Gawain confesses, 'Thorow my wylfulnes I was causer of myne owne dethe…And thorow me and [my] pryde ye have all thys shame and disease' (3:1230). The mortally wounded Arthur says, 'A, sir Launcelot!…thys day have I sore myssed the! And alas, that ever I was ayenste the! For now have I my dethe, whereof sir Gawayn me warned in my dreme' (3:1238). Lancelot regrets that, in having wounded Gawain, he was ultimately responsible for his death (3:1249–50), and at the tomb of Arthur and Guenevere he blames himself for both of their deaths: 'Whan I remembre me how by my defaute and myn orgule and my pryde that they were bothe layed ful lowe…wyt you wel…this remembred, of their kyndenes and myn unkyndenes, sanke so to myn herte that I myght not susteyne myself' (3:1256). Malory's conception of tragedy seems almost Aristotelian; but he would not have had to read Aristotle to know that good people often make terrible mistakes and realize it only after it is too late to do anything about it.

Although Malory follows the stanzaic *Morte Arthur* closely in his adaptation of the scene between Lancelot and Guenevere, he adds reminders of Lancelot's failure on the Grail quest in the earlier Tale VI. There is nothing in the immediate sources to correspond to Lancelot's response when Guenevere doubts his conversion and says that she believes he 'woll turne to the worlde agayne.' Lancelot replies:

> 'For in the queste of the Sankgreall I had that tyme forsakyn the vanytees of the worlde, had nat youre love bene. And if I had done so at that tyme with my harte, wylle, and thought, I had passed all the knyghtes that ever were in the Sankgreall except sir Galahad my sone' (3:1253).

Thus a major intertext for Malory's depiction of Lancelot and Guenevere at the convent is Malory's own sixth tale, his account of the quest for the Holy Grail.

The allusion to Galahad recalls that he, in Malory's version, had given Lancelot a warning at the end of the quest similar to the one Guenevere gives him. Galahad had said to Bors, 'My fayre lorde, salew me unto my lorde sir Launcelot, my fadir, and as sone as ye se hym bydde hym remembir of this worlde unstable' (2:1035). And indeed Bors conveys the warning to Lancelot in the last lines of the tale: 'Sir Galahad prayde you to remembir of thys unsyker worlde as ye behyght hym whan ye were togydirs more than halffe a yere.' Lancelot replies, 'I truste to God hys prayer shall avayle me' (2.1036). Unfortunately, Galahad's prayer does not help Lancelot, for at the beginning of the following tale:

> sir Launcelot began to resorte unto quene Gwenivere agayne and forgate the promyse and the perfeccion that he made in the queste; for...had nat sir Launcelot bene in his prevy thoughtes and in hys myndis so sette inwardly to the quene as he was in semynge outewarde to God, there had no knyght passed hym in the queste of the Sankgreall. But ever his thoughtis prevyly were on the quene, and so they loved togydirs more hotter than they dud toforehonde (2:1045).

At the end of the final tale Guenevere fears that he will again forget 'the promyse and the perfeccion.'

What is at issue here is Lancelot's instability, his inability to renounce the unstable world that he must abandon if he is to be saved. Related to the theme of instability and stability is that of disloyalty and loyalty, one of the major concerns of medieval literature. Derek Brewer has suggested that loyalty 'creates the stability which Malory so much cherishes.'[14] Yet Lancelot's loyalty to Guenevere leads to instability in the kingdom because that loyalty to Guenevere leads to Lancelot's disloyalty to Arthur and to Lancelot's own instability, his forgetting the promise he had made on the Grail quest to renounce the world and Guenevere. At the end of Malory's book that same loyalty to Guenevere, not to Arthur or to the promise he had made on the Grail quest, leads to stability and salvation. His loyalty to her makes him reject her admonition to return to his kingdom and marry and causes him to follow the same path she has taken. As Felicity Riddy has observed, Lancelot's 'conversion is not born out of penitence, as Guinevere's is, but is initiated by her rejection of him.'[15] Similarly, Carol Hart writes that Malory's 'heroine elevates his hero to the spiritual plane,'[16] and Lori Walters describes Guenevere as having 'ultimate responsibility…as the keeper of morality.'[17] In rejecting him, Guenevere becomes his guide; and she succeeds where Galahad had failed.

P.J.C. Field and Derek Brewer have commented on the general lack of irony in *Le Morte Darthur*. Although both have observed that while characters may at times use irony in speaking to one another, one does not find a narrator with an 'ironic superiority' over the other characters nor, in Brewer's words, does one find an 'ironic culture' in Malory.[18] For the most part, these observations are true. However, there is a major irony in the presentation of Guenevere as the one who is able to lead Lancelot to salvation. Galahad was the perfect knight who saved those imprisoned in the Castle of Maidens, who restored the sight of the blind king Mordrain, who healed the maimed King Pelles, and who saw the wonders of the Grail. Yet the Galahad who performed miracles and saved so many was unable to cause his father to turn permanently from the world and was thus incapable of saving him.

This irony, of course, is present in the French source as well. His name in the French Vulgate was Galaad and echoed the name Mt. Galaad in the Vulgate Old Testament (Mt. Gilead in the King James Version and the Revised Standard Version), the mountain of witness representing the covenant between Laban and Jacob.[19] According to commentators such as Isidore of Seville and the Venerable Bede, Mt. Galaad prefigured the great covenant between God and the human race that was represented by God's sending His son into the world. It became a figure of Christ.[20] The correspondence between Lancelot and Galaad in the French Vulgate *Queste* parallels the correspondence between Adam and Christ, the perfect man flawed by sin contrasted with his successor, the sinless son of God who through the harrowing of Hell was able to save Adam. The correspondence in the French source also breaks down at this point: for Galaad does not cause Lancelot to renounce the world. However, in the French source, neither does Guenevere. In the French Vulgate *Mort Artu* Lancelot becomes a monk after experiencing suffering and losses of various types, only one of which is the giving up of Guenevere by returning her to Arthur. And that is a major difference between

Malory's book and the thirteenth-century French romance. In Malory's *Le Morte Darthur*, a book that with its emphasis on knighthood might appear to have been written by an author primarily interested in masculine loyalties, it is remarkable that a woman was able to achieve what Galahad had not.

This is particularly arresting when one considers that on the Grail quest women had been depicted as a stumbling-block on the road to salvation. In both the French Vulgate *Queste* and in Malory's adaptation of it, when the knights are to depart on the Grail quest an old man tells the knights 'none in thys quest' is to take 'lady' nor 'jantillwoman with hym.'[21] Lancelot on the quest confesses 'how he had loved a quene unmesurabely and oute of mesure longe' and promises to come no more into that queen's fellowship.[22] But even though he repents, because of his past love for Guenevere, Lancelot cannot approach the Grail and does not rank with Galahad, Perceval and Bors as one of the Grail knights.

Ironically because of his love for and loyalty to Guenevere, at the end Lancelot forsakes the world. By following her example, he achieves a stability that he had been unable to achieve earlier. Initially this is not so much because he has religious conviction but because he could not be disloyal to Guenevere. He could not, as she suggested, return to his own kingdom and marry someone else. He withdraws from the world only because she has done so. He becomes a monk, serves 'God day and nyght with prayers and fastynges' (3.1254), and becomes a model for the other knights to follow:

> Thus they [Lancelot and his knights] endured in grete penaunce syx yere. And than syr Launcelot took th' abyte of preesthode of the Bysshop, and a twelve-monthe he sange masse. And there was none of these other knyghtes but they redde in bookes and holpe for to synge masse, and range bellys, and dyd lowly al maner of servyce. And soo their horses wente where they wolde, for they toke no regarde of no worldly rychesses; for whan they sawe syr Launcelot endure suche penaunce in prayers and fastynges they toke no force what payne they endured, for to see the nobleste knyght of the world take such abstynaunce that he waxed ful lene (3:1255).

On the night of Lancelot's death, the former Bishop of Canterbury tells Bors of a vision he had: 'Truly...here was syr Launcelot...with mo angellis than ever I sawe men in one day. And I sawe the angellys heve up syr Launcelot unto heven, and the yates of heven opened ayenst hym' (3:1258).

Maureen Fries, in writing of the final meeting between Lancelot and Guenevere, observes that Guenevere's rejection of Lancelot's offer of marriage and of his request for a final kiss 'casts her into a heroic mold, but it is a male-inspired one: that of the repentant worldly woman, on the model of

Mary Magdalene, Mary of Egypt and other formerly sexual females.'[23] Male authors from Geoffrey of Monmouth and the later chroniclers to the authors of the French and English romances that tell of the death of Arthur believed that the convent was the best place for Guenevere. The authors of the French Vulgate Cycle who added the story of Lancelot's love for Guenevere, however, must have been egalitarian-minded individuals who also believed that if Guenevere belonged in a convent at the end, Lancelot belonged in a monastery. And the author of the final meeting of Lancelot and Guenevere that was added to the Palatinus manuscript and the author of the English stanzaic Morte gave Guenevere the dignity of leading Lancelot to repentance, a holy life, and salvation. What Malory added to what he found in his sources was the allusion to Galahad with its reminder of two failures: Lancelot's failure to achieve the Grail and Galahad's failure to save his father. Guenevere does what Galahad, that knight created for the Vulgate cycle and idealized by the French Cistercian author who wrote the Queste, could not do: she who had caused Lancelot's downfall now leads him to salvation.

Galahad, because of his perfection, was sometimes exalted as an ideal by nineteenth-century authors and artists, but he has had less appeal in the twentieth century. Guenevere, on the other hand, continues to fascinate as one who has gone through sin, suffering, acknowledgment of sin, and repentance. For Guenevere the ending of Le Morte Darthur is not the tragic one that it is for the Arthurian kingdom as a whole. She achieves salvation for herself and enables Lancelot to achieve it. The ending for them is that of a Divine Comedy. Guenevere becomes, as T.H. White describes her, 'a woman who had grown a soul.'

UNIVERSITY OF NORTH CAROLINA, CHAPEL HILL

Edward Donald Kennedy is Professor of English and Chair of Comparative Literature at the University of North Carolina at Chapel Hill. His work includes Chronicles and Other Historical Writing (vol. 8 of A Manual of the Writings in Middle English, gen. ed. Albert E. Hartung), King Arthur: A Casebook, and numerous articles and reviews, primarily on Arthurian subjects and chronicles. He is editor of Studies in Philology and on the editorial boards of Arthuriana and of the series Medieval Chronicles.

NOTES

1 T.H. White, The Once and Future King (1958; New York: Berkeley Publishing Corporation, 1971), p. 564.

2 Derek Brewer, ed., Malory: The Morte Darthur: Parts Seven and Eight, York Medieval Texts (London: Edward Arnold, 1968), p. 18.

3 Thelma S. Fenster, Arthurian Women: A Casebook, Arthurian Characters and Themes 3 (New York: Garland Publishing, 1996), p. xxiv; Terence McCarthy,

Reading the Morte Darthur, Arthurian Studies 20 (Cambridge: D.S. Brewer, 1988), pp. 121–24.

4 Sir Thomas Malory, *The Works of Sir Thomas Malory*, ed. Eugène Vinaver, rev. P.J.C. Field, 3d edn., 3 vols. (Oxford: Clarendon Press, 1990), 2:669–70. Subsequent quotations from Malory's work will appear within parentheses in the text.

5 Brewer, ed., *Malory: The* Morte Darthur: *Parts Seven and Eight,* p. 19.

6 Derek Brewer 'Malory: The Traditional Writer and the Archaic Mind,' *Arthurian Literature* 1 (1981): 108 [94–120].

7 *La Mort le Roi Artu,* ed. Jean Frappier, 3d edn. (Geneva: Droz, 1964), pp. 157–58, 254.

8 Jean Frappier, *Étude sur La Mort le Roi Artu,* 3d edn. (Geneva: Droz, 1972), pp. 229–43.

9 *La Mort le Roi Artu,* ed. Frappier, pp. 216–19.

10 Jean Frappier, 'Sur un remaniement de *La Mort Artu* dans un manuscrit du XIVe siècle: Le Palatinus Latinus 1967,' *Romania* 57 (1931): 214–22.

11 Frappier includes this scene as an appendix in his edition of *La Mort le Roi Artu,* pp. 264–66.

12 See my 'The Stanzaic *Morte Arthur*: The Adaptation of a French Romance for an English Audience,' in *Culture and the King: The Social Implications of the Arthurian Legend,* ed. Martin B. Shichtman and James P. Carley (Albany: State University of New York Press, 1994), pp. 102–104 [91–112].

13 *Le Morte Arthur: A Romance in Stanzas of Eight Lines,* ed. J. Douglas Bruce, EETS ES 88 (1903; repr. London: Oxford University Press, 1959), lines 3622–3745.

14 Brewer, 'Traditional Writer and the Archaic Mind,' 109.

15 Felicity Riddy, *Sir Thomas Malory,* Medieval and Renaissance Authors (Leiden: E. J. Brill, 1987), p. 157.

16 Carol Hart, 'Newly Ancient: Reinventing Guenevere in the *Morte Darthur,*' in *Sovereign Lady: Essays on Women in Middle English Literature,* ed. Muriel Whitaker (New York: Garland Publishing, 1995), p. 18 [3–20].

17 Lori J. Walters, ed., *Lancelot and Guenevere: A Casebook,* Arthurian Characters and Themes 4 (New York: Garland Publishing, 1996), p. xxxi; similarly Sarah J. Hill, 'Recovering Malory's Guenevere,' *Proceedings of the Medieval Association of the Midwest* 1 (1991): 148 [131–48]; rep. in Walters, *Lancelot and Guenevere,* p. 277 [267–77].

18 P.J.C. Field, *Romance and Chronicle: A Study of Malory's Prose Style* (London: Barrie & Jenkins, 1971), pp. 111–12, 147–48; Brewer, 'Traditional Writer and the Archaic Mind,' 108.

19 Gen. 31:25–54

20 See Albert Pauphilet, *Études sur* La Queste del Saint Graal (1921; rep. Paris: Champion, 1980), pp. 135–38; Pauline Matarasso, *The Redemption of Chivalry: A Study of the* Queste del Saint Graal (Geneva: Droz, 1979), p. 38.

21 *Works,* 2:869; similarly, *La Queste del Saint Graal,* ed. Albert Pauphilet (1923; rep. Paris: Champion, 1972), p. 19.

22 *Works,* 2:897; *Queste,* ed. Pauphilet, pp. 66–67.

23 Maureen Fries, 'Female Heroes, Heroines, and Counter-Heroes: Images of Women in Arthurian Literature,' in *Arthurian Women,* ed. Fenster, p. 66 [59–73].

Gilding the Lily (Maid): Elaine of Astolat

JAMES NOBLE

Misogynist that he was, Malory appears to have taken some pains to reconstruct the Elaine of his source text into the embodiment of what he defines as the 'erthely woman.' Tennyson also sees things to admire in Malory's Elaine but ultimately represents her as a 'false' woman in the making. (JN)

Whether I'm teaching Malory's Arthuriad or Tennyson's, I have come to expect a spirited class discussion the day we deal with the figure known to both Malory and Tennyson as Elaine of Astolat. Elaine invariably finds sympathetic support from some members of the class who see her as a tragic figure, a woman who dies for love when Lancelot rejects her offer of marriage. Students less affected by the romantic circumstances surrounding Elaine's death are more inclined to see her as a caricature of the submissive woman who kills herself when rebuffed by the man to whom she hopes to subjugate herself for the rest of her life. I have heard Malory's Elaine described as a woman committed to spending her life as Lancelot's 'doormat' and Tennyson's Elaine as 'a noisy drama queen' who ought to have been silenced by death a couple of hundred lines earlier than she is.

My concern in this paper, however, is not the different ways we may be inclined to read Elaine of Astolat today but how Malory and Tennyson would seem to have read her in their respective source texts and chosen to inscribe her into the culture of their respective Arthuriads as a particular *type* of woman. To compare the Elaine of Malory's text with her counterpart in *La Mort le Roi Artu* is to discover evidence of a good deal of reconstruction on Malory's part, reconstruction that serves to transform Elaine into a figure sufficiently secure in her identity as a woman to take to task no less influential an authority figure in her culture than the churchman who has come to administer the last rites to her. To compare Tennyson's Elaine with Malory's, the figure from whom she derives, is to see similarities between the two women but also differences which speak to Tennyson's conviction that women come in only two varieties—*fair* and *false*—and that as fair as the lily maid of Astolat might *appear* to be, she is actually a false woman in the making.

That both Malory and Tennyson should have devoted particular attention to the figure of Elaine of Astolat is, in itself, noteworthy, given that she plays a relatively minor role in the grand scheme of the Arthurian story and given that neither Malory nor Tennyson seems to have been a particular admirer of women to begin with. For more than it is anything else, the world of Malory's Arthuriad is a world of knights and tournaments, a world where men prove their worth by engaging in feats of arms with other men, a world where the ultimate loyalty a man owes is not to a female partner but to his (male) God, his (male) king, and his fellow knights—i.e., to other men. That women should emerge as marginalized figures in such a social construct is almost inevitable. That they should be perceived and portrayed as an ever-present threat to the stability and welfare of the hegemony, however, speaks directly to a misogyny that informs Malory's telling of the Arthurian story and his treatment of the female characters who participate in it.

That Malory believed his knights would have profited by avoiding women altogether is clearly reflected in Lancelot's famous speech in 'The Book of Sir Launcelot' concerning his choice to remain unattached to a woman as either a husband or a lover:

> 'Fayre damesell...I may nat warne peple to speke of me what hit pleasyth hem. But for to be a weddyd man, I thynke hit nat, for than I muste couche with hir and leve armys and turnamentis, batellys and adventures. And as for to sey to take my pleasaunce with peramours, that woll I refuse : in prencipall for drede of God, for knyghtes that bene adventures sholde nat be advoutrers nothir lecherous, for than they be nat happy nother fortunate unto the werrys; for other they shall be overcom with a sympler knyght than they be hemself, other ellys they shal sle by unhappe and hir cursednesse bettir men than they be hemself. And so who that usyth peramours shall be unhappy, and all thynge unhappy that is aboute them.'[1]

Whether or not Lancelot is practicing what he preaches at this point in his relationship with Guenevere has been the subject of some debate,[2] but the misogynous perception underpinning the speech—the perception that woman is an ever-present threat to the success of knightly endeavors—is reflected elsewhere in Malory's text: in the injunction that knights must forswear all dealings with women in the pursuit of the holy grail (2:868–69), for example; in the repeated eremitical utterances to the effect that Lancelot can never hope to achieve the grail until he atones for the sin of having 'loved a quene unmesurably and oute of mesure longe' (2:897); and in the devil's decision to test the faith of both Percival and Bors by assuming the guise of a seductive female (2:915–19, 2:964–68). Equally misogynous is the notion that the various enchantresses of Malory's text—Morgan le Fay, Dame

Brusen, the mother of Sir Urry, Hellewes the Sorceress, and Aunowre, for example—are an ever-present threat to the welfare of Arthur and his knights because their knowledge of magic and their complete disregard for the sexual mores of the dominant culture make it impossible for the men of that culture to control them.[3] Finally, the destructive effect of women on the lives of even the best of Arthur's knights is to be seen in the madness that afflicts both Lancelot and Tristram as a consequence of having fallen in love; in the untimely deaths of such distinguished knights as Tristram, Accolon, and Lamorak, all of whom die for the sake of a woman; and in the despair over Iseult that debilitates Palomides and, for a long time, prevents him from measuring up fully to his potential as a knight.

Yet in the midst of all this misogyny emerges Elaine of Astolat, a figure to whom Malory evidently devoted some thought and seems to have taken some pains to treat sympathetically. Malory may well have found it safer to accord Elaine a more sympathetic treatment than he was inclined to afford the more influential women of his text—the Gueneveres, the Iseults, the Morgans, the Morgauses to which I have just alluded—for, in his source, Elaine is a shadowy figure whose primary function is to serve as a foil for Guenevere. In her unswerving devotion to Lancelot throughout the episode, the Maid of Astolat emerges as the antithesis of the raging and faithless Guenevere who wishes Lancelot shamed and dead, who swears to hate him all the days of her life, and who drives him and his kin from the court.[4] Although she functions to some extent in this same capacity as foil in Malory's text, Elaine emerges as a woman quite different from her prototype.

The woman Malory was to name Elayne le Blanke is nameless in his source text and referred to only as 'the girl' or 'the vavasour's daughter.' When Lancelot arrives at her father's home requesting lodging for the night but refusing to disclose his identity, the vavasour's daughter presses Lancelot's squire until he finally identifies Lancelot as the finest knight in the world. Once she is in possession of this information, 'the girl' goes directly to Lancelot and tricks him into agreeing to wear her sleeve at the tournament at Winchester. Kneeling before him, she asks him for a gift by the faith he owes to whatever he loves most in the world.[5] When Lancelot grants her request and discovers that he has been duped into wearing the maiden's sleeve into battle, he is annoyed but feels compelled to keep his promise. Before he has any chance to change his mind, 'the girl straight away brought him her sleeve attached to a plume, and begged him to carry out feats of arms at the tournament for her love, so that she could consider that her sleeve had been put to good use.'[6]

In Malory's version of the story, Elaine is introduced as a young woman awed by the presence of the knight who has sought lodging at her father's home but refused to disclose his identity. Unlike her French prototype, Malory's maiden makes no attempt to find out who Lancelot is. Instead, Malory informs us, 'ever she behylde sir Launcelot wondirfully' (2:1067). Like her French counterpart, she falls hopelessly in love with Lancelot and asks him to wear her token into battle: 'So thus as she cam to and fro, she was so hote in love that [she] besought sir Launcelot to were uppon him at the justis a tokyn of hers' (2:1067). Reluctant to grant the request 'because he had never aforne borne no maner of tokyn of no damesell' (2:1067), Lancelot ultimately complies when he realizes that the sleeve will assist him in maintaining his disguise at the tournament. That evening Lancelot leaves his shield in the maid's keeping and departs for Winchester.

The decisiveness exhibited by the maid of the French text in her efforts to get Lancelot to wear her sleeve in the tournament at Winchester is evidenced again in the conversations she has with Gawain and Lancelot later in the romance. Notwithstanding the fact that he has identified himself as the king's nephew and therefore her social better, Elaine unhesitatingly rebuffs Gawain's professions of love and declares unequivocally that the only man she will ever love is Lancelot. She is equally straightforward in her dealings with Lancelot when she discovers that he is about to leave the house where he has been recuperating after his injury in the tournament. Telling him that she has been unable to eat or drink, rest or sleep, and that she has suffered every kind of pain and grief imaginable for his sake, the maid announces that she will die if Lancelot does not return her love. When Lancelot rebukes her for her madness in loving him although he has already informed her that he is committed to another, the vavasour's daughter takes to her bed and dies. In the letter found in her purse when her body arrives in Camelot, she tells Arthur's knights that she has 'died for the noblest man in the world, and also the wickedest.' 'He is the wickedest,' she explains, 'as far as I know because however much I begged him with tears and weeping he refused to have mercy on me, and I took it so much to heart that as a result I died from loving faithfully' (94).

Although the Elaine of Malory's text also asks Lancelot to wear her sleeve into battle, her request, as we have already seen, has none of the duplicity about it that characterizes the request of her prototype. Instead, Malory would have us see the maid's request as that of a naive young woman awed by the presence of Lancelot in her father's house. Further evidence of the naiveté with which Malory attempts to invest his Elaine is to be discerned in the episode having to do with the disclosure of Lancelot's shield. When Gawain asks to see the shield in the French text, 'the vavasour's daughter' accompanies him to the bedroom where it is being stored. When she offers to take Gawain to the shield in Malory's text, her father intervenes and tells Elaine to send a servant to fetch the shield; sensing, as she obviously does not, the dangers inherent in her being alone in a bedroom with the lecherous Gawain, Elaine's father compensates for the maid's naiveté and lack of experience with the opposite sex (2:1078).

In Malory's source, the maid of Astolat happens entirely by accident upon the ailing Lancelot and, although she is said to have remained with him until he recovers, nothing is made of her tending to Lancelot's welfare in the way her English counterpart does. As soon as she hears that Lancelot has been injured in the tournament, Malory's Elaine requests her father's permission to go looking for Lancelot, saying that she will go mad unless she is able to find him. When she manages to do so, she twice faints at the sight of Lancelot lying 'so syke and pale in hys bed' (2:1082). Once she has recovered from the shock of seeing Lancelot so ill, however, Elaine becomes his nurse, tending him day and night for almost a month. Bors cannot fail to notice the maiden's devotion to Lancelot, remarking that her attentiveness suggests that she loves him 'intyerly' (2:1084). Indeed, the narrator himself takes pains to applaud Elaine's devotion to Lancelot by remarking 'that there was never chylde nother wyff more mekar tyll fadir and husbande than was thys Fayre Maydyn of Astolat' (2:1085).

When a recovered Lancelot announces his intention to return to Camelot, the Elaine of Malory's text asks him to marry her with a directness comparable to that of her French counterpart. Unlike the latter, however, who immediately resigns herself to the prospect of an imminent death when her proposal is rebuffed, Malory's Elaine shocks Lancelot by making a second request—that he make her his paramour instead. Lancelot's response reflects in every way patriarchy's conviction that woman is a male possession denied the right to chart her own course: '"Jesu deffende me!" seyde sir Launcelot. "For then I rewarded youre fadir and youre brothir full evyll for their grete goodnesse"' (2:1089). In a homoerotic twist, Elaine's brother, who professes himself to be as unwilling and unable as his sister to be separated from Lancelot, is invited by Lancelot to accompany him to Camelot.

Although Elaine's death comes as quickly in Malory's text as it does in his French source, Malory's Elaine attains in the last moments of her life an identity that sets her apart from both her French prototype and her Victorian protégée. For in these final moments, in what amounts to her 'swan song,' she becomes the embodiment of what she herself defines as the 'erthely woman.' Chastised by her confessor for mourning the loss of an earthly lover when she ought to be contemplating heavenly love instead, Elaine in no uncertain terms defends her right to love whom she chooses:

> "Why sholde I leve such thoughtes? Am I nat an erthely woman? And all the whyle the brethe ys in my body I may complayne me, for my belyve ys that I do none offence, thou[gh] I love an erthely man, unto God, for He fourmed me thereto, and all maner of good love comyth of God. And othir than good love loved I never sir Launcelot du Lake. And I take God to recorde, I loved never none but hym, nor never shall, of erthely creature; and a clene maydyn I am for hym and for all othir. And sitthyn hit ys the sufferaunce of God that I shall dye for so noble a knyght, I beseche The, Hyghe Fadir of Hevyn, have mercy uppon me and my soule, and uppon myne unnumerable paynys that I suffir may be alygeaunce of parte of my synnes. For, Swete Lorde Jesu," seyde the fayre maydyn, "I take God to recorde I was never to The grete offenser nother ayenste Thy lawis but that I loved thys noble knyght, sir Launcelot, oute of mesure. And of myselff, Good Lorde, I had no myght to withstonde the fervent love, wherefore I have my deth!" (2:1093)

It is significant, I believe, that this defense of human love should stand unchallenged in Malory's text. As C. David Benson has remarked, 'Any moral theologian could find holes in Elaine's argument,' but her confessor remains silent.[7] In providing Elaine with such a spirited defense of herself and her actions, Malory would seem to be putting the final touches on the portrait of a woman he sees as different from other women in the Arthurian story. In his efforts to feminize the Elaine of his source text by making her naive rather than willful, maternal in her concern for Lancelot's health, and an 'erthely woman' so in love with Lancelot that she cannot bear to live without him, Malory would seem to be celebrating the prospect of earthly love as a viable option for knighthood, albeit only under special circumstances. The circumstances, of course, require that the woman be an Elaine, a woman prepared to subject herself completely to the needs and desires of her knight, lover, or husband. Such a woman is not the threat to knighthood that, from Malory's perspective, women in general tend to be because her primary concern is not her own welfare but her lover's; indeed, Malory seems to be saying that, unlike Guenevere, for example, who is at this point so caught up in her jealousy, anger, and self-pity that she is prepared to destroy Lancelot, the 'erthely woman' properly motivated is a potential asset to knighthood.

The passivity and willing subservience of Malory's Elaine could hardly have failed to appeal to Tennyson, given that his ideal woman is she who is prepared to efface herself completely for the sake of serving her husband.

The embodiment of the 'erthely woman' in Tennyson's text is not Elaine, however, but the long-suffering Enid, a woman who unquestioningly endures the verbal and psychological abuse, not to mention the physical dangers, to which Geraint subjects her when he suspects her of having been unfaithful to him. Her reward for having proven herself a 'fair' woman, as opposed to the 'false' woman Geraint thinks her to be, is what Tennyson clearly perceived to be the thing women want most—bourgeois domesticity. With evident satisfaction, Tennyson concludes the tale of Geraint and Enid with 'Enid the Good' living happily with her husband in their home amid 'The cry of children, Enids and Geraints / Of times to be.'[8] Clearly, it is precisely this kind of domesticity that Tennyson's Elaine also longs for once she falls in love with Lancelot. Tellingly, Elaine exhibits the same desire to be 'sweet and serviceable'[9] to Lancelot that Enid exhibits in her relationship with Geraint. Although her love for Arthur's greatest knight is not reciprocated, Elaine tirelessly and without thought for her personal welfare tends an ailing Lancelot in the way Enid cares for the wounded Geraint. When pain occasions Lancelot to speak discourteously to Elaine, she 'Sweetly forbore him ever, being to him / Meeker than any child to a rough nurse, / Milder than any mother to a sick child.'[10] When her proposal of marriage to Lancelot is rebuffed, the maid declares that a life of service outside of marriage will suffice. Denied the option of becoming Lancelot's paramour, a role her medieval prototype proposes for herself, Tennyson's Elaine offers to become Lancelot's squire: '"No, no," she cried, "I care not to be wife / But to be with you still, to see your face, / To serve you, and to follow you thro' the world".'[11]

That a woman so eager to serve him might well have made Lancelot a good wife is recognized by the ultimate authority figure in Tennyson's text—Arthur himself:

> ...but now I would to God,
> Seeing the homeless trouble in thine eyes,
> Thou couldst have loved this maiden, shaped, it seems,
> By God for thee alone, and from her face,
> If one may judge the living by the dead,
> Delicately pure and marvellously fair,
> Who might have brought thee, now a lonely man
> Wifeless and heirless, noble issue, sons
> Born to the glory of thy name and fame,
> My knight, the great Sir Lancelot of the Lake.[12]

How much more succinctly could Tennyson have summarized the qualities of what he perceived to be a 'fair' woman? She is virtuous, beautiful, faithful, domestic, and maternal; capable, it should be noted, of producing not simply 'issue,' but '*sons* / Born to the glory of [a man's] name and fame.' Arthur's sadness that Elaine proves incapable of assuaging 'the homeless trouble' in Lancelot's eyes is echoed by the narrator who speculates that 'peradventure had he seen her first / She might have made this and that other world / Another world for the sick man.'[13] Such is the power of 'maiden passion for a maid,' as Arthur declares on another occasion:

> ...for indeed I knew
> Of no more subtle master under heaven
> Than is the maiden passion for a maid,
> Not only to keep down the base in man,
> But teach him high thought, and amiable words
> And courtliness, and the desire of fame,
> And love of truth, and all that makes a man a man.[14]

Because Lancelot's days of 'maiden passion' are long past by the time he encounters the Maid of Astolat, she is unable to effect for him the kind of regeneration Enid successfully facilitates for Geraint. We are left to conclude that, as regrettable as Elaine's death is, it is a greater misfortune that the 'sweet and serviceable' Elaine proves incapable of distracting Lancelot from the passion that is destroying him and that, at the end of the idyll, leaves him wracked with despair.

Her 'sweet and serviceable' qualities notwithstanding, his Elaine is endowed with two traits of character that prevent Tennyson from admiring her in the way Malory seems to have admired her prototype. The first of these is what Tennyson terms the maid's 'fantasy,'[15] an intellectual capacity that manifests itself in Elaine's ability to imagine herself into Lancelot's life. The reader is introduced to Elaine sitting in her tower guarding the shield Lancelot has left in her keeping and for which she has made a silken cover embroidered with 'All the devices blazon'd on the shield' and to which she has added '...of her wit, / A border fantasy of branch and flower, / And yellow-throated nestling in the nest.'[16] That Elaine fancies herself the flower to Lancelot's branch is suggested by Gawain's reference to her as a 'wild flower,'[17] by her reference to herself as a 'blossom,'[18] and by her arrival at Camelot with a lily clutched in her cold hand.[19] She is also the nestling embroidered on the shield cover, of course, given that she later in the idyll describes herself as 'a little helpless innocent bird.'[20] By virtue of what Tennyson terms 'her wit,' in short, Elaine succeeds in ingratiating herself into Lancelot's life by making herself a part of his life story as the latter is inscribed on the shield cover.

Elaine's propensity for maintaining the fantasy she has constructed for herself manifests itself elsewhere in the idyll: it is to be witnessed, for example, in her mistaken assumption that 'a sudden-beaming tenderness / Of manners and of nature' that Lancelot displays at her father's table to disguise his melancholy is 'all, perchance, for her.'[21] Similarly, when she arrives to find him near death and her sleeve still attached to his helmet, Elaine's immediate assumption is that Lancelot 'meant once more perchance to tourney in it.'[22] When she tells Lancelot that she has brought him the diamond won in the tournament and Lancelot's eyes glisten in anticipation of his being able to give it to Guenevere, Elaine misreads the gleam in Lancelot's eyes and 'fancied "Is it for me."'[23] Finally, we see her fantasizing unrealistically about the reverential reception she, a virtual unknown, will be accorded at Camelot when her corpse arrives there:

> There will I enter in among them all,
> And no man there will dare to mock at me;
> But there the fine Sir Gawain will wonder at me,
> And there the great Sir Lancelot muse at me;
> Gawain, who bade a thousand farewells to me,
> Lancelot, who coldly went, nor bad me one:
> And there the King will know me and my love,
> And there the Queen herself will pity me,
> And all the gentle court will welcome me,
> And after my long voyage I shall rest![24]

Indeed, when Elaine asks her father to dress her like a queen and to deck her funeral barge '"like the Queen's"' because she wants to '"go in state to court, to meet the queen,"'[25] she is suggesting how distanced from reality she has become by virtue of having been permitted to live for so long in the fantastical construct she has devised for herself and for Lancelot. As Arthur L. Simpson has observed, Elaine is too deeply immersed in her fantasy world by this point in the idyll to be deterred in any way: 'In addition to making up her own pretty histories and creating a private and erroneous image of Lancelot,' Simpson argues, 'Elaine is so assured of the accuracy of her private fantasies and so unquestioning in her presumption of rectitude that she is simply unable to turn away from her path of self-indulgent self-destruction.'[26] Clyde de L. Ryals makes a comparable claim when he suggests that 'To [Elaine], love and death are inextricably intertwined, for her will is to merge herself with the symbol of her identity and vanish into nothingness.'[27]

Although he has her father attempt to 'blunt or break her passion,'[28] initially by having Lancelot behave discourteously to the maid and, when that action fails, by attempting to disabuse Elaine of her high opinion of

Lancelot by disclosing to her the true nature of Lancelot's relationship with the queen,[29] Tennyson would seem to be suggesting in his treatment of Elaine that even patriarchy's influential sway over a dutiful daughter will prove insufficient in the wake of a female imagination left to its own devices. Patriarchal intervention that might (and in Tennyson's opinion clearly should) have come earlier than it does fails to restore Elaine's sanity. To the news that Lancelot is the queen's lover, Elaine responds that Lancelot has obviously been maligned and that "'now it is [her] glory to have loved / One peerless, without stain… / …God's best / And greatest'" knight.[30]

His failure to 'blunt or break her passion' speaks to another of the failings of Elaine's father, however, for Tennyson is clearly of the opinion that Elaine dies not only because she has been permitted to exercise her imagination too freely but also because she has been allowed to exercise her will too freely. In the world of Tennyson's Arthuriad, women are expected to subjugate their wills to those of the male authority figures in their lives—their fathers, brothers, or husbands. Arthur makes this quite clear in announcing his intention to marry in the first idyll:

> …for saving I be joined
> To her that is the fairest under heaven,
> I seem as nothing in the mighty world,
> And cannot will my will, nor work my work
> Wholly, nor make myself in mine own realm
> Victor and lord. But were I join'd with her,
> Then might we live together as one life,
> And reigning in one will in everything
> Have power on this dark land to lighten it,
> And power on this dead world to make it live.[31]

Although the union Arthur is proposing for himself and Guenevere purports to be a partnership, it is clear from the personal pronouns he uses that the *one life* and *one will* in question are his, not theirs as equal partners. With a wife to complement and complete him, Arthur believes that he will be able to will *his* will and work *his* work wholly, become 'victor and lord' in *his* own realm. It is her willingness to subjugate her will to Geraint's in precisely this fashion that renders Enid the fairest of Tennyson's *fair* women.

Elaine's unwillingness to submit to the will of her father by divesting herself of the passion she feels for Lancelot ultimately relegates her to the ranks of the *false* woman in Tennyson's binary schema. For like her false counterparts in *Idylls of the King*, Elaine is shown to be possessed of a willfulness that is always dangerous in a woman and often destructive to the welfare of patriarchy. Her willfulness is noted early in the idyll when Elaine's father jokingly tells Lancelot that if Lavaine were to win the diamond in the tournament and give it to his sister to adorn her hair, the gesture would "'make her thrice as willful as before.'"[32] Elaine admits to her willfulness and her father's failure to curb this defect of character when she prefaces her request to go in search of the wounded Lancelot with the remark, "'Father, you call me willful, and the fault / Is yours who let me have my will.'"[33] Her father concedes to the request with a statement that he repeats four lines later in the text: "'Being so very willful you must go.'"[34] What Elaine hears her father say as he grants her permission to exercise her will, however, is "'Being so very willful you must die.'"[35] That Elaine in fact wills herself to die when Lancelot refuses to have her as either wife or squire is reflected in the mantra she adopts when she realizes that she will not be accompanying him to Camelot: 'And "Him or death," she mutter'd, "death or him" / Again and like a burthen, "Him or death."'[36] The efforts of her father and brothers notwithstanding, Elaine refuses to be dissuaded from exercising her will. Indeed, in defiance of their wishes, she declares "'Now shall I have my will'"[37] as she proceeds to make arrangements for her funereal voyage to Camelot.

Although it could be argued that Elaine does no real damage to patriarchy in willing herself to die, her determination to exercise her will despite the wishes of the male authority figures in her life renders her a potential threat to the well-being of the hegemony and thus the antithesis of the dutifully submissive 'erthely woman' of Malory's text. Instead, Tennyson's Elaine dies a Vivien, an Isolt, an Ettare, or a Guenevere in the making, for as Simpson has argued, 'her willful egocentricity becomes, one way or another, manipulative of other people: she uses them as means, as objects, for accomplishing varieties of self-aggrandizement.'[38]

Although Malory and Tennyson are perhaps not to be censured too harshly for treating her in the way their respective cultures traditionally responded to women, the fact remains that both writers are guilty of objectifying Elaine of Astolat in the way patriarchy has traditionally objectified women—by representing them as means, rather than ends. In Malory's hands, Elaine becomes, on her deathbed, a woman in her own right prepared to stand up for what she believes in. But, ultimately, in Malory's representation of her Elaine remains only a means, to either Lancelot's or some other knight's happiness. One is never given the sense that she is capable of making her own way in the world. Tennyson's Elaine fares even less well, for beneath her 'sweet and serviceable' veneer she is revealed to be manipulative and self-interested—poor qualities in 'a servant'—as well as subject to 'typically female' behavior: bouts of hysteria. 'She shrilling, "let me die!,"'[39] Tennyson's Elaine is a far cry from the equally distraught but much more self-possessed and selfless Elaine of Malory's text. Ultimately, however, by killing her off, both Malory and Tennyson prevail over the threat of femininity posed by even as timid a figure as Elaine of Astolat. Only when she is safely dead is she accorded her allotted 'fifteen minutes of fame;' in both texts, but especially in Tennyson's version of her funeral, patriarchy buries the fair maid of Astolat with far more fanfare than any of its representatives had ever seen fit to bestow on her while she lived.[40]

THE UNIVERSITY OF NEW BRUNSWICK, SAINT JOHN

James Noble is Professor of English at the Saint John Campus of The University of New Brunswick. He has published articles on a variety of Arthurian texts, both medieval and modern, and is currently working on a book that focuses on images of women in the Arthuriads of Malory, Tennyson, and five contemporary female novelists.

NOTES

1 Sir Thomas Malory, *The Works of Sir Thomas Malory*, ed. Eugène Vinaver, rev. P.J.C. Field, 3d edn., 3 vols. (Oxford: Clarendon Press, 1990), 1:270–71. Subsequent quotations from Malory's work will appear within parentheses in the text.

2 See Maureen Fries, 'Commentary: A Response to the Arthuriana Issue on Adultery,' *Arthuriana* 7.4 (1997): 94–96 [92–96].

3 For a discussion of these women as 'female counter-heroes,' see Maureen Fries, 'What Tennyson Really Did to Malory's Women,' *Quondam et Futurus: A Journal of Arthurian Interpretations* 1.1 (1991): 45–47 [44–55].

4 *La Mort le Roi Artu,* trans. James Cable as *The Death of King Arthur*, (Harmondsworth, Middlesex, England: Penguin Books, 1971), pp. 49–52 and 61.

5 Cable, *The Death of King Arthur*, p. 30.

6 Cable, *The Death of King Arthur*, p. 30.

7 C. David Benson, 'The Ending of the *Morte Darthur*,' in *A Companion to Malory*, ed. Elizabeth Archibald and A.S.G. Edwards (Cambridge, UK: D.S. Brewer, 1996), pp. 224–25 [221–38].

8 Alfred, Lord Tennyson, *Geraint and Enid,* in *Idylls of the King,* ed. J.M. Gray (London: the Penguin Group, 1983), ll. 964–65.

9 Tennyson, *Lancelot and Elaine*, in *Idylls of the King*, ed. Gray, ll. 762.

10 Tennyson, *Lancelot and Elaine*, ll. 851–53.

11 Tennyson, *Lancelot and Elaine*, ll. 933–34.

12 Tennyson, *Lancelot and Elaine*, ll. 1353–62.

13 Tennyson, *Lancelot and Elaine*, ll. 867–68.

14 Tennyson, *Guenevere*, in *Idylls of the King*, ed. Gray, ll. 474–80.

15 Tennyson, *Lancelot and Elaine*, ll. 27, 396.

16 Tennyson, *Lancelot and Elaine*, ll. 10–12.

17 Tennyson, *Lancelot and Elaine*, ll. 640.

18 Tennyson, *Lancelot and Elaine*, ll. 965.

19 Tennyson, *Lancelot and Elaine*, ll. 1141.

20 Tennyson, *Lancelot and Elaine*, ll. 889.

21 Tennyson, *Lancelot and Elaine*, ll. 326–28.

22 Tennyson, *Lancelot and Elaine*, ll. 805.

23 Tennyson, *Lancelot and Elaine*, ll. 817.

24 Tennyson, *Lancelot and Elaine*, ll. 1045–54.

25 Tennyson, *Lancelot and Elaine*, ll. 1111–17.

26 Arthur L. Simpson, Jr., 'Elaine the Unfair, Elaine the Unlovable: The Socially Destructive Artist/Woman in *Idylls of the King*,' *Modern Philology* 89 (1992): 346–47 [341–62].

27 Clyde de L. Ryals, *From the Great Deep: Essays on Idylls of the King* (Athens, OH: Ohio University Press, 1967), p. 134.

28 Tennyson, *Lancelot and Elaine*, ll. 968.

29 Tennyson, *Lancelot and Elaine*, ll. 1075–77.

30 Tennyson, *Lancelot and Elaine*, ll. 1083–87.

31 Tennyson, *The Coming of Arthur*, in *Idylls of the King*, ed. Gray, ll. 84–93.

32 Tennyson, *Lancelot and Elaine*, ll. 205.

33 Tennyson, *Lancelot and Elaine*, ll. 745–46.

34 Tennyson, *Lancelot and Elaine*, ll. 772, 776.

35 Tennyson, *Lancelot and Elaine*, ll. 778.

36 Tennyson, *Lancelot and Elaine*, ll. 897–98.

37 Tennyson, *Lancelot and Elaine*, ll. 1040.

38 Simpson, 'Elaine the Unfair,' 358.

39 Tennyson, *Lancelot and Elaine*, ll. 1019.

40 For a useful discussion of representations of the dead Elaine in Tennyson's poem and the visual arts, see Bram Dijkstra, *Idols of Perversity: Fantasies of Feminine Evil in Fin-de-Siècle Culture* (Oxford: Oxford University Press, 1986), pp. 39–42.

Malory's Other(ed) Elaine

ELIZABETH S. SKLAR

Because of the ethical ambiguity of 'The Tale of Lancelot and Elaine,' the figure of Elaine of Corbyn, Malory's "other" Elaine, has been marginalized by both modern Arthurian fiction and contemporary Arthurian scholarship, despite her thematic and narratival significance. (ESS)

> No one can help feeling the pathos of [Lancelot's] sojourn with Elaine, the acknowledged mother of his son, an honored, sad, figure, *kept wisely in the background.*[1]

Elaine of Corbyn, who shares center stage with Lancelot in the tale of 'Lancelot and Elaine,' the penultimate episode of Malory's 'Book of Sir Trystram,' is arguably second only to Guenevere as the most interesting and complexly-rendered female figure in the entire *Le Morte Darthur.* As Lancelot's seducer, lover, healer, and common-law wife, she serves a multiplicity of important narratival and thematic functions, of which her bearing of Galahad, the ordained 'enchever' of the Holy Grail, is only one. Her character is as various as her narratival functions; alternately selfish and compassionate, stubborn and compliant, bold and submissive, she is at once the victim of the entrenched patriarchal system and a remarkably successful manipulator of that system. She is also arguably the most othered of all Malory's major female figures; underservedly (if understandably) eclipsed by the more socially presentable 'lily maid of Astolat,' this Elaine has suffered denigration and suppression in the post-medieval literary canon, having been undeservedly patronized and decisively marginalized by the critical and scholarly establishment as well. What I want to argue here is that the othering of Malory's 'other' Elaine probably has more to do with the problematics of the tale itself, the ethical discomfiture it engenders, and residual post-Victorian ideologies on the part of modern writers and critics, than it does with Malory's own figuring of Elaine. Indeed, there is ample evidence, I shall suggest, from Malory's treatment of his source material that he took pains to foreground Elaine of Corbyn by more fully rendering her character and amplifying her role in the important episode in which she is featured.[2]

I

Since the tale of 'Lancelot and Elaine,' as well as its female protagonist, has tended to get short shrift in the history of Malory studies, a summary is probably in order here.[3] The narrative concerning the relationship between Elaine of Corbyn and Lancelot occurs in three passes. The first of these revolves around an event described by J.D. Bruce as 'the cardinal episode of the Grail romances'[4] and certainly one of central thematic import to the remainder of Malory's Arthuriad: the begetting of Galahad. It transpires thus: In the course of his wanderings, Lancelot arrives at the Castle of Corbyn, where, after accomplishing two 'strange adventures,' both supernatural, both earmarked for 'the beste knyght of the worlde' (2:792), he is welcomed by Pelles, 'kynge of the forayne contre' and temporary guardian of the Grail. Knowing that 'sir Launcelot shulde gete a pusyll uppon his doughtir, whyche shulde be called sir Galahad'(2:794), Pelles calls upon Dame Brusen, 'one of the grettyst enchaunters that was that tyme in the worlde' (2:794), for advice on how to get Lancelot into bed with his virgin daughter, Elaine. Through a combination of trickery—Lancelot is led to believe that Guenevere is near by, requesting his company—and witchery—Brusen gives Lancelot a 'kupp of wyne' laced with a fast-acting aphrodisiac (2:795)—Lancelot is brought to bed with Elaine, happily believing that he is coupling with Guenevere. The morning after, however, is anything but blissful. Affronted by the deception, Lancelot draws his sword on Elaine threatening to kill her, but is dissuaded when Elaine informs him that she is the daughter of his host and already carries in her womb the child who will become 'the most nobelyste knyght of the worlde' (2:796). In a stunning *volte face*, not necessarily to his credit, Lancelot relents and, as the tale telleth, 'toke her up in his armys and kysed her' forthwith, 'for she was a fayre lady, and thereto lusty and yonge...' (2:796).

The second pass, which occurs after an unspecified lapse in narrative time, recounts the disastrous results of Elaine's decision to attend a 'grete feste' mounted by King Arthur (2:802–808). Having followed her father's advice to 'be well beseyne in the most rychest wyse' (2:802)—if nothing else, Pelles knows how to package his daughter—she is unanimously acknowledged the 'fayrest and the beste beseyne lady that ever was seyne in that courte' (2:803). But Lancelot is so ashamed at having drawn his sword on her that he will neither greet her nor speak with her. Distressed by his neglect—indeed 'so hevy she wente her harte wolde have to-braste' (2:803)—Elaine complains to Dame Brusen, who promises that Lancelot will be in her bed that very night. And so it comes to pass, as it had at Corbyn, that Lancelot is again tricked into Elaine's arms in the belief that he is embracing the queen, who has, in fact, cannily invited him 'to hir chambir that nyght' for the explicit purpose of keeping him out of Elaine's bed (2:804). Unfortunately for all concerned, including the kingdom at large, Elaine happens to be lodged in the queen's own chambers. Upon hearing Lancelot 'clatir in his slepe' from another woman's bed, and already angered by Lancelot's failure to keep his rendez-vous with her, Guenevere confronts him, and summarily banishes him from her chamber and forever from her sight (2:805). After recovering from the swoon into which shock has sent him, Lancelot leaps 'oute at a bay-wyndow,' *sans* both clothing and wits. The episode concludes with a spiteful argument between Elaine and Guenevere, each blaming the other for Lancelot's madness, and the scene culminates in a terse indictment of both women by Sir Bors: '[B]etwyxt you bothe,' he exclaims, 'ye have destroyed a good kynght' (2:807).

The final encounter of Lancelot with Elaine takes place after a period of approximately five years, during which time Lancelot has run 'as wylde woode as ever was man' (2:806). Blundering his way back to the Castle of Corbyn, Lancelot is adopted as court 'foole' by the castle's inhabitants, who supply him with straw to sleep on and daily 'throw hym mete and set hym drynke' (2:823). Eventually, he is discovered sleeping in a garden by Elaine, who recognizes him and asks her father's help in restoring him to health. Lancelot is carried into the Grail chamber, and 'by vertu of that holy vessel' he is 'heled and recoverde' (2:824). With the return of memory comes return of shame and the desire for exile and anonymity. At Lancelot's request, Elaine secures from her father an isolated island castle (2:826), and, expressing undying love for and devotion to Lancelot, she leaves her paternal home and follows him to his remote retreat. There they live for many years, until Lancelot is drawn back to Camelot by the news that the queen desires his return (2:831); and thus he parts from Elaine, abandoning his common-law wife, healer, and long-time companion with not so much as a backward glance, and a singular lack of regret.

II

The tale of 'Lancelot and Elaine' is unquestionably a problem piece. Erupting into the narrative at a most improbable point—immediately before the conclusion to the notoriously protracted 'Book of Sir Tristram'—it derails narrative momentum and defers closure, consigning Tristram and Palomydes, the protagonists of the preceding and concluding episodes, to a kind of narrative limbo. It is disruptive in other respects as well. Into a narrative that has been relentlessly secular and militaristic, it interjects the mysterious, the holy, the spiritual, abruptly transporting us from the familiar territory of socio-cultural pragmatics and power politics into a liminal space situated on the cutting edge of the Other World and partaking of its characteristic surreality, misdirection, and supernatural eructations. The tale as a whole nibbles away at the tenets of the chivalric value system until it is in tatters. Sir Lancelot is successively duped, humiliated, banished, degraded, and pronounced spiritually inadequate. It is not, all told, a pretty picture. No one behaves very well (with the exception of Sir Bors), or emerges entirely untarnished. Foregrounding sexuality and bespeaking the dangers of female empowerment, the tale of 'Lancelot and Elaine' is an exercise in demystification, unleashing the latent gynophobia that underpins the romance genre in general and Malory's rendering in particular; in a damning representation of the consequences of female autonomy, Guenevere, Elaine, and Dame Brusen, like a triad of malignant fates, manage to short-circuit the patriarchal structure and subvert the stability of the realm. The narrative mode caroms unnervingly from the discourse of spirituality on the one hand to the sensationalistic and downright pornographic on the other. The material itself, the fictive history, poses an unresolvable ethical conundrum: there is no getting around the fact that the conception of Galahad, that 'cardinal event' of the Arthuriad, also entails cardinal sin. A father panders to his own daughter. However virtuous the end-product of Lancelot and Elaine's coupling, and however unwittingly Lancelot participates in the event, the fact remains that Lancelot is guilty of violating a virgin because of his adulterous love for the Queen, and of betraying his lady-love in the process. And Lancelot's abandoning Elaine with nary a by your leave may give pause as well.

Given the anomalous placement of this narrative, its moral ambiguities, its anti-heroic ambiance, and what we might call the sleaze factor, it is no wonder that the Victorian fathers of the Arthurian revival did not want anything to do with either the tale of Galahad's conception or his less-than-model maternal parent. Tennyson finessed the awkward issue of Galahad's origins by simply ignoring it (thereby banishing Elaine of Corbin from the master-narrative), and others followed his lead. While nineteenth-century Arthurians in both literature and the visual arts embraced Elaine of Corbyn's more congenial and conventionally feminine namesake, Elaine of Astolat, who at least managed to negotiate her brief existence as *virgo intacta*, they not only turned their backs on, but succeeded in radically and permanently marginalizing her functionally more important and infinitely more interesting namesake: better a dead Elaine than a live and sexually active one. The inevitable outcome of this marginalization is that the modern literary tradition—when it does not exclude her from the master-narrative altogether—has irreparably muddled her fictive history and subjected her to a variety of textual abuses.[5] She has been fused more than once with Elaine of Astolat (Parke Godwin's *Firelord*, for example), and, of all things, with Morgawse (Nicole St. John's *Guinevere's Gift*). Twice she has been summarily married off, once to Lancelot (Lord Ernest Hamilton, *Lancelot* [1926]) and once to Sir Bors (Charles Williams, *Taliessin*). Even her canonical maternal role has been traduced: Richard Hovey (*Birth of Galahad*) perversely impregnates Guenevere with Galahad, demoting Elaine to the status of foster mother, while St. John afflicts her with a nasty changling in the person of Mordred. The one constant in modern representations of Elaine of Corbyn is that she is almost uniformly represented as singularly unpleasant. T.H. White's Elaine has been described as 'a vulgar and almost repulsive figure' who deprives Lancelot of his much-treasured virginity, and Godwin's as 'unattractively pious, humorless, and dull.'[6] Alternately manipulative and hysterical, this modern Elaine deliberately gets pregnant to trap Lancelot in one account (John Erskine's *Galahad*), and in another accuses Lancelot of rape to keep him from abandoning her (Thomas Berger's *Arthur Rex*).

In many ways, Malory's 'other' Elaine has been even more othered and systematically marginalized by the scholarly and critical Arthurian establishment than she has been in the literary products of the Arthurian revival. Despite its pivotal role in Malory's narrative (and in the Arthurian master-narrative), centering as it does on the conception of the future Grail knight and functioning crucially as a bridge to the quest narrative,[7] the tale of 'Lancelot and Elaine' has attracted remarkably little scholarly attention. Tellingly, in his sixty-five-page discussion of the 'Book of Sir Trystram,' the most detailed source study we have for Malory's Book v, Thomas Rumble does not so much as mention the tale of 'Lancelot and Elaine' and most other Malory scholars have attended to it only in passing.[8] Inevitably, Elaine of Corbyn gets lost in the shuffle. To my knowledge, the only detailed discussion of this Elaine is Jerome Mandel's 1984 'Constraint and Motivation in Malory's "Lancelot and Elaine."'[9] The composite portrait of Elaine of Corbyn that emerges from the otherwise rare, and for the most part cursory discussions—although it tends to be less uniformly negative than Elaine's literary representations—is piecemeal and not very coherent. Where Mandel comments upon Elaine's hypocritical and cynical manipulation of political ideology for selfish reasons,[10] Larry Benson gives us an Elaine who, in her devotion to Lancelot and her 'generosity of spirit' sounds suspiciously like another, more popular Elaine.[11] For Charles Moorman she is little more than a brood mare ('Lancelot conceives Galahad on Elaine'[12] is his sole observation on her), while both Terence McCarthy and Benson rather patronizingly limn her as a medieval version of the plucky little lady or the brave little woman, commending her temerity in standing up to Guenevere after the latter has banished Lancelot.[13] McCarthy's emphasis on Elaine's 'purity' and the 'honor involved' in her selection as Galahad's progenetrix, her sacrifice of virginity for a 'higher cause'[14] stands in interesting contrast to Maureen Fries's passing observation that the incident serves, rather, to 'slake Elaine's lust.'[15] Edmund Reiss is in the same camp: his Elaine is simply a deceitful, self-indulgent girl whose sole mission in life is to trick Lancelot into her bed.[16] Can this be the same Elaine as Scudder's 'honored, sad, figure'—or McCarthy's pure maiden or Benson's generous lass, for that matter?

III

This saga of contradiction, suppression, marginalization, and distortion indicates, if nothing else, that the figure of Elaine of Corbyn and the matter in which she is embedded has been abidingly problematic for the majority of the post-medieval readers and writers who have chanced upon it. It seems equally obvious that the problematic centers on the confrontation between her fictive history, as represented by Malory, and traditional patriarchal gender politics. The freewheeling tampering with her narrative in modern literary treatments of Elaine, the social-worker stratagems and maneuvers deployed thereto—removing her son from a dysfunctional home environment or making an honest woman of her by getting her properly married off— point to one element that sticks in the craw: as an unwed mother who not only voluntarily bedded a man with whom she had no legitimate relationship for the express purpose of becoming pregnant, but compounded her flauting of valorized female behavior by contriving yet another (semi-public) sexual encounter with him—and this after giving birth to the future Grail knight— Malory's other Elaine is simply not socially acceptable. She is an embarrassment to the Arthurian establishment, and an affront to the sacred concept of Motherhood. The unpleasant character accorded her modern composite in fictional representations, where she appears to have become a receptacle for all sorts of gynophobic *angst*, undoubtedly stems from the same impetus; perhaps we are not as distant from the ideologies of our Victorian forbears as we might like to believe. I think it goes beyond residual prudery and patriarchal hi-jinx, however. Underlying this collective exercise in denial there seems to be a scramble on the part of writers and scholar-critics, possibly because of preconceptions about medieval gender politics, to reduce Elaine of Corbyn to an acceptable, or at least a familiar, female cultural stereotype by pinning her, still wriggling, on the good woman/bad woman continuum: mother/maiden, virgin/whore, seducer/victim, helpmeet/harridan. Hence the piecemeal nature of her modern manifestations. She comes to us in fragments.

IV

Turning from our Elaine to Malory's, those fragments coalesce into an interesting and unusual assemblage. Among other things, it becomes immediately evident that Malory's other Elaine stubbornly resists traditional taxonomy; she refuses to submit to any cultural or literary stereotype, medieval or modern, because she is a complex aggregate straddling both sides of the dyadic formula and thereby transcending it. On the face of it, her disdain for normative behavior, her overt sexuality, her excesses, and the general lack of 'mesur' that those excesses entail (she has a decided flair for the histrionic) would seem to mark her as the quintessential Malorian woman, subversive and disruptive, a threat to the status quo and to the stability of the realm: in effect, she manages to do more actual damage to the kingdom's well-being than Morgan le Fey does (although narcissism and insouciance, rather than malice guide her behaviors). But Elaine of Corbyn only partially and temporarily fits the gynophobic profile of Malory's Female Other, for her antisocial behavior at court is more than counterbalanced by other, positive typologies—the 'whore,' as it were, is contained by the virgin and the helpmeet. Like a parodic Mary, impregnated through no will of her own, she is the vehicle for producing a savior, a precious vessel bearing a preordained and sacred cargo. And when she willingly forsakes the security of her paternal home to follow her beloved into exile, the analogue that comes to mind is the biblical Ruth; surely the echoes we hear in Elaine's 'And where ye be...doute ye nat but I woll be wyth you' (2:826) are not merely fortuitous. Thus, in the most abstract terms, Elaine of Corbyn is an anomaly—an othered Other, a typological composite whose multivalence defies the binary thinking we habitually invoke in our negotiations with premodern female figuration.

Malory's other Elaine is more, however, than a compendium of female typologies; she is what we formerly had permission to call a 'dynamic character': initially a commodified virgin, without agency, she makes her way through a rebellious adolescence to emerge a mature, autonomous, proactive, self-actualizing individual. This proto-novelistic character representation is itself anomalous in Malory's *oeuvre* for a non-recursive figure. Also anomalous is the degree to which her actions influence fictive history: only Guenevere and, to a lesser extent, Nyneve are similarly empowered with regard to the cycle of cause and effect in Malory's Arthuriad. Moreover, she is no mere French import. This is beyond question *Malory's* Elaine. In the process of consolidating and dramatically condensing material casually interlaced through some 300-print-pages of Old French prose, Malory has foregrounded an originally minor and vaguely delineated figure, allocating a full fifty percent of his narrative to Elaine of Corbyn.[17] He has, moreover, strategically situated the three passes in which Elaine functions as co-protagonist in initial, medial, and closing positions, so that they comprise, in effect, the organizing principle of this tale.

Malory has also radically modified her representation. Elaine's Old French counterpart is barely individuated, the merest whisper of a character, a good girl, as far as we can tell, pious, passive, obedient, all but voiceless, and utterly nameless, her identity circumscribed by and limited to her *parage* ('la fille au roy pelles' or 'la bele fille le roy de la terre foraine').[18] From this preliminary sketch, Malory fashions a fully-rendered, colorful portrait, endowing Elaine with a fictive history of her own by transforming the shadowy 'fille au roy pelles' into an Elaine animated with a distinctive identity and a distinctive voice. In contrast to her French prototype, who is more often seen than heard, Malory's Elaine, with an impressively expanded speaking role, is a vocal, outspoken lass, who says what's on her mind with little or no regard for social niceties, etiquette, or protocol, whether triumphantly announcing her pregnancy to an outraged Lancelot, sword drawn for the kill (2:795), or bluntly taking the queen to task for ruining Lancelot and forgetting where her political and spousal obligations properly belong:

> Madame, ye ar gretly to blame for sir Launcelot, for now have ye lost hym...and therefore, alas! madame, ye have done grete synne and yourselff grerte dyshonoure, for ye have a lorde royall of youre owne, and therefore hit were youre parte for to love hym; for there ys no quene in this worlde that hath suche another kynge as ye have (2:806).

The passivity of Elaine's prototype is transmuted into activity, obedience into agency. It is Elaine, not her father, who explains to a befuddled Lancelot how he finds himself at Corbyn as he recovers from a lengthy bout of amnesia (2:825); it is to Elaine, not Pelles, that Lancelot addresses his petition for a penetential retreat (2:825);[19] and unlike her OF sister, who meekly requests her father's permission to accompany Lancelot in his exile, Malory's Elaine forthrightly announces her intention to follow Lancelot into retreat and quickly translates words into action.

Malory allows Elaine physical as well vocal presence. Maidenly modesty cedes to healthy sexuality. Where 'la fille de pelles' emerges from bed the morning after the first tryst decorously draped in 'sa chemise,' humbly begging Lancelot to grant her mercy, just as 'diex eut de marie magdalaine,'[20] Elaine skips 'oute of her bed all naked.' Her plea for mercy has imperative undertones ('I requyre you to have mercy uppon me'), and is distinctly subordinate to her fairly immodest announcement of the conception that has just occurred: 'for I have in my wombe bygetyn of the that shall be the moste nobelyste knyght of the worlde' (2:796). The OF narrator, indeed, takes considerable pains to deflect attention from the sexual nature of both this encounter and the maiden herself, who submits to her father's plan not, we are specifically admonished, 'pour la biaute de lui ne pour escauffement de char'[21] but for purely patriotic motives—to restore the fertility of the land laid waste by the dolorous *coup*. There is no mistaking the motives of Malory's Elaine: a 'fayre lady, and thereto lusty and yonge...' (2:796), she openly rejoices in her first sexual encounter, 'glad...that she had gotyn sir Launcelot in her armys' (2:795), and yearns for the second more 'than all the golde that ys abovyn erthe' (2:803).

Oddly enough, for all his apparent reservations about female sexuality, Malory seems to approve his handiwork—the Pygmalion effect, perhaps. Or, to put it a tad less unfashionably, the narrative tenor here is one of forbearance towards, even a rather parental indulgence of Elaine in her lesser moments, and admiration for her finer ones. She is the 'feyre Elayne' (2:807) whose breathtaking beauty melts away Lancelot's postcoital rage, stuns the court, and impresses even the queen herself: 'And whan she cam to Camelott kynge Arthure and quene Gwenyver seyde wyth all the kynghtes that dame Elayne was the fayrest and the beste besyne lady that ever was seyne in that courte' (2:803). 'Wyse,' as well as 'lusty and younge' (2:796), she transforms an angry, scolding Sir Bors into an instant ally through her eloquence (2:807). More significantly, she serves as a kind of touchstone of false and true values in society almost obsessively concerned with appearances, and a tale equally obsessed with shifting value systems: by igniting the fuse of Guenevere's instability, she inadvertantly orchestrates the public exposure of a fissure in the structural fabric of Logres—Lancelot's relationship with the queen— that will ultimately widen into an irreparable breach, simultaneously exposing, even as she exploits it, the flawed nature of 'the floure of kynghthode' himself (2:791). And by healing Lancelot physically, mentally, and spiritually, nurturing him until such time as he is ready to resume his role at the center of Arthur's government, she crucially supports Lancelot in the penitential exercise that serves, unbeknownst to either of them, as preparation for his imminent spiritual quest. Above all, once she understands the consequences of her youthful sexual adventuring, Elaine of Corbyn—standing in eloquent contrast to Guenevere's increasingly hysterical possessiveness—becomes the exemplar of what human, heterosexual love should be, or could be if the world were less corrupt: faithful, loyal, self-sacrificing, and redemptive, willing to die if necessary, for the well-being of the other: "'Sir,'" she says to Lancelot, "'I woll lyve and dye wyth you, only for youre sake, and yf my lyff myght nat avayle you and my dethe myght avayle you, wyte you well I wolde dye for youre sake'" (2:825–6).[22] With these words, which immediately precede Lancelot's penitential retreat, Elaine serves as midwife to the New Age of Christian spirituality, already hovering in the wings.

In sum, Malory's Elaine of Corbyn, in her singular otherness, demands our attention. Although not always attractive—'Elaine the loveable' she's not—this Elaine is always compelling. Vividly rendered, vital both in her own right and to the narrative at large, she challenges our preconceptions even as she interrogates the righteousness of the Arthurian enterprise and exposes its inadequacies. And although such a cursory discussion as this can hardly aspire to do her justice, perhaps it may serve to compensate in part for the history of marginalization, suppression, and misrepresentation that has hitherto obscured Malory's other, and othered, Elaine.

WAYNE STATE UNIVERSITY

Elizabeth Sklar is on the English faculty at Wayne State University, where she teaches Old and Middle English language and literature. She has published on a variety of Arthurian subjects and has served on the Advisory Board for the International Arthurian Society. She is Area Chair for Arthurian Legend in the Popular Culture Association.

NOTES

1   Vida D. Scudder, *Le Morte Darthur of Sir Thomas Malory & Its Sources* (New York and London: E.P. Dutton & Co.; J.M. Dent & Sons, 1917), p. 270 (emphasis mine).

2   The question of Malory's sources for 'Lancelot and Elaine' is a vexed one. The common position is that Malory drew upon some version of the OF *Tristan en Prose*; Vinaver posits BNfr99, Add5474, and Vienna 2542 as the most likely exemplars. However, since the narrative concerning Elaine is imported into the Tristan story from the Prose *Lancelot*, and since it is, moreover, contiguous with the materials of Malory's Book 3 ('The Noble Tale of Sir Launcelot du Lake'), it

is equally likely that the *Lancelot* comprised Malory's source here.

3   All citations from *Le Morte Darthur* will appear within parentheses in the text. They are taken from Sir Thomas Malory, *The Works of Sir Thomas Malory*, ed. Eugène Vinaver, rev. P.J.C. Field, 3d edn., 3 vols. (Oxford: Clarendon Press, 1990).

4   J.D. Bruce, *The Evolution of Arthurian Romance: From the Beginnings down to the year 1300*, 2d ed. 2 vol. (Gloucester, MA: Peter Smith, 1958), 2:349.

5   The following discussion of treatments of Elaine in contemporary fiction are based on accounts thereof in Beverly Taylor and Elisabeth Brewer, *The Return of King Arthur* (Cambridge: Boydell and Brewer, 1983) and Raymond Thomson's *The Return from Avalon: A Study of the Arthurian Legend in Modern Fiction* (Westport, CN: Greenwood Press, 1978). References to Parke Godwin, Nicole St. John, and Lord Ernest Hamilton come from Thomson, pp. 129, 25, and 65 respectively. From Taylor and Brewer, references to Williams, Hovey, White, Erskine, and Berger are found on pages 249, 177, 293, 200, and 352, respectively.

6   Taylor and Brewer, *Return of King Arthur*, p. 319.

7   Larry D. Benson, *Malory's Morte Darthur* (Cambridge, MA: Harvard University Press, 1976), p. 128; see also my 'Malory's "Lancelot and Elaine": Prelude to a Quest,' *Arthurian Yearbook* 3 (1993): 127–40.

8   Significantly, while the index for *Malory's Originality* (ed. R.M. Lumiansky, Baltimore: Johns Hopkins,1964), in which Rumble's study appears, contains six entries for Elaine of Astolat, there is not a single entry for Elaine of Corbyn. At best, the tale of 'Lancelot and Elaine' has stirred only minor interest in scholarship that offers readings of the 'hoole book.' In *The Book of Kyng Arthur: the Unity of Malory's Morte Darthur* (Lexington KY: University of Kentucky Press, 1965), Charles Moorman, for example, mentions it only in passing, pp. 9, 31, once in connection with narrative chronology, once to dispute an eminently disputable Vinaverian dictum concerning Malory's treatment of the Grail material. Benson's brief discussion of the tale of 'Lancelot and Elaine' (*Malory's Morte Darthur*, pp. 128-133) focuses on its relation to the larger narrative, while Terence McCarthy concentrates on rationalizing the fairly nasty circumstances surrounding the begetting of Galahad: McCarthy, *An Introduction to Malory* (Cambridge: Boydell and Brewer, 1991), pp. 37, 61.

9   Jerome Mandel, 'Constraint and Motivation in Malory's "Lancelot and Elaine,"' *Papers in Language and Literature* 20.3 (1984): 243–58.

10 Mandel, 'Constraint and Motivation in Malory's "Lancelot and Elaine,"' p. 257.

11 Benson, *Malory's Morte Darthur*, pp. 132, 133. The extent to which the marginalization of Elaine is almost reflexive is perhaps indicated by the fact that although Benson mentions Elaine by name eleven times in the course of his discussion, she is completely absent from his index.

12 Charles Moorman, *The Book of Kyng Arthur*, p. 311.

13 McCarthy, *Introduction to Malory*, p. 37; Benson, *Malory's Morte Darthur*, p. 132.

14 McCarthy, *Introduction to Malory*, pp. 37,61.

15 Maureen Fries, 'Indiscreet Objects of Desire: Malory's "Tristram" and the Necessity of Defeat,' in *Studies in Malory*, ed. James W. Spisak (Kalamazoo: Western

Michigan University Press, 1985), p. 103.

16 Edmund Reiss, *Sir Thomas Malory* (New York: Twain, 1966), pp. 114, 119.

17 The 'Tale of Lancelot and Elaine' runs for thirty-six pages, of which narrative involving Elaine occupies eighteen.

18 All citations from the OF are from H. Oskar Sommer, *The Vulgate Version of the Arthurian Romances,* vol. 3 (rep. New York: AMS Press, 1969). Significantly, in G.D. West, *An Index of Proper Names in French Arthurian Prose* (Toronto: University of Toronto Press, 1978), there is no entry for this figure under any of the variant spellings of the OF version of 'Elaine' (Helains, Heliene, Helaine); in fact, she doesn't appear under any entry of her own, but rather is subsumed by her father even here, the entry for Pelles reading in part, 'The daughter, unnamed in most texts, is called Amite in *Gal*; see also Helizabel.' The cross-reference takes us to the single instance of her naming in the Prose *Tristan* (l. 300). A remote possibility exists that Malory chose her name through misreading a passage from the Prose *Lancelot*, which says that there were only two women in Britain as beautiful as Guenevere, one, from Norgales 'ot non heliene sans peir…et lautre fu fille au roi mahaignie, che fu li rois pelles' (Sommer 3:29.3–5).

19 In the OF, the king takes charge of the explanation to Lancelot (401), and Lancelot asks Pelles, not his daughter, for advice on securing a retreat (402).

20 Sommer 3:112.3.

21 Sommer 3:110.28.

22 This is the second occasion on which Elaine has stated her willingness to die for Lancelot's sake; earlier in the tale, she has told Sir Bors 'I wolde lose my lyff for hym rathir than he shulde be hurte.'

Elemental Goddesses:
Nymue, the Chief Lady of the Lake,
and Her Sisters

SUE ELLEN HOLBROOK

Approached within the paradigm of Goddess study, Malory's Nymue
and her counterparts invite re-readings of their relationship to Merlin,
inspire recognition of early religious rituals, and offer myths of
transformation for our time. Associated with the Nymue-figure's goddess
functions are landscape elements of multivalent meanings, namely,
water, woods, and (surprisingly) stones. Regarded in such Goddess
environment, Nymue may be seen not so much as defeating Merlin as
initiating a cyclic transformation. (SEH)

Nymue, the Chief Lady of the Lake in Sir Thomas Malory's *Morte
Darthur*, and her counterparts in related texts attract infamy as women
who take advantage of Merlin's sexual desire for them to learn from him the
very magic that they then turn against him. Thus, they join the queue of
deceptive temptresses. Yet this misogynist vein is only fool's gold: a richer
understanding may be gained by approaching their stories through the lenses
of Goddess mythology. A Goddess outlook highlights, as Prudence Jones
and Nigel Pennick explain, the 'female divine principle.'[1] It also recognizes,
in Juliette Wood's ecumenical phrase, 'intermediary beings,' that is, particular
goddesses and their human avatars.[2]

In Arthurian tales, supernatural women with goddess connections, as
Nymue and her counterparts have, are no strangers to students of fairy
mythology, such as Lucy Allen Paton, who was concerned with rooting
Arthurian literature in Celtic mythology,[3] and Laurence Harf-Lancner, who
has traced the development of fairy women in French romance.[4] Nor have
Nymue and her counterparts been underestimated by contemporary novelists
remaking the legend, such as Marion Zimmer Bradley.[5] Still, annexed to
Merlin as they have been, Nymue and her analogues do seem overshadowed
by, in Peter Goodrich's words, 'his aura of wizardry.' As Goodrich claims,
the fascinating figure of Merlin, in a 'myriad of guises as well as under his
own name,' is 'more alive today than ever. His story and Arthur's has for

centuries been more than the national myth of Britain; it may eventually prove to be *the* myth of Western culture.'[6] Approached within a G/goddess paradigm, however, Nymue and her sisters are as protean in their potential meanings as are Merlin and Arthur.

In approaching the Nymue-figure here, I will bring forward what has been said about her in several previous studies, some aimed at amateurs, i.e. lovers of Arthurian legend, others at academic professionals. Varying in their use of supporting evidence, these studies are, as we shall see, alike in treating literary texts as repositories of information for purposes other than literary explication. Regardless of their validity for literary history or critical interpretation, the readings such studies produce appeal to the imagination. Moreover, whatever their shortcomings from the perspective of traditional scholarship, such studies may stimulate attention to certain details and patterns, which in turn may serve literary scholars in making sense of the fictive worlds in which Nymue and her sisters move, especially Malory's Arthuriad and Geoffrey of Monmouth's two Merlin works, *Historia regum Britanniae* and *Vita Merlini*.

Specifically, then, I will set forth the various associations the Nymue-figure may be seen to have with goddesses, from fairy godmothers and spirits of the place to cultic priestesses and facets of the Great Mother. In doing so, I will also consider the landscape elements in her stories, for to look at goddesses is to contemplate the telluric or celestial phenomena entailed by their names, acts, and locales. In the case of our Ladies of the Lake, I will show that woods and (especially intriguingly) stones are as significant and multivalent as water. Furthermore, while viewing the Nymue-figure and her landscapes in terms of her goddess penumbra, I will question the character of her relationship to Merlin. On the one hand, this relationship has been interpreted as oppositional, that is, the power of the Nymue-figure conflicts with Merlin's power, and her opposition results in his defeat. On the other hand, it has also been seen as complementary, that is, her capacities augment or balance his. Concurring with some other writers, I will suggest that their relationship should be regarded as a degree beyond complementary, as transformational. Although others may prefer to find conflict and disruption, this point of view has allowed me to reconsider my own interpretation of the first two episodes in which Nymue figures in Malory's *Morte Darthur*. Whereas I once saw Nymue's inaugural role only as that of a 'mortal woman…distressed by men,'[7] I now see her also as initiating a cycle of transformation.

To cast attention on the Nymue-figure's[8] goddess manifestations, we begin with five fairly recent, eclectic books, which vary in aim from recovering past religious beliefs to providing a means of change for individuals and society. Eclecticism marks goddess interests just as it does Arthuriana. As Wood observes of Robert Graves's 'influential and oft-quoted' *The White Goddess*, 'fascinating' work conducted with faulty methodology, such as 'poor philology, inadequate texts, and out-of-date archaeology,' may 'follow personal imagination rather than provide insight into the culture from which the data comes.'[9] With this caveat in mind and also respect for the authors' intentions, let us find the fascinating.

Relying on archaeology and etymology, John Darrah, in 1994, searches through French Arthurian romances in order to uncover Bronze Age paganism. He categorizes the 'Damsel of the Lake' as one of the 'organizing' damsels, who are aspects of a dimly perceptible 'multifaceted goddess.'[10] More specifically, Darrah interprets Merlin's fate at the hands of the Damsel of the Lake as a 'defeat.' This defeat marks an historical change from a belief system in which megalithic cult sites and the 'position of the sun on the horizon' predominate to one in which watery cult sites prevail.[11]

Nikolai Tolstoy, in 1985, argued that Merlin was a late sixth-century historical prophet, who first served as an avatar of the Celtic god Lug, presiding as a druidical priest for a cult at Lochmabenstane in Dumfriesshire, Scotland. After a 'dynastic crisis' precipitated by the battle of Arderydd, Merlin became instead a shamanistic priest as a Cernunnos-like Lord of the Forest and Beasts in the area of Hart Fell.[12] Working primarily with the Welsh Myrddin poems and Geoffrey of Monmouth's *Historia* and *Vita Merlini*, Tolstoy does not have a Nymue, as such, to account for, but he does briefly hypothesize the role of Merlin's sister, identified as Gwenddydd in the Welsh poems. As Lug's incarnation, Merlin was the son (Mabon) of the Virgin Mother Goddess (Modron, Matrona), officiating at rites of divine kingship. Along with him in these rituals was his sister, who may have personified Modron.[13]

Like Tolstoy, Norma Lorre Goodrich, in 1988, reconstructed a sixth-century, historical Merlin located in Scotland. Goodrich's Merlin, however, was a Christian priest whose sacred precincts lay on the Whithorn peninsula near the Rhinns of Galloway. 'Niniane/Vivian' was a 'real young woman' whom he educated and who then became his beloved as well as the 'most powerful female personage of her time,' evidently as a priestess of a moon cult.[14] Goodrich concluded that she lovingly helped Merlin enter the cave in which he died after performing an initiatory and penitential rite during an eclipse of the sun.[15]

It is not for historical ritual practices that Jean Markale, in a work first published in 1972, examined Celtic myth, folklore, and courtly romance, but for the expression of an ideal that can fire social revolution through a 'revolution in the structure of human thought.'[16] Specifically, he registered the desire to return women to the status of respect they held in a past era. In voicing this desire, Markale's call is a vivid instance of what Wood calls the 'elegiac quality' of many Goddess studies. Yet, although Wood does not mention his work, the gendered socio-economic critique of contemporary European society that frames his view of this better time past locates his interpretations within a conceptual frame where, as Wood puts it, 'the past becomes a template for possible renewal in the future.'[17] As Markale sees the feminine ideal expressed in the Merlin and 'Vivienne' story, Vivienne is one face of the mother goddess, who is both good-willed and spiteful, giving and withholding. As a giver, Vivienne is the initiating, transforming woman who compels a willing male subject to be contained in her and sheltered by her as their fusion transforms them both.[18]

Caitlin and John Matthews, writing in 1992, also studied myth as a source for changing awareness within the present-day reader. Calling upon water as their organizing image, they arrange nine Arthurian women in a star reflecting the major aspects of the Goddess as defined by the effect on 'us.' [19] Among these aspects, 'Nimue' is the Initiator, or Keeper of the Ways, who opens doors concerned with rebirth. Similar to Tolstoy's reading is their interpretation of Nimue as Merlin's sister. As his 'spiritual sister,' she is a priestess prepared by Merlin not only to become his lineal successor but also to accompany him into the otherworld to enable his rebirth.[20]

In these various approaches to goddesses, we find the Nymue-figure viewed as a prestigious practitioner with special powers having to do with healing or rebirth, natural and/or psychic. In addition, sharing an impulse also felt by some literary scholars, most explain her as benevolent. The exception is Darrah's understanding of the 'defeat' dealt by the Damsel of the Lake. To Tolstoy, N.L. Goodrich, and the Matthews, she is a well-meaning colleague complying with Merlin's wish that she participate in a ritual. That ritual seems to require a feminine presence along with a masculine one; with the inclusion of both genders in a cooperative relationship Markale's view agrees. Essential to all these interpretations however, including Darrah's, are certain elements of the landscape suggested by the stories. As we turn to these elements, we will see not only more goddess associations but also further ways of characterizing the Nymue-figure's relationship to Merlin.

Trees and woodland are prominent in the settings of Merlin's retreat and/ or demise in nearly all versions but Malory's. Similar to the apple tree in Celyddon Wood in one set of the Welsh Myrddin stanzas, is the Calidonian forest, replete with ash, oak, and hazel as well as apple, in Geoffrey's *Vita*

Merlini. There Merlin withdraws while mad and, restored, lives out his days in a windowed house built for him by his sister, Ganieda.[21] First a manor park with an orchard garden and then a large hawthorn bush, all in the forest of Broceliande, constitute the scenes of courtship and imprisonment in the *Estoire de Merlin* and its Middle English translation, while in the *Suite*, Merlin's encounter with Niviane in the park in Brittany is followed by their trip to Britain where they ride through a boulder-strewn ravine in the Perilous Forest.[22]

It may be the forest of the *Suite* version that misleads Corinne Saunders into assuming that, in Malory's tale, it is 'in the forest' that 'Merlin entrusts Nenyve with his magical powers, teaching her of an enchanted cave,' in which she imprisons him, thus 'transforming the forest into the landscape of abduction and betrayal.'[23] However, in Book IV chapter 1, Malory, whose story of Merlin's demise deviates from that in the *Suite*, does not mention forests when Merlin follows Nymue 'ouer the see vnto the Land of Benwyck' or 'by the waye' as they 'cam into Cornewaill.'[24] True, later in Book IV, Bagdemagus, angry at not being made a knight of the Round Table, rides away from Camelot (at Winchester) directly into a forest where he and his squire find a prophetic cross. But after that episode, Malory's narrative takes Bagdemagus out of this forest, riding to 'see many aduentures' before he comes to the 'roche [where] the Lady of the Lake had put Merlyn vnder the stone' in Cornwall (chapter 5).

Nevertheless, when she is not connected with Merlin, Malory's Nymue has certain sylvan associations. She enters his Arthuriad as the woman on the white palfrey whose white brachet is chasing the white hart that runs into the hall at Arthur and Guenever's wedding (Book III chapter 5), hence as the 'cacheresse' [huntress], as his source, the *Suite*, explicitly calls her.[25] Too, it is in a forest that Pellinor searches for her, finding her 'yonder bynethe in a valey' being fought over by two knights, and it is under a tree that she revives from her fall during the journey back (chapters 12–13). Moreover, forests are the settings for two later episodes Malory devises for Nymue. At the end of Book IV, she is the supreme fairy mistress. A knight walking 'in the forest' takes her to the despondent Pelleas, whom, after she has punished the lady who has maltreated him, Nymue commands to 'come forthe with me' and lives with in love and guardianship for the rest of their lives (chapter 23). And in Book IX chapter 16, she rides into the 'Forest Perillous, that was in North Walys' to find Lancelot or Tristram to save Arthur from the sorceress Annoure, whose tower is located there. In these appearances, Nymue has a 'woodland deity' presence, like many of the fairy women, traced by Harf-

Lancner, who mingle with humans in French romance. More particularly, as a savior of Arthur and Pelleas, she falls into Harf-Lancner's category of 'fairy-godmother.' In the Pelleas story, as Thelma S. Fenster observes, her fairy godmother function is conflated with the 'fairy-lover figure.'[26]

Although not at all concerned with wood sprites or romance, Tolstoy gives trees importance in his reconstruction of Merlin. He hypothesizes Merlin's ascent of a world-tree in a ritual journey to the otherworld in order to be reborn as a shaman. Tolstoy likens the Welsh 'fair wanton maid…slender and queenly' at the 'foot' of the apple tree growing on the 'river-bank' to the belief (expressed in Scandinavian and Siberian lore) in a 'young girl of the forest' who comes at night 'to sleep with a fortunate shaman.' This girl is a 'protectress of birds and…a Guardian of the Animals.'[27] Moreover, Merlin may have climbed through the forest covering the slopes of Hart Fell in a ritual passage to his sacrificial death. The forest, Tolstoy says, is a 'real place' in Merlin's sacred precinct yet also a 'symbol of immanent unconsciousness.'[28] However, this forest becomes significant after Merlin leaves the cult of Lug in which his sister also officiated, and he enters his Wild Man stage.

For the Matthews, on the other hand, the Wild Man has his 'perfect counterpart' in Nimue, whose 'wild woodland' and huntress associations suggest 'remnants' of a native, pre-Celtic Deer Goddess.'[29] They take note too of the *Vita Merlini* story of Merlin's prophetic power diminishing while he and his sister, Ganieda, dwell in the woods.[30] Woodland is also important to Markale's understanding of the Mother Goddess visible in Vivienne. Drawing upon the *Estoire de Merlin* tradition, he emphasizes the 'magnificent orchard' in which Merlin sees her, a 'place outside' on 'earth.' The forest, he notes, is a 'feminine, maternal symbol,' like caves.[31]

Caves and stones are critical in most of these interpretations of Nymue's goddess work. The Matthews are interested not so much in caves as in chambers with doors, such as the iron doors in the *Suite* version. Following Robert Graves, they link 'Nimue' with Cardea, a goddess of doorways as well as a huntress.[32] Thus, she initiates Merlin's entrance into the chamber of his rebirth. In contrast, Norma Lorre Goodrich has in mind a specific cave as the location of Merlin's interment, one named St. Niniane's cave on the Whithorn peninsula in Scotland eighteen miles from the northern tip of the Isle of Man.[33] 'Lavishly sculpted,' Goodrich postulates, it was intended by Merlin as the tomb he would share with 'Niniane/ Vivian,' for she 'planned to sleep beside her beloved teacher.'[34] Darrah, reaching back farther into the Bronze Age, hypothesizes that Merlin's burial cave was an underground chamber hewn out of rock and located within the boundaries of a megalithic cult stretching over the Severn Valley to Salisbury Plain.[35] Darrah points out as well the likelihood that the 'perron' Merlin is 'shut under' is one of the many standing stones associated with him.[36]

Megalithic stones are important to the cult of Lug that Tolstoy envisions for the historical Merlin and his sister in Dumfriesshire. He points out that the Clochmabenstane, a huge, round, granite boulder at Gretna, was once surrounded by a stone circle.[37] He observes too that the landscape in Merlin's region by the Solway Firth is full of 'passage graves, court cairns, portal dolmens and other mighty relics of a forgotten religion.'[38] In placing an historical Merlin in this landscape, Tolstoy imagines stone circles as Omphalos temples and envisions the Lug cult rituals, in which the divine king marries the land, as 'necessary to preserve the harmony of the natural order.'[39] Quite another conjunction between goddess and stones is suggested by Markale's discussion of the erotic tenor of the power over Merlin held by Vivienne in the *Estoire de Merlin*. Reviewing folklore customs in which a woman compels a man to desire her, he reports that she might sit on a hollow stone; sit with lifted skirts on a menhir (monolith) or climb or slide on one; rub against a sloped rock; or clench a stone between the knees. 'Absolutely essential,' he points out, is the 'contact between the naked flesh and the stone.'[40]

Although Markale's point is about eroticism, it is the stones in these customs that stand out, particularly menhirs. But stones need not be male. 'The scholar seeking beliefs in supernatural women in megalithic folklore has much from which to choose,' remarks Samuel Pyeatt Menefee, who settles on the stone circle in Little Salkeld in Cumbria known as Long Meg and her Daughters.[41] It is with the 'Goddess of the Stones' that Cheryl Straffon opens her study of the earth goddess. Straffon identifies prehistoric stone structures in Britain and Ireland as sites allied with land configurations and icons denoting a Neolithic and Bronze Age all-encompassing Goddess who gives life, nurtures a people, and watches over the dead.[42] She includes Long Meg and her Daughters in her gazetteer, pointing out that Long Meg, an eleven-foot sandstone inscribed on the circle-facing side with a spiral, is 'reputed to bleed if a piece is broken off.' The 'bleeding woman' and 'mystic spiral' are 'elements of Goddess,' she observes, as are the legend that a wizard turned witches into these stones and their alignment with the spring and autumn equinoxes.[43] Furthermore, Straffon appends a description of a 'Neolithic site with Goddess stones' discovered in Wessex by Terence Meaden, who calls it a 'vast religious area glorifying Goddess,' with hardly any 'masculine contribution.' The Goddess stones filling this area consist of 'megaliths forming circles, sanctuaries, sacred enclosures, standing stones and stone rows.'[44]

Straffon's Goddess stones may broaden our view of Nymue's role in sealing Merlin under a stone. A supernatural woman's petrifaction story does occur in Malory's Book IV, but the goddess it belongs to is Morgan le Fay. When chased by Arthur for having stolen his scabbard in an attempt to replace him with her lover Accolon, Morgan rides into a valley having 'many grete stones' where she 'shope [shaped] herself hors and man by enchauntement vnto a grete marbyl stone' and thus escapes. 'Telle [Arthur],' she boasts, 'I fere hym not whyle I can make me and them that ben with me in lykenes of stones' (chapters 14–15). In contrast to the triumphant Morgan, Nymue is injured by a fall when her horse stumbles in another valley 'ful of stones' through which she is escorted back to Arthur's court by Pellinor (Book III chapter 13).

Although Darrah does not consider this adventure, he includes Pellinor among other males having Pel-names, which he identifies with 'Belenus the Brilliant,' the name of a Celtic solar deity. Darrah associates these Pel-figures with personages having names of the goddess Elaine. These Elaine names, he hypothesizes, point to the 'name of an office' filled in 'successive generations' by the 'goddess…descended to earth…in the shape of her priestess…assisted by the heroes who likewise carry the same name from father to son.'[15] While I hesitate to turn Nymue into an Elaine-priestess, Darrah's interpretation of Pellinor does prompt me to rethink the first episode in which Malory includes her. As noted earlier, in my previous work on Nymue I had regarded her narrative role in this initial episode to be that of a mortal damsel in distress, as Paton does the huntress in the analogue in the *Suite*. But with Darrah's argument in mind, I now see as well a suggestive pattern of goddess associations.

When Nymue, not yet named, arrives at Arthur's court, she is a sylvan equestrian in pursuit of a white hart. In other texts, a white hart connotes not simply a mysterious adventure but a theme of marriage and sovereignty, equally appropriate at the wedding of Guenevere and Arthur. Upon being abducted, she cries with conspicuous vocal energy, a noisiness suggesting a desperate wrong. Out in the forest valley, her two male cousins attempt to protect her: Bryan of the Ilys, who withholds himself in one pavilion, where she also seems to be waiting; and Meliot of Logurs, who intends to take her back to her people and combats the abducting knight. Then come Pellinor's search, assistance, and retrieval, and her injury during the return, not her return to her people but to Arthur's court. In so far as uses of megalithic constructions involve solar phenomena and therefore Belinus, as Darrah surmises, we may apply his theory to Pellinor's role here. Pellinor's assignment to bring Nymue back and his intervention in the fight between her cousin and her abductor may be read as a transition between cultic sites and rituals, as solar orientation is superseded or complemented by water veneration. As told by Malory, the story does at least suggest the search for a new agency of supernatural energy.

Indeed, Nymue's passage with Pellinor through the stony valley forms an intriguing prelude to her studies with Merlin from whom she learns how to enclose him 'in a roche...vnder a grete stone.' In the elaborate rendition of this enclosure in the *Suite*, the situation is a 'rocky cliff' approached by a narrow path from the road through the rocky defile Merlin and Niviane are taking in the Perilous Forest. Merlin's reference to a chamber 'carved out of the rock' suggests an enhanced cliff-side cave, yet the architectural details point to a Neolithic chambered barrow, a type of burial site constructed of megaliths for walls and roof and turfed over, making either a long or round shape, and (like the chamber in the *Suite* story) attracting later beliefs that legendary lovers lay therein.[46] Though terser, Malory's account of a rock in Cornwall in which there are 'merueilles' that have been 'wroughte by enchauntement' (Book IV chapter 1) under a stone 'so heauy that an C men myght not lyfte hyt vp' (chapter 5) conjoins Nymue with a megalith, recumbent or upright, as well as a rock chamber. However, the contact between Nymue and the stone is not of her flesh, as in Markale's folklore, but of her 'craft.' In Malory's version, Nymue wishes to repel Merlin, not to compel him to her. Indeed, through putting him under the stone in the rock she herself does not enter, she substitutes, as it were, the rock for herself. Thus, she succeeds in protecting her 'maydenhode,' which we may understand to be the integrity, or concentration, of the power gathering within her, while Merlin's sexual obsession with her may result in the waning of his power, as he withdraws into the 'erthe quyck' (Book IV chapter 1).

Functioning as a goddess, Nymue has overseen Merlin's need for renewal, and she has transmuted his mantic energy. On the narrative level, then, just as Ganieda gains a prophetic voice when her brother is content to lose his in their house in the Calidonian woods of the *Vita Merlini*, so does Nymue gain skills of bespelling, insight, and foresight when Merlin descends willingly but without her, into the rock whose opening and closing stone she now controls. As Markale observes of Vivienne and the Matthews of their composite Nimue, she initiates the move into a transformative cycle.[47] We can see, then, that Malory's text indicates a cyclical change in the agency of magic. Geraldine Heng also perceives the 'structure of cyclical replacement,' as 'Nyneve...supplants [Merlin], as spring replaces winter.'[48]

Yet the antagonistic note coloring the transference of power in Malory and the *Suite*'s tradition of Merlin's withdrawal does return us to Darrah's point of view, that the Lady of the Lake's cult replaces one involving stones. Three issues seem to be embedded in Darrah's hypothesis: conflict between megalithic sites and water sites; between celestial, particularly sun, worship and water worship; between masculine and feminine divine principles.

That such historical change occurred is evident, though not necessarily how and why. The watery loci that were among the Celts' sacred spaces, such as bogs and springs, and the ritual deposits made in these places, seem on archaeological evidence to be of the Iron Age, though some lake deposits are earlier.[49] On the other hand, megalithic chambered tombs, stone circles, and isolated standing stones distinguish the people occupying Ireland, Britain, and Brittany during the millennia of the Neolithic and Early Bronze ages. According to Rodney Castleden, the chambered tombs, which replicated the construction of homes, served as 'houses for the dead,' at which various, complex funeral rituals were enacted, including burning, while some isolated monoliths (standing stones not adjacent to a circle) seem also to have functioned in funeral ceremonies. As for the circles, although they have been interpreted as astronomical observatories, Castleden proposes that they are instead 'celestial temples,' 'expressions' of a community's 'relationship with the cosmos,' stages for numerous collective rites, including death, and 'liminal refuges during solsticial crises.' Remarkable is the sustained commitment to quarrying, moving, importing (in the case of the blue stones of Stonehenge), dressing, erecting, arranging and rearranging huge stones over many generations. But as Castleden concludes of the tombs as well as such circles as Avebury and Stonehenge, 'making and unmaking' are themselves 'ritual acts.' That the sky, sun, and some stars were integral to the rituals and symbolism of the stone circles is not to be doubted. But Castleden also emphasizes the 'dedication' to the earth as well as to the sky at some sites, notably Stonehenge, which he interprets as a structure symbolizing the union between the sky-god and the earth-goddess.[50]

The megalithic structures of the Stonehenge people do differ decidedly, then, from the type of sacred spaces used by Iron Age Celts, which include shafts into the earth and enclosures as well as water. The advent of the Celts is now regarded as a gradual process with geographical variants developing among indigenous cultures rather than a sharp imposition, through conquest, of a national way of life.[51] But (Tolstoy's fascinating story of Merlin standing in a line of successive generations of Druid priests associated with Stonehenge notwithstanding), present-day archaeology suggests it unlikely that the ancient megalithic monuments remained in use as temples throughout this process of 'Celticization,' or that Iron Age Druids resorted to them.[52] Indeed, stonework in Celtic sacred space is rare, apart from the Celto-Ligurian structures at Entremont, Roquepertuse, and Glanum in Provence.[53] In considering the abandonment of megalithic monuments and the apparent preference for water worship among the Celts, we might note that Britain and Europe became wetter as well as colder in the later Bronze Age.[54] Nevertheless, archaeological study of the east-facing entrances of round houses as well as of sacred sites indicates that solar movement, solstices, and other astronomical principles influenced Celtic religious concepts, spatial arrangements, and rites.[55]

Given this archaeological backdrop, the Lady of the Lake's enclosure of Merlin in a megalithic structure becomes a text that not only has potency as symbolic discourse but, as Darrah perceives, may also hint at a cultural memory of an historical shift in ritual sites and practices. Within (pre-)history, however, this shift would seem to have been a gradual one in which megalithic monuments may have been forsaken but sun and water both signify. The possibility of confluence, rather than conflict, between sun and water veneration may yield new readings of the Arthurian stories in which an astronomer and stone-circle architect Merlin is immured by a Lady of the Lake. However, the matter of the mysterious megalithic monuments and the relationship of masculine and feminine divine principles still require explanation.

From a Goddess perspective, megalithic formations harmonize rather than clash with sacred waters, for both are Goddess elements. Castleden points out that the earlier stone circles, which in Britain are in Cumbria, usually stand next to water. Long Meg and her Daughters, for instance, are situated on a terrace above the east bank of the River Eden. He also reports a suggestion in which barrows, stones, and streams cooperate: 'stone settings' on Exmoor may have led the spirits of the dead down from the barrows on the ridge to the source of the streams, which then became the conduits for moving the spirits into the sea.[56] The vitalizing interaction of stone and water is acknowledged in Merlin's account, in Geoffrey's *Historia*, of the medicinal properties of the standing stones in Ireland he would transport to make up the Stonehenge circle. These stones are washed with water mixed with herbs; this solution then pours down the stones to be collected in baths, for immersing ill people and for making poultices.[57] Another attraction of stone to water is indicated in a folkloric theme attached to standing stones in Finistère, Brittany, southern England, and Wales. According to Leslie V.

Grinsell, these stones move to a 'neighboring river, stream, loch, pool, spring or well, usually to drink or bathe.' In numerous instances, this movement of stone to water happens at certain hours or on certain holidays—Easter, Midsummer Eve, All Hallows Eve, Christmas, and New Year's Eve, thus suggesting, Grinsell remarks, 'calendar customs.'[58]

The funerary guiding of spirits by stones to springs, the ceremonial drinking and bathing of stones in nearby water, and the wetting of them to elicit a curative liquor lead us to discover the significance of water. With regard to Merlin, water is associated with an apparent ritual of regeneration and prophetic inspiration in the story Geoffrey tells to introduce him in the *Historia*. A subterranean pool causes the mortared stones laid by Vortigern's masons for the foundation of his tower to disappear night after night, thus, we might infer, destabilizing and resisting the imposition of Vortigern's power. This pool contains, womb-like, 'hollow stones with two sleeping dragons in them.' When the water is drained to reveal these gestating creatures, in what seems to me to be a ritual-like birthing scene, the boy Merlin enters the supernatural zone of prophecy.[59]

Whereas the onset of prophecy comes with the draining of water in that story, the cessation of Merlin's prophecies in *Vita Merlini* is marked by the outbreak of running waters that restore him to sanity. As he finishes reciting to Taliesin the 'savage battles' he has foreseen, report arrives that a 'new fountain has broken out at the foot of the mountains and was pouring out pure waters which were running through all the hollow valley and swirling through the fields as they slipped along.' After Merlin imbibes the fountain water and moistens his temples with it, 'all madness departed,' for which he gives thanks to the Lord for the 'water which I hitherto lacked.' Taliesin then goes on to extol the healthful properties of various fountains, lakes, and rivers.[60]

In his recreation of an historical Merlin, Tolstoy does not tap Geoffrey's remarkable associations of water with prophecy. He does, however, follow the *Historia* in associating Merlin with a spring. For Tolstoy, this 'holy spring' arises in a 'rocky crevice on Hart Fell,' and to it Merlin makes his ritual ascent in order to participate in a sacrificial three-fold death symbolized by 'Tree, Spear, and Water.'[61] Furthermore, Tolstoy does draw upon the Welsh stanzas in which Gwenddydd's questions elicit Myrddin's foretellings, to hypothesize that incarnated as a prophetess (rather than as Modron) Gwenddydd represents the Morning Star, Venus, source of prophetic inspiration. Tolstoy's description of the 'still waters of Loch Maben as they reflect the glittering Morning Star' implies the lake's presence in the 'solemn ceremonies taking place' within the sanctuary as Lug's avatar, Merlin, prophesied a king's 'fruitful reign.'[62]

In the *Estoire de Merlin*, Vivienne is not called a lady of the lake, but she does have a fountain, lives next to a lake, hears a story about a bath, and learns to conjure a river as well as make the mist that envelops Merlin. Neither the *Suite* nor Malory mentions water in the location of Merlin's demise. Nor does water emerge in the settings of Malory's other Nymue episodes until, of course, the final one. There, Nymue appears among the 'many fayr ladyes,' including Morgan le Fay, who are wearing black hoods and weeping on the barge that takes the wounded Arthur to the Vale of Avalon (Book xxi chapter 5). Although Malory, not his English or French sources, creates this ultimate role for Nymue, we may see here the Celtic goddess of the dead, exemplified by Morgan le Fay's Celtic forebears. We also see another instance of Nymue's function as the 'fairy godmother.' According to Harf-Lancner's exposition of the development of fairy women in medieval French romance, the fairy godmother derived from the Latin Parcae, goddesses of fate.[63] Finally, in *Le Morte Darthur*, the epithet Malory gives Nymue, the Chief Lady of the Lake, connotes the broad significance of water as well as her kinship with other fairy women of romance who evanesce from water deities.

To illustrate yearning for the lost goddess, Markale draws upon mermaid and 'drowned princess' stories in the beginning of his study. However, in looking at the goddess in Vivienne's story in the *Estoire de Merlin*, Markale does not respond to its aquatic features. Instead, he is attracted to Vivienne's luminosity and tyrannical character. To him, these attributes make her a solar deity.[64] On the other hand, accepting Graves's identification of Niniane/ Vivian as a moon goddess, Norma Lorre Goodrich envisions her occupying a temple by the sea and looking like Botticelli's blonde Venus floating on a clamshell.[65]

Among the range of studies I have brought forward, the potency of water is best expressed by writers at two ends of the spectrum of G/goddess studies, mythographers who reweave stories for spiritual use now, exemplified by Caitlin and John Matthews, and mythologists who scrutinize epigraphy, iconography, and material remains to interpret belief systems of the past, exemplified by Miranda Green. In the Matthews' vision of the meaning Ladies of the Lake have for those seeking the Goddess within their inner beings, water is the predominant Otherworld element from which their nine Arthurian women draw their power. Emphasizing the 'feminine symbolism' of water, they describe it as flowing, weaving, uncontainable, invading, and moistening, thus emotive, dangerous, and overwhelming as change in an inner voyage may be.[66]

   The Matthews also refer to the numerous wells, springs, rivers, and lakes linked with sacred females,[67] towards which Darrah's theory that water sites succeeded megalithic structures associated with solar movement also leads. Green, among others, has studied some of these waterworks in connection with Celtic healer-goddesses, such as the continental Sequana and insular Sulis, neither of whom took mates, and Nemetona, another insular goddess, who did accept a consort. Sulis, Green points out, was also an avenger of wrongs, a role evidently overlapping her function as healer. In explaining concepts fundamental to these healer goddesses, Green says that the 'perception of the numinous in water is important. There is abundant evidence...from at least the later Bronze Age...that water was a focus of ritual activity.' Indeed, sanctuaries sited at springs are linked to both healing and fertility, and, as Green remarks, the 'most interesting' of the healing-cults 'were those centered upon the goddesses, to whom the relationship between healing and fertility is specific.'[68]

   Bringing all points of reference to bear on the meaning of water in stories about Nymue, the Chief Lady of the Lake, we may see her as an active force, protective and generative, fairy lover and fairy godmother, avenger of wrongs and initiator of change. In taking Arthur to Avalon, as she does in Malory's *Le Morte Darthur*, she is a goddess who promises to heal, watches over the dead, and enables rebirth. Regarded as Merlin's mate or as his successor, she is an 'uncontainable' agent of transformation.

   As manifestations of goddesses, Nymue and her counterparts in Arthurian legend have invited rereadings of their relationship to Merlin, inspired recognition of early religious rituals, and offered myths of transformation for our time. Merlin may well, as Peter Goodrich avers, have entered 'the public domain' as "the wizard with a thousand faces."'[69] Yet, among the elements of water, trees, caves, and stones in stories, studies, and nature, the many faces of a Great Goddess shine in Nymue and her sisters.

SOUTHERN CONNECTICUT STATE UNIVERSITY

Sue Ellen Holbrook is Professor of English at Southern Connecticut State University. Among her publications are studies of Malory's *Le Morte Darthur*, Margery Kempe, and text and image in Wynkyn de Worde's editions of Jerome's *Vitas Patrum* and Bartholomew's *De Proprietatibus Rerum*. Current projects include virility and property in *Kulhwch and Olwen*, illustrations of Bartholomew's book on time, vernacularity in four de Worde incunables, and consciousness and landscape in *The Flower and the Leaf*.

NOTES

1 Prudence Jones and Nigel Pennick, *A History of Pagan Europe* (London: Routledge, 1995), p. 2.

2 Juliette Wood, 'The Concept of the Goddess,' in *The Concept of the Goddess*, ed. Sandra Billington and Miranda Green (London: Routledge, 1996), p. 8.

3 Lucy Allen Paton, *Studies in the Fairy Mythology of Arthurian Romance* (Boston: Ginn & Co., 1903).

4 Laurence Harf-Lancner, 'Fairy Godmothers and Fairy Lovers,' in *Arthurian Women: A Casebook*, ed. Thelma S. Fenster (New York: Garland Publishing, Inc., 1996), pp. 135–51.

5 Marion Zimmer Bradley, *The Mists of Avalon* (New York: Del Rey, 1982). On Bradley, see Thelma S. Fenster, 'Introduction,' in *Arthurian Women*, pp. xxxii–xxxiii, xxxvii; Marilyn R. Farwell, 'Heterosexual Plots and Lesbian Subtexts,' in *Arthurian Women*, ed. Fenster, pp. 319–30; and Diane L. Paxon, 'Marion Zimmer Bradley and *The Mists of Avalon*,' *Arthuriana* 9:1 (1999): 110–26, esp. 119–20, 125 on Viviane.

6 Peter Goodrich, 'Introduction,' *The Romance of Merlin: An Anthology* (New York: Garland Publishing, Inc., 1990), p. xiii, xvii.

7 Sue Ellen Holbrook, 'Nymue, The Chief Lady of the Lake, in Malory's *Le Morte Darthur*,' *Speculum* 53.4 (1978): [761–77]; rep. *Arthurian Women: A Casebook*, ed. Thelma S. Fenster (New York: Garland Publishing, Inc., 1996), p. 178.

8 'Nymue' is the name and spelling most frequently occurring in William Caxton's edition of Malory's *Le Morte Darthur*. For spellings in the Malory (Winchester) manuscript, British Library MS Additional 59678, and in other works, see Holbrook, 'Nymue, The Chief Lady of the Lake, in Malory's *Le Morte Darthur*,' in *Arthurian Women: A Casebook*, ed. Fenster, pp. 172–73, 188 n2–3, 5–6. In the present essay, I will give the name as used by the writers under discussion, but otherwise use the name 'Nymue.' Not all Ladies of the Lake are the equivalent of Nymue. Malory differentiates two ladies of the lake, and in the Middle English prose *Merlin* and its French source, the *Estoire de Merlin*, Merlin's beloved nemesis is not given the epithet 'Lady of the Lake.' On the various lake ladies in French prose romance, see Lucy Allen Paton, 'La Dame du Lac,' *Studies in the Fairy Mythology of Arthurian Romance*, pp. 167–203; Anne Berthelot, 'From the Lake to the Fountain: Lancelot and the Fairy Lover,' in *Arthurian Women*, pp. 153–69, 'Merlin and the Ladies of the Lake,' *Arthuriana* 10.1 (2000): 55–81, and also her chapter in this volume.

9 Wood, 'The Concept of the Goddess,' in *The Concept of the Goddess*, ed. Sandra Billington and Miranda Green, pp. 10, 12.

10 John Darrah, *Paganism in Arthurian Romance* (Woodbridge, UK: Boydell Press, 1994), p. 87.

11 Darrah, *Paganism in Arthurian Romance*, p. 103.

12 Nikolai Tolstoy, *The Quest for Merlin* (Boston; Little, Brown and Company, 1985), pp. 87–99, 210–11.

13 Tolstoy, *Quest for Merlin*, pp. 204–9. Gwenddydd appears in stanza 5 of 'Yr Afallennau: The Apple Tree Stanzas,' and she is called Myrddin's sister in the final stanza of another early poem, 'The Prophecy of Myrddin and Gwenddydd, His Sister,' both translated by John K. Bollard, *The Romance of Merlin*, ed. Peter Goodrich, pp. 22–24, 30–46. Bollard points out that Gwenddydd may 'originally have been Myrddin's mistress' (p. 20). In Geoffrey of Monmouth's *Vita Merlini*, in which Merlin has a wife as well, his sister is Ganieda. While not a lady of the lake, the sister-figure is, as Anne Berthelot says, the 'prototype of the feminine figure whose presence runs parallel to Merlin's story,' 'Merlin and the Ladies of the Lake,' *Arthuriana* 10:1 (2000): 58.

14 Norma Lorre Goodrich, *Merlin* (New York: HarperPerennial, 1988), pp. 270, 217, 275.

15 Norma Lorre Goodrich, *Merlin*, pp. 272, 317, 326.

16 Jean Markale, *Women of the Celts*, trans. A. Mygind, C. Hauch and P. Henry (Rochester, VT: Inner Traditions International, Ltd., 1986), p. 255.

17 Wood, 'The Concept of the Goddess,' in *The Concept of the Goddess*, ed. Billington and Green, pp. 22, 15.

18 Markale, *Women of the Celts*, pp. 133, 138, 227.

19 Caitlin and John Matthews, *Ladies of the Lake* (London: the Aquarian Press, 1992), p. xxxii.

20 Matthews, *Ladies of the Lake*, pp. xxxix, 123–25, 120, 129.

21 'Yr Afallennau: The Apple Tree Stanzas,' trans. John K. Bollard, in *The Romance of Merlin*, ed. Peter Goodrich, pp. 22–24.

22 The *Estoire de Merlin* may be found in H. Oskar Sommer, *The Vulgate Version of the Arthurian Romances* (1908) and the relevant portions of the Middle English translation in 'Middle English Prose Merlin,' *The Romance of Merlin*, ed. Peter Goodrich, pp. 149–51, 162–64. For the *Suite du Merlin*, see the edition by Gaston Paris and Jacob Ulrich (Paris: Firmin Didot, 1886), and for translation of the relevant portions, Samuel N. Rosenberg, 'From the *Suite du Merlin*,' *The Romance of Arthur II*, ed. James J. Willhelm (New York: Garland Publishing, 1986), pp. 252–66.

23 Corinne J. Saunders, *The Forest of Medieval Romance: Avernus, Broceliande, Arden* (Cambridge, UK: D.S. Brewer, 1993), pp. 168–69.

24 Citations of Malory are from *Caxton's Malory: A New Edition of Sir Thomas Malory's* Le Morte Darthur, ed. James W. Spisak (Berkeley: University of California Press, 1983), given by book and chapter number and henceforth cited in parentheses.

25 See Paton, 'La Damoisele Cacheresse,' in *Studies in the Fairy Mythology of Arthurian Romance*, pp. 228–47; Samuel N. Rosenberg, 'From the *Suite du Merlin*,' in *The Romance of Arthur II*, p. 252.

26 Harf-Lancner, 'Fairy Godmothers and Fairy Lovers,' in *Arthurian Women*, p. 144; Fenster, 'Introduction,' in *Arthurian Women*, p. lii.

27 Tolstoy, *Quest for Merlin*, p. 151.

28 Tolstoy, *Quest for Merlin*, pp. 123, 131, 143, 152, 168, 170, 185, 249.

29 Matthews, *Ladies of the Lake*, pp. 125–26.

30 Matthews, *Ladies of the Lake*, p. 128.

31 Markale, *Women of the Celts*, pp. 239, 297 n7.

32 Matthews, *Ladies of the Lake*, pp. 128–29.

33 Norma Lorre Goodrich, *Merlin*, p. 278.

34 Norma Lorre Goodrich, *Merlin*, p. 274–75.

35 Darrah, *Paganism in Arthurian Romance*, pp. 171, 205; also p. 182 on cromlechs.

36 Darrah, *Paganism in Arthurian Romance*, p. 172.

37 Tolstoy, *Quest for Merlin*, pp. 206, 210; illustration 15 of the Clochmabenstane.

38 Tolstoy, *Quest for Merlin*, p. 126.

39 Tolstoy, *Quest for Merlin*, pp. 121, 127, 99.

40 Markale, *Women of the Celts*, p. 220.

41 Samuel Pyeatt Menefee, 'Meg and Her Daughters: Some Traces of Goddess-Beliefs in Megalithic Folklore,' in *The Concept of the Goddess*, ed. Billington and Green, pp. 78–79.

42 Cheryl Straffon, *The Earth Goddess: Celtic and Pagan Legacy of the Landscape* (London: Blandford, 1997), p. 21.

43 Straffon, *Earth Goddess*, p. 156. On the petrifaction legend, see also Leslie V. Grinsell, *Folklore of Prehistoric Sites in Britain* (London: David & Charles, 1976), pp. 164–65; Grinsell reports the earliest version, of 1690, to say that the stones are 'unlawful lovers' that have solicited Meg (Mag). For an engraving of the spiral on Long Meg, see Evan Hadingham, *Circles and Standing Stones: An Illustratted Exploration of Megalith Mysteries of Early Britain* (New York: Anchor Press, 1976), p. 137 (upper left). For a photograph of Long Meg while the sun breaks over her, see Andrew Rafferty (photographs) and Kevin Crossley-Holland (text), *The Stones Remain: Megalithic Sites of Britain* (London: Rider, 1989), p. 31.

44 Straffon, *Earth Goddess*, p. 212.

45 Darrah, *Paganism in Arthurian Romance*, pp. 271–77.

46 Chambered barrows are known as cromlechs, dolmens, and quoits when the mounded up cover of soil and vegetation has worn away to expose the stones; see Grinsell, *Folklore of Prehistoric Sites in Britain*, pp. 79–80. On construction and uses of chambered barrows, see Rodney Castleden, *The Stonehenge People: An Exploration of Life in Neolithic Britain, 4700–2000 BC* (London: Routledge & Kegan Paul, 1987), pp. 157–90; and on 'trysting' place belief, pp. 189–90.

47 Matthews, *Ladies of the Lake*, p. xxxix; Markale, *Women of the Celts*, p. 201.

48 Geraldine Heng, 'Enchanted Ground: The Feminine Subtext in Malory,' *Arthurian Women*, pp. 104, 112 n33.

49 Jane Webster, 'Sanctuaries and Sacred Places,' in *The Celtic World*, ed. Miranda J. Green (London: Routledge, 1995), pp. 449–51.

50 Rodney Castleden, *The Stonehenge People*, pp. 163, 187–89 on tombs; p. 153 on monoliths; pp. 131, 152, 155, 241 on circles; pp. 93–112 on building Stonehenge; p. 188 on ritual acts; pp. 111, 150–54 on sky, sun, stars, earth. In contrast to Castleden's union of sky-god and earth-goddess, Michael Dames understands Stonehenge, like the hill of Uisnech (in County Westmeath) with which an 'exchange of *some* kind'

must have taken place, to be a 'centre of a prehistoric sun goddess religion.' *Mythic Ireland* (London: Thames and Hudson, 1992), pp. 201, and pp. 194–242 for elaboration of his theory of Uisnech.

51 See Miranda J. Green, 'Introduction: Who Were the Celts?' in *The Celtic World*, ed. Green, pp. 3–7.

52 Tolstoy, *Quest for Merlin*, p. 115. On the issue of whether Celts, specifically Druids, worshipped at megalithic circles, see Rodney Castleden on the end of the Neolithic as a warrior ethos developed in the Bronze Age, *The Stonehenge People*, pp. 259–60; and Evan Hadingham, *Circles and Standing Stones*, pp. 168–77.

53 On stone-built sanctuaries, see Jane Webster, 'Sanctuaries and Sacred Places,' in *The Celtic World*, ed. Green, pp. 452–53.

54 See Martin Bell, 'People and Nature in the Celtic World,' in *The Celtic World*, ed. Green, pp. 146–47.

55 On the sun, see Bell, 'People and Nature in the Celtic World,' in *The Celtic World*, ed. Green, p. 155; and Jane Webster, 'Sanctuaries and Sacred Places,' in *The Celtic World*, ed. Green, pp. 459–60.

56 Rodney Castleden, *The Stonehenge People*, pp. 141–42; p. 154, 224 Plate 37 of Watersmeet, and p. 226 Plate 38 of the Longstone. Evan Hadingham also notes that 'many cursus monuments, earth circles and stone rings do seem to be sited close to fresh water,' *Circles and Standing Stones*, p. 178.

57 Geoffrey of Monmouth, 'History of the Kings of Britain,' trans. Aubrey Gaylon and Zacharias P. Thundy, in *The Romance of Merlin*, ed. Peter Goodrich, p. 69.

58 Leslie V. Grinsell, *Folklore of Prehistoric Sites in Britain*, pp. 58–60. See also Evan Hadingham, *Circles and Standing Stones*, pp. 178–79, esp. the photograph of Le Menec.

59 Geoffrey of Monmouth, 'History of the Kings of Britain,' trans. Gaylon and Thundy, in *The Romance of Merlin*, ed. Peter Goodrich, pp. 59–60.

60 Geoffrey of Monmouth, '*Vita Merlini*,' trans. John Jay Parry, *The Romance of Merlin*, ed. Peter Goodrich, pp. 89–93.

61 Tolstoy, *Quest for Merlin*, pp. 183, 185; illustration 10 of the chalybeate spring. With regard to the dragons in the pool, Tolstoy considers the animals important, not the water (p. 113).

62 Tolstoy, *Quest for Merlin*, pp. 209–10.

63 Harf-Lancner, 'Fairy Godmothers and Fairy Lovers,' in *Arthurian Women*, pp. 136, 140.

64 Markale, *Women of the Celts*, pp. 43–84 (with mention of Merlin and Vivienne on p. 63); p. 323; pp. 239–41.

65 Norma Lorre Goodrich, *Merlin*, p. 275.

66 Matthews, *Ladies of the Lake*, pp. xxiv–xxv.

67 Matthews, *Ladies of the Lake*, p. xxiv.

68 Miranda Green, 'The Celtic Goddess as Healer,' in *The Concept of the Goddess*, ed. Billington and Green, pp. 28–33, 35, and 37. See also Miranda J. Green, 'The Gods and the Supernatural,' in *The Celtic World*, p. 474. Nemetona is paired with Mars Loucetius at Aquae Sulis (Bath), where Sulis presided.

69 Peter Goodrich, 'Introduction,' in *The Romance of Merlin*, p. xiii.

From Niniane to Nimüe:
Demonizing the Lady of the Lake

ANNE BERTHELOT

Starting as a rather vague figure in Chrétien's *Chevalier de la Charrette*, the Lady of the Lake goes through a number of mutations in later texts. Since she is related to Lancelot, she has to be innocent of a sinful Otherworldly origin. However, even the texts which tend to erase her mermaid or fairy nature have to admit a connection with Merlin, the 'devil's son.' Whether the Lady of the Lake loves Merlin or not, she is eventually demonized as a formidable enchantress, or forgotten as the cause of Merlin's destruction. (AB)

When, in Chrétien de Troyes' *Chevalier au Lion* the Lady of Noroison finds Yvain lying naked in the forest, she remembers an unguent given to her by 'Morgue la sage' [the wise Morgan], and decides to heal the knight's madness with this magical remedy. In later texts, Morgue undoubtedly plays a more important part, but her reputation tends to degenerate from one romance to the next. Similarly, in the *Chevalier de la Charrette*, one learns that a *fee*, a fairy without any other definition, has raised the hero and given him a magical ring that allows him to see whether there are enchantments threatening him. A few hundred lines later, this 'best knight in the world' is given a name: he is called Lancelot del Lac. Although the form 'Lac' appears as a personal name, that of Erec's father, King *Lac*, in Chrétien's *Erec et Enide*, critics have tended to choose the variant 'of the Lake,' in Lancelot's case suggested by the definite article. Lancelot's prestige is enhanced by this mysterious association of a knight coming from nowhere with a magical place belonging to a *fee* who gives enchanted gifts. Nothing more is said about these two characters in the *Charrette*: the romance tells the story of Lancelot's love for Queen Guenevere, but says nothing more about Lancelot's birth and youth.

Since the Prose *Lancelot*, written some forty years later, focuses on the character whose first appearance in Chrétien's romance apparently met with huge success, it expands on every detail of the few elements that suggest a 'biography' of Lancelot in the *Charrette*. Accordingly, the figure of the Lady of the Lake, previously mentioned in passing, is given considerable

importance. Originally, she is a mermaid, or an ondine—a water fairy, who
has a rather tarnished reputation among the numerous supernatural creatures
haunting the borders of the civilized world.[1] Such creatures take pleasure in
making men drown by luring them into deep waters. They are also
exceedingly fond of human children, whom they steal away to their underwater kingdom. The trouble is that most children who undergo this fate
disappear forever. If Lancelot survived an education in a submarine kingdom,
it means he himself is at least partly of supernatural stock. However, Lancelot
'du Lac' may have a fairy origin in Chrétien's text, where his past remains an
enigma, but this blemish on his character must be glossed over, and he has
to be given a perfectly human, albeit glorious, lineage, in a more prosaic (in
every sense of the word) narrative. Consequently, if Lancelot is introduced
as King Ban of Benoïc's son, a descendant (through his mother) of King
David, and as such a 'collateral' member of the Grail family, the Lady of the
Lake who has raised him also acquires at least a veneer of respectability that
suppresses the suspicion that she is a vulgar mermaid.

The *Lancelot* depicts the Lady of the Lake in a very positive manner,
working very hard to erase all suspicion of her connection to the supernatural:
the lake is but a mirage, the lady but a courtly damsel who happens to have
pursued a course of study allowing her to know the *vertus des plantes et des
pierres*. Nothing other-worldly in that, since the formula is almost exactly
the one employed by Bartholomeus Anglicus in his *De proprietatibus rerum*.
If such a distinction might be considered valid during the first half of the
thirteenth century, one might say that the Lady of the Lake is a scientist, not
a witch or an enchantress. Whenever she or one of her damsels accomplishes
any undoubtedly magical feat, the word used to describe it is always *ars* or at
most *sors,* and never *nigremance*. In fact, the whole episode is a study in
character rehabilitation wherein the narrative tries to skirt the issue of the
supernatural origin or nature of the Lady of the Lake. For the first time, a
text uses the wonderful argument of 'naive people believing that any
intelligent and well-read woman is a "*fee*," a fairy.' This opens the way to a
long tradition of rhetorical denials by characters as widely disparate as
Esclarmonde, in the *Huon de Bordeaux* sequels, and the 'Reine-Fee' [the 'Fairy
Queen], of the *Roman de Perceforest*. In order to encourage the reader's
sympathy for the Lady of the Lake, the *Lancelot* confuses the issue by linking
the Lady to Merlin, in what is probably the first implementation of this
story-line in a French text.[2] By making the beautiful and virtuous damsel
the gifted pupil of the prophet-enchanter, the text achieves two goals: on the
one hand, it demonstrates the scientific nature of the future Lady of the

Lake's knowledge; on the other hand, it displaces the blemish of a supernatural origin from the damsel to her would-be lover: Merlin is the devil's son, but his reluctant *amie* is a very human girl. Consequently, the *Lancelot* depicts the Lady of the Lake in a most favorable light at that early stage of her career, even if her dealings with Merlin do not quite bear close examination.

Her *enfance*, however, is not dwelt upon very long, since the important element here is Lancelot's *enfance* and his involvement with the Lady of the Lake. The narrative glosses rather quickly over the odd scene of a silent woman carrying off a little boy and jumping into a seemingly real lake. The Lady of the Lake's motives are never explained, since the only reason that she abducted Lancelot is indeed her ambiguous mermaid nature. Nevertheless, this surprising and somewhat questionable behavior is more or less redeemed by the Lionel and Bohort episode: certainly, the Lady is not a fairy stealing a human child, but a noble damsel doing her best to thwart Claudas de la Deserte's cruel and uncourtly goals. Amusingly enough, though, an earlier passage describing Lancelot's departure from his 'foster-mother' betrays the deep drive hidden behind purported noble intentions: the Lady, crying bitterly about the loss of her dearest child, comforts herself with the knowledge that after his departure she will still have Bohort and Lionel, and even when Lionel leaves, she will be able to keep Bohort for an undetermined period of time.

The euhemerization of the water fairy is never quite complete, however, since a few elements betray her dubious origins. Although the Lady of the Lake herself does not currently practice magic, she is surrounded by damsels whose function is to *jeter des sors*, to use enchantments to help the Lady reach her goals. Such is, of course, the elaborate game Saraïde plays with the two greyhounds and the two sons of King Bohort. The text states clearly that the whole episode has been organized, even dictated, to Saraïde by her Lady. Moreover, the enchantment that makes the boys appear as dogs and the greyhounds appear as boys is not only a narrative trick, forgotten as soon as the damsel has taken the children away from Claudas. It also has further consequences since the masquerade is discovered at Claudas's court when Saraïde undoes the enchantment at night to allow the children to eat dinner. Since Pharien and the lords of Gaunes have not been informed of the Lady of the Lake's interference, they believe Claudas has tricked them, and their war with him recommences.

On the other hand, the motif of the lake as the abode of a water fairy— obviously a difficult element to insert in even a moderately realistic narrative—is constantly downplayed to the point that it almost disappears completely. The Lady lives in everyday settings, enriched with all the trappings of aristocratic life, and takes great care that no one discovers this supposedly magical place. The 'lake' is supposed to be nothing more than a mirage, an illusion that hides not only the Lady's manor but also a fairly large area from the notice of any passer-by. However, Lancelot, while hunting, is prone to meet with *vavasours* and other knights, inhabitants of the normal world who do not seem to realize they have crossed an invisible border. In later retellings, the Lake is no more nor less than the Lady's dominion, without any pointed reference to a real lake. One must remember that the Vulgate does not employ the motif of the sword of the lake: it gains eminence in what is known as the Post-Vulgate. Consequently, the Lady of the Lake has no immediate connection to Arthur, nor (despite a hurried '*replâtrage*') to Merlin and the damsel Niniane. In fact, the only remaining trace of the supernatural origin of the Lady's lake is that those who are privileged to come to the lake proper cannot leave: such is the fate of Pharien, Pharien's wife, and Lambegues. However, the precautions the Lady takes to avoid any chance discovery or any deliberate betrayal of the royal children's whereabouts to Claudas do not completely mask the otherworldly nature of a place no one can leave once admitted.

Conversely, the total 'whiteness' of the Lady's cortège while accompanying Lancelot to Arthur's court may be interpreted as a simple indicator of sophisticated elegance, or as the unmistakable proof of the supernatural origin of the water fairy and her changeling child.[3] There is an element, however, which tends to humanize the Lady of the Lake and to attenuate her fairy characteristics: she has an *ami* who is part of this cortège. In fact, while this character is never given much attention in the *Lancelot*, he tends to become more prominent in later texts that tend to downplay the parallel between the Lancelot/Guenevere relationship and the relationship the young *fils de roi* enjoys with 'his lady.'[4]

In the late-thirteenth-century romance the *Prophecies de Merlin*, for instance, the Lady of the Lake's *ami* is Meliadus, a brother or half-brother of Tristan de Leonois, and he is one of the causes of the Lady of the Lake's desire to dispose of Merlin. When he threatens that he will 'never sleep with her anymore' if she does not lead him to the place where she has buried Merlin, the Lady agrees to take him to the '*montagne qui debat*,' although she has previously sworn never to return there. She even travels with him dressed as 'a wedded woman' and willingly acquiesces to the jokes of some of her old acquaintances regarding her change of status. Although the focus of the *Prophecies* is on Meliadus and not on the Lady of the Lake, who serves mainly to introduce a character who will act as Merlin's posthumous messenger, the choice of the Lady's *ami* for this role is nevertheless representative of a significant tendency in the late romances to expand his role. The *Livre d'Artus* goes still further in this direction, since it establishes from the beginning a love interest on the Lady of the Lake's part, one which causes her to get involved with Merlin so that she can steal his wisdom and ultimately destroy him.[5]

However, in both texts, 'Lady of the Lake' or 'Damsel of the Lake' are just titles applied to Merlin's *amie*. There is no lake, no reminder of the lady's supernatural origin—or if there is one it comes from another source. The *Prophecies de Merlin* character stems from the same Diana prototype as the Post-Vulgate *Suite*'s Nivième, although it somewhat softens the Blanche Serpente's hatred for Merlin. In fact, the existence of Meliadus, the Lady of the Lake's *ami*, may be closer to the Diana story of the Post-Vulgate *Suite*, in which we have a female figure who seeks amorous liaisons, than to Nivième's characteristic persistent refusal of love and sex. On the other hand, the *Livre d'Artus* character goes further back indeed, to Chrétien de Troyes—but not to the 'Lady of the Lake' subliminally present in the *Chevalier de la Charrette*. On the contrary, she is an analogue, and even, technically, a family relation, of another 'water fairy,' the Lady of the Fountain featured in the *Chevalier au Lion*.[6] (In fact, Merlin's friend in the *Livre d'Artus* is the cousin of the Lady of the Fountain, but the Lady of the Fountain is called Lunette, like the Lady's maid in the *Chevalier au Lion*.) This brilliant intertextual rearrangement causes the reader to forget the true nature of the 'Niniane' character—although, to be accurate, the *Livre d'Artus* neither names her nor calls her 'Lady of the Lake.'

Nevertheless, she has been called Niniane earlier in this family of texts that bridges the gap between Arthur's coronation at the end of the French *Merlin* and the 'war of Gaule' at the opening of the *Lancelot*. The Niniane of the Vulgate *Suite* is created as a plausible mirror image of the Lady of the Lake in the *Lancelot*: a reflection created to offer a convincing background for the earlier figure. The chronological and logical aspects are at odds in the Vulgate *Suite*, a transition text that is never able to overcome its contradictions. Even the cyclic manuscripts which try most earnestly to erase the divergences between the *Merlin* proper and the *Lancelot* cannot reconcile the account of Merlin's birth and nature with the depiction of an evil devil's son given in the *Lancelot*. Similarly, there is an unbridgeable gap between the precocious child Niniane and the mature Lady of the Lake. Niniane's first appearance, in any case, takes us far from any lake, and back to Roman mythology:

Merlin's future *amie* is the daughter of Dyonas, a *vavasour* who happens to be the goddess Diana's godson—which is *per se* something of a paradox.[8]

There is no direct relationship between the pseudo-Diana and the child Niniane, but the latter acquires through a kind of semantic proximity some traits of the dryad. She lives, and will always live, in the heart of the 'Brecheliant' forest in Brittany, far from the Arthurian world. She is, however, just a bright child—except for Diana's 'gift' of prophecy about her. Because of the great love the *divesse* feels for her godson, she arranges for his first-born daughter to be loved by the wisest man in the world. Although this gift is explicitly mentioned as a blessing, one is likely to understand it as a curse. The story of the *divesse*, despite its apparent lack of connection to Niniane, in fact prepares the way for Niniane's appearance. The Lady of the Lake-to-be owes her singularity to the ambiguous relationship between her father and his godmother: their two names, Diane and Dyonas, are closely related, while Niniane's name belongs to a separate linguistic paradigm.[7]

Niniane, a name probably inherited from a Celtic tradition, is artificially enriched with an exotic meaning that brings Chaldean wisdom to Brittany. Niniane means, supposedly, 'Neant n'en feray' [I will do nothing of it], and the character behaves in a manner consistent with her name. A few centuries before Goethe's Mephistopheles, Niniane is 'der Geist, der stets verneint,'[9] the embodiment of negation. Nevertheless, since as far as I know there is no Chaldean word with such a meaning, nor any sounding like 'Niniane,' this naming is arbitrary, doing nothing to reconcile the 'wonder-child' Niniane of Brecheliant with the later Lady of the Lake, foster-mother to Lancelot. For one thing, this character has no name, even in a romance that tends to name a number of secondary figures. The 'damsel of the lake' whom the Lady sends to Trebes to rescue Lionel and Bohort from Claudas by an enchantment is named Saraïde, but her mistress is never named. Besides, there is a world of difference between, on one hand, the fourteen-year-old girl who asks Merlin to teach her how to 'make' a river—the key-element of any *locus amoenus*, and an apt symbol of a water fairy—and a cadre of handsome knights and beautiful ladies,[10] and on the other hand the powerful enchantress who abducts Lancelot (and later 'acquires' his two cousins). In effect, and as usual in a thirteenth-century text, there is no 'psychology' in the Vulgate *Suite*, no explanation of Niniane's motives, feelings, or goals. Everything is represented without extraneous comment. Merlin first hesitates to approach Niniane, since he knows what will then happen. Niniane herself is somewhat astonished by her would-be lover's persistence, since he knows the future. Both, nevertheless, play their parts in exact conformity to an ancient pattern, one that has nothing to do with the story of the 'Lady of the Lake.' The Vulgate *Suite* version of Merlin's ultimate deception avoids any reference to a lake or a water fairy, except for the aforementioned allusion to a magical river created by the wizard to please his new love.

The prison in which Niniane encloses Merlin is a 'prison of air,' a transparent castle, the threshold of which is a hawthorn tree. Niniane's Diana ascendancy again surfaces in this link between the fairy and the magical tree, traditionally used to signal the door to the Otherworld. Admittedly, the hawthorn tree is often situated near a river, or even a ford, since the frontier to the Otherworld has almost always something to do with water— running water, at that. But in the Vulgate *Suite*, no river is mentioned in this episode, not even a fountain, and certainly no lake, mirage or not. Moreover, the Vulgate *Suite* states very clearly that Niniane encloses Merlin in this quite literally 'magical circle' to avoid his tendency to stray, in effect preventing him from leaving her after he has slept with her. But then, once he is her prisoner, she agrees to love him, and promises to spend a lot of time with him in the castle of air that nobody can see from outside. And the text does add that Niniane keeps her promise, going in and out at will, but staying most nights with her lover. This almost happy ending not only gives a very original twist to the story of Merlin and his *amie*, but also creates a state of things which cannot be reconciled with the opening sequence of the *Lancelot* mentioned earlier.

Contrary to the Post-Vulgate *Suite*, where Merlin and Niviène's visit to King Ban de Benoïc and his queen prepare the reader for the Lady of the Lake's infatuation with Lancelot, the Vulgate *Suite* does not introduce Niniane to Ban's son. In fact, Niniane is instead the somewhat distant cause of Hector des Mares' birth, since Merlin loves Niniane too much to sleep with Agravain's daughter and therefore 'gives' her to Ban de Benoïc instead. Nevertheless, the rather precise chronology at the end of the Vulgate *Suite* underscores the lack of continuity between this text and the *Lancelot*, even while trying to suppress it. The quick retelling of the Merlin-and-Niniane story at the beginning of the 'Marche de Gaule' suggests a long interval between the Lady of the Lake's disposal of Merlin and her abduction of Lancelot.[11] However, the Vulgate *Suite* tells the story of Ban de Benoïc's return to his wife and of Lancelot's conception a bare few weeks or months before Merlin's disappearance. In so doing, it drastically reduces the interval, and fails in its primary objective of reconciling two heterogeneous narratives. Despite the efforts of the Vulgate *Suite*, Niniane (Merlin's *amie*) and the 'Lady of the Lake' remain two different characters, who apparently share enough elements to be fused in one synthetic figure, but continue to present specific traits impossible to reconcile.

At first glance, the situation seems vastly different in the Post-Vulgate *Suite*, but the results are globally the same as far as the Lady of the Lake's mystique is concerned. Technically, Nivlène is not a Lady, or even a damsel, of the Lake. Introduced in the narrative through her role of an adventure— one of these numerous adventures that keeps the knights busy and only acquires significance through the systematic decoding of the world the Post-Vulgate *Suite* happily provides—Nivlène is only a *damoiselle cacheresse* [a damsel-huntress], whose surprising decision to stay at Arthur's court is the first indication of her importance. Nevertheless, the reader remains somewhat perplexed: normally, this kind of damsel does not remain on the narrative scene after playing her—usually mute—*figurante's* part. (Otherwise, the prose romances would suffer from a plethora of damsels.) Nivlène gets her reprieve partly because of Merlin's sudden, or suddenly revealed, interest in her. From the beginning, however, her continuing presence is based on a paradox: since she fears and hates the devil's son's attentions, why should she choose to remain on the spot, in the only place where she is indeed the object of these attentions? Nivlène stays at Arthur's court only in order to provoke Merlin's love and consequently leads him to his ultimate destruction.

Conversely, Merlin chooses this damsel whose first appearance does not reveal her as anything special, in order to engage in the lethal game of seduction that constitutes, in most literary texts, the author's best and only way of getting rid of him. Nivlène, the damsel-huntress, is but a 'shifter,' her apparent importance in fact a delusion: she is still a minor character whose entire function revolves around Merlin. Since she is fated to remain in the spotlight somewhat longer than other damsels of her kind, she has to be given, as quickly as possible, something of the richness of a primary, or at least secondary, character. Accordingly, because she must stay at Arthur's court, she rapidly acquires a familial and geographical genealogy: she is a king's daughter, and she (like Niniane) comes from Brittany ('Bretaigne la Menor'). At this point, however, she is not yet linked to the Lake or its Ladies, whose function in the Post-Vulgate *Suite* is both reduced and essential.

Indeed, while the Vulgate *Suite* is satisfied with identifying Excalibur with the 'Sword in the Stone,' thus saving itself the trouble of 'inventing' an encounter between Arthur and the Lady of the Lake, the Post-Vulgate *Suite* insists on the necessity of Arthur winning an extraordinary sword, including an extraordinary scabbard, since he is an extraordinary king. The acquisition of Excalibur takes place through Merlin's mediation; the Lady, however, does not become a part of the Arthurian world, although she reserves the right, quite naturally, of exacting a payment from Arthur through the gift of an unnamed boon. She stays in or under the Lake, the ambiguous nature of which Merlin rapidly glosses over. When somewhat later a lady, or damsel of the Lake comes to court, her visit has to do with the strange and dark motive of Balin, the Knight with the Two Swords; there is no immediate relationship between this adventure and the one in which the damsel-huntress plays a part. In fact, one may doubt there is any relationship between the two, until a *coup-de-force* of the narrative binds them together, because it is by then too well known that Merlin meets his end at the hand of a 'lady of the Lake' for the Post-Vulgate *Suite* to reject this motif entirely.

However, Niviène, contrary to the Lady of the Lake in the *Lancelot*, is not primarily a mermaid or a water fairy. She is rather, quite openly, an avatar of the goddess Diana although the text is intent on dispelling all evidence of supernatural elements in its material, erasing any suggestion of direct relationship between 'Diane la divesse' and Niviène. Indeed, in the Post-Vulgate *Suite*, Diana has been dead a long time, and besides she never was a goddess; Merlin tells her story as a kind of etiological legend when he happens to visit a beautiful place where Diana lived. It is a very dark and tragic story, including the cold-blooded murder of Diana's first lover by her own hand because she wishes to clear the way for a second lover. It does, however, make wonderful sense from an anthropological point of view, as well as providing adequate material for a misogynist exemplum. The paradox in this episode is that the author unambiguously condemns Diana for an action that will give her 'spiritual daughter' the means to get rid of Merlin—a feat clearly considered sympathetically by the Post-Vulgate *Suite*. Moreover, this Diana-figure is strangely deprived of the most preeminent trait of the original goddess: her chastity. Diana, in this story, is the lecherous individual who deserves death as punishment for her betrayal—while Niviène's obsessive preoccupation with her virginity is presented as a positive response to Merlin's wily seductions.

In fact, Niviène's terror of and revulsion at the very idea of sex is much closer to the Diana-prototype than the euhemerized character associated with Faunus (another Roman deity, but a rather lecherous one) and Felix. The Post-Vulgate *Suite* in effect blackens the Diana-figure it uses as a model or inspiration for Niviène in order to offer a positive reading of Niviène's character. The pseudo-goddess serves also to create an (admittedly) fragile link between Niviène and the lake—or, more modestly, a lake. Her story is the origin of the numerous occurrences of a 'Lac Diane' in various later texts, especially the *Prophecies de Merlin*. Nevertheless, Nivième remains closer to the wood dryad than to the water fairy, and she considerably improves upon her predecessors. Despite her hatred for the devil's son, to escape her father's authority, she uses Merlin's power after feigning her obedience to her father's wishes in order to escape the confinement of Arthur's court.[12] The Diana story not only provides a way of getting rid of Merlin (which is then implemented later in a different place, far from the lake), but also creates a space of feminine freedom for the damsel-huntress, who is to have her own place and people from then on, without having to submit to masculine authority.

The 'Lac Diane' also gives her a new name, so that she becomes *de jure* a 'Damsel of the Lake,' even if it is definitely not the same lake as the one from which Arthur got Excalibur from the unnamed water fairy. Through this means, the transition is successfully accomplished, the Merlinesque tradition is respected, and the Nivième figure acquires her independence. In fact, the last elements revealing the discrepancy between two very different Ladies of the Lake may be seen in Nivième's aiding Arthur after Merlin's disappearance. In these episodes, Nivième opposes Morgue, another lover of Merlin and the embodiment of *bad* magic. While she had nothing to do with the gift of the sword Excalibur, she is involved in the theft of Excalibur's scabbard in a positive, albeit rather ineffectual, way. Her disposing of Merlin is consequently vindicated from the point of view of the narrative, as it has already been vindicated from a moral perspective. Whatever the sins and responsibilities of both characters might be, it would be difficult to present the newly created 'Damsel of the Lake' as a positive figure (which is undoubtedly the case) if she had deprived Arthur of a perhaps diabolical, but nevertheless useful and trustworthy, counselor without offering any compensation for the removal of Merlin.

By assuming Merlin's function of supernatural advisor at Arthur's court, Nivième justifies her acts and becomes respectable. However, the main question remains unanswered: the text expends great energy and relatively sophisticated narrative strategies in developing a character who, at the beginning, is but one of the numerous damsels haunting the adventure-filled forests and kingdoms. And then, after going to all this trouble, it completely ignores this new Damsel of the Lake, despite all her potentially useful attributes. We do not, of course, possess the complete Post-Vulgate Cycle, so we have no way of knowing whether or not the damsel-huntress, a.k.a. Nivième the 'Lady of the Lake,' would have played a part in the following romances analogous to the one Niniane plays in the Vulgate *Lancelot*.

What we do have depicts Nivière's disappearance shortly after she has disposed of Merlin, as if disposing of him was her only function. This pattern is brought to its logical conclusion in Malory's *Le Morte Darthur*, when Nimüe is only mentioned in passing as 'one of the damosels of the lake,' in a very short section devoted to Merlin's removal from the narrative scene. This, of course, deals efficiently with the difficulty of merging two or more different figures, more or less connected with various elements of the supernatural world. It also saves the trouble of inventing a plausible background for Nimüe, who is indeed a rather skeletal variant in this series of Ladies of the Lake. Nimüe, in fact, is needed in Malory's text only to help kill Merlin; however, as Malory did not choose to describe Merlin's birth or his first adventures, he does not care either to detail the circumstances of Merlin's death or disappearance. Merlin 'falls in a dotage' on Nimüe, and she takes advantage of it to *erase* him, as if he had never existed. She then disappears herself: whatever else she may be in this text, she is certainly not Lancelot's fairy foster-mother, the traditional Lady of the Lake.

It is all the more interesting, under these circumstances, to note how this character—and this somewhat strange name—fascinate later writers and audiences, even to the point where Merlin's betrayal by his beautiful *amie* is nowadays one of the best-known surviving elements of the Arthurian legends.[13] This extraordinary success is, in fact, rather paradoxical in view of the very little space dedicated to the character by Malory. When reading *Le Morte Darthur,* it seems that, at the end of the Middle Ages, the Lady of the Lake—reduced to the position of a 'Damsel of the Lake'—loses her independence as a fairy or a magician. She becomes only Merlin's bane, the traditional embodiment of 'the woman who conquers the wisest man in the world'—whether Aristotle, Solomon, or Merlin. The water fairy, the enchantress, has renounced her specific nature and/or her original function: she survives only as an element of a couple—the lesser element at that—in what remains basically a moral exemplum. When Merlin is ousted from the narrative, this downgraded Lady of the Lake endures the same fate. In the Post-Vulgate *Suite*, or to a lesser extent in the *Prophecies de Merlin*, Merlin's *amie* inherits in part the wizard's power and function, but in Malory Nimüe has no other part to play than to ensure Merlin's expulsion from the narrative. There is no question of transmutation of power, no hint of a feminine magic succeeding to Merlin's more disruptive manipulation of the structure of the story. As opposed to Nivière, Nimüe seems to be nothing but an appendage of Merlin's, and she does not appear again on the narrative scene.

In other words, while the accession of a secondary character (a water fairy gifted with a few magical talents) to an apparently promising position (that of Merlin's *amie*) would seem to amplify the Lady of the Lake's role, it has a perverse result: first this feminine figure is demonized, and then eventually erased. The Lady of the Lake is a victim of her success as well as of her superficial resemblance to Morgue, Arthur's half-sister and Merlin's lover in a number of versions. At the most, the story can absorb one enchantress, one 'Queen of Air and Darkness.'[14] Two of them would be redundant, even if a few versions do attempt to differentiate between a 'good' and a 'bad' enchantress, black and white magic. To some extent, the aforementioned *Livre d'Artus* illustrates the difficulty of keeping both characters separate: there, Morgue and Niniane almost exchange their places, the latter being depicted somewhat negatively. Uniquely among the manuscripts, this story does not address the problem of an enchantress helping—or, on the contrary, trying to destroy—Arthur. However, it becomes clear elsewhere, for instance in the Post-Vulgate *Suite*, that Morgue and the Lady of the Lake are impossible to distinguish, and that one such character should be enough: a feminine character whose knowledge underlines her dangerousness, a supernatural creature whose real nature has to be glossed over, a fairy whose femininity must be subjected to masculine power—or reduced to the traditional role of an evil seductress. Nimüe, the last medieval avatar of the Lady of the Lake, is also a radical negation of this character's primary traits. Demonized as a new Eve, she serves to ensnare Merlin and she remains the symbol of feminine falsehood—a sad, all too frequent ending for this medieval mermaid.

UNIVERSITY OF CONNECTICUT, STORRS

An alumna of the French École Normale Supérieure, Anne Berthelot earned her Doctorat d'Etat at the Sorbonne (Paris IV) and is now Professor of French at the University of Connecticut. She has published several books and a number of articles about Arthurian prose romances; she is currently part of the *Pleiade* Gallimard team preparing a complete edition-translation of the Vulgate Cycle (from the *Estoire dou Graal* to the *Mort le roi Artu*).

NOTES

1   See Françoise Morvan, *La douce vie des fées des eaux* (Arles: Actes Sud/Babel, 1998).
2   In Welsh texts like the *Afallenau* or the *Oianau*, Myrddin, Merlin's prototype or avatar, regrets the loss of a beautiful maiden, called Gwenddydd or left nameless, sometimes presented as his sister and sometimes as his lover, who has turned against him for reasons unclear. On the other hand, the *Vita Merlini* surrounds Merlin with at least two feminine figures, his sister and his wife.

3 Again, these traits are more clearly readable in the German *Lanzelet*, whose Lady of the Lake has chosen the hero as a tool to ensure her own son's deliverance, and engages him in a series of obviously supernatural adventures. See Ulrich von Zatzikhoven, *Lanzelet*, ed. and trans. in NHD, W. Spiewok (Greifswald: Reineke-Verlag, 1997).

4 Lancelot as a young knight recently dubbed shows the same overwhelming respect to any wish, or fancied desire, of 'sa dame la reïne' and 'sa dame du Lac.'

5 Probably written before the most developed version of the *Prophecies*.

6 It is certainly not insignificant that both characters appear in the two romances which Chrétien supposedly wrote simultaneously, at least in part. However, the two types of supernatural women linked to water and the Otherworld are not completely analogous.

7 Of course, the traditional euhemerization technique is employed on behalf of this 'Diane la divesse,' but the attempt to Christianize such a character is somewhat forced.

8 It would be difficult not to see in this Diana figure an image of the fairy lover, choosing as her *ami* a very young man whom she initiates into love.

9 That is, 'the spirit which always says no,' or 'always negates everything.' See Goethe's *Faust*, trans. with an introduction by Philip Wayne (Baltimore: Penguin, 1958–59).

10 Which reminds the reader of a number of enchanted places in the earlier Arthurian literature, and looks much like a barely softened version of the *Val sans Retour* [The Valley Without Return].

11 That is the name currently given to the first part of the *Lancelot*.

12 She leaves the court to answer her father's summons, but when she discovers the beautiful lake of Diane, she asks Merlin to build a palace for her in this place and decides to remain there forever, renouncing her duty as a daughter and, in fact, all family ties.

13 In addition to classical texts, like Tennyson's *Idylls of the King* (New York: Bantam Books, 1965) some of the newest versions of the story continue to demonize Nimüe. A very good example of this tendency appears in Irene Radford's *Guardian of the Balance: Merlin's Descendants* (New York: DAW Books, 1999), which invents a new character, Wren, Merlin's daughter, but reuses the motif of Merlin's seduction and quasi-murder by Nimüe (in this volume, she is the incestuous daughter of Caradoc, Wren's husband).

14 To use the title made famous by T.H. White in *The Once and Future King* (New York: G.P. Putnam's Sons, 1958).

Morgan le Fay at Hautdesert

MICHAEL W. TWOMEY

The toponymic *Hautdesert* 'high wilderness' in *Sir Gawain and the Green
Knight* is here considered as a clue to Bertilak's feudal relationship with
Morgan le Fay in light of the Arthurian commonplace of Morgan as
ruler of the wilderness. Acting in the belief that Morgan is marginal to
the poem, editors of *SGGK* obscure this relationship in transcribing
Bertilak's speech about Morgan's role in lines 2445 ff. (MWT)

In her essay 'From the Lady to the Tramp: The Decline of Morgan le Fay,'
Maureen Fries, struck by the minor role that Morgan le Fay played in
Malory, observed that Morgan appears 'literally near the narrative margins
of the book' because 'Malory's *Morte*, after all, like all Arthurian romances,
is not really about women, but about aristocratic men and their adventures,
feuds, and often hazardous exchanges of females.'[1] This marginalization is
evident in terms of narrative space devoted to her and the cultural ideologies
that underwrite the use of females in Arthurian literature. Morgan's
appearances in Arthurian romances are quite limited as compared to
Lancelot's and Gawain's, and when they do occur, her textual moments are
overdetermined by her complementary functions as the benevolent healer
who conducts Arthur to Avalon and as the malevolent hag bent on undoing
him and his court. However, Maureen's metaphor also implies that to be
marginal is still to be on the page, if only at the edges, and thus vital to the
text.

A quite literal case in point is in MS Royal 12.C.ix in the British Library,
a collection of astronomical/astrological treatises and tables copied in the
thirteenth and fourteenth centuries which, like many medieval manuscripts,
bears marginalia by various hands. Among these is a letter in French scrawled
across the bottom of a set of solar and lunar tables on folios 165v and 166r.
The letter, in a late-fourteenth- or early-fifteenth-century secretary hand, is
to a bachelor of Morgan's court, reporting on an audience with another
knight and inviting the bachelor to visit her in her castle. The salutation of
the letter identifies Morgan thus: 'Morgayne, *par* la grace deu emp*er*isse de
desert' [Morgan, by the grace of God empress of the desert (=wilderness)].[2]
Although a letter purporting to be from Morgan le Fay may seem incongruous

in the margins of a set of astrological tables, perhaps the writer was remembering that according to the Prose *Merlin*, Morgan had been put to school to study the arts, astrology, and medicine when she was young.[3]

The letter is very interesting in its own right as an example of Arthurian reception, but since transcribing it poses some difficulties that I shall have to deal with in another space, in this essay I want to call attention only to the notion of Morgan le Fay as ruler of the wilderness. The title 'empress of the desert' in Royal 12.C.ix may call to mind images of antipodal drag queens roaming the Outback, but whoever wrote the letter in Royal 12.C.ix managed to epitomize one of the main attributes of Morgan le Fay in Arthurian literature, that she presides over the unknown world—the world that circumscribes and frames the known world, like the margins surrounding a text.[4] Taking Maureen's comment about the marginality of Morgan as a geographical metaphor, then, whether she is sailing in from Avalon to remove the wounded King, or whether she is imprisoning Lancelot in one of her wilderness castles, Morgan fills the spaces left empty by Arthur, which even in terms of a Eurocentric medieval *mappa mundi* constitute a huge area—one that Lydia the Tattooed Lady would have envied.[5]

Considering the late-medieval English context in which Royal 12.C.ix was written, the title 'empress of the desert' also recalls a familiar and fictional place-name found in *Sir Gawain and the Green Knight* [henceforth *SGGK*]. In line 2445, in reply to Gawain's request to know the name of his host at the castle where he has stayed, the Green Knight identifies himself as 'Bertilak de Hautdesert':

> "Bot on I wolde yow praye, displeses yow neuer:
> Syn ʒe be lorde of þe ʒonder londe þat I have lent inne
> Wyth yow wyth worschyp—þe Wyʒe hit yow ʒelde
> Þat vphaldez þe heuen and on hyʒ sittez—
> How norne ʒe yowre ryʒt nome, and þenne no more?"
> "Þat schal I telle þe trwly," quoþ þat oþer þenne,
> "Bertilak de Hautdesert I hat in þis londe,
> Þurʒ miʒt of Morgue la Faye, þat in my hous lenges,
> And koyntyse of clergye, bi craftes wel lerned—
> Þe maystrés of Merlyn mony ho hatz taken.
> For ho hatz dalt drwry ful dere sumtyme
> Wyth þat conable klerk; þat knowes alle your knyʒtes
>   At hame.
>   Morgue þe goddes
>   Þerfore hit is hir name.
>   Weldez non so hyʒe hawtesse

Þat ho ne con make ful tame—." (2439–55)[6]

["But I would pray you of one thing, may it never displease you:
Since you are the lord of that yonder land where I have stayed
Worshipfully with you—may the Man repay it you
Who holds up the heavens and sits on high—
How do you properly call yourself, and that's all (I want to know)?'
"That shall I tell you truly," said the other then,
"Bertilak de Hautdesert I am called in this land.
Through the might of Morgan le Fay, who dwells in my house,
And the skill of learning, by crafts well learned—
The many arts of Merlin has she acquired.
For once she had a most pleasant love affair
With that excellent sage; as all your knights know
                At home.
        Morgan the goddess
        Therefore is her name.
        No one has such high pride
        That she can not completely tame him—"].

Since Gawain has asked only for the Green Knight's proper name, and
'no more,' Bertilak's additional revelation about Morgan le Fay along with
his own toponymic identity in the following lines comes as a surprise.
Although in the following stanza (2456–71) Bertilak will explain Morgan's
role in the adventure, for the moment there is no apparent reason why Bertilak
must reveal Morgan's name as soon as he reveals his own. The passage therefore
raises questions that I shall discuss in this essay in light of the implications
of the epithet 'empress of the desert' from Royal 12.C.ix. One is about the
possible function of the toponymic *Hautdesert* as a geographical revelation
of Morgan's presence in Bertilak's castle.[7] Following from that, another
question concerns how the relationship between Bertilak and Morgan le Fay
that is implied in 2446–51 has been marginalized, to apply Maureen's
metaphor in yet another sense, by editions of the poem.

The place-name *Hautdesert* has been variously explained. Both elements
of the name are French, and the crux of the name is the element *desert*, a
noun found in both Old French and Middle English that corresponds to
Latin *desertum* and means, as defined in the *Middle English Dictionary*, '1a. a
barren area, wooded or arid, and hence uninhabitable or sparsely inhabited;
wasteland, wilderness, a desert; 1b. a (specified) desert or wilderness; 2a. the
wilderness as a retreat for religious conversion; 2b. applied to this world; 2c.
desolation.'[8] Together, *haut* and *desert* would form a compound meaning
'high wasteland' or possibly 'high hermitage.' The elements *haut* and *desert*
are found singly or in combination in a number of French and English
place-names, but aside from this occurrence the compound *Hautdesert* does

not occur in France or England.[9] It is a fictional name that invites the question of what in the poem it may identify.

According to one interpretation, *Hautdesert* refers to the Green Chapel where Gawain meets the Green Knight. Exemplifying this view, G.V. Smithers, who read Gawain's encounter at the Green Chapel as a palimpsest of encounters with hermits in the Vulgate *Queste del saint Graal*, suggested that Hautdesert was a 'direct translation of [*le*] *haut hermitage* in the *Queste*.'[10] What underwrites this possibility is the extended sense of a *desert* as a place inhabited by hermits. A more widely accepted view is that the element *desert* bears only the base meaning 'wasteland,' a region uninhabited or uninhabitable. Thus Norman Davis maintained that *Hautdesert* 'the high wasteland' could not refer to the Green Chapel, which was in a valley rather than on a height, and that since Gawain had asked specifically for his host's name 'in the yonder land,' Bertilak understood him to be referring to the castle, not to the chapel.[11] Peter Lucas, who noted the existence of an analogous medieval place-name *Beaudesert* in Warwickshire and Staffordshire as a possible inspiration for *Hautdesert*, took issue with Davis's notion that *Hautdesert* referred to the castle, since the castle is in a park ('Pyched on a prayere, a park al aboute,' 768) rather than a wilderness, and he suggested instead that *Hautdesert* could refer only to the high hill (2199; cp. 2166, 2221) where Gawain saw the Green Knight.[12] An objection to Lucas's objection, however, is that the Beaudesert in Staffordshire, four miles west of Lichfield, was a mansion and park together that were enclosed from the surrounding Cannock Forest—hence, an example of a toponymic in the form X + *desert* that refers to a house and park in a forest, very much like Bertilak's castle.[13]

The possibility that *Hautdesert* refers to the castle after all has been argued cogently by Ralph Elliott, whose scrupulous examination of the language and geography of the poem places Hautdesert at the site of Swythamley Grange in Staffordshire, on the property of the Cistercian abbey at Dieulacres. Just as Bertilak's castle is only two miles from the Green Chapel (1078), the grange is only two miles from Ludchurch, a possible candidate for the site of the Green Chapel. Swythamley sits on a height looking south over the Leekfrith valley towards Dieulacres, east towards a rocky escarpment called the Roaches, and west towards Gun Hill. Once known as 'Knight's Low,' a name that recalls the poet's word *lawe* to describe its setting in line 765, it is surrounded by a wilderness forest known in the Middle Ages as the High Forest, which was used for hunting, just as Bertilak hunted in the area around his castle. If the name *Hautdesert* refers to the castle, then it would have been chosen because of the castle's situation above the valley and because of the surrounding wild countryside, whose name, the High Forest, could even have suggested the castle's name.[14]

The original audience of *SGGK* would probably have been amused to recognize a place on the local map masquerading as the lodging of the famous Sir Gawain. But as Gawain's journey takes the reader from the fictional landscape of Camelot to the very real landscape of fourteenth-century Staffordshire, it takes Gawain from the known world of Arthur to the unknown world of the Green Knight. *SGGK* is a fictional narrative superimposed over a realistic geography. As such, its landscapes, though they may have given the poem's original audience the pleasure of recognizing familiar territory, are part of that fiction. As it happens, the wilderness location identified by Elliott as the location of castle Hautdesert is also ideally suited to Morgan le Fay as 'empress of the desert,' ruler of the wasteland.

The poet carefully highlights the wilderness location of the castle from the time he describes Gawain's journey along the deserted Welsh coast. The landscape along the way is undifferentiated until Gawain comes to the first named location, North Wales (697), a site associated in Arthurian literature with the King and Queen of North Wales, she being one of Morgan le Fay's companions in attempting to seduce Lancelot in the Prose *Lancelot* and in Malory.[15] North Wales would thus be the first hint that Gawain's journey will take him to Morgan le Fay. From there, Gawain passes Anglesey and the Holy Head, then enters the wilderness of the Wirral (698–701), appropriately a lawless region known in the fourteenth century for crime and insurrection.[16] On Christmas Eve he passes 'by a mount. . ./ Into a forest full deep, which was marvelously wild, / High hills on each side and holt-woods below' [Bi a mount…/ Into a forest ful dep, þat ferly watz wilde, / Hiȝe hillez on vche a halue and holtwodez vnder] (740–42), where the trees and bushes are gnarled together to make an almost impenetrable barrier, and are relieved only by swamps and bogs (740–49). This rugged landscape so thoroughly discourages Gawain that he utters a desperate prayer to God and to Mary for a place where he might hear Mass, and no sooner has he crossed himself when he looks up, and there above him is not a hermitage or a monastery but a castle, as if materialized out of thin air (763–70). It is 'The handsomest castle ever owned by a knight' [A castel þe comlekost þat euer knyȝt aȝte] (767), where Gawain is courteously received and lavishly entertained.

Poets as widely separated in time as Marie de France, William Dunbar, and John Keats knew that fairies could be found almost anywhere at the liminal, marginal spaces of the world, and the poet of *SGGK*, like the writer

who devised the salutation in Royal 12.C.ix, knew it, too. As Helen Cooper
has observed, Gawain 'has to confront…a series of adventures that are never
quite what they seem, and in which neither he nor the reader is quite sure
what elements belong to the natural world and what to the worlds of magic
and the supernatural.'[17] However much the topography of *SGGK* evokes
the Staffordshire countryside, the wilderness setting of the castle and its
mysterious appearance out of nowhere are clues that Gawain has entered
the realm not of the Cistercians at Dieulacres but of Morgan le Fay.
Retrospectively placed at the end of the poem, the element *desert* in the
name *Hautdesert* would signify not only the local topography but the presence
of Morgan le Fay at the place to which Gawain had come when he saw the
castle in Fitt II.

The abundant indications of fairy magic present in the Green Knight's
appearance and in the landscape surrounding Hautdesert have received their
share of attention,[18] but so far the name of the castle has not been considered
one of them. There is warrant to raise this possibility, though, not only
because of the name of the castle, but also because of the very grammar of
Bertilak's speech. Editors and translators confronting this passage must decide
whether 'through the might of Morgan le Fay' (2446) functions as an adverbial
phrase modifying 'Bertilak de Hautdesert I am called in this land' (2445) or
whether it is grammatically unconnected. The difference is that if the lines
are connected, Bertilak is saying that 'in this land' his name comes from the
power of Morgan le Fay. This reading of the lines suggests that Bertilak's
explanation of Morgan's powers and her role in the adventure is a function
of his self-identification, perhaps out of anxiety to avoid lese-majesty.
However, editorial practice has been to put a full stop after 2445 and to
make the best of the grammatical confusion that follows from treating 2446–
51 as an aside rather than as part of Bertilak's self-identification. The standard
editions of Tolkien and Gordon (rev. Davis) and Andrew and Waldron both
illustrate this approach:

> "Bertilak de Hautdesert I hat in þis londe.
> Þurȝ miȝt of Morgue la Faye, þat in my hous lenges,
> And koyntyse of clergye, bi craftes wel lerned—
> Þe maystrés of Merlyn mony ho hatz taken,
> For ho hatz dalt drwry ful dere sumtyme
> Wyth þat conable klerk; þat knowes alle your knyȝtes
> At hame." (2445–51)

The grammatical construction that results from this punctuation becomes what Andrew and Waldron in their note to these lines charitably call a 'loose conversational structure' that they translate thus:

> [Through the might of Morgan le Fay, who dwells in my house,] and (her) skill in learning, (she who is) well-instructed in magic arts—she has acquired many of the miraculous powers of Merlin, for she has formerly had very intimate love-dealings with that excellent scholar, as all of your knights at home know.

This rendering is unable to connect line 2446 to line 2447 without supplying additional words, and it is unable to connect the result to the following lines at all, inserting a dash to provide the illusion of hypotaxis that would connect the subordinate clause created out of 2447 and 2448 with a main clause beginning in 2449. Thus, by this reading, 'Through the might of Morgan le Fay' is left dangling, modifying nothing.[19]

In an earlier era, editors faced with difficulties in single-witness texts often resorted to emendation. For example, in order to make sense of 2446–51, in his EETS edition Gollancz 'solved' the grammatical problem by suggesting that a line had been dropped between 2445 and 2446 by which Bertilak explains that through the power of Morgan le Fay he had been changed into the Green Knight. Gollancz even provided his own Middle English filler: "'Bertilak de Hautdesert I hat in þis londe, / [þat þus am aȝlych of hwe & al ouer brawden] / þurȝ myȝt,'" etc. [Bertilak de Hautdesert I am called in this land, / Who am thus terrible in hue and thus transformed / Through the might, etc.]. There is no doubt that the scribe of Cotton Nero A.x nodded occasionally. In 2448, for example, the scribe wrote 'ho taken,' which editors emend either to 'hatz taken' or to 'ho hatz taken.' It is well for readers to recall that they encounter *SGGK* in an editorial rather than an authorial form. In the manuscript, there is neither punctuation nor capitalization (except for the large capitals) to guide the reader. Especially because *SGGK* exists in only one manuscript, quite often editors must make decisions based on their construction of authorial intention. Traditionally, editing precedes criticism, with the critics depending on the editions for what the text actually 'says.' However, editorial practice tends to be conservative, with editors repeating one another sometimes for decades. Once a reading is established it wields authority long after the critical presumptions that guided it have disappeared, and the text can easily be regarded as clear and unambiguous when it is anything but.[20]

In fact, there is no grammatical reason not to link 2445 and 2446 so that the lines read "'Bertilak de Hautdesert I hat in þis londe / þurȝ miȝt of Morgue la Faye, þat in my hous lenges.'" Here I would like to propose two alternative solutions to 2446–51 that make this connection and, I think, make better grammatical sense of the passage than the standard editions, without the use of textual prosthetics. First:

"Bertilak de Hautdesert I hat in þis londe
Þurȝ miȝt of Morgue la Faye, þat in my hous lenges,
And koyntyse of clergye, bi craftes wel lerned—
Þe maystrés of Merlyn; mony ho hatz taken,
For ho hatz dalt drwry ful dere sumtyme
Wyth þat conable klerk, þat knowes alle your knyȝtes
            At hame." (2445–51)

[Bertilak de Hautdesert I am called in this land
Through the might of Morgan le Fay, who dwells in my house,
And the skill of (i.e. her) education by crafts well learned—
The arts of Merlin; many has she acquired,
For once she had a most pleasant love affair
With that excellent sage, who knows all your knights
            At home.]

In this transcription, 'þurȝ' (2446) governs two objects, 'miȝt of Morgue la Faye' (2446) and 'koyntyse of clergye' (2447), one expressing Morgan's power (which could be magical or seigniorial), the other her education (obtained in the Prose *Merlin*—see above, at note 3). The next phrase in 2447, 'bi craftes wel lerned,' modifies 'koyntyse of clergye,' which is restated as the appositive phrase 'þe maystrés of Merlyn' (2448). The full stop in 2448 makes a natural caesura at the mid-point of the long alliterative line, a common feature in both narrative and dialogue in *SGGK*.[21] All together, 2445–48a would say that Bertilak is called 'de Hautdesert' in this land by virtue of the power and the learning of Morgan le Fay, who practices the arts of Merlin. Where she learned these arts is alluded to in the following lines, which refer to the love affair between Merlin and Morgan that occurred when Morgan was expelled from court for her affair with Guenevere's cousin Gui[g]omar. The story of how Morgan acquired Merlin's magic is cited by the Prose *Lancelot* in a passage containing all of the biographical information about her that is found subsequently in Bertilak's speech—i.e., the epithet 'goddess' (2452), her genealogical relationship to Gawain (2467) and to Arthur and Igerne (2464–67), plus her narrative relationships with Merlin (2447–51) and Guenevere (2459–62).[22]

One ambiguity that remains is the reference of 'mony ho hatz taken' (2448b). If it refers to 'maystrés of Merlyn' in the same line, as this first transcription implies, then Bertilak is saying that Morgan acquired many (but implicitly not all) of the arts of Merlin when she had her affair with him. But on the other hand, 'mony' could refer to men such as Bertilak whom Morgan has taken into her service—an anticipation of his disclosure about how Morgan "'wayned me vpon þis wyse to your wynne halle / For to assay þe surquidré...'" [sent me in this appearance to your beautiful hall / In order to test the surquidry...] (2456–57). Perhaps abashed at having to admit his subordination to Morgan, Bertilak mitigates his embarrassment by making himself one of many—the same exculpatory tactic employed by Gawain, only explicitly, in his *blasme des femmes* about Adam, Solomon, Samson, and David (2414–28). The connection to 2449–50a, which mentions Morgan's affair with Merlin, would make sense, then, as an explanation of how and when Morgan acquired the magic by which she accomplished this feat.

The second transcription emphasizes this latter possibility by placing a full stop after 2447a and a hyphen after 2448a:

> "Bertilak de Hautdesert I hat in þis londe,
> Þurȝ miȝt of Morgue la Faye, þat in my hous lenges,
> And koyntyse of clergye. Bi craftes wel lerned—
> Þe maystrés of Merlyn—mony ho hatz taken,
> For ho hatz dalt drwry ful dere sumtyme
> Wyth þat conable klerk, þat knowes alle your knyȝtes
>   At hame." (2445–51)

> [Bertilak de Hautdesert I am called in this land,
> Through the might of Morgan le Fay, who dwells in my house,
> And the skill of (i.e. her) education. By crafts well learned—
> The arts of Merlin—many has she taken,
> For once she had a most pleasant love affair
> With that excellent sage, who knows all your knights
>   At home.]

Both transcriptions not only make far better sense of the passage than the 'loose conversational structure' proposed by Andrew and Waldron, they offer a better solution to the noun-verb agreement problem in 2550b, by construing Merlin as the subject and the knights of the Round Table as the object of 'knowes.' Although plural verbs ending in -es do occur in the manuscript, -en is the norm, with -es reserved for the third person present singular.

Probably the main reason why editors have not proposed solutions such as these to the grammar of the passage is that even though the grammar works, it has been difficult to understand how Bertilak de Hautdesert could be so called 'in this land' through the power of Morgan and through the skill of (her) education. This has more to do with editorial presumption than with grammar. If Morgan is presumed to be marginal to the narrative, then she could not possibly have anything to do with Bertilak's lordship in the land from which he derives his name. Editorial decisions must of course always depend on linguistic, paleographical, and codicological facts, but they do not take place in isolation from literary concerns. The editions that we use were all completed at a time when critics tended to dismiss Morgan from *SGGK*, in the extreme regarding her appearance as some kind of bizarre obeisance to a now-lost source.[23] Although a number of recent historicist and feminist readings have retrieved Morgan from the margins of the poem, editors have yet to catch up.[24] Even the third edition of Andrew and Waldron (1996) does not take account of recent scholarship about Morgan's role.[25]

Editorial thinking seems largely to be prompted by Bertilak's speeches to Gawain in the beheading scene. In these speeches, playing the role of father-confessor, Bertilak maintains the pretense that the testing was his by carefully restricting his explanation of the adventure to the exchange of winnings. In this account of the adventure, first person nominative and possessive pronouns figure heavily, as for example in Bertilak's explanation of the girdle and the wooing:

> "For hit is my wede þat þou werez, þat ilke wouen girdel.
> Myn owen wyf hit þe weued, I wot wel forsoþe.
> Now know I wel þy cosses and þy costes als,
> And þe wowyng of my wyf. I wroȝt hit myseluen;
> I sende hir to asay þe " (2358–62)

> [For it is my garment that you are wearing, that same woven girdle.
> My own wife gave it to you, I know it well in truth.
> Now I know well your kisses and your behavior also,
> And the wooing of my wife—I contrived it myself;
> I sent her to test you...]

Bertilak's version of his role changes when he names himself and then Morgan le Fay, offering a radically different account of the adventure. In this second revelation, even Bertilak's language destabilizes his earlier proprietary claims. His use of the possessive with regard to Hautdesert and its people ('my house' 2446, 2468; 'my retinue' 2468) brackets his revelation of Morgan's role. As Bertilak stands there in the figure of the Green Knight, explaining his enchantment by Morgan le Fay, his identities clash and his sense of self slips, for he refers to the Green Knight in the third person when citing his visit to Camelot (2461–62). This slippage extends to his reference to the Round Table as 'your knights' (2450) and to Camelot as 'your fine hall' (2456), as if the retinue and the castle were Gawain's, not Arthur's. Whereas the first account of the adventure makes Bertilak the subject, the second account makes him the object, emphasizing Morgan's agency:

> "Ho wayned me vpon þis wyse to your wynne halle
> For to assay þe surquidré, ȝif hit soth were

Þat rennes of þe grete renoun of þe Rounde Table;
Ho wayned me þis wonder your wyttez to reue,
For to haf greued Gaynour and gart hir to dyȝe
With glopnyng of þat ilke gome þat gostlych speked
With his hede in his honde bifore þe hyȝe table.
Þat is ho þat is at home, þe auncian lady;
Ho is euen þyn aunt, Arþurez half-suster,
Þe duches doȝter of Tyntagelle, þat dere Vter after
Hade Arþur vpon, þat aþel is nowþe.
þerfore I eþe þe, haþel, to com to þyn aunt.
Make myry in my hous: my meny þe louies
And I wol þe as wel, wyȝe, bi my faythe,
As any gome vnder God, for þy grete trauþe." (2456–70)

[She sent me in this appearance to your fine hall
In order to test the surquidry, if it were true
What circulates about the great renown of the Round Table.
She made me this wonder to rob you of your wits,
In order to afflict Guenevere and cause her to die
With horror of that same man who mysteriously spoke
With his head in his hand before the high table.
That is she who is at home, the ancient lady;
She is even your aunt, Arthur's half-sister,
The daughter of the duchess of Tintagel, upon whom dear Uther later
Begot Arthur, who now is noble.
Therefore I urge you, knight, to come to your aunt.
Make merry in my house. My retinue loves you
And I will (love you) as well, man, by my faith,
As any man under God, for your great faithfulness.]

It was Morgan who made him into the Green Knight in order to test the surquidry of the Round Table and (unsuccessfully) frighten Guenevere to death (2445–62); moreover, Bertilak informs Gawain of his blood relationship to Morgan, who is Gawain's aunt (2463–66), and he invites Gawain to return with him for the New Year holiday (2467–70)—an invitation that Gawain flatly refuses (2471). He may wear the green girdle and the nick on the neck on his body, but he carries Morgan in his body, in his blood. Whereas earlier (357) Gawain believed that his worth came from the blood of his uncle, Arthur, now he learns that the same blood is Morgan's.[26] Although this final revelation is surely the greatest surprise for Gawain, because it brings the foreign, female, magical Morgan from a wilderness castle called Hautdesert to lodge within Gawain himself, Bertilak has at the same time admitted something equally momentous about himself: that just as Morgan resides in Gawain's blood, she also resides in Bertilak's feudal identity.

Considering Morgan as 'empress of the desert' helps to explain her relationship to Bertilak, but however attractive it may be to see Morgan as the only begetter of the whole adventure, it will not do. To define their roles in terms of the traditional plot elements in *SGGK*, according to Bertilak's account—the only one we have to go on—the 'beheading game' was Morgan's scheme, while the 'exchange of winnings' was his. In one sense she and Bertilak are collaborators, while in another sense his is the social power as owner of the castle, and in yet another sense hers is the underlying power as magician and moral force that sets the adventure in motion. Bertilak's insistence that the girdle, the wife, the wooing, and the castle are his is not simply male puffery. The narrative calls Bertilak the 'lord of the lede' [lord of the people] (833) when he is introduced in Fitt iii. Yet it is also the narrative that makes Morgan one of only three characters in Bertilak's household who share Gawain's social status. She is introduced when she emerges from evensong with Bertilak's wife (947–69), whom she leads by the hand; she is 'highly honored by the men all around' (949); and when dinner is served, it is Morgan who sits at the high seat on the dais, courteously attended by the lord of the castle: 'Þe olde auncian wyf, heȝest ho sittez; / Þe lorde lufly her by lent as I trowe' [The old ancient woman, highest she sits; / The lord courteously took his place beside her, as I think] (1001–02). If naming a character privileges that character, then Morgan is more significant than the lady, despite the fact that the lady does so much talking in Fitt iii and Morgan never utters a line in the poem. Morgan is a VIP presence, one called 'goddess' (2452) who can tame the pride of any man (2454–55) and who turned Bertilak into the Green Knight and sent him to Camelot as her errand boy. If Bertilak holds his land 'þurȝ myȝt of Morgue la Faye, þat in my hous lenges,' the feudal relationship is such that he is her vassal: to conceal Morgan's seigniorial authority would be an act of the very surquidry that it is Morgan's specialty to probe.

ITHACA COLLEGE

Michael W. Twomey is Professor of English and Chair of the English Department at Ithaca College, where he teaches medieval literature and the Bible. In 1996–97 he was Fulbright Senior Lecturer at the Institut für Anglistik und Amerikanistik, Technische Universität Dresden. He writes about Middle English literature, especially the *Gawain*-poet, and about medieval encyclopedias. Currently he is producing a reception study of medieval encyclopedias in England and is part of an international collaboration, based in Münster and Orléans, to edit the *De proprietatibus rerum* of Bartholomeus Anglicus.

NOTES

1 Maureen Fries, 'From the Lady to the Tramp: The Decline of Morgan le Fay in Medieval Romances,' *Arthuriana* 4.1 (Spring 1994): 15 [1–18].

2 The manuscript is described in Sir George F. Warner and Julius P. Gilson, eds., *Catalogue of Western Manuscripts in the Old Royal and King's Collections*, 4 vols. (London: British Museum, 1921), 2:26. Punctuation, expansion of abbreviations, and translation mine. I am grateful to Nicole Clifton, Northern Illinois University, for calling the manuscript to my attention.

3 See *Lestoire de Merlin* in *The Vulgate Version of the Arthurian Romances*, ed. H. Oskar Sommer, 7 vols., Carnegie Institution of Washington Publications 74 (Washington, DC: Carnegie Institution, 1908), 2:73; Modern English trans. Rupert T. Pickens, *The Story of Merlin*, in *Lancelot-Grail: The Old French Arthurian Vulgate and Post-Vulgate in Translation*, ed. Norris J. Lacy, 5 vols. (New York: Garland, 1993–96), 1:208. Morgan also figures in the corresponding passage of the Middle English version [ca. 1450], *Merlin: A Prose Romance*, ed. H.B. Wheatley, EETS o.s. 10, 21, 36, 112 (London: K. Paul, Trench, Trübner, 1865–99), p. 86.Cf. the version attributed to Robert de Boron: *Merlin: roman du XIIIe siècle*, ed. Alexandre Micha, Textes Littèraires Français 281 (Geneva: Droz, 1979), p. 245.

4 I refer to the film, 'The Adventures of Priscilla, Queen of the Desert,' written and directed by Stephan Elliott (1994). Narratives about Morgan are surveyed in Fanni Bogdanow, 'Morgain's Role in the Thirteenth-Century French Prose Romances of the Arthurian Cycle,' *Medium Ævum* 38 (1969): 123–33; Wolfgang Fauth, 'Fata Morgana,' in *Beiträge zum romanischen Mittelalter*, ed. Kurt Baldinger, Zeitschrift für Romanische Philologie, Sonderband zum 100-Jährigen Bestehen (Tübingen: Niemeyer, 1977), pp. 417–54; Eberhard W. Funcke, 'Morgain und ihre Schwestern: Zur Herkunft und Verwendung der Feenmotivik in der mittelhochdeutschen Epik,' *Acta Germanica: Jahrbuch des Germanistenverbandes im südlichen Afrika* 18 (1985): 1–64; Laurence Harf-Lancner, *Les Fées au moyen âge. Morgane et Mélusine: La naissance des fées*, Nouvelle Bibliothèque du Moyen Âge 8 (Paris: Champion, 1984); Roger Sherman Loomis, 'Morgain la Fee and the Celtic Goddesses,' *Speculum* 20 (1945): 183–203, rep. in *Wales and the Arthurian Legend* (Cardiff: University of Wales Press, 1956), pp. 105–30; Loomis, 'Morgain la fée in Oral Tradition,' *Romania* 80 (1959): 337–67; Loomis, 'A Survey of Scholarship on the Fairy Mythology of Arthurian Romance Since 1903,' in Paton (below), pp. 280–307; Loomis, 'The Legend of Arthur's Survival,' in *Arthurian Literature in the Middle Ages: A Collaborative History,* 2d. edn. (Oxford: Clarendon, 1961), pp. 64–71; Lucy Allen Paton, *Studies in the Fairy Mythology of Arthurian Romance*, 2d edn., Burt Franklin Bibliographical Series 18 (1903; rep. New York: Burt Franklin, 1960); Jeanne Wathelet-Willem, 'La fée Morgain dans la chanson de geste,' *Cahiers de Civilisation Médiévale* 13 (1970): 209–19.

5 'Lydia the Tattooed Lady,' music by Harold Arlen and lyrics by E.Y. Harburg, performed by Groucho Marx in 'At the Circus' (1939) and by Virginia Weidler

in the film version of 'The Philadelphia Story' (1940), was a favorite of Maureen's. Examples of Morgan as ruler of the wilderness, besides Avalon: *La Bataille Loquifer*, ca. 1170 (Harf-Lancner, *Les Fées*, pp. 275–77); Wolfram's *Parzival* (Fauth, 'Fata Morgana,' p. 437); *Ogier le Danois*, fourteenth century (Harf-Lancner, *Les Fées*, pp. 279–88); *Floriant et Florete*, ca. 1250 (Loomis, 'The Legend,' pp. 67–68); *Tavola Ritonda*, 1325–50 (Fauth, 'Fata Morgana,' p. 435); *Le Bastard de Bouillon*, ca. 1350 (Loomis, 'The Legend,' p. 68); Jean d'Outremeuse, *Myreur des Histors*, fourteenth century (Loomis, 'The Legend,' p. 68); *Pulzella Gaia*, fifteenth century (Fauth, 'Fata Morgana,' p. 436). In Chrétien's *Erec*, a very early reference, Morgan lives in the *Val Perilleus* (lines 2352–76; Guiot MS. only): Chrétien de Troyes, *Erec et Enide*, in *Les Romans de Chrétien de Troyes, I*, ed. Mario Roques, Classiques Français du Moyen Age 80 (Paris: Champion, 1970). Lope García de Salazar's summary of the Post-Vulgate *Roman du Graal* relocates Morgan's Avalon on the Island of Brasil, west of Ireland, adapting stories told by sailors from Bristol: see Harvey L. Sharrer, ed., *The Legendary History of Britain in Lope García de Salazar's 'Libro de las bienandanzas e fortunas'* (Philadelphia: University of Pennsylvania Press, 1979), pp. 72–73, and also Sharrer, 'The Acclimatization of the Lancelot-Grail Cycle in Spain and Portugal,' in *The Lancelot-Grail Cycle: Texts and Transformations*, ed. William W. Kibler (Austin, TX: University of Texas Press, 1994), p. 184 [175–90], and the sources mentioned therein. In a fifteenth century *Fastnacht* play Morgan is the queen of Cyprus (Fauth, 'Fata Morgana,' p. 434). For Lancelot as Morgan's prisoner, see *Lancelot: roman en prose du XIIIe siècle*, ed. Alexandre Micha, Textes Littéraires Français, 9 vols. (Geneva: Droz, 1978–83), vol. 1, sections xxv–xxxi, vol. 5, sections lxxxvi–lxxxviii; *Le roman de Tristan en prose*, ed. Philippe Ménard et al., Textes Littéraires Français, 9 vols. (Geneva: Droz, 1987–97), vol. 3, sections 167–82, vol. 6, sections 35, 67–68; Malory's 'Tale of Sir Launcelot du Lake.'

6 Citation is to the edn. of Malcolm Andrew and Ronald Waldron in *The Poems of the Pearl Manuscript*, York Medieval Texts, 2d series, 3d edn. (1978; Exeter: Exeter University Press, 1996). Unless otherwise indicated, all re-punctuation and translations are my own. On reading Morgan's name as *Morgue*, see my article, 'Is *Morgne* la Faye in *SGGK*—Or Anywhere in Middle English?' *Anglia* 117 (1999): 542–57.

7 In the following discussion I hew to the majority opinion that *Hautdesert* is a toponymic; for the notion that it may pun on 'great merit' or 'high reward,' see Avril Henry, 'Temptation and Hunt in *SGGK*,' *Medium Ævum* 45 (1976): 119, n29 [187–99].

8 MED, s.v. *desert*. The Middle English sense of the word parallels the French: 'souvent employé au moyen âge dans le contexte religieux de la retraite des ermites et cénobites, il [*désert*] acquiert bientôt des sens metaphoriques (v. 1278 ce mondain désert), fréquents dans la rhetorique religieuse où le *désert* s'oppose au *monde*': Alain Rey et al., eds., *Dictionnaire historique de la langue française* (Paris: Dictionnaires Robert, 1992), s.v. *désert, -erte*. At one time, the element *desert* in *Hautdesert* was thought to be Celtic, but its combination with French *haut* would

militate against that possibility: see Norman Davis, note to line 2445 in *SGGK*, ed. J.R.R. Tolkien and E.V. Gordon, rev. Norman Davis (Oxford: Clarendon, 1967).

9 Eilert Ekwall, *Oxford Dictionary of English Place-Names*, 4th edn. (Oxford: Oxford University Press, 1960), s.v. *Beaudesert*; Ernest Nègre, *Toponymie générale de la France*, 3 vols., Publications Romans et Français 103–05 (Geneva: Droz, 1991), s.v. *Désert* (nos. 24082–87) plus, e.g., *Hautmont* (no. 5264) and CA. 50 other compounds beginning in *haut*. I am grateful to Alice Colby-Hall for directing me to Nègre.

10 'What *SGGK* is About,' *Medium Ævum* 32 (1963): 178 [171–189].

11 *SGGK*, ed. Tolkien and Gordon, rev. Davis, note to line 2445.

12 Peter J. Lucas, 'Hautdesert in *SGGK*,' *Neophilologus* 70 (1986): 319–20.

13 See 763–72; plus Michael Paffard, 'Staffordshire Place-Names,' *Staffordshire Studies* 8 (1996): 10 [1–23], and W.H. Duignan, *Notes on Staffordshire Place-Names* (London: Frowde, 1902), p. 12.

14 R.W.V. Elliott, *The Gawain Country*, Leeds Texts and Monographs, n.s. 8. (Leeds: University of Leeds School of English, 1984), summarized in 'Landscape and Geography,' in Derek Brewer and Jonathan Gibson, eds., *A Companion to the Gawain-Poet*, Arthurian Studies 38 (Cambridge: D.S. Brewer, 1997), pp. 105–17. For an alternate suggestion that the castle is modeled after Beeston Castle, Cheshire, see M.W. Thompson, 'The Green Knight's Castle,' in *Studies in Medieval History Presented to R. Allen Brown*, ed. Christopher Harper-Bill, Christopher J. Holdsworth, and Janet L. Nelson (Woodbridge: Boydell, 1989), pp. 317–25. Ludchurch is the site for the Green Chapel preferred by Elliott, but the topography best fits Wetton Mill, the site suggested by Mabel Day in the preface to the edn. of Sir Israel Gollancz, *SGGK*, EETS o.s. 210 (London: Oxford University Press, 1940), p. xx, and further supported by R.E. Kaske, 'Gawain's Green Chapel and the Cave at Wetton Mill,' in *Medieval Literature and Folklore Studies: Essays in Honor of Francis Lee Utley*, ed. Jerome Mandel and Bruce A. Rosenberg (New Brunswick, NJ: Rutgers University Press, 1970), pp. 111–21.

15 For examples, see Robert W. Ackerman, *An Index of the Arthurian Names in Middle English*, Stanford University Publications, University Series, Language and Literature 10 (Stanford, CA: Stanford University Press, 1952), s.v. *North Wales*. For the Queen of North Wales in the French Prose *Lancelot* see the edn. of Micha, vol. 4, section lxxviii. See also Malory's 'Tale of Sir Launcelot du Lake.' In Malory she is also one of Morgan's companions on the barge that conducts Arthur to Avalon.

16 Michael J. Bennett, *Community, Class, and Careerism: Cheshire and Lancashire Society in the Age of SGGK* (Cambridge: Cambridge University Press, 1983), pp. 93–95, 208–09, and H.L. Savage, 'A Note on *SGGK* 700–2,' *MLN* 46 (1931): 455–57. For a recent explanation of Gawain's itinerary see J. Eadie, 'Sir Gawain's Travels in North Wales,' *Review of English Studies*, n.s. 34 (1983): 191–95.

17 Cooper, 'The Supernatural,' in *Companion*, eds. Brewer and Gibson, pp.285–86 [277–91].

18 One of the valuable contributions of the Celtic school of Arthurian interpretation was the uncovering of numerous motifs and themes that might loosely be called 'fairy symptoms.' For example, the Otherworld quality of the whiteness of the castle (798, 799) was noted by J.R. Hulbert, 'Syr Gawayne and the Grene Knyght,' *Modern Philology* 13 (1915): 458 [433–62]; for a more exhaustive study of 'fairy symptoms' see Martin Puhvel, 'Art and the Supernatural in *SGGK*,' *Arthurian Literature V*, ed. Richard Barber (Cambridge: D.S. Brewer, 1985), pp. 1–69.

19 Two popular student texts, by John Burrow (in normalized Middle English) and Marie Borroff (in modern English translation) also reflect the grammatical confusion of the standard editions. Burrow: "'Bertilak de Hautdesert I hat in this londe. / Thurgh myght of Morgne la Faye, that in my house lenges, / And koyntyse of clergye by craftes wel lerned, / The maystryes of Merlyn mony has taken; / For ho has dalt drury ful dere sumtyme / With that konable clerk, that knowes all your knightes / At hame.'" [Bertilak de Hautdesert I am called in this land. / Through the agency of Morgan le Fay, who dwells in my house / and through learned skills well and artfully mastered, / many people have experienced the magic powers of Merlin; / For she formerly had a very intimate love-affair with that excellent scholar / as all your knights at home know]; *SGGK*, Penguin English Classics (London: Penguin, 1972), trans. from n. to 2446–51, p. 123. Borroff: "'Bercilak de Hautdesert this barony I hold, / Through the might of Morgan le Fay, that lodges at my house, / By subtleties of science and sorcerers' arts, / The mistress of Merlin, she has caught many a man, / For sweet love in secret she shared sometime / With that wizard, that knows well each one of your knights / and you,'" *SGGK* (New York: Norton, 1967).

20 For a brief analysis of spelling, the expansion of abbreviations, and word-division in three popular modern editions, see N.F. Blake, 'Reflections on the Editing of Middle English Texts,' in *A Guide to Editing Middle English*, ed. Vincent P. McCarren and Douglas Moffat (Ann Arbor: University of Michigan Press, 1998), pp. 61–77. Generally on the ways the edition of Tolkien and Gordon, revised by Davis, implies its own critical reading of *SGGK*, see Arthur Lindley, 'Pinning Gawain Down: The Misediting of *SGGK*,' *JEGP* 96 (1997): 26–42. For a discussion of the manuscript see A.S.G. Edwards, 'The Manuscript: British Library MS Cotton Nero A. x.,' in *Companion*, eds. Brewer and Gibson, pp. 197–219.

21 Other full stops, editorially marked by periods, colons, semicolons, dashes, and question marks, occur at the same point in lines 87, 91, 194, 376, 404, 434 (possible), 452, 546, 654, 701, 1029, 1038, 1108, 1197, 1210, 1304 (possible), 1379, 1591, 1633, 1653 (possible), 1701 (possible), 1704, 1793 (possible), 1811, 1847, 1863, 1944, 2287, 2322, 2335, 2341, 2346, 2361, 2368, 2378, 2383, 2409, 2471 (possible), 2491. Interjections are excluded.

22 Ed. Micha, vol. 1, sections xxii, xxiv. On this passage as a possible source for *SGGK*, see my article, 'Morgain la fée in *SGGK*: From Troy to Camelot,' in *Text and Intertext in Medieval Arthurian Literature*, ed. Norris J. Lacy (New York: Garland, 1996), pp. 96–98 [91–115]. Morgan's expulsion from court is foretold in the Prose *Merlin* but it never becomes a separate narrative in the Vulgate Cycle.

23 Twomey, 'Morgain la fée in *SGGK*,' 92–96.

24 Three groundbreaking examples of feminist criticism that argue for Morgan's centrality in *SGGK* are Sheila Fisher, 'Leaving Morgan Aside: Women, History, and Revisionism in *SGGK*,' in *The Passing of Arthur: New Essays in Arthurian Tradition*, ed. Christopher Baswell and William Sharpe (New York: Garland, 1988), pp. 129–51, rep. in *Medieval English Poetry*, ed. Stephanie Trigg, Longman Critical Readers (London-New York: Longman, 1993), pp. 138–55; Sheila Fisher, 'Taken Men and Token Women in *SGGK*,' in *Seeking the Woman in Late Medieval and Renaissance Writings: Essays in Feminist Contextual Criticism*, ed. Sheila Fisher and Janet E. Halley (Knoxville: University of Tennessee Press, 1989), pp. 71–105; and Geraldine Heng, 'Feminine Knots and the Other *SGGK*,' *PMLA* 106 (1991): 500–14. At this writing, Ad Putter of the University of Bristol is preparing a new edition of the poem.

25 The one edition that acknowledges Morgan's seigniorial power is William Vantuono's, *SGGK*, rev. edn. (Notre Dame, IN: University of Notre Dame Press, 1999), but unfortunately its reading of 2445–46 depends on a lexical error: 'Bercilak de Hautdesert. I hot [hold sway, command] in þis londe / Þurȝ miȝt of Morgne la Faye,' etc., emends *hat* to *hot*, which it takes as the 3 pres. sg. of *hōten*, citing *MED* v.1, 3a. As the *MED* entry makes clear, this verb requires an object and cannot mean 'to rule.'

26 Here I follow Cooper, 'The Supernatural,' *Companion*, eds. Brewer and Gibson, p. 289.

The Hag of Castle Hautdesert: The Celtic Sheela-na-gig and the *Auncian* in *Sir Gawain and the Green Knight*

LORRAINE KOCHANSKE STOCK

The Celtic Sheela-na-gig is an analogue for the construction of Morgan le Fay's character in *SGGK*. Supporting this identification are: the poem's debt to its Celtic sources/analogues; affinities between the Sheelas, Celtic goddess figures, literary loathly ladies, and Morgan the 'goddes'; and the location of several Sheela-na-gigs in Northern Wales. (LKS)

Visual analogues or direct illustrations[1] are available for almost all major characters in *Sir Gawain and the Green Knight*;[2] even the Virgin Mary, the unembodied, but ever-present, divine patroness of the hero, is a familiar subject of medieval art for her role in the Nativity. However, visual depiction of Morgan le Fay, Gawain's ultimate tester who orchestrates the entire plot of *SGGK*, not only is omitted for this particular poem, but is infrequent in manuscripts of other Arthurian romances in which she plays a crucial role.[3] To compensate for the rarity of medieval images of Morgan, I suggest the Celtic Sheela-na-gig as a visual prototype or analogue for both Morgan le Fay and related literary hags and loathly damsels.[4] This difficult-to-date medieval category of stone sculpture was extant in the British Isles, especially Ireland, and arguably on the Continent.[5] My essay presents the case for regarding the Sheela-na-gig[6] as an iconographic model/analogue for the *Gawain*-poet's construction of Morgan le Fay.[7] In her role as 'goddes' in *SGGK*, Morgan competes with the Virgin Mary for sacral authority and power over Gawain and perhaps even shares culpability with her for bringing Gawain to a castle and a chapel, the two sites of Gawain's testing in the poem and, significantly, the two most common structures on which Sheela-na-gigs are located.

SHEELA-NA-GIGS

The etymological provenance and meaning of the term *Sheela-na-gig*—the type-name by which this sculpture is designated by anthropologists,

Plate 1: Killinaboy Church wall

folklorists, and art historians—are uncertain. Jørgen Andersen and Eamonn Kelly adduce various possible meanings: 'Sheela on her hunkers,' referring to the squatting posture; 'an immodest woman,' alluding to her genital display; a generalized term for 'woman'; 'Sheela of the paps,' a reference to the dug-like breasts on some; 'hag,' referring to the witch-like facial features, and 'Hag of the Castle,' referring to a frequent location.[8] The name may be an anglicized corruption of variant spellings of the Gaelic *Síle na gCíoch*. The *Sí* of *Síle* suggests the Irish word for 'fairy' or 'otherworld creature' whose underground dwelling or 'fairy hillock' was known as a *sídh*.[9]

Stella Cherry defines Sheela-na-gigs as 'carvings of naked females exposing their genitalia.'[10] From this accurate but most neutral of descriptions, however, one could call any classical female nude a Sheela-na-gig. Eamonn P. Kelly offers a more specific, though 'constructed,' definition: 'Sheela-na-gigs are *grotesque* carvings of naked females posed in a manner which displays and emphasises the genitalia' (my emphasis).[11] Indeed, in many of the

Plate 2: Closeup of Killinaboy

examples found in England, Wales, Scotland, and especially Ireland, the naked Sheela-na-gig represents a hideously ugly, often physically misshapen, obviously old woman. In addition to extreme age, the other distinguishing characteristic is the gender of these sculptures, because the Sheelas' blatant display of disproportionately oversized female genitalia emphasizes their 'femaleness.' The characteristic physical features of Sheelas include an oversized bald head; glaring eyes; disfigured facial features; pulled up shoulders; small, flat, or lop-sided breasts; long arms and prominent hands; and diminutive, foreshortened legs emerging from oversized buttocks.[12] Sheela-na-gigs were positioned on the exteriors of two kinds of architectural structures primarily—religious buildings such as chapels, small churches, convents, abbeys, or monasteries, and secular structures such as castles, tower houses, and civic walls.

Three Irish Sheela-na-gigs I observed *in situ* illustrate the physical attributes and classic locations noted above. Situated in the wall over an arched doorway

Plate 3: Closeup of Ballynahinch

on the south side of the now-ruined ca. twelfth-century 'Old Church' in Killinaboy, Co. Clare, is a Sheela-na-gig that has been identified with St. Inghean Bhaoith, the founder, first abbess, and namesake of the original monastic site, whose name may be a deliberately Christianized version of originally pagan goddess figures, either Bóand/Boann/Innam Buidhe or Brigit, two sovereignty goddesses associated with fertility and the cow (see Plate 1: Killinaboy Church wall).[13] Like the Fetherd Wall Sheela described below, this grim-looking carving conveys the ambivalence presumably at the root of the meaning of all Sheelas (see Plate 2: Closeup of Killinaboy). Noting the Killinaboy Sheela's bald head, emaciated torso, and fierce facial expression, Andersen claims that despite the carver's intention 'to achieve an effect of repellence,' in her hand gesture that solicits attention to her genitalia, there is also apparent enticement, leading him to conclude, 'threat and

Plate 4: Fetherd Wall

invitation combine in this image.'[14] Sheelas above entrances to or windows of various Irish castles or tower houses include the one at Ballynahinch Castle, a remote, now nearly-inaccessible site near Cashel in Co. Tipperary, located in what are now unmarked farm fields between an abandoned cemetery and the bank of the river Suir. Situated high on the wall over the doorway of the tower of the castle ruin, this 'witch on the wall' and 'hag of the castle' would have presented (as I can attest) a formidable apotropaic effect to those entering the tower (see Plate 3: Closeup of Ballynahinch). Most notable are this Sheela's staring eyes, open mouth, deeply wrinkled brow, and joined hands displaying her vulva. Finally, exemplifying most of the characteristics of these carvings listed above, is the 'witch' of the old medieval town wall of Fetherd, established in the fourteenth century in Co. Tipperary (see Plate 4: Fetherd Wall). The wall faced a bridge at the Watergate over the Clashawley River, the original

Plate 5: Closeup of Fetherd Sheela

medieval entry to the town, a strategic apotropaic position (see Plate 5: Closeup of Fetherd Sheela). Glaring at potential visitors/intruders are the piercing eyes and wide, tooth-filled grimace of the Fetherd Wall Sheela, whose grotesque face conveys old age, largely through the chevron-like wrinkles incised on her cheeks and the vertical striations (either wrinkles or veins) that score her neck. Deep horizontal lines etched across both sides of her chest suggest emaciated ribs. Her elongated arms reach below her buttocks between the splayed legs and her fingers join between the buttocks, pulling apart the labia of the vagina. From my own observation, the claw-like grip of the fingers forms spaces suggesting the toothy 'mouth' of the *vagina dentata*, which mirrors the toothy grin or grimace of her hideous face. The relation of these figures' vulvic display with the *vagina dentata* will be relevant in my interpretation of Morgan's Green Chapel in *SGGK*.

As these examples attest, Sheela-na-gigs occupied architectural thresholds or the physical boundaries between inside and outside, between us and them, between the self and the other. Whether serving as keystones of doors, squatting astride or beside windows, presiding over entrances such as gates and doorways, or looming on the external face of town walls, the grim-looking figure and her impudent genital display certainly gave pause to onlookers or perhaps even deflected intruders.[15] Positioned thus, they were icons of both figurative and literal liminality. As a category of extreme female otherness, they earned nicknames such as 'witch on the wall' or 'hag of the castle' and in the opinion of some scholars, they represent or allude to goddess figures.

On the other hand, Anthony Weir and James Jerman's designation of the Sheelas as icons of the deadly sin of *luxuria* reflects medieval patristic and patriarchal constructions of all females as sexual temptresses who lure unsuspecting males to spiritual perdition by succumbing to the sin of lechery. This approach invokes the medieval period's obsessive fearfulness about human corporeality, which, in the prevailing discourse of medieval misogyny, was inevitably gendered female. Page Du Bois characterizes this 'intense misogyny and the witch-hunting contemporaneous with it' as being 'center[ed] on women's bodies,' with the vagina, the particular body part most prominent on the Sheelas, troped as the 'devil's gateway.'[16] The location of these figures over or near various types of architectural *entrances* produced a marriage of form and content that was likely not accidental. However, as useful as the catalogues of Sheela-na-gigs produced by Andersen and Weir and Jerman may be, their constructions of the cultural meaning of the Sheelas are univalent. Taking a different perspective, Roberts defines the Sheelas more positively as:

> *religious* carvings of women, special women, the symbolical representation of femininity and/or actual female deities or Goddesses. They were placed on churches, castles, and other important buildings of the medieval period where, until quite recently in some instances, they acted as dedicatory or protective symbols promoting good luck and fertility....They were a very potent and powerful image, obviously the primary religious belief of the people of that era of Christianity.[17]

Viewing the Sheelas in the context of the authority wielded by both goddess figures and literary versions of similar physically-repellent female figures—and the *Gawain*-poet's characterization of Morgan le Fay operates within such a context—helps to recuperate the Sheelas' potential for connoting power, as well as abjection, for the gender they so blatantly represent.

LITERARY HAGS AND LOATHLY LADIES

The repellent, aged appearance of the Sheela-na-gig renders her an appropriate candidate to illustrate the established medieval literary character-type of the 'hag' or (more decorously-labelled) 'loathly damsel,' occurring in stories such as Chaucer's 'Wife of Bath's Tale,' its Middle English analogues,[18] and Irish Sovereignty analogues.[19] Cathalin Folks analyzes the old 'wyf' of the 'Wife of Bath's Tale'and Morgan the 'auncian' of *SGGK* within the context of all these various loathly ladies.[20] Although these tales usually are discussed as analogues of the 'Wife of Bath's Tale,' rather than as *aventures* of Sir Gawain comparable to the one he has in *SGGK*, given the poet's inclusion of the description of Morgan as 'auncian' discussed below, there is good reason to read *SGGK* as an example of the loathly damsel tale-type.[21] Moreover, in the analogues of Chaucer's tale, the hero who promises to marry the hag is nearly always Sir Gawain, sometimes acting on behalf of or at the request of King Arthur, a situation quite similar to that in *SGGK*. Similarly, in the Irish Sovereignty stories the rulership over the land can only be attained by the future king through sex with or marriage to a repulsive crone, representing the female-personified land of Ireland herself (as territorial goddess, Ériu *is* Ireland).[22] In some Sovereignty stories the most noticeable physical characteristic of the hag figure, whose euphemized 'lower mouth' droops down as low as her knee, is the size of her genitalia, which suggests to Máire Bhreathnach the Sheela-na-gig figures.[23] In the thirteenth-century German romance about Gawain, *Diu Krône*, by Heinrich von dem Türlin, Gawain is attacked by a female Other whose grotesque appearance replicates the features of other literary loathly ladies, the Sovereignty hag, and the Sheela-na-gig:

> Her ostrich eyes burned like fire; her nose was hideous—wondrously broad and flat—...the wide, thick-lipped mouth turned up toward the ears, and from it protruded sharp, broad, teeth that met in four places like a boar's....The wrinkled jowls of the devilish woman hung down to her chin....The hands and arms of the wild woman were fully as strong as pillars; she had long claws that were sharp and powerful....Below the waist, around the pelvis, she resembled nothing but an ape, and the place below was hideous, looking like a horse collar. Her skin hung on her as wrinkled and folded as a sack, while her sinews beneath were as large as wagon ropes.[24]

Upon sexual union or marriage to the potential king, the Irish sovereignty hag suddenly transformed herself into a beautiful, young bride. Helen Wood's analysis of women in the Irish texts provides suggestive links between the Irish hag tales and aspects of *SGGK*: she identifies the war goddesses, Morrígan and Macha, with the sacrificial offering of severed human heads; she associates the territorial and sovereignty goddess Ériu with passage graves, which resemble the cave structure of the Green Chapel; and she correlates the growth of the cult of the Virgin Mary in Ireland with the twelfth-century appearance of the carvings representing *luxuria*, including Sheela-na-gigs.[25] For sharing several common aspects—a loathsome appearance, an ability to shapeshift mutually from alluring beauty to grotesque ugliness, and an association not only with blatant sexuality and/or fertility but also with death, especially a hero's death by decapitation—this generalized literary hag figure suggests the territorial goddess as well as several Celtic war-goddesses including Macha and the Morrígan,[26] prompting anthropologists and scholars of Celtic literature and myth to draw explicit analogies between these 'divine hag figures' of the Celtic pantheon and the Sheela-na-gigs.[27] Margaret Murray even claims divinity or at least divine attributes for the English versions of the Sheela-na-gig because 'the figures are almost invariably found on Christian churches.'[28] The apotropaic function of the Sheela—guarding castles or towns; warding off threats by brazen vulvic exhibition; or conveying fertility upon women who rubbed the carvings for luck—endowed these figures with a power parallel to, and perhaps derived from, the force attributed to various Celtic goddess figures, foremost among which is the war goddess Morrigain. By viewing the *Gawain*-poet's characterization of Morgan le Fay in *SGGK* through the prism of the above-established iconographic characteristics of the Sheela-na-gig and the textual category of the literary hag figures, in the remainder of this essay I shall adduce evidence to support my nomination of the Sheela-na-gig as a visual analogue for Morgan le Fay, especially in her depiction as the 'auncian' of *SGGK*.[29]

WHAT'S IN A NAME?: MORGAN LE FAY AND *Síle na Gcíoch* OR SHEELA-NA-GIG

Admittedly, at least by her usual nominal designation, Morgan is absent from *SGGK* until the Green Knight's late revelation that, disguised earlier as the loathly-looking 'auncian' [ancient one] (l. 948), Morgan the goddess has instigated the entire adventure of Gawain, including his testing at Castle Hautdesert. The generic term 'auncian,' by which she is first identified, and later the more explicit phrase indicating her extreme age—'Þe olde auncian wyf heʒest ho syttez' [the old ancient woman sits highest] (l. 1001)— encourage analogy between Morgan and the Sheela-na-gig since in many Sheela figures still in their original sites, the carving of an old, hag-like woman could be said to 'sit' on her squatting haunches *high* above the viewer's gaze, whether on the wall of a chapel, the tower of a castle, or a public town wall.[30] Further, not only do the adjectives of the designation 'olde auncian wyf' mirror the typically advanced age of the Sheela-na-gig, but the noun 'wyf,' the Middle English word for generic 'woman,'[31] emphasizes her representative femaleness, which corresponds to the Sheela-na-gig's iconic representation of that sex.[32] The specific name of Arthur's ambivalently evil/ benevolent sister, spelled variously as Morgan, Morgaine, Morguein, Morganz, or Morgue, has prompted several scholarly explanations. Partly because of the similarity between their names, partly because of their dangerous character profiles, the Irish triple war goddess the Modron/Macha/ Morrígan has been suggested as a prototype for the medieval romancers' characterization and naming of Morgan, whom the poet has the Green Knight refer to as 'Morgne þe goddes' (l. 2452) in *SGGK*.[33] This connects Morgan generally with the Celtic goddess figures, who themselves have been associated with Sheela-na-gigs. Thus, indirectly, Morgan le Fay may be related to the Sheelas through their common behavioral and physical resemblance to these formidable goddesses. The actual names of Morgan and the Sheela-na-gig share an analogous provenance as well. Recall that in one likely derivation of 'Sheela' from the Gaelic *Síle*, the *Sí* refers to the Old Irish word for 'fairy' or 'Otherworld creature' whose underground dwelling or 'fairy hillock' was known as a *sidh*. Significantly, the epithet 'fay' or *fée*, by which Morgan is designated, is the French equivalent of the Irish *Sí*, meaning 'faery.'[34] Moreover, according to tradition, when the Sons of Mil (the Gaels) invaded Ireland, the indigenous divine race of the Tuatha dé Danann were forced underground beneath the hills of Ireland and each mound, called a *sidh*, was assigned to its respective divinity. One of the major female divinities, the Morrígan, emerged from her *sidh* to destroy Cú Chulainn.[35] This fairy mound resembles the barrow or naturalistic 'green chapel' presided over by Morgan the goddess in *SGGK*. Thus, another link between Morgan and the Sheela figure is their mutual association with the world of faery through their respective fanciful names and cave-like sites.

Weir and Jarman classify the Sheela-na-gigs as signifiers of or reminders against the deadly sin of *luxuria*. This provides another link with the medieval conception of Morgan le Fay. Although there are almost as few literary portraits of Morgan in the Continental romances that feature her as there are medieval visual imagings of her, when narrators do describe her physical appearance, they present an ambivalent rather than a consistent picture— alternating between the traditionally young and beautiful *fée* [fairy] and the wrinkled, *laide* [ugly] loathly damsel.[36] Her portrait in the Vulgate *Merlin*, the 'most complete description of Morgain that has come down to us,'[37] exemplifies this ambivalence:

> This Morgan was a young lady, very cheerful and merry, but her face was somber; she had a rounded build, not too thin, not too plump. She was quite clever and comely in body and in features....But she was the most lustful woman in all Great Britain and the lewdest [Mais ele estoit la plus chaude feme de toute la grant bertaigne & la plus luxurieuse]. Yet she was a woman of wondrous learning…which Merlin had taught her....Afterwards she was called Morgan the Fay [morgain la fee], sister of King Arthur, because of the wonders she worked throughout the country. She…had the fairest head…, the most beautiful hands, and wondrously well-made shoulders, and…she had a sweet, soft way of talking, and…as long as she was in her right mind, she was more courteous than any, but when she was angry with anyone, there was no need to try to reconcile them.[38]

Note that she is pretty, though sober-faced, and hot and lecherous, in fact the most lustful woman in Britain. The adjectives *chaude* and *luxurieuse* denote the deadly sin of *luxuria*, of which Weir and Jerman claim the Sheela-na-gig was an icon. The portrait emphasizes the beauty of Morgan's head, hands, and shoulders, all body parts that are grotesquely exaggerated physical attributes of the Sheela-na-gig. When this sweet-talker is crossed, no one is more formidable an opponent. Stone carvings cannot talk, but the apotropaic powers attributed to Sheela-na-gigs evince an equivalent formidability in the insular sculptures. Another brief but graphic description of Morgan in the Vulgate Cycle comes from a section of the *Lancelot* notable not only for its reference to Morgan as a goddess, but for the misadventures of many knights, including Lancelot, whom she held captive in the Val sans Retour, a perilous landscape in the magical Forest of Broceliande in Brittany. Resembling her father, Morgan 'was also ugly; and when she came of age, she was so lustful and wanton that a looser woman could not have been found.'[39] Thus, whether she is beautiful or exceedingly ugly, an important component of Morgan's job description is to be an icon of the sin of *luxuria*, which also describes Sheela-na-gig figures.

Although Morgan's character occurs in both the ugly and the beautiful paradigms in *SGGK*, the Cotton Nero A.x manuscript contains no obvious pictorial representation of Morgan either as 'auncian' or as 'goddes.' As in the case of the Vulgate Cycle's depictions of Morgan, we must settle for a vivid verbal imaging of the 'auncian' and her double in a joint-portrait of them that conflates the beautiful and the ugly guises of Morgan.[40] The passage (ll. 943–69) describes them as they emerge from a Christian chapel in Castle

Hautdesert, with the older 'oþer lady' [other lady] leading the younger by the left hand 'þurȝ þe chaunsel' [through the chancel] (ll. 946–47). In Gawain's opinion, with her attractive, lowcut costume, her youthful vitality, her snowy coloring, Bertilak's wife is 'þe fayrest in felle, of flesche and of lyre, / And of compas and colour and costes, of alle oþer, / And wener þen Wenore' [the fairest in complexion, and skin, and visage / and her proportions, coloring, and manners exceeded all others, / making her more beautiful than Guenevere] (ll. 943–45).

On the other hand, in the guise of the 'auncian,' Morgan is the quintessential literary 'loathly damsel' in a graphic portrait of feminine otherness whose details also suggest the classic attributes of the Sheela-na-gig as described above: 'ȝolȝe' [withered] skin; 'Rugh ronkled chekez' [rough, wrinkled cheeks]; she is so thoroughly covered by a wimple that except for 'hir blake chyn' [her black chin], 'noȝt watz bare of þat burde bot þe blake broȝes, / Þe tweyne yȝen and þe nase, þe naked lyppez, / And þose were soure to se and sellyly blered' [nothing was bare on that damsel except her black eyebrows, two eyes, a nose, and naked lips, and those were sour to see and marvelously bleared] (ll. 951, 953, 958, 961–63). Moving from the hideous face of the 'auncian' to her lower parts, we see further parallels with the Sheela-na-gig: 'Hir body watz schort and þik, / Hir buttokez balȝ and brode,' [her body was short and thick, / her buttocks were swollen and broad] (ll. 966–67). In their combined *effictio*, Bertilak's lady and the 'auncian' co-preside in great honor over a *castle* after emerging from a *chapel*, the two most frequent locations of Sheela-na-gigs. Together Bertilak's Lady and 'that other,' the 'auncian,' display the bare breast, the wrinkled cheeks, the misshapen eyes, nose, and especially sour-looking and ferocious mouth of the Sheela. Like the Sheela, the 'auncian' is noted for having a foreshortened, thick body and prominent haunches or buttocks. Were this not a courtly poem, the front side of those prominent buttocks, the most striking aspect of the Sheela, might next be mentioned.

After this passage establishes her role as 'hag' of Bertilak's Castle, over which, like the the Sheela-na-gig, she is 'mensk' [honored] (l. 964), the 'auncian' does not play a significant part in the plot again until near its end, when the Green Knight reveals to Gawain the crucial role she has played in his test and her identity as his aunt, Morgan le Fay (ll. 2445–66). Here, because of her complicity in Gawain's *rendezvous* with the Green Knight at the Green Chapel, Morgan is even more categorically associated with the second site where Sheela-na-gigs were located, churches or chapels, despite the fact that earlier in the text, the title by which Gawain's otherworldly antagonist first identified himself was the 'Þe knyȝt of þe grene chapel' [the knight of the Green Chapel] (l. 454).[41] Thus for the character whom most have come to think of as the Green Knight, his own notion of personal identity is firmly tied to the chapel to which he must, as Morgan's agent, draw Gawain. As Gawain prepares himself to journey toward the assignation with what he himself thinks of as the 'gome of þe grene' [the green man] (l. 549), others at court muse that Gawain's required beheading by an 'aluisch mon' [elvish man] (l. 681), whom they classify among 'knyȝtez in *caue* loumȝ'[42] [knights with cave-weapons] (l. 683, my emphasis) is a waste of a valued knight. Somehow, the people at Camelot intuit the extent to which the Green Knight's 'elvish'-ness (connoting the world of faery) and his association with a cave (suggesting a site of 'female geography') not only inform his identity as 'knight of the Green *Chapel*,' the subordinate of Morgan the goddess, but ultimately feminize him. This second chapel (the first being the chapel in the Castle) now has to be seen as *her* Green Chapel rather than the Green Knight's.

To the surprise of the literal-minded Gawain, the site to which he has been directed by Bertilak's guide is hardly the 'chapel' (l. 2132, 2169) or architectural edifice he has been expecting. All along, the goal of Gawain's search has been a physical 'kyrk' [church] (l. 2196) or ecclesiastical structure, rather than the metaphoric 'chapel *grene*' (l. 2003, my emphasis) that awaits him in the midst of a 'wylde' [wild] (l. 2163) landscape full of steep hills, jagged rocks, roiling streams, and overgrown foliage. That Green Chapel, which one critic calls 'the true focal point' of all of *SGGK*,[43] is no ordinary chapel but instead is 'a lawe as hit were; / A balȝ berȝ bi a bonke' [a mound as it were; / A rounded barrow on a stream bank] (ll. 2172–73). Rather than a church, this earth mound in the landscape with a grotto-like declivity is a natural structure, 'nobot an olde caue, / Or a creuisse of an olde cragge' (ll. 2182–83) [nothing but an old cave / or a fissure in an old crag]. The subterranean passage is described in great detail: 'Hit hade a hole on þe ende and on ayþer syde, / And ouergrowen with gresse in glodes aywhere, / And al watz holȝ inwith...Þis oritore is vgly, with erbez ouergrowen' [It had a hole at the end and on either side, / And was all overgrown with patches of grass, / And was all hollow inside;...This oratory is gruesome, with grass overgrown] (ll. 2180–82, 2190). Perhaps not quite as literally as Gawain sought an architectural 'church' to fulfill his mission, various scholars have nevertheless persisted in their own quests to identify an actual geographical site, usually a cave, on which the poet modeled the location and topography of the Green Chapel.[44]

Other scholars have followed a more metaphorical path toward the identity of the Green Chapel, and these respective paths lead, as I shall finally argue, to an association between *SGGK*'s Morgan and the Sheela-na-gig. For John Speirs, the fact that the chapel of the green man is nothing but a cave, 'that immemorial symbol and sacred place....the hidden, secret source of life,' has more profound significance than if it were an actual ecclesiastical structure: 'If the cave is the entrance to the underworld, that entrance is in our poem realized not as the devourer of life but as the source of life, the entrance through which life *returns* to the earth. The place...is felt as holy, enchanted, taboo; it is *sacer*.'[45] In another metaphorical reading of that topographic site, Robert J. Edgeworth, who interprets the the features of the Green Chapel and its setting as a 'piece of sexual geography' provided by the poet, and who suggests that these topographical peculiarities 'are readily identifiable with the features of the female genitalia,'[46] supports a reading of *SGGK* that seeks to discover what Geraldine Heng calls its 'feminine nexus.'[47]

The cave in *SGGK* is also suggestively reminiscent of passage graves that were believed in Irish folklore to be sites of fairy mounds or the *sidhe*,[48] whose name resonates linguistically with the name of the Sheela-na-gig. Here, in her tomb-like chapel-cave, using powers she acquired from Merlin, Morgan who (prophetically) is designated 'þat oþer' [that Other] in the dual portrait, and whose extreme otherness mirrors that of the repulsive Sheela-na-gig—culminates Gawain's test. This test, involving the threat of a ritual beheading on January 1 (designated in the liturgical calendar as the feast of Christ's Circumcision) thus corresponds to the implicit physical threat of castration signified by the visual subtext of the Sheela's toothy grin, which often is mirrored in her vaginally-dentative vulvic display.[49]

The analyses of Kelly and other scholars suggest that the medieval Sheela-na-gig exemplifies the 'female grotesque.' Wolfgang Kayser notes that, as a stylistic category, the 'grotesque' etymologically derives from *grotta,* the Italian word for 'grotto' or 'cave.'[50] Mary Russo elaborates by associating all caves with the feminine because they are 'low hidden, earthy, dark, material, immanent, visceral. As bodily metaphor, the grotesque cave tends to look like (and in the most gross metaphorical sense be identified with) the cavernous anatomical female body.'[51] Russo reminds us that attitudes toward the female grotesque are inevitably gendered. From the viewpoint of 'cultural feminism,' which 'posits a natural connection between the female body (itself naturalized) and the "primal" elements, especially the earth,' such a black hole is valorized as earth mother, crone, or fairy queen.[52] On the other hand, from the perspective of patriarchal (and medieval) misogyny, this 'hidden inner space…down there in that cave of abjection' contains 'all the detritus of the body that is separated out and placed with terror and revulsion on the side of the feminine.'[53] The literal 'black hole' of the 'female grotesque' certainly provides a useful analogy for the equally grotto-esque black hole of the vulva, flaunted or pointed to, both invitingly and threateningly, by the Sheela-na-gig. It cannot be accidental that in one of the four 'significant moments' chosen for illustration in the unique manuscript of *SGGK*— Gawain's arrival at the long-sought and heretofore-elusive Green Chapel, the lower right register of the manuscript illumination (Cotton Nero A.x, fol. 129v)—depicts Morgan's cave as a deep, dark, suspiciously vulvic-shaped 'black hole.'[54] James Dunn characterizes the meaning of the Sheelas and analogous war goddesses as a 'convergence of opposites: life and death, fertility and war,'[55] the blatant sexual nature of which elicits 'male fantasies of the devouring mother.'[56] Early medieval glosses for the Irish war goddesses attest their witch-like character. In a ninth-century gloss, 'the words, *lamia, monstrum in femine figura,* are explained by the word *morrigain.*'[57] Like the Morrígan, the *lamia* was known for vanishing out of sight; shape-shifting from ugliness to beauty; enervating, seducing, and sucking the blood of young men in the manner of a succubus, and devouring them.[58] Through her relation to the Morrígan, this same signification may be assigned to Morgan le Fay.

Morgan's identification with such threats to male autonomy and physical integrity is made plain in the name of the geographic domain in Brittany over which she famously ruled in the French Arthurian romances, the *Val sans Retour* [Valley of No Return]. Morgan's valley, deep in the wild Breton Forest of Broceliande, is unique for its ubiquitous purplish-colored rocks, out of which scrubby vegetation fights its way alongside a running streambed and a lake piquantly named the '*mirroir des fées.*' It is a beautiful but confusingly undifferentiated landscape in which (as I can attest from personal experience) modern tourists, as well as their predecessors, Arthurian knights, can get lost for a while. In my own pilgrimage to the 'Val sans Retour' in 1994, I was struck by the similarities between the description of the topography of the Green Chapel in *SGGK*—hyʒe bonkkez…And ruʒe knokled knarrez with knorned stonez' [high hills…and rough, knobby crags with jagged stones] (ll. 2165–66)—and Morgan's primal 'green dungeon' for unfaithful lovers. The name 'Valley of No Return' does not idly threaten its visitors, for in the Vulgate Cycle many knights were transformed into unwilling slaves to *eros* by 'chaude' [hot] Morgan. This renders the Val sans Retour a physical/symbolic locus suggesting sexual enslavement and physical bondage similar to that practiced by the *lamia*. In such contexts, the Green Chapel, the cave over which Morgan presides in *SGGK*, can be interpreted similarly as a locus of male susceptibility to female power. In light of this, it is hardly accidental that Gawain invokes that very 'Power of Women'[59] in his 'Blasme des Femmes' antifeminist tirade,[60] which he offers as an excuse for his failure to resist succumbing to the third temptation of Bertilak's Lady by keeping the Green Girdle (ll. 2414–28). This gendered power, whether in the apotropaic power of the Sheela-na-gig or in the erotic hegemony of Morgan the *dominatrix,* provides yet another parallel between these two formidable female figures, Morgan and the Sheela.

THE EVIDENCE OF MATERIAL CULTURE

I have tried to offer evidence of affinity between the Celtic Sheela-na-gig and the *Gawain*-poet's construction of Morgan le Fay, 'the goddess' in SGGK. Against my suggestion, it might be argued that the sculpture category in question is found more in Ireland than in Great Britain, and that the poem in question is composed in fourteenth-century Middle English of North-west Midlands provenance, not Irish. However, the editors have described the author as someone 'who seems to know a good deal about the geography of North Wales and the Wirral, and to expect that his audience will be interested in the district.'[61] Although the Irish/Celtic literary motifs that offer parallels or analogues to the plot elements of *SGGK* suggest that the author was at least familiar with some significant aspects of Irish culture, I cannot prove that the *Gawain*-poet ever went to Ireland and saw a Sheela-na-gig there. However, one does not have to venture far from what Elliott calls 'the Gawain Country' to find examples of English or Welsh Sheela-na-gigs that the author may well have actually seen. The most widely reproduced[62] and the 'most typical' example of a Sheela-na-gig is part of a corbel table decorating the Norman Church of St. Mary and St. David at Kilpeck, in Herefordshire in the Welsh borderland, located tantalizingly close to the geographic territory described in *SGGK*. Further south in Wales, in the town of Llandrindod Wells, is one of the fiercest-looking Sheelas in Britain, certainly the best preserved example in Wales.[63] This carving, originally in the old medieval church, has the features typical of the Sheela-na-gig: incised ribs; a big pendulous head with sagging jowls, prominent eyes and heavy eyebrows, a large nose, a pointy chin, and a toothy slit of a mouth; the usual squatting legs and vulvic display; and unlike many other specimens, high, prominent breasts that parallel those of the *auncian*'s double, Bertilak's wife, whose 'brest and hir bryȝt þrote [were] bare displayed' [breast and bright throat were boldly displayed] (l. 955).

Tolkien and Gordon's reference to the poet's deep knowledge of 'the geography of North Wales' is no doubt prompted by the catalogue of places that Gawain passes through in his search for the Green Chapel:

> Til þat he neʒed ful neghe into þe Norþe Walez.
> Alle þe iles of Anglesay on lyft half he haldez,
> And farez ouer þe fordez by þe forlondez,
> Ouer at þe Holy Hede, til he hade eft bonk
> In þe wyldrenesse of Wyrale (ll. 697–700)

> [Until he ventured well enough into North Wales.
> All the Isles of Anglesey he passes on the left
> And fares over the fords near the promontories,
> Over at the Holy Head[64] until he reached the bank
> In the wilderness of Wirral].

Among the place names specifically mentioned is the Island of Anglesey,[65] located off the Northwest coast of Wales. This island had longstanding connections with Ireland, going back to neolithic times, and was a haven for Celtic druids, both male and female priestesses, whose activities there Patrick Ford cites to demonstrate the 'importance of the female Celtic religion.'[66] The whole island is dotted with the remains of neolithic passage graves and burial chambers—the interiors of some contain carvings of spiral designs signifying Goddess worship—the kind of mounds that were identified in Ireland as *sidhe* or fairy mounds and that are reminiscent of the cave of the Green Chapel in *SGGK*. On the north-east coast of Anglesey, just above Beaumaris Castle, one of the last royal fortifications built by Edward I, is a monastery established by St. Seiriol in the sixth century at Penmon, a promontory overlooking the Menai Strait between the island and the mainland of North Wales. Penmon was the location of an Augustinian priory, a twelfth-century church, and Saint Seiriol's Well, a shrine visited by pilgrims for the healing waters throughout the Middle Ages and into modern times. Penmon is the part of Anglesey physically nearest to the mainland of Wales. Given the area's close proximity to the coast, to a major royal fortification nearby, and to a monastic site and popular pilgrimage destination, it is likely that the Gawain-poet's personal experience of Anglesey would have included a visit to the Penmon headland and its environs. Significantly, the now-partially-ruined Norman church at Penmon Priory contained at least one and possibly three Sheela-na-gigs, all of which are currently housed inside the twelfth-century Church of St. Seiriol.[67] The first very worn example (see Plate 6: Penmon Sheela 1) shows a female gesturing with her left arm toward the area of the vulva, her long, bent-kneed legs stretched wide apart to form a larger than usual 'black hole.'[68] The second example (see Plate 7:

Plate 6: Penmon Sheela 1

Plate 7: Penmon Sheela 2

Penmon Sheela 2) is dominated by an oversized head with large staring eyes and a long nose, a short, squat body pulled up toward the head, and long arms gesturing down toward the pudendum. Both crude figures categorically illustrate the 'female grotesque.'

CONCLUSION

Support for the identification between Morgan in *SGGK* and the Sheela-na-gig figures includes the poem's debt to its Celtic sources/analogues, the affinity between the Sheelas and Celtic goddess figures and their connections to Morgan le Fay, and the location of several Sheela-na-gigs, which the poet himself may have seen, in the environs of the story's geographic locale in North Wales. If the *Gawain*-poet knew Anglesey at all, and Tolkien and Gordon claim that he did, he would have been aware of the presence of numerous passage grave/caves situated on the island as well as the two Sheela-na-gig figures then exhibited somewhere on the outer walls of Penmon Priory. Both aspects of the material culture of Anglesey support my suggestion of the Sheela-na-gig as an analogue for the *Gawain*-poet's construction of Morgan le Fay's character in *SGGK*.

UNIVERSITY OF HOUSTON

Lorraine Kochanske Stock has published many essays on Chaucer, Langland, the *Gawain*-poet, Dante, French Arthurian romances, and other topics in medieval English and Continental literature. Recent publications include articles on the *Roman de Silence*, the Wild Man, the Wild Woman, the Green Man and Robin Hood, Lady Godiva, the *Nuremberg Chronicle*, the *Bal de Ardents*, and the charivari. She is completing three interdisciplinary book projects: about ambivalent constructions of the Wild Man as reflected in late medieval material culture and literary texts; about the use of the mythic Wild Man by contemporary artists and writers to deconstruct fourteenth-century monarchs such as Charles VI, Wenceslas IV, and Richard II; and about constructions of the medieval Female Other— Wild Women, warrior women, and witches. She serves as the President of Southeastern Medieval Association in 2001–03.

NOTES

1   In the unique manuscript of the poem, *Sir Gawain and the Green Knight* itself is illustrated by four miniatures that collectively depict the main characters multiple times: London, British Library Cotton Nero A.x, fol. 94v, fol. 129r, fol. 129v, fol. 130r. The manuscript illuminations are discussed by Jennifer A. Lee, 'The Illuminating Critic: The Illustration of Cotton Nero A.x,' *Studies in Iconography* 3 (1977): 17–46; Sarah M. Horrell, 'Notes on British Library, MS Cotton Nero A.x,' *Manuscripta* 30 (1986): 191–98; A.S.G. Edwards, 'The Manuscript: British Library MS Cotton Nero A.x,' in *A Companion to the Gawain-Poet*, ed. D.S.

Brewer and Jonathan Gibson (Cambridge, UK: D.S. Brewer, 1997), pp. 197–219.

2 *Sir Gawain and the Green Knight*, ed. J.R.R. Tolkien and E.V. Gordon, 2d. edn. rev. Norman Davis (Oxford: Clarendon Press, 1967), l. 2366. Unless another edition's reading is noted as preferable, all subsequent references to the text of *Sir Gawain and the Green Knight*, hereafter *SGGK*, will be to this edition, cited parenthetically by line number. Translations are my own and are intentionally very literal.

3 In Roger Sherman Loomis and Laura Hibbard Loomis, *Arthurian Legends in Medieval Art* (New York: Modern Language Association of America, 1938; rep. New York: Kraus Reprint Corporation, 1966), an exhaustive catalogue of medieval Arthurian images, Morgan does not merit even a listing in the index. Muriel A. Whitaker, *The Legends of King Arthur in Art* (Cambridge, UK: D.S. Brewer, 1990), a more recent treatment of visual Arthuriana, discusses only nineteenth-century depictions of Morgan.

4 My understanding of the definition and characteristics of the Sheela-na-gig figure is informed by Margaret A. Murray, 'Female Fertility Figures,' *The Journal of the Royal Anthropological Institute of Great Britain and Ireland* 64 (1934): 93–100 with Plates viii–xii; Jørgen Andersen, *The Witch on the Wall: Medieval Erotic Sculpture in the British Isles* (Copenhagen: Rosenkilde and Bagger, 1977); James H. Dunn, 'Síle-na-gCíoch,' *Éire/Ireland* 12.1 (1977): 68–85; Anthony Weir and James Jerman, *Images of Lust: Sexual Carvings on Medieval Churches* (London: B.T. Batsford, 1986); Stella Cherry, *A Guide to Sheela-Na-Gigs* (Dublin: National Museum of Ireland, 1992); Eamonn P. Kelly, *Sheela-na-Gigs: Origins and Functions* (Dublin: County House/The National Museum of Ireland, 1996); Jack Roberts, *The Sheela-Na-Gigs of Britain & Ireland: An Illustrated Guide* (Skibbereen, Ireland: Key Books, undated, ca. 1995); Jack Roberts and Joanne McMahon, *The Sheela-na-Gigs of Britain & Ireland: An Illustrated Map/Guide* (Ireland: Bandia Publishing, 1997), for which I thank Bonnie Wheeler, who thoughtfully gifted me with this useful gazetteer.

5 Dating is problematic; although many of the figures are now found in structures that date from the twelfth century or after, the figures are stylistically crude, and may have been created earlier and incorporated into medieval buildings. Andersen devotes a chapter to the related figures of exhibitionists and acrobats and examples of what he believes are genuine Sheelas in France (*Witch on the Wall*, pp. 48–57). In *Images of Lust*, Weir and Jerman view the Sheela-na-gig as one of several types of Continental and British exhibitionist figures. Malcolm Jones, 'Sheela-na-Gig,' in *Medieval Folklore: An Encyclopedia of Myths, Legends, Tales, Beliefs, and Customs*, eds. Carl Lindahl, John McNamara, and John Lindow, 2 vols. (Santa Barbara, Denver, and Oxford: ABC-CLIO, 2000), 2:912–14, disagrees with Weir and Jerman on the Romanesque dating and continental provenance. After viewing some of these exhibitionist figures in France, I was struck by the very different appearance and context of these continental examples, and I am not persuaded that their functions are the same as the insular specimens, since the mermaids and sirens

seem part of a larger program of grotesqueries decorating the outside of twelfth-century churches in Brittany and Normandy. In contradistinction, the insular Sheelas were usually singular both in appearance and position, the carving is much cruder than on Continental examples, and their effect is disconcerting rather than entertaining.

6 I visited Ireland in 1994 to observe and photograph *in situ* Sheela-na-gigs on both religious and secular buildings; directly afterwards I visited the Forest of Broceliande in Brittany, especially the Val sans Retour, the famed area controlled by Morgan le Fay, a touring juxtaposition that was richly suggestive for purposes of this argument. In 1999, I searched for Sheela-na-gigs in Wales, especially on Anglesey. On both these *aventures*, I was accompanied by my husband Tom and my son Andrew, whose tolerance of my quest for 'just one more Sheela' I deeply appreciate; their cheerful help in locating and photographing the carvings made possible the material research for this project. All photographs used to illustrate this essay were taken by its author.

7 I chose this topic for this volume because it reflected various scholarly interests of Maureen Fries as demonstrated in several of her most recent publications: 'Shape-shifting Women in the Old Irish Sagas,' *Bestia: The Yearbook of the Beast Fable Society* 3 (1991): 15–21; 'Women and Sexuality in the Old Irish Sagas,' *Celtic Connections, Acta* 16 (1993, for 1989): 19–28; 'From the Lady to the Tramp: The Decline of Morgan le Fay in Medieval Romance,' *Arthuriana* 4.1 (1994): 1–18. Those interests enjoy a serendipitous concatenation in my correlation between Morgan and the Celtic Sheela-na-gig. I think Maureen would have enjoyed the connection between these medieval 'bad girls.'

8 Andersen, *Witch on the Wall*, pp. 22–23; E. Kelly, *Sheela-na-Gigs*, p. 5.

9 Roberts, *Sheela-na-Gigs* (ca. 1995), p. 8; Roberts, *Illustrated Guide/Map*, under the rubric 'Sheela-Na-Gigs,' column 2. This etymology was also suggested by a Gaelic-speaking guard at the Athlone Castle Museum, who discussed with me the meaning of the name in Old Irish while I photographed two Sheelas on display.

10 Cherry, *Guide to Sheela-na-gigs*, p. .

11 Eamonn P. Kelly, 'Sheela-na-gigs: A Brief Description of Their Origin and Function,' in *From Beyond the Pale: Art and Artists at the Edge of Consensus* (Dublin: Irish Museum of Modern Art, 1994), p. 45 [45–51]. Two years later, Kelly's almost identical definition in *Sheela-na-Gigs* omits the adjective 'grotesque' (p. 5).

12 My catalogue of physical characteristics conflates the attributes found on most, but not all, Sheelas. Using a representative sample of British and Irish Sheelas, Murray emphasizes common features such as frontality, blatant display of an enlarged vulva, grotesque or distorted facial features, malformed limbs, and lack of emphasis on the breasts ('Female Fertility Figures,' 95–99).

13 Andersen, *Witch on the Wall*, p. 149; Roberts, 'Tradition and Folklore,' in *Illustrated Map*, uses the Killinaboy carving, which he identifies as Innam Buidhe or St. Buidhe, to illustrate his contention that some Sheelas 'are regarded as being actual images of the saints and in each instance these are Christianised Pagan

Goddesses whose worship goes back far beyond the Christian era.' Mary Condren, *The Serpent and the Goddess: Women, Religion, and Power in Celtic Ireland* (San Francisco: Harper SanFrancisco, 1989), p. 65, identifies the Killinaboy Sheela as Brigit in the role as Mother Goddess whose 'image, a sheela-na-gig (a figure holding the entrance to her womb wide open) is carved on the top of the arch to the door, effectively allowing the congregation to enter the church through her womb.'

14 Andersen, *Witch on the Wall,* p. 98.

15 For theorizing of the cross-cultural implications for gender studies of the apotropaic threat symbolized by such vulvic display, see Shirley Ardener, 'A Note on Gender Iconography: The Vagina,' in *The Cultural Construction of Sexuality,* ed. Pat Caplan (London: Tavistock, 1987), pp. 113–42.

16 Page Du Bois, '"The Devil's Gateway": Women's Bodies and the Earthly Paradise,' *Women's Studies* 7 (1980): 45, 47.

17 Roberts, *Sheela-Na-Gigs: Guide* (1995), p. 3.

18 For the relations between the 'Wife of Bath's Tale' and its various analogues, see G.H. Maynadier, *The Wife of Bath's Tale: Its Sources and Analogues* (London: David Nutt, 1901); Sigmund Eisner, *A Tale of Wonder* (New York: Burt Franklin, 1957); Meredith Cary, 'Sovereignty and the Old Wife,' *Papers on Language and Literature* 5 (1969): 375–88; Robert Shenk, 'The Liberation of the "Loathly Lady" of Medieval Romance,' *Journal of the Rocky Mountain Medieval and Renaissance Association* 2 (1981): 69–77.

19 On the Irish Sovereignty stories see: A.H. Krappe, 'The Sovereignty of Erin,' *American Journal of Philology* 63 (1942): 444–54; R.A. Breatnach, 'The Lady and the King: a Theme of Irish Literature,' *Studies* 42 (1953): 321–36; Proinsias Mac Cana, 'Aspects of the Theme of the King and the Goddess in Irish Literature,' an article published in three installments in *Études Celtiques* 7 (1955): 76–114; 7 (1955–56): 356–413; 8 (1958): 59–65; J.K. Bollard, 'Sovereignty and the Loathly Lady in English, Welsh and Irish,' *Leeds Studies in English* 17 (1986): 41–59.

20 Cathalin Buhrmann Folks, 'Gentle Men, *Lufly* and *Loothly* Ladies, *Aghlich Maysters*: Characterizations in the *Wife of Bath's Tale* and *Sir Gawain and the Green Knight,*' in *Noble and Joyous Histories: English Romances, 1375–1650,* ed. Eiléan Ní Cuilleanáin and J.D. Pheifer (Dublin: Irish Academic Press, 1993), pp. 59–85.

21 White was one of the first to suggest that the Auncian is a type of the loathly lady: 'As we meet her here, Morgan La Faye has obvious connections with the "Loathly Lady," Celtic in origin and herself a victim of enchantment as she appears in the "Wife of Bath's Tale" and in Gower's story of "Florent," and not only the Loathly Lady whom a kiss cures of the ugliness of age, but the portrait of Elde herself as it was painted on the wall of the beautiful garden that contained at its centre the Rose of the Lover's desire.' Beatrice White, 'Cain's Kin,' in *The Witch Figure: Folklore Essays by a Group of Scholars in England Honouring the 75th Birthday of Katherine M. Briggs,* ed. Venetia Newell (London: Routledge & Kegan Paul, 1973), p. 189 [188–99].

22 Anne Ross, 'The Divine Hag of the Pagan Celts,' in *The Witch Figure*, ed. Newell, 139–64.

23 Máire Bhreathnach, 'The Sovereignty Goddess as Goddess of Death,' *Zeitschrift für Celtische Philologie* 39 (1982): [243–60], esp. 246, 251 n59. The grotesquely elongated pudendum (in this case hanging almost to her feet!) of the Sheela on the outside of the Church in Oaksey, Wiltshire, England illustrates this feature of the Sovereignty figure; see Andersen, *Witch on the Wall*, fig. 82, p. 121.

24 J.W. Thomas, trans., *The Crown: A Tale of Sir Gawain and King Arthur's Court by Heinrich von dem Türlin* (Lincoln: University of Nebraska Press, 1989), p. 104.

25 Helen Lanigan Wood, 'Women in Myths and Early Depictions,' in *Irish Women: Image and Achievement. Women in Irish Culture from Earliest Times*, ed. Eiléan Ní Chuilleanáin (Dublin: Arlen House, 1985), pp. 15–16, 21–22 [13–24].

26 Bhreathnach, 'Sovereignty Goddess'; Vivian Mercier, 'The Sheela-na-gig,' in *The Irish Comic Tradition* (Oxford: Clarendon Press, 1962), pp. 53–56; Patrick K. Ford, 'Celtic Women: The Opposing Sex,' *Viator* 19 (1988): 416–33; Peter Berresford Ellis, *Celtic Women: Women in Celtic Society and Literature* (Grand Rapids, MI: William B. Eerdmans Publishing, 1995) especially chapter 1, 'The Mother Goddess,' pp. 21–39 and chapter 2, 'Women in Myth,' pp. 40–75; Miranda Green, 'Sovereignty, Sexuality and the Otherworld in Irish Myth,' in *Celtic Goddesses* (New York: George Braziller, 1995), pp. 70–88.

27 See Ross, 'The Divine Hag of the Pagan Celts,' in *The Witch Figure*, ed. Newell; Bhreathnach, 'Sovereignty Goddess,' p. 251 n 50; Lisa M. Bitel, *Land of Women: Tales of Sex and Gender from Early Ireland* (Ithaca, NY: Cornell University Press, 1996) especially chapter 9, 'Warriors, Hags, and Sheelanagigs,' pp. 204–34; Catherine E. Karkov, whom I thank for generously sharing a pre-publication copy of her essay, 'Sheela-na-gigs and Other Unruly Women: Images of Land and Gender in Medieval Ireland,' forthcoming in *From Ireland Coming...*, ed. Colum Hourihane (Princeton: Princeton University Press, 2000).

28 'Fertility Figures,' 97.

29 The role of Morgan in *SGGK* has been one of the most contested aspects of the poem. For an excellent examination of the intertextuality of the *Gawain*-poet's construction of Morgan and a thorough review of previous scholarship about Morgan, see Michael W. Twomey, 'Morgain La Fée in *Sir Gawain and the Green Knight*: From Troy to Camelot,' in *Text and Intertext in Medieval Arthurian Literature*, ed. Norris J. Lacy (New York: Garland, 1996), pp. 91–115, and his essay in this volume.

30 E. Kelly emphasizes that the Sheela carvings found on churches and castles are 'generally placed high up on the walls' ('Sheela-Na-Gigs: A Brief Description,' p. 49).

31 Here I read 'wyf' as 'female-gendered human,' a category of gender, as opposed to '*married* woman,' a category of socio-economic status. There is no indication of the marital status of the 'auncian' per se; however, I infer that she represents some form of the unmarried state, either maid or widow, from the fact that

when Bertilak subsequently refers to the younger 'Lady' of the double portrait, he calls her 'my clere wyf' (l. 2351), 'myn owen wyf' (l. 2359) and 'my wyf' (l. 2404), all indicating her status not only as a woman, but as a married woman.

32 This is also true of the hag figure in the 'Wife of Bath's Tale,' whom Chaucer never has the Wife of Bath actually call a 'hag,' instead referring to her merely as a 'wyf' or an 'olde wyf.'

33 See Roger S. Loomis, 'Morgain la Fee and the Celtic Goddesses,' *Speculum* 20 (1945): 183–203; Lucy Allen Paton, *Studies in the Fairy Mythology of Arthurian Romance*, 2d. ed. (New York: Burt Franklin, 1960), pp. 148–54; Edith Whitehurst Williams, 'Morgan la Fee as Trickster in *Sir Gawain and the Green Knight*,' *Folklore* 96.1 (1985): 38–56.

34 On Morgan's association with the medieval French *Fée* figure, see Margaret Jennings, "'Heavens Defend Me From That Welsh Fairy" (*Merry Wives of Windsor*, V, v. 85): The Metamorphosis of Morgain La Fee in the Romances,' in *Court and Poet: Selected Proceedings of the Third International Courtly Literature Society, Liverpool, 1980*, ed. Glyn Burgess et al. (Liverpool: Francis Cairns, 1981), pp. 197–205; Kathryn S. Westoby, 'A New Look at the Role of the Fée in Medieval French Arthurian Romance,' in *The Spirit of the Court: Selected Proceedings of the Fourth Congress of the International Courtly Literature Society, Toronto, 1983* (Cambridge, UK: D.S. Brewer, 1985), pp. 373–85.

35 See *sídh* in Miranda J. Green, *Dictionary of Celtic Myth and Legend* (London: Thames and Hudson, 1992), p. 190.

36 In fact, referring to Morgan's ability to shapeshift back and forth between beauty and repulsiveness, Paton posits that 'the difference of opinion in regard to her beauty that evidently existed among the narrators who described her appearance looks as if there had been some story that is lost to us, which represented her as assuming the form of a loathly lady' (*Studies in the Fairy Mythology*, p. 151, including notes 1–4, which contain passages from the Vulgate Cycle that support this ambivalence).

37 Paton, *Studies in the Fairy Mythology*, p. 63.

38 *The Story of Merlin*, trans. Rupert T. Pickens, in *Lancelot-Grail: The Old French Arthurian Vulgate and Post-Vulgate in Translation*, gen. ed. Norris J. Lacy (New York: Garland, 1993), 1:354. Phrases from the Old French original, which are bracketed within the passage, are from *Lestoire de Merlin*, in *The Vulgate Version of the Arthurian Romances Edited from Manuscripts in the British Museum*, ed. H. Oskar Sommer (Washington, DC, Carnegie Institution of Washington, 1908–16; reprint New York: AMS Press, 1969), 2:338.

39 *Lancelot*, Part III, trans. Samuel N. Rosenberg, in *Lancelot-Grail: The Old French Arthurian Vulgate and Post-Vulgate in Translation*, 2:311. For the Old French text see *Le Livre de Lancelot del Lac*, in Sommer's *The Vulgate Version of the Arthurian Romances*, 4:124. The text reads, '& elle fu laide & chaude de luxure.'

40 This passage is analyzed in many treatments of Morgan in SGGK. See especially: Folks, 'Gentle Men'; Elisa Marie Narin, "'þat on…þat oþer": Rhetorical Description and Morgan La Fay in *Sir Gawain and the Green Knight*,' *Pacific*

Coast Philology 23 (1988): 60–66.

41 Before this moment in the text, the narrator had referred to him simply as 'aghlich mayster' [terrifying master] (l. 136), 'Half etayn in erde' [half a giant on earth] (l. 140), 'gome' [knight] (ll. 151, 178, 179), until finally he summarily designates him by the title by which most readers know him, the 'grene knyȝt' [the green knight] (l. 390), a descriptor that categorizes him by the color of his costume and hair, rather than by an identifying *name*.

42 Here I prefer Vantuono's unemended manuscript reading. See his note to l. 683 in *Sir Gawain and the Green Knight: A Dual-Language Version*, ed. and trans. William Vantuono (New York: Garland, 1991), p. 170.

43 Florence M. Weinberg, 'Monster-Cave or Sacred Grotto? The Green Chapel in *Sir Gawain and the Green Knight*,' in her *The Cave: The Evolution of a Metaphoric Field From Homer to Ariosto* (New York: Peter Lang, 1986), p. 231 [231–57]. Weinberg's treatment of the Green Chapel as cave does not anticipate any of the ideas I have suggested here.

44 For a summary of various suggestions of the actual model for the Green Chapel, see notes to ll. 709–43 and ll. 2171–84 in Vantuono, *Sir Gawain and the Green Knight*, pp. 172–73; 205–06. See also Ralph W.V. Elliott, *The Gawain Country*, Leeds Texts and Monographs, n.s. 8, ed. Stanley Ellis and Peter Meredith (Leeds, UK: University of Leeds School of English, 1984), pp. 43–72, on the realism of the landscape of the Green Chapel in general and the identification of the chapel with Lud's Church in particular. For my purposes, a precise identification of the particular cave is not necessary; the fact that the 'chapel' is a *cave* is of primary significance.

45 John Speirs, *Medieval English Poetry: The Non-Chaucerian Tradition* (London: Faber and Faber, 1957, rep. 1971), p. 246.

46 Robert J. Edgeworth, 'Anatomical Geography in *Sir Gawain and the Green Knight*,' *Neophilologus* 69 (1985): 318–19.

47 Geraldine Heng, 'Feminine Knots and the Other *Sir Gawain and the Green Knight*,' PMLA 106.3 (1991): 501 [500–514].

48 Green, *Dictionary of Celtic Myth and Legend*, p. 190, says of the *sidhe*, 'The burial mounds of the Neolithic and Bronze Ages were long believed to be the dwelling place of the Irish gods.'

49 Mercier, *The Irish Comic Tradition*, p. 56, makes the connection between the Sheela and fear of castration.

50 Wolfgang Kayser, *The Grotesque in Art and Literature*, trans. Ulrich Weisstein (Bloomington: Indiana University Press, 1963; rep. New York: Columbia University Press, 1981), p. 19.

51 Mary Russo, *The Female Grotesque: Risk, Excess, and Modernity* (New York: Routledge, 1994), p. 1.

52 Russo, *Female Grotesque*, pp. 1 and 29, where she identifies the grotto or cave 'with the womb, and with woman-as-mother.'

53 Russo, *Female Grotesque*, p. 2.

54 Edwards, in summarizing the intent of the illuminations of the Cotton Nero

manuscript, notes, 'While some of the pictures contain obscurities or inconsistencies, they all show conscientious efforts to reflect the texts and significant moments within them' ('The Manuscript,' 219). The image of the Green Chapel is reproduced as pl. 11, p. 216.

55 Dunn, 'Síle,' 72.

56 John Sharkey, *Celtic Mysteries* (London: Thames and Hudson, 1975), p. 6, as cited by Dunn, 'Síle,' 72.

57 As cited from W. Stokes and J. Strachan, *Thesaurus Paleohibernicus* (Cambridge, 1922), 1:2 in Charles Donohue, 'The Valkyries and the Irish War-Goddesses,' *PMLA* 56 (1941): 6 [1–12].

58 For constructions of the *lamia*, see: Gertrude Jobes, *Dictionary of Mythology, Folklore and Symbol*, vol 2. (New York: Scarecrow Press, 1961), pp. 967–68; Katherine Briggs, *An Encyclopedia of Fairies: Hobgoblins, Brownies, Bogies, and Other Superntural Creatures* (New York: Pantheon Books, 1976), pp. 260–62; Katherine Briggs, *The Fairies in English Tradition and Literature* (Chicago: University of Chicago Press, 1967), p. 127; Rosemary Ellen Guiley, *The Encyclopedia of Witches and Witchcraft* (New York: Facts of File, 1989), p. 191; *The Age of the Marvelous*, ed. Joy Kenseth (Hanover, NH: Hood Museum of Art, 1991) is a catalogue of an art exhibition and the material on the *lamia* comes from a woodcut of a *lamia* from Edward Topsell's *The History of Four-Footed Beasts* that shows a picture of a *lamia*, complete with female head, cloven hindfeet, clawed feline front paws, reptilian scales, bushy tail, bare breasts, and a penis: p. 327.

59 Gawain in *SGGK* is one of many examples of this *topos* discussed by Susan L. Smith, *The Power of Women: A Topos in Medieval Art and Literature* (Philadelphia: University of Pennsylvania Press, 1995).

60 This passage has been discussed at length by Mary Dove, 'Gawain and the *Blasme Des Femmes* Tradition,' *Medium Ævum* 41 (1972): 20–26; Catherine Batt, 'Gawain's Antifeminist Rant, the Pentangle, and Narrative Space,' *Yearbook of English Studies* 22 (1992): 117–39.

61 Tolkien and Gordon, ed., 'Introduction,' *SGGK*, p. xxvi.

62 See Andersen, *Witch on the Wall*, p. 32; the Kilpeck Sheela is reproduced as fig. 12, p. 36.

63 Andersen, *Witch on the Wall*, p. 142; for the Llandrindod Sheela and its original site, see: <http://www.jharding.demon.co.uk/SheelaLlandrindod.htm>; for other sheelas in Great Britain, see <http://www.jharding.demon.co.uk/SheelaNaGigIndex.htm>.

64 For various scholars' theories about the exact locations alluded to, see the notes to the passage in Vantuono, *SGGK*, pp. 171–72. It has been suggested that Holy Head refers either to the town on the west coast of Anglesey or to Holy*well*, site of the shrine to St. Winifred, who was beheaded. If the *head* in 'holy head' does denote a well, it is equally possible that the well being alluded to in the passage is not that of St. Winifred, but of St. Seiriol, at Penmon Priory on Anglesey, as described below.

65 My information about Anglesey derives from Lesley Macinnes, *Anglesey: A Guide*

to Ancient and Historic Sites on the Isle of Anglesey (Cardiff: Cadw: Welsh Historic Monuments, 1994).

66 Ford, 'Celtic Women,' 421.

67 Roberts, *Sheela-na-Gigs Map/Guide* (1997), under 'Penmon,' lists the two Sheelas discussed here and mentions possibly a third, which I omit because it seemed to me more like a siren or mermaid figure than a traditional Sheela.

68 Andersen, *Witch on the Wall*, pp. 142–43. Stylistically the Penmon Sheela is similar to the Sheela that originally was situated on the eleventh-century tower of the Church of St. Michael at the Northgate, Oxford (the church is the oldest extant building in Oxford).

Malory's Morgause

DORSEY ARMSTRONG

In Malory's version of the adulterous relationship between Arthur and
his half-sister, it is Morgause's actions, not Arthur's, that are the most
socially destructive. (DA)

We are all familiar with the series of tragic events that mark the
concluding pages of Malory's *Le Morte Darthur*: the violent escape of
Lancelot from Guenevere's chamber and his equally bloody rescue of her
from the stake; the unceasing wrath of Sir Gawain that compels Arthur to
attack Lancelot's homeland in a quest for vengeance; the attempt of the
duplicitous Sir Mordred to usurp both throne and queen in Arthur's absence;
the king's rout of Mordred's forces at Dover, where Gawain receives his death
wound; the parley between Arthur and Mordred undone by the appearance
of an adder; and the final battle between Arthur and Mordred in which each
mortally wounds the other on Salisbury Plain.

While seemingly just one in a series of tragic events, I contend that
Gawain's death at Dover is a highly significant occurrence, a moment that
lays bare the foundation of the Arthurian social order and reveals that
foundation to be deeply flawed. Arthur mourns his nephew's impending
death with significant words:

> 'Alas! sir Gawayne, my syster son, here now thou lyghest, the man in the
> worlde that I loved moste. And now ys my joy gone! For now, my nevew, sir
> Gawayne, I woll discover me unto you, that in youre person and in sir Launcelot
> I moste had my joy and myne affyaunce. And now have I loste my joy of you
> bothe, wherefore all myne erthely joy ys gone fro me!'[1]

Malory has altered this speech as he found it in his source, the *Mort Artu*. In
the French, Arthur exclaims "'Biax niés, grant domage m'a fet vostre felonnie,
car ele m'a tolu vos, que ge amoie seur touz hommes, et Lancelot après'";[2]
[Dear nephew, your treachery has done me great harm, because it deprived
me both of you, whom I loved more than anyone else, and also of
Lancelot…].[3] Arthur's choice of words in the Arthuriad is notable; while in
both the *Mort Artu* and the Stanzaic *Morte*, Arthur refers to Gawain as his
'nephew,' there is no reference to the mother who bore him. The ghost of
Queen Morgause here conjured by the phrase 'syster son' reveals much about

the system of values upon which the Arthurian community is founded, and why that system fails. Mother of both Arthur's ally, Gawain, and Arthur's enemy, Mordred, Arthur's half-sister suddenly becomes pivotal to an understanding of the rise and fall of Arthur's kingdom. The moment when Arthur laments over the body of his 'syster son' both exalts and condemns a system of social order founded upon a kin-based patriarchal structure in which the bodies of women form the locus of masculine homosocial relationships. When seen through the lens of Morgause, the idealized patriarchal order of the chivalric community is revealed to be undone by its refusal to recognize that the exchange of women on which its structure depends may be threatened by those very objects of transaction, should they resist their identity construction as commodities to be exchanged.

I

In seeking to explain how and why Malory's Arthuriad ends the way it does, scholars have returned again and again to an episode in the first tale of the text: the moment when Arthur incestuously and adulterously begets Mordred upon his half-sister Morgause, wife of his enemy King Lot.[4]

> And thydir com unto hym kynge Lottis wyff of Orkeney in maner of a message, but she was sente thydir to aspye the courte of kynge Arthur, and...she was a passynge fayre lady. Wherefore the kynge caste grete love unto hir and desired to ly by her. And so they were agreed, and he begate uppon hir sir Mordred. And she was syster on the modirs syde Igrayne unto Arthur...(But all thys tyme kynge Arthure knew nat that kynge Lottis wyff was his sister.) (1:41.16–29).

It would seem that the seeds of destruction are sown early in Malory's text. Yet, significantly—and perhaps understandably—when critics speak of this scene, the primary focus and emphasis appears to be on *Arthur* and his actions; Morgause is little discussed. Most of the attention given to this episode is devoted to establishing which is the king's greater sin—adultery or incest. For example, in a recent issue of *Arthuriana* devoted to the topic of 'Arthurian Adultery,' David Scott Wilson-Okamura focuses on Malory's source for the 'Tale of King Arthur,' the French *Suite du Merlin*, and states 'My primary goal is to correct what seems to me an oversight on the part of the *Suite's* previous critics, who have consistently emphasized the incestuous aspect of Mordred's conception, neglecting its adulterous aspect altogether.'[5] In the same issue, Beverly Kennedy similarly focuses on the *king's* sin, arguing that Arthur's act of adultery with Morgause does not result in any loss of honor for the king because 'the woman is willing and the adulterer is not honor-bound to be loyal to her husband.'[6] Scholars have also looked to the first example of adulterous activity in Malory and his sources—Uther Pendragon's seduction of Igrayne while disguised as her husband, the Duke of Cornwall— and sought to draw parallels and connections between the two events. The implications seem both logically symmetrical and clear: the Arthurian order, born out of an adulterous relationship, will similarly be destroyed by such an affair. Speaking of Malory's source text, Victoria Guerin attempts to pare the nature of the Arthurian tragedy down to its core elements:

> Uther's adultery with Igerna, and Arthur's own consequent birth, now become a realization of the biblical threat of 'visiting the iniquity of the fathers upon the children unto the third and fourth generation.' Arthur is doomed to repeat, in all innocence, his father's sin of adultery in a far more serious form and, in so doing, to sow the seeds of his own downfall.[7]

While Arthur's act of adultery with Morgause may hardly be referred to as an act committed 'in all innocence,' Guerin's succinct description of the factors that produce the final social collapse suggests that the ending of the *Le Morte Darthur* has been foretold from its opening pages. Arthur and the other characters have in some sense been nothing more than puppets, seemingly unable to avoid fulfilling the destiny that Uther's acts of deception and conception have created.

The sin of incest, then, is seemingly subordinate to that of adultery. Although Mordred had from the time of Geoffrey of Monmouth been portrayed as Arthur's enemy, the nephew who attempts to usurp the throne while the king is away, it is not until the thirteenth century and the composition of the earliest sections of the French Vulgate that the story of Mordred includes his incestuous conception.[8] We see little of Mordred's relationship with his biological mother, Queen Morgause of Orkney, she who unknowingly conceives a child with her own half-brother. Indeed, while the incestuous aspect of Arthur's relationship with Morgause effectively renders Mordred a more horrific, inherently evil villain for both medieval and modern audiences, what is of greatest importance here is that Arthur is apparently the author of his own undoing, whether it be the sin of incest or adultery that ultimately brings about the destruction of his realm.[9]

Though critics have rightly looked to Arthur's incestuous and adulterous relationship with Morgause as a source of the collapse of the Arthurian community, their focus has been misplaced. The chivalric social order is not brought down by the actions of the king in begetting the traitorous Mordred. It is not even Mordred, villainous as he is, who is to blame: ultimately, the collapse of the patriarchal Arthurian community may be attributed to the actions of Morgause.

How and why Morgause's actions lead to the undoing of chivalric community is most clearly demonstrated through a comparison of her relationship with Arthur to that of Uther and Igrayne. Such a comparison reveals that the Uther-Igrayne and Arthur-Morgause episodes follow in many ways a similar pattern; however, the outcome of each is strikingly different. While Uther's semi-rape of Igrayne produces the noble Arthur, Arthur's consensual yet adulterous liaison with Morgause results in the evil Mordred. What is to account for these different outcomes? One answer is in the role that the feminine plays in each of these encounters, and how each of these women conforms to or resists chivalric ideals of femininity. Igrayne, described by Malory as a 'passyng good woman,' never knowingly consents to the betrayal of her lord, while in the case of Morgause, Lot's wife is a willing participant in the cuckolding of her husband: 'Wherefore the kynge caste grete love unto hir and desired to ly by her. *And so they were agreed*, and he begate uppon hir sir Mordred (italics mine).'[10] The agreement between Arthur and Lot's wife, while implied in Malory's source text—the *Suite du Merlin*—is not given the emphasis found in *Le Morte Darthur*. We see no evidence of Morgause's agency:

> Moult fist li rois Artus grant joie de la dame et moult le festia et li et ses enfans Li rois vit la dame de grant biauté plainne, si l'ama durement, et la fist demourer en sa court deus mois entiers. Et tant qu'en chelui terme il gut a li et engenra en li Mordrec, par cui tant grant mal furent puis fait en la terre de Logres et en tout le monde.[11]

> [King Arthur received the lady and her children with rejoicing and feasting. He saw that the lady was beautiful and loved her passionately and kept her at his court for two whole months, until finally he lay with her and begat on her Mordred, by whom such wrongs were later done in Logres and in all the world.][12]

The most significant difference between Arthur and Mordred's conceptions is not the fact that Mordred is conceived incestuously or adulterously, but rather that Malory's Morgause is cited as an *active* player in the adultery— she is not seduced, or deceived as Igrayne was, but she *agrees* to commit the sin of adultery. It is her agreement, her active role in the exchange of her body, that subverts and threatens the patriarchal social order of Arthur's kingdom.

The work of Claude Lévi-Strauss has relevance here in understanding the foundation and structure of the Arthurian social system in Malory's text. In his discussion of kinship systems (an important preoccupation of medieval literature, specifically chivalric romance literature), Lévi-Strauss identifies the transfer or exchange of women as the means by which such systems generate broader social structures such as patriarchy:

The total relationship which constitutes marriage is not established between a man and a woman, but between two groups of men, the woman figures only as one of the objects in the exchange, not as one of the partners...This remains true even when the girl's feelings are taken into consideration as, moreover, is usually the case. In acquiescing to the proposed union, she precipitates or allows the exchange to take place, she cannot alter its nature.[13]

Lévi-Strauss further identifies the incest taboo as an important element in the formation of kinship systems, arguing that such a constraint amplifies the possibilities for wide-ranging social relationships and linking of kinship groups:

The prohibition on the sexual use of a daughter or sister compels them to be given in marriage to another man, and at the same time it establishes a right to the daughter or sister of this other man...The woman whom one does not take is, for that very reason, offered up.[14]

Gayle Rubin, engaging Lévi-Strauss in her now-classic essay 'The Traffic in Women: Notes on the "Political Economy of Sex,"' points out that in the distinction between 'gift and giver' in such a system, it is those who are the 'givers' who enjoy the benefits of social linkage with one other, and that as 'gifts' women cannot derive any benefit from their own circulation: 'As long as the relations specify that men exchange women, it is men who are the beneficiaries of the product of such exchanges—social organization.'[15] In *Le Morte Darthur*, the social organization effected by such exchanges is dependent upon the construction of the feminine as silent, passive, and malleable—a commodity to be exchanged.

Malory's Morgause resists this commodification, the implications of which become clear when her narrative is compared with that of Igrayne. Upon learning that her husband, the Duke, has not only been killed, but passed away hours before her sexual encounter with Uther in the likeness of the Duke, Igrayne 'mourned pryvely and held hir pees' (1:9.29–30). She offers no objection when the nobles of the land decide to wed her to Uther, the man responsible for the death of her husband; when Uther reveals to her his deception and that he is in fact the father of the child she is carrying, Malory tells us that 'Thenne the quene made grete joye whan she knewe who was the fader of her child' (1:10.30–31). Upon the death of her second husband Uther, Malory relates that as was the case with the passing of her first, 'fayre Igrayne made grete sorowe and alle the barons' (1:12.9–10). Although it might seem at first that she is partially to blame for Arthur and Morgause's incestuous relationship (for withholding the information that both are her children), Malory makes clear that Igrayne is unaware that her son and King Arthur are one and the same person until after Mordred's conception:

Ryght so com in Ulphuns and seyde opynly, that the kynge and all myght
hyre...
"...that thys quene Igrayne ys the causer of youre grete damage and of youre
grete warre, for and she wolde have uttirde hit in the lyff of Uther of the birth
of you, and how ye were begotyn, than had ye never had the mortall warrys
that ye have had...and she that bare you of hir body sholde have made hit
knowyn opynly..."
Than spake Igrayne and seyde..."Merlion knowith well...how kynge Uther
com to me...in the lyknes of my lorde...and there begate a chylde that nyght
uppon me...And by his commaundemente, whan the chylde was borne, hit
was delyvirde unto Merlion and fostred by hym. And so I saw the childe
neveraftir, nothir wote nat what ys hys name; for I knew hym never yette"
(1:45.8–36; 1:46.1–3).

Indeed, Igrayne's ignorance of Arthur's identity underscores her
unquestioning obedience to the wishes of her husband, who orders her to
give up her child to Merlin. Igrayne stands out as *the* exemplary female in
Malory's text, quickly and silently adapting to the needs and wants of the
men who fight over and exchange her.

The fact that Igrayne protests and resists Uther's advances while still the
wife of the Duke of Cornwall emphasizes her characterization as the
exemplary representation of femininity in terms of patriarchy. Malory tells
us that she 'wold not assente unto the kynge,' and she calls her husband's
attention to the threat of Uther's overtures in interesting terms: "'I suppose
that we were sente for that *I* shold be dishonoured. Wherfor, husband, *I*
counceille yow that we departe from hens sodenly, that we may ryde all
nyghte unto oure owne castell." And in lyke wyse as she saide so they
departed...' (emphasis mine; 1:7.15–19). Although Igrayne seemingly focuses
on her potential dishonor, not that of her husband, her expression of concern
for her own honor neatly coincides with Cornwall's own interests: namely,
preserving his control over access to his wife's reproduction and maintaining
his genealogical and hereditary interests. Even though she articulates her
concern in terms of her own dishonor, as the 'gift' by which Cornwall has
presumably acquired some measure of land, status, or mutually beneficial
relationship with other men, any threat to Igrayne is a threat to his own
integrity of identity and social position. Possession of women within the
patriarchal order also means possession of the concerns of lineage and ancestry,
and Uther's interest in his wife threatens the stability of Cornwall's control
over these matters.

When word comes that Cornwall has been defeated by Uther's forces,
Malory tells us that 'alle the barons by one assent prayd the kynge of accord

betwixe the lady Igrayne and hym' (1:9.31–32), to which request the King accedes, and charges Sir Ulfius to make the arrangements for the wedding:

> "Now wille we doo wel," said Ulfyus; "our kyng is a lusty knyght and wyveles, and my lady Igrayne is a passynge fair lady; it were grete joye unto us all and hit myghte please the kynge to make her his quene."
> Unto that they were all well accordyd and meved it to the kynge. And anone, lyke a lusty knyghte, he assentid therto with good wille, and so in alle haste they were maryed in a mornynge with grete myrthe and joye (1:9.36–39; 1:10.1–4).

While the King's assent to the will of his barons is important to the re-establishment of order, Igrayne's explicit consent is deemed unnecessary for the act of reintegrating her first husband's realm into that of her second. Igrayne is the gift or object exchanged for peace, property, and a means of establishing male homosocial bonds within this patriarchal, kin-based social order.

In a striking example of community solidarity, several other important unions are consecrated at the same time that Uther and Igrayne wed:

> And kynge Lott of Lowthean and of Orkenay thenne wedded Margawse…and kynge Nentres of the land of Garlot wedded Elayne: al this was done at the request of kynge Uther. And the thyrd syster, Morgan le Fey, was put to scole in a nonnery…And after she was wedded to kynge Uryens of the lond of Gore…(1:10.5–12).

This is the first time that the theme of 'wedding proliferation' occurs in Malory; it is a pattern that he insistently repeats in the text, each time underscoring the importance of such unions in affirming social bonds, and the critical role that women play in this exchange and alliance of power and kinship.

The series of marriages that occur in this first section of the 'Tale of King Arthur' illustrates Lévi-Strauss's theorization of the function of marriage within kin-based social systems: rather than a union between a man and a woman, a marriage is in fact a union between groups of men, in which women are the object of a transaction in return for masculine friendship, support, and alliance. This exchange function is the result of the incest taboo, which renders a woman valuable to her close male relatives only in that she may be exchanged for something else of worth—yams, land, money, power, status, or occasionally, another woman.

Thus exchanged by her stepfather, Uther Pendragon, to secure an alliance with King Lot of Orkney, Morgause clearly serves her function as a commodity in the patriarchal chivalric community of Le Morte Darthur, a system in which loyalty is indeed first established by blood, and then extended in alliance with other kin groups through a practice of exogamy. Once married, Morgause produces four sons, thus gaining in the terms of Luce Irigaray 'use value.'[16] Therefore, she can no longer participate in the marketplace of patriarchy: 'mothers, reproductive instruments marked with the name of the father and enclosed in his house, must be private property, excluded from exchange.'[17]

But as Morgause's relationship with Arthur demonstrates, patriarchy can succeed only when those commodities exchanged—women—are stringently controlled as property under the name of the father or husband to whom they 'belong' or have been 'gifted,' and when men acknowledge the right of another man to possess a woman, seeking access to her only through the proper channels. As Rubin points out, 'kinship systems do not merely exchange women. They exchange sexual access, genealogical status, lineage names and ancestors, rights and *people*—men, women, and children—in concrete systems of social relationships.'[18] Morgause and Arthur have transgressed patriarchal systems of social relationships by breaking the incest taboo and committing adultery, but what is of greatest import here is the active role Morgause plays in the exchange of her body.[19]

In agreeing to the relationship with Arthur, Morgause effects a transaction of feminine sexuality that subverts the dominant paradigm. No man contracts access to Morgause's body, or exchanges it for power, wealth, or status; Morgause is both gift *and* giver, a stark contrast to her mother. Igrayne resists Uther's overtures as long as she is married to another man; upon Cornwall's death, Igrayne's resistance dissipates, and she silently permits herself to be the object of masculine exchange, thereby strengthening the chivalric social and political order. Morgause's behavior runs contrary to the greater communal good, and her agreement to commit adultery threatens not only her husband, King Lot, but her transgression also poses a danger to the larger Arthurian community, in that the product of that adultery is Mordred. Although it is Mordred's adulterous and incestuous conception that critics repeatedly invoke as one of the primary causes of the destruction of the chivalric community, the larger issue of proper feminine behavior overshadows those of adultery and incest. It is Morgause's *agreement*—as was the case with Igrayne's *resistance*—that is critical to an understanding of the destructive impact of this act on the rest of the community.

III

It is through Morgause, then, that Arthur acquires one of his greatest allies— his nephew Gawain—as well as his greatest enemy—his nephew/son

Mordred. Significantly, Morgause herself is destroyed by her own kin, killed by her son Gaheris when he catches her in bed with Sir Lamorak:

> So whan sir Gaherys sawe his tyme he cam to there beddis syde all armed, wyth his swerde naked, and suddaynly he gate his modir by the heyre and strake of her hede. Whan sir Lameroke saw the blood daysshe uppon hym all hote...wyte you well he was sore abaysshed and dismayed of that dolerous syght (2:612.9–16).

Significantly, Gaheris does not slay Lamorak, although he is naked and unarmed at the time of Gaheris's attack on Morgause: "'Alas, why have ye slayne youre modir that bare you? For with more ryght ye shulde have slayne me!'" exclaims Lamorak. Gaheris's response—"'And now is my modir quytte of the, for she shall never shame her chyldryn'" (2:612.18–35)—reveals the hierarchy of transgressions and values around which the ideology of the Arthurian community is ordered. Morgause's behavior clearly poses a greater threat to the social order than does Lamorak's. Her refusal to adhere to the structures of kin-loyalty and submit to the sanctioned circulation of women between and among groups of men—a system of exchange that serves to cement homosocial and patriarchal bonds—identifies Morgause as the single greatest threat to the Arthurian community. Indeed, Gaheris's act is an attempt to rescue the threatened social order, but it comes far too late. In stepping outside the prescribed role of the feminine in agreeing to a relationship with Arthur, Morgause has already compromised the foundation of the Arthurian community years before her relationship with Lamorak. It is her willing participation in the conception of Mordred—not the adultery or the unintentional incest—that prepares the reader for Arthur's nephew/son to be such a monster, a figure who has no respect for the structure of patriarchy.

In the final battle on Salisbury plain, father and son at last meet face to face late in the day on the corpse-strewn field. Spying Mordred still standing, Arthur commands Sir Lucan "'now, gyff me my speare...for yondir I have aspyed the traytoure that all thys woo hath wrought'" (3:1236.25–27). In gruesome detail, Malory then relates how Arthur and his son meet their ends:

> there kyng Arthur smote sir Mordred undir the shylde, with a foyne of hys speare, thorowoute the body more than a fadom. And whan sir Mordred felte that he had hys dethys wounde he threste hymselff with the myght he had upp to the burre of kyng Arthurs speare, and ryght so he smote his fadir, kynge Arthur, with hys swerde holdynge in both hys hondys, upon the syde of the hede, that the swerde perced the helmet and tay of the brayne. And therewith Mordred daysshed downe starke dede to the erthe (3:1237.14–22).

In the masculine arena of combat, Arthur has simultaneously slain both his enemy and his heir, literally impaling Mordred on the spear of his status as father and king. In destroying the greatest threat to his kingdom, however, Arthur has also paradoxically put the chivalric community in peril, as he has destroyed any possibility of effecting the patrilineal transference of wealth, status, and name so essential to the functioning of the kin-based patriarchy over which he rules.[20] Mortally wounded, his son and heir dead, Arthur realizes that there is no one to whom the sword Excalibur—the violent symbol of patriarchal power and authority—may rightfully be given. He asks Bedivere to return it to the water from whence he received it.

Thus, when Arthur stands over the mortally wounded Gawain and offers up a lament for his 'syster son,' he is mourning not only the loss of his nephew and ally, but also the collapse of the entire community, a collapse in part precipitated by *another* 'syster son,' Mordred. Ultimately then, both the establishment and destruction of the Arthurian social order can be traced back to the 'syster' herself: Queen Morgause. It is her transgression against the structures of patriarchy, kinship, and homosocial bonding—structures that are revealed to be incredibly fragile in their absolute dependence upon a definition of the feminine as passive, malleable, and objectified—that in fact dooms Malory's Arthurian community.

CALIFORNIA STATE UNIVERSITY, LONG BEACH

Dorsey Armstrong received her Ph.D. in Medieval English Literature from Duke University. She has published 'Gender in the Chivalric Community: The Pentecostal Oath in Malory's "Tale of King Arthur,"' in BBIAS 52 (2000) and 'Holy Queens as Agents of Christianization in Bede's *Ecclesiastical History*: A Reconsideration' in *Medieval Encounters* 4:3 (1998). She is currently working on a book, *Gender and the Chivalric Community: Sir Thomas Malory's Arthuriad*.

NOTES

1   Sir Thomas Malory, *The Works of Sir Thomas Malory*, ed. Eugène Vinaver, rev. P.J.C. Field, 3d. edn., 3 vols. (Oxford: Oxford University Press, 1990), 3:1230.11–17. Subsequent parenthetical in-text citations to Malory refer to this edition.
2   Jean Frappier, ed., *La Mort le Roi Artu* (Geneva: Droz, 1964), p. 212.
3   Norris Lacy, ed., *Lancelot-Grail: The Old French Arthurian Vulgate and Post-Vulgate in Translation*, 5 vols. (New York and London: Garland, 1995), 4:146.
4   See Martha Asher's introduction to the translation of Malory's source for this scene, the thirteenth-century *Suite du Merlin* in Lacy, ed., *Lancelot-Grail*, 4:163–65.
5   David Scott Wilson-Okamura, 'Adultery and the Fall of Logres in the Post-

Vulgate *Suite du Merlin*,' *Arthuriana* 7.4 (1997): 18 [16–46].
6 Beverly Kennedy, 'Adultery in Malory's *Morte Darthur*,' *Arthuriana* 7.4 (1997): 67 [63–91].
7 Victoria Guerin, 'The King's Sin: The Origins of the David-Arthur Parallel,' in *The Passing of Arthur: New Essays in Arthurian Tradition*, ed. Christopher Baswell and William Sharpe (New York: Garland, 1988), p. 23 [15–30].
8 See Elizabeth Archibald, 'Arthur and Mordred: Variations on an Incest Theme,' in *Arthurian Literature VIII*, ed. Richard Barber (Cambridge: D.S. Brewer, 1989), pp. 1–28. In this article, Archibald argues that the insertion of Mordred's incestuous conception into the Arthurian legend reflects 'a contemporary vogue for incest stories,' tracing the development of this theme through the well-known incest legends of Judas, Gregorious, Roland, and Charlemagne. Although this revision of the Arthurian legend could be said in some sense to reflect the popularity of incest stories in medieval Europe, the double-incest theme played out in the Arthuriad departs from the traditional tale, in which an incestuously conceived child returns from exile and unknowingly duplicates his parents' sin by innocently marrying a woman who turns out to be his sister or mother. In Malory's text, the tale is turned on its head—the product of unwitting incest, Mordred deliberately and perversely seeks to marry his father's wife, and thereby secure his claim to the throne. The best known example of the incest story is, of course, the myth of Oedipus. Archibald points out the two major innovations in medieval incest stories: 'the double incest theme, the conception of the hero in a knowingly incestuous liaison which motivates his exposure, followed by his unwitting incest with his mother; and the Christian elements of contrition, penance, and a spiritually happy ending. The Arthurian legend borrowed from the first innovation, the double incest, but not the second' ('Variations on an Incest Theme,' p. 11).
9 In claiming that the significance of the adultery of Arthur with Morgause has been overshadowed by the sin of incest in Malory's source, the *Suite du Merlin*, Wilson-Okamura traces the figure of the adulterous hero-king back to the biblical figure of David, arguing that Arthur's status as adulterer and ruler is best understood in light of this tradition. See Wilson-Okamura, 'Adultery and the Fall of Logres.' Guerin also calls attention to this parallel; see Guerin, 'The King's Sin,' in *The Passing of Arthur: New Essays in Arthurian Tradition*. For a critical response to Wilson-Okamura's contention that adultery, not incest, is the more significant of the two sins committed by Arthur and Morgause, see Maureen Fries, 'Commentary,' *Arthuriana* 7.4 (1997): 92–96.
10 Malory, *Works*, ed. Vinaver, 1:41.17–20. Rosemary Morris argues that Malory 'establishes a parallel between Uther's conscious sin of lust, from which comes good (Arthur's birth) and Arthur's unconscious sin of incest, from which comes evil (Mordred's birth)'; see Rosemary Morris, 'Uther and Igerne: A Study in Uncourtly Love,' in *Arthurian Literature IV*, ed. Richard Barber (Cambridge, UK: D.S. Brewer, 1985), p. 87 [70–92]. While Morris and other critics have pointed to the similarities between these acts of sinful lust, no one has yet fully

appreciated the differences between them.

11 Gaston Paris and Jacob Ulrich, eds., *Merlin: roman en prose du XIIIeme siecle*, 2 vols. (Paris: Didot, 1886), 1:147.

12 Lacy, ed., *Lancelot-Grail*, 4:167.

13 Claude Lévi-Strauss, *The Elementary Structures of Kinship* (Boston: Beacon Press, 1969), p. 115.

14 Lévi-Strauss, *Elementary Structures of Kinship*, p. 51.

15 Gayle Rubin, 'The Traffic in Women: Notes on the Political Economy of Sex,' in *Toward an Anthology of Women*, ed. Rayna Reiter (New York: Monthly Review Press, 1975), pp. 157–210; rep. in *The Second Wave: A Reader in Feminist Theory*, ed. Linda Nicholson (New York and London: Routledge, 1997), p. 37 [27–62].

16 See Luce Irigaray, *This Sex Which is Not One*, trans. Catherine Porter with Carolyn Burke (Ithaca: Cornell University Press, 1985), p. 170.

17 Irigaray, *This Sex Which is Not One*, p. 185.

18 Rubin, 'The Traffic in Women,' in *The Second Wave*, ed. Nicholson, p. 38.

19 For more on medieval concepts of adultery, see Vern L. Bullough and James A. Brundage, eds., *Sexual Practices and the Medieval Church* (Buffalo: Prometheus, 1982); James A. Brundage, *Law, Sex and Christian Society* (Chicago and London: University of Chicago Press, 1987); Vern L. Bullough, *Sexual Variance in Society and History* (New York: Wiley, 1976). In a recent article Bullough has pointed out that 'obviously, a man who had sexual relations with someone else's wife violated *another man's property...*'(emphasis added); see Vern L. Bullough, 'Medieval Concepts of Adultery,' *Arthuriana* 7.4 (1997): 8 [5–15].

20 As many scholars have noted, Sir Borre, Arthur's son fathered on Lyonors at the beginning of the text, has disappeared from the narrative. It seems clear that Lyonors, like Morgause, is a willing participant who knowingly accedes to the king's overtures. The difference is Lyonors's unmarried state. While fornication is a sin as surely as adultery, the lack of anxiety over this coupling and its offspring, Borre, is clearly located in the fact that genealogy is here not a question. The fact that Arthur is Borre's sire does not compromise the integrity of another man's identity and power as Arthur's parentage of Mordred compromises Lot's stable identity, nor does it pose a threat in terms of claims of inheritance, at least from the position of Lyonors's father. Although as an unmarried woman Lyonors is still considered the property of her father, Earl Sanam, in the terms of patriarchy, her union with Arthur—far from shaming her father, who has control only *over* (and not access to) her sexuality (as a husband would)—brings her father into closer relationship with the king, and thereby benefits her father.

Arthurian Wonder Women: The Tread of Olwen

JO GOYNE

Though introduced as a curse placed upon her suitor, Olwen, the most beautiful giant's daughter in Welsh folklore, brings to this tale wisdom and an aura of enchantment worthy of the most exemplary Arthurian heroines. (JG)

The tale of 'Culhwch ac Olwen' is certainly one of the loveliest in the collection of Welsh folk tales known as *The Mabinogion*. Rachel Bromwich and D. Simon Evans speculate that the form in which we see the story today was probably first recorded at a monastic center in southwestern Wales, in the midst of a period of interest in and revival of folk tales, approximately in the year 1100. Bromwich and Evans characterize 'Culhwch ac Olwen' as 'the oldest Arthurian tale.'[1] In it the activities and reputation of Arthur and the members of his court are very much the major focus of the story, while the tale adapts one of the oldest folk-tale forms—'six go through the world.'[2] The characters of Culhwch and Olwen are grafted onto the form as well. Though only a minor player in the action of the tale, the beautiful Olwen nevertheless casts a sensual and memorable glow over the whole 'aventure.'

Olwen enters her story in the form of what may appear to be a curse put on the boy Culhwch by his stepmother after he has rejected the suggestion that he marry her daughter: "'I put a curse on you," she said, "that your flesh shall not touch woman's till you get Olwen daughter of Ysbaddaden Chief-giant!"'[3] But if the queen's remark is a curse, it is equally a promise of Culhwch's destiny, a destiny articulated and framed by these two women. The boy blushes at his stepmother's prediction and 'love for the girl entered every limb, though he had never seen her' (123). He is infused with her, and she is at once seen as an object of magic, someone whose life force can pervade another across both time and space. As a cousin of Arthur, Culhwch is an appropriate candidate for a magical match, and he will, on the advice of his father, go to Arthur for help in winning Olwen, daughter of a fearsome giant. Here we see Olwen as a representative of the folk-tale motif of the 'giant's daughter.'[4]

In a magnificent passage of description, an *oratio,* Culhwch, appropriately fitted out in purple mantle secured with golden apples at the shoulders and accoutered with grey steed, axe and sword, and a pair of greyhounds, makes his way to Arthur's court. While getting a trim of hair and beard from the king himself, Culhwch asks for the traditional boon from his cousin and lord, to which Arthur replies: "'My heart inclines toward you: I know we are of the same blood…Claim what you will and you shall have whatever your head and tongue may claim'" (126). Culhwch replies: "'I request that you get for me Olwen daughter of Ysbaddaden Chief-giant. And I invoke her in the name of your warriors'"(126). Bromwich and Evans inform us that '[t]hese names [men and women assembled at Arthur's court] are invoked by Culhwch as guarantors of the…privileged gift which he demands from Arthur on the occasion of his acceptance by the king as his kinsman' symbolized by Arthur's cutting of his hair.[5]

Arthur professes ignorance of this special maiden but sends messengers to seek her for the traditional year—but to no avail. Culhwch threatens to leave Arthur's court without the promised boon, thus taking Arthur's honor with him. But Cei intercedes, offering to lead a search party including Culhwch himself that will seek Olwen until Culhwch acknowledges that "'the maiden does not exist, or until we find her; we shall not forsake you'"(132). Cei is not herein the ill-tempered and ineffectual malcontent we often see in Arthurian literature, but a truly magical personage, and he boasts attributes needed for the task at hand: as Ford describes him, Cei can last nine days and nights underwater, holding his breath; when he wishes he can become as tall as the tallest tree of the forest; he can inflict wounds no physician can heal; and he has such body heat that he can keep dry in the rain for a hand's breadth on all sides as well as be kindling for his comrades in the cold (132). Cei and Culhwch are joined by the most handsome Bedwyr, who would never shirk any quest undertaken by Cei; Cynddylig, the guide *par excellence*; Gwrhyr, the translator who knows all tongues; Gwalchmei, the best walker and rider in the world and Arthur's nephew as well; and Menw, a magician whose specialty is invisibility (132–33). These are, of course, the 'six who go through the world,' a search party of true superlatives who are appropriate for the task of finding the equally magical Olwen.

Such a group, of course, should have no trouble finding the object of its quest, and shortly after crossing a wide plain, the searchers find themselves at a great fort whose gate is guarded by a shepherd who has been ruined by Ysbaddadan Chief-giant, father of Olwen. This shepherd's wife is none other than Culhwch's aunt. Both the shepherd and his wife know Olwen, but lament that no one who has sought her previouly has returned alive, much less in her company. Culhwch learns that Olwen comes regularly to a place nearby every Sunday to wash her hair. She leaves her golden rings in the wash basin and never returns for them or sends anyone to reclaim them—implying great generosity on Olwen's part. After extracting Culhwch's promise that Olwen will not be harmed, the woman sends for her. The text tells us simply that 'She came in…' (135) without time passing or entourage or preparation of any kind. She appears before Culhwch almost as if she had been conjured by his desire for her.

The passage that follows in which Culhwch and readers first view Olwen is appropriately magical and symbol-laden, employing beautifully imagistic language. Its tone is one of revelation rather than the unrestrained exuberance we see in the exaggerated, even comical, lists of courtiers or in the abilities of Cei. The language here is mystical but restrained and clearly a companion piece to the earlier *oratio* about Culhwch himself. The parallels between these rhetorical set pieces reinforce the reader's sense of Culhwch and Olwen as an appropriately matched pair.

In the Welsh, the tone of this passage is soft and poetic, and all the sections describing Olwen's parts rhyme as little units. According to Bromwich and Evans, this passage is an early instance of rhetoric or *araith* (the latin *oratio*)—that is, 'passages of heightened prose in rhythmical periods in which substantives may be welded into unfamiliar compounds and governed by a series of alliterating compound adjectives.'[6] Such passages are related to the stylistic feature known as 'runs' in Gaelic folktales and they 'signify the arrival of a significant point in the story…,'[7] and this is indeed such a moment—the impulse upon which all following action is based.

> She came in wearing a flaming-red silk robe with a reddish-gold torque studded with precious stones and red gems about her neck. Her hair was yellower than the flowers of the broom; her skin whiter than the foam of a wave, her palms and fingers whiter than the blooms of the marsh trefoil amidst the sands of a gushing spring. Neither the eye of a mewed hawk nor the eye of a thrice-mewed falcon was brighter than her own. Her breasts were whiter than a swan's; her cheeks redder than fox-glove: whoever saw her was filled with love of her. Four white clovers would spring up in her track wherever she went. Because of that she was called Olwen (White-track). (135)

Olwen enters wearing a 'flaming red silk robe with a reddish-gold torque studded with precious stones and red gems about her neck' (135). The Welsh terms for these reds are each subtly different: the red silk robe would be a red-purple garment accented by the copper-gold or ruddy-gold of the torque, while the red gems would be blood red, like garnets.[8] Olwen fairly glows with warmth and wealth. 'Her hair was yellower than the flowers of the broom,' a golden, warm yellow, not pale, but robust and glowing as well. '[H]er skin [was] whiter than the foam of the wave,' the translucently fair skin of her face, again subtly different from the whiteness of her palms and fingers, which were 'whiter than the blooms of the marsh trefoil amidst the sands of a gushing spring.' These little marsh trefoils are the first flowers to bloom in the Spring and do so in areas that are the source of a spring's fertility, the gushing waters. We notice the inherent contrast in these two images—the delicacy of the flower and of Olwen herself, and the power and potency of the gushing waters and the warm and lively reds—which nevertheless coexist amiably in one being.

'Neither the eye of a mewed hawk nor the eye of a thrice-mewed falcon was brighter than her own.' Captured birds have an intense stare, an almost hypnotic brilliance to the eyes, and here we see that brightness and intensity implied, interestingly, instead of any reference to color. 'Her breasts were whiter than a swan's'—the author delineates yet another degree of whiteness, suggesting the softness of down. Royal status is also conveyed in the comparison of Olwen to the noble swan. And 'her cheeks redder than fox-glove'—foxgloves are little red flowers, and again the glowing red imagery appears. The images the author uses convey delicacy and smallness, yet also vibrancy and warmth. And lastly, the element unique in folk literature to Olwen: 'Four white clovers would spring up in her track wherever she went. Because of that she was called Olwen (White-track).' Here the Welsh word for this white means 'bright,' yet another dimension of color and energy. Not only does wealth remain behind as Olwen passes—the golden rings—but beauty and fertility as well. The narrator need hardly tell us that 'whoever saw her was filled with love of her' (135).

Culhwch's love for her is already in full flower, and in the tradition of true love, when she enters the house, he knows her to be Olwen, and asks her to come with him. Olwen explains that she cannot comply because of a promise she made to her father, the Chief-Giant. The day his daughter takes a husband will be the day of her father's death: '"My father has extracted a pledge from me that I will never go without his counsel, for he can live only until I go with a husband"' (135). But she counsels Culhwch, perhaps sensing a difference in this suitor, in the only other words spoken by Olwen herself: '"I will give you some advice, if you will take it: go to my father to ask my hand, whatever he may ask of you, promise to get it and you shall have me. If you hesitate about anything, however, you shall not have me and you will be lucky to escape with your life"' (135). In her admonition that Culhwch take care that her father have no cause to doubt him—his prowess, his dedication, his ability to perform the duties of a king responsible for not only his love Olwen, but for her people as well—we see Olwen asserting that in order to win her and her kingdom, he must prove himself capable of being a king, a fulfillment of destiny beyond just the wishes of his own heart. And here emerges a far larger and more significant dimension to Culhwch's quest. Olwen knows and understands what will be required of Culhwch far more clearly than he at this moment; in sharing that knowledge with him, she allows readers an understanding of these requirements as well. Olwen warns him of the price to be paid if he cannot meet the challenge, implying that were he to ascend to the kingship unable or unprepared, the results for her and her kingdom could be disastrous.

This said, Olwen retires to her chamber while Culhwch and the faithful band of six, with readers in tow, are off on a series of hair-raising adventures, both literally and figuratively, beginning with their braving her father at his own table. Culhwch disappears from the story at this point, and the tasks are engaged by Arthur and his representatives. After a truly remarkable number and variety of seemingly impossible tasks are demanded and many are accomplished, Culhwch reappears and gathers together everyone who bears Ysbaddaden ill will—a sizeable group—before they proceed to the Chief-Giant's fortress once more. He demands Olwen, and her father must oblige. Though Culhwch apparently gets credit for passing the tests and thus earning the giant's kingdom, Ysbaddaden thrusts a final and truthful barb: "'but don't thank me for that, thank Arthur who brought it about for you. If I'd had my own way you never would have got her...'"(157). Even now, her father remains unconvinced that this youth is a worthy husband for his daughter, but will not or cannot challenge the fact that the deeds have been accomplished, albeit by Arthur. As all fathers are forced to accept their daughter's departure into the arms of another man, and often one less worthy in their opinion, so must Ysbaddaden. The giant's head is cut off and stuck on the baily-stake, not by Culhwch but by one of Arthur's men, while Culhwch takes possession of his fort and lands—the king is dead; long live the king.

And 'that night [Culhwch] slept with Olwen' (157), implicitly confirming his kingship. The text closes by telling us that 'as long as he lived she was his only wife' (157). As the culmination of the tale, such a statement is remarkable. Does it mean simply that Olwen outlived her husband—or that his fidelity to her (unlike his father's to his mother) outlived death itself? The latter certainly seems appropriate for such a memorable woman. And with this final comment, we are brought full circle, back to the issue of fidelity with which the tale began. Olwen never appears elsewhere in Welsh or Arthurian literature, yet her presence in *The Mabinogion* haunts us with its mystical qualities, like a beautiful fragrance, once smelled and never quite forgotten.

I find it appropriate to remind us all of the lovely Olwen in a paper honoring Maureen Fries. Just as Olwen's tread symbolizes her great generosity in the beautiful trefoils that sprung up when she passed, so also has Maureen sown the path of her career with the many aspiring Arthurian students who emerged in response to her equally incredible generosity of both knowledge and spirit. Maureen was wise and knowing and as full of pertinent instruction as Olwen, and was just as loyal once she had vested herself in a friend or student. And, like Olwen who blossoms beautifully but all too briefly, Maureen will forever remain with us in spirit as a true Arthurian wonder woman.

SOUTHERN METHODIST UNIVERSITY

Jo Goyne, Associate Editor of *Arthuriana*, is a Senior Lecturer and Director of the First-Year Writing Program at Southern Methodist University. She has published several articles on medieval literature and thought as well as on gender/women's issues in Malory and Chaucer.

NOTES

1   *Culhwch and Olwen: An Edition and Study of the Oldest Arthurian Tale*, eds. Rachel Bromwich and D. Simon Evans (Cardiff: University of Wales Press, 1992), titlepage.
2   Bromwich and Evans, *Culhwch and Olwen*, p. xliii.
3   *The Mabinogi and Other Medieval Welsh Tales*. trans., ed., with intro., Patrick K. Ford (Berkeley: University of California Press, 1977), p. 123. All in-text citations are to this translation.
4   Bromwich and Evans, *Culhwch and Olwen*, p. xxvi.
5   Bromwich and Evans, *Culhwch and Olwen*, p. xxxvii.
6   Bromwich and Evans, *Culhwch and Olwen*, p. lxxiii.
7   Bromwich and Evans, *Culhwch and Olwen*, p. lxxiv.
8   I am immensely grateful to Chris Grooms, Welsh scholar and folklorist *extraordinaire*, for his lovely and loving explication of the Olwen *oratio*. The analysis and interpretation of colors I cite here are his entirely and came to me in his 'Tales of Wales' course taught at Southern Methodist University (Fall 1997). This chapter is slightly revised from one that appeared in *Arthuriana* 9.2 (Summer, 1999).

Chrétien's Enide: Heroine or Female Hero?

MARGARET JEWETT BURLAND

Romance heroines are often seen as lacking in subjectivity and significance, yet a crisis in Enide's subjectivity can be seen as the primary motivation for the adventures in the second part of Chrétien de Troyes's *Erec et Enide*. Examining Enide's self-perception enhances one's appreciation for Maureen Fries's models of Arthurian heroines and for Chrétien's complex treatment of gender roles. (MJB)

What is a 'heroine'? The term appears to be simply the feminine form of 'hero,' but like some other feminine forms (such as 'poetess,' and increasingly 'actress'), 'heroine' suggests to many a lesser status than its masculine form. Generic descriptions of the 'typical' heroine of medieval romance usually express disdain for and/or disappointment in this character type.[1] Those critics who continue to use 'heroine' to describe some medieval literary characters also tend to disqualify many other characters from the category on the grounds that they are too passive or that they are portrayed too negatively to be considered as heroic as male protagonists in the same texts. Other critics use the term but choose to define it to encompass passivity or negative traits.[2] Still others, who dislike the term, tend to avoid it by calling such characters 'women,' which is accurate within the fictional universe, but which, applied from outside the fiction, tends to blur the line between literary creations and actual human beings. The controversies surrounding the heroic nature of female Arthurian characters, in particular, led Maureen Fries to examine the 'heroine' category more closely, 'to determine whether such negative images are universal or whether there are other female images—both heroic and positive—to be discovered.'[3]

Fries devised three categories to describe the functions of female characters in Arthurian literature: 'heroines,' 'female heroes,' and 'counter-heroes.' One virtue of Fries's approach was that she considered not only descriptions of these characters' appearance and actions, the two criteria most important to other critics, but also the characters' own intentions, which contributed most decisively to placing them into one category or another. If a character's intentions were to undermine the hero's efforts or the stability of the society in which he lived, she would be considered a 'counter-hero,' since her intentions ran counter to those of the hero. If, instead, she sought to uphold society and fulfill a traditional female role within it, she would be considered a 'heroine.' If she sought to uphold society but had to step out of traditional female-gendered behavior in order to do so, she would be considered a 'female hero.'[4] This refinement of the category 'heroine' into three sub-categories provides a welcome antidote to other discussions of 'heroines' that define them so generally or so specifically that the term becomes useless. Within Fries's study, however, one character stood out as unclassifiable: Chrétien de Troyes' Enide.

While all the other characters mentioned by Fries could be neatly classified into one category or another, she offered Enide as a representative example for two categories between which Enide's behavior alternates at different points in the romance. Fries called these different manifestations of the character 'Enide I' (Enide as 'heroine' in the first section of the romance) and 'Enide II' (Enide as 'female hero' when she defies Erec's command to remain silent during their adventures in the second section). Fries concluded that Enide returns to the 'heroine' role as soon as she and Erec are reconciled: 'Impressed by such heroism, Erec assures her he now knows her love is perfect. But his kiss turns her again, as in the archetypal fairy tale, into a heroine.'[5]

Fries has not been the only modern reader to perceive Enide's multiplicity or Erec's influence over each of her transformations. Several other critics have emphasized Enide's dual role as *fame* (wife) versus *amie* (lover), a distinction inspired by the scene in the romance in which Enide is asked which role she occupies in relation to Erec (vv. 4648–49). Barbara Sargent-Baur and Joan Brumlik both stress Erec's agency in determining which of the two roles Enide is allowed to play at each given moment of the romance.[6] Michel-André Bossy also notes the unusual variety of qualities demonstrated by Enide and suggests that, in forming Enide, Chrétien was drawing upon the established functions of several identifiable female characters from previous French narratives.[7] Bossy provides a key to the types of agency being exerted by Erec and by Enide in the second section of the romance by highlighting the fact that the narration of these adventures encourages readers to identify with Enide, since she rides in front of Erec and therefore is the first to see and narrate new events in monologues heard only by the reader: 'The upshot of this narrative stratagem is that the narrator becomes aligned with Enide, the wondering and anxious outrider, while the author's position as plot contriver becomes analogous to that of Erec driving Enide ahead without revealing his specific intentions.'[8] Bossy's association of Erec with the author enhances the notion of Enide's heroic status, since one way to identify the hero or protagonist of a medieval verse romance is to determine whose adventures the reader is watching and whose perspective the reader shares. If Erec is allied with the author during the second section of *Erec et Enide*, while the reader is sympathetic to Enide and sees what she is doing even when Erec is not present, then it seems clear that Enide has shifted into the traditional heroic *narrative* function during the time when Fries considered her to be a 'female hero.'

Bossy's observations provide further support for Fries's view of Enide as a heroic figure in the second section of the romance, but they also raise the possibility that it is the audience's interior view of Enide, as much as her actions in service to Erec, that places her in the heroic role. By further examining Enide's interiority, I will demonstrate that the apparent transformation of Enide from 'heroine' to 'hero' and back again actually expresses Chrétien's consistent underlying intention to dramatize a female heroic crisis. As Norris Lacy describes the hero's crisis in Chrétien, 'the crisis necessitates a personal renewal, in which the hero constructs for himself an identity in accord with his expanded or perfected comprehension of his purpose. His adventures thus constitute both a moral and a psychological rebirth.' Lacy adds that the 'only character who receives any psychological development is the hero (and, in the first two romances, the heroine).'[9] I believe that Enide's heroism is an essential part of her nature throughout the romance, rather than a temporary condition through which she passes: her noticeable 'psychological development' as a character provides an indication of her participation in the heroic function, and thus it is worthwhile to examine what we know of her inner life.

Enide's crisis does not take place entirely within herself, any more than the male heroes' crises do. In fact, what often sparks a hero's inner crisis is a tension between private concerns (the hero's love relationship) on the one hand and public concerns (his political allegiances and homosocial activities) on the other. While some critics have seen the public/private conflict as an issue only for male characters in medieval romance,[10] it is a defining feature of Chrétien's female characters as well. The nature of the public/private conflict is particularly complex for romance heroines in that the private is made public and vice versa: their personal security rests on their allegiances to men by family lineage and marriage. These allegiances involve personal relationships as well as a public persona, with both public and private roles largely defined for them by the expectations of others. Chrétien deliberately intensifies this public pressure for his heroines by making them queens or major land-holders: the public identity of these female characters is hardly incidental, but rather exerts a profound influence on their everyday circumstances as well as their adventures. For Chrétien's heroines public and private life are simultaneously fused together and in conflict with each other, thus allowing him to create unusually complicated resolutions to his romances.[11] This double bind can be traced in two of Chrétien's female characters. Both Enide and Fénice, the two heroines from Chrétien's romances in whom Lacy observes an unusual degree of psychological development, are young brides assuming new public identities, Fénice as an empress and Enide as a princess soon to become a queen. Like Chrétien's heroes, then, they are both forced to develop a new concept of themselves in order to integrate this public persona into their psychological framework.

If Enide is undergoing an identity crisis analogous to those of Chrétien's heroes, why have critics not subjected her perception of herself to closer examination?[12] One reason is that Enide's interiority might be considered a questionable object of study, since her 'thoughts' were created by a medieval male author whom some critics have characterized as misogynist.[13] Enide, in particular, has been read as one of Chrétien's more menacing creations from the point of view of female audiences: just as romances are assumed to be primarily about male heroes, they also often are assumed to have been written for male audiences with voyeuristic tastes which Enide has been thought to satisfy. Indeed, most critics have agreed that one of Enide's primary characteristics is that of being objectified by the gaze of others.[14] Enide has been considered too perfect, the youthful Chrétien's own fantasy girl.[15] Building on this critical tradition of Enide as the victim of every man around her, from husband to author to audience, E. Jane Burns reads Enide's speeches as a subversive rebellion against the silencing of women practiced in and by the courtly, chivalric universe that contains her.[16]

While I do not agree with the characterization of Chrétien de Troyes as misogynist, neither would I claim that his female characters demonstrate a profound, compassionate understanding of women: Chrétien's female characters are *not* women, but literary characters in highly unusual situations. Indeed, Chrétien was similarly disadvantaged in regard to his male characters, since he was in all likelihood not knight, king, brigand, nor Welsh country boy, and so it is unlikely that Chrétien's purpose in creating female literary characters would have been to reveal the nature of real women. Instead, like Chrétien's male characters, these female characters were created to portray (within a fictional universe imagined by a medieval male mind) the uncomfortable intersection between one's gender and one's individual identity and experience.

Chrétien's narratives are perpetually conscious of the physical, emotional, and political constraints caused by gender, constraints within which both men and women live, and they therefore present the resulting problems from the point of view of each gender simultaneously and consistently.[17] At the same time, Chrétien's romances also portray the quandaries facing individual heroes and heroines whose experiences have been designed to provoke specific crises of identity development as well as interesting plot twists. In other words, Chrétien incorporates into his fictional universe certain contemporary social pressures for each gender (for example, the constant threat of attack for women or the constant performance anxiety experienced by men). I would not venture to judge whether or not observations about human nature (male or female) based on Chrétien's characters are accurate; instead, my aim is to look more closely at what we know about the perspective of one of his characters, Enide, and how we know it.

On the surface, Enide does not seem to be the troubled person in her marriage: the dynamics of that marriage have been analyzed many times, but the question is usually whether or not Erec is abusive toward Enide and whether or not Enide deserves this treatment in any way.[18] Yet Enide does experience an inner conflict because of her marriage: she perceives a problematic fusion of herself with Erec, whereas other characters perceive her and attempt to validate her as a separate person. For readers who may find it objectionable that the fusion of public and private roles is held up as the ideal for female characters in other romances by Chrétien de Troyes, an ideal that often creates double binds for them, Enide's example is important because it shows that Chrétien began his series of romances by setting up a clear distinction between that fusion of roles and an actual lack of subjectivity or self-worth.

The prologue to *Erec et Enide* can be read as an indication that Enide's worth, including the worth she assigns to herself, is meant to be a central concern of the rest of the narrative:

> Li vilains dit an son respit
> que tel chose a l'an an despit
> qui molt valt mialz que l'an ne cuide;
> por ce fet bien qui son estuide
> atorne a bien quel que il l'ait;
> car qui son estuide antrelait,
> tost i puet tel chose teisir
> qui molt vandroit puis a pleisir.

[The common man says in his proverb that something that one holds in contempt is worth far more than one thinks; and so he does well who puts his

effort into making the most of whatever he has; for he who relaxes his effort,
before long can silence something that would have come to be greatly pleasing
later] (vv. 1–8).[19]

These lines are deliberately and even explicitly vague about their subject,
called only *tel chose* [something]. This 'something' may be Enide or the
romance itself, with Erec or Chrétien as the agent. Enide can also be
considered, along with the romance itself, the subject of the final section of
the prologue, where Chrétien criticizes the way this story is usually told (vv.
19–22). Here Chrétien associates the supposed 'story about Erec' with the
abridging and corrupting of which he accuses other tellers of the tale.[20]
Perhaps he means that the story should not really be about Erec alone, but
rather about both Erec and Enide, as the last line of the romance indicates:
'Explycyt li romans d'Erec et d'Enyde' [here ends the story of Erec and of
Enide].

The silencing of Enide is a unifying theme of the whole prologue, in
which Erec and other storytellers are the most apparent agents of silencing.
The undervaluing of Enide is the first concept presented in the prologue,
and one that deserves careful scrutiny. It might be said that Erec does not
value her enough when he orders her to be silent during their adventures,
but at the same time her value is the very currency of their adventures, since
these adventures consist of Erec displaying Enide in front of men who will
want to fight him for her. In a more respectful sense, Erec affirms Enide's
value before they even set out on their adventures: when Erec says goodbye
to his father, at the moment when his anger at Enide would have been at its
height, he nevertheless demands in strong terms that his father give his
inheritance to Enide if Erec should be killed along the way (vv. 2721–27).[21]
Furthermore, Erec values Enide by trusting her: during their adventures he
agrees to sleep while she keeps watch (vv. 3084–89), and he does not for a
moment question her story when she announces to him in the middle of the
night that another man will soon be arriving to kidnap her because, in an
effort to protect Erec, she had pretended that she wanted to leave with this
other man (vv. 3474–86). Finally, a brief glimpse of Erec's thoughts provided
by the narrator shows that they are loving, in spite of his forbidding
appearance (vv. 3751–55).

If anyone in this romance fails to value Enide, it is not her husband but
Enide herself. Although Erec does, of course, order Enide to remain silent
when their adventures of the second section begin, no limits were placed on
Enide's speech throughout the first section, and yet she chose not to speak.
Moreover, like the rival storytellers evoked by Chrétien in the prologue,

Enide edits herself during all of her early speeches to Erec: she announces her thoughts to the audience in spoken monologues, but then she rephrases those thoughts for Erec.

The most famous case of Enide's self-editing is her first speech, in which she reveals the criticism she has been hearing of Erec's *recreantise*, the fact that he no longer seeks to prove his knightly prowess after marrying Enide. Erec responds by ordering Enide to set out with him on a series of adventures. Enide's subjective perception of this gossip, rather than the gossip itself, causes Erec to leave on the road to adventure and to take Enide with him. Erec never confronts the gossip directly, nor does he seek to demonstrate his knightly prowess in front of those who demeaned him; indeed, the romance ends before Erec makes his way home to his own kingdom, so the resolution of the romance does not rely on Erec's disproving the gossip. Instead, it is Enide's distorted self-concept in this first speech, immediately apparent to Erec, that constitutes the heroic crisis to be resolved by the couple's adventures. It is no accident that Erec has so often been aligned with the author in critical commentaries: having proven his own worth in the first section, Erec's primary purpose in the second section is to create a meaningful framework for Enide's heroic process of self-development, and this is more an authorial function than a heroic one. Before examining Erec's treatment of Enide as a helpful solution to her problem, however, it is necessary to examine the problem. Although the speech that causes them to leave on their adventures is the first direct discourse by Enide, Chrétien had already laid the groundwork in the first section of the romance for Erec and the audience to understand the problematic nature of Enide's self-perception as revealed in this speech.

Up to the moment when Enide heard the gossip about Erec's *recreantise*, she had been receiving continuous praise from everyone around her. In spite of her family's relative material poverty, her father had been unwilling to accept noble and wealthy suitors from the area because he adored Enide so much that he wanted to wait for an even better match, a man more worthy of her many good qualities (vv. 525–46). In Enide's first public appearance, she won the sparrowhawk contest because she was the most beautiful, wise, and purehearted of the ladies present. The nature of this contest places Erec in the role of praising and encouraging Enide from the start of their relationship, telling her why she alone is worthy to claim the sparrowhawk (vv. 830–36). This speech allows Chrétien to show Erec's immediate appreciation of Enide's multiple good qualities: her beauty, honesty, honor, and overall worth. Erec does not just appreciate her sex appeal, as has been argued,[22] and his description of Enide is far richer than his opponent's description of his own lady as simply 'bele et gente' [beautiful and noble] (v. 810). In the only interior view of Enide in this first section, the narrator communicates to the audience the way in which Enide is contemplating her future with Erec: she sees Erec as a worthy man to be given to, and she knows that she will be honored because she is married to him (vv. 684–90). In other words, she sees her own honor as entirely dependent upon the honor that is shown to Erec. Her parents view her future life in the same way (vv. 1448–55). Finally, although the narrator offers the opinion that Erec and Enide are equally good, beautiful, and wise (vv. 1484–92), Enide is flustered by public attention at Arthur's court (vv. 1707–14) in a way that the self-confident Erec is not.

Chrétien's portrayal of Enide in this section is often considered a non-portrayal in the sense that she does not speak and is constantly the object of the gaze of others, but it is Enide herself who chooses this role by not speaking. Furthermore, her discomfort when she is presented at court suggests her desire to avoid the scrutiny of others. Whether in rags or in the queen's own gown, Enide does not enjoy being conspicuous. Erec offers Enide not only a husband whose social status impresses even her proud father, but also a refuge from difference in the 'mirror stage' of courtly romance, in which the two lovers seem to be perfect images of each other.[23] The mirror is evoked as soon as Erec and Enide meet, in a description of Enide's beauty: 'Ce fu cele por verité / qui fu fete por esgarder, / qu'an se poïst an li mirer / ausi com an un mireor' [In truth she was one who was made for looking, for one could look at oneself in her just as in a mirror] (vv. 438–41). This passage has often been used as evidence that Enide's role in life is to be the object of others' admiring gazes, but the ambiguity of the grammar suggests that Enide could also be the agent of *esgarder,* in which case Chrétien would be telling us something here about how Enide chooses to view the world: 'she was made so that she looked [at one] in such a way that one could look at oneself in her as in a mirror.' Read in this way, this comment indicates that Enide deliberately keeps her own gaze blank so that others will not be able to see anything about her by looking in her eyes: instead, they will simply see themselves projected onto her. Once Enide is betrothed to Erec, she does not mind his admiring gaze because she can look back at him in exactly the same way (vv. 1466–96): their reciprocal gaze suggests not only equality but also, potentially, the erasure of difference. It has been observed that a frequent characteristic of heroines is precisely that of not seeing themselves as subjects, but rather as objects or reflections of the people around them.[24] This may also make it more difficult for readers to recognize the subjectivity of heroines. Yet that subjectivity is manifested precisely in the distance between Enide's self-perception and the way in which others perceive her. Enide is described and praised so many times throughout the first section in order to ensure that the audience will see Enide's negative perception of herself in the second section as an aberration.

The shock produced by Enide's first speech results in part from the bleakness of her outlook on her own life, following the many rosy descriptions of her throughout the first section. Her despair is the result of a basic error: not believing in her own honor, she is invested entirely in the honor shown toward her husband. When Enide realizes that Erec's behavior is viewed by people in his household as dishonorable and as a result of his marriage to her, she experiences this realization as a hostile force capable of destroying her personhood, a rupture in the previously clear purpose of her own life: 'Lasse, fet ele, con mar fui! / de mon païs que ving ça querre? / Bien me doit essorbir la terre' [Wretched woman, she said, woe is me! what did I come here from my own land to look for? Really, the earth should swallow me up] (vv. 2492–94). She does not understand her function in the marriage, sees herself as the problem in Erec's life, and believes that the solution would be for her to be magically removed from the situation, either annihilated or transported back to a moment before she left home to be married. In other words, this scene is as much about a crisis in the development of Enide's subjectivity as it is about Erec's reputation or about a communication gap between the two of them: if Enide wishes to be swallowed by the earth every time she hears a rumor about her husband, she will not be an effective queen or wife. Such psychological abdication would create a void where a person needs to be: for the sake of her future queenship, her marriage, and herself, Enide must learn to resolve this problem.[25]

The proof of Enide's distorted subjectivity emerges not only in the way she articulates her situation to herself but also in the difference between what Enide hears about Erec's *recreantise* and how she herself retells it to him. The narrator tells the audience that what Enide heard was that Erec had made a regrettable decision to devote all of his attention to love, using several verbs to emphasize that Erec was fully responsible for this decision: spending time with Enide was what Erec wanted (*volt*, v. 2434), where he invested his attention (*a mise s'antendue*, v. 2436), what was appealing to him (*lui estoit bel*, v. 2444). Yet Enide invents for Erec an overheard narrative in which she is the gendered vilain: 'blasmee an sui, ce poise moi, / et dïent tuit reison por coi, / car si vos ai lacié et pris / que vos an perdez vostre pris' [I am blamed for it, which weighs heavily upon me, and they all say the reason for it, for I have so tied you up and taken you over that you have lost your worth] (vv. 2557–60). Enide claims to be viewed as an overbearing sexual temptress, but the narrator has specifically and repeatedly told the audience that this is not how she is perceived by anyone else. Instead, everyone admires her for her moral qualities as well as for her beauty: just before Enide's speech, the narrator emphasizes at great length that no one ever criticized Enide because there was nothing in her to criticize (vv. 2397–2429). Erec does not criticize her here either: although Erec is understandably upset to learn that his reputation has been attacked, he never expresses a desire to be rid of Enide and he never implies that she has caused his problem. On the contrary, he describes the people whose accusations Enide overheard as 'cil qui m'an blasment' [those who blame me for it] (v. 2573), which suggests that he does not believe Enide's self-accusing narrative.

Enide continues to criticize herself as soon as Erec leaves the room: she believes that her words showed that she has an excess of pride(vv. 2602 and 2604), and she imagines that Erec intends to send her away and never see her again (vv. 2592–94). It is interesting to note that when Erec tells Enide to put on her best dress, she sees that as the prelude to his abandoning her. For Enide, to be conspicuous is to be separate from Erec, and to be attractive leads to punishment. Here the narrator emphasizes Enide's excessive self-punishment with a proverb comparing her to a goat who has scratched itself so much that it can no longer comfortably lie down (vv. 2582–84). By poking fun at Enide in this way, the narrator is also emphasizing that her attitude is inappropriate, a problem to be remedied. Enide closes her speech with another proverbial statement that can be seen to describe both her own self-sabotage and the nature of the difficult work of identity transformation that lies ahead of her: 'ne set qu'est biens qui mal n'essaie' [Whoever does not test out the bad does not know the good] (v. 2606). Enide has been presented as someone who has no faults and who therefore is incapable of appreciating her own good qualities. Since praise has not convinced her to think highly of herself, the only way for her to recognize her own good qualities will be to put her supposed bad qualities to the test. In order to gain an appreciation of her own value, Enide will have to experience criticism and learn to judge its validity for herself: this is exactly the treatment she will experience during her adventures with Erec. As Joan Grimbert put it, 'Enide will have to depend entirely on her own judgment to interpret not only the individual adventures that come their way, but also the aventure that they are living as a couple in crisis.'[26]

Whether Erec had an insight into the nature of Enide's problem or whether Chrétien manipulated his hero into supporting his heroine's quest for self-understanding, the rules Erec imposes on Enide during their adventures help her to grow precisely because they set her up to fail and then to be forgiven. Critics have often noted the irony of the abusive Erec proclaiming late in the couple's adventures that he is ready to forgive Enide for all her faults (what faults?), but this moment makes sense if Erec is viewed as formally concluding the game by placing Enide's 'test' in terms appropriate to her during her period of self-criticism. The link between Enide's view of herself at the outset and Erec's process of testing her is emphasized by the use of the verb *essaier* by Enide here and by Erec in the scene of their reconciliation ('bien vos ai de tot essaiee' [I have truly tested you in everything], v. 4883). According to the terms of this 'test' of Enide, however, no failure on her part would cause her to be abandoned by her husband. With Erec's parting speech, insisting that Enide be supported as his wife even if Erec should die, he affirms before the couple's round of supposed 'testing' adventures begins that Enide's public and private role as his wife is guaranteed and non-negotiable. In fact, he stipulates that Enide's claim to his inheritance must be upheld, 'que qu'il aveigne' [whatever might happen] (v. 2721). What critics have taken to be a series of episodes in which Erec tests Enide's obedience therefore might as easily be viewed as a series of episodes in which Erec makes it possible for Enide to understand her true identity as a person who is allowed to make mistakes and as a wife who will be protected and loved 'no matter what happens.'

It might be objected that, if Erec loves Enide unconditionally, barking orders and reproaches at her is a strange way for him to show it. Yet in order for Enide's understanding of herself to change, she must experience herself as separate from her husband and reach the point where she is capable of articulating her own will and her own worth.[27] The fact that the adventures are constructed in such a way that Enide must continually face her own fears and misperceptions indicates that a major purpose of the adventures is to externalize these aspects of Enide's inner life and force Enide to proclaim their falsehood. It is for this reason that Erec continually threatens Enide (voicing her fear of rejection) and in the same moment says explicitly that he is forgiving her (drawing her attention to the possibility that her faults might not result in rejection). This pattern is repeated several times (vv. 2846–52, 2993–3003, 3553–60, 3751–55), each time with clearer indications from the narrator that Erec is not speaking in this way in order to be selfish or to hurt Enide. In one instance, Erec himself hints at a desire to drop the game when he says that he will punish her later for speaking out of turn, *unless* his attitude changes ('se corages ne me remue' [if my thinking does not change], v. 3560). Indeed, through repetition these threats become so clearly commonplace and empty that the narrator gives them less and less textual space, finally reducing the last confrontation to a single line of indirect discourse: 'ele li dit; il la menace' [she talks to him; he threatens her] (v. 3751).

The repetitious nature of Erec's reproaches to Enide has been discussed by critics many times, but the repetitious nature of Enide's self-critical discourse has been examined less closely.[28] When the couple's adventures are viewed as a testing process through which Enide is meant to overcome her negative view of herself, however, it can be argued instead that each successive adventure represents a renewed effort to teach Enide to let go of her distorted self-image, but the adventures keep coming because her perception does not change. Another case of the couple's adventures externalizing Enide's inner conflict is her conversation with the lecherous count, in which he voices Enide's own fear that Erec does not love or value her any more (vv. 3322–23). Since the loyal Enide inevitably will refute the count's words, this would be an opportunity for her to insist that in fact Erec does love and value her. Instead, however, she manages to put into her rejection of the count yet another vivid depiction of her own destruction: "'Sire, de neant vos penez, / fet Enyde, ce ne puet estre. / Hé! mialz fusse je or a nestre, / ou an un feu d'espines arse, / si que la cendre an fust esparse, / que j'eüsse de rien fausse / vers mon seignor'" [Sir, you are suffering over nothing, said Enide, this cannot be. Oh! it would be better if I had never been born, or if I were burned in a fire of thorns, and the ashes of it scattered, than if I did any wrong toward my lord] (vv. 3326–32). When the count threatens to hurt Erec because Enide has not said what he wants to hear, Enide misrepresents herself by responding with a speech in which she claims that she really does want to become the count's lover (vv. 3356–93). As in her first speech to Erec, Enide chooses to portray herself as a wily seductress rather than to stay true to herself and allow Erec to defend himself against attack, as he has shown he is quite capable of doing.

In her next monologue, Enide claims to have learned a lesson through the series of adventures that she now understands as having been a proving ground for that purpose; unfortunately, the lesson she has learned is the wrong one: she thinks she has learned that she should not speak, for silence never hurt anyone, and she adds 'ceste chose ai bien essaiee / et esprove an mainte guise' [this I have truly tested and proved in many ways] (vv. 4594–95, emphasis mine). Instead, Enide should have learned through her testing that her own judgment about when it is appropriate to speak is more trustworthy than Erec's rule. What is truly distressing about this speech is that she begins it with the same desire for self-annihilation that, according to my reading, made her initial inner crisis a sufficient cause for the second round of adventures. In the bedroom scene, she had wished to be swallowed up by the earth; in this scene, in which she believes that Erec is dead, she asks to be killed along with him (vv. 4580–82). This is a commonplace of medieval laments, but here it appears alongside a number of other specific references to her earlier discourses of self-blame, the whole scene serving to demonstrate that Enide is not receiving the messages the adventures were designed to send her. The end of this scene when God intervenes in order to prevent Enide from killing herself with Erec's sword strengthens this impression: 'Dex la fet un petit tarder, / qui plains est de misericorde' [God made her delay a little, who is full of mercy] (vv. 4634–35).

This divine intervention confirms that Enide's attitude is not only inaccurate but in conflict with God's will for her. In fact, Enide's stubborn refusal to change her distorted view of her proper place in the world brings to mind Perceval, whose stubborn five-year pursuit of mindless chivalric adventures finally had to be ended by explicit religious instruction on Good Friday. Divine intervention and religious instruction are not frequent features of Chrétien's plots, but they become a necessary last resort for questing characters as self-absorbed as Enide and Perceval. Since the appearance of the Count of Limors prevents Enide from killing herself, the narrator suggests that the entire episode with the malevolent Count is actually meant as a final attempt to teach Enide to assert herself not only against Erec's bad temper, but in defense of her own integrity as a sovereign subject. Enide truly believes that Erec is dead, and therefore her refusal to marry the Count of Limors shows not only her desire to remain faithful to Erec but also her decision to live out the rest of her life alone, as a separate person, rather than to be fused with another man simply because he appears to offer her a socially advantageous match. Enide endures threats and physical abuse in a situation from which it appears that she will be unable to escape, but yet she continues to assert her own will. What is particularly striking about this scene is that there is no difference between what Enide thinks and what she says: she is no longer misrepresenting herself in an effort to placate the other person, as she had done previously with Erec and with the first count who had hoped to take her away with him. The narrator tells us that Enide actually is not afraid of the Count, not even within her own mind: 'Cele ne li vialt mot respondre, / car rien ne prisoit sa menace' [She was not willing to respond with a single word, for she considered his threat worthless] (vv. 4786–87). This represents a profound change from Enide's reaction to the accusations of Erec's *recreantise*, which were less hostile and not even directed at her personally. Having consciously recognized within herself both her own will and her capacity to be the best judge of her own behavior, Enide is then able to verbalize a defiant subjectivity to the Count: "'Ahi! fet ele, ne me chaut / que tu me dïes ne me faces: / ne criem tes cos ne tes menaces'" [Oh! she said, it doesn't matter to me what you say or do to me: I am not afraid of your blows or of your threats] (vv. 4806–8). Once Enide has passed this test of her subjectivity, Erec (awakened by these words from Enide) removes her from this dangerous situation. The narrator emphasizes humorously the miraculous nature of Erec's awakening by showing that the members of the Count's household believe he has risen from the dead, but this same discourse of the miraculous serves as a reminder that it was God who initiated this episode, and perhaps it is therefore God who puts an end to it when its purpose has been achieved.

Although Fries claimed that the couple's reconciliation transformed Enide back into a 'heroine' it is really Erec who announces at this point that his attitude toward Enide has changed (vv. 4882–90). The following episode, in which Enide confronts Guivret, shows her stepping farther outside a traditional feminine role than ever before, grabbing Guivret's horse by the reins and lecturing Guivret on proper chivalric conduct (vv. 4983–5008). Here she experiences her emotions in familiar terms ('quant son seignor a terre voit, / morte cuide estre et mal baillie' [when she sees her lord on the ground, she thinks that she is dead and without protection] (vv. 4984–85), but she is able to act and speak bravely nevertheless. This speech is important because she is not only defying Erec in order to protect him, as usual, but she is also articulating a reasoned world view based on ethics. Brave though they were at times, Enide's previous speeches had revealed a perspective dominated by her own isolation and pessimism: she now speaks as a member of a larger chivalric society in which she and Erec have a right to expect fair treatment.

Although Enide does not play a leading role in the *Joie de la Cort* episode, she does have an opportunity to talk to someone else about her experiences when her cousin asks her how she came to be married to Erec. The way in which she finishes that story suggests that she has 'rewritten' in her own mind the real nature of her transformation after her marriage to Erec. She describes her material poverty before the marriage, but then also describes herself at that time as having been *desconseillee* (v. 6261), which suggests that she was fundamentally mistaken about herself as well. Two meanings of this adjective are 'a person without advice, helpless, crippled, discouraged' or 'without direction, lost.'[29] Both of these meanings describe Enide's state of mind before her testing adventures: because of her problematic self-perception, she was discouraged, misguided, and unable to believe the good opinions of her expressed by others. Significantly, Enide then introduces the story of the couple's shared adventures as the story of "'comant *je* ving a tel hautesce'" [how *I* arrived at such a height] (v. 6265, emphasis mine). Her adventures have finally taught her to form an appropriately 'high' opinion of herself as separate from Erec and as an important member of her society. Perhaps this central lesson about the development of Enide's subjectivity and self-esteem is what makes this narrative inspiring to her cousin. When Maboagrain, the lover of Enide's cousin, hears Enide's story and approves of it (vv. 6283–86), Enide's cousin takes heart, even though her fear of being abandoned by her lover had made her seem inconsolable a few minutes before (vv. 6140–73). Thus within the fiction, Enide's story is offered as an inspiring *exemplum* to another female character whose desire to remain with her lover in a closed universe of their own suggested her low self-esteem and her fear of assuming adult responsibilities.[30] Maboagrain's approval of the story suggests that there might be hope for reconciliation in their relationship and also that Enide's story is one from which both male and female characters can learn something. That Enide has no trouble assuming her own adult responsibilities as queen is indicated by the narrator's focus on the exterior of the coronation scene and on its symbolic meanings: with the inner crises of hero and heroine resolved, the characters' perceptions of themselves match their triumphant appearance.

Having considered the extent to which Enide and the resolution of her problems dominate this romance and the form the couple's adventures take, what have I concluded about her status as 'heroine' or 'female hero'? She is a 'female hero' in that she is a protagonist engaged in a heroic conflict, and yet she sees herself as a 'heroine' and deliberately plays that role, to the point where the two roles coexist throughout the romance. Does this negate the validity of Fries's categories? Not at all: Fries herself anticipated Enide's return to her customary 'heroine' role at the end of the romance by stating that 'If completely successful, female (like male) heroes return to their original societies with the prized gift of renewal.'[31] If Enide returns to her society at the end, then her conformity to the gender norms of her society in the final scenes is no surprise. Renewal can take many forms, but in this romance it is represented by the coronation scene: it seems to feature the same hero and heroine as the earlier wedding scene, but in fact both the new king and queen have become stronger people than the new bride and groom had been. This shared renewal explains Chrétien's emphasis on the striking similarity of the two thrones (vv. 6651–61). The case of Enide as a heroine in a hero's role therefore shows not a weakness in the model proposed by Fries but rather a strength in Chrétien de Troyes: his awareness of the complexity of female characters' roles in the developing romance genre. He did not see the female protagonist as excluded from the heroic realm, but at the same time he was aware that gender expectations, including those of the character herself, would lead her to manifest that heroism through actions and attitudes different from those of a male hero.

Chrétien's heroes learn how to be more fully themselves by rising above the stereotypes by which others judge them.[32] In the case of Enide, she must rise above her own stereotypical perceptions of what it means to be a woman with a life in the public eye: at first she believes that it means being judged for her inadequacies and penalized for her sexual attractiveness, as were other female romance characters such as Yseut. Enide seeks to escape this gendered fate by hiding behind her husband, but this solution causes a more profound crisis when criticism of Erec causes Enide to believe that her unworthiness is actually contaminating him. Each time Enide is forced to face the reality of her own subjectivity, she feels shame and contemplates her own annihilation, but her love for Erec gives her the courage to defend him and herself whenever he is threatened. When Enide remains faithful to Erec even after his apparent death, she faces and refutes her own fears. She then stops worrying about how others judge her and, in her confrontation with Guivret, assumes the role of judging others and demanding her rights appropriately. By shedding her own misconceptions about how women inevitably will be treated, she becomes able to assume comfortably a most conformist female role in her society: that of a queen. As other critics have pointed out with dismay, Enide plays her societal role perfectly in the closing scenes of the romance, and we see no more of her thoughts or her words. Yet this apparent effacement is actually a fulfillment according to Enide's own standards: she sees herself as occupying a 'high' place in her society that she has no desire to leave. Again, Yseut had demonstrated convincingly that leaving the role of queen to pursue one's own desires in the forest was not a viable solution to the social problems of women in the Arthurian world. As a final consideration of the role of 'heroine,' then, it is worthwhile to return to a central issue of Fries's study: the extent to which female characters carry out their own intentions. Perhaps Enide's goal of harmonious social conformity would not be considered admirable by many women today, but she does have to overcome daunting obstacles in order to achieve it. As a tribute to that achievement, I will

CHRÉTIEN'S ENIDE: HEROINE OR FEMALE HERO

therefore identify Enide as a 'heroic heroine,' particularly in the context of Chrétien de Troyes's model of heroism, but only in the hope that a similar compassion for other conformist heroines may eventually make that adjective superfluous.

Margaret Jewett Burland is Assistant Professor of French at Dartmouth College, and holds a Ph.D. from the University of Chicago. Her research focuses on French and Occitan adaptations of the Roland legend from the twelfth to fifteenth centuries, as well as on twelfth- and thirteenth-century French verse romance and on modern medievalism in literature and film.

NOTES

1 For example: 'In the typical romance, little attention is given to the characterization of the lady, who exists mainly as a motivating force or source of inspiration for the knight...The medieval heroine may be a temptress or a virgin, disdainful or unaware, but she rarely plays an active role.' Diane Bornstein, *The Lady in the Tower: Medieval Courtesy Literature for Women* (Hamden, CT: Archon Books, 1983), pp. 9–10.

2 Penny Schine Gold cautioned against the possible 'anachronism and ethnocentricity' of labelling images of women from past cultures as wholly 'positive' or 'negative' in the introduction to *The Lady and the Virgin: Image, Attitude and Experience in Twelfth-Century France* (Chicago: University of Chicago Press, 1985), pp. xviii–xx.

3 Maureen Fries, 'Female Heroes, Heroines, and Counter-Heroes: Images of Women in Arthurian Tradition,' in *Arthurian Women: A Casebook*, ed. Thelma S. Fenster (New York: Garland, 1996), p. 59 [59–73].

4 These definitions summarized in Fries, 'Female Heroes, Heroines, and Counter-Heroes,' pp. 60–61.

5 Fries, 'Female Heroes, Heroines, and Counter-Heroes,' p. 66.

6 In 'Erec's Enide: "sa fame ou s'amie?,"' *Romance Philology* 33 (1980): 373–87, Barbara Sargent-Baur sees the two roles as determined by Erec's perspective rather than by Enide's behavior: she is his (courtly) lover when Erec has the time and inclination to play the game of courtly love, and the rest of the time he treats her as his wife, ordering her around as he pleases. In 'Chrétien's Enide: Wife, Mistress, and Metaphor,' *Romance Quarterly* 35 (1988): 401–14, Joan Brumlik suggested that Erec imposed the rule of silence upon Enide in an effort to transform her back into the compliant beauty she had appeared to be before their marriage.

7 Michel-André Bossy, 'The Elaboration of Female Narrative Functions in *Erec et Enide*,' in *Courtly Literature: Culture and Context*, ed. Keith Busby and Erik Kooper (Philadelphia: John Benjamins, 1990), pp. 24–26 [23–38].

8 Bossy, 'The Elaboration of Female Narrative Functions,' p. 29.

9 Norris J. Lacy, *The Craft of Chrétien de Troyes: an Essay on Narrative Art* (Leiden:

Brill, 1980), pp. 27 and 28. See also his complete examination of the heroic crisis in the first chapter, pp. 1–14.

10 Gold, *The Lady and the Virgin*, p. 41.

11 For a discussion of the public/private conflict for another of Chrétien's heroines, as well as the way in which Chrétien's complex endings rely on the inner struggles of his female and male characters, see A.R. Press, 'Chrétien's Laudine: A Belle Dame Sans Mercy?' *Forum for Modern Language Studies* 19 (1983): 158–71.

12 While many critics have acknowledged that readers are given an interior view of Enide in some scenes of the romance, most have not considered her self-perception as a central issue. For example, in *The Individual in Twelfth-Century Romance* (New Haven: Yale University Press, 1977), pp. 67–79, Robert Hanning discusses at length the way in which Enide's unique perspective is narrated in one particular scene, but does not speculate about the significance of Enide's perspective for the romance as a whole. Myrrha Lot Borrodine wrote nearly an entire chapter of *La Femme et l'amour au XIIe siècle d'après les poèmes de Chrétien de Troyes* (Geneva: Slatkine Reprints, 1967), pp. 22–76, on *Erec et Enide* in sympathy with Enide's 'heroic' point of view as she understood it, but she saw Enide's problem as one of overcoming her fear of Erec rather than changing her perception of herself.

13 The issue of Chrétien's misogyny has been raised more or less explicitly by many studies, but one of the first explicit discussions of this issue appeared in Marie-Noëlle Lefay-Toury, 'Roman breton et mythes courtois: l'évolution du personnage féminin dans les romans de Chrétien de Troyes,' *Cahiers de civilisation médiévale* 15 (1972): 193–204 and 283–93. See also Z.P. Zaddy, 'Chrétien misogyne,' *Marche Romane* 30 (1980): 301–7, and Lynn Tarte Ramey, 'Representations of Women in Chrétien's *Erec et Enide*: Courtly Literature or Misogyny?' *Romanic Review* 84 (1993): 377–86.

14 This is a passing comment in many studies, but for a particularly sophisticated discussion of the male- and female-gendered gaze in *Erec et Enide*, see Sarah Stanbury, 'Feminist Film Theory Seeing Chrétien's Enide,' *Literature and Psychology* 36 (1990): 47–66.

15 See Lefay-Toury, 'Roman breton et mythes courtois,' 292. Much has been made of Enide's semi-clothed state during the early scenes of the romance, in which she is wearing rags with such large holes that her alluring body easily can be seen through them (vv. 401–10, 1475–77). Kathryn Gravdal has suggested the erotic titillation that would have been provoked in male audience members not only by Enide's torn clothing but also by the more overt threat of rape that seems to hang over her repeatedly when she is coveted by lecherous counts or by brigands contemplating attacking her because she appears to be riding alone through the forest. See Kathryn Gravdal, *Ravishing Maidens: Writing Rape in Medieval French Literature and Law* (Philadelphia: University of Pennsylvania Press, 1991), pp. 55–59.

16 E. Jane Burns, 'Enide's Disruptive Mouths,' in *Bodytalk: When Women Speak in Old French Literature*, New Cultural Studies Series (Philadelphia: University of

Pennsylvania Press, 1993), pp. 151–202, esp. p. 158.

17 While others have perceived medieval romances as containing a masculine narrative and a feminine narrative, they have also perceived the masculine narrative as the validated one and the feminine narrative as threatening to female readers or as disruptive to the hegemonic male-gendered universe of medieval romance. See Burns, 'Enide's Disruptive Mouths'; Roberta Krueger, *Women Readers and the Ideology of Gender in Old French Verse Romance* (Cambridge: Cambridge University Press, 1993), for example pp. 34–35; Laurie Finke, 'Towards a Cultural Poetics of the Romance,' *Genre* 22 (1989): 112 [109–27].

18 For a summary of this critical debate, see René Menage, 'Erec et Enide: quelques pièces du dossier,' *Marche Romane* 30 (1980): 203–21.

19 Line numbers cited or referenced correspond to the edition of *Erec et Enide* by Mario Roques, Classiques français du Moyen Age, (Paris: Champion, 1981). All translations are my own.

20 'D'Erec, le fil Lac, est li contes / que devant rois et devant contes / depecier et corronpre suelent / Cil qui de conter vivre vuelent' [About Erec, the son of Lac, is the story which, before kings and counts, those who want to make a living by storytelling have a habit of cutting into pieces and corrupting, vv. 19–22].

21 That this request contradicts the notion that Erec wishes to punish Enide has also been noted by Joan Trasker Grimbert, 'Misrepresentation and Misconception in Chrétien de Troyes: Nonverbal and Verbal Semiotics in *Erec et Enide* and *Perceval*,' in *Sign, Sentence, Discourse: Language in Medieval Thought and Literature*, ed. Julian N. Wasserman and Lois Roney (Syracuse, NY: Syracuse University Press, 1989), p. 65 [50–79].

22 This argument was presented most forcefully in Sargent-Baur, 'Eric's Enide,' 377–78.

23 Brumlik, 'Chrétien's Enide: Wife, Mistress, and Metaphor,' 404. See also Frederick Goldin, *The Mirror of Narcissus* (Ithaca, NY: Cornell University Press, 1967) and Joan Ferrante, *Woman as Image in Medieval Literature*, 2d edn. (Durham, NC: Labyrinth Press, 1985) for extensive treatments of this aspect of courtly love, usually ascribed to male lovers.

24 Nadya Aisenberg, *Ordinary Heroes: Transforming the Male Myth* (New York: Continuum, 1994), pp. 16–17.

25 Chrétien already suggested the importance of Enide's separate identity at the moment of her marriage when he stressed that no woman can be married without being named by her own name (vv. 1973–76).

26 Grimbert, 'Misrepresentation and Misconception in Chrétien de Troyes,' p. 65.

27 The interpretation of the couple's adventures as assertiveness training for Enide was proposed by Z.P. Zaddy in *Chrétien Studies: Problems of Form and Meaning in Erec, Yvain, Cligés and the Charrette* (Glasgow: University of Glasgow Press, 1973), pp. 26–38, but the focus was still on Erec and his intimidating temper, rather than on Enide's own need for transformation.

28 For example, Glyn Burgess has suggested that Chrétien agrees with Enide's self-

reproaches, and has her repeat them simply as reminders to the audience that she is not blameless. See Glyn Burgess, *Chrétien de Troyes: Erec et Enide*, Critical Guides to French Texts 32(London: Grant and Cutler, 1984), p. 53. Lacy also stated that pride was Enide's principal flaw (p. 44).

29 My translations of the definitions in Algirdas Julien Greimas, *Dictionnaire de l'ancien français*, 2d edn. (Paris: Larousse, 1992), p. 163.

30 When Enide's cousin recounts the circumstances through which she and Maboagrain came to live in the garden together (vv. 6207–37), she emphasizes that she was very young at the time, probably not yet of conventionally marriageable age. In Maboagrain's account, he stresses that they left her father's house as soon as he was knighted (vv. 6018–28).

31 Fries, 'Female Heroes, Heroines, and Counter-Heroes,'p. 60.

32 This is most obviously true for Perceval, but it is also applicable to Lancelot as the initially shamed 'knight of the cart' and even more to Yvain, who at first tries to live up to generic expectations of knighthood put forth by Gauvain and other members of Arthur's court but who eventually achieves a much higher standard of chivalry.

Belacane: Other as Another in Wolfram von Eschenbach's Parzival

SUSANN T. SAMPLES

Wolfram von Eschenbach strongly affirms Other as Another in *Parzival*, by having his first hero-knight, Gahmuret, fall in love with the black Moorish queen, Belacane, who is shown to be a member of the universal chivalric-knightly ethos and is thus worthy of this Christian knight. (STS)

Wolfram's depiction of a shared chivalrous knighthood transcending the barriers of religion and skin color may, in part, mirror the social change occurring in German-speaking areas in the thirteenth century. The rise of the knightly class in medieval German-speaking areas coincided with the ascent of the new nobility, the ministerial class. According to Joachim Bumke:

> Although there were great social differences within the ministerial class, we can say that as early as around 1200, the leading ministerials could hardly be distinguished from the old nobility in regard to their lifestyle. Subsequently, the extinction of many families of the old nobility in the thirteenth century led to a steady increase in the percentage of ministerials within the free holding nobility (*landsässiger Adel*). Legally, however, the *nobiles* and the ministerials remained separated for quite some time.[1]

Although biographical information on Wolfram von Eschenbach is scarce, it is believed that he was probably of this ministerial rank, which could help explain his expansive and inclusive vision of knighthood. Chivalrous knighthood as a literary ideal had little in common with the harsh realities of medieval life, but its exalted image gave the German nobility a goal and a more positive self-image.

My study of Wolfram's *Parzival* (Book One) offers a new image of the Other in a medieval literary setting. Wolfram's use of skin color as Other-defining needs further explanation. As we shall see, Wolfram effectively uses the black skin color of Belacane and the other Moors to stress difference and exoticism. Gahmuret's initial discomfort with Moors was probably shared by Wolfram's medieval audience. The black skin color, however, had no moral status for Wolfram; that is, it did not connote intellectual inferiority and moral deficiency. Therefore racism, as Appiah describes it, is absent in Wolfram's *Parzival:* '[the belief] that racial essence entails certain morally relevant qualities. The basis for this extrinsic racists' discrimination between people is their belief that members of different races differ in a respect that warrants the differential treatment' (p. 13).² Keeping in mind that race, racialism, and racism are later conceptions, arising from European nationalism, Wolfram's depiction of Other is still unusual and thought-provoking.

Both Islamic and Christian accounts of the Crusades (1095–1291) typically ignored any commonality between Islam and Christianity and depicted members of the other group as infidels or demons, suggesting that the experiences and encounters with the Other during the Crusades were largely negative.³ In *The Song of Roland* the Islamic forces are at times depicted negatively, as prey to be hunted down by the Christian forces: 'As the stag runs before the hounds / So the pagans flee before Roland.'⁴ While the Crusades fostered religious fanaticism and intolerance, in *Parzival* Wolfram portrays an idealized courtly society in which Christians and non-Christians engage in harmonious social intercourse. In view of intolerance of religious otherness on both sides, one might expect that Wolfram's *Parzival*, a Germanic Arthurian romance written ca. 1210 (in the midst of the Crusades), would depict Muslims in a less than flattering fashion. However, his portrayal of the Other in *Parzival* is highly sympathetic. Wolfram strongly affirms Other as Another by having his first hero-knight, Gahmuret, fall in love with Belacane, a black non-Christian. Despite the differences of skin color and religion, black non-Christian figures are shown to possess a commonality with white Christian nobles, namely a courtly culture. The various courtly situations depicted in the Moorish kingdom of Zazamanc could easily take place in any medieval European court. With his favorable and sympathetic portrayal of these black non-Christian Moors, Wolfram attempted to show his audience the shared human condition of noble Christians and non-Christians. In this respect Wolfram reveals a considerable level of cross-cultural oneness and engaged tolerance for a thirteenth-century poet.

Significantly, the two belief systems, Christianity and 'paganism,' coexist peacefully in *Parzival*. Wolfram's depiction of 'paganism' is especially vague, with no description of gods or ritual. Moreover, Wolfram portrays the Moors' religion without any censure:

> si taeten sînen boten kunt,
> ez waere Pâtelamunt.

daz wart im minneclîche enboten.
si manten in bî ir goten
daz er in hulfe: es waere in nôt,
si rungen niht wan umben tôt (17, 3–8).

[They told his envoys that it was Patelamunt and sent their message with
friendly tokens, imploring him by their gods to aid them—they were in
great need, fighting for survival] (p. 22).[5]

His description of Moorish townspeople is similarly neutral: 'Si brâhten
opfers vil ir goten, / die von der stat....' [The townsfolk brought rich offerings
for their gods] (45, 1–2; p. 34). Wolfram's rather terse description of the
Christian knight Gahmuret is entirely consistent with his tendency to de-
emphasize the significance of religious difference:

der gap dennoch niht liethen schîn.
dô solt och dâ bereite sîn
zer messe ein sîn kappelân:
der sanc si got und im sân (36, 5–8)

[It had not begun to glow before he told his chaplain to make ready for
Mass, which the latter sang for God and his master] (p. 30).

In effect, Wolfram simply allows the figures to practice their own respective
religions. This tendency reflects Wolfram's unorthodox views about religion.

Because of their shared understanding of the rules of chivalry, Gahmuret,
the Christian knights, and the Moors have little or no trouble interacting
with one another since all are familiar with and embrace these rules. The
knights of both sides adhere to a knightly code in their fighting: fair play,
honor, and courtesy are observed. In its exalted state, knighthood is shown
to transcend the barriers of religion and skin color. Therefore, courtly love
(*minne*), not religion, is the cause of the current hostilities. Indeed, Christian
and non-Christian knights are found on both opposing sides. Non-Christians
also occupy positions of respect in Gahmuret's huge entourage:

dâ hinden nâch den knappen riten,
an guoter zuht, mit süezen siten.
etslîcher was ein Sarrazîn (18, 27–29)

[After the squire rode twelve noble pages, some of whom were Saracens,
well-bred and with engaging manners] (p. 23).

Therefore, Wolfram did not simply retell Chrétien's *Perceval*, but rather
reshaped and completed the romance, imbuing it with his own unique vision
of Christianity and knighthood. Wolfram's intention is to show that Parzival's
knighthood possesses a strong Christian component, which ultimately enables

him to become the Grail King. However, Gahmuret, a Christian knight, experiences *no* difficulties in offering his service for hire throughout the Muslim world. Since he distinguished himself in the service of the 'Baruc of Baghdad,' it appears that fighting ability and courage matter, not religious belief. In his description of Gahmuret's many travels, Wolfram mentions locations such as Persia, Morocco, Damascus, and Arabia, which his audience would have probably identified with the Muslim world. It is also noteworthy that he never criticizes Gahmuret for fighting for non-Christian clients because knights are knights regardless of faith system or skin color. Consequently, when Wolfram creates Books One and Two (depicting the adventures of Parzival's father Gahmuret), he reveals Gahmuret's unease with racial difference, but that discomfort does not preclude Moors from being honorable knights.

When Gahmuret arrives in the city of Zazamanc, Wolfram stresses Gahmuret's initial discomfort at seeing that 'liute vinster sô diu naht/wârn alle die von Zazamanc' [And the people of Zazamanc were all as dark as night]—a human reaction to something new or different (17, 24–25; p. 22). His first impulse is to reject them: 'bî den dûht in diu wîle lanc' [he had had enough of their company] (17, 26; p. 22), and he likewise notes the dark skin of 'manege tunkele frouwen…nâch rabens varwe was ir schîn' [many dusky ladies…whose colour resembled the raven's] (20, 4–6; p. 23). In the course of this episode Wolfram makes frequent references to the skin color of the Moors, employing words which translate into English as 'dusky,' swarthy,' 'dark,' and 'black.'

However, Wolfram makes one derogatory remark about the black skin color of the Moors, despite their nobilty: he describes some Moors as they are moving toward the Palace as 'swaz dâ fürsten was,' [of princely rank] with 'die nâch der helle wârn gevar,' [their faces black as Hell] (51, 24–25; p. 37). In light of what we shall see as Wolfram's generally favorable depiction of black characters, we should view this passage as an aberration. In general, although skin color defines Otherness for Wolfram, Other simply means different, not bad. For example, when Belacane and Gahmuret consummate their love, Wolfram notes their difference in skin color, but does not mark that difference as a problem (44, 27–30; p. 34).

It is worth noting that Wolfram also depicts the lovers' inherent differences, skin color and religion, from Belacane's perspective. She, too, is quite aware of their differences.

> durch die zäher manege blicke
> si schamende gastlîchen sach

an Gahmureten: dô verjach
ir ougen dem herzen sân
daz er waere wol getân.
si kunde ouch liehte varwe spehen:
wan sie het och ê gesehen
manegen liehten heiden.
aldâ wart undr in beiden
ein vil getriulîchiu ger:
si sach dar, und er sach her (28, 28–30–29, 1–8)

[The lady fell to sighing. Through her tears she cast many a shy glance at Gahmuret, as between strangers, and her eyes told her heart he was well made. She was a judge of fair complexions, too, since before this she had seen many a fair-skinned heathen. With this there was born between them a steadfast longing—she gazed at him, and he at her] (p. 27).

Wolfram shows a great deal of tolerance here in that he allows Belacane to employ the word 'heiden' (heathen) to describe Gahmuret's Christianity. It is also noteworthy that Belacane's behavior is like that of any other romance heroine:

durch die zäher manege blicke
si schamende gastlîchen sach
an Gahmureten: dô verjach
ir ougen dem herzen sân
daz er waere wol getân.
Si kunde ouch liehte varwe spehen:
wan sie het och ê gesehen
manegen liehten heiden.
aldâ wart undre in beiden
ein vil getriulîchiu ger:
si sach dar, und er sach her (28, 28-29.8)

[Through her tears she cast many a shy glance at Gahmuret as between strangers, and her eyes told her heart he was well made. She was a judge of fair complexions, too, since before this she had seen many a fair-skinned heathen. With this there was born between them at steadfast longing—she gazed at him, and he at her] (p. 27).

Other-defining in Book One of *Parzival* occurs on two levels: skin color and religion—the Moors depicted in *Parzival* are black and 'pagan.' In his description of Belacane, Wolfram notes her skin color but depicts her as a courtly and beautiful lady:

ist iht liehters denne der tac,
dem glîchet niht diu künegin.
si hete wîplîchen sin,

> und was abr anders rîterlîch,
> der touwegen rôsen ungelîch.
> nâch swarzer varwe was ir schîn (24, 6–11)

[If anything is 'brighter than the day' the Queen does not resemble it. She had a woman's heart and was all that a knight could want in other ways, but not 'like the dewy rose'—she was of a swarthy aspect] (p. 25).

Despite his recognition of her other qualities, by defining her as a pagan (28, 10–11; p. 27), Wolfram falls into the common trap in the thirteenth century of equating Islam with paganism. However, while Wolfram is stressing the Otherness of Belacane and her subjects, that is, their black skin color, and, to a greater degree, their religion, he also affirms their shared human condition by describing the suffering that the inhabitants of Zazamanc have endured:

> der hêrre schouwen began
> manegen schilt zebrochen,
> mit spern gar durchstochen:
> der was dâ vil gehangen für,
> an die wende und an die tür.
> si heten jâmer unde guft.
> in diu venster gein dem luft
> was gebettet mangem wunden man,
> swenn er den arzât gewan,
> daz er doch mohte niht genesen (19, 20–28)

[The knight saw a profusion of battered shields pierced through and through by spears, many of them hanging on doors and walls. There was weeping there, and wailing. Numbers of men had been laid on beds in the windows for the fresh air, so badly wounded that even when they had the doctor they could not recover] (p. 23).

Here and elsewhere the Moors are portrayed as human beings, having the same concerns, fears, and hopes as the Christian European Gahmuret.

Wolfram juxtaposes Belacane's blackness and 'paganism' with her undeniably womanly virtue, which is further underscored by her enormous grief. In *Parzival* weeping or tears is a recurring feminine attribute that confirms the capacity for compassion and hence inherent goodness. The very reason for Isenhart's death affirms Belacane's womanly virtue since her refusal to reward him stems from her naiveté and, especially, her overmodesty. In fact, her remorse is so great that she does not consider marriage:

> daz klag ich noch, vil armez wîp:
> ir bêder tôt mich immer müet.
> ûf mîner triwe jâmer blüet.
> ih enwart nie wîp decheines man' (28, 6–9)

[Wretched woman, I mourn it still, nor shall I ever cease to regret their deaths. The affection I bear them blossoms forth in grief. I was never yet wife to any man] (p. 27).

With this declaration, Belacane demonstrates the capacity for unwavering and self-sacrificing faithfulness which establishes her kinship with other exemplary courtly ladies in *Parzival* such as Herzeloyde, Sigune, and Orgeluse. In light of the numerous laudable ladies appearing in *Parzival*, it is indeed significant that the first courtly lady whom Wolfram chooses to embody his ideal of the *gutiu wîp* is Belacane, a black non-Christian. Belacane demonstrates a sincere *minne* (courtly love) and a steadfast faithfulness, two integral components of Wolfram's concept of the *gutiu wîp*.[6] Wolfram's selection of and emphasis on these two attributes confirms that for him good and laudable womanhood is based on the courtly lady's submission to her knight. Belacane's belonging to the knightly-chivalric society is further stressed in the feast scene in which Belacane serves her guest Gahmuret and is extremely attentive to his pages who likewise are impressed by her generosity, a mark of her courtliness (34, 5–6; p. 29). She lives in a courtly setting in which her ladies engage in typical courtly feminine activities (17, 30 and 18, 1–4); she is described as 'diu süeze vlasches âne' ['sweet and constant Belacane…'] (16, 8; p. 22); and she reads French (which Wolfram presents as a major accomplishment) (55, 17–19; p. 39), making her the embodiment of Wolfram's ideal of the courtly lady. Because Belacane is shown to be a member of this universal chivalric-knightly ethos, the poet dispels the readers' doubts of her worthiness to receive Gahmuret's service and win his love.

The revelation of Belacane's worthiness also dispels Gahmuret's lingering misgivings and he, too, acknowledges her worthiness. As Wolfram demonstrates, this shared human condition is most apparent when the two protagonists, Gahmuret, a white Christian knight, and Belacane, a black non-Christian queen, fall in love. Wolfram is at his best in their first scene together (24, **6–11?).** As Gahmuret falls in love with Belacane, he not only loses his misgivings about the dark skin color of these Moors but also offers his service to Belacane. As a knight he is supposed to assist the vulnerable, the helpless; therefore, Gahmuret's help is color-blind and religion-neutral. Moreover, by depicting Belacane's weeping over Isenhart's death, Wolfram not only is able to demonstrate her womanly virtue but also to speak of her 'provisional' baptism which probably helped to soften his audience's misgivings about her 'paganism:'

Gahmureten dûhte sân,

> swie si waere ein heidenin,
> mit triwen wîplicher sin
> in wîbes herze nie geslouf.
> ir kiusche was ein reiner touf,
> und ouch der regen der sie begôz,
> der wâc der von ir ougen flôz
> ûf ir zobel und an ir brust.
> riwen phlege was ir gelust,
> und rehtiu jâmers lêre (28, 10–19)

[It seemed to Gahmuret that although she was an infidel, a more affectionate spirit of womanliness had never stolen over a woman's heart. Her modest ways were a pure baptism, as was the rain that fell on her—the flood descending from her eyes down to her sabled breast. Her pleasures in life were devotion to sorrow and grief's true doctrine] (p. 27).

If Belacane is capable of such devotion to a knight whom she did not love, her faithfulness will be all the greater when it is accompanied by a fierce and absolute love. In addition, the emphasis Wolfram puts on this pseudo-baptism suggests that for him Belacane's non-Christian status is more important than her skin color.

Wolfram again stresses Belacane's apparent Otherness when he employs the words 'swarze' (dusky) and 'Moerrine' (Moor) (35, 21; p. 30), but within the context of love, these apparent differences become meaningless. Wolfram presents Belacane and Gahmuret as behaving like any other pair of courtly lovers, struggling to conquer their mutual frustration through following proper social etiquette (29, 9–16; p. 27). As a knight, Gahmuret would have offered his service since Belacane was a vulnerable courtly lady, but their mutual love radically transforms this service for him. By defeating her enemies, he can claim her as his reward: 'sîn dienest nam der minnen solt: / ein scharpher strît im ringe wac' [He served for Love's wages: thoughts of a fierce battle left him unmoved] (37, 8–9; p. 31). Not surprisingly, Belacane begins to assume a much more subordinate role after Gahmuret has vanquished her opponents, thereby winning her and her kingdom. Her public serving of him at the meal is the first indication of this change. Upon his return from the battle scene, she publicly acknowledges his role now as *her* king when she leads him back to the palace:

> diu küneginne im widerreit.
> sînen zoum nam si mit ir hant,
> si entstricte der fintâlen bant.
> der wirt in muose lâzen.
> sîne knappen niht vergâzen,

sine kêrten vaste ir hêrren nâch.
durch die stat man füeren sach
ir gast die küneginne wîs,
der dâ behalden het den prîs (44, 2–10)

[The Queen came riding out to meet him. She took his bridle and unlaced his
ventail. Gahmuret's host had to surrender him. But Gahmuret's squires kept
close to his heels. The subtle Queen led her guest through the town for all to
see—the champion!] (p. 34).

Although a queen, Belacane represents the traditional female role of the
'threatened woman' who is in need of an errant knight to rescue her. Later,
because of his victories on the battlefield, Gahmuret wins both Belacane
and her kingdom. Afterwards Belacane assumes a much more passive role as
his wife-queen. Consequently, Belacane never transgresses the acceptable
boundaries of feminine conduct. By stressing these very differences—her
black skin color and her non-Christian religion—Wolfram actually reveals
her humanness, or in the case of this narrative, her belonging to the courtly
world and value system. Her very precarious situation—her kingdom is under
siege by two hostile armies of her slain knight, Isenhart—almost immediately
confirms her status as a courtly lady whose rescue makes Gahmuret's prowess
shine all the more brightly. As a courtly lady, although a queen, she is
prevented by her gender from actively leading her army. Coupled with her
gender and the obvious vulnerability it brings, Belacane's apparent youth
and inexperience affirm her connection to the courtly world in *Parzival*, a
world that appears to transcend the normal barriers of skin color and religion.
These qualities also facilitate the arrival of her future rescuer, the distinguished
knight Gahmuret. Since Wolfram's medieval audience probably was intended
to identify with Gahmuret, the European Christian knight, his reaction most
likely was designed to prompt a similar reaction in them.

Although Wolfram continues to calls Belacane 'queen' in the subsequent
reconciliation scene, this designation no longer reflects reality. Indeed, their
mutual love has harmful consequences for Belacane, who as Gahmuret's
wife must now defer to him both in private and in public:

diu ê hiez magt, diu was nu wîp;
diu in her ûz fuorte an ir hant.
si sprach 'mîn lîp und mîn lant
ist disem rîter undertân,
obez im vînde wellent lân' (45, 24–28)

[She who had been called maiden but who was now a woman, led him out by
the hand. 'I and my lands are subject to this knight,' she said, 'if enemies will
concede it'] (p. 35).

As his queen and wife, she assumes the role of hostess in that she kisses her former enemies. In short, her role of queen is now largely ceremonial. In this respect, the black and non-Christian Belacane conforms to Wolfram's ideal of a courtly lady that is predicated on absolute and willing submission to the knight (the husband-lover), which precludes any self-assertiveness or self-identity. Once their love has been consummated and the roles of husband and wife established, little more is said about their marriage until Gahmuret's departure, when Wolfram tells us that Belacane grieves his loss, but does not go into great detail. Wolfram simply tells us that because of her intense love for Gahmuret, she remains faithful to him and never remarries. When Belacane proves herself a true courtly lady by dying of grief, her greatest virtue is shown to be her all-consuming and steadfast devotion to Gahmuret, whose own conduct is not held to such high standards.[7]

At the end of Book One, however, Gahmuret suddenly employs their religious differences to explain his abandonment of Belacane:

> frouwe, in mac dich niht verheln,
> waer dîn ordn in mîner ê,
> sô waer mir immer nâch dir wê
> und hân doch immer nâch dir pîn (55, 24–27)

> [Madam, I cannot conceal it that did you but live within my rite, I would long for you to all eternity…Madam, you can still win me, if you will be baptized] (p. 39).

Since Wolfram has Gahmuret raise the issue of religious differences relatively late in his relationship with Belacane, this statement does not seem justified by the way Gahmuret's value system has been depicted up to this point. Moreover, he departs without waiting for her response. We should probably view this matter as a narrative device to move the plot along. After all, Gahmuret must leave Belacane in order to marry Herzeloyde so that the romance's hero, Parzival, can be born. While Gahmuret blames her 'paganism' for his departure, he never cites her skin color as a probable cause. Therefore, Wolfram consistently presents religious difference as more problematic than racial difference.

Although, on one level, Wolfram's vision of knighthood is inclusive, minimizing religion and/or skin color, knighthood itself is an exclusive social institution, based on social rank. A careful examination of *Parzival* reveals a continuing preoccupation with social rank. For example, the burgrave has to assure Belacane that Gahmuret is indeed of royal ancestry and therefore worthy of her attentions:

"ist er mir dar zuo wol geborn,
daz mîn kus niht sî verlorn?'
"frowe, erst für küneges künne erkant:
des sî mîn lîp genennet phant" (22, 15–18).

["Is he near enough to me in birth for my kiss not to be thrown away?" "He is known to be a scion of royal stock, let my life be pledge for it, ma'am"] (p. 24).

Not surprisingly, Wolfram does not depict the interaction between Christian and non-Christian commoners, who are largely peripheral.[8] However, more important for our purposes is the way in which the chivalric ideal elides racial and religious difference.

Chivalrous knighthood, a literary ideal stressing 'material splendor and ceremonial etiquette,'[9] fosters recognition of a shared human condition between the Moors and the Christians in *Parzival*. In effect, Wolfram presumes that *all* aristocratic classes possess and share this knightly-chivalric self-image. Consequently, there is *no* conflict between religious beliefs and cultural practices, since knighthood is an integral and universal social institution. Because of their presumably *shared* knightly chivalric culture, the white Christian and black non-Christian social structures are almost indistinguishable from each other. The Moorish nobility are depicted as members of this courtly culture. The brotherhood of knighthood makes possible the praise Wolfram lavishes on a black non-Christian knight that is emblematic of his tolerant attitude towards racial difference:

ein fürste Razalîc dâ hiez.
deheinen tac daz nimmer liez
der rîcheste von Azagouc
(sîn geslehte im den niht louc,
von küneges frühte was sîn art),
der houp sich immer dannewert
durh tjostieren für die stat (41, 9–15)

[There was a prince named Razalic, the mightiest man of Asagouc. Day after day he never failed to set out for the town in search of jousting. In this his race did not belie him, he was a scion of royal stock] (p. 32).

The sharp contrast between this description and parts of *The Song of Roland* and the *Arab Histories,* in which the enemy has no honor, reveals how unique Wolfram's attitude toward the Other is among medieval authors.[10]

MOUNT SAINT MARY'S COLLEGE

Susann T. Samples received her M.A., M.Phil., and Ph.D. from Yale University. She is currently Morrison Professor of International Studies and Chair of Foreign Languages at Mount Saint Mary's College. Her most recent articles include 'The Rape of Ginover in Heinrich von dem Türlen's *Diu Crône*' in *Arthurian Romance and Gender*, ed. Friedrich Wolfzettel (1995), and 'Afro-Germans in the Third Reich,' in *Afro-German Experience: Critical Essays*, ed. Carol A. Blackshire-Belay (1996). She has also co-authored a book with Edward R. Haymes entitled *The Nibelungs and Dietrich of Bern: The Historical Legends of Medieval Germany and Scandinavia* (1996).

NOTES

1   Joachim Bumke, *Courtly Culture*, trans. Thomas Dunlap (Berkeley, Los Angeles, and London: University of California Press, 1991), p. 35.
2   Kwame Anthony Appiah, *In My Father's House* (New York and Oxford: Oxford University Press, 1992), p. 35.
3   For example, an Islamic historian refers to the Christian Crusaders as follows: 'In less time than it takes to tell the enemy [Crusaders] was completely overwhelmed and the fighting was over. Almighty and all-conquering God had sent His virtuous supporters victory and condemned the infidel rebels to hell.' (Francesco Gabrieli, *Arab Histories of the Crusades*, trans. E.J. Costello [Berkeley and Los Angeles: University of California Press, 1957], p. 67.)
4   *The Song of Roland*, in *Classics of Western Thought*, ed. Karl F. Thompson, 4th edn. (New York: Harcourt, Brace and Jovanovich, 1986), p. 21.
5   In-text quotations in German refer to Wolfram von Eschenbach, *Parzival*, ed. Karl Lachmann. Studienausgabe (Berlin: Walther De Gruyter & Co., 1965). In-text English translations of Wolfram are cited by page number from Wolfram von Eschenbach, *Parzival*, trans. A.T. Hatto (Harmondsworth: Penguin Books, 1980).
6   For further information, see the Prologue of *Parzival* in which Wolfram explains his concept of the *gutiu wîp*.
7   Blake Lee Spahr vigorously attacks Gahmuret's role as hero-knight: 'In point of fact, Gahmuret is a cad, a vain show-off, and a profligate spendthrift. He is a womanizer, a liar, and a deceiver. His only real virtue is an enormous talent for fighting. This and his great sensuous beauty are the sources of his attractiveness to women (and to at least one woman critic!) See 'Gahmuret's Erection: Rising to Adventure,' *Monatshefte* 83.4 (1991): 403 [403–13].
8   In a conference paper, 'The Image of the Non-Noble Figures in the German Courtly Epic,' I examined the non-noble figures as Other.
9   Bumke, *Courtly Culture*, trans. Dunlap, p. 275.
10 For example: 'He strikes Oliver from behind full in the back' (*The Song of Roland*, in *Classics of Western Thought*, ed. Thompson, p. 22, l. 145) and 'They [the Crusaders] took the money, but did not make peace and attacked Tunisia...' (Gabrieli, *Arab Histories of the Crusades*, trans. Costello, p. 303).

The Beaten Path:
Lancelot's Amorous Adventure at the
Fountain in *Le Chevalier de la Charrete*

ELLEN LORRAINE FRIEDRICH

The essay interprets the 'comb' episode in Chrétien de Troyes's *Chevalier de la Charrette* as an erotic exchange between Lancelot and the damsel. (ELF)

The curious 'comb' episode in Chrétien de Troyes's *Le Chevalier de la Charrete* takes place at a fountain—or spring, or source—found in a field by Lancelot and the desiring *dameisele* he escorts.[1] The interlude serves to highlight both the knight's obsession with Queen Guenevere and his supposed obliviousness to the charms of the young woman who had lodged him the previous night. While I do not intend to dispute Lancelot's devotion to his lady love, I will argue that the knight's resistance to the seduction attempts of the young lady he accompanies may not be as complete as previously thought.[2]

In the introduction to his facing-page Old and Modern French edition of the romance, Jean-Claude Aubailly characterizes the *Charrete* as 'un roman lourd de sens multiples' [a romance loaded with multiple meanings] having 'significations voilées' [veiled meanings].[3] Numerous critics have attempted to address the problems in the poem, citing, for example, the enigmatic nature of the main character and the ambiguity of the author's narrative strategies; the contradictions between feudal and courtly values and the resulting paradox of Lancelot's service to both his lady and his lord; and even the incoherence and incompleteness of the text.[4] Several scholars focus on the otherworldliness of the romance, pointing to the underworld-like realm of Gorre and its anti-hero Meleagant; to the super-knight Lancelot who has the strength of many men; to the 'fairylike atmosphere' of symbols and magical sites; and finally to the fantastic female figures characterized by Aubailly, among others, as 'fées.'[5] Medievalists also notice comic elements in the work. Their observations range from a passing reference to Chrétien's sense of humor, to statements about the possible presence of parody and satire in the *Charrete*, to a declaration that the *Lancelot* contains high comedy.[6]

These three aspects of Chrétien's text—the impenetrability of the author's 'intention,' the poem's mystery and *merveille*, and the range of wit in the work—combine to confound our understanding of a number of passages, including that of Lancelot and the lady at the fountain. The same three features also join forces to encourage an audience to suspend its disbelief and to accept Chrétien's imaginary world with all its possibilities. The problematic poem may thus permit the multiple meanings alluded to by Aubailly. The alternate interpretation I propose of the fountain episode rests on recognizing the effects the enigmatic elements of Chrétien's text have on the underlying eroticism in the romance in general, and more specifically, on the sexuality suggested in Lancelot's interlude with the desiring *dameisele*.

Perhaps the feature of the work most written about (other than the love story itself)—one to which I will devote little space—is the *sens*, i.e., the sense, direction, or meaning of the romance, the subject of numerous articles and book-length studies. Taken with the narrative strategies of the author and the structure of the *Charrete*, the significance of the poem has been studied by Old French scholars such as F. Douglas Kelly and Norris Lacy.[7] Kelly refers to the work as 'poorly conceived, badly constructed, and unworthy of the ideas expressed in most of Chrétien's writings,' and mentions another critic's identification of 'inconsistencies, omissions, and improbabilities in the plot.'[8] In 'The Unity of Chrétien's *Lancelot*,' Elaine Southward, while recognizing the genius of Chrétien de Troyes, characterizes the romance as 'incomplete,' a 'failure,' as having 'manifest faults,' and as lacking an artful closing.[9] The question of the nature of the love story, the role of love in courtly culture, and the implications of adultery as the motivating force behind the actions of the poem's protagonist have also been the subject of debate.[10] These and other difficulties in the text invite infinite interpretation by Chrétien's past and present audiences, of which the writer of this essay and its readers form a part.

In the introduction to his edition and translation of *Le Chevalier de la Charrete*, William W. Kibler refers to the otherworldy and fairylike atmosphere of the story, pointing out the 'magnificent deeds, hideous dwarfs, fair damsels, wicked giants, and the like' in the tale, as well as the 'magic rings, the mysterious tomb, the vision of lions, the swift-flying rumor, and the invisible boundary of the kingdom of Gorre.'[11] Z.P. Zaddy notes the 'atmosphere of mystery' inherent in elements such as the sword bridge.[12] Other scholars list locales identified as magical or supernatural, including the first castle in which Lancelot lodges with its flying flaming lance; the second castle belonging to the desiring *dameisele*, its extreme splendor

contributing to a sense of otherworldliness; the ford at the river into which
Lancelot falls in deep reverie before coming upon the seductive damsel; the
forest he traverses with her; the cemetery he comes across with the same
lascivious lady; and so forth.[13] The sites serve to remind us that almost
anything is possible in the world of Arthurian romance. David Shirt argues
that Chrétien makes use of a literary device referred to by E.R. Curtius in
European Literature and the Latin Middle Ages as 'World Upside Down.'[14]
This inversion of the normal order suggests that we suspend not only our
disbelief, but also our moral judgment, and that we 'interpret positive
evidence negatively'—that we understand the obverse of what the text tells
us.[15] Thus, indeed, things may not always be as they seem. Scenes in the
Charrete shift from the real to the unreal, and magic moves mountains—or
at least the marble slab covering a certain tomb.[16]

Jacques Ribard employs Jean Frappier's expression, 'frontières humides,'
in pointing out how water often signals the entrance into 'another world.'[17]
The young lady of the fountain episode first appears in the forest after the
ford episode, which serves as a transitional interlude in itself. Lucienne
Carasso-Bulow, author of *The Merveilleux in Chrétien de Troyes' Romances*,
asserts that the forest represents an intermediary zone, a place for magical
occurrences, 'a zone of wildness, darkness and mystery.'[18] Folklorist Judy
Grahn points out that a forest often signals a site for sexual escapades.[19]
Carasso-Bulow identifies still 'other elements that usually precede [or
accompany, I would add] fantastic worlds: water, fountains, mirrors, castles
surrounded with water,' and so on. Moreover, she categorizes the anonymous
damsels in Chrétien's romances as possible 'former fairies,' belonging to the
merveilleux.[20]

As noted, *le gué* [the ford] represents an important boundary. Lancelot's
encounter with the knight guarding it may not count as the first instance
that the Knight of the Cart tends to lose himself in thought, but it does
likely portray one of the most extreme and comical cases of the knight's
careless contemplation, and presages a later reverie as he rides with the
dameisele towards the fountain. Chrétien describes the danger of the lover's
losing himself in thought as his horse wanders towards the ford:

> et ses pansers est de tel guise
> que lui meïsmes en oblie;
> ne set s'il est, ou s'il n'est mie;
> ne ne li manbre de son non;
> ne set s'il est armez ou non,
> ne set ou va, ne set don vient.

De rien nule ne li sovient (vv. 714–20)

...

Li chevax voit et bel et cler

le gué, qui molt grant soif avoit;

vers l'eve cort quant il la voit (vv. 738–40).

...

et li chevax eneslepas

saut an l'eve et del chanp se soivre,

par grant talant comance a boivre (vv. 754–56).

...

Si li cheï tot a un vol

la lance et li escuz del col.

Quant cil sant l'eve, si tressaut;

toz estormiz an estant saut

ausi come cil qui s'esvoille (vv. 765–69).

[and his 'thinking' is of such a manner

that he forgets himself;

he doesn't know if he is, or if he is not;

neither does he remember his name;

nor does he know if he is armed or not,

nor know where he goes, nor know whence he comes.

Nothing at all does he remember

...

The horse sees the fine and clear water

at the ford, had very great thirst;

runs toward the water when he sees it.

...

and the horse immediately jumps in the water and from the field moves

away, with great desire begins to drink.

...

And from him [Lancelot] fall away suddenly

his lance and his shield from his neck.

When he feels the water, he startles;

all stunned, in a standing leap

just as one who awakens].

Given the description of the confusion in the mind of the 'hero,' and the ridiculous predicament in which he finds himself, as noted by Kelly,[21] it is for good reason that D.D.R. Owen ascribes a burlesque character to the poem and to the protagonist he refers to as a 'mock-heroic figure.'[22]

The Catalan medievalist Martín de Riquer recognizes a medieval topos of horseback reverie similar to Lancelot's *pansers*. Riquer finds related reveries in works such as the late twelfth-century Provençal romance *Jaufre*; in the *Libre de l'orde de cavalleria* of the thirteenth-century Catalan mystic, the Doctor Illuminatus Ramon Llull; in the fifteenth-century *Tirant lo Blanch*;

and in the well-known poem 'Farai un vers de dreit nien' by none other than Guilhem, Duke of Aquitaine and Count of Poitou, and, of course, great-grandfather of Marie de Champagne, Chrétien's patroness.[23] As in the *Lancelot*, the horse in Llull's book heads for a drink, at which point the rider awakes. The narrator of Guilhem's poem finds himself as confused as Lancelot:

> qu'enans fo trobatz en durmen
>   sus un chivau.
> No sai en qual hora.m fui natz,
> no soi alegres ni iratz,
> no soi estranhs ni soi privatz,
>   ni no.n puesc au,
> qu'enaisi fui de nueitz fadatz
>   sobr'un pueg au.
> No sai cora.m sui endormitz (vv. 5–13, Riquer ed.).

> [for it (the poem) was composed while sleeping
>   on a horse.
> I don't know at what hour I was born,
> I'm not happy nor sad,
> I'm not withdrawn or sociable,
>   nor can I be otherwise,
> for thus I was at night enchanted
>   on a high hill.
> I don't know by what time I am asleep.]

In the above song, Guilhem mentions having a female friend, and in another composition, "'Farai un vers, pos mi sonelh'" [I will make a poem, for I fall asleep], his dream-like state is a prelude to a wild sexual adventure with two women he encounters.

Some one hundred and sixty lines after the reverie at the ford in the *Charrete*, Lancelot comes across 'une dameisele venant, / molt tres bele et molt avenant, / bien acesmee et bien vestue' [a young lady coming, / very beautiful and very comely / well adorned and well dressed] (vv. 933–35). There exists no doubt of her desirability, nor of her desire, as she declares to Lancelot, 'avoec moi vos coucheroiz' [with me would you sleep] (v. 944) . Although it apparently pains him to do so, Lancelot, in fact, agrees to sleep with her (v. 957), suggesting a potential, eventual, sexual liaison. Sarah Melhado White agrees that the 'bed-motif' implies 'erotic possibilities.'[24] The couple spends a pleasant evening at her curious castle, during which time Lancelot's speech and the *Charrete* narrator's commentary repeatedly assure the audience, the lady, and the protagonist himself that the knight will keep the agreement: 'Je vos tendrai / vostre covant' [I will uphold / your covenant] (vv. 1043–44); 'car covant tenir li covient' [for it suited him to uphold his covenant] (v.

1049); 'An quel leu qu'ele soit / je la querrai tant que je l'aie' [In whatever place that she be / I will search for her until I have her](vv. 1054–55); 'et ce estoit meïsmes cele / avoec cui couchier se devoit' [and she was the same one / with whom he was to lie](vv. 1060–61).

During the dramatic night at the castle, Lancelot—after hesitating while he observes the partly nude body of his hostess being ravaged by a man—successfully defends the lady from the pseudo-rape she had apparently staged. In the midst of the passage recounting the assault, the *Charrete* narrator inserts a strange statement to the effect that Lancelot will keep the promise and his covenant, leaving the audience to wonder 'When?' 'Randre li porra la promesse / et son covant einz qu'il s'an aut' [He will be able to render to her the promise / and the covenant before he goes away](vv. 1154–55).

For the desiring *dameisele*, alas, it does not come to pass that night. But I suspect the lady has not entirely given up in *her* quest, for in the morning she convinces the knight to accompany her on a journey. According to the damsel's explanation of the customs of the region during their ride, Lancelot will have to defend her against any knight they might come upon who would fight for the 'right' to take sexual advantage of her, while if she travels alone, as a question of honor, she would be safe from assault (vv. 1295–1320). Inexplicably, Lancelot agrees to go with her, setting himself up for another scenario with erotic overtones. With his promise to lie with her as yet unfulfilled, he sets out to ride through the forest knowing that he may have to defend the demanding *dameisele* from an amorous aggressor, foreshadowing still one more titillating trial for the hero.

Aubailly insists on the initiatory quality of the romance, and on the eroticism of the tests the *Charrete* hero undergoes.[25] According to Aubailly, one can consider the *Charrete* a compendium of courtly thought following the code of sexual desire developed by the troubadours.[26] He points out that the lance of the first castle Lancelot visits symbolizes power and force. Charles Muscatine, writing in *The Old French Fabliaux*, lists 'lance' as one of the Old French metaphors for the penis, and Étienne de Fougères, in his ca. 1174–78 (approximately contemporary to the *Charrete*) *Livre des manières*, uses *lance* as a phallic metaphor.[27] As Matilde Tomaryn Bruckner asserts in her article 'Why Are There So Many Interpretations of Chrétien's *Chevalier de la Charrette?*' 'a close reading of Chrétien's work [and, I think, of romance in general] reveals a world where the ambiguities of signs may require an inexhaustible series of interpretations.'[28] Carasso-Bulow notes that the whole scene of the burning lance is ambiguous and that the lance is personified.[29] In 'Love in Chrétien's *Lancelot*,' David Fowler, concurring with Chaucerian scholar D.W. Robertson, Jr., recognizes that the fire may be an emblem for lust, awakened in the hero.[30] Therefore, I suggest, might the ardent lance not symbolize the erect penis/phallus? Aubailly maintains that the nights Lancelot spends in the two castles serve to stimulate the knight's sexual appetite.[31] So although he resists acting on his desire, Lancelot may be in an aroused state as he rides with his seductive hostess, an enchantress identified as a 'fée,' as previously noted. Here again the Knight of the Cart easily enters a hypnotic-like state, 'pansers li plest' (v. 1335), akin to that of the ford episode. At this point, he and his companion draw near the fountain, spring, or source in the middle of a meadow:

> La fontainne est enmi uns prez
> et s'avoit un perron delez.
> Sor le perron qui ert iqui
> avoit oblïé ne sai qui
> un peigne d'ivoire doré (vv. 1347–51).

> [The spring is in the midst of a field
> and there was a big stone alongside.
> On the stone someone who was here
> had left—I know not who—
> a comb of gilded ivory.]

Horseback riding, the water source, the field, as well as the *perron* and the *peigne*, all function as the crucial, and erotic, elements of the episode. The fountain, a site of romantic rendezvous in Latin literatures in general, and the field, 'the *pre[z]*,' together comprise a *locus amoenus*.[32] Mariantonia Liborio, writing on 'Rhetorical *Topoi* as "Clues" in Chrétien de Troyes,' studies the ways 'Chrétien involves his hearer or reader by giving him clues, setting strategies to direct his attention to the most important knots of his narrative.'[33] She notes how Chrétien 'plays' with the *locus amoenus* topos, the typical setting for love, and an 'erotic stereotype,' the appearance of which in a text lets the reader, 'who must interpret everything,' know what to expect. Liborio concludes, '[t]hrough the rhetorical *topoi*…the audience finds the keys to that special sort of puzzle which a literary text is.'[34]

Terence Scully has examined the role of the fountain in Chrétien's *Chevalier au lion*. As Scully points out, 'the medieval fountain is not necessarily a spring; it could be, and is commonly, just a hole in the ground, and that is its…sexual value…The female…, being conceived in Galenic humoral theory as fundamentally cold and moist, had a natural affinity with water; her genital area, set in its grassy *préau*, was the definitive source of this element. The symbolic sense of the fountain was appropriate.'[35] Its placement in a field reminds us that Chrétien placed the fountain Lancelot comes upon in the midst of a field. Muscatine identifies the *fontaine* or *fontenele* as metaphors for the *con*, the female genitals, while the historical French dictionary of Sainte-Palaye demonstrates that *fontaine* had a 'sens obscène.'[36]

As for the *perron*, the stone slab, and the *peigne*, the comb of ivory, both may refer to the male genitals. Although translators often take the *perron* to be a flat stone, in fact, according to the Old French dictionary of Godefroy, the term may refer to an upright sort of herm or statue.[37] The *perron* may also be understood as phallic or priapic in nature.[38] A herm, as defined by Eva C. Keuls in *The Reign of the Phallus*, was originally 'a statue of the god Hermes, consisting of a stone slab topped by a sculpted head and with testicles and an erect penis…The penis in most cases protruded from the slab and must have been extremely susceptible to damage.'[39] Keuls explains that the penis was often broken off and she mentions 'altars topped with phalluses,'[40] perhaps equivalent to the *perron* that the travelers find with the *peigne* sitting on top. Furthermore, Hermes was the god of travelers[41]—like Lancelot and the lady—and his form, a type of boundary marker, was found in fields, on roads, and in gardens.

The allusion to rocks should not be lost on us. J.N. Adams, in *The Latin Sexual Vocabulary*, notes that words (like *perron*) for 'stones' and 'rocks' serve as metaphors for the testicles.[42] Moreover, the Latin word for comb, *pecten*, as well as its Romance derivatives, has for some time held sexual currency.[43] Michael Camille, in his book *The Medieval Art of Love: Objects and Subjects of Desire*, notes that a medieval comb fits snugly into its leather pouch, and that ivory is a 'substance suggestive of the flesh…[it is among the] most fleshlike of all artistic media.'[44] Significantly, the desiring *dameisele* demands the hard, pointy object of Lancelot: 'Donez le moi' [Give it to me] (v. 1389). He gives it to her 'willingly'—'Voluntiers' (v. 1390), as he replies.

Critics such as Fowler who credit Chrétien with a considerable use of comedy in his composition[45] might recognize in the *Charrete* a medieval—and perhaps earlier—topos of encountering disembodied genitals—especially, but not exclusively, male ones. In fabliaux and in other tales folk find male genitalia in markets or by the side of the road.[46] Chaucer's Pardoner carries his 'reliques' around with him, as does Brother Cipolla in Boccaccio's *Decameron*.[47] We learn that the *peigne* on the *perron* had belonged to Guenevere. Lancelot too (as well as his body, and its parts, presumably) 'belongs' to the queen. Might the misplaced object, separated from its owner (Guenevere and/or Lancelot?), stand for the penis the knight cannot, has not, used? Lancelot, of course, chooses to give the relic-like *peigne*, or, in its alternate spelling, *pigne*, both terms similar in sound to *pene* and *pine*, words for the penis, to the damsel with whom he is travelling. But, according to traditional interpretations, he retains the hair of Guenevere, keeping it close to his body, almost as a buffer between himself and the lady (v. 1457 ff.). Nevertheless, the narrator uses ambiguous language to describe the scene:

> Et cil, qui vialt que le peigne ait,
> li done et les chevox an trait
> si soëf que nul n'an deront (vv. 1457–59)

> [And he, who wants that she have the *peigne*,
> gives it to her and pulls the hair (parts it?)
> so softly that none is broken.]

Chrétien seems to suggest that Lancelot gives the *dameisele* what she has so desperately wanted as he gently enters her. At this point, the knight proceeds to enter a near orgiastic, orgasmic state, beginning to adore 'them,' the hairs (v. 1462; 'il les comance a aorer').

The lady had approached Lancelot to seek the object: 'Je ving cest peigne querre' [I come to get this comb](v. 1453). Now she is ready to ride. Just as the narrator refuses to elaborate on the action taking place in the later love scene between Lancelot and the Queen (v. 4680–81), so he demurs now in his description of what happens once the damsel gets the comb: 'Et que feroie ge lonc conte?' [And why should I make a long story?](v. 1465). As with the later love liaison, he rapidly brings the episode to a climax before someone else appears:

> La pucele molt tost remonte
> atot le peigne qu'ele an porte;
> et cil se delite et deporte
> es chevox qu'il a en son saing.
> Une forest aprés le plaing
> truevent et vont par une adresce
> tant que la voie lor estresce,
> s'estut l'un aprés l'autre aler,
> qu'an n'i poïst mie mener
> deus chevax por rien coste a coste.
> La pucele devant son oste
> s'an vet molt tost la voie droite.
> La ou la voie ert plus estroite
> voient un chevalier venant.
> La dameisele maintenant,
> de si loing com ele le vit,
> l'a coneü et si a dit... (1496–1512)

> [The girl very soon remounts
> with the *peigne* that she holds;

and he takes his delight and plays the game of love
in the hair he has at his breast.
A forest after the plain
they find and go by the right way
so much that the way narrows for them,
it was necessary for one after the other to go,
for one could not at all lead
two horses in any way side by side.
The girl before her host
goes very soon the right way.
There where the way was the narrower
they see a knight coming.
The damsel now,
from so far as she sees him,
recognized him and said....]

All of this activity takes place, of course, while mounted or dismounted—
or in the act of mounting. Equine events have long been associated with the
sex act, as noted by both Adams and Muscatine.[48] Adams, and William Paden
writing on Bernart de Ventadorn, both interpret the man—his body—as
the horse.[49] The woman is the rider.[50] Muscatine designates *remonte* as one
of the terms for *foutre*, the sex act.[51] Thus the damsel 'mounts' her escort.
The knight 'delights'—another sexual euphemism, according to Muscatine—
and the two take an *adrece* or *la voie droite* [the right way], metaphors for the
con [vagina].[52] Unable to ride side by side, they must double up, so to speak,
forming, after a fashion, 'the beast with two-backs,' to which Shakespeare
refers in *Othello* 1.1. It should come as no surprise then, that where the way
was narrowest, the lady saw a knight 'coming.' In the last line, *L'a coneü*, a common
pun on *con* recognized by Old French scholars such as Muscatine, Sarah Melhado
White, and Robert Harrison, we understand that she 'blanked' him—'cunted'
him.[53] The demanding *dameisele* has finally had her way with the formerly
resisting knight.

   The 'Beaten Path' of the title of this essay, then, represents the *chemin*,
voie, or *sentier batu[z]* that Lancelot prefers and takes.[54] The terms *chemin batu*
(v. 1379), *fontaine*, and *fontenele* comprise some of the most common metaphors
for the female genitals,[55] which when joined with terms for the masculine
sex symbols, the *perron* and *peigne*, symbolize the ancient act that brings a
woman and man together. Chrétien de Troyes has indeed furnished us with
the clues to place the pieces of the puzzle that form his poem into a new
pattern—different from that of traditional interpretations of the romance—
but one that nevertheless tells an old story. The 'well-worn way' Lancelot
chooses has long been used, but we, Chrétien's audience, are well advised to

take paths less traveled by as we endeavor to understand the enigmatic *Chevalier de la Charrete.*

PRESBYTERIAN COLLEGE

Ellen Lorraine Friedrich is Assistant Professor of Romance Languages at Presbyterian College, South Carolina. Her research has focused on a homoerotic reading of Guillaume de Lorris's *Roman de la rose.* In addition, she has done work on the Provençal troubadours, the Galician-Portuguese *cantigas d'escarnho e mal dizer,* the fabliaux, Ovid, and Alain de Lille.

NOTES

1 I use the edition by William W. Kibler, ed., *Lancelot, or, The Knight of the Cart (Le Chevalier de la Charrete)* [New York: Garland, 1981], and the Old French citations are from this edition. Translations are my own, unless otherwise noted, and are deliberately literal because of the philological nature of my study.

In my attempt to understand the *Chevalier de la Charrete* better, I am much indebted to Mrs. Teresa Inman, Presbyterian College Head of Circulation and Interlibrary Loans, for the many materials she obtained for my use, to Ms. Victoria Koger, Reference Librarian, for her readiness to assist in this and other projects, and finally to Sarah Bufter, *assistante extraordinaire,* for her efficiency in daily details.

2 A version of this essay was given as a paper with the same title at the 35th International Congress on Medieval Studies, Kalamazoo, MI, May 7, 2000, in a special session sponsored by the Friends of Maureen Fries entitled 'The "Bad" Girls of Arthurian Literature.'

3 Chrétien de Troyes, *Lancelot, ou Le Chevalier de la Charrette,* ed., trans. and intro. Jean-Claude Aubailly (Paris: Flammarion, 1991), pp. 9, 48, 14.

4 Matilde Tomaryn Bruckner, 'Why Are There So Many Interpretations of Chrétien's *Chevalier de la Charrette?' Romance Philology* 40.2 (1986): 159 [159–80] reviews some of the problems with the poem; David J. Shirt, 'Chrétien de Troyes and the Cart,' in *Studies in Medieval Literature and Languages in Memory of Frederick Whitehead,* ed. W. Rothwell et al. (New York: Manchester University Press/Barnes and Noble, 1973), p. 279, summarized by Z.P. Zaddy in the chapter entitled 'The Structure of the *Charrete,*' in *Chrétien Studies: Problems of Form and Meaning in* Erec, Yvain, Cligés *and the* Charrete (Glasgow: University of Glasgow Press, 1973),p. 110 [110–58].

5 See, for example, the introduction to Kibler's edition, p. xviii; F. Douglas Kelly, *Sens and Conjointure in the* Chevalier de la Charrette (The Hague: Mouton, 1966), esp. pp. 116–21; Kibler's term, p. xviii. Aubailly (p. 29 and n44, 34) also cites Charles Méla, *La Reine et le Graal* (Paris: Seuil, 1984), p. 265. The second, and to a lesser extent, the third, chapters of Lucienne Carasso-Bulow's study *The Merveilleux in Chrétien de Troyes' Romances* (Geneva: Droz, 1976), identify elements and levels of the *merveilleux* in the *Charrete.*

6 Humor: Tom Peete Cross and William Albert Nitze, *Lancelot and Guenevere: A*

Study on the Origins of Courtly Love (Chicago: University of Chicago Press, 1930), p. 73; parody: David C. Fowler, 'Love in Chrétien's *Lancelot*,' *Romanic Review* 63 (1972): 6 [5–14]; and satire: Fowler, 'Love,' 14; high comedy: Fowler, 'Love,' 7. See also Claudine Dubois, 'L'humour,' in *Analyses et réflexions sur Chrétien de Troyes: Lancelot, le Chevalier de la Charrette*, ed. Christophe Carlier (Paris: Ellipses, 1996).

7 F. Kelly, *Sens*, and his introduction to the collection of essays he edited, *The Romances of Chrétien de Troyes* (Lexington: French Forum, 1985); Norris Lacy, *The Craft of Chrétien de Troyes* (Leiden: E.J. Brill, 1980).

8 F. Kelly, *Sens* (reference to Wendelin Foerster), p. 1.

9 Elaine Southward, 'The Unity of Chrétien's *Lancelot*,' *Mélanges de linguistique et de littérature romanes offerts à Mario Roques par ses amis, ses collègues et ses anciens élèves de France et de l'étranger* (Paris: Didér, 1950–52), pp. 281, 282, and 290 [281–90].

10 See, for example, Gustave Cohen, *Un grand romancier d'amour et d'aventure au XIIème siècle: Chrétien de Troyes et son oeuvre* (Paris, Boivin, 1931; rep. 1948); Cross and Nitze, *Lancelot and Guenevere*; Peter S. Noble, *Love and Marriage in Chrétien de Troyes* (Cardiff: University of Wales Press, 1982); Pietro Beltrami, 'Racconto mitico e linguiaggio lirico: Per l'interpretazione del *Chevalier de la Charrete*, *Studi mediolatini e volgari* 30 (1984): 5–67; and Fowler, 'Love.'

11 Kibler, 'Introduction,' p. xvii; Carasso-Bulow, *The Merveilleux*, also examines fantastic elements.

12 Zaddy, *Chrétien Studies*, p. 146.

13 See, for example, Kibler, p. xvi–xvii; and the following three essays in *Analyses et réflexions sur Chrétien de Troyes: Lancelot, le Chevalier de la Charrette*, ed. Christophe Carlier (Paris: Ellipses, 1996): Catherine Blons-Pierre, 'Espace et lieux,' pp. 41–45; Marie-Françoise Minaud, 'Le Merveilleux "Mervoilles li sont avenues,"' pp. 65–70; and Emmanuèle Baumgartner, 'Lancelot et les "demoiselles,"' pp. 60–64. See also David Shirt, '*Le Chevalier de la Charrete*: A World Upside Down?' *Modern Language Review* 76 (1981): 811–22; and Carasso-Bulow, *The Merveilleux*.

14 Shirt '*Le Chevalier*,' 811.

15 Shirt, '*Le Chevalier*,' 822; he also cites Jean de Meun in the *Roman de la Rose*, vv. 21543–46, ed. Félix Lecoy, *Le roman de la rose par Guillaume de Lorris et Jean de Meun*, 3 vols. (Paris: Honoré Champion, 1973–75).

16 I refer, of course, to the scene in the cemetery where Lancelot, exhibiting the strength of several men, raises the slab covering the tomb in which he will eventually lie (vv. 1855–1919).

17 Jacques Ribard, in *Le Chevalier de la Charrette: Essai d'interprétation symbolique* (Paris: Nizet, 1972), pp. 65–66, cites Jean Frappier's expression, 'frontières humides,' from Frappier's *Chrétien de Troyes* (Paris: Hatier, 1968), p. 57.

18 Carasso-Bulow, *The Merveilleux*, p. 39.

19 Judy Grahn, *Another Mother Tongue: Gay Words, Gay Worlds* (Boston: Beacon, 1984), p. 208.

20 Carasso-Bulow, *The Merveilleux*, p. 39, p. 61 n36.

21 Kelly, *Sens*, p. 115.

22 D.D.R. Owen, 'Profanity and Its Purpose in Chrétien's *Cligés* and *Lancelot*,' *Forum for Modern Language Studies* 6 (1970): 47 [37–48]-.

23 Martín de Riquer, *Los Trovadores: Historia literaria y textos*, 3 vols. (Barcelona: Planeta, 1975), 1:113–17.

24 Sarah Melhado White, 'Lancelot's Beds: Styles of Courtly Intimacy,' in *The Sower and His Seed: Essays on Chrétien de Troyes*, ed. Rupert T. Pickens (Lexington: French Forum, 1983), p. 119–26.

25 'Introduction,' *Lancelot*, ed. Aubailly, esp. pp. 19, 21, 31.

26 'Introduction,' *Lancelot*, ed. Aubailly, pp. 9–10, cites Emmanuèle Baumgartner, *Histoire de la littérature française: Moyen Âge, 1050–1486* (Paris: Bordas, 1987), p. 86.

27 Charles Muscatine, *The Old French Fabliaux* (New Haven: Yale University Press, 1986), p. 112 and p. 188, n15; I am grateful to Robert L.A. Clark for pointing out this occurrence in Étienne de Fougères, *Le Livre des manières*, ed. R. Anthony Lodge (Geneva: Droz, 1979), p. 97, v. 1110.

28 Bruckner, 'Why,' 160. She sends the reader to Howard Bloch, 'Tristan, the Myth of the State and the Language of the Self,' *Yale French Studies* 51 (1974): 61–81.

29 Carasso-Bulow, *The Merveilleux*, pp. 46, 49.

30 Fowler, 'Love in Chrétien's *Lancelot*,' 9, citing D.W. Robertson, Jr., *A Preface to Chaucer* (Princeton: Princeton University Press, 1963), p. 450.

31 Aubailly, 'Introduction,' pp. 33–34.

32 See, for example, Ernst Robert Curtius, *European Literature and the Latin Middle Ages* (Princeton, NJ: Princeton University Press, 1952), pp. 192–200. For a specific reference to Chrétien, see Baumgartner, 'Lancelot,' p. 63.

33 Mariantonia Liborio, 'Rhetorical *Topoi* as "Clues" in Chrétien de Troyes' in *Rhetoric Revalued*,' ed. Brian Vickers (Binghamton, NY: Center for Medieval and Early Renaissance Studies, 1982), p. 173 [173–78].

34 Liborio, 'Rhetorical *Topoi*,' esp. 175–77.

35 Terence Scully, 'Love and the Fountain: Chrétien's *sen*,' paper read at the 31st International Congress on Medieval Studies, Kalamazoo, MI, May 1996. I thank Professor Scully for sending me a copy of his paper.

36 Muscatine, *Old French Fabliaux*, pp. 113–114; p. 189, n23; Sainte-Palay (Jean Baptiste de La Curne), et al., *Dictionnaire historique de l'ancien langage français*, 10 vols. (Niort: L. Favre, 1875–82), 6:255.

37 Frédéric Godefroy, *Dictionnaire de l'ancienne langue française*, 10 vols. (Paris: Librairie des sciences et des arts, 1937–38), 6:110. See also Amy Richlin, *The Garden of Priapus: Sexuality and Aggression in Roman Humor* (New York: Oxford University Press, 1992), esp. pp. 63, 66.

38 Richlin, *Garden*, esp. pp. 63, 66; and cf. Walter F. Otto, *Dionysus: Myth and Cult*, trans. Robert B. Palmer (Bloomington: Indiana University Press, 1965), p. 164.

39 Eva C. Keuls in *The Reign of the Phallus: Sexual Politics in Ancient Athens* (Berkeley: University of California Press, 1985), p. 385.

40 Keuls, *Reign of the Phallus*, pp. 385, 78.

41 Keuls, *Reign of the Phallus*, p. 31.

42 J. N. Adams, *The Latin Sexual Vocabulary* (Baltimore: Johns Hopkins, 1982), pp. 22.

43 Adams, *Latin Sexual Vocabulary*, pp. 76–77. Nobel laureate Camilo José Cela documents the diminutive of Spanish *peine* 'comb,' *peinecito*, as 'penis,' in *Diccionario secreto*, 2 vols. (Madrid: Alianza, 1974), vol. 2, part 2, p. 393.

44 Michael Camille, *The Medieval Art of Love: Objects and Subjects of Desire* (New York: Harry N. Abrams, 1998), pp. 56–57.

45 Fowler, 'Love in Chrétien's *Lancelot*,' esp. 6–7, 10–11, 13–14.

46 Sarah Melhado White details a number of these fabliaux in her article 'Sexual Language and Human Conflict in Fabliaux,' *Comparative Studies in Society and History* 24.1 (1982): 191, 197–202 [185–210].

47 For the sexual symbolism of the Pardoner's 'relics' see Monica E. McAlpine's 'The Pardoner's Homosexuality and How It Matters,' PMLA 95 (1980): 8–22; *Decameron* 6:10.

48 Adams, *Latin Sexual Vocabulary*, p. 165; Muscatine, *Old French Fabliaux*, p. 110, p. 186 n7.

49 Adams, *Latin Sexual Vocabulary*, p. 165; William D. Paden, '*Utrum Copularentur: Of Cors*,' *L'Esprit Créateur* 19:4 (Winter 1979): 74–75.

50 Adams, *Latin Sexual Vocabulary*, p. 165.

51 Muscatine, *Old French Fabliaux*, p. 110; p. 186, n7.

52 See Muscatine, *Old French Fabliaux*, Chapter 5, for an explanation of sexual metaphor and lists of terms; and Adams, *Latin*, Chapter 3, for the classification of female genitalia.

53 Muscatine, *Old French Fabliaux*, p. 115 and pp. 189–90, nn24–27; White, 'Sexual,' 195; and Robert Harrison, *Gallic Salt* (Berkeley: University of California Press, 1974), p. 187.

54 The terms appear throughout the passage, for example, at vv. 1344–45.

55 Muscatine, *Old French Fabliaux*, pp. 113–14; p. 189 n23.

Lyonet, Lunete, and Laudine: Carnivalesque Arthurian Women

MELANIE MCGARRAHAN GIBSON

The perverse voices and behavior of three Arthurian women—Chrétien's Lunete and Laudine and Malory's Lyonet—are illuminated when seen in relation to Mikhail Bakhtin's theory of carnival. The perversity of Lyonet and Lunete makes them mediators in their worlds. (MMG)

Below the surface of Sir Thomas Malory's happily resolved tale, 'The Tale of Sir Gareth of Orkney,'[1] one finds dark elements that contrast with the tale's comedy. These are elements of carnival and magic, embodied in the characters of Lyonet, her sister, and Gareth himself. [2] This tale places the ability to manipulate language above the ability to fight well. This is true also of Chrétien de Troyes's *Yvain* (*Le Chevalier au Lion*), which, as Faith Lyons and others have pointed out, contains several parallels to Malory's tale.[3] R.W. Hanning has examined Chrétien's theme of the value of love and mercy over violence.[4] This theme surfaces in 'The Tale of Sir Gareth' mainly in the stock elements of medieval carnival plays, while in *Yvain* the theme is more overtly illustrated in the characters of Lunete and Laudine and in the penultimate episode. In both tales, I will argue, female characters speak perversely, in carnivalesque voices.

CARNIVAL THEORY AND LIMINALITY

In *Rabelais and His World*, Mikhail Bakhtin expounds his theory of carnival, tracing it from the Saturnalia plays of the ancient world, through the 'feast of fools' and carnival plays of the medieval world, up to an examination of Rabelais's novels and other works of the Renaissance. 'Carnival,' as Bakhtin describes it, expresses the laughter of the people, and it creates a space for other voices. Carnival laughter is ambivalent, directed at the object and at the one who laughs.[5] Carnival exposes the arbitrariness of hierarchies in its mocking laughter and in its insistence on grotesque realism—the material reality of the body.[6] Carnival celebrates all aspects of the physical body, the whole of life.[7]

Clifford Flanigan, in 'Liminality, Carnival, and Social Structure,' says that the 'popular festivities' of carnival, according to Bakhtin, 'had little or nothing to do' with the official celebrations to which they were connected.[8] Instead, these celebrations allowed people to criticize the establishment.[9] At carnival time, rules no longer apply and 'the prevailing order of things' is threatened.[10] It is a performance in which roles are reversed. 'The Tale of Sir Gareth' begins with a disguised Gareth coming to Arthur's court during the sacred feast of Pentecost. This is appropriate for a tale with carnival motifs: the feast is a communal event; it involves eating, drinking, and celebrating the physical body; Gareth, by hiding his true identity, marginalizes himself by reversing his role from that expected of a knight to that of a knave.

This marginal status is what Victor and Edith Turner call 'liminality,' a period when one separates from the group and becomes an 'outsider,' between what was one's ordinary life before and the later reincorporation into the group and return to ordinary life.[11] They group the terms '[l]iminality, marginality, and inferiority' together, all characteristics of Gareth at the beginning of the story.[12] While Gareth chooses his outsider status, Lyonet, the Savage Damsel in Malory, and Lunete, the damsel on the margins in *Yvain*, are outsiders both because they have access to magical powers and because their well-being is threatened. Gareth's ultimate goal is reincorporation into the court and an enhanced return to his previous status. The status of the liminal characters Lyonet and Lunete, on the other hand, differs considerably from Gareth's. Laudine, the lady Lunete serves in *Yvain*, is marginalized for still other reasons: first she is widowed, then she is abandoned by Yvain.

LYONET, THE SAVAGE DAMSEL, AND GARETH ON THE MARGINS

When Gareth arrives at the feast of Pentecost, the stage is set for carnival disruption—deviation from official speech—to enter the story. In this case, disruption is reflected in abusive language.[13] First Sir Kay's and then Lyonet's abusive language is carnivalesque. It revives and renews Gareth, while the laughter Lyonet inspires directs itself at all. This laughter fills in the gaps between conventional and actual behavior in the story.

Lyonet violates with apparent impunity the rules that govern her sister's behavior, and she transgresses the boundaries that contain women in her society. She is free to leave the besieged castle to find someone to rescue her sister. When she arrives at Arthur's court, she refuses to identify herself or her sister when the king asks the sister's name, and Arthur becomes angry.

This contrasts greatly with his response to Gareth when he also refused to give his name upon arrival at court: Arthur responded to him with surprise. He expressed wonder that the young man did not know his name. Gareth's actual words are "'I can nat tell you,'" but the king interprets this differently from the way he does Lyonet's answer.[14] Her response is not so different— "'that shall nat ye know for me as at thys tyme'"—but this time Arthur reacts with outrage. Because of her response, he refuses her the assistance of his knights, while he granted Gareth's request.[15]

Lyonet enters the story speaking perversely (or, more precisely, like the knights in her world usually speak). She will not follow the social conventions expected of most females of her time; she refuses to acknowledge the 'word of the fathers.'[16] Instead she uses words as her own tools and speaks what she chooses, even though this seems to defeat her purpose since she ends up not with one of Arthur's knights to fight for her sister but with the young man who has been working in the kitchen (where Gareth has taken up residence). Because of her disgust with this apparently lower-class servant, Lyonet continues to speak perversely and abusively to Sir Gareth throughout the journey to her sister's castle.

On their trip they encounter several knights, each of whom Lyonet incites to fight Gareth. To the Black Knight she says:

> "Sir, I can not be delyverde of hym, for with me he rydiyth magre my hede. God wolde," sayde she, "that ye wolde putte hym from me, other to sle hym and ye may, for he is an unhappy knave, and unhappyly he hath done this day thorow myssehape."[17]

Gareth kills the Black Knight, so when they meet his brother, the Red Knight, Lyonet again tries to get rid of Gareth. She urges him to "'be revenged [for his brother's sake], for I may nevir be quyte of hym.'"[18] Encouraging Gareth's opponents while constantly abusing Gareth, Lyonet actually succeeds in rousing Gareth to fight harder.

Lyonet wields words skillfully, eloquently insulting Gareth. Like Sir Kay, she calls him Sir Bewmaynes because of his large white hands. She berates him because he refuses to leave her and because he stinks: "'What doste thou here? Thou stynkest all of the kychyn, thy clothis bene bawdy of the grece and talow.'"[19] She also cautions Gareth before each battle to turn back and save himself (an insult to a knight). They encounter various opponents for Gareth, and Lyonet warns him each time:

> [Two knights guarding the river] "What seyst thou?" seyde the damesell. "Woll you macche yondir two knyghtis other ellys turne agayne?"[20]

[The Black Knight] "I sey hit for thyne avayle, for yett mayste thou turne ayen with thy worshyp; for and thou folow me thou arte but slayne."[21]

[The Green Knight] "But hereby is one that shall pay the all thy paymente, and therefore yette I rede the flee."[22]

Lyonet also tempts Gareth to flee when he faces the Red Knight and the Blue Knight, but her tone changes to one of concern with the Blue Knight. She urges Gareth to "'save thyself and thou may, for thyne horse and thou have had grete travayle...here I drede me sore last ye shall cacche some hurte.'"[23] By overcoming this last temptation to run away, couched in language of concern (but still another form of insult), Gareth proves to Lyonet his nobility:

> "A, Jesu! Mervayle have I," seyde the damesell, "what maner a man ye be, for hit may never be other that ye be com of jantyll bloode, for so fowle and shamfully dud never woman revyle a knyght as I have done you, and ever curteysly ye have suffyrde me, and that come never but of jantyll bloode."[24]

Lyonet begs Gareth to forgive her for insulting him, but Gareth says, "'all youre evyll wordys pleased me.'"[25] Her words have acted as a magical incantation, humiliating Gareth but at the same time reviving and renewing him. The result of this behavior is carnival perversion, urging Gareth on to greater glory with each joust. Lyonet delivers her remarks with complete seriousness. Her disapproval of Gareth is social, not moral, and although we laugh at Gareth, we must also laugh at Lyonet.

Lyonet's verbal assaults on Gareth are made even more amusing by his mild, forbearing, and ironic responses to them. When he approaches the Green Knight, Gareth refuses to heed Lyonet's warning, "'for ever ye sey that they woll sle me other bete me, but howsomever hit happenyth I ascape and they lye on the grounde.'"[26] After Gareth forces Lyonet into begging him to spare the Green Knight's life, he says, "'Damesell...your charge is to me a plesure.'"[27] Gareth is also clever in his speech, and he too is capable of verbal manipulation. After the trenchant Lyonet is finally subdued by Gareth's gentle answers, the reader may miss her abusive comments.[28]

During his fight with Sir Ironside at Lyoness's castle, Lyonet provokes Gareth at a crucial moment as her sister watches from the window: "'A, sir Bewmaynes! Where is thy corryage becom? Alas! My lady sistir beholdyth the, and she shrekis and wepys so that hit makyth myne herte hevy.'"[29] Again, Lyonet seems to doubt Gareth's abilities, but the result is that Gareth rushes forward with renewed strength and defeats Sir Ironside.

Unlike her sister Lyoness, who has a magic ring but apparently no other magical qualities, Lyonet's magic and supernatural knowledge are pervasive. Lyoness, until Gareth lifts the siege, is confined to the space she has inherited, her castle, which has led to the problem with Sir Ironside. Lyonet, who lacks the benefits of the elder sister—land ownership—nevertheless has something Lyoness cannot have: the freedom to move about and to travel to Arthur's court. Lyoness's magic ring, which gives Gareth special abilities, cannot help Lyoness; the ring's power is only available when she gives it to another.

Just as Lyonet's movements are unrestricted, so is her magical ability. Lyonet prevents her sister and Gareth from consummating their love prior to marriage by sending a conjured knight to interrupt their tryst. Gareth must fight him; he defeats him and cuts off his head. In the midst of the uproar over Gareth's injuries, Lyonet

> toke up the [knight's] head in the syght of them all, and anoynted hit with an oyntemente thereas hit was smyttyn off, and in the same wyse she ded to the other parte thereas the heade stake. And than she sette hit togydeirs, and hit stake as faste as ever hit ded.[30]

Everyone is shocked, and Gareth expresses his dismay. But she does it again, this time reconstructing the knight's head from the little pieces Gareth has chopped it into. In this way she protects her sister's and her family's honor. Her magic encompasses the elements of Bakhtin's carnival body: dismemberment, disintegration, renewal, and rebirth.

Although she appears to be an unlikely force for reconciliation, Lyonet is the one who prevents Gareth and Gawain from fighting each other to the death. Here she plays a role similar to the one Lunete plays in *Yvain*; their clever manipulation of situations with their quick tongues makes them both good diplomats and mediators. Lyonet's diplomatic role continues when she advises Gareth to summon the knights he previously defeated to join his party in a tournament. At the tournament—the Arthurian world's great communal event—Gareth gathers around him the men whose loyalty he has won through his skill with the help of Lyonet's disruptive language. Bakhtin's communal event is a feast or outdoor spectacle; tournaments also end with feasting. Frequently they were settings for weddings. The tournament would bring together the community to resolve differences through both love and controlled conflict. The conflict happened to involve death and dismemberment for some, great honor and reconciliation for others. Gareth proves himself at this communal event before the entire court and his family, just as he hoped from the beginning when he first asked Arthur to grant his request.

Conversely, Lyonet in the context of this tale has never been a part of the 'ordinary life' her sister leads. Her status in her family may have marginalized her at first, but her behavior and her magic have kept her marginalized. Lyonet is called the Savage; she bears this name from the beginning of the tale, so she enters as a liminal character, one between two worlds, the lady and the hag. Even though there has been no mention of Lyonet as love object, Arthur marries her off to Gareth's brother at the same time Lyoness marries Gareth. Lyonet thus is safely reincorporated back into court society; contained within acceptable bounds, she becomes a wife and a lady of Arthur's court.

But the story has let loose the Savage Damsel and her words. In all of her actions within the story, she has reversed expected female roles: she is not mild or meek, she answers the king the way privileged knights answer one another, and she influences the outcome of the tale. She acts as a catalyst for bringing Gareth out of the kitchen at court; her abuse helps make possible Gareth's perilous deeds on his quest. She acts as a go-between, adviser, and chaperone for Gareth and her sister, and she makes the peace in the end between the two brothers, Gawain and Gareth, reuniting Gareth and Lyoness with the rest of the court. Her unusual, carnivalesque behavior makes the happy outcome of this story possible. Lyonet and Gawain may be the only characters who do not get what they want. It seems unlikely that what she wants is to become just like her sister and most of the other women in her society.

Malory's tale explores the problems of trial by combat, concealment of identities, and violence as a social mediator in different ways from Chrétien's. Gareth establishes a pattern of dispensing mercy to his defeated opponents that forces Lyonet to acknowledge him as one capable of granting mercy. After he defeats the Green Knight, Gareth agrees to spare his life only if Lyonet requests it. She finally gives in when the Green Knight again calls for mercy and Gareth appears willing to kill him:

> "Sir knyght," seyde Bewmaynes, "all this avaylyth the nought but yf my damesell speke to me for thy lyff," and therewithall he made a semblaunte to sle hym. "Lat be," seyde the damesell, "thou bawdy kychyn knave! Sle hym nat, for and thou do thou shalt repent hit."[31]

After the defeat of the Red Knight, Gareth again says he will spare his foe's life only if Lyonet asks him to do so. This time, she responds less acidly but no more willingly.[32] When he defeats the Blue Knight, Lyonet asks Gareth to spare his life without any prompting from Gareth. This ritual allows Gareth to win from Lyonet a sign of her respect, by taking her weapon of choice—her speech—and making her use it as *he* wishes, rather than against him.

At the battle with Sir Ironside, another Red Knight, Gareth must decide for himself whether or not to grant mercy to his defeated opponent. At first he refuses the Red Knight's plea. But then he allows the Red Knight to explain his shameful behavior. Sir Ironside's speech persuades Gareth to show mercy.[33] This passage illustrates not only the value of speech over violence in determining the proper course of behavior but also ties mercy to justice. Gareth displays his sense of justice when he tells Ironside to go to Lyoness and, if she will forgive him, then Ironside must "goo unto the courte of kyng Arthur and that he aske sir Launcelot mercy and sir Gawayne for the evyll wylle he hath had ayenst them."[34] Ironside must seek mercy, and the method he must use is speech: he must ask forgiveness from exemplars of the entire community. In this manner, Gareth shows he has overcome his own violence as well as Ironside's.[35] Gareth's mercy transforms Sir Ironside into a knight worthy to sit at the Round Table and demonstrates that he has internalized one of the precepts of the Pentecostal Oath. This transformation is a kind of chivalric magic Gareth has wrought as he has become the embodiment of the ideal knight. This chivalric magic parallels carnival magic in the tale.

Changing of identities and reversal of expectations based on appearances are parts of carnival behavior, and they are part of Gareth's story as well. Gareth changes identities several times in the story, from his decision to live in Arthur's kitchen, to his changing of shields each time he defeats an opponent, to his hiding his identity at the tournament with Lyoness's magic ring. In his final disguised state, Gareth unknowingly fights his brother Gawain; they are only saved from destroying each other by Lyonet's fortuitous appearance.

Gareth's actions follow a ritualistic pattern; through this ritual he seeks to create himself as a being separate from his family. Gareth tells Lyonet that he lived in Arthur's kitchen "for to preve my frendys."[36] The jousts and the tournaments of this society are another ritual the participants perform in order to make themselves knights. Although Gareth cannot escape from his family, and the concealing of his identity nearly causes the tragedy of brother killing brother, Gareth succeeds in creating his own identity. The magic, the changing of identities, and the role reversal contribute to the privileged status of love, mercy, and a skillful rhetorical style in this story.

The tale ends with several marriages that are raucous in the mode of charivari. Instead of being anti-structural (the usual expectation of carnival), this is a kind of carnival as fulfillment of social structures. This is a moment of social reintegration when everything is reinforced: the Round Table, monogamous marriage, love in marriage, families. But one brother, Gawain, is left out. Arthur does not marry him off. This darkens the picture because of our knowledge of the tragedy to come in later tales. But for now, in the happiest ending of all of Malory's tales, love and marriage triumph.

LUNETE AND LAUDINE: POWER THROUGH WORDS

'The Tale of Sir Gareth,' as is well known, shares many characteristics with Chrétien de Troyes's *Yvain* (*Le Chevalier au Lion*). It is likely that *Yvain* was one of Malory's sources for his tale. The most obvious parallel between the two tales is the damsel who assists the hero in his quest and guides him to his lady. Even their names are similar: Lyonet and Lunete. Both share similar characteristics; both use magic and traverse the social boundaries of their worlds. There is also the connection between the two women of the moon and the lion: in an essay on 'The Tale of Sir Gareth,' Bonnie Wheeler points out this similarity and notes that in medieval alchemical treatises, the lion symbolizes the union of the sun and moon.[37] Lyonet (little lion) marries Gaheris. Lunete becomes Gawain's 'amie' [his sweetheart] (*Yvain*, v. 2424); Chrétien describes this union as the 'privé consoil/entre la lune et le soloil' [meeting/that occurred in private/between the moon and the sun] (*Yvain*, vv. 2400–02).[38] And, of course, Yvain's closest companion is the lion he rescues; for much of the tale Lunete and the lion are his only friends.

Lyonet's skill with words is similar to Lunete's, but the latter uses her skill for different purposes. Whereas Lyonet seeks reconciliation only once (between Gareth and Gawain), and for most of the story she encourages physical combat between Gareth and other knights, Lunete does not usually encourage physical combat. Instead she continually seeks to reconcile her lady Laudine to Yvain, using her words skillfully to accomplish what she wants. When she discovers Yvain, the murderer of her lady's husband, in her lady's castle, she hides him so that the people of the town will not kill him. She tells Yvain:

> "Une foiz, a la cort le roi
> m'envoia ma dame an message;
> espoir, si ne fui pas si sage,
> si cortoise, ne de tel estre
> come pucele dëust estre
> me onques chevalier n'i ot
> qu'a moi deignast parler .i. mot

fors vos, tot seul, qui estes ci.
Mes vos, la vostre grant merci,
m'i enorastes et servistes;
de l'enor que vos m'i fëistes
vos randrai ja le guerredon."

[Be assured that, if I am able,
I will render you service and honor,
for you have already done so for me.
Once my lady sent me with a message
to the court of the king;
perhaps I was not as prudent
or courteous or proper
as a maiden should be,
but there was not a knight there
who deigned to speak a single word to me,
except you alone, who stand here now.
But you, to your great credit,
honored and served me there;
for the honor you paid me then
I'll now give you the reward.] (*Yvain*, vv. 1004–15).

Lunete, perhaps previously another Savage Damsel, did not behave the way
the court expects maidens to behave. Yvain, however, was courteous to her,
proving his great nobility and earning Lunete's eternal gratitude. She gives
him a magic ring to keep him hidden while Laudine's people are searching
for him. Then Yvain sees Laudine and falls in love with her. Lunete, who is
grateful for an opportunity to make Yvain happy, agrees to help him win
Laudine.

The narrator says that 'La dameisele estoit si bien / de sa dame, que nule
rien / a dire ne li redotast, a que que la chose montast, / qu'ele estoit sa
mestre et sa garde' [The damsel was in such favor / with her lady, that there
was nothing / she was afraid to tell her, / no matter what it might concern,
/ for she was her advisor and confidante] (*Yvain*, vv. 1593–97). She uses this
position to convince Laudine of the logic of accepting the man who has
killed her husband as her new spouse. First, she reminds Laudine that her
mourning will not bring her husband back, that she can find a better husband,
and Lunete will prove it to her. Then she tells Laudine they have received a
message that King Arthur is coming to Laudine's spring within a week, and
she asks who will defend the spring. She then reminds Laudine that her
knights are all cowards, and not one will step forward to defend the spring.
Laudine angrily forbids her to speak any more of this.

Although Laudine is angry, she soon decides she wants to know who could be a better husband than the one she has just buried. Lunete takes the opportunity to remind her there are hundreds of valorous men. This is all to provoke Laudine, who rises to the bait and tells Lunete to name one. This is the opening Lunete has been waiting for. She points out that the man who defeats another man in combat is the more worthy man. Laudine suspects she is being tricked, but Lunete continues:

> "Par foi, vos pöez bien entandre
> que je m'an vois parmi le voir,
> et si vos pruef par estovoir
> que mialz valut cil que conquist
> vostre seignor, quë il ne fist."

> ["By my faith, you can clearly understand
> that I'm following the line of truth,
> and I am proving to you irrefutably
> that the one who defeated your husband
> is more worthy than he was."] (*Yvain*, vv. 1706–10).

Laudine is furious, and Lunete withdraws again. But Laudine begins to worry about her spring, and soon begins to believe what Lunete has told her. Laudine argues the case within herself much in the same way as Lunete had argued it to her, but imagining the responses to her accusations from the man who defeated her husband. And so she persuades herself that Lunete is right. In other words, Lunete has used rhetoric to trick her mistress into marrying the man she should hate more than any other. And Laudine has enabled her in this task.

Lunete happily sends for Yvain and next gives him advice on how to handle her people so that they will not be shocked that she has remarried so quickly. Laudine gets the people to beg her to marry again immediately because of the threat to their land:

> Et trestuit jusqu'aus piez li vienent;
> de son voloir an grant la tienent;
> si se fet preier de son buen,
> tant que, ausi com maugré suen,
> otroie ce qu'ele fëist
> se chascuns li contredëist.

> [They all fell at her feet,
> urging her to do what she already desired;
> and she let herself be begged to do her wish,
> until, as if it were against her will,

she agreed to what she would have done
even if they had all opposed her.] (*Yvain*, vv. 2111–16).

So Laudine perhaps has learned something from Lunete about manipulating
people through words.

It is in this space that most of Laudine's power lies. She is tied to her space
(much as Lyoness was a prisoner of her space), a country which has the
added burden of a spring that must be defended if they are to survive.
Although she is the lady of the land, she must please her nobles and gain
their approval for her decisions, or she may find herself in trouble. In addition,
as Lunete points out, her nobles are cowardly. Although they greatly fear not
having a defender for the spring, they themselves are afraid to do the job
(*Yvain*, v. 1635). Laudine, on the other hand, because she is a woman, cannot
take up arms to defend the spring even if she were willing; her only real job
is to marry a man who *can* defend the spring. Through the artfulness of
Lunete, Laudine is convinced of the absolute necessity of marrying the man
who killed her husband as he is the best possible defender of the spring. She
must therefore persuade her people that Yvain is the proper husband for her
without incurring their contempt or worse. Again, Lunete steps in, supplying
the means for getting the people to agree to this marriage without seeming
to do so, in fact by seeming to ask for their advice. In her limited area of
wielding power, then, Laudine at least becomes mistress of her words, thanks
to Lunete.

Laudine also possesses a ring, much like Lyoness's, which does not seem
to offer her any particular benefit, but helps the one she gives it to, provided
he follows Laudine's incantation when she lends it:

> "Vos voel dire tot en apert:
> prison ne tient ne sanc ne pert
> nus amanz verais et leax
> ne avenir ne li puet max;
> mes qui porte et chier le tient,
> de s'amie li resovient,
> et si devient plus durs que fers."

> ["...I mean to explain
> to you all about the stone:
> no true and faithful lover, if he wears it,
> can be imprisoned or lose any blood,
> nor can any ill befall him;
> but whoever wears and cherishes it
> will remember his sweetheart,
> and will become stronger than iron."] (*Yvain*, vv. 2607–14).

The magical protective qualities should keep Yvain safe; the rest of the spell should ensure his return within the time deadline Laudine has set. The first part works, the second does not.

Laudine tells Yvain she has never lent anyone this ring. This first-time gift of her only magical talisman raises some interesting issues. Perhaps she gives it to her current husband because he is placing her in a position her first husband never did: he has asked permission to go away and fight in tournaments. Once more Laudine's power is limited to her own will and speech—to her promise that she will never forgive him if he does not return to her by the end of the year. The ring is the symbolic token of this promise. Surely he cannot forget. But he does.

Laudine is humiliated by Yvain's failure to keep his promise. She begins to agree with some in her land who accuse Lunete of treason, since Lunete is the one who persuaded her to marry Yvain. Lunete is sentenced to burn at the stake. Yvain happens to arrive just in time, and, disguised as the Knight with the Lion, he fights three knights and wins. Lunete and Laudine are reconciled. But Yvain will not allow Lunete to reveal his identity to Laudine. When the opportunity comes, though, Lunete again acts as mediator, obtaining a pledge from Laudine. She promises to do her best to effect a reconciliation between the Knight with the Lion and his lady if he saves her spring. Lunete knows that Laudine will be forced to forgive Yvain for breaking his oath. Once more she guides the lovers to a happy reunion through her subtle use of argument.

In another episode, the power of words is again shown to be the better way to resolve conflict in a culture that sanctions violence.[39] In the final section of *Yvain*, a younger sister sought redress against her elder sister at Arthur's court, but the elder sister arrived before her sister and secured the services of Gawain, the best knight of the court. The younger sister tells King Arthur that she would gladly submit to her elder sister out of love, but she refuses to surrender under duress.[40] Her comment on her own situation highlights the fine line between love and force; the younger sister wants to be assured of protection should she relinquish her inheritance. The preferred method for resolving disputes—trial by combat—underscores its inherent problem: it can be used by either the just or the unjust to effect the outcome. In this case, the disguised Gawain and the disguised Yvain (who would never knowingly fight one another) could kill one another, and still the outcome may not be the just one.[41] King Arthur, who could speak and decide the outcome, is caught in a system which requires him to balance a complex hierarchy of powers, including both the knights, the two sisters, and his own power. He resolves the conflict through manipulative language—a method sometimes scorned as a woman's method—thus bringing about justice, keeping the two knights unhurt, and protecting his own position. His manipulation of words takes the place of and is stronger than magic. Both Lunete and Arthur exhibit keen rhetorical ability: through their quick minds and tongues, they make possible the happy and just outcomes in their respective courts—in Arthur's case, between the sisters, and in Lunete's, between Laudine and Yvain. In other words, Chrétien in his tale created an effective model of diplomacy.

The manipulation, or perversion, of language is a facet of Bakhtin's carnival theory. Lunete's and Arthur's manipulative words create the space for acceptable resolutions without resorting to violence, just as Bakhtin argues the rituals and laughter of carnival do. Carnival performances also expose the arbitrariness of power structures, something King Arthur recognizes and respects. Carnival performances incorporate role reversals and disorder; Arthur, Lunete, and Laudine see to it that order is restored through their rhetorical skill.

SOUTHERN METHODIST UNIVERSITY

Melanie McGarrahan Gibson teaches First-Year Rhetoric at Southern Methodist University. She discusses many of these same issues in her graduate thesis, which she completed in 1999. She spends her spare time reading and playing with her two children.

NOTES

1   Sir Thomas Malory, 'The Tale of Sir Gareth of Orkney that was Called Beawmaynes,' in *The Works of Sir Thomas Malory*, ed. Eugène Vinaver, rev. P.J.C. Field, 3d edn., 3 vols. (Oxford: Clarendon Press, 1990), 1:289–363. Subsequent quotations from Malory's work refer to this edition.

2   Bonnie Wheeler, 'The Prowess of Hands: The Psychology of Alchemy in Malory's *Tale of Sir Gareth*,' in *Culture and the King: The Social Implications of the Arthurian Legend*, ed. Martin B. Shichtman and James P. Carley (Binghamton: State University of New York Press, 1993), p. 181.

3   Faith Lyons, 'Malory's *Tale of Sir Gareth* and French Arthurian Tradition,' in *The Changing Face of Arthurian Romance: Essays on Arthurian Prose Romances in memory of Cedric E. Pickford*, ed. Alison Adams, Armel H. Diverres, Karen Stern, and Kenneth Varty (Cambridge: D.S. Brewer, 1986), pp. 137–47.

4   R.W. Hanning, 'Love and Power in the Twelfth Century, with Special Reference to Chrétien de Troyes and Marie de France,' in *The Olde Daunce*, ed. Robert R. Edwards and Stephen Spector (Albany: State Univ. of New York Press, 1991), pp. 87–103.

5 Mikhail Bakhtin, *Rabelais and His World*, trans. Helene Iswolsky (Bloomington: Indiana University Press, 1984), p. 7.

6 Bakhtin, *Rabelais and His World*, p. 18.

7 Bakhtin, *Rabelais and His World*, p. 7. Bakhtin calls this the cycle of 'copulation, pregnancy, birth, growth, old age, disintegration, dismemberment.'

8 C. Clifford Flanigan, 'Liminality, Carnival, and Social Structure: The Case of Late Medieval Biblical Drama,' in *Victor Turner and the Construction of Cultural Criticism: Between Literature and Anthropology*, ed. Kathleen M. Ashley (Bloomington: Indiana University Press, 1990), pp. 54–5. Flanigan says, '[T]he immediate ancestors of [Renaissance] carnival were the popular celebrations which surrounded officially sanctioned ecclesiastical holidays in the late Middle Ages.' Thus for Bakhtin official culture promulgated these days as holidays, but the popular festivities which marked its often raucous celebration had little or nothing to do with the event that was officially commemorated.

9 Flanigan, 'Liminality, Carnival, and Social Structure,' p. 55. Flanigan says Bakhtin focuses on the tension in festival 'between cultural phenomena which are rigidly ideological and cultural phenomena which allow many voices to surface without trying to reconcile or level them.'

10 Flanigan, 'Liminality, Carnival, and Social Structure,' p. 55.

11 Victor W. and Edith Turner, *Image and Pilgrimage in Christian Culture: Anthropological Perspectives*, Lectures on the History of Religions, 11 [n.s.] (New York: Columbia University Press, 1978), p. 2.

12 Turner and Turner, *Image and Pilgrimage*, p. 251.

13 Bakhtin, *Rabelais and His World*, p. 16: 'Abusive expressions are not homogeneous in origin; they had various functions in primitive communication and had in most cases the character of *magic* and *incantations*...These abuses were ambivalent: while humiliating and mortifying they at the same time revived and renewed' (emphasis mine).

14 Malory, 1:293.27.

15 Malory, 1:296.27.

16 Mikhail Bakhtin, *The Bakhtin Reader: Selected Writings of Bakhtin, Medvedev, Voloshinov*, ed. Pam Morris (London: Edward Arnold, 1994), pp. 78–79. Bakhtin calls authoritarian discourses the authoritative word: 'The authoritative word demands that we acknowledge it, that we make it our own; it binds us,...we encounter it with its authority already fused to it...It is, so to speak, *the word of the fathers*. Its authority was already acknowledged in the past (emphasis mine).

17 Malory, 1:303.18-22.

18 Malory, 1:309.19-20.

19 Malory, 1:300.7-8.

20 Malory, 1:301.32-33.

21 Malory, 1:302.28-30.

22 Malory, 1:304.30-31.

23 Malory, 1:312.13-14.

24 Malory, 1:312.29-34.

25 Malory, 1:313.16-17.

26 Malory, 1:304.35-36.

27 Malory, 1:306.34-35.

28 Dhira Mahoney has discussed these comical aspects of the tale and how many of them hinge on class. See Dhira B. Mahoney, 'Malory's *Tale of Gareth* and the Comedy of Class,' in *The Arthurian Yearbook I*, ed. Keith Busby (New York-London: Garland Publishing, Inc., 1991), pp. 165–89.

29 Malory, 1:324.12-14.

30 Malory, 1:334.20-25.

31 Malory, 1:306.29-33.

32 Malory, 1:310.9-11.

33 Malory, 1:325.24-25.

34 Malory, 1:325.30-32.

35 Wheeler, 'The Prowess of Hands,' p. 181.

36 Malory, 1:313.8.

37 Wheeler, 'The Prowess of Hands,' p. 181.

38 Chrétien de Troyes, *The Knight with the Lion, or Yvain* (*Le Chevalier au Lion*), ed. and trans. William W. Kibler (New York–London: Garland Publishing, Inc., 1985). All subsequent in-text references refer to *Yvain*.

39 Hanning, 'Love and Power', p. 90. Hanning argues that the romance puts forward alternatives to the culture of violence of the twelfth century. He points out that Chrétien here condemns force as a means of obtaining justice.

40 Hanning, 'Love and Power,' p. 92.

41 Hanning, 'Love and Power,' p. 92. Hanning argues that Chrétien makes clear verbal wit combined with love can change a system based on trial by combat.

A Bad Girl Will Love You to Death: Excessive Love in the Stanzaic *Morte Arthur* and Malory

JANET KNEPPER

The Stanzaic *Morte Arthur* and Malory's *Le Morte Darthur* demonize the passion and agency of two female characters, the Maid of Ascolot (Stanzaic *Morte*) and Hellawes (Malory) by representing their love as excessive, transgressive, and disruptive. But while female agency and passion are demonized, the knights of the Round Table prove to be implicated in a similar economy of excess and death. (JK)

The discourse of 'fin amor' or courtly love writes love as an ennobling passion for the male lover. When combined with the ideology of chivalry, courtly love (ideally) creates a knight whose passion increases both his virtue and prowess. The discourse of courtly love also casts the male lover as aggressor and an idealized woman as the passive (or defensive) object of desire. In romances or romance episodes that feature Lancelot, however, Lancelot often finds himself the object—or victim—of female desire. This female desire, as is often the case in the Middle Ages, is depicted as transgressive and thus in some way evil; the women who pursue Lancelot are often 'bad girls' who threaten the hero's identity and the adventures on which that identity is based. This paper discusses two 'bad girls' whose excessive love for Lancelot creates an unholy communion of love and death.

The first bad girl I wish to examine is the Stanzaic *Morte Arthur*'s Maid of Ascolot, who suffers from unrequited love for Lancelot. The Maid is described in terms that usually refer to the male courtly lover: she falls in love from excessive looking and meditation on the object of her love. The narrator explains that: 'Mikel Lancelot she beheld'; and that because 'so mikel on him her herte gan helde,' she now spends her time suffering and weeping (ll. 178, 183–84).[1] Interestingly, if the stricken courtly lover is male, the suffering is acceptable. In fact, as Louise Fradenburg points out, suffering underwrites the superior nature of his love: 'The finamen (courtly lover)' not only 'wills his own passion,' but also 'possesses a special body capable of deferral and lack; it can endure, because it so chooses, and its endurance marks…its power of alteration over its own flesh.'[2] In the Maid, however, and in women in general, this passionate loving is seen as excessive. Passion and excess are seen in the Middle Ages as being special vices of womankind. The *Malleus maleficarum*, for example, states that 'it is a natural vice in [women] not to be disciplined, but to follow their own impulses without any sense of what is due.'[3] The Stanzaic *Morte* presents the Maid's infatuation as undisciplined, that is, as excessive, foolish, and histrionic: in the space of eleven lines, the Maid progresses from staring at Lancelot, to weeping constantly, to running to her bedroom and falling on her bed with her heart nearly 'brast in two' (ll. 178–89).

Desire is, according to Alexandre Kojève, the desire to be loved or recognized, and the Maid's histrionic passion is driven by the need to be desired and recognized by Lancelot.[4] The introduction of the Maid in the Stanzaic *Morte* shows her to be marginalized, barely recognized at all, for she is not even given a name. She is simply the earl's daughter; her introduction, 'Th'erl had a doughter that was him dere' (l. 177) places the father, not the daughter, in the subject position. The Maid, this daughter, is not even accorded the full romance *effictio*. Instead, her *effictio* is truncated and dismissive: 'Her rode was red as blossom on brere / Or flowr that springeth in the feld' (l. 179). No blond hair, no shining grey eyes, no skin as white as lily flower—the Maid's *effictio* basically just gives her a red face. Further, this mini-*effictio* is sandwiched between a line about her staring at Lancelot and another about how happy she is to just to sit by him. The Maid's identity is constituted only by her relationship to her father and her excessive desire for Lancelot; the Maid and her passion are both devalued.

The Maid's excessive desire, however, quickly turns her from a foolish girl into a 'bad girl,' for in her determination to be recognized as Lancelot's lover, she connives, manipulates, and lies, successfully interfering with the sign-system of courtly love and causing trouble and shame for both Gawain and Lancelot.

The Maid is an object of pity for Lancelot, and she plays on this pity by first stating her love as a case of life or death: 'Sir, but yif that ye it make, / Save my life no leche may' (ll. 199–200). She then asks that Lancelot wear in the tournament 'some sign of mine that men might see' (ll. 211–12). The Maid seems at this point willing to trade recognition by Lancelot for recognition by the court as a whole: even if Lancelot does not desire her, others will think that he does. Lancelot accedes to her request, and wears her sleeve at the upcoming tournament. She later persuades Lancelot to leave his armor behind, as, she claims, an object of comfort for her love-struck gaze. She wails, 'Sithe I of thee ne may have more, / Some thing ye wolde beleve me here, / To look on when me longeth sore' (ll. 457–59).

Both of these requests cause disruption and confusion in the sign-system of courtly love and chivalric identification. In this culture, certain signs are assigned certain meanings: the color and crest of one's shield signifies identity, and a favor worn by a knight betokens and identifies a lover. Further, the exchange of gifts or tokens traditionally signified that two people were lovers—clearly not the case here—and since Lancelot, as the spectators of the tournament point out, has never worn a favor other than Guenevere's, his fidelity to Guenevere becomes suspect. Lancelot had planned to attend both tournaments in disguise, so it suited his purpose to wear the Maid's sleeve at one and leave his armor behind for the other, but interestingly, the text completely elides any mention of such a motivation on Lancelot's part and instead states that he is simply acceding to her requests out of pity.[5] What we see is the Maid using her Lancelot-armor-collection as 'proof' of a lie, for the Maid tells Gawain that Lancelot has taken her 'for his leman,' and offers to show Gawain Lancelot's armor (ll. 582–83). Gawain looks at this ocular proof (he will know Lancelot's shield by its colors, he says), and verifies the Maid's claim (ll. 592–606). The Maid, depicted as a foolish, besotted young girl, deliberately misuses the signs of courtly culture, and her manipulations and lies cause grief and disruption: Gawain's later report to Guenevere that the Maid is Lancelot's lover causes Guenevere to languish in sorrow and then to send Lancelot away; later, when Gawain's report is found to be untrue, Gawain suffers a thorough public upbraiding and humiliation at Guenevere's hands.

The Maid seems to think that displaying the signs of love will cause Lancelot to love her, or that public acknowledgment of desire will substitute or compensate for Lancelot's lack of desire for her. But the Maid cannot replace or control his desire, so she kills her own desire by dying. Ironically, the Maid achieves both value and recognition through her death, for the next time we see her, she has become an object of value and admiration for the Round Table.

A little boat appears on the river below Camelot. Arthur and Gawain are drawn to the boat; its rich furnishings and shape have captured their attention and their curious gaze, and the narrative action pauses for a lengthy description of the boat: it is covered richly, 'in manner of a vout with clothes ydight / All shinand as gold….' Arthur wonders at the sight of the 'rich apparail' that adorns the boat, and Gawain pronounces, 'This bote is of a rich entail' (ll. 968–73). The scene has the mark of cinematic spectacle, where the narrative action pauses and the camera lingers on a display whose very lavishness creates pleasure.[6] And indeed, important action has been interrupted: Guenevere has been accused of murder and Arthur was busy, until the appearance of the boat, trying to find a knight who would defend her by serving as her champion in a judicial duel. But now Arthur and Gawain are drawn by this scene of visual excess, the business of court forgotten in the wonder at the 'rich apparail' of the boat. And this stasis is foregrounded because it is one of very few in this text; the Stanzaic *Morte* has cut most of its French source's descriptions.

The boat and its rich furnishings are inert objects, seemingly subject here to Arthur and Gawain's curious and controlling gaze; they are invited to penetrate the mystery of the canopied bier, and offer their interpretation of it as the authoritative one. But, as I will argue below, the iconographic valences of the boat—particularly its vault—undermine this control and disrupt masculine interpretative certainty. What appears to be an invitation to penetrate and control turns out to be a seduction with unforeseen consequences.

The boat is a mystery whose meaning and import are not readily apparent. The boat is also described as covered, 'ydight' (adorned or dressed) in 'rich apparail.' That the boat's meaning is not readily accessible and that it is veiled or clothed make the boat an allegorical text to be read and deciphered: the boat/text has an outer layer of meaning that covers the 'true' meaning underneath. The boat's adornment is also a reminder of the association of women with texts to be read and deciphered. Because women in the Middle Ages were associated with deceptive façades, one paradigm for the act of reading in the Middle Ages was the stripping and rape of the female text by the male reader.[7] The act of interpretation is figured as an erotics of control, for interpretation is associated with controlling the semantic instability or 'play' of a text, and this control is figured as a masculine controlling of a female body.[8] The boat with its vault is, as the text makes clear with its *effictio*, one such clothed and adorned body and thus like the adorned female to be stripped and penetrated. Arthur and Gawain seem to be invited to rend the curtain, to penetrate the mystery of the boat, and to read, interpret, and control.

Arthur and Gawain appear to be in control of the reading project and to have the necessary interpretive tools. Arthur in particular shows himself an experienced reader of romance; he recognizes the convention of the well-dressed boat/tent: to Arthur the richly decorated cloth vault can only mean 'adventures.' Arthur's certainty is underscored by having him state twice in one stanza that they will surely find 'aunters' or adventures in the boat (ll.976–83). He would, then, appear to have the authoritative reading of this text, and he and Gawain thus seem to be in control of this romance fantasy.[9]

This masculine control, however, is less fixed and certain than would appear. The significations of the vault suggest that the invitation to penetrate is more of a seduction, and that the vault does contain 'adventures,' but not the sort that Arthur has in mind. The associations of the boat with curiosity, desire, and women make it dangerous and destabilizing.

The vault of cloth functions much like the cinematic veil which conceals the face of a woman in a close-up shot. The veil, by the very fact of concealing, creates a secret and thereby provokes curiosity. That is, the veil creates a secret by seeming to hide one: the covering must cover *something*.[10] Not only, then, does the 'wonder' and richness of the boat attract Arthur and Gawain's gaze. The secret created by the veil or curtain incites their curiosity, arouses their desire to know and to find adventure or pleasure. Curiosity, though, is a form of desire, and desire, whether in the form of curiosity or sexual desire, is inherently destabilizing, because desire in and of itself takes rational control away from the subject.[11] Even though Arthur and Gawain are depicted as agents of action, it is the veiled secret that acts on them, for it provokes and incites. Arthur and Gawain are actually animated by curiosity, the desire to uncover the mystery.[12]

That this mystery is figured as female is suggested not only by connection of women with ornamentation and with veils, but also by the configuration of the vault. The vault is a clothed or curtained structure, and the narrator reports that a cloth, curtain-like, covers the vault to form an entrance. As Michael Camille has shown, the curtain (particularly the parted curtain) was a common trope in medieval art for women's genitalia.[13] The clothed or curtained vault signals the uncanny presence of the 'original home' and invites entrance into the unknown country of the female. But while the vault is inviting, offering a secret to be penetrated, an adventure to be accomplished, the association of the vault with the female also suggests a darker, more sinister side to the secret. Woman, as Hélène Cixous suggests, is still man's great unsolved enigma, man's 'dark continent' and thus an 'adventure' that is never completed, never accomplished.[14] Arthur and Gawain will not find a call to adventure there in the vault; instead, the vault *is* the adventure, and its association with woman signals danger, for if the curtain on the vault suggests women's genitalia, the vault itself is a representation of the womb. While the entrance to the womb invites penetration, it also invites horror, for the womb can signify not just pleasure and safety but also engulfment and death.[15] That the bedecked vault also resembles a shrine further heightens the sense that the men are impinging on the private and the forbidden, perhaps the taboo, thus inviting retribution.

The overtones of fetish that accompany the lavish display of the boat also suggest that this beautiful object of desire has a dangerous underside. The fetish, while offering itself to erotic contemplation, also serves as a diversion and disavowal, a decoration that distracts from, masks, or hides 'ugliness and anxiety with beauty and desire.'[16] In this case, the fetish diverts from, and seems to allow the men to disavow, the corruption at the core of the Round Table. This scene provides a diversion from the issue of Guenevere's trial; it also serves as a 'time-out' from other problems that are bubbling to the surface at Camelot: Lancelot and Guenevere's treasonous adultery and the failure of the sign-system of the chivalric community to contain and control (by rendering legible) Lancelot's adventures in field, forest, or bedroom. Perhaps the most important issue that the fetish covers over is one that is typically associated with it: absence or lack. The Stanzaic *Morte* by this point has begun to reveal that there is no 'center' in Camelot, for Arthur is increasingly depicted as unable—unable to see what is going on around him, unable to prosecute justice, unable to control his 'best knight' or his wife.

But we have left our heroes about to lift the cloth that covers the opening of the vault. What the veil veils and the fetish covers is woman, and that is what Arthur and Gawain find after Gawain lifts the cloth and the two men enter the vault. The text spends several more moments describing the lavish display inside the tent. The knights see, amongst the rich furnishings, a fair bed with 'a dede woman' on it, 'The fairest maid that might be fand' (ll. 998–99). Gawain looks more closely, and pronounces that 'the Maid of Ascolot was she' (l. 1009–11). On the surface, the text presents us with another moment of erotic contemplation with Arthur and Gawain seemingly in control: the Maid displayed on her bed with her 'rich apparail' is totally passive, completely at the mercy of the scrutinizing gaze and the predations of Arthur and Gawain.[17] Dead, the Maid poses no threat—she has no agency that might come into conflict with any knight's agenda, no 'selfish' motives of her own. Dead, she seems simply an exotic and sumptuous object, an object of 'delectation' for the viewer.[18] As Regina Barreca writes, 'death, like adultery, makes women's lives interesting to men because it renders exotic what is otherwise seen as domestic.'[19] Dead, the Maid is both safe *and* intriguing.

If the gaze on the boat's exterior carried sinister undertones, the investigation of the Maid's bier proves to be far more unsettling for readers.

First, this scene is troubling because the Maid is presented as far more beautiful, desirable, and lovable in death than she was in life. Alive, she was a conniving, lying fool who caused all kinds of grief for the heroes of the Round Table. Alive, the Maid was given only a truncated, begrudging *effictio*, but now that she is dead, the text spends many lines on a careful *effictio* of the boat, the corpse, and its accouterments. Dead, floating by on her burial bed, arrayed for scopophilic pleasure, the Maid is looked upon lovingly, almost reverently, by Arthur and Gawain. In fact, it is almost easy to forget that the object of their worshipful desire is a corpse, but it is. And this is the second reason that the scene is troubling: the lingering descriptions of the dead Maid in her array (seen as though through the eyes of Arthur and Gawain) implicate the Round Table in an economy of excess, death, and necrophilia. The text devalues the court even further, however, by portraying Gawain and Arthur as meddling with a corpse. They poke about the bed and her belongings, and Gawain even rifles through her purse: 'Then Sir Gawain, the goode knight, / Sought about her withoute stint / And fand a purse full rich aright' (ll. 1032–34). The men have no respect for the dead, nor any concern for the Maid; instead they are motivated by prying curiosity.

The Maid, bad girl that she is, has the last laugh, however, for even though she seems to have completely elided herself as subject, her disruptive agency does not cease with her death. As discussed above, the Maid's corpse, on display, seems to be the passive object of Arthur and Gawain's violating male gaze. John Berger notes that because women know they are the objects of the male gaze, they turn themselves 'into an object, most particularly an object of vision: a sight.'[20] This displaying of the self, I would argue, denotes agency, and can be put to use by women. That is precisely what the Maid has done. Clearly this trip down the river to Camelot was planned; the Maid knew her lavish and artful display would attract attention, and it does. Arthur and Gawain hurry down to it expecting to find adventures. What do they find? First, a corpse. Second, a letter, an item that seems at first marginal, a trifle. The letter, however, rewrites Arthur's script. Instead of adventures, he finds shame. The letter makes a lengthy formal complaint of a wrong: the Maid asserts that she died because Lancelot, in spite of her prayers and weeping, refused to love her. She charges him with 'churlish manners' and lack of 'gentilness.'[21] In a statement laden with dramatic irony, for Arthur has yet to find out about Lancelot's treasonous adultery, Arthur proclaims that Lancelot 'was greatly to blame' and has won himself reproving 'forever' and wicked fame. 'Sithe she died for grete loving, that he her refused it may him shame' (ll. 1099–1103). The Maid, then, gets the last word. This has been a staged production: she has staged this display of her corpse to get some measure of revenge.

The Maid of Ascolot reappears in Malory's *Le Morte Darthur*, but this time considerably tamed, and the 'bad girl' roles fall to other female characters. One of these bad girls is Hellawes the sorceress and, like the Maid in the Stanzaic *Morte*, she suffers from excessive love, a love to the death, for Lancelot.

Malory's text is loaded with gratuitous violence, a violence that might be characterized, as Marion Wynne-Davies puts it, 'by its proclivity to excess.'[22] Lancelot's encounter with a 'fair damosel' stands out not, however, for its representation of violence, but instead because the love the damsel cherishes for Lancelot is excessive, transgressive, and ultimately disgusting. In this scene, Lancelot has just come from the Chapel Perilous. In the Chapel, he did as he had been instructed by a damsel: he cut away a piece of the silk cloth covering a corpse and took the sword lying next to the corpse. As he hies himself away from the churchyard, the thirty knights who are apparently in residence there tell him to leave the sword. He does not. Lancelot then meets another fair damsel, who twice tells him that if he does not leave the sword he will die. When he refuses, she tells him he made the right choice, for if he had left the sword he would never have seen Guenevere again. The damsel then says, 'Now, jantyll knyghte…I requyre thee to kysse me but onys.' Lancelot refuses. This refusal turns out to be a good thing as well, because, as the damsel confesses, 'and thou haddyst kyssed me thy lyff days had be done.' The damsel then gives a chilling explanation:

> "And, sir Launcelot, now I tell the: I have loved the this seven yere, [but] there may no woman have thy love but quene Guenyver; and sytthen I may not rejoyse the nother thy body on lyve, I had kepte no more joy in this worlde but to have thy body dede. Then wolde I have bawmed hit and sered hit, and so to have kepte hit my lyve dayes; and dayly I sholde have clypped the and kyssed the, dispyte of quene Gwenyvere."[23]

The damsel who offers the kiss of death turns out to be Hellawes the sorceress; she dies within a fortnight.

On the surface, the scene validates Lancelot's heroism by showcasing his bravery and by placing his (masculine) silence and steadfast refusal in contrast to Hellawes's peremptory commands and (womanish) compulsion to confess.[24] The scene also confirms Lancelot's status as object of love and desire. Unfortunately, Hellawes's love is so excessive that she wants to remove him from the economy of desire in the mortal world and, covetously, keep him for herself alone. That the damsel/sorceress would keep Lancelot's dead body on hand signals Lancelot's status as an object of veneration; like the saint's body, Lancelot's body, not subject to decay, is to be worshipped. But that worship is transgressive; it is not appropriate to create a holy relic by killing a man, and handling a corpse as if it were a doll, kissing and 'clipping' it, is taboo and revolting.

Positing Lancelot as an object to be worshiped signals his placement in the realm of the sacred; thus alive he is taboo as well. He is already off limits for Hellawes, since his heart is with Guenevere; Hellawes's fantasy, though, reveals the desire that this double taboo elicits. Lancelot is in some sense sacred—his prowess places him beyond the pale of the other knights; further, for women he is the most desired, but least accessible object. Hellawes's excessive love has made her resolve, in Bataille's words, 'to trespass into a forbidden field of behavior.'[25] Hellawes's is an unholy love, one that unites love with death, or that confounds the sex act with killing; her excessive love creates an erotics of death.

Hellawes's crossing into a forbidden field of behavior is perhaps an attempt by Malory to put the killings by males into 'proper' perspective: necrophilia is far worse, far more disgusting than plain killing. One of the things that makes her love transgressive is that she does not feel the proper sense of fear, disgust, and revulsion at the sight of a corpse. She has instead planned to make love to it. Lancelot, on the other hand, has felt the proper fear of the taboo. When he cut the piece of cloth away from the corpse's covering, he felt as if the earth quaked a little and 'therewithall he feared.'[26] Further, Lancelot's license with the knight's corpse was licensed and necessary: he was ordered by a maiden to fetch that sword to heal her brother.

Hellawes's desired act of love reveals the connection between love, control, and possession. Hellawes cannot control Lancelot's will or desire when he is alive, but dead, he would be all hers—she would even replace his bodily fluids with those supplied by her. Hellawes's reason for inflicting the 'kiss of death' may be, as Bataille puts it, to end her isolation, her sense of discontinuity by uniting herself with Lancelot; she may also want to end the frustration and restlessness created by lack and desire. But, as mentioned above, she had no control over the live Lancelot's body and desire. As Bataille writes, 'If the lover cannot possess the beloved he will sometimes think of killing her; often he would rather kill her than lose her.'[27] But notice the pronouns. Bataille's comments make clear who should be doing the killing and possessing. He writes, 'in the process of dissolution [common to both the sex act and to death] the male partner generally has the active role, while the female partner is passive. The passive, female side is essentially the one that is dissolved as a separate entity.'[28] Therefore, our damsel has not only decided to transgress the bounds of morality and of taboo, but she also desires to transgress the prerogatives of gender, and dissolve Lancelot as a separate (living) entity. She is truly a medieval 'bad girl.'

Hellawes clearly falls into Maureen Fries's category of 'female counter-hero.' First, she exhibits agency, and it is far from the heroine or female hero's selfless agency that supports patriarchal purposes. Second, she 'holds values which are not necessarily those of the male culture in which she must exist'—or does she?[29] That is a question to which I shall return.

As is often the case with women in Arthurian romance, female agency that is seen as working for its own purposes rather than as a helper or tool for the patriarchy is coupled with evil, and with that particularly female evil, excess. Literature on the proper place of women in the Middle Ages abounds.[30] One example, however, is particularly pertinent to my discussion here. Michael Camille, discussing manuscript illustrations that demonstrate the normal copulative position (man on top, oftentimes pinning the woman underneath), explains how important it was that the male partner be the active one in heterosexual coupling. The 'woman on top' was, as Camille puts it, 'viewed with horror by theologians and by medical practitioners.' This reversing of the 'natural' order was such an abomination 'that it caused God to bring the biblical flood (Romans 1:26–27), and its consequences were still thought dire....' Camille reproduces an illumination of David and Bathsheba in bed and one from the prose *Merlin* illustrating the conception of Mordret. In both illuminations, the woman is on top. About David and Bathsheba, Camille notes that 'David is literally effeminized in this sexual position. The active partner is Bathsheba.'[31] The point here is that these couples and couplings are illegitimate, and are products and producers of passion, sin, and evil. What these representations suggest, then, is that the woman on top, in the active position, is associated with excessive passion and with abomination and evil. Hellawes's necrophilia only underscores the disgust with which an active, predatory sexuality on the part of woman was viewed.

As I suggested above, though, Lancelot, particularly as courtly lover, is implicated and tainted by this scene. That Lancelot's robbing of a corpse placed in a chapel is followed immediately by Hellawes's necrophilic plans, suggests that Lancelot's graveyard adventure falls in the category of trangression and taboo as well. But more important, I think, is the connection between dead Lancelot, victim of a kiss, and Lancelot, victim of courtly love. Hellawes's necrophilia, as stated above, reveals the connection between love, possession, and control, and in so doing, points to a major contradiction for the courtly lover: while knightly identity is, as David Aers asserts, associated with being active and predatory,[32] courtly love places him in subjection and submission to 'Love,' and the medieval habit of personifying 'Love' and making 'him' a general, is just a way to mask the fact that the knight submits not only to his desire, but also to a woman. In order to 'win' the lady, that is, the male lover is subject to and controlled by the lady's desires.[33] And as romances repeatedly show, the precepts of chivalry that order the knight to aid maidens and honor their requests, make him subject to the bizarre commands of all maidens. Lancelot, in his subscription to the tenets of chivalry and courtly love, repeatedly places himself in the service of damsels, doing their bidding.[34] Even though Malory attempts to divert the reader from Lancelot's lack of volition by putting him perpetually in action and by presenting a scene that equates lack of volition with untimely death (at the hands of a woman, of course), Lancelot, object of desire, and object of 'Love,' is in some sense already a zombie before he meets Hellawes.

Both *Le Morte Darthur* and the Stanzaic *Morte Arthur* create seeming oppositions between the male hero and the 'bad girl.' The hero is presented as a figure of masculine control, of acceptable aggression, while the bad girl's feminine agency and desire are demonized by being depicted as motivated by undisciplined passion. The bad girls indulge in excess and attempt to disrupt masculine adventure, identity, and social structures. But both texts also taint their knight-heroes; Lancelot in Malory, and Gawain and Arthur in the Stanzaic *Morte* rob graves and meddle with corpses. They are also less in control than they or the text might have us believe: Gawain and Arthur dance to the tune of curiosity, while Lancelot's brush with necrophilia reveals him to be a puppet of courtly love. The hero's adventures are tainted as well: instead of retaining their value and centrality in the text, they are revealed to be mere fetishes, masks or diversions that temporarily distract the hero and the plot from the real problems that plague the Round Table.

CLARION UNIVERSITY, PENNSYLVANIA

Janet Knepper is Instructor of English at Clarion University of Pennsylvania, where she teaches Medieval and Renaissance literature. This essay is part of a project on women and death in medieval narrative.

NOTES

1   The text of the Stanzaic *Morte Arthur* cited parenthetically is in *King Arthur's Death*, ed. Larry D. Benson (Exeter: University of Exeter Press, 1986), pp. 3–111. For medieval 'fin amor,' consult Andreas Capellanus, *The Art of Courtly Love*,

trans. John Jay Parry (New York: Columbia University Press, 1990), p. 28.

2 Louise O. Fradenburg, 'The Love of Thy Neighbor,' in *Constructing Medieval Sexuality*, ed. Karma Lochrie, Peggy McCracken, and James A. Schultz (Minneapolis: University of Minnesota Press, 1997), p. 141 [135–57].

3 Heinrich Kramer, *Malleus Maleficarum* (1487) in *Witchcraft in Europe 1100–1700: A Documentary History*, ed. Alan C. Kors and Edward Peters (1972; rep. Philadelphia: University of Pennsylvania Press, 1986), p. 124 [113–189].Classical, patristic, and medical authorities on womankind's shortcomings find that women's weaker powers of reason make them far more susceptible to being ruled by their passions. See Ian Maclean, *The Renaissance Notion of Woman: A Study in the Fortunes of Scholasticism and Medical Science in European Intellectual Life* (1980; rep. New York: Cambridge University Press, 1988), pp. 15, 41–43. According to Maclean, even some typically female virtues are felt to be the result of passion rather than reason (see pp. 20–21, for example). Women were also, as Natalie Zemon Davis has shown, felt to be 'naturally' lawless and disorderly. See Davis, *Society and Culture in Early Modern France* (Stanford: Stanford University Press, 1975), p. 124.

4 Kojève, as Cynthia Chase explains, defines human desire as the desire for recognition: 'Desire is human only if the one desires, not the body, but the Desire of the other…that is to say, if he wants to be "desired" or "loved," or rather "recognized" in his human value.' See Alexandre Kojève, *Introduction to the Reading of Hegel: Lectures on 'The Phenomenology of Spirit,'* assembled by Raymond Queneau, ed. Allan Bloom (Ithaca: Cornell University Press, 1980), p. 6. Cited by Cynthia Chase, 'Desire and Identification in Lacan and Kristeva,' in *Feminism and Psychoanalysis*, ed. Richard Feldstein and Judith Roof (Ithaca: Cornell University Press, 1989), p. 68 [64–83].

5 After much weeping on the Maid's part, Lancelot is described as visiting the Maid's chamber 'for the Maiden's sake' and speaking 'courtaisly' in order 'to comfort that faire may.' He instructs her to cut off a sleeve for a 'sign' and says, 'I will it take for the love of thee' (ll. 184, 193–214).
   The scene where Lancelot leaves his armor behind is described in similar terms: 'The Maiden wept for sorrow and care,' and then asks that he leave something for her to look at when she 'longeth sore.' Again, Lancelot is described as acting 'For to comfort that lady hende' when he leaves his armor (ll. 555–62).

6 On cinematic spectacle, see Laura Mulvey, *Visual and Other Pleasures* (Bloomington: Indiana University Press, 1989), pp. 16–21.

7 Pertinent here is Carolyn Dinshaw's formulation of the allegorical text as clothed or adorned female body, a text/body that is to be, as Suzanne Klerks puts it 'undressed or unveiled' or 'penetrated' for the truth by the male reader. See Suzanne Klerks,'The Pain of Reading Female Bodies in Marie de France's "Guigemar,"' *Dalhousie French Studies* 33 (1995): 2 [1–14], and Carolyn Dinshaw, *Chaucer's Sexual Poetics* (Madison: University of Wisconsin Press, 1989), pp. 3–51.

8 Robert Hanning discusses how glossing, or exegetical reading, is an attempt to determine and to fix interpretation. See Hanning, "'I Shal Finde It in a Maner

Glose": Versions of Textual Harrassment in Medieval Literature,' in *Medieval Texts and Contemporary Readers*, ed. Laurie A. Finke and Martin B. Shichtman (Ithaca: Cornell University Press, 1987), pp. 28–30 [27–50]. Hanning describes glossing as a 'textual harassment…a forcible imposition of special meanings on single words or entire verbal structures' (p. 27). That the text to be fixed or made stable is female, and that the act of interpretation is, for the male reader, figured as an erotics of control, are points Dinshaw makes in her discussion of Criseyde in *Sexual Poetics*, pp. 28–52.

9 Mulvey writes that 'the split between spectacle and narrative supports the man's role as the active one of advancing the story, making things happen. The man controls the film fantasy….' (*Visual and Other Pleasures*, p. 20).

10 I have borrowed and modified the concept of the veil as theorized by Mary Ann Doane. Doane writes that 'the veil's work would seem to be that of concealing, of hiding a secret,' and that the 'veil functions to hide an absence…and thus to incite desire.' My argument is that the veil, in seeming to conceal something, incites curiosity, and that curiosity is a form of desire. See Mary Ann Doane, 'Veiling over Desire,' in *Feminism and Psychoanalysis*, ed. Richard Feldstein and Judith Roof (Ithaca: Cornell University Press, 1989), p. 110 [105–41].

11 One need only recall Andreas Capellanus's discussion of love, in which he defines love as an excessive desire for the opposite sex. Love begins with the subject in command of the gaze, but control is soon transferred to the object: viewing the object creates desire, and desire takes over from there, leading to longing, suffering, sleeplessness, and illness, the body at the mercy of the passion. This loss of control is figured in the medieval commonplace of Love piercing the man through the eye with an arrow that passes to his heart. Agency clearly lies with 'Love.'

12 Lady Mede's appearance in Langland's *Piers Plowman* illustrates most clearly the power of the beautiful and intriguing object. When the dreamer turns to look at her, he reports, 'Hire array me ravysshed, swich richesse saugh I nevere. / I hadde wonder what she was…' (B.2.17–18). See A.V.C. Schmidt, ed., *William Langland: The Vision of Piers Plowman* (London: J.M. Dent & Sons Ltd., 1978), p. 17. See also Maclean, *Renaissance Notion*, p. 17.

13 Michael Camille, 'Manuscript Illumination and the Art of Copulation,' in *Constructing Medieval Sexuality*, p. 69 [58–90].

14 Hélène Cixous, 'The Laugh of the Medusa,' trans. Keith Cohen and Paula Cohen, in *The Signs Reader: Women, Gender and Scholarship*, ed. Elizabeth Abel and Emily K. Abel (Chicago: University of Chicago Press, 1983), pp. 280, 282, 289 [279–97]. See also Mary Jacobus, *Reading Woman: Essays in Feminist Criticism* (New York: Columbia University Press, 1986), p. 115, and Sarah Kofman, *The Enigma of Woman: Woman in Freud's Writings*, trans. Catherine Porter (Ithaca: Cornell University Press, 1985), pp. 39, 101–5.

15 On the fear of the womb as a place of engulfment, suffocation, and death, see Janet Adelman, *Suffocating Mothers: Fantasies of Maternal Origin in Shakespeare's Plays*, Hamlet *to* The Tempest (New York: Routledge, 1992), pp. 3–4. See also Jacobus, *Reading Woman*, pp. 115–16.

16 Laura Mulvey, *Fetishism and Curiosity* (Bloomington: Indiana University Press, 1996), pp. 4–6.

17 Mulvey writes that woman as spectacle '[freezes] the flow of action in moments of erotic contemplation' (*Visual and Other Pleasures*, p. 19). Rosalind Coward writes that 'the ability to scrutinize is premised on power. Indeed the look confers power; women's inability to return such a critical and aggressive look is a sign of subordination, of being the recipients of another's assessments.' See Coward, *Female Desire* (St. Albans: Paladin Press, 1985), p. 75. To David Aers '"masculine identity"' is 'active, free, predatory' and 'dependent on the simultaneous construction of "feminine" identity as passive, powerless object.' See Aers, *Community, Gender and Individual Identity. English Writing 1360–1430* (London: Routledge, 1988), p. 120.

18 On the woman displayed as an object of 'delectation,' see A.C. Spearing, *The Medieval Poet as Voyeur: Looking and Listening in Medieval Love-Narratives* (New York: Cambridge University Press, 1993), p. 46.

19 Regina Barreca, 'Writing as Voodoo: Sorcery, Hysteria, and Art,' in *Death and Representation*, ed. Sarah Webster Goodwin and Elisabeth Bronfen (Baltimore: The Johns Hopkins University Press), p. 175 [174–91].

20 As Berger puts it, 'women watch themselves being looked at' that is, they look at themselves (and at other women) to a certain extent through the male gaze. Berger's conclusion is that the woman 'turns herself into an object, and most particularly an object of vision: a sight.' John Berger, *Ways of Seeing* (London: BBC and Penguin, 1972), pp. 46–47.

21 The text emphasizes the charges and the wrong by having the Maid mention Lancelot's 'churlish manners' twice; she also asserts that there is no one 'so unhende of thewes' as Lancelot (ll. 1072–95).

22 Marion Wynne-Davies, *Women and Arthurian Literature: Seizing the Sword* (New York: St. Martin's Press, 1996), p. 60.

23 Sir Thomas Malory, *The Works of Sir Thomas Malory*, ed. Eugène Vinaver, rev. P.J.C. Field, 3d edn., 3 vols. (Oxford: Clarendon Press, 1990), 1:281.3–20. Subsequent quotations from Malory's work refer to this text.

24 The subtext of misogyny, which draws a binary opposition between male virtues and female vices, is at work here. In the misogynist's view, men use language judiciously and are stable and steadfast; women, on the other hand, are unstable and garrulous. On the female as the opposite or negative of the male, see Maclean, *Renaissance Notion*, pp. 8–9, 30–34, 40–42. On female garrulity, see Maclean, *Renaissance Notion*, p. 16; R. Howard Bloch, *Medieval Misogyny and the Invention of Western Romantic Love* (Chicago: University of Chicago Press, 1991), pp. 14–16, and Lee Patterson, *Chaucer and the Subject of History* (Madison: University of Wisconsin Press, 1991), p. 290.

25 Georges Bataille, *Erotism: Death and Sensuality*, trans. Mary Dalwood (San Francisco: City Lights Books, 1986; rep. of *Death and Sensuality: a Study of Eroticism and the Taboo*, New York: Walker and Company, 1962), p. 79. Bataille also explains that the taboo excites awe, fear, disgust, and desire, and that the

barrier of the taboo invites transgression (pp. 37–48, 66–67).
26 Malory 1:280.22.
27 Bataille, *Erotism*, p. 20.
28 Bataille, *Erotism*, p. 15.
29 Maureen Fries, 'Female Heroes, Heroines, and Counter-Heroes: Images of Women in Arthurian Tradition,' in *Arthurian Women: A Casebook*, ed. Thelma Fenster (New York: Garland Press, 1996), p. 68 [59–73] (rep. from *Popular Arthurian Traditions*, ed. Sally K. Slocum [Bowling Green, OH: Bowling Green State University, Popular Press, 1992], pp. 5–17).
30 For a discussion of women's conduct, see Margaret Hallissy, *Clean Maids, True Wives, and Steadfast Widows: Chaucer's Women and Medieval Codes of Conduct* (Westport, CT: Greenwood Press, 1993), chapter 2 (pp. 9–24).
31 Camille, 'Manuscript Illumination,' pp. 77–78, 75.
32 Aers, *Community*, p. 120.
33 See Capellanus, *Art*, pp. 28–32.
34 In fact, one wonders if perhaps Lancelot would have dropped the sword at Hellawes's request, had he not been commanded by another woman to fetch that sword for her.

Malory's Lancelot
and the Lady Huntress

Lancelot's encounter with a lady huntress near the end of *Le Morte Darthur* reveals fissures in his chivalric identity, and in Malory's nostalgic ideology. (MBM)

> It is not uncommon for large parts of a novel to go virtually unread; the less manifest portions of its text (its secrets) remain secret, resisting all but abnormally attentive scrutiny... (Frank Kermode, 'Secrets and Narrative Sequence,' in *On Narrative*).

Malory's *Le Morte Darthur* is not a novel, although there is a powerful temptation to see it as looking forward to that undeniably modern form from the older genres of romance and chronicle. Nevertheless, few narratives guard their secrets more jealously or have gone more consistently 'unread' in Kermode's sense of the word. Indeed, the vast bulk of Malory studies until very recently has consisted of source criticism—arguments about which French texts Malory was 'translating,' whether he also used English material, whether there is such a thing as originality in Malory. Source criticism is an essential component of what medievalists do; all too often, however, it has the unfortunate side effect of foreclosing the very possibility of the kind of close reading which forces a text to reveal its secrets, or at the very least, to demonstrate that it has secrets which it intends to keep. In this essay, I will attempt an 'abnormally attentive' reading of a passage from 'The Book of Lancelot and Guenevere' which has gone 'virtually unread.' I will glance briefly at its possible sources, but only in order to emphasize the very curious nature of the episode in which Lancelot gets shot in the buttocks by a lady huntress. I am interested less in where this episode came from than in what it betrays about Malory's attitude towards a series of bodies: the corpus of Arthurian tales that he calls the 'Freynshhe booke,' the body of his hero Sir Lancelot, and the disturbing and dangerous bodies of the women who inhabit and threaten the masculine world of chivalry.

The episode in question begins at a point when Lancelot has left the court with his companion Sir Lavayne in order to rest up for a great tournament at which he has promised to wear, for the first time, the Queen's favor. The two knights lodge with a hermit in the forest, and every afternoon Lancelot rests in the woods by a fountain. One day, he suffers an accident:

> So at that tyme there was a lady that dwelled in that foreyste, and she was a grete huntresse, and dayly she used to hunte. And ever she bare her bowe with her and no men wente never with her but allwayes women, and they were all shooters and cowde well kylle a dere at the stalke and at the trest...the lady, the huntresse, had abated her dogge for the bowghe at a barayne hynde and so [this barayne hynde] toke the flyghte over hethys and woodis....And so hit happed the hynde came to the same welle thereas sir Launcelot was by that welle slepynge and slumberynge. And so the hynde, whan he came to the welle, for heete she wente to soyle and there she lay a grete whyle. And the dogge came after and unbecast aboute, for she had lost the verray parfyte fewte of the hynde. Ryghte so cam that lady, the hunteres, that knew by thy dogge that the hynde was at the soyle by that welle, and thyder she cam streyte and founde the hynde. And anone as she had spyed hym she put a brode arow in her bowe and shot at the hynde, and so she overshotte the hynde, and so by myssefortune the arrow smote sir Launcelot in the thycke of the buttok over the barbys.[1]

For some reason, few critics have paid any attention at all to this misadventure. The omission is even stranger since the last two books of *Le Morte Darthur*—'The Book of Launcelot and Guenevere' and 'The Most Piteous Tale of the Morte Arthur Saunz Guerdon'—are universally acknowledged to be Malory's finest creations, and have thus been the recipients of more critical ink than any other part of his work. Most of the attention, however, has been focused on how Malory reordered the events of the story as he inherited it from his sources. He does this, according to many, to increase the elegiac quality of the ending by emphasizing the death of Gareth, a minor figure in the French tradition but a major one in Malory. Another, not exclusive, possibility, is that Malory, as a secularizing writer, is working to redeem the figure of Lancelot: redemption was necessary because in the Cistercian tradition of the *Queste del Saint Graal*, the failure of the 'best knight in the world' was the whole point, intended to turn the minds of readers away from this world altogether and towards the spiritual realm. Both of these effects are without a doubt intentional on Malory's part. To concentrate exclusively on such effects, however, is to be seduced by what Kermode calls 'narrative sequence'—causality, intelligibility, tradition, plot.[2]

Vinaver's three-volume critical edition suggests two possible French sources for this episode, although it occurs in a chapter ('The Great Tournament') which he admits has no precise parallel in the Vulgate Cycle. In the first possible source (*La Mort le Roi Artu*), Lancelot falls asleep by a fountain, unaware that the King's huntsmen are in the woods; the stag goes to ground near the sleeping knight and is pursued by 'un archiers qui estoit montez seur un grant destrier' [an archer mounted on a great war horse] who shoots Lancelot by accident through the left thigh [*parmi la cuisse senestre*]. Feeling himself struck, Lancelot seizes his sword and tries to attack the huntsman, who flees in abject terror.[3] In the second possible source, the Prose *Lancelot*, another knight tells Lancelot the story of how he, pursuing a wounded opponent, stumbled upon two beautiful young women bathing; one of them shoots him 'parmi la cuisse' [through the thigh]; he faints and is told upon waking (by a third beautiful and mysterious maiden passing by) that he can only be healed by the best knight in the world. He stubbornly fails to recognize Lancelot as the best knight in the world, and is forced to spend the next sixty pages or so jouncing around the countryside in a litter, trying to catch up with the famous knight errant.

Before returning to Malory's passage, I would like to note just a few ways in which plot elements of these two proposed sources have entirely different implications from those of Malory's text. The accident in *La Mort le Roi Artu* occurs right before Lancelot returns to Camelot in order to fight on Guenevere's behalf when she has been accused of poisoning an innocent knight; this is the moment when Arthur is forced into the most impossible of situations, that of either watching his wife burn at the stake or watching her lover rescue her. The fact that it is an agent of Arthur's who shoots Lancelot at this moment can be read as a manifestation of Arthur's own well-repressed anger at his best knight and best friend, and in fact Lancelot himself seems to interpret the incident in this way. When asked who has injured him, he replies that all he knows is that it was someone from Arthur's household.[4] The Prose *Lancelot* episode is also markedly different from Malory's (and not just because in the French text it is not Lancelot himself who is wounded); again, the primary difference is one of agency: the knight is in some sense responsible for what happens to him; he unchivalrously pursues a wounded opponent, and he bursts in rudely upon the naked maidens. He is not, like Malory's Lancelot, the entirely passive victim of mysterious forces.

In *Le Morte Darthur*, not only is the archer female, but so are most of the other participants in the scene—or are they? The fundamental gender switch, from the King's huntsman to a lady huntress, is echoed by other, more subtle confusions. In Malory's text, the intended prey is not a stag, as it is in the French, but a 'barren hind.'[5] Even more curiously, Malory's pronouns are radically unstable. The hynde is he and she in the space of a single sentence: 'when he cam to the welle, for heete she wente to soyle.' The dog too is called 'she.' Vinaver explains the apparent confusion as to the hynde's gender by reference to the fluidity of Middle English forms of the feminine nominative: 'he' can mean 'she' by derivation from the Old English *heo*; Vinaver points out other instances in the later books *of Le Morte Darthur* where women are identified with the pronoun 'he.' Another explanation would, of course, be scribal error: an *s* was lost in the copying of the manuscript, turning *she* to *he*. More problematic, however, is the occurrence of the pronoun 'hym' a few lines later: '...thyder she cam streyte and founde the hynde. And anone as she had spyed hym she put a brode arow in her bowe and shot at the hynde, and so she overshotte the hynde, and so by myssefortune the arrow smote sir Launcelot....' The grammar of Middle English simply does not allow for the substitution of the feminine objective pronoun *hire* with the masculine *hym*. Nor is it so easy to imagine a scribal error in this sentence since to do so would require the miswriting of not one but two letters. Either the hynde has changed its sex or the lady spies not the hynde but Sir Lancelot, and shoots him accidentally on purpose. Her response to his reproach also suggests that she is less than entirely innocent: '"Now, mercy, fayre sir!" seyde the lady, "I am a jantillwoman that usyth here in thys foreyste huntynge, and god knowyth I saw you nat but as here was a barayne hynde at the soyle in thys welle. And I wente that I had done welle, but my hande swarved."'[6] It is a rather casual excuse, given that Lancelot's wound is not only embarrassing (more embarrassing than his wounding in the French texts since a buttock is not a thigh) but 'six inchys depe and inlyke longe.'[7]

The possibility that the shooting of Sir Lancelot is intentional is never more than implied; it is reinforced, however, by the fact that the lady does not operate alone. Rather, she is the leader of an entire hunting party of women, which invites us to see her as a sort of Diana figure, hostile to men in general. The world of *Le Morte Darthur* is in fact populated by a consortium of otherworldly women who exist outside of the boundaries limiting the agency of courtly ladies, wives, and lovers of knights. They appear regularly but almost always inexplicably in the forests, in places where 'decent' women clearly should not be, and they weaken the argument of critics like Andrew Lynch, who maintains that 'Malory's women...are denied the field except as spectators.'[8] Lynch insists, in an article which is otherwise very persuasive, but which overlooks the existence of this lady huntress, that women in Malory are denied 'dedys full actuall,' that is to say the self-expression through combat which is the primary mode of signification for knights; ladies must therefore resort to other forms of activity, especially treachery, poison, and magic.

Hunting, however, should be added to this list, although it is a curiously marginal activity. It is more active and aggressive than those deeds Lynch notes, falling somewhere between combat and treachery, and not exclusive to women. Archers were condemned by the Second Lateran Council and often thought of as wild men living on the fringes of society and engaged in an inherently devious form of military activity. Beverly Kennedy notes that Malory 'never portrays Sir Lancelot as a hunter' except when 'he is, quite literally, out of his mind.'[9] Kennedy goes on to argue that while hunting was certainly popular among the upper classes in fifteenth-century England, it was also considered to have a limited value for knights. Sir Gilbert Hay, a Scottish contemporary of Malory's who wrote a handbook of knightly behavior, considered hunting to be a useful training ground for young knights, but also a potential distraction that might divert the adult knight from his duty to the order of knighthood: 'Hay leaves little doubt that he would expect a "veray" knight never to indulge in such frivolity,'[10] and Malory's Lancelot is certainly a 'veray' knight. The lady huntress's occupation thus marks her as an active threat to true knighthood.

Her gender, of course, marks her even more clearly as dangerous. Women are consistently represented in *Le Morte Darthur* as the greatest threat to chivalry. In 'The Noble Tale of Sir Launcelot du Lake,' which shows us a sort of pre-lapsarian hero not yet tainted by adultery and still an irreproachable admirer of the queen, Lancelot is constantly threatened by wicked women. Early in the book, he falls asleep under an apple-tree, where 'four queenys of a grete astate,'[11] one of whom is Morgan le Fay, find and kidnap him in order to force him to take one of them as a lover. Lancelot is able to escape with the help of King Bagdemagus's daughter, an eminent example of the 'safe' woman in Malory, nameless, docile, and defined exclusively through her relationship to her father. Later on, Lancelot encounters another dangerous and magical lady, the sorceress Hallewes of the castle Nygurmous, whose passion for him proves to be necrophiliac in nature. Even less clearly magical women are dangerous; the wife of Sir Phelot convinces Lancelot to take off his armor and climb a tree in order that he be vulnerable to attack by her cowardly husband. It is no wonder that the Lancelot of 'The Noble Tale' pronounces the following credo:

> Knyghtes that ben adventures sholde nat be advoutreres nother lecherous, for than they be nat happy nother fortunate unto the werrys; for other they shall be overcom with a sympler knyght than they be hemmself, other ellys they shall sle by unhappe and hir cursednese bettir men than they be hemself. And so who that usyth peramours shall be unhappy, and all thynge unhappy that is aboute them.[12]

Ironically, the Lancelot of 'The Book of Lancelot and Guenevere' has become precisely what he preached against. He is not fortunate in the wars; he has been, during the Grail Quest, overcome by a simpler knight than himself—his own son, Galahad—and he will, very soon, slay by mischance and cursedness (in an incident directly provoked by the adultery plot) a better man, the knight he loves more than any other, Sir Gareth. Many critics before me, including Maureen Fries, have noted just how hard Malory works to confuse the issue of whether or not the relationship between Lancelot and Guenevere has been consummated, with his extraordinary renunciation of authorial omniscience in the very last book: 'For as the Freynshhe booke seyth, the quene and sir Launcelot were togydirs. And whether they were abed other at other maner of disportis, me lyste nat thereof make no mencion, for love that tyme was nat as love ys nawadayes.'[13] The fulfillment of Lancelot's own prophecy, however, gives the answer Malory cannot stand to give: the best knight in the world has become an adulterer and a lecher, and suffers accordingly. It is as though the author himself cannot bear the fate that the narrative imperative has reserved for his beloved hero, and so distances himself from it in any way possible. The lady huntress thus comes to seem like an agent of the punishment the author knows he must inflict, but cannot bear to inflict in his own authorial and authoritative persona.

At this point, we might do well to take a different kind of look at the 'Freynshhe booke' that Malory was using. I have argued that the narratives of the Vulgate Cycle do not provide adequate explanation for the infliction of Lancelot's humiliating wound. There is, however, more to a book than its narrative. The marginalia of the manuscripts of the Cycle are aswarm with archers firing arrows at inappropriate targets. In *Image on the Edge*, art historian Michael Camille provides several examples of marginal drawings, including one from the Prose *Lancelot,* in which knights are shot not 'parmi la cuisse' but much more explicitly in the buttocks. According to Camille, 'arrows [may] be seen as metaphors for God's punishment of sinners, where the victims are monsters or monkeys…but arrows are also signs of evil doers.'[14] In Malory's text, the arrow is functioning both ways at once; the lady is an evil doer ('the devill made you a shoter,'[15] Lancelot reproaches her) but Lancelot is a sinner, an adulterer, being punished by a woman who comes as close as never mind to castrating him for his sexual transgression.

At this point it may begin to sound as though the 'secret' I am pointing at in this passage is Malory's misogyny, but that would hardly be much of a revelation. Malory's *Le Morte Darthur* is clearly among the most misogynist of the major texts of the Arthurian corpus. Malory's Guenevere is significantly more bad-tempered and unreasonable than any of her foremothers, and Elayne is an embarrassment and an annoyance in Malory's text. While the *Mort Artu* allows Lancelot to treat her with a degree of courtesy, Malory makes it clear that her attentions are unwanted if not positively annoying: 'thys damesell Elayne was ever aboute sir Launcelot all the whyle she might be suffirde.'[16] Lancelot even complains rather churlishly of her nursing to his cousin Bors. "'But sir, ys thys she," seyde sir Bors, "that ys so busy aboute you, that men calle the Fayre Maydyn of Astolat?" "Forsoothe, she hit ys," seyde sir Launcelot, "that by no meany[s] I cannat put her fro me!"'[17] Bors is mildly shocked by this, but one suspects that Malory feels as Lancelot does; his Elayne, in contrast to her French counterparts and the Elaine of the Stanzaic *Morte Arthur*, is unpleasantly vocal, almost shrewish: she 'rebukes'[18] knights, she 'shryke[s] shirly' and makes 'overmuche sorrow' when Lancelot refuses to marry her,[19] and she even argues with her priest on her deathbed.

More significantly, Elayne's love for Lancelot, represented by Malory as both annoying and inappropriate, reveals by contrast what ought to be the only kind of truly appropriate love: that of one knight for another. Sir Barnard, Elayne's father, drops a serious hint to Lancelot that he ought to make Elayne an honest woman: 'I cannat se but that my doughtir woll dye for your sake.'[20] Lancelot appeals to Elayne's brother, Lavayne, to uphold his contention that he never encouraged Elayne in any way, and Lavayne rises to the occasion: 'I dare make good she ys a clene maydyn as for my lorde sir Launcelot; but she doth as I do, for sythen I saw first my lorde sir Launcelot I cowde never departe frome hym, nother nought I woll, and I may folow hym.'[21] This declaration veers dangerously close to the homoerotic rather than the homosocial considering that the last offer Elayne made to Lancelot was that she should become his paramour if he will not have her as his wife. Lavayne's determination to follow Lancelot is thus virtually inseparable ('but she doth as I do') from Elayne's determination to sleep with him.

Nor is this the only place in the narrative where the idealized homosocial bond is shadowed by the specter of the homoerotic. If we cast a glance back once again to 'The Noble Tale of Sir Lancelot du Lake,' we find the clearest indication of the way the two categories can slide together. Exhausted from a long day of adventuring, Lancelot happens on an empty pavilion pitched in the forest and decides to sleep there. He disarms himself and falls wearily into bed and is sleeping soundly when the rightful occupant arrives:

> Than within an owre there com that knyght that ought the pavylyon. He wente that his lemman had layne in that bed, and so he leyde hym adowne by sir Launcelot and toke hym in his armys and began to kysse hym. And whan

sir Launcelot felte a rough berde kyssyng hym he sterte oute of the bedde
lyghtly, and the other knyght after hym. And eythir of hem gate their swerdys
in their hondis, and oute at the pavylyon dore wente the knyght of the pavylyon,
and sir Launcelot folowed hym.[22]

In an article entitled 'Malory's Body Chivalric,' Kathleen Coyne Kelly
argues that what is happening here is that the erotic impulse aroused when
the sleeping Lancelot becomes the object of the gaze of the four queens is
spilling over into a much more problematic context. In a system in which
the gaze itself is always masculinized and its object feminized, she asks, what
happens when the object of the male gaze is the male body? Having become
feminized by Sir Belleus' mistaken amorous advances, Lancelot must
reconstitute his knightly identity by feminizing Sir Belleus in his turn, by
penetrating him with a sword, in order to avert the threatened homoerotic
and feminizing sexual penetration.[23] However, Sir Lavayne's declaration
enunciates an even more problematic version of the same uncomfortably
revealing situation. Elayne is a woman; it is not only understandable, it is
inevitable that she should fall in love with Sir Lancelot, since almost any
woman who lays eyes on him does. But this very laying on of eyes feminizes
its object within the universe of courtly love, and when the lover is a man
(Sir Lavayne) the implicit feminization of the beloved is even more strongly
felt. Thus, by confessing his love in words that seem to feminize himself, to
make him like his sister, Lavayne paradoxically succeeds in feminizing the
object of his love, Sir Lancelot, as well. In the case of Sir Belleus, the situation
can be rectified by combat: the two knights encounter each other first in the
feminine confines of a bed, stripped of their armor and thus their knightly
identity. By resuming their arms and fighting almost to the death, they are
able to reinstate an appropriately masculine, armored identity. Once they
have convinced themselves that they are both good knights but that Sir
Lancelot is the better, they become firm friends and allies.

Sir Lavayne's declaration is more insidious, because it occurs after Lancelot
and he have become brothers in arms; the homoerotic cannot thus be laid to
rest by combat since to do so would shatter the homosocial bond between
the two men. So Lavayne and Lancelot ride off to Camelot, the Fair Maid of
Astolat dies, her body floats down the river, following them; immediately
afterwards, Lancelot retires to the woods and it is here that the erotic impulse
of Lavayne's confession overflows into violence and humiliation, when
Lancelot feels himself shot in the buttock: 'he whorled up woodly and saw
the lady that had smytten hym. *And whan he knew she was a woman* he sayde
thus: "lady, or damesell, whatsomever ye be, in an evyll tyme bare ye thys

bowe.'"[24] Because his assailant is female, the Lancelot of *Le Morte Darthur* is denied the satisfaction of the Lancelot of *La Mort le Roi Artu*, who terrifies the King's huntsman and only fails to kill him because the huntsman is well mounted and the knight is on foot. Malory's Lancelot, on the other hand, has suffered the ultimate humiliation. Being revealed as defenseless before a male gaze is bad enough, but it can be rectified through combat. Being shot in the posterior by a woman is irredeemable. Lancelot cannot fight her without destroying his own chivalric identity; to do so would make him into the worst kind of recreant, the kind he himself has so often reviled as a shame to the Order of Knighthood, a man who 'dystressis ladyes and jantlewoman,'[25] a traitor like the cowardly Sir Pedyvere who 'swaps' off his wife's head in a memorable moment in 'The Noble Tale.'[26]

Again, it may seem that the 'secret' I am pointing at is not much of one. It has become a commonplace to argue that the world of chivalry is one energized by explicit homosocial and implicit homoerotic currents. Something more complicated, however, is at issue in the encounter with the lady huntress. If violence is what happens in *Le Morte Darthur* when one man becomes the object of another's eroticized gaze, it becomes necessary to ask who is controlling the gaze in this passage. The arrow of the lady huntress performs the same directive function as the arrows in marginal illustrations; it draws the gaze of the reader to Lancelot's humiliation, to a humiliation that appears to be occurring at precisely the wrong moment: at the beginning of a chapter which will end in yet another triumphant tournament, in the middle of a book which will lead up to Lancelot's one true miracle, the healing of Sir Urry, which Malory invents to allow his hero at least partial redemption from the shame of the Grail Quest. Critics overlook the incident because they don't want to see it, just as art historians for years overlooked Camille's marginalia in favor of the miniatures whose meaning the marginalia seem so often to criticize or subvert. For Camille, the marginalia represent the return of the repressed, the only place in the manuscripts of the courtly tradition where we can see 'the class code in crisis, as cowardly knights flee from snails and get it from behind, their nobility usurped, sodomized, by inferiors in the social order.'[27] The very same artist who produces the heroic figures of the miniatures also parodies them in the margins. In the episode of the lady huntress we can see a similar return of the repressed in Malory; here we can see, suddenly and graphically, the author turning against the hero whom he elsewhere seems to idolize. I suggested above that the lady's profession of innocence is disingenuous, that she may have seen Sir Lancelot—hym—perfectly clearly and not mistaken him for the hynde. What seems equally possible is that Malory allows himself to entertain here, just for a moment, a much more ridiculous and much more disturbing possibility: that a knight, and not just any knight but Sir Lancelot himself, may not in the final analysis be distinguishable from a barren hynde. The arrow parodies the amorous gaze, the kind of look which causes pain to Palamon in the 'Knight's Tale' when he first sees Emelye, or to Troilus when he first sees Criseyde, turning it here against a masculine object in a way that is both a feminization and a violation. What we witness in this episode is a sudden eruption of scorn and disgust on the part of the author for his deeply beloved subject.

This reading inevitably raises the question of just what Lancelot means to Malory. How is Malory's investment in his hero different from that of the authors of the Vulgate Cycle? As I suggested above, for the Cistercian or Cistercian-influenced author of the *Queste del Saint Graal*, it is absolutely essential that Lancelot fail in the Grail quest. Martin Shichtman takes us a step further, proposing that the *Queste* 'reflects Cisctercian skepticism about the knightly classes as well as the monastic order's struggles to define the parameters of a network with members of these classes.'[28] According to Shichtman, the *Queste* proposes to instruct knights, both within and outside the text, on the truly important things in life: spiritual things. Malory's text, on the other hand, emphasizes precisely how difficult it is to determine what *is* truly important; as Shichtman puts it, 'the *Tale of the Sankgreal*…suggests that meaning and stability may not be accessible at any price, and that truth is never absolute.'[29] I am less convinced than Shichtman appears to be that Malory is fully in control of the confusion he conveys; still, I am inclined to agree with his assessment of that confusion as emanating from Malory's role in the political events of his day.

Most of those interested in establishing a biography for the author of *Le Morte Darthur*, who tells us of himself only that he was once a 'knyght presoner'[30] and that he finished his book in 'the ninth yere of the reyngne of Kyng Edward the Fourth,'[31] would like him to have been imprisoned unjustly for noble political reasons, for taking one side or the other in the Wars of the Roses. Sir Thomas Malory of Newbold Revel, however, who is the most likely candidate for our author, was imprisoned repeatedly for much less high-minded crimes. His life records have been published in full, and they reveal a wonderfully complicated man, who was imprisoned for cattle stealing, horse stealing, raiding an abbey, ambush and attempted murder, and rape twice upon the person of the same lady. He was also a Member of Parliament, and a turncoat during the Wars of the Roses. Plenty of admirers of *Le Morte*

Darthur have found this fellow a completely inappropriate author for the 'noble' tale of king Arthur and his knights, and even Vinaver austerely announced that what is known of his life 'does not contribute much to the understanding of his character.'[32] On the contrary, it seems to me that there is no one more likely to have written this particular version of the Arthurian tale—with its rejection of the spiritual values of the *Queste del Saint Graal,* its romanticization of the secular order of knighthood, and its idolization of Sir Lancelot (the best knight in the world)—than a man whose own career looks remarkably like that of a misguided knight errant, riding around the countryside, attacking other knights for no apparent reason, carrying off women, and behaving in short very much like Tristan or Lancelot himself.

It is tempting to see Thomas Malory as an anachronism rather in the style of Bernard Goetz, a man whose personal code of morality was simply hopelessly out of step with the times he inhabited. By 1470, when an old man in prison was writing *Le Morte Darthur,* the 'verray' order of knighthood was quickly being rendered redundant by new modes of warfare that would give the real power in battle first to infantry and then to artillery, and by the increasingly Machiavellian politics of the age. Malory, I think, loved Sir Lancelot, not exactly as Sir Lavayne does within the story, but because Lancelot was the model embodying what a true knight should be, what the author himself wanted to be. Lancelot, however, is not Malory's creation but part of a long tradition, encumbered by a narrative from which Malory could not free him. The adultery plot, which Malory tries so hard to undo, to work against—love was not then as love is now—was an insurmountable obstacle. It is there, it is part of the story, but Malory hates it, and hates what it does to his hero. True knights should not be adulterers, they should not have paramours. For Malory, who has fallen as thoroughly in love with Lancelot as everyone else in *Le Morte Darthur* does, from Guenevere to King Bagdemagus's daughter to Gareth to Sir Belleus, Lancelot's inevitable fall because of his love affair with the queen is not just a moral lapse or lesson; it is a personal betrayal. Therefore, what the attack by the lady huntress reveals, finally, is the erotic charge of the gaze the author casts upon his hero. That dangerous gaze, reflecting back and forth between Sir Lancelot and Sir Thomas Malory, disrupts the relationship between the text and its source narratives. It requires the humiliation of the hero in order to save the chivalric identity—already all too tenuous—of the author. It is only the humiliation of the one by the other which allows Lancelot to re-emerge, in the rest of the last two books, as a tragic and beloved figure. Sir Ector, speaking Lancelot's eulogy at the very end, speaks for Malory:

Thou, Sir Launcelot, there thou lyest, that thou were never matched of erthely knyghtes hande. And thou were the curtest knyght that ever bare shelde! And thou were the truest frende to thy lovar that ever bestrade hors, and thow were the trewest lover of a synful man that ever loved woman, and thou were the kyndest man that ever strake wyth swerde. And thou were the godelyest persone that ever cam emonge prees of knyghtes, and thou was the mekest man and the jentyllest that ever ete in halle emonge ladyes, and thou were the sternest knyght to thy mortal foo that ever put spere in the rest.[33]

Truest lover of a sinful man— read either way, it describes Malory as neatly as it does Lancelot.

HAVERFORD COLLEGE

Maud Burnett McInerney, Assistant Professor of English at Haverford College, is the editor of *Hildegard of Bingen: A Book of Essays* (1998). She writes on medieval constructions of gender. Her most recent publication concerned Troilus' dubious masculinity, and she is at work on a book on saints' lives.

ACKNOWLEDGEMENTS

An early version of this paper was presented to the members of the Delaware Valley Medieval Association, whose comments contributed much to its final form. James McNelis straightened me out on some points to do with hunting, and the essay would never have been finished without the help of David Kuhn, Bill Harris, Bonnie Wheeler, and the Bibliothèque Municipale de Dijon. Finally, I would never have paid much attention to the episode of Lancelot and the lady huntress had it not been for the reactions of my undergraduate seminar in the Legend of Arthur.

NOTES

1 Sir Thomas Malory, *The Works of Sir Thomas Malory*, ed. Eugène Vinaver, rev. P.J.C. Field, 3d edn., 3 vols. (Oxford: Clarendon Press, 1990), 3:11040. Subsequent quotations from Malory's work refer to this text.

2 Undergraduates, almost entirely unhampered by generic expectations in their reading of Malory, never fail to notice or even to fixate upon this episode. The first question they pose is often 'what's the deal with Lancelot getting shot in the butt?' It is sometimes productive to follow the lead of the naive reader.

3 *La Mort le Roi Artu*, ed. Jean Frappier (Geneva: Droz, 1954), 64.27–52.

4 *La Mort le Roi Artu*, 64.23–25.

5 The hind, or doe, is described as barren because it was (and still is) against the rules of hunting to pursue a doe who might be either pregnant or lactating. Thus does could only be hunted in the autumn, when their fawns would have grown to maturity.

6 Malory 3:1105.

7 Malory 3:1114.

8 Andrew Lynch, 'Gesture and Gender in Malory's *Le Morte Darthur*,' in *Arthurian Romance and Gender: Selected Proceedings of the XVIIth Annual International Arthurian Congress*, ed. Friedrich Wolfzettel (Amsterdam; Atlanta, GA: Rodopi, 1995), p. 286 [285–95].

9 Beverly Kennedy, *Knighthood in the Morte Darthur*, 2d edn. (Cambridge, UK; Rochester, NY: D.S. Brewer, 1992), p. 309.

10 Kennedy, *Knighthood in the Morte Darthur*, p. 310.

11 Malory 1:256.

12 Malory 1:270–71.

13 Malory 3:1165.

14 Michael Camille, *Image on the Edge* (Cambridge, MA: Harvard University Press, 1992), p. 106.

15 Malory 3:1104.

16 Malory 2:1068.

17 Malory 2:1084.

18 Malory 2:1086.

19 Malory 2:1090.

20 Malory 2:1090.

21 Malory 2:1091.

22 Malory 1:259–60.

23 Kathleen Coyne Kelly, 'Malory's Body Chivalric,' *Arthuriana* 6.4 (1996): 54–66.

24 Malory 3:1104.

25 Malory 1:269.

26 Malory 1:285.

27 Camille, *Image on the Edge*, p. 111.

28 Martin Shichtman, 'Politicizing the Ineffable: The *Queste del Saint Graal* and Malory's "Tale of the Sankgreal"' in *Culture and the King: The Social Implications of the Arthurian Legend*, ed. Martin B. Shichtman and James P. Carley (Albany: State University of New York Press, 1994), p. 166.

29 Shichtman, 'Politicizing the Ineffable,' p. 167.

30 Malory 1:180.

31 Malory 3:1260. For a succinct account of the controversies about the historical Malory, see Terence McCarthy, *An Introduction to Malory* (Cambridge: D.S. Brewer, 1996), pp. 156–67.

32 Eugène Vinaver, Introduction to Sir Thomas Malory, *Works*, 2d edn., 1 vol. (Oxford: Oxford University Press, 1971, rep. 1977), p. v.

33 Malory 3:1259.

Merlin's Mother in the Chronicles

CHARLOTTE A.T. WULF

An examination of the changes in the way Merlin's Mother is portrayed
in chronicle histories from the twelfth through the fifteenth centuries
illuminates attitudes toward women and their proper role in society,
and also raises the issue of how scholars might approach the study of
Unnamed Characters, many of whom happen to be female. (CATW)

With these words, '...neminem agnoui qui illum in me generauit' [I have known no man who begat that child in me],[1] Merlin's Mother[2] confronts King Vortigern to save the life of her son, bravely and skillfully handling a dangerous situation. This woman is well worth a closer look, but she has rarely been studied. Merlin's Mother appears briefly in Geoffrey of Monmouth's *Historia Regum Britannie* and Wace's *Roman de Brut,* and then in later chronicles written by their successors. Playing a small but pivotal role in the story of Merlin and Vortigern, this character is unusual among the women in those chronicle histories which follow Geoffrey. An examination of the changes in the way she is portrayed in the various versions of the story to be considered in this study not only illuminates the attitudes of chronicle authors toward women and their proper role in society, but also raises the issue of how scholars might approach the study of unnamed characters, many of whom happen to be female.

Since the *Historia Regum Britannie* is the history of the *kings* of Britain, it is not surprising that women tend not to play large roles.[3] Geoffrey of Monmouth tells us the names of only nineteen women in the entire narrative. The named women are (not surprisingly) the wives, mothers, daughters, and/or mistresses of kings.[4] Many remain anonymous. Although some of these women play significant roles, they are mentioned by function or affiliation but are never named. Ironically, of the women who are named, most are not given the opportunity to speak—not even such important women as Guenevere. Therefore, Merlin's Mother and Helena's Nurse are unusual as the only two women in the *Historia* who speak but are not named.[5] The primary reason for Helena's Nurse to speak is to tell Bedivere what has happened to Helena, but she is not herself involved in the action. In contrast, Merlin's Mother is involved in the action, and her speech directly affects events.

Prior to the introduction of Merlin's Mother, after attempts to build a defensive tower have failed repeatedly, Vortigern consults his wizards, who tell him that he must find a fatherless boy, then kill the boy and mix his blood with the mortar and stones—this will make his foundation stand. One of Vortigern's search parties finds young Merlin in the town of Carmarthen playing with other children, one of whom is overheard saying to Merlin, 'De te autem nescitur quis sis cum patrem non habeas' [Nothing is known about who you may be, since you do not have a father.]⁶ Inquiries of local people result in the following information: 'Quibus illi dixerunt quia nesciebatur quis pater cum progenuerat. Mater uero filia fuerat regis Demetie, que in ecclesia sancti Petri in eadem urbe inter monachas degebat' [They said that no one knew who the father was who begat the child. Merlin's Mother was the daughter of the King of Demetia (South Wales) and she lives with the nuns at St. Peter's Church in the same city].⁷ Merlin and his mother are found and sent to Vortigern, who separates the two of them in order to question each of them individually. When he asks her by whom she had conceived Merlin, she replies:

"Uiuit anima mea et vivit anima tua, domine mi rex, quia neminem agnoui qui illum in me generauit. Unum autem scio quod, cum essem inter consocias meas in thalamis nostris, apparebat mihi quidam in specie pulcerrimi iuuenis et sepissime amplectens me strictis brachiis deosculabatur. Et cum aliquantulum mecum moram fecisset, subito euanescebat ita ut nichil ex eo uiderem. Multotiens quoque alloquebatur, dum secreto sederem, nec usquam comparebat. Cunque me in hunc modum frequentasset, coiuit mecum in specie hominis sepius atque grauidam in aluo deseruit. Sciat prudentia tua, domine mi, quod aliter uirum non agnoui qui iuuenen istum genuerit."⁸

[May my soul live, my lord king, and may your soul live, for I have known no man who begat that child in me. At one time, however, I know that when I was among my fellow maidens in our bedchambers, there appeared to me a certain person in the form of a most handsome young man, who quite often, encircling me with tight arms, used to kiss me passionately. And when he had tarried with me for a short time, he would suddenly vanish so that I saw nothing of him. Time and again he would address me while I was sitting apart, nor would he appear in any way. Whenever he would visit me in this way he lay with me in human form, and he impregnated me. Let it be known in your wisdom, my lord, that other than the one who begat this youth, I have known no other man.]

Despite the simplicity of the speech itself, this scene in Vortigern's court is all about power: who has it, who wants it, who is afraid of it, and who is trying to manipulate it for their own ends.⁹ Vortigern has power, but he is afraid of losing it to the invading Saxons, hence the importance of the defensive tower he is trying to build and the apparent necessity of killing the fatherless boy. Vortigern's wizards want it—they are trying to gain a measure of power for themselves by finding a solution to the king's problem. Merlin's Mother is afraid of Vortigern's power over her son's life and her own, and she is courageously trying to escape this threat to her son's life and to her reputation. Merlin himself will manipulate events for his own ends as soon as he has an opportunity. Although Merlin's Mother has good reason to be fearful, she demonstrates great courage and presence of mind, choosing her words carefully so that neither she nor her son can be accused of any sin or crime. She speaks only once, but for this one brief period she has Vortigern's entire court hanging on her every word.

After she speaks, Vortigern's wise man Maugantius verifies that this apparent 'virgin birth' could indeed be possible, noting that half-human incubus-demons are capable of assuming human form and consorting with human women. Merlin then proves he has more than human powers by providing the explanation for the collapsing tower that Vortigern's own wise men could not, thus saving his own life. Although Merlin's Mother does not appear in the narrative again, Geoffrey of Monmouth highlights her role in British history just as he highlights the actions and/or speeches of other praiseworthy mothers who act in the best interests of their children, women like Guendolena,[10] Marcia,[11] and Tonuuenna.[12] Merlin's Mother's story, as told by Geoffrey, is one of a strong woman who is able to defend herself from the power of Vortigern and his wizards, refusing to become a victim. The information she provides, combined with Maugantius's, explains Merlin's unusual abilities, while still keeping him within the Christian purview, and helps to save his life—as well as her own good name.

In Wace's *Roman de Brut*,[13] Merlin's Mother remains unnamed, even though, as in Geoffrey's *Historia*, she plays an active role in defending herself and her son. Wace, however, makes several small but significant changes to her story. First, when he introduces her, he emphasizes her presence as an individual rather than a member of a community of nuns. He notes that 'Nunaine esteit de mult bone vie' [She was a nun of exemplary life],[14] but he does not include Geoffrey's information that the nuns she lives with are at St. Peter's Church.[15] In the scene in which Vortigern questions her about her son, Wace adds a few details describing her actions as she is about to speak which make this scene more vivid.[16] By noting that 'La none tint le chief enclin; / Quant ele out pensé un petit:...' [The nun bowed her head. After reflecting a while:...],[17] Wace stresses both her holy vocation and her humility, traits which he apparently thought appropriate for a woman addressing a king in this situation.

Among differences in tone and emphasis between Wace's version and Geoffrey's, three changes Wace makes stand out. The first is that Wace has Merlin's Mother describe herself as 'alques grant nurrie' [a full-grown novice] when her relationship with the mysterious stranger developed.[18] In contrast, Geoffrey has her 'inter consocias meas in thalamis nostris' [among my fellow maidens in our bedchambers], meaning she was still living at home in her father's castle when her male visitor came to spend time alone with her. Since Geoffrey later has Arthur address his knights as 'consociis,'[19] it seems unlikely that Merlin's Mother in the *Historia* is referring to fellow nuns by this term. In the *Roman de Brut*, however, Wace makes it clear that she is not living at home, and is older and already a novice, which means she was in the process of dedicating her life to God when she became pregnant with Merlin. If, as Neil Wright believes, Wace used the First Variant Version of the *Historia* as the basis of his *Roman de Brut*, the change he makes is even more significant, since the First Variant Version text is more explicit than the Vulgate Version of the *Historia*, reading 'cum essem in thalamo parentum puella' [when I was a girl living in the bedchambers of my parents' home].[20]

The second change Wace makes is to leave out the reference to the physical attractiveness of the mysterious visitor whom Geoffrey describes as 'pulcerrimi' [very handsome] in the Vulgate Version, while the First Variant Version uses the similar 'in specie formosa' [beautifully formed],[21] and this deletion makes Merlin's Mother appear to be a victim of rape. A third change is in the immediate circumstances surrounding her speech: in Geoffrey's version Merlin and his mother are separated so that each one can be questioned alone, while Wace has them kept together. Thus, Wace always presents Merlin's Mother as accompanied by a male (even though he is a young boy); therefore she never has to stand up on her own against Vortigern as she does in Geoffrey's *Historia*.

In both the way Wace describes her as she speaks and in what she says, she appears to be crafting her response to Vortigern carefully in order to deny any responsibility she has for the relationship and the resulting pregnancy. There is no hint of any attraction or pleasure on her part, but neither is there any direct accusation of her being overpowered by her visitor. However, Wace creates moral ambiguity regarding this event, just as he does in many situations throughout the *Roman de Brut*. Where Geoffrey's Merlin's Mother is an active participant in events, in Wace she seems passive and isolated.

A number of later versions reduce the amount of time Merlin's Mother has 'on stage,' thus suggesting her relative lack of importance in the narrative. While scholars have noted that, on the whole, women's roles expand in many of the romances over time, in the chronicle histories after the twelfth century their roles tend to diminish in importance.

However, there are two notable exceptions: the first is Lawman's *Brut* (ca. 1200)[22]; the second is Robert Mannnyng of Brunne's *Chronicle*, which he finished in 1338. Just as Wace translated, adapted, and expanded Geoffrey's Latin prose into French verse, Lawman and Mannyng translated, adapted, and expanded Wace's French verse into English verse, but each author produced a version of Merlin's Mother consistent with his view of women and their proper role in society. Lawman's *Brut* is nearly twice as long as Wace's *Roman de Brut*, its primary source, because he adds descriptive details to scenes and gives characters more direct speech than did either Geoffrey or Wace.[23] Thus his scenes are often more dramatic than they those found in either of his predecessor's versions, and the story of Merlin's Mother is no exception. Because Lawman tends to categorize woman as either Marys or Eves,[24] he portrays Merlin's Mother as sheer innocence, in contrast to Wace's less categorical, more neutral character, who carefully provides no information that could implicate either herself or her son. In fact, she provides no information beyond the bare minimum necessary. Thus, Merlin's Mother becomes even more passive than she is in Wace, but this passivity fits Lawman's definition of a feminine ideal.

Lawman develops a conversation between Merlin's Mother and Vortigern, a dramatic scene in which she announces that her father, named Conan, was once a great leader of warriors and a ruler of a large country (ll. 7818–24). Lawman heightens the suspense in this scene by not revealing who her father is before this moment; and, more importantly, this announcement implies that Merlin's Mother has a powerful male protector. Lawman creates a portrait of a young, innocent girl living with a loving family, visited by a mysterious yet glorious being, who then finds herself pregnant by him. When Vortigern asks Merlin's Mother who the boy's father is, Lawman greatly expands and changes her reply from Wace's version. Rather than open with a standard Christian phrase such as 'God help me,' she says that "'mi fader Conaan þe king luuede me þurh alle þing'" [my father King Conan loved me very dearly],[25] continuing with a description of herself as a fifteen-year-old living at home, visited late at night while she slept by "'þe fæireste þing þat wes iboren, / swulc hit weore a muchel cniht al of golde idiht'" [the fairest creature ever born, in the guise of a tall warrior all arrayed in gold].[26] She describes her visitor as embracing her, kissing her, and so forth, and says she did not understand what was happening when her body felt strange and her food tasted unpalatable, but finally she realized that she was with child. She gave birth to Merlin, she says, but has no idea who or what his father is. She concludes by saying, "'La, swa ich ibedde are, nat ich namare / to suggen þe of mine sune, hu he to worulde is icume'" [So, pray you excuse me, I know nothing more to tell you about my son, of how he came into the world],[27] after which she bows her head and composes herself.

Now a nun, as she is in Geoffrey's *Historia*, she tells her story with dignity, but is careful not to offend the king, and to portray herself as a naive, innocent recipient of the tall warrior's advances. Lawman is clearly sympathetic to Merlin's Mother, adding only positive details to his story. With the details about her father, more description of her attractive stranger, mention of the pregnancy itself, and reiteration of her lack of knowledge about who her visitor might have been, it would be difficult for a reader not to feel sympathy toward this woman. However, by giving names both to her father and to the magistrate of Carmarthen, but not to Merlin's Mother, Lawman suggests that although she deserves the reader's sympathy, she is still not as important as the male characters.

Like Lawman, Mannyng often adds interesting descriptive details to the portraits of the women in his *Chronicle*, frequently making them more sympathetic characters than they had been in his source, the *Roman de Brut*. When his Merlin's Mother is introduced, Mannyng notes the King of Demetia's high position and that she is a nun at St. Peter's Church, and then changes both the wording and the tone of her speech to Vortigern, making her seem to be more of a victim. As a result of these changes, she deserves the reader's sympathy based on her situation rather than on her specific words or actions. Following Wace, Mannyng has Merlin's Mother pause and think about her response before she speaks. As in both Geoffrey's and Wace's versions, she begins with a standard Christian phrase, but where Wace had her begin simply with "'Se Deus me aït'" [God help me],[28] this time she says—appropriately, invoking a prior virgin birth—"'Bi Ihesu in Mari light'"[By Jesus who arrived in Mary].[29] Unlike earlier versions of her speech in which she concludes by saying that she does not know who or what her visitor was, here she begins by stating her ignorance of her visitor's identity.

The most significant change in her speech is in her description of her relationship with the mysterious visitor, whose physical appearance is not mentioned at all. She says that, "'One come to my bed I wist, / with force he me halsed & kist'" [I knew that someone came to my bed, / and with force he embraced me and kissed me].[30] In both Geoffrey's and Wace's versions, the descriptions of the relationship between Merlin's Mother and her mysterious visitor are carefully phrased so that there is no clear indication one way or another as to whether she actually enjoyed the attentions of her visitor or not (although Geoffrey may have given out a slight hint that she did by describing him as very attractive; Wace leaves this out); the fact that she is not describing the visits in negative terms in the *Historia* leaves the possibility open that she was not repelled by his attentions. In the *Roman de Brut*, the relationship is described in carefully neutral terms, while in Lawman's *Brut* the visitor is once again described as attractive but powerful (which implies that it is difficult to for a young girl to resist his attentions).

Mannyng's terminology is different from all three prior versions: here the visitor has forced his attentions on Merlin's Mother, which changes the tone of their relationship to a negative one. By describing it in this way, Mannyng makes her an entirely innocent victim of unwanted attentions who could not possibly have derived any pleasure from the visits from this incubus-demon; thus Merlin's Mother appears absolutely blameless of anything even approaching sin. She is clearly innocent, but rather than appearing youthfully passive as she does in Lawman's *Brut*, in this version she becomes an object of pity.

In contrast to the amount of narrative space and sympathy female figures receive in Lawman's *Brut* and Mannyng's *Chronicle*, the fifteenth-century French and English *Brut* chronicles have a decided tendency to reduce women's roles drastically. However, the narrative about Merlin and his mother includes one significant addition to the story: she is finally given a name. This is surprising first because she is not given a name in any other version of this story before the sixteenth century,[31] in chronicle history or in romance, and second, the name itself in both versions is unusual—no source for it has yet been found. Most surprising, though, is adding a name for a female character at this point in time, when in rest of the *Brut* chronicles most women's roles are diminishing or even disappearing completely.

The Middle English *Prose Brut* chronicle, although it does not identify either her father or the location of her convent, gives her a name: 'a grete gentilwoman him bare in Kermerdyne, þat me callede Adhan, but neuere myȝt men wete who was þe childes fader' [a great noblewoman bore him in Carmarthen, that men called Adhan, but never might men know who was the child's father].[32] The author of the *Brut* chronicle takes a practical approach to Merlin's Mother's speech. He may have wondered at a young noblewoman apparently being left alone a great deal, as not only does he include the mention of 'others of noble birth' being often in Adhan's company, but he also finds it necessary to explain why she did not go outside—she was avoiding the 'burning of the sun'—a sensible reason in a time when poets frequently praised the whiteness of a lady's skin. The author also describes the doors as being heavily barred: having the power to get to Adhan despite this gives further evidence of the supernatural powers of her mysterious visitor, which further implies that it would be very difficult for her to resist him. One other change this author makes is in the way he introduces her speech, showing her weeping hard. This weeping marks her as not having the power to 'defend' herself from him, as in Mannyng's version, as does her not knowing who or what he was, where he was from, or his name as in all the other versions of the story. Thus, the *Brut* chronicle author portrays Adhan as a weak, innocent victim of supernatural forces:

> The lady ansuerede, ful tender wepyng, and saide she had neuer company of man worldely; "but, sire," quod shee, "as y was a ʒonge maiden in my faderes chambre, and oþere of grete lynage were in my company, þat ofte were wont to playe and to solacen, I belefte allone in my chaumbre of my fader, and wolde nouʒt gon out, for brennyng of þe sone. And oppon a tyme þere come a faire bachiler, and entrede into my chaumbre þere þat I was allone; but how he come into me, & wher, I wist neuer, ne ʒitte wote, for þe dores were fast barrede; and wiþ me he dede game of loue, for I nade noþer myʒt ne power him to defende fro me; and ofte he came to me in the forsaide maner, so þat he bigate one me þis same childe; but neuer myʒt y wete of him what he was, ne whens he come, ne what was his name"[33]

> [The lady answered, weeping hard, and said that she had never known the company of a man of this world; "But, Sire," she said, "As I was a young maiden in my father's home, and others of noble birth were in my company, who often used to play with me and comfort me, I was sometimes left alone in my room in my father's home, and would not go outside, because of the burning of the sun. And one time there came a handsome young man, and he entered into my room when I was alone; but how he was able to come to me, and where, I never knew, nor do I yet know, for the doors were heavily barred; and with me he played the game of love, for I did not have the power to defend myself from him; and often he came to me in the aforesaid manner, so that he begat on me this same child; but never was I able to know what he was, where he came from, or what his name was"].

In the French Prose *Brute*, Merlin's Mother is introduced as in the English *Brut* as 'une gentile famme qui avoit nom Asehanne…' [a noble young woman whose name was Asehanne]. Once again she does not know who Merlin's father is. As in the English *Brut*, Asehanne is weeping when she responds to Vortigern and companions are mentioned (although not in quite as much detail as the English version), and Asehanne's handsome and mysterious visitor enters through heavily barred doors. She, too, mentions not being able to defend herself against him and the phrase 'game of love' is used here also: 'Il me fist le jeu d'amours car je n'avoye poer de moy deffendre' [He played the game of love with me because I did not have the power to defend myself]. Finally, the last few phrases are virtually identical, a similarity that should not surprise us since the French *Brut* derives from the English. (The French version's omission of Adhan's fear of sunburn is a minor difference).

Therefore, the *Brut* chronicle authors seem to agree with Lawman and Mannyng that women are weaker than men and should not play prominent roles in political history, yet they work against the general trend of reducing her importance by giving Merlin's Mother a name. This allows the reader to recognize her as a person in a way that she had not been recognized before. However, as we examine the various versions of Merlin's Mother's speech, we perceive a general trend: she is rendered more passive and weaker than the strong figure Geoffrey of Monmouth created.

These names, Adhan and Asehanne, are still a mystery. No prior trace in any other medieval narratives, Arthurian or otherwise, has yet been found.[34] Puzzling in a different way, however, are the questions of why Merlin's Mother is named in both the French and English Prose *Brut* chronicles, and why then in the late fourteenth or the early fifteenth century. No one else gives her a name before this, and with the exception of the Lambeth manuscript, she is not named again until Elizabethan times.[35] When she does appear with a name in later times, there is no consistency—each author gives her a different one.

I hope that this brief examination of Merlin's Mother will prompt scholars to consider studying many neglected, unnamed female figures in medieval literature. Perhaps the single biggest hindrance to the inclusion of these female characters in critical studies, discussions, and, most importantly, reference books, is the lack of a standard mode of reference—therefore such female figures are rarely included in lists and indices.[36] I suggest that we agree to give these unnamed women a capitalized referent according to their function or affiliation, like 'Merlin's Mother'; we already use such referents for 'The Green Knight,' and 'The Lady of the Lake.' By giving these unnamed figures standard referents, we can work to bring them in from the margins of medieval studies. I firmly believe Maureen Fries would support this practice and the broadening of scholarly interest it would bring.

THE PENNSYLVANIA STATE UNIVERSITY

Charlotte A.T. Wulf is a lecturer in English and Religious Studies at The Pennsylvania State University. She is currently teaching Business Writing, Freshman Composition, and Early and Medieval Christianity.

ACKNOWLEDGMENTS

I wish to thank Jeanne Krochalis and Suzanne Thomas for the generous suggestions and helpful comments they made while I was working on this project. I made use of many of their suggestions, but any errors or infelicities are my own responsibility. I also want to thank Bonnie Wheeler and Fiona Tolhurst for their patience, encouragement, and editorial expertise.

NOTES

1　This and later citations from Geoffrey of Monmouth are to *The Historia Regum Britannie of Geoffrey of Monmouth I: Bern, Burgerbibliothek, MS 568, Section 107*, ed. Neil Wright (Cambridge: D.S. Brewer, 1985), p. 72. Unless otherwise noted, all transations are my own.

2　Since she is not given a name in the twelfth-, thirteenth-, and fourteenth-century texts, I have chosen to refer to her as 'Merlin's Mother,' capitalized, as if it were a proper name.

3　Composed ca. 1138; for a discussion of Geoffrey of Monmouth's life and works, see Wright's introduction to his edition of the Bern MS (above, n1), pp. ix–xx; see also Wright's bibliography, pp. lx–lxv.

4　These nineteen are the following: associated with Arthur are Anna (his sister), Helena (his niece), Ygerna (his mother), and Guenevere; associated with Lear are his daughters Cordelia, Goneril, and Regan; associated with Locrinus are Gwendolen (his wife), Estrildis (his mistress), and Habren (her daughter); Renwein is married to Vortigern; Ignoge is Brutus' wife; Helen is the daughter of King Coel; Genvissa is the wife of Arvirargus; Judon is the wife of Gorboduc; Marcia is the wife of Guithelin; Tanguesteaia is the mistress of Danius; Tonuuenna is the mother of Belinus and Brennius; and Galaes is queen of the last Britons in Wales (whose name Geoffrey tells us the word *Welsh* may have come from). This count does not include the thirty daughters of Ebraucus, who are named, but play no individual part in the story, or the three named goddesses (Diana, Minerva, and Freia).

5　Nearly all of the unnamed women are also the wives, mothers, daughters, and/or mistresses of kings; the exception, besides Merlin's Mother, is Helena's Nurse (found in section 165).

6　Geoffrey of Monmouth, *Historia I*, 106.

7　Geoffrey of Monmouth, *Historia I*, 106. For more on Carmarthen, St. Peter's Church, and Geoffrey's knowledge of the area, see J.S.P. Tatlock, *The Legendary History of Britain* (Berkeley: University of California Press, 1950), pp. 67–68 and n284.

8　Geoffrey of Monmouth, *Historia I*, 107. While most of the narrative about Vortigern and the fatherless boy is based on Nennius's story of Vortigern and Ambrose (the boy's name—it is not 'Merlin' in Nennius's account), this speech is entirely Geoffrey's creation. In the *Historia Britonum*, the only words said by Ambrose's mother are a denial that she has ever had intercourse with any man.

Later Ambrose tells Vortigern that his father was a Roman consul. See chapters 40–42 of the *Historia Britonum*; an English translation is available online at Paul Halsall's Medieval Sourcebook, <http://www.fordham.edu/halsall/source/nennius.html>. Tatlock discusses the relationship between Geoffrey's account and that of Nennius at length in his chapter on Merlin, pp. 171–77.

9 As Stephen Knight says, 'The Arthurian legend...is about power in the real world' (*Arthurian Literature and Society*, [London: Macmillan, 1983], p. xiv).

10 For a discussion of Guendolena, see Fiona Tolhurst, 'The Britons as Hebrews, Romans, and Normans: Geoffrey of Monmouth's British Epic and Reflections of Empress Matilda,' *Arthuriana* 8.4 (1998): 79–81 [69–87].

11 See Tolhurst, 'The Britons as Hebrews, Romans, and Normans,' 82.

12 For more on Tonuuenna in the *Historia* and in Wace's *Brut*, see Fiona Tolhurst, 'The Once and Future Queen: The Development of Guenevere from Geoffrey of Monmouth to Malory,' *Bibliographic Bulletin of the International Arthurian Society*, L (1998): 277.

13 Composed ca. 1155; for a discussion of Wace's life and works, and his *Brut*'s relationship with Geoffrey's *Historia*, see *Wace's Roman de Brut: The History of the British, Text and Translation*, ed. and trans. Judith Weiss (Exeter: University of Exeter Press, 1999), pp. xi–xxiv, and Weiss's bibliography, pp. 374–78.

14 Wace, *Roman de Brut*, l. 7399, pp. 186–87.

15 Wace says only that she lives 'En la ville en une abeïe' ['in an abbey in the town']. Wace, *Roman de Brut*, l. 7400, pp. 186–87.

16 Robert H. Fletcher was the first to note the way Wace describes her holding her head down and thinking a little before answering Vortigern, in his *The Arthurian Material in the Chronicles* (repr. New York: Burt Franklin, 1966), p. 131.

17 Wace, *Roman de Brut*, ll. 7412–13.

18 The *Anglo-Norman Dictionary*, ed. Louise W. Stone and William Rothwell, Fascicle 4: M–O/U, (London: Modern Humanities Research Association, 1985) lists this as the third meaning for *nurrie*; the first is 'dependent, retainer' and the second is 'ward, adopted child.' Since we are told she is the daughter of the King of Demetia, 'novice' does seem the only possible meaning here.

19 Geoffrey of Monmouth, *Historia I*, 159.

20 Geoffrey of Monmouth, *The Historia Regum Britannie of Geoffrey of Monmouth II: The First Variant Version: A critical edition, Section 107*, ed. Neil Wright (Cambridge: D.S. Brewer, 1988), p. 99.

21 Geoffrey of Monmouth, *Historia II*, 107.

22 The dates usually given for Lawman's *Brut* are 1189–1204, although Françoise Le Saux argues for extending the range to 1185–1216 in *Laȝamon's Brut: The Poem and Its Sources* (Cambridge: D.S. Brewer, 1989), pp. 1–10.

23 Quotations from and translations of Lawman's *Brut* are from *Laȝamon's Brut, or Hystoria Brutonum*, ed. and trans. with textual notes and commentary by W.R.J. Barron and S. Weinberg (New York and Harlow: Longman, 1995). Running from line 7745–855, Lawman adds details to Vortigern's search for the boy without a father, including a conversation between Merlin's men and the magistrate of

Carmarthen, whom Lawman names Eli (lines 7783–804), and more details about bringing Merlin's Mother from the convent where she was living to Vortigern (lines 7805–17).

24 For more on Lawman's female characters, see Maureen Fries, 'Women, Power, and (the Undermining of) Order in Lawman's *Brut*,' *Arthuriana* 8.3 (1998): 23–32.

25 *Laȝamon's Brut*, ed. and trans. Barron and Weinberg, l. 7833. For more about Lawman's *Brut* see above, n 22; also *The Text and Tradition of Laȝamon's Brut*, ed. Françoise Le Saux (Cambridge: D.S. Brewer, 1994); and Elizabeth J. Bryan, *Collaborative Meaning in Medieval Scribal Culture: The Otho Laȝamon* (Ann Arbor: University of Michigan Press, 1999).

26 Lawman, *Laȝamon's Brut*, ll.7839–40.

27 Lawman, *Laȝamon's Brut*, ll.7853–54.

28 Wace, *Roman de Brut*, l. 7414.

29 Robert Mannyng of Brunne, *Robert Mannyng of Brunne: The Chronicle*, ed. with introduction, notes, and glossary by Idelle Sullens (Binghamton: Medieval & Renaissance Texts & Studies, State University of New York Press, 1996), ll. 7932. See also Najaria Hurst Esty, 'Wace's *Roman de Brut* and the Fifteenth-Century Prose *Brut Chronicle*: A Comparative Study,' unpub. diss. (The Ohio State University, 1978).

30 Robert Mannyng of Brunne, *The Chronicle*, ll. 7939–40.

31 Christopher Bruce cites three names from Elizabethan and later times in *The Arthurian Name Dictionary* (New York: Garland, 1999), p. 360, two of which have listings of their own: Joan Go-too't (see below, n. 35), Marinaia (in Paolino Pieri's *La Storia di Merlino*, p. 345), and Optima (not listed).

32 Anonymous Chronicler, *The Brut, or the Chronicles of England*, ed. Friedrich W.D. Brie, EETS Original Series 131 (London: Oxford University Press, 1906; rep. EETS, 1960), p. 56.

33 English Prose *Brut Chronicle*, ed. Brie, p. 57.

34 Lister Matheson, in 'The Arthurian Stories of Lambeth Palace Library MS 84,' *Arthurian Literature* V (Cambridge: D.S. Brewer, 1985), 70–91, notes that Merlin's Mother is named 'Adhan' in Lambeth Palace Library MS 84, which he believes derives from the *Brut Chronicle* tradition (the wording in the MS is virtually identical—see his p. 78).

35 She is named Joan Go-too't in *The Birth of Merlin: or The Childe hath found his Father*, by William Rowley. This play, probably written ca. 1620, was once thought to have been written by Shakespeare. The earliest and only known edition is from 1662; today it is available as part of the Microbook Library of English Literature.

36 With the important exception of Alexandre Micha's ed. of *Lancelot* (vol. 10 contains an index of anonymous characters, including 101 unnamed 'damoiseles'), indices in various editions of Arthurian texts do not list unnamed women, and neither do such reference books as Norris Lacy's *Arthurian Encyclopedia* or Christopher Bruce's *Arthurian Name Dictionary* (cited above). Once a referent is commonly accepted, however, listing can take place, as with the eight different 'Ladys' and seven different 'Maidens' Bruce includes in his *Arthurian Name Dictionary*.

Hard(l)y Tristan

The essay considers Hardy's late drama as a reflection of the Tristan
legend informed by the themes of Hardy's novels and Ibsen's theater.
(DLH)

Although Thomas Hardy may be little more than a footnote in Arthurian
literature, his peculiar play, *The Famous Tragedy of the Queen of Cornwall*,
stands as the culminating work of his distinguished career, and as a striking
new direction in his *oeuvre*. Strange, indeed, that the last composition of a
novelist famous for his naturalist studies of provincial England should turn
out to be a verse drama with a courtly Arthurian subject.

Hardy's version, if not entirely successful, attempts a radical revision of
the legend that tries to connect with Shakespearean and pre-Shakespearean
theater in both the traditions of the Tudor Interludes and the folk tradition
of the Mummers' plays, which had survived into his own time. This attempt
is reinforced by Hardy's stage directions which recall the pre-Shakespearean
theater of the Tudor interludes and the tradition of the Mummers' plays:

> *The Stage is any large room; round or at the end of which the audience sits. It is
> assumed to be the interior of the Great Hall of Tintagel Castle: that the floor is
> strewn with rushes: that there is an arch in the back-centre (a doorway or other
> opening may counterfeit this) through which the Atlantic is visible across an outer
> ward and over the ramparts of the stronghold. [...]*

> *The costumes of the players are the conventional ones of linen fabrics, made gay
> with knots and rosettes of ribbon, as in the old mumming shows; though on an
> actual stage they may be more realistic.*[1]

In his omnibus aims, however, Hardy attempts to connect with the ancient
Greeks as well. His stress on 'the Time covered by the events is about the Time of
representation'[2] calls attention to his desire to reproduce the notorious 'Unities'
of Time, Place, and Action. He confesses these Attic aspirations in a letter to
Harold Child on November 11, 1923:

> My temerity in pulling together into the space of an hour events that in the
> traditional story covered a long time will doubtless be punished by reviewers
> of the book. But there are so many versions of the famous romance that I felt

free to adapt it to my purposes in any way—as, in fact, the Greek dramatists did in their plays, notably Euripides.[3]

Despite Hardy's hopes, no one, I imagine, has found *The Famous Queen* the equal of *Medea*. Nevertheless, his attempt to confine the Tristan narrative within the limits of the unities is not without interest. Much, as one would expect, is lost in the compression, but the tension between the two Isoldes is quite possibly more dramatically explored in this version than in any other. Oddly, and mainly due to the fact that she is the only one to survive, the winner of the conflict seems to be Isolde of the White Hands with her concluding claim of the rights of the legal wife. Her claim, in fact, seems to be endorsed by Hardy, who has Isolde the Queen kill herself by leaping off the castle into the sea rather than expiring on Tristan's dying body. This revision of the scene enforces a separation of the lovers in death (a dramatic rethinking, if not simple contradiction, of the tradition) and leaves the stage to Isolde of the White Hands, the sole survivor and the final speaker, who can, therefore, conclude the narrative with her particular 'spin.'

She enters, having witnessed her rival's suicide:

> I heard her cry. I saw her leap! How fair
> She was! What wonder that my brother Kay
> Should pine for love of her....O she should not
> Have done it to herself! Nor life nor death
> Is worth a special quest.
> (*She sees TRISTRAM's body.*)
>   What's this — my husband?
> My Tristram dead likewise? *He* one with *her?*
> (*She sinks and clasps TRISTRAM.*)
> . . . .
> And she beholding? *That* the cause wherefor
> She went and took her life? He was not hers....
> Yet did she love him true, if wickedly!
> . . . .
> (*seeing MARK's body*)
> And the King also dead? My Tristram's slayer?
> Yet strange to me. Then even had I not come
> Across the southern water recklessly
> This would have shaped the same—the very same.
> (*Turning again to TRISTRAM.*)
> Tristram, dear husband! O!
> (*She rocks herself over him.*)
> What a rare beauteous knight has perished here
> By this most cruel craft! Could not King Mark

If wronged, have chid him—minded him of me,
And not done this, done this! Well, well;
      she's lost him,
Even as have I.—This stronghold moans with woes,
And jibbering voices join with winds and waves
To make a dolorous din!…
(*They lift her.*)
                       Aye, I will rise —
Betake me to my own dear Brittany —
Dearer in that our days there were so sweet,
Before I knew what pended me elsewhere!
These halls are hateful to me! May my eyes
Meet them no more!
(*She turns to go.*)
          BRANGWAIN

   I will attend you, Madam.

*Exit ISEULT THE WHITEHANDED assisted by BRANGWAIN and
Bowerwomen. Knight, retainers, etc., lift the bodies and carry them out. A
Dirge by the Chanters.*[4]

Despite the trapping of ancient legend, Isolde's complaint takes up themes
that had haunted Hardy all his life. There is a sense of fate, a claim of the
futile, but legal, victory of the bonds of matrimony (and 'bonds' in Hardy is
far more often a concrete reality rather than a metaphor), and the focus on
the central suffering woman. There is even the last painful betrayal, which
could go almost unnoticed (and may simply be motivated by the need to
clear the stage), but, nevertheless, reveals a subtle treachery, when Brangwain's
simple "'I will attend you, Madam,'" signals her abandonment of her queen
to become the handmaid of her mistress' rival, and turns her back without a
tear on the famous Queen of Cornwall.

It is not, perhaps, surprising that Hardy's last work, however different its
setting and subject, would reprise themes that had obsessed him throughout
his career. What is more intriguing is Hardy's statement on the occasion of
the play's production in 1923 that it had been '53 years in contemplation.'[5]
Fifty-three years earlier in 1870, Hardy made his first visit to the site of *The
Famous Tragedy*, Tintagel Castle in Cornwall, and it was on that trip that he met
Emma Gifford, the woman who would be his first wife. While very little of the
'fairy princess' hovered about Emma, Hardy returned from his visit dazzled by
the setting and the young woman he met there. He rapturously writes:

   When I came back from Lyonesse
      With magic in my eyes,

> All marked with mute surmise
> My radiance rare and fathomless,
> When I came back from Lyonesse
> With magic in my eyes![6]

Those musical verses probably capture more of the spirit of romance than the leaden iambics of the later tragedy, but they certainly identify the intensity of Hardy's associations with Tintagel both at his first sight and fifty-three years later. With this assumption, that Tintagel haunted Hardy from 1870 to 1923, it becomes possible to suggest that not only was his Tristanian work infused with his life-long themes, but that Tristanian themes may have subtly influenced his earlier works as well. I should like to argue that in the case of at least one of his novels, *Jude the Obscure*,[7] there are indeed echoes of the Tristan legend.

There are to begin with evocations of a mystical Middle Ages throughout the book, primarily in Jude's early fantasies and later disillusions about his own Grail kingdom, the academic Sarras of the city of Christminster. As a boy, he climbs a ladder to join some tilers on a roof in the hope that he can see in the distance the city that looks to him like 'the heavenly Jerusalem.' Like visionary cities from Sarras to Brigadoon, Christminster seems to Jude to rise magically from topaz points of light only to disappear, invisible, veiled in mist. It is a vision that encourages Jude's aspirations toward the knowledge enclosed in Christminster and his nearly spiritual quest for learning. When he arrives there, however, the actuality of the city has quite a different effect, medieval, to be sure, but not quite the shining 'city of light and lore.' There are 'sprocketed pinnacles, and indented battlements, [...] oriels, [and] doorways of enriched and florid middle age design, their extinct air being accentuated by the rottenness of the stones' (84). A young man like Jude, trained in that medieval mystery of stonecutting, whose world is bounded by *Mary*green and *Christ*minster, can hardly evade being touched by a pervasive religiosity with medieval roots.

In this provocatively, if negatively, medieval setting, Jude's erotic life develops with peculiar, if less than literal, echoes of Tristanian themes, particularly themes of love and marriage, and, especially, love versus marriage. Tristanian echoes emerge, first of all, dramatically and oddly, in the controversial scene of Jude's first encounter with the woman who will be his first wife, Arabella.

Lost in thought and reviewing his acquaintance with the Fathers of the Church, Roman and English history, and his intention to read Livy, Tacitus, Herodotus, Æschylus, Sophocles, Aristophanes…, he is interrupted by voices giggling, 'Ha, ha, ha! Hoity-toity!' (39). He is only slightly distracted, until after rehearsing a few more Greek and Latin authors, and renewing his intention to read the Fathers along with 'Bede and ecclesiastical history generally' (40), he is interrupted by a few more 'hoity-toities' and a more substantial object:

> On a sudden something smacked him sharply in the ear, and he became aware that a soft cold substance had been flung at him, and had fallen at his feet.
>
> A glance told him what it was—a piece of flesh, the characteristic part of a barrow-pig, which the countrymen used for greasing their boots, as it was useless for any other purpose. Pigs were rather plentiful hereabout, being bred and fattened in large numbers in certain parts of North Wessex (40).

Hardy's information about animal husbandry in North Wessex is almost comically anticlimactic, and may have been meant, in part, as a comic deflation of the grossness of the scene; it may also have been meant as a kind of authentication of his fictional reality that might serve to deflect some of the harsher criticism of the episode. If so, it did not work. Arabella and her pig parts have offended some readers for just over a century now.

It may merely be fortuitous, depending on just how persevering a Tristan scholar Hardy could be shown to be, but there is a suggestive echo, if not straight parody, of the pig power of the original Tristan legend. The triads, after all, witness one of the earliest episodes of the 'Drystan' legend in which he disguises himself as a swineherd and tends the royal pigs, while the real pig-tender carries a message to Isolde.[8]

Apart from the fact that Jude falls unhappily in love with her and that she is surrounded by pigs, there may be little to identify Arabella with the Queen of Cornwall. But Arabella provokes Jude's first desires and has an elemental force that echoes an idea of Isolde. For the moment that is enough. Suggestively, however, when much later in the book Arabella is courted by a young collegian, he overtly refers to the Tristan legend. 'That philtre is operating, you know,' claims the amorous scholar, recollecting the drink that provokes the love of Tristan and Isolde.

Tristanian themes particularly coalesce about the figure of Sue Bridehead, who has features of both Isoldes. Like Blanchemain she is belated (the hero's second love), but, like the Queen, her previous marriage becomes an impediment and her husband becomes very much a husband in the mold of Mark. Sue, an ambiguous and doubled Isolde, is also one of the most irritating women ever invented. She claims to be a rather advanced sort of being 'more ancient than medievalism' (142), but proves this to herself by buying tacky ten-shilling statues of Venus and Apollo (very large and very naked statues, they seem to her) that she tells her landlady are images of St. Peter and Mary

Magdalene. Unjustifiably proud of her learning and her modernity (despite her equally bogus claims to pagan roots), in the picture gallery she ignores Carlo Dolci, Guido Reni, and Andrea del Sarto, in order to wait for Jude before a Lely or Reynolds. Not utterly wretched taste, perhaps, but a taste that is obviously determined by her idea of what a picture ought to be rather than by any particular ability to actually look at a picture. Her reading is similarly narrow:

> "I know most of the Greek and Latin classics through translations, and other books too. I read Lemprière, Catullus, Martial, Juvenal, Lucan, Beaumont and Fletcher, Boccaccio, Scarron, De Brantôme, Sterne, De Foe, Smollett, Fielding, Shakespeare, the Bible, and other such; and found that all interest in the unwholesome part of those books ended with its mystery." (155)

But, despite her claims, she has read little, and has read less well. Her belief that she is loftily unaffected by 'the unwholesome parts' is particularly suggestive because it is so utterly unnecessary. It suggests, among other things, that rather than being removed from the naughty bits, she has been more intrigued by them than she cares to admit. But, ever the *poseuse*, she prefers to adopt an attitude rather than express an honest reaction. And it is the attitude that is problematic. It is the attitude of one who claims to be modern and above superstition, while her 'modernity' is both affected and out of date. Jude's medievalism may, in fact, be more in tune with the spirit of the Late Victorian Age than Sue's supposed modernity, which doesn't seem to go much past the eighteenth-century novel. In the Age of Wilde and Whistler, it is a 'modernity' that seems decidedly old-fashioned.[9]

The tale of Sue and Jude's love, like that of Tristan and Isolde, pivots around the problems of love and marriage and society vs. passion. Their union is forbidden because of Jude's marriage to Arabella, which Sue refuses to overlook even though Arabella has absconded to Australia and the marriage is a technicality that might have been gotten around. Much as in the way she looks at paintings, her idea of what she ought to focus on makes it difficult for her to actually see what is there. As Tristan and Isolde, wrapped in passion, endure the rigors of the forest in Béroul, so Jude and Sue in their irregular relationship endure the trials of poverty and the scorn of priggish townsfolk. Jude exacerbates the problem with his occasional bouts of drunkenness, which can be read as a sad and ironic commentary on the archetypal love philtre that makes the original Tristan drunk with love. While it may seem far-fetched, turning the famous love-drink into problems of love and drunkenness seems precisely the sort of ironic deflation of the legend that would have appealed to Hardy.

The couple's difficulties are intensified by the arrival of children. Here, too, one can imagine Hardy supplying the obvious omission in the original. Traditionally, adulterous couples in romance are never encumbered by children, which, in a period obsessed by issues of inheritance, could be seen as a curse, but is probably more often seen as a remarkable bit of luck. But in viewing the trials of Jude and Sue as an imagining of what would have happened if Tristan and Isolde had to deal with the problems of 'real' people, supporting children, paying the rent, etc., one sees the poignancy of the drama of thwarted romance that underlies the novel, but sees also how the tragedy of the original is enabled by an erasure of innumerable distractions.

The examination of marriage is far more intense, complex, and painful in *Jude* than in the Tristan legend. In the original, Mark ranges from reasonable to villainous, but the marriage never exercises the oppressive power that it does in the novel. That power is, however, dependent on the assumptions and conventions of provincial life, on Jude's capacity to imagine ideal worlds at the expense of being able to negotiate with any skill in the real one, and especially on Sue's choices and, at the end, on her willful capacity to choose a tragically stupid course of action. She is a woman of limited intellect in possession of an implacable will.

The ending of the novel also presents a pessimistic deflation of the passion of the original, a deflation that is analogous to the love potion being transformed into pots of pub ale leading to Jude's embarrassing drunken scenes. At the end, reversing roles slightly, Arabella becomes at last the wife, the analogue of Isolde of the White Hands. (Even that hint returns us to Hardy's deflation of the romance, as we try to join in our memories the image of the White Hands and her entrance into the novel using those delicate instruments to slaughter pigs and sling their pizzles at passing idealists.) As White Hands attempted to cheat Tristan of his deathbed reunion with the queen, Arabella even more cruelly leaves Jude dead in the bedroom while she goes out to attend a college festival; ironically, it is at this festival that young Vilbert makes reference to the love philtre.

Two brief exchanges prior to Jude's death clarify the contrast between Jude's two strange Isoldes. After his exposure to Sue along with damp and chilly weather, Jude acquires the illness that kills, but must first take the train back to Christminster where Arabella waits for him on the platform.

'You've done for yourself by this, young man,' said she. 'I don't know whether you know it.'

'Of course I do. I meant to do for myself.'

'What—to commit suicide?'

'Certainly.'

'Well, I'm blest! Kill yourself for a woman!' (413).

With almost comic clarity, Arabella and Jude define opposing notions of love, romance, and tragedy. For Jude, the desire 'to see a particular woman, and then to die,' and to accomplish both of these wishes 'by taking this journey in the rain' (413) seems a reasonable plan. Absurd as it is romantic, it defines Jude as a man of intense, if misplaced, passions, and lets us know that, in crucial moments, he shares with Sue the implacable will to carry out a plan, and that the stupider the plan the more intensely it is likely to be carried out. This kind of mad intensity is dramatically countered by Arabella's straightforward deflationary common sense: 'Well, I'm blest! Kill yourself for a woman!' Vulgar peasant woman that she is, Arabella the pig girl often turns out to be the oddly sensible center of the novel.

No one could be less like Arabella than Jude's beloved Sue, who, as a kind of ascetic exercise, embraces an unhappy marriage as a form of punishment and penitence, an undertaking that amazes the sensible housekeeper, Mrs. Edlin:

'Lord, lov 'ee, what do ye do that yourself for, when I've come o' purpose! You knew I should come.'

'Oh—I don't know—I forgot! No, I didn't forget. I did it to discipline myself. I have scrubbed the stairs since eight o'clock. I *must* practise myself in my household duties. I've shamefully neglected them!'

'Why should ye? He'll get a better school, perhaps be a parson, in time, and you'll keep two servants. 'Tis a pity to spoil them pretty hands.'

'Don't talk of my pretty hands, Mrs. Edlin. This pretty body of mine has been the ruin of me already!'

'Pshoo—you've got no body to speak of! You put me more in mind of a sperrit' (415).

For all her pretenses to paganism and modernism, Sue creates for herself the life of a medieval penitent, choosing a life of pain and arduous exercises, eschewing the care of the body. But there remains an unpleasant streak of vanity in her rejection of her 'pretty body' (which, by the way, is her own elaboration of Mrs. Edlin's limited praise of her 'pretty hands'). Mrs. Edlin makes two important points, however. When she focuses on Sue's 'pretty hands,' she almost consciously evokes the sobriquet of Isolde of the White

Hands, confirming, it would seem, that Hardy intentionally plays with shifting indicators of Isolde the wife and Isolde the mistress. But again, as Mrs. Edlin makes clear, the difference between the two women in Jude's life is a difference between body and 'sperrit.' The contrast between body and spirit is not, however, precisely symmetrical with the contrast between wife and lover.

Both wives, Arabella and Iseult of the White Hands, are forced to look on the corpses of their husbands, but what a difference there is between Iseult's "'What a rare beauteous knight has perished here'" and Arabella's "'Yes. He's a 'andsome corpse'" (430). The difference in tone reflects a difference in class between the princess and the peasant, but also reflects Arabella's determinedly antiromantic view of life. One thing the two widows do share, however, is the proprietary view summed up in Iseult's '*He* one with *her?*' Hardy refuses, despite the precedent of the legend, to allow either set of lovers the kind of union in death that suggests that love transcends mortality and the claims of ordinary bonds, like marriage. The entire liberatory, if perhaps delusional, thrust of the legend is denied not only in the determinedly bleak view expressed in *Jude the Obscure*, but in Hardy's elevated tragedy as well. And, in both cases, it is the wife who wins.

While the impetus of the legend is toward reunion and transcendence, the novel consciously avoids these consolations. It is unnecessary for the wife to impede the return of the lovers, since the lovers themselves, having internalized a sense of guilt from the community and from their own interpretations of their behavior, impose their own isolation.

More interesting from a Tristanian perspective, however, is the text's refusal of erotic transcendence. The notion of transcendence seems so out of tune with the bleakness of *Jude* that it is not surprising that there is no such resolution here; the fact such a notion is banished also from *The Famous Tragedy*, however, suggests that Hardy is consciously writing the crucial Tristanian theme out of the Tristan legend. The legend itself imposes limits on what he can do in the tragedy, but it is still remarkable that he has Tristan's body on the stage, while Iseult leaps over the cliffs. They both die, but they die separately. In *Jude*, where Hardy is obviously freer to invent, he rejects the Tristanian theme completely. It is not love, but the tragic view of marriage that survives.

This refusal of transcendence and a denial of the salvific power of erotic passion may be read merely as the Victorian realist demystifying some hoary traditional ideas. In rejecting absolutely the idea of reunion in death and transcendence in love, Hardy has not misunderstood, not updated, but undermined and attacked the essential meaning of the legend. He has created a text that is consciously and ruthlessly anti-Tristanian.

While my primary arguments have been in a sense proleptic, arguing from the influence of a text that Hardy did not write until thirty years after he completed *Jude*, there is another text that may have influenced him more immediately. In the week ending June 10, 1893, Hardy spent a great deal of time at the theater, attending performances of *Hedda Gabler, Rosmersholm,* and *The Master Builder*, the last in the company of Florence Henniker.[10] For some years, also, he had been a close friend of Edmund Gosse, one of Ibsen's earliest translators and supporters.

It is not too difficult to see the influence of Hedda Gabler on the character of Sue Bridehead. Both are neurotic, manipulative women, who have destructive effects on the men in their lives, especially the ones who love them most. And both manage to be both passionate and frigid, daring and cowardly, eager to shock and deeply conventional.

Hedda and Sue have both been claimed as members of that peculiar species, 'the New Woman.' It is irrelevant here to argue this point at any length, but I should like to pause briefly to suggest that the vulgar Arabella (rather like Ibsen's Thea) is, in fact, a more reasonable role model for the New Woman than either Sue or Hedda. She takes action and responsibility and is in control of her life, whatever the consequences to others may be, in a way that the neurotic and essentially dependent Sue never is. She is also free of the pretense, cant, and hypocrisy in which Hardy allows Sue to wallow.[11]

There is, however, a little more to the influence of *Hedda Gabler* than Sue's neuroses. If Sue is a displaced ascetic, Hedda is a displaced romantic. Both characters are haunted, somewhat subliminally to be sure, by images from the Middle Ages. Hedda, however, is haunted by, and the play is structured by, a reminiscence of the Tristan legend even more precise and direct than what is found in *Jude*. In *Hedda*, Ibsen reflects the marriage-mistress structure that is central to the legend, with dreary old Tesman as the long-suffering Mark-figure, and Eilert as the ever-desirable Tristan torn between his companionate relationship with the adoring Thea and his passionate, unsatisfied relationship with the married and unattainable Hedda. That Ibsen did not merely accidentally reflect the Tristanian structure is, I think, made certain by the name of the poet-lover in the play. The name Eilert Lovberg is surely intended to echo the name of the first German Tristan poet, Eilhart von Oberge, who composed his *Tristrant* sometime between 1170 and 1190, and which is 'the earliest complete account of the tragic love story of Tristan and Isolde and the version which, according to many scholars, most closely resembles the lost original.'[12] Ibsen's slight change of the last name does not, I think, vitiate the allusion, but clarifies it. The mere placename is intensified by its enuniciation of love, and the resulting compound, which suggests 'Love Mountain,' may also evoke another medieval, or, more accurately, post-medieval, reference to the Venusberg in Wagner's *Tannhauser*. In addition to the name, Hedda's determination to see that her lover dies *beautifully* reflects, although in an utterly perverted sort of way, the crucial connection between love and death essential to the *Tristan*. Hedda further clinches this reference by her vision of Eilert 'with vine leaves in his hair,' an allusion that is certainly Bacchic, but also recalls the vine leaves that grow over Tristan's grave and intertwine with the roses growing from Isolde's grave. Finally, like Isolde (and unlike Sue), Hedda joins her lover in death. While her means of doing so both reflects and denies Tristan as a model, Ibsen maintains features of the legend that Hardy rejects. Ibsen's lovers both die, and are, at least theoretically, if ironically, united in death. And there is the desire, however grimly it is carried out, to die beautifully.

There is, in conclusion, a clear trajectory of Hardy's interest in the legend from 1870 to the production of *The Famous Tragedy* in 1923. And it seems likely that Ibsen's *Hedda Gabler* triggered these themes that are then reflected and revised in *Jude*. If this argument of a Tristan component to *Jude* is accepted and the influence of Ibsen acknowledged, a further conclusion can be drawn. Hardy manages to be the sole Victorian writer to be involved with the Tristan legend while remaining untouched, untainted, and totally uncontaminated by any trace of influence from the nineteenth-century Tristanian mammoth, Wagner's colossal opera. If for nothing else, Hardy deserves our admiration for escaping those Wagnerian tentacles and creating a Victorian meditation on the Tristan legend that is bleak, unromantic, and as original as it is disturbing.

NORTHEASTERN ILLINOIS UNIVERSITY

Donald L. Hoffman of Northeastern Illinois University is the immediate Past President of the North American Branch of the International Arthurian Society. He has published on Arthurian influences in a variety of literatures ranging from twelfth-century Italian prophecy to the postmodern African-American novel and surrealist film.

NOTES

1 Thomas Hardy, *The Famous Tragedy of the Queen of Cornwall at Tintagel in Lyonesse: A new version of an old story arranged as a play for mummers in one act requiring no theater or scenery* (New York: MacMillan, 1923), p. 4.

2 Hardy, *The Famous Tragedy of the Queen of Cornwall*, p. 3.

3 Martin Seymour-Smith, *Hardy* (London: Bloomsbury, 1994), p. 854.

4 Hardy, *The Famous Tragedy of the Queen of Cornwall*, pp. 72–76.

5 Seymour-Smith, *Hardy*, p. 854.

6 Quoted in Seymour-Smith, *Hardy*, p. 108, from Thomas Hardy, *Collected Poems of Thomas Hardy* (New York: MacMillan, 1925), p. 294.

7 Hardy, *Jude the Obscure* (1896; rep. New York: Bantam, 1996). All subsequent references to *Jude the Obscure* will be parenthetical.

8 Gertrude Schœpperle Loomis, *Tristan and Isolt: A Study of the Sources of the Romance*, 2d. edn., 2 vols. (rep. New York: Burt Franklin, 1970), p. 2.

9 Her taste in art and her taste in literature are similar. Both are less than up-to-date and reflect the taste of a slightly earlier period. She is unaware that Andrea del Sarto and his pre-Raphaelite predecessors (whom she scorns) are far more fashionable than the work of Lely and Reynolds who are rapidly going out of fashion.

10 Seymour-Smith, *Hardy*, p. 480.

11 There are, of course, other approaches to Sue. For example, in *Thomas Hardy* (New York: Macmillan, 1967), p. 403, Irving Howe seems more taken with her than even Jude was:

> Sue is that terrifying specter of our age, before whom men and cultures tremble: she is an *interesting* girl. She is promethean in mind but masochist in character; and the division destroys her, making a shambles of her mind and a mere sterile discipline of her character. She is all intellectual seriousness, but without that security of will which enables one to live out the consequences of an idea to their limit. She is all feminine charm, but without body, flesh or smell, without femaleness. Lacking focused sexuality, she casts a vaguely sexual aura over everything she touches. Her sensibility is kindled but her senses are mute.

It seems to me that Howe gives undue credit to Sue's intelligence, which is limited, superficial, and cluttered with bizarre *idées reçues*. She does not have ideas; she is possessed by them. Her will, on the other hand, while it may lack 'security,' is, nevertheless, relentless. Above all, as Howe suggests, there is her pansexual fear of sexuality. As in her unnecessary reassurance that she is unaffected by the naughty bits in the books she reads, she is, in fact, obsessed by the erotic, but displaces and represses it. Her repressed erotomania reinforces an impression of her as a displaced (medieval) ascetic. She is, then, not so much a 'new' as an 'anachronistic' woman with a vocation for suffering, but with no structure or institution to validate her suffering. In her extreme abjection, Sue is a far more serious case than Hedda, but, as Rutland pointed out over half a century ago, 'it is easy to see that *Jude the Obscure* owes something to Ibsen.' In W.R. Rutland, 'Hardy, Parnell, and Isben,' in *Thomas Hardy: Jude the Obscure*, ed. Norman Page (New York: Norton, 1978; rep. from Rutland, *Thomas Hardy, a Study of his Writings and their Backgrounds* [1938; rep. New York: Russell, 1962]), p. 375. That 'something' is the neurasthenic character of Sue Bridehead derived from Hedda Gabler. See Howe, 'A Distinctly Modern Novel,' in *Thomas Hardy: Jude the Obscure*, ed. Norman Page (New York: Norton, 1978; rep. from Howe, *Thomas Hardy* [New York: Macmillan, 1967]), pp. 395–405; and W.R. Rutland, 'Hardy, Parnell, and Isben,' pp. 373–76.

12 Eilhart von Oberge, *Tristrant*, trans. J.W. Thomas (Lincoln, NE: University of Nebraska Press, 1978), p. 1.

'No—I am out—I am out of my Tower and my Wits': The Lady of Shalott in A.S. Byatt's *Possession*

Possession is preoccupied with Tennyson's 'Lady of Shalott' and how she has been interpreted as representing the literary imagination. While Christabel LaMotte and Maud Bailey manage to break out of the Lady's tower, neither transcends the Lady's destiny: to remain always the object of poetic and critical discourse, never the subject. (KCK)

Female visionaries are poor mad exploited sibyls and pythonesses. Male ones are prophets and poets.[1]

I grew up on 'The Lady of Shalott' and the 'Morte d'Arthur.' I must have been about six years old when I was given fat colouring books containing both poems [sic], full length. As a result I find the rhythms, and the images, and even whole sentences, haunting everything I write, irrelevantly and relevantly....Eliot said that Tennyson did not feel his thought as immediately as the odour of a rose, but I think increasingly that that is what he most precisely *did* do—more than any other English poet. He thought with images, and they act on the blood and the mind together.[2]

A S. Byatt describes *Possession* (1990) as a study of 'the life of the mind';[3] indeed, it is a virtuoso study of the fully-examined and critical life—of the 'sibyls and pythonesses' and 'prophets and poets,' of the first epigraph, and of those capable of 'acting on the blood and the mind together' of the second. There is much to work with in this 555-page novel, but in this essay, I want to pull on just one thread, which is the novel's preoccupation with the figure of the entowered, enclosed maiden and how she has been used or interpreted as representing the literary imagination and the problem of subjectivity. Malory's Fair Maid is here, but it is Tennyson's Lady of Shalott who serves as the model for both the nineteenth-century poet Christabel LaMotte and the twentieth-century feminist scholar Maud Bailey, the two central female characters in the novel. In her poetry, Christabel is obsessed with thresholds and boundaries and violations thereof; in turn, the scholar Maud writes about Christabel's use of such images. Both women struggle with boundaries in their own lives; both attempt to make space for creative work in their respective worlds, generally hostile to such work by women. But Christabel and Maud are just two of many confined and constricted women, literal and metaphorical, whom we meet throughout the novel. For example, Byatt puts Maud's cousin Jean in a wheelchair, and includes a tale about a living woman enclosed in a glass coffin.[4] Byatt also makes references to women in towers, prisons, and convents—and to woman/Woman as egg, both whole and broken (151, 492, 549, 309). Byatt even structures the novel as an enclosed, tautological space, beginning and ending with references to that famous historian of the cyclical, Giambattista Vico (8, 510, 512, 548).

Traditional critics have long been concerned with degendering and circumscribing Tennyson's Lady, making her *stand in for* the male poet rather than *taking her for* a female poet.[5] Byatt is certainly aware of this critical tradition: Byatt dedicated *Possession* to her friend, Victorian scholar Isobel Armstrong, who in 1989, one year before *Possession* was published, wrote a definitive article on the Lady of Shalott.[6] As she develops her very original argument about Tennyson's understanding of and use of myth, Armstrong furnishes a thorough survey of scholarship on 'The Lady of Shalott' to date. In fact, one might productively read Armstrong's essay as a kind of critical commentary on *Possession* and on Byatt's representation of the Lady and her avatars. Byatt is able to turn critical arguments into compelling, resonant fiction, as in, for example, her characterization of Ellen Ash. Ellen, outwardly steadfast but possessed by a secret sorrow, writes in her diary of her adolescent wish to be 'a Poet and a Poem' and of her unhappiness that she is neither (136). This is, in effect, the Lady's dilemma in traditional readings of Tennyson's poem, in which expressions of feminine desire have no place. Certainly, the Lady's status in the Anglo-American canon as the quintessential 'mad exploited' literary heroine can be traced to Tennyson, who speaks of the Lady as experiencing the 'new born love for something, for someone in the wide world from which she has been so long secluded,' which 'takes her out of the region of shadows into that of realities.'[7] (And given the ending of the poem in which the Lady floats down to Camelot on her funeral boat, 'reality' is death, as Armstrong notes.)[8] Yet how we read the Lady today is also the result of an accretion of readings spanning more than one hundred years, as the following gendered interpretation, found in a popular college anthology, demonstrates:

The tower, the loom, the Lady herself, have no consistent figurative meaning, but the reader is tempted to consider the Lady in her tower as representing the poet, the loom as art, and the mirror as poetic imagination....The poem suggests that the artist must remain in aloof detachment, observing life only in the mirror of the imagination, not mixing in it directly. Once the artist attempts to lead the life of ordinary men his poetic gift, it would seem, dies.[9]

Thus Byatt exploits literary *history* as much as she exploits the *literary* in her highly nuanced, allusive use of the Lady of Shalott. The Lady serves Byatt well, allowing her to make explicit the bonds among the many women who populate her novel and to explore their often-troubled relations to creative work and identity. As we shall see, while both Christabel LaMotte and Maud Bailey manage to break out of the Lady's tower as it has been constructed by Tennyson and his readers, neither woman fully transcends the Lady's destiny, which is to remain always the object of poetic and critical discourse, never the subject.

Before I continue, a summary of the novel may be helpful. Roland Mitchell, a research assistant to scholar and editor James Blackadder, is busily hunting down material for an edition of a nineteenth-century poet Byatt has invented, Randolph Henry Ash. (Ash is a cross between Browning and Tennyson, with bits of Wordsworth, Arnold, Morris, Ruskin, and Carlyle, and George Henry Lewes thrown in.) Mitchell discovers a letter suggesting that the married Ash had an affair with the equally-imaginary poet, Christabel LaMotte, a composite of Emily Dickinson, Christina Rossetti, and Elizabeth Barrett Browning, with dashes of George Eliot and the Brontës. Their affair ends when LaMotte finds herself pregnant and chooses not to tell Ash. As Mitchell attempts to verify his find, he meets Maud Bailey, a feminist scholar who specializes in LaMotte's poetry. Together, they make a series of discoveries about Ash and LaMotte that take them on a number of adventures— adventures that begin to parallel the lives of the poets. (A major structuring device of *Possession* is the repetition of scene, action, phrase, object, color, and even character; the nineteenth-century Christabel-Randolph-Blanche-Ellen characters mirror the twentieth-century Maud-Roland-Leonora-Val characters.) Maud, it is revealed at the end of the novel, is Christabel's great-great-great-granddaughter. Byatt shuttles her readers between the present-time narrative and the journal of Ash's wife Ellen; the journal of Blanche Glover, Christabel's lesbian companion; the standard biography of Ash; a number of scholarly articles about the poets; and, most crucially, the letters and poetry of Randolph Ash and Christabel LaMotte. Every one of these texts-within-the-text is a stunningly convincing invention of Byatt herself.[10]

Byatt subtitles *Possession* 'A Romance,' and chooses for an epigraph an excerpt from Nathaniel Hawthorne's preface to *The House of the Seven Gables*, in which he says: 'When a writer calls his work a Romance, it need hardly be observed that he wishes to claim a certain latitude, both as to its fashion and material.' The sort of latitude Byatt claims is now almost a cliché: *Possession* is very much a *postmodern* romance in the most conventional, generic sense. Roland, for example, comes to the highly self-conscious conclusion that he

> was in a Romance, a vulgar and a high Romance simultaneously; a Romance was one of the systems that controlled him, as the expectations of Romance control almost everyone in the Western world, for better or for worse, at some point or another (460).

Such narratorial comments mark *Possession* as an example of what we have come to call *metafiction*; that is, fiction about fiction. John Fowles's *The French Lieutenant's Woman* and Julian Barnes's *Flaubert's Parrot* and *History of the World in 10 Chapters* are good examples of such fiction—and, proof that metafiction is not a modern invention, Chaucer's *House of Fame* and *The Canterbury Tales* also serve as examples of a preoccupation with the literary within the literary. I would argue, moreover, that *Possession* represents, if not inaugurates, a particular sub-genre of metafiction: like Byatt's later novellas *The Conjugal Angel* and *The Djinn in the Nightingale's Eye*, *Possession* is a cross between fiction and literary criticism—'critafiction,' or even 'fictcrit.'[11] Think of Terry Eagleton's engaging *Literary Theory* and imagine a novel wrapped around it: this is a fair description of *Possession*.

Metafiction may lead us to meditate on the making of fiction, but Byatt's critafiction gives us a more explicit and self-conscious interpretation of the text at hand, as we are shuttled between Byatt's imaginative plot and her literary-theoretical exposition thereof. Byatt ventriloquizes an array of critical voices that represents the range of contemporary literary criticism, a trick that teaches us how to position her work in the canon of contemporary British literature. Byatt, in effect, has written her own *Cliff Notes*.

Not only does Byatt give us a map for reading *Possession*, but we are also supplied with directions for reading the novel's myriad intertexts. Most of these intertexts supplement or parallel 'The Lady of Shalott' plot line in that they are concerned with the figure of the female visionary as she has been variously represented in Western, mainly Anglo-American, literature and art. Enclosed and entowered female figures are part of a larger female/feminine mythos that Byatt weaves throughout *Possession*: women are represented as homemakers, mothers, lovers, scholars, weavers, monsters, and mediums (461). We find allusions, direct and oblique, extended and fleeting, not only to the Lady of Shalott (205, 206), but to Coleridge's Christabel (193, 196); Tennyson's Maud; Keats's La Belle Dame Sans Merci (555); the medieval Jean D'Arras's Melusine (180, 192, 312, 436); the Princess and the Pea (160, 307), the Princess Dahud (378), and princesses in general (65, 459); Emily Dickinson; the feminized muse (211); witches, lamias, undines (266-67); the Little Mermaid (404); mermaids in general; selkies (305), water-pixies (488), Celtic whiteladies (191), sirens (Christabel 'sang like Goethe's sirens and Homer's [310]); Christina Rossetti's heroines in 'Goblin Market'; Ariadne, Arachne (194, 360, 340, 368), and women in general as spiders (198); Pandora (217), Proserpina, Pomona (511, 512), Medusa (342), Maia (543, 553-54); Vivien (382), Malory's Elaine (in the figure of Blanche Glover, who is also an Ophelia figure), Eve (511), Martha and Mary (373); Rapunzel (LaMotte's poem 40, Maud's growing of her hair 64); and even woman reborn as the Phoenix (214). Byatt's zaftig American critic Leonora Stern speaks of 'every archetype' and, indeed, they are all here (461).

Yet in spite of such a plentitude, it often seems as if 'The Lady of Shalott' was the sole palimpsest upon which *Possession* was written. Tennyson's poem surfaces in the novel explicitly through allusion, and implicitly as half-remembered lines and shadowy images. One quick example: the name *LaMotte*, itself a pun on enclosure, resonates nicely with *Shalott* and *Camelot*, and returns us to Tennyson's repetitive rhyme scheme. (Maud's last name also suggests enclosure, as in the *bailey* of a castle.) [12]

But Byatt goes beyond mere allusion to 'The Lady of Shalott.' As I suggested above, she exploits the history of the reception of Tennyson's poem and provides us with a reading of her own, accomplishing both critical tasks through character development and plot, supplemented by critical exposition in the various conversations, letters, poems, and excerpts from ersatz scholarship that give *Possession* its distinctive character. For example, Byatt captures an important moment in the history of literary criticism by bringing to life her most famous teacher at Cambridge, F.R. Leavis. Leavis, along with his fellow contributors to *Scrutiny*, managed to exile Tennyson from the canon in the 1930s. (He's back in, of course.) Byatt makes Blackadder a former student of Leavis's who has never quite got over Leavis's influence. Blackadder recalls how Leavis used his 'analytic brilliance in distinguishing fake from authenticity, Victorian alienation from the voice of true feeling' in order to condemn Ash's poetry. Ash, a generic Victorian poet who happens to write very much like Tennyson and Browning, is 'duly exposed and found wanting' (32).[13] Byatt not only desires to reaffirm Tennyson's place in the canon (thus resisting Leavis's judgment), but also critiques Tennyson's mostly male exegetes (ca. 1842 to 1972) who have conventionally read the Lady as the feminine Muse or as a figure for masculine creativity.

Let us turn to Byatt's refashioning of the Lady as Christabel LaMotte and Maud Bailey, both of whom seem to have stepped out of a painting by Pre-Raphaelite painter William Holman Hunt. Byatt weaves the symbols of the Lady of Shalott's isolation—her island, her tower, the tapestry of the world distorted through a mirror—into her descriptions of both women, who themselves mirror each other.

Our first introduction to Christabel LaMotte comes through a letter that Roland Mitchell discovers in Randolph Ash's copy of Vico's *Principi di una Scienza Nuova* (*Principles of the New Science*). 'I know you go out in company very little,' Ash writes to her (8; see also 97). It is a small detail, but one that will take on significance later, as the nature of Christabel's isolation becomes clearer. (She replies: 'I live circumscribed and self-communing' [97].) Ash sees Christabel as 'distant and closed away, a princess in a tower' (301). Just as the Lady of Shalott is compelled to leave her tower once she gazes upon Lancelot, Christabel breaks with social convention and her own self-imposed seclusion once she falls in love with Ash. At one point, she writes to Ash, 'No—I am out—I am out of my Tower and my Wits,' and continuing, 'the Muse has forsaken me—as she may mockingly forsake all Women, who dally with Her—and then—Love—' (215, 216). By alluding to the Lady in her Tower—by identifying with her—Christabel reproduces the dominant reading of Tennyson's poem, and foreshadows her own end.

At one point, Christabel writes to William Rossetti:

> In these dim November days I resemble nothing more than that poor Creature of [Ash's] Fantasy, immured in her terrible *In-Pace*, quieted perforce and longing for her Quietus. It takes a Masculine Courage to find pleasure in constructing Dungeons for Innocents in his Fancy, and a Female Patience to endure them in sober fact (48).

That 'poor Creature' to whom Christabel refers is the main character in Ash's poem, 'The Incarcerated Sorceress,' of which we get only one small snippet (77), but that we may take as Ash's version of, or companion piece to, Tennyson's 'Lady of Shalott.' We may well apply Christabel's comment on 'Masculine Courage' to Tennyson, who did indeed construct a prison-house for the Lady of Shalott.

Like the Lady of Shalott, Christabel is bound by a 'curse': her adulterous affair with Randolph Ash and the resulting pregnancy certainly violate Victorian social mores. Afterward, Christabel withdraws completely from the world—she dies a social death—and settles in the tower of 'Seal Court,' the family manor. In essence, she seals herself off, becomes an anchoress in a cell. At the end of her life, Christabel describes herself to Ellen as living 'in a Turret like an old Witch' (489; see also 543).[14]

We meet Maud Bailey immediately after the episode in which Roland discovers Christabel. This early, strategic juxtaposition helps to underscore the affinities developed throughout the novel between the two women. And, just as we first saw Christabel through Roland's questing gaze, we see Maud through Roland's eyes. Maud's hair, we are told, is 'wound tightly into a turban of peacock-feathered painted silk, low on her brow' (44). She covers her head because she is ashamed of her emphatically blond hair, out of keeping, she feels, with her feminist sensibilities (64). There is an economy, a purity about Maud, in the way she holds herself, thinks, and speaks. She is entowered within herself. At one point, she wonders: 'Why could she do nothing with ease and grace except work alone, inside these walls and curtains, her bright safe box?' (151).

Maud teaches at the fictitious Lincoln University, which the narrator describes as having 'white-tiled towers, variegated with violet tiles and orange tiles' (44). Tennyson grew up in Lincolnshire, and as the narrator puts it, '[f]rom there he made the cornfields of immortal Camelot' (77). This particular passage, in which Byatt describes Lincoln University and then goes on to invoke Tennyson's biography, illustrates Byatt's tendency to give us not only the allusion or the association, but the obvious cue for making the correct connection.

Maud's office is at the top of 'Tennyson Tower,' the front door of which is glass, and walled with books on three sides and with glass on the fourth side (45, 46). Maud often sits, the narrator says, behind 'the barrier of the desk' (46). At one point, the narrator describes Maud standing inside the mirrored, bronzed elevator in Tennyson Tower, in which 'she flash[es]...from wall to wall' (45). I find it hard to resist imagining Maud as caught within a mirror, deflecting the world in a very Lady-like way. And like the Lady, Maud 'weaveth steadily': as a poststructuralist feminist critic, Maud is a weaver—and unweaver—of narratives.

When (Childe) Roland to Tennyson Tower comes, he trips on the threshold, 'the floor lifting beneath him' (45). He has moved into a liminal space, crossed a threshold into an Otherworld of women, of feminist scholarship: in short, into the Lady's tower (see 65 for another example). Just as Randolph Ash is Christabel's Lancelot, Roland is Maud's, moving into her field of vision and upsetting her tidy world—though it must be said that, while Lancelot remains impervious to the Lady in Tennyson's poem,

Christabel changes Ash's personal and creative life profoundly, as does Maud change Roland's.

Unlike Christabel, Maud Bailey has no Gothic scandals in her life; rather, her problems are strictly of the 1990s variety, as seen in her complicated relationship with her ex-lover Fergus Wolff, a man described by Roland as a 'devourer' (550). The Lady of Shalott's tower is invoked in a roundabout way when Fergus writes to Maud about his plans for a scholarly paper, titled 'The Queen of the Castle: What is kept in the Keep?' (153). Fergus even calls this proposal his 'siege-paper'—an offensive aimed at Maud, and, by extension, at Christabel and her poetry.

Byatt ties the two women together in a number of descriptive passages. Maud's cousin Jean describes Maud as 'stand-offish or shy, maybe both. What my mother used to call a chilly mortal' (159). In fact, Fergus Wolff, quoting Coleridge, says of Maud that 'she thicks men's blood with cold' (39). Christabel is also called 'a chilly mortal' by her Yorkshire landlady (310). Both women wear the same heraldic colors: Maud is described as tall, clothed in a 'green and white length' (44). She wears green shoes. She has a 'clean, milky skin,' with features 'largely composed' (44). When Maud blushes, we are told how '[r]ed blood stained the ivory' (57). The narrator tells us that Christabel is 'very fair, pale-skinned, with eyes...of a strange green colour which transmuted itself as the light varied' (298). She wears emerald green boots, and 'everything about her was...neat' (298). Ash sees Christabel this way as well: he notes 'the whiteness of her' and 'the green look of those piercing or occluded eyes' (301). Maud quotes from Christabel's poetry: 'Outside our small safe place flies Mystery' (315). This is as much a comment about Christabel as it is about herself. Maud says later, "'I feel as she did. I keep my defences up"' (549; Maud quotes this line, 290).

I want to juxtapose two passages; in the first, Christabel writes to Ash (and here we find Byatt's most explicit use of the Lady of Shalott figure); in the second, Maud speaks to Roland:

1) Think of me if you will as the Lady of Shalott—with a Narrower Wisdom— who chooses not the Gulp of outside Air and the chilly river-journey deathwards—but who chooses to watch diligently the bright colours of her Web—to ply an industrious shuttle—to make—something—to close the Shutters and the Peephole too—(205)

2) I wrote a paper on Victorian women's imagination of space. Marginal Beings and Liminal Poetry. About agoraphobia and claustrophobia and the paradoxical desire to be let out into unconfined space, the wild moorland, the open ground, and at the same time to be closed into tighter and tighter impenetrable small

spaces—like Emily Dickinson's voluntary confinement, like the Sibyl's jar (61).

Though Christabel eventually takes a version of the Lady's 'chilly river-journey' in *Possession*, she does achieve the status of a speaking subject, a status denied Tennyson's Lady of Shalott. Remember that the Lady sings 'her last song…mournful, holy, / Chanted loudly, chanted slowly' on the way to Camelot.[15] But we are never given her actual words—no one hears her. On the other hand, Christabel leaves behind a rich legacy of poems and original fairy tales. Compared to Christabel, Maud is that lesser being, a scholar, and gives us not poetry, but an abstract for a scholarly paper *about* poetry—an abstract that reveals as much about Maud and her personal fears as it does about her feminist project. In their own ways—ways very much dictated by their respective cultural moments—both women attempt to write themselves out of the Lady of Shalott's predicament. But do they succeed?

At a first reading, it seems as if Christabel avoids the Lady's fate. After all, Christabel lives again through Maud Bailey, for Maud's scholarship brings Christabel's work to a new and appreciative audience, thus securing Christabel's place in the canon. Moreover, Christabel lives again quite literally: as we discover at the climax of the novel, Maud is Christabel's great-great-great-granddaughter. Yet it strikes me that this romantic conclusion is cast in masculinist terms in which the value of the immortal word and the importance of genealogy is made primary. I would argue that Christabel is indeed subject to the imperatives of conventional romance, and a tragical romance it is, for Christabel must give up her work, love, and, finally, her child. Christabel is nothing more than another iteration on the theme of the entowered, doomed maiden. Her story is not a *revisioning*, but simply a *revisiting* of the tantalizing tale of 'The Lady of Shalott,' fleshed out for modern readers greedy for a fuller, more detailed narrative.

And Maud's liberation? At the end of the novel, Roland and Maud make love:

> And very slowly and with infinite gentle delays and delicate diversions and variations of indirect assault Roland finally, to use an outdated phrase, entered and took possession of all her white coolness that grew warm against him, so that there seemed to be no boundaries, and he heard towards dawn, from a long way off, her clear voice crying out, uninhibited, unashamed, in pleasure and triumph (550–51).

This passage might be found in any one of the better-written romance novels on the market today. Are we to take this seriously, as a classic romantic ending signifying coherence and closure? Or is this passage a parody of the genre? Perhaps a parody of coherence and closure? A parody of our own desire for such?

The allusions to Vico at the beginning and end of the novel suggest that *Possession* (as in other narratives in shape of an 'o,' from the medieval *Pearl* onwards) is intended to resist closure at the same time that it encloses. *Possession* thus ends ambiguously enough for any postmodern reader, yet not because Byatt has fully embraced the postmodern project, but because, I would argue, she finds herself at odds with it.

Possession oscillates between two contradictory philosophical positions— on the one hand, it stages a desire to acknowledge the situatedness of subjectivity and the implications of such situatedness, and on the other, it argues for transcending the constraints of such situatedness. I would describe the overall thrust of the novel as a self-conscious return to traditional humanist literary values, a declaration of a *post* postmodern aesthetic (a New *Humanist* Criticism, perhaps). Trained as a New Critic—Leavis's student, remember— Byatt has made it her business to learn about poststructuralist theory, which she finds exhilarating but alarming. (As an author, Byatt certainly hopes that the reports of her death are much exaggerated.) Byatt's use of Tennyson's Lady represents a struggle between a knowing and self-reflective postmodernism and an allegiance to received narrative. For a moment, the stories of Christabel and Maud reposition the feminine as autonomous subject. We begin to imagine a different ending to Tennyson's poem, but what we get in *Possession* is the same, but new-fashioned: Christabel abandons her life work and suffers grave loss; Maud loses her self in passion and sexual possession—like Rapunzel, she is set free, but only through masculine agency. Byatt thus fulfills Christabel's argument about the imperatives of narrative; Christabel says

> All old stories…will bear telling and telling again in different ways. What is required is to keep alive, to polish, the simple clean forms of the tale which *must* be there…And yet to add something…of the writer, which makes all these things seem new and first seen…(379).

Perhaps to give the Lady of Shalott and her descendants and analogues a happy ending is to eviscerate the tale: what '*must* be there,' it seems, is separation and loss and death. And surely the power, if not the heart, of *Possession* lies in the tale of the doomed love affair between Randolph Ash and Christabel LaMotte. Yet I long to rewrite Tennyson's Lady, perhaps in the same way that Hélène Cixous so artfully recuperates the Medusa by writing against myth: 'You only have to look at the Medusa straight on to see her,' says Cixous. 'And she's not deadly. She's beautiful and she's laughing.'[16] After all, as Cixous might ask, *what must be there, and according to whom?*

Perhaps it is not fair to accuse Byatt of not going far enough in her treatment of the Lady of Shalott figure. Perhaps she intends to remind us of the degree to which we are always already embedded in the culture we inhabit, unable to escape its terms—and that we are the most ensnared by culture when we attempt to critique it. On the other hand, perhaps Byatt has simply hit some sort of cultural glass ceiling, as gallingly unavoidable and distorting as is the Lady's mirror—and eerily reminiscent of it.

NORTHEASTERN UNIVERSITY

Kathleen Coyne Kelly (www.dac.neu.edu/english/kakelly) is Associate Professor of English at Northeastern University. Her most recent book is *Performing Virginity and Testing Chastity in the Middle Ages* (Routledge), and she is currently working on a monograph tentatively titled 'Malory's Desire for History and the History of Desire.'

NOTES

1 A.S. Byatt, new introduction to *Shadow of the Sun* (1964; rep. London: Vintage, 1991), p. x.

2 A.S. Byatt, 'A Hundred Years After: Twelve Writers Reflect on Tennyson's Achievement and Influence,' in *Times Literary Supplement*, 4670 (2 October 1992), p. 8.

3 As quoted in 'A.S. Byatt,' *Contemporary Authors*, N.R.S. 33 (Detroit, MI: Gale Publishing, 1991), p. 70.

4 A.S. Byatt, *Possession: A Romance* (New York: Random House, 1990), p. 65. Henceforth, all page numbers will appear in the body of the text.

5 See Kathleen Coyne Kelly, 'The Lady of Shalott: Malory, Tennyson, Pynchon,' in *Modern Retellings of Chivalric Texts*, ed. Gloria Allaire (Aldershot, England, and Brookfield VT: Ashgate Press, 1999), pp. 25–38, for a discussion of this tradition.

6 Isobel Armstrong, 'Tennyson's "The Lady of Shalott": Victorian Mythography and the Politics of Narcissism,' in *The Sun is God: Painting, Literature, and Mythology in the Nineteenth Century*, ed. J.B. Bullen (Oxford: Clarendon, 1989), pp. 49–106.

7 As quoted in Christopher Ricks's headnote to the poem. *The Poems of Tennyson*, ed. Christopher Ricks, 2d. edn. (University of California Press, 1987).

8 Armstrong, ' 'Tennyson's "The Lady of Shalott,"' p. 51.

9 Walter E. Houghton and G. Robert Stange, ed., *Victorian Poetry and Poetics*, 2nd edn. (Boston: Houghton Mifflin, 1968), p. 16, n4.

10 I take this summary, somewhat revised, from my *A. S. Byatt* (New York: Prentice-Hall/Twayne, 1996), pp. 78–79.

11 Marilyn Butler calls Byatt's hybrid of fiction and criticism 'ficticism.' See 'The Moth and the Medium,' *Times Literary Supplement* (16 October 1992): 22. Byatt continues to be interested in writing critafiction, as her latest novel, *The Biographer's Tale* (London: Chatto and Windus, 2000), amply demonstrates.

12 At the end of the novel, Byatt, who, as I have said, can never resist explicating her own work, includes a letter from Christabel to Ash in which she says: 'if I had kept to my closed castle, behind my motte-and-bailey defences—should I have been a great poet—as you are?' (545).

13 See also *Possession*, p. 483, where Byatt quotes an imaginary article by Leavis on Ash in *Scrutiny*.

14 Byatt invokes another compelling female figure, the Lamia, through these and other descriptions. Maud's bathroom is a 'chill green glassy place...full of watery lights' (*Possession, 63*)—a suitable place for a lamia and a Lady who looks at the world reflected through a glass. And see *Possession*, p. 396. We can profitably read Keats's two poems, 'Lamia' and 'La Belle Dame Sans Merci' along with *Possession*. Also see Byatt's short story, 'A Lamia in the Cévennes,' for a more explicit working out of the lamia myth in *Elementals: Stories of Fire and Ice* (New York: Random House, 1998), pp 81–111.

15 Ricks, *The Poems of Tennyson* , ll. 143, 145–46.

16 Hélène Cixous, 'The Laugh of the Medusa,' in *New French Feminisms: An Anthology*, ed. Elaine Marks and Isabelle de Courtivron (New York: Schocken, 1981), p. 255.

Women Illustrators of the Arthurian Legends

ALAN LUPACK

Some male illustrators of the Arthurian legends have received considerable recognition, unlike some women who have also produced fascinating Arthurian images. One example is Dora Curtis, whose unclichéd images and use of borders to reflect the theme of the image make her illustrations worthy of note. She and other women illustrators reward further study. (AL)

The best known and most often reprinted Arthurian illustrations have been created by men. This is particularly true of illustrated editions of Malory's *Le Morte Darthur*, the first modern example of which was done by Aubrey Beardsley for Dent in 1893–94 and reissued in 1909 and again in 1927 (and reprinted in facsimile in 1972). The unmistakable style of Beardsley's black and white illustrations, his hermaphroditic knights and ladies, and his bizarre decorations make his edition memorable. His depictions of Merlin being sealed up by Nimue, of Tristram and Isolt drinking the love potion, and of Bedivere returning Excalibur to the water are among the most distinctive and recognizable of Arthurian images. Also remarkable are the illustrations to an edition of Malory in 1910–11 by W. Russell Flint. Flint's illustrations often have a grandeur and a perceptive attention to detail: the swirling water from which a hand raises Excalibur while the Lady of the Lake floats serenely on the surface captures the momentous and magical qualities of the event; the young Morgan le Fay in the nunnery conjuring up an apparition to frighten a nun hints at the future character of the enchantress; and the look that Guenevere gives Lancelot as he rescues her from the stake speaks volumes about their relationship. Even better known are the illustrations by Arthur Rackham to Alfred W. Pollard's 1917 edition of Malory, such as the Grail maiden bearing the sacred cup, the strange image of the Questing Beast, and the depiction of the final struggle between Arthur and Mordred, which seems to reflect the desolation of World War I as well as that of the civil strife that ended Arthur's glorious realm.

When one thinks of illustrations of Tennyson's *Idylls of the King*, it is again a male illustrator, Gustave Doré, who first comes to mind. Doré's

Romantic and Gothic interpretations of Tennyson's epic are justly famous. His Vivien curling serpentine at Merlin's feet echoes the imagery of the poem; however, the ancient oak in Doré's illustration goes beyond anything in the poem: the roots and branches are as sinuous as Vivien's body and seem almost like the tentacles of a living creature about to grasp an unknowing victim. In other of Doré's illustrations—'The Remorse of Lancelot' or 'Vivien and Merlin Disembark,' for example—the sublime landscape dwarfs to insignificance the problems of the denizens of Camelot. In still others, such as 'Cloister Scene,' which depicts Guenevere in the nunnery, the dark Gothic interior parallels the gloom that has spread over Camelot. The receding corridor suggests the problem of foreseeing the consequences of actions but the funereal image on the floor and the crucifix looming above Guenevere's head signal that consequences and moral judgments about one's actions are inescapable. No doubt Doré reflected much of what made the *Idylls* a mirror of its age.

Even among illustrators of Arthurian books for children, it is men who are best known. Howard Pyle's four Arthurian books (*The Story of King Arthur and His Knights*, *The Story of Sir Launcelot and His Companions*, *The Story of the Champions of the Round Table*, and *The Story of the Grail and the Passing of Arthur*) are some of the most popular retellings of the tales. Pyle's illustrations, imitating the woodblocks of early printing, create an archaic feel that matches the language of his stories. His portraits of major figures throughout the four books bring the characters alive, and the interaction between text and illustration makes the pictures an essential part of the retelling. Pyle trained a whole generation of illustrators, including N.C. Wyeth, whose renditions of scenes from *The Boy's King Arthur* by Sidney Lanier are so memorable as to have remained with novelist Walker Percy from his youth and to have influenced his writing of the novel *Lancelot*.[1]

While the works of all of these male artists deserve the recognition and the reprinting that they have received, there are some wonderful Arthurian illustrations by women that have not achieved similar status. Perhaps one reason for this neglect is that no woman has ever been commissioned to illustrate a major edition of Malory, as Beardsley, Flint, and Rackham were— though a few women have illustrated a portion of Malory's masterpiece.[2] Margaret Gere did some of the illustrations for the Ashendene Press edition of Malory, but the majority were done by Charles Gere.[3] Catherine Donaldson provided 'illustrations designed and engraved on wood' for *The Death of King Arthur*.[4] The engravings for the book include some excellent depictions of events from Malory's tale, including a striking picture of

Ill. 1: 'Gawaine found in a great boat' by Catherine Donaldson

Gawaine found in a great boat, lying more than half dead'[5] (see illustration 1). And Helen Urquhart illustrated Malory's tale of the Grail.

Some retellings of tales from Malory for children have, however, been richly illustrated by women artists; and although these types of books are usually thought of as children's literature and their illustrations accordingly deemed less worthy, some of them merit serious consideration. Among these are the illustrations done by Dora Curtis for Beatrice Clay's *Stories from King Arthur and His Round Table*. A reworking of an earlier version of this book, *Stories from Le Morte Darthur and the Mabinogion* (1901), the 1905 edition includes retellings of tales from the *Mabinogion* as well as from Malory. But there are some differences between the editions, the main one being the inclusion by Clay of additional material on Morgan le Fay and the reflection of this expansion in Curtis's illustrations. Clay says of Morgan that 'the difficulty of handling this somewhat unpleasant character was so great that, practically, she did not appear in the first edition of this little work. It was pointed out to me, however, that Arthurian stories that had nothing to tell about this great sorceress were somewhat in the case of a "Hamlet" without the Ghost, and so I have now endeavored to include her story by treating it with a boldness that, I trust, may not be inexcusable' (viii).[6] Indeed the inclusion of Morgan is part of a pattern in the early sections of this book of focusing on wicked but powerful women who are given prominence in the illustrations. While there are also some fine images of male characters, Curtis's emphasis on women in the illustrations reflects Clay's emphasis on them in the text. In both the images of women and those of men, the text and illustrations complement each other in such a way as to suggest a true collaboration between writer and artist.

The color frontispiece that depicts Morgan holding Excalibur highlights the bold inclusion of her story (see illustration 2). Her rich forest green dress, with all of the symbolic ambiguity of the Green Knight in *Sir Gawain and the Green Knight,* suggests her audacity and her prominence, especially as the dress is fringed in gold to match her gold cape and crown and enhanced with a red jewel. The opulent image implies luxury in several of its meanings, and this symbolism is fostered by various elements of the picture. The Moor who attends Morgan is dressed exotically, with black and white striped tights, a bold orange cloak, a white turban, a gold earring, and a scimitar at his side. The blue parrot with yellow head and a flash of yellow on its wings adds another exotic touch. Even the border of the picture is significant. The lower of the two shields in the right border contains a chevron and roundel that are suggestive of lechery. Similarly suggestive is the device of the goat on the shield across the page on the lower left.

A black and white illustration of Morgan later in the text (45) shows her riding with her band of knights after stealing the scabbard to Excalibur. Her head faces boldly, almost defiantly, toward the viewer. Again the border details are important. In this case, the lower portion of the picture is flanked by peacocks, the richness they connote consistent with the imagery associated with Morgan in the frontispiece. A chapter heading (27)—and Curtis's chapter headings are often more than decorative—also depicts Morgan, this time clutching Excalibur, hugging it almost as if it were a loved one. She desires to possess Excalibur, not to have it in safekeeping for Arthur but so that she can 'have it for her own, to bestow as she would' and so she might never 'have need to fear his justice for the wrong she had done' (28–29). Yet

Ill. 2: 'Morgan le Fay with Excalibur' by Dora Curtis

Beatrice Clay finds redemption for Morgan: 'in the end, she repented her of her malice, for she was of those that came to bear Arthur to the Delightful Islands from the field of his last bitter conflict; but that was long after' (28). And indeed in a chapter heading depicting 'The Three Queens' (310) who take Arthur to be healed, one of the queens, the central one, is clearly recognizable as the Morgan of the earlier illustrations. But this is 'long after,' and the early impression of her character is of a powerful woman who will use whatever means necessary to gain what she wants.

The audacious wickedness of Morgan is not the only example of women challenging male power in this collection of stories. In fact, the images of women in the early part of the book call to mind Maureen Fries's comment on women in Lawman's *Brut*: 'Shut off from the manly oaths of feudal loyalty and knightly reciprocity, they are capable of turning their supposed weakness(es) into (illicit) strength as they find their own, unexpected and unorthodox means of undermining the male order.'7 Among the other women depicted by Curtis are three more sorceresses.

Ill. 3: 'Vivien Imprisons Merlin' by Dora Curtis

Annoure tries to tempt Arthur from his service to his people. She calls him a fool and asks 'why should one that may command be at the beck and call of every hind and slave within his realm?' (18).[8] Curtis portrays Annoure and Arthur standing on a tall battlement overlooking her magnificent castle. When Arthur refuses all the power and possessions she offers, she uses her magic to imprison him until a combination of his resolve and his 'cross-hilted sword' convinces the evil woman to free him, but only to follow a path dictated by her magic arts that leads him to a near fatal conflict with Pellinore.

Curtis also illustrates the entombment of Merlin by Vivien, who is described as 'a damsel of the Lady of the Lake—her whose skill in magic, some say, was greater than Merlin's own' (50). That the Lady of the Lake is said to be greater than Merlin is just another indication of the book's emphasis on female empowerment. Vivien is presented in the text as a manipulative sorceress who wins her way into Merlin's heart 'thinking it should be fame for her, by any means whatsoever, to enslave the greatest wizard of his age'

(50). Clay's account makes it clear that Merlin was sealed up 'through the treachery of a damsel' (53). Curtis's image of Vivien imprisoning Merlin depicts her power and treachery (51) (see illustration 3): one of Vivien's hands is raised as if drawing potency from the heavens; the other is pointed towards Merlin and seems to force his head and body into the rocks that have already begun to surround him. The treachery that Clay suggests is represented by the serpents winding through the stylized flowers at the bottom of the border.

The third sorceress other than Morgan whose story is represented in text and image is the woman called by Clay 'the sorceress of the Chapel Perilous,' Malory's Hallewes, who tries to trap Launcelot into actions that would doom him to death as he tries to retrieve a sword and a piece of cloth, needed to cure Sir Meliot, from the body of a knight in the Chapel Perilous. Once again the hands are significant. As the sorceress reaches towards Launcelot, he pulls back, placing the hands that hold the curative cloth and sword behind him. His body language bespeaks the rejection of the sorceress that is his salvation, hers the grasping desire for the knight.

An interesting feature of Dora Curtis's illustrations, and indeed of those of the best of the other women illustrators, is that they are often unclichéd in their choice of subject matter and treatment. Curtis's extension of the theme of her illustrations to the borders, for example, is as original as her choice of unconventional subjects like Annoure and Hallewes. Similarly, when Curtis turns to the Tristram story, she illustrates several dramatic moments that artists seldom portray. Her first illustration in this section, a chapter heading, is of the birth of Tristram (76). Curtis shows Tristram's mother Elizabeth cradling in one arm her newborn son, her other hand raised to her head, perhaps in pain and grief. Trees, representing the forest in which she has been searching for her husband, fill out the graphic block. Rabbits look on and birds hover nearby, apparently in sympathy with the natural processes of birth and death occurring before them. In a later illustration, Tristram's father King Meliodas, another unusual subject, is about to drink the poison that his new queen has prepared for Tristram so that upon his death one of her own sons will become the heir to the throne (79) (see illustration 4). The Queen, who loves her husband more than her stepson, has raised her hands to prevent Meliodas from consuming the poison. The Queen, unnamed in Clay's version, is another of the powerful but wicked women who populate the early stories in this retelling. While this scene is full of dramatic tension and is of great importance to the plot, only one other illustrator that I can think of, Arthur A. Dixon (in Doris Ashley's *King Arthur and the Knights of the Round Table*), has chosen to represent it visually.

Ill. 4: 'Meliodas and the Poisoned Drink' by Dora Curtis

Curtis's illustration captures the very moment at which Meliodas is about to
meet his doom and the moment that reveals not only the treachery of the
Queen but also her love for her husband, since she exposes her own crime
rather than allow him to die. The episode is also significant to the plot since
it reveals Tristram's nobility when he pleads for the life of the woman who
would have killed him and it prompts Meliodas to send his son to France to
learn courtly ways. Curtis again uses her borders to comment on the scene.
Centered below the picture is a chalice or cup, like the one containing the
poison; it is entwined by thorny brambles that spread beneath the picture
and halfway up its length. From the brambles drip drops of some liquid,
perhaps representing the poisoned drink or perhaps blood to symbolize the
intended death.

A little later in the story, Curtis depicts the scene in which King Anguish
of Ireland hands Isolt over to Tristram (103) (see illustration 5). The transfer
of Isolt for Tristram 'to wed or to give to your uncle, King Mark, as seems
good to you' (102), takes place on the deck of the ship that is to bear her to

Ill. 5: 'King Anguish Entrusts Isolt to Tristram' by Dora Curtis

Cornwall. Few illustrators of the Tristram story can resist portraying the drinking of the love potion; but Curtis forgoes this typical scene and instead focuses on what is for Isolt the crucial moment in which she is transferred as property from one man to another. In Curtis's rendition of this moment, Anguish opens his arms in a gesture of generosity while Isolt's hand rests on top of Tristram's as a sign that she is being entrusted to him. But surely this placement of the hands also foreshadows the bond that will develop between them. Isolt maintains her dignity in this degrading situation by staring ahead without expressing any emotion. Once again the border is thematically linked to the picture. Fish swim in swirling water along the bottom and partway up the side while the water itself extends to the top of the image. The fish and the water are reminders of the sea voyage that is so integral to the Tristram story and that becomes a central image in retellings of it from the Middle Ages to the twentieth century. The swirling water also symbolizes the swirling passions that will engulf the tale's central figures.

Ill. 6: The Rescue of Guinevere" by Dora Curtis

Isolt is just one of several women in the retelling who are described and depicted as victims, usually of love of one sort or another, or of male values or power—another theme that seems to run throughout the book and that is highlighted in Curtis's illustrations. Palamides finds Isolt weeping in the forest for Bragwaine, and the Saracen knight extracts a rash promise from her in exchange for Bragwaine's safe return. Palamides requests that Isolt follow him and do his bidding, a fate from which she is saved by Tristram. Curtis shows the grief-stricken Isolt (108) being discovered by Palamides, a knight marked as different from other knights by the curved feathers in his helmet and the strange armor he wears. Isolt lies on the ground, her face covered with one hand, at the feet of Palamides, in a position reminiscent of that of Guenevere groveling at Arthur's feet in Tennyson's *Idylls*. Clearly, she is at the mercy of the knight.

Other women who are victims of men include the lady whom Sir Gawain accidentally kills when on the quest for the white hart; she is represented in a chapter heading with her severed head tied by her hair around Gawain's neck (148), a penance imposed on him by the ladies who spare his life. Another tragic lady is the one whose husband has been slain by three wicked knights and who is met by Geraint and the long-suffering Enid (191). Curtis also depicts Elaine in the barge—not one of the more original illustrations in the volume but part of the pattern of victimized women. The final female victim in the volume is Guenevere herself, who is seen being carried off by Launcelot after being rescued from the stake (287) (see illustration 6). She clutches his neck, her head bowed as they dash off over the cobblestoned street; the sword of a knight in armor is thrust aside by one of Launcelot's companions, and two unarmed figures—perhaps Gareth and Gaheris about to be slain— are in the background. At the top of the border is the crown of the queen and at the bottom the shield and helmet of a knight. The two symbols are separated by the entire space of the picture, suggesting the separation that will inevitably come between Launcelot and Guenevere even as they seem closest together, the two figures almost merging into one in the image. In the bottom portion of the frame is a thorny bramble similar to that in the frame around the depiction of Meliodas about to drink from the poisoned cup. Here again the bramble represents death and separation. Guenevere is seen a final time in the depiction of her dead body (320) with Lancelot leaning over her, in the end unable to save her. (An earlier image of Guenevere as a queen crowned and magnificently gowned [280], the epitome of nobility, contrasts with the presentation of her as a victim.)

Depictions of women make up more than half of the illustrations in the volume. This may be indicative of a different perspective by a woman illustrating a text by a woman or merely of the significance of women in the Arthurian story in general. In the end, perhaps more important than the actual number of illustrations of women is their quality and originality. Even some of the depictions of males in this volume are striking. The religious passion of Palamides as he gazes at a glorified crucifix at the moment of his conversion, for instance, captures his religious ardor. The portrayal of Galahad flanked by Bors and Percival after he has seen the Grail reflects a similar, almost mystical ardor (259). As Clay writes, 'they went to Sir Galahad where he still knelt in prayer, and behold, he was dead; for it had been with him even as he had prayed; in the moment when he had seen the vision, his soul had gone back to God' (258). The look of perfect contentment on Galahad's face suggests the joy he feels in leaving a troubled world for heavenly bliss. This transportation is reflected in the border where rays emanating from the sacred cup spread through stars, and the picture has at its four corners angelic wings to represent the spiritual nature of Galahad's life and death.

Ill. 7: 'Arthur Entrusts Excalibur to Bedivere' by Dora Curtis

A final illustration worthy of note is the depiction of Arthur entrusting Excalibur to Bedivere after being wounded in the final battle with Mordred (313) (see illustration 7). Barely conscious, Arthur hands the sword to his last surviving knight. The battle is indicated only by the wounded Arthur lying on the ground and by the body of Sir Lucan at his feet. One of Lucan's hands lies across his chest, over a fatal wound; the other clutches a clump of grass in a pathetic death grip. On the right side of the border are three queens, each with a shield, the lowest of the three clearly Morgan le Fay. The queens imply the passing of Arthur to Avalon, though the text leaves open whether he goes there to die or to have his wounds healed.

I have dwelt at such length on Dora Curtis because she seems typical of a whole group of women illustrators who are virtually unknown yet who present often unclichéd depictions of important moments from Arthurian story—women who deserve further attention either because of their style or because of the subjects of their illustrations, which can focus attention on certain characters or themes in the legend and thus suggest interpretations of or approaches to reading the Arthurian stories. A book illustrated by Ann D. Alexander, for example, is an early attempt to focus on the women of the legend. In *Women of the Morte Darthur* (1927), subtitled 'Twelve of the Most Romantic of the World's Love Stories Selected from Malory's Morte Darthur,' Alexander obviously wants to make the women central, but calling the book a collection of love stories is something of a ruse. While some of the tales are stories of romance in the modern sense, others can be seen as *love* stories only by taking the widest interpretation of the word. The account of Sir Percivale's Sister, for example, is not a tale of love, though she does consider herself 'one of the blessed maidens of the world'[9] when she girds upon Galahad the Sword with the Strange Girdles.

An interesting visual device that suggests the book's agenda of bringing women into prominence is the depiction of arms and seals not just for the knights but for the women as well. These heraldic representations, like the illustrations themselves,[10] are in a striking Art Nouveau style. At the end of the chapter on Percivale's Sister, Alexander illustrates the arms of Galahad and of Percivale's Sister.[11] Earlier in the book Alexander depicts the arms of Uther and Igraine,[12] the arms of the three Elaines,[13] the arms of Colombe,[14] the arms of the two queens of Liones,[15] and the arms of Sir Urre's Mother,[16] as well as the seals of Dame Lionesse,[17] La Beale Isoud,[18] La Beale Alice,[19] and even the Damosel of the Lake[20] (see illustration 8)—a list that suggests some of the women whose stories are told in the volume. The inclusion of a figure like Sir Urre's Mother again demonstrates that the volume's purpose is not only to narrate love stories. Her tale does tell of Lavaine's love for and marriage to 'Sir Urre's fair sister' but only in one sentence, a clear indication that it is not Alexander's main concern.

Malory is not the only Arthurian author illustrated by women deserving of more attention; another is Tennyson. Perhaps the finest illustrator of the *Idylls of the King* was Eleanor Fortescue Brickdale (1872–1945). As Debra Mancoff has noted, in 1911 Brickdale 'presented thirty-seven watercolors at the Leicester Gallery, inspired by the poems of Tennyson. As a result selections from this exhibition were published to illustrate two editions of the *Idylls of the King* (1911–12), the first a de luxe volume with twenty-one plates and the second a smaller, less expensive book of twelve plates illustrating the first four *Idylls*.'[21]

What makes Brickdale such an excellent artist is the way that she interprets the tales anew in her watercolors and the resulting illustrations. Instead of depicting Elaine dead in the barge, the image that was so popular in the late-

Ill. 8: 'The Seal of the Lady of the Lake' by Ann D. Alexander

nineteenth and early-twentieth centuries, she portrays Elaine's brothers carrying her to the barge, a scene fraught with emotion.[22] The grief of Elaine's brothers and father gives the lie to the notion that the death of a beautiful woman is in any sense romantic. Another image, of Elaine sewing the cover for Lancelot's shield, conveys symbolically the devotion of the young woman to the knight who has captured her heart.[23] Not only does Elaine toil with a radiant smile, but she has positioned Lancelot's shield so that the light from the window before which she works will strike it in the morning and so that it will be the first thing she sees when she awakes and draws the curtains from her bed.

Brickdale's inventive approach to her choice of subjects is evident in a remarkable depiction of a scene from Tennyson's 'Vivien' idyll (later 'Merlin and Vivien'). Brickdale focuses on one of the most original passages in the idyll and one generally overlooked by illustrators. Tennyson tells brilliantly— or rather has Merlin tell to Vivien—the history of the book of magic that contains the spell that will ultimately be the mage's undoing. It is the story of an Eastern potentate who has acquired the most beautiful woman in the world as his wife and who wants to make her inaccessible to all but himself. Finally, a magician is found who can provide the spell that will prevent anyone from seeing her and prevent her from seeing anyone but her husband. The magician's book is ultimately passed on to Merlin. Although this part of Tennyson's narrative is rarely illustrated, Brickdale, captivated by the story, lavishly depicts the beautiful maiden, richly robed and leaning on plush pillows.[24] She gazes at a chess piece she has lifted from the board that rests on a splendid Oriental table. The piece is, symbolically, the king (suggesting the king who is all to her now), but her glazed look warns of the dangers of this sort of entrapment, particularly for the object of the entrapment—for as Tennyson says, 'she lay as dead / And lost all use of life.'[25] The opulence of her surroundings, even the servant offering her a huge platter of fresh fruits, are of little use to her, just as the wealth offered to the magician is of little use to him. The potentate has led the magician to the top of a stairway from which he sees the province and palace that could be his; but rather than accept the riches the king would give him for his service, he goes back to living in the wild and eating grass. The Oriental splendor of the dress of the king and his bride and of the furnishings around her are contrasted in Brickdale's image with the simpler garb of the magician who clutches the book that is more precious to him than all the wealth he might possess. Brickdale thus calls attention to an important part of the poem and provides her visual interpretation of the incident, as one would expect a good illustrator to do.

A final image from Brickdale, one that exemplifies better than almost any other her interpretative powers, depicts Guenevere in the nunnery.[26] Debra Mancoff observed that this image is an example of how Brickdale can use a detail, in this case 'the basket of bread Guenevere carries as she serves out her days as a nun,' to 'increase the sentiment' and to 'impart a genuine humanity to the legendary characters....'[27] But the bread does more than humanize Guenevere; it symbolizes the life that goes on, that must go on, after the tragedy. In fact many of the details of this very tactile illustration combine to convey this idea. One can almost feel the varied textures of the image: the tiles of the roof behind Guenevere, the stones of the low wall behind her, the rough rope of her cincture, the woven basket she carries. And like the breads themselves, the orange and blue flowers almost suggest real smells and tastes.

Besides Dora Curtis and Eleanor Fortescue Brickdale, there are many other women artists whose Arthurian illustrations merit further study. Perhaps the most prominent of these is Jessie King (1875–1949), who illustrated William Morris's *Defence of Guenevere and Other Poems* and Sebastian Evans's 1903 translation of *The High History of the Holy Graal.*[28] But still others need to be studied—like Florence Harrison, who illustrated Tennyson's *'Guinevere' and Other Poems*;[29] Katharine Cameron, who illustrated Mary MacGregor's *Stories of King Arthur's Knights Told to the Children*;[30] and the modern children's illustrator Carol Heyer,[31] to name just a few. Further analysis of women artists such as these and of their place in Arthurian illustration can only increase our understanding and appreciation of the Arthurian tradition.

UNIVERSITY OF ROCHESTER

Alan Lupack, current President of the North American Branch of the International Arthurian Society and creator of The Camelot Project, is co-author of *King Arthur in America*, author of numerous articles on medieval and modern Arthurian literature and popular culture, and editor of *Sir Tristrem* and *Lancelot of the Laik* as well as of several volumes of modern Arthurian literature.

NOTES

1   For a discussion of this influence, see Alan Lupack and Barbara Tepa Lupack, *King Arthur in America* (Cambridge: D.S. Brewer, 1999), pp. 229–30.
2   A new edition of Malory is illustrated by a woman artist, Anna-Marie Ferguson: Sir Thomas Malory, *Le Morte d'Arthur*, ed. John Matthews, ill. Anna-Marie Ferguson (London: Cassell, 2000).
3   For information about these illustrations, see Barry Gaines, *Sir Thomas Malory: An Anecdotal Bibliography of Editions 1485–1985* (New York: AMS Press, 1990), p. 35.
4   Gaines describes Donaldson's woodcuts as 'dark and brooding yet delicately wrought' (*An Anecdotal Bibliography of Editions*, p. 64).
5   Gaines, *An Anecdotal Bibliography of Editions*, p. 7.
6   All in-text citations refer to Beatrice Clay, *Stories from King Arthur and His Round Table*, ill. Dora Curtis (New York: E.P. Dutton, n.d. [1905]).
7   Maureen Fries, 'Women, Power, and Order in Lawman's *Brut*,' *Arthuriana* 8.3 (Fall 1998): 31.
8   This and six other illustrations from the 1905 edition were redone in color for later editions, but the other black and white illustrations, except for the chapter headings, were omitted.
9   Ann D. Alexander, *Women of the Morte Darthur: Twelve of the Most Romantic of the World's Love Stories*, ill. Ann D. Alexander (London: Methuen, 1927), p. 178.
10 See, for example, 'Sir Gareth and Dame Lionesse,' Alexander, *Women of the Morte Darthur*, p. 76.
11 Alexander, *Women of the Morte Darthur*, p. 192.
12 Alexander, *Women of the Morte Darthur*, p. 9.
13 Alexander, *Women of the Morte Darthur*, p. 76.
14 Alexander, *Women of the Morte Darthur*, p. 118.
15 Alexander, *Women of the Morte Darthur*, p. 124.

16 Alexander, *Women of the Morte Darthur*, p. 198.

17 Alexander, *Women of the Morte Darthur*, p. 112.

18 Alexander, *Women of the Morte Darthur*, p. 155.

19 Alexander, *Women of the Morte Darthur*, p. 161.

20 Alexander, *Women of the Morte Darthur*, p. 23.

21 Debra N. Mancoff, *The Arthurian Revival in Victorian Art* (New York: Garland, 1990), p. 272.

22 Alfred Lord Tennyson, *The Idylls of the King*, ill. Eleanor Fortescue Brickdale (London: Hodder and Stroughton, n.d.), opposite p. 134; see The Camelot Project [http://www.lib.rochester.edu/camelot/images/efbdead.htm] for a reproduction of this image.

23 Tennyson, *Idylls of the King*, ill. Brickdale, opposite p. 102; see The Camelot Project [http://www.lib.rochester.edu/camelot/images/efbsew.htm] for a reproduction of this image.

24 Tennyson, *Idylls of the King*, ill. Brickdale, opposite p. 86; see The Camelot Project [http://www.lib.rochester.edu/camelot/images/efbeast.htm] for a reproduction of this image.

25 Tennyson, *Idylls of the King*, ill. Brickdale, p. 84.

26 Tennyson, *Idylls of the King*, ill. Brickdale, opposite p. 172; see The Camelot Project [http://www.lib.rochester.edu/camelot/images/efbnun.htm] for a reproduction of this image.

27 Mancoff, *The Return of King Arthur: The Legend through Victorian Eyes* (New York: Harry N. Abrams, 1995), p. 143.

28 Jessie King receives brief mention in Debra N. Mancoff's two books (see notes 21 and 27) and in Muriel Whitaker's *The Legends of King Arthur in Art* (Cambridge: D.S. Brewer, 1990).

29 Tennyson, *'Guinevere' and Other Poems*, ill. Florence Harrison (London: Blackie and Son, 1912).

30 Mary MacGregor, *Stories of King Arthur's Knights Told to the Children*, ill. Katharine Cameron (London: T.C. & E.C. Jack, n.d. [1905]).

31 Carol Heyer, *Excalibur*, retold and ill. Carol Heyer (Nashville, TN: Ideals Children's Books, 1991).

A Note on Maureen Fries, Morgan le Fay, and Ugo Falena's 1911 Film *Tristano e Isotta*

KEVIN J. HARTY

Ugo Falena's little-known 1911 film *Tristano e Isotta* offers an interesting treatment of the oft-retold legend of the two lovers. Clearly, the film is indebted to the several medieval versions of that legend, but Falena also adds new details, including a role for Morgan le Fay, to create a more effective reading than some more modern films have offered of the story of Tristan and Isolde. (KJH)

The study of what I have elsewhere called 'cinema Arthuriana' is greatly indebted to Maureen Fries. Maureen's decision to commission an essay on film for her jointly edited volume for the Modern Language Association on *Approaches to Teaching the Arthurian Tradition* lent the study of the cinematic reinterpretations of the Arthuriad a legitimacy and cachet it had not previously had.[1] Seven years later, Maureen's final published essay would give the study of Arthurian film her own personal imprimatur as she lamented 'the reduction of Morgan's otherworldly powers and ambiance'[2] at the hands of modern filmmakers. In that final essay, Maureen catalogued a pattern of cinematic underestimations and distortions of the figure of Morgan and looked forward to a more sympathetic portrait of a character who has been central to the story of Arthur since at least the twelfth century when Geoffrey of Monmouth presented 'a positive and even androgynous portrait of a powerful ruler of an island paradisial in its fecundity.'[3]

I can think of no better way to celebrate Maureen's scholarly career in general and her contribution to the study of Arthurian film in particular than to comment briefly on a screen appearance of Morgan in, and on other unique features of, Ugo Falena's 1911 *Tristano e Isotta*, one of the earliest films to tell what is arguably the most famous and enduring love story that has come down to us from medieval times. Celtic in its origins, the story of Tristan and Isolde in verse form seems to have passed through Brittany to France in the middle of the twelfth century, spreading thereafter to Germany and Norway. Separately, a prose tradition of the legend developed in the

second half of the thirteenth century that saw Tristan as a member of the
fellowship of the Round Table, often second only to Lancelot in his prowess.
The successive versions of the Prose *Tristan* in turn influenced later romances
in Spain, Portugal, Denmark, and Russia. In condensed form, the Prose *Tristan*
became the centerpiece of Sir Thomas Malory's late fifteenth-century *Le Morte
Darthur*.

Twentieth-century treatments of Tristan and Isolde often owe a debt to
Joseph Bédier's conflation of the legend first published in 1900. The film
tradition has admittedly been uneven. That tradition began in 1909 with
Albert Capellani's unsuccessful attempt to present a screen version of Wagner's
opera, *Tristan et Yseult*, for France's Pathé Frères. Falena's 1911 and Maurice
Mariaud's 1920 films looked to the medieval legend rather than to Wagner
as a source, as did later film versions such as Jean Delannoy's 1943 *L'Éternal
retour*, Luis Buñuel's 1970 *Tristana*, Tom Donovan's 1979 *Tristan and Isolt*, François
Truffaut's 1981 *La Femme d'à côté*, Veith von Fürstenberg's 1981 *Feuer und Schwert*,
Hrafn Gunnlaugsson's 1988 *I Skugga Hrafnsina*, and Jytte Rex's 1989 *Isolde*.[4]

The first Tristan films reflect a widespread interest among filmmakers
and audiences alike in historical and pseudo-historical spectacle as the basis
for early cinematic plot lines. The Italian director Ugo Falena (1875–1931)
specialized in such costume dramas bringing to the screen the stories of
Carmen, Othello, and Camille (all in 1909), Beatrice Cenci and Lucretia
Borgia (both in 1910), Shylock (in 1911), and Francesca da Rimini and Marco
Visconti (both in 1913), among others. Falena's film on Tristan and Isolde
was produced by La Film d'Arte Italiana, the Italian subsidiary of France's
Pathé Frères.[5] Running approximately thirty minutes, Falena's film falls into
two parts, each with five scenes introduced by a title. No records survive
listing a direct source for the version of the legend that the film presents, but
some version of Bédier's conflation seems to lie behind the film's plot,
although Falena offers some surprises in his film.

In the film's opening sequence, King Mark of Cornwall (Serafino
Mastracchio) sends his nephew Tristan (Giovanni Pezzinga) to Ireland to
ask for the hand of the Princess Isolda (Francesca Bertini) in marriage.[6] Two
things are notable about this first sequence. The film uses elaborate sets and
costumes that accurately suggest the medieval period,[7] and Mark, who falls
in love with Isolda after seeing her picture, is much older than either Tristan
or Isolda. Such a disparity in ages—Mark appears well in his sixties; Tristan,
in his late forties; and Isolda, in her late twenties—necessarily skews the
romantic triangle. And while characters in medieval romances are often ageless
or fail to grow old despite the passage of great chunks of time, Mark's lust

for Isolda has here perhaps an unintentional nod toward the figure of the *senex amans* from the medieval fabliau, as the film's Mark ends up playing January to Isolda's May.

In the film's second sequence, Tristan sets out for Ireland accompanied by his favorite female slave, Rosen (Bianca Lorenzoni). This curious detail is decidedly unmedieval—homosocial bonding practices in the Middle Ages dictated that noble ladies be accompanied by handmaidens and ladies-in-waiting and knights by squires and fellow knights—but it does allow for an interesting plot twist later in the film. In the film's third sequence, Isolda watches the arrival of Tristan's ship from the terrace of her palace. The princess is a reluctant bride, in part because she seems clearly smitten with Tristan at first sight—just as Rosen is jealous of the princess's affection for her master.

On the journey back to Cornwall which informs the film's fourth sequence, Rosen's jealousy plays itself out as she pours poison into the wine goblets intended for Tristan and Isolda. As the two are about to drink the lethal mixture, Morgan le Fay—here called the Fairy Morgan in a costume more suggestive of Greek mythology than of medieval romance—appears and changes the poison into a love philtre. Morgan's unexpected appearance in the film is a bit startling and not found elsewhere in other treatments of the legends. However, it has two significant effects. First, it clearly anchors the story of Tristan and Isolda in the Arthurian world, and second it introduces a key element from the legend, the love philtre that the two lovers drink, into the film. That philtre, which traditionally the lovers accidentally drink on their return voyage, is intended for the bridal couple and traps Tristran and Isolda in a love for each other from which neither can escape. Here, immediately after quaffing their drinks, Tristan and Isolda embrace.

Rosen's presence in the film and her reaction to Isolda's love for Tristan add complication and depth to the film's plot. Suddenly there is not one but two love triangles. By the time Malory came to incorporate parts of the Prose *Tristan* into his *Le Morte Darthur*, the two different yet parallel love triangles in Cornwall and Camelot show, as Thomas C. Rumble pointed out more than thirty years ago, that 'the tragic fall of King Arthur's noble realm is not the result of the action of individuals taken separately…; rather, it is the result of excesses of…[the] whole chivalric system of social and sexual relationships.'[8] Falena's film offers a less global, but nonetheless effective, view; Tristan and Isolda find their love thwarted from below by the hero's slave and from above by the hero's uncle and king.

Seemingly resigned to her fate, Isolda arrives at the court of King Mark in the film's fifth sequence. Despite her resignation, Isolda is less than subtle in her reaction to Mark when they first meet. She practically swoons in his presence, and she repeatedly engages in a fair amount of eye rolling—as is typical of the style of acting in silent films—to express the emotions she is feeling. Rosen is no less expressive of her continuing love for Tristan in the film's sixth scene, a feast given by Mark to celebrate his impending marriage to Isolda. In an interestingly authentic costuming note, the robes worn by everyone in this scene feature intricately embroidered designs that clearly suggest the Celtic.

But the influence of the philtre remains strong, and Tristan and Isolda escape from court in the film's seventh sequence. In the film's eighth sequence, the lovers flee on foot across a barren wasteland as Rosen runs to inform Mark of their flight. Mark is at first reluctant to believe Rosen—he even physically threatens her for lying—until he finds Tristan's crown and sword in Isolda's bedchamber and Isolda's cloak in the castle forecourt. Suddenly, Mark is as emotionally overwrought over Isolda's flight as she was over marrying him, and as Rosen was over Isolda's love for Tristan. Again, in keeping with the style of acting in silent films, all three give way to sweeping gestures and what today would qualify as overacting to express the depths of emotion they feel.

In the film's ninth sequence, Mark, who with three retainers has been following the lovers on horseback, comes upon them sleeping. At first, he raises his sword to strike them dead, but then, moved out of pity for their youth, he pardons them, placing his sword upright in the ground and his crown between them as they continue to sleep. When they awake and kiss, the lovers discover the sword and crown. Clearly overwrought, they go off once again into an inhospitable wilderness where Isolda swoons and faints. In the film's final sequence, recognizing that their love is insurmountable, Tristan and Isolda decide to take refuge, and seek union, in death. They climb a mountain together and leap into the sea.

As unorthodox as the film's resolution may at first seem—in conflicting traditions Isolde dies from grief when she hears about or witnesses Tristan's death; Tristan dies as the result of Mark's treachery or from a poisoned arrow wound—the film's last two sequences clearly nod in the direction of scenes from several medieval versions of the legend. In the twelfth-century Anglo-Norman verse Tristan romances attributed to Thomas D'Angleterre and Béroul, Mark does stumble upon the lovers in a garden. However, the sword that rests between them is Tristan's. Seeing the sword between them, Mark wrongly concludes that the two lovers are without sin. In the episode in the legend which Bédier labels 'The Chantry Leap,'[9] the captured Tristan does leap from a cliff, though not to his death. Rather, he 'fell upon a smooth rock at the cliff's foot, which to this day the men of Cornwall call "Tristan's Leap."'[10]

Even more fluid than the legend of Arthur, of which it would eventually become a part, the medieval legend of Tristan and Isolde offered later continuators a wealth of plot details to develop for their own purposes. Ugo Faleno's 1911 film *Tristano e Isotta* is a good case in point. Probably the first film to be based directly on some version or collation of the medieval legend rather than on Wagner's opera, *Tristano e Isotta* is true in incident and spirit to the medieval legend. At the same time, it introduces two new characters to the legend, Morgan le Fay as a positive character and Tristan's female slave, Rosen, rather than Isolde's long-suffering servant, Brangwain, as a jealous suitor for Tristan's affection. The result is a skillful cinematic treatment of the oft-retold legend of Tristan and Isolde.

LA SALLE UNIVERSITY

Kevin J. Harty is Professor of English at La Salle University in Philadelphia and Associate Editor of *Arthuriana*. He has published widely on screen adaptations of the medieval.

NOTES

1   See Kevin J. Harty, 'Teaching Arthurian Film,' in *Approaches to Teaching the Arthurian Tradition*, ed. Maureen Fries and Jeanie Watson (New York: Modern Language Association, 1992), pp. 146–50.

It was a well-known hallmark of Maureen's career that she was vigorous in her support of other scholars, especially younger scholars, constantly encouraging them to pursue their own research and urging them to share the results of their research in the form of conference papers and published essays. I am grateful to have been the beneficiary of her encouragement.

2   Maureen Fries, 'How to Handle a Woman, or Morgan at the Movies,' in *King Arthur on Film: New Essays on Arthurian Cinema*, ed. Kevin J. Harty (Jefferson, NC: McFarland, 1999), pp. 69–80.

3   Fries, 'How to Handle a Woman,' p. 67. Maureen had earlier written about Morgan a number of times, most notably in her essay, 'From the Lady to the Tramp: The Decline of Morgan le Fay,' *Arthuriana* 4.1 (1994): 1–18.

4   On the varying artistic merits of the film versions of the legend of Tristan and Isolde, see Barthélemy Armengual, *Le Mythe de Tristan et Yseult au Cinéma* (Algiers: Travail et Culture, 1952); Joan Tasker Grimbert, 'Truffaut's *La Femme d'à côté* (1981): Attenuating a Romantic Archetype—Tristan and Iseult?' in *King Arthur on Film*, pp.183–201; Kevin J. Harty, 'The Arthurian Legends on Film: An Overview,' in *Cinema Arthuriana: Essays on Arthurian Film*, ed. Harty (New York: Garland, 1991), pp. 3–28; Harty, 'Lights! Camelot! Action!' in *King Arthur on Film*, pp. 5–37; Harty, *The Reel Middles Ages: American, Western and Eastern*

European, Middle Eastern, and Asian Films About Medieval Europe (Jefferson, NC: McFarland, 1999); Donald L. Hoffman, 'Tristan la Blonde: Transformations of Tristan in Buñuel's *Tristana*,' in *King Arthur on Film*, pp. 167–82; Norris J. Lacy, '*Lovespell* and the Disinterpretation of a Legend,' *Arthuriana* 10.4 (Winter 2000): 5–14; and Meradith T. McMunn, 'Filming the Tristan Myth: From Text to Icon,' in *Cinema Arthuriana*, pp. 169–80.

5   On the history of Pathé's Italian subsidiary, see Aldo Bernardini, 'La Film d'Arte Italiana,' in *Pathé, Premier Empire du Cinéma* (Paris: Éditions du Centre Georges Pompidou, 1994), pp. 112–19.

6   I use the spelling for the names of the principals from the British release of the film. In Italy, the title was *Tristano e Isotta*; in France, *Tristan et Yseult*; and in Spain, *Tristán é Isolda*—see Aldo Bernardini, ed., *Archivo del Cinema Italiana*, vol. 1 of *Il Cinema Muto 1905–1931* (Rome: Edizioni Associazione Nazionale Industrie Cinematografiche e Audiovisive, 1991), p. 319. For a contemporary review of the film in English, see *Bioscope* 28 September 1911; supplement v.

7   The copy of the film that I viewed in the Library of Congress lacks credits indicating where it was shot, but a number of scenes appear to have been staged in the courtyard of Florence's Bargello, which dates from 1250, or in the courtyard of a similar structure.

I am grateful once again for the help of Madeline F. Matz at the Library of Congress who arranged for me to view the Library's copy of *Tristano e Isotta*.

8   Thomas C. Rumble, '"The Tale of Tristram": Development by Analogy,' in *Malory's Originality*, ed. R.M. Lumiansky (Baltimore: Johns Hopkins, 1964), p. 183.

9   Jospeh Bédier, 'The Chantry Leap,' in *The Romance of Tristan and Iseult*, trans. Hilaire Belloc (1945; rep. New York: Vintage, 1965), pp. 58–66.

10 Bédier, 'The Chantry Leap,' p. 61.

PART TWO:

ON WOMEN ARTHURIANS

The 'Mabinogion'
and Lady Charlotte Guest (1812–1895)

RACHEL BROMWICH

For thee, of English birth but British heart,
Our bardic harp neglected and unstrung
Moved to the soul, and at thy touch there start
Old harmonies to life; our ancient tongue
Opens, its buried treasure to impart.
Rowland Williams (Goronva Camlan) ca. 1850

Today we regard the 'Mabinogion' as the foremost Welsh prose classic of the Middle Ages. But this is very far from having been the case in the past; indeed it would seem that up till the end of the eighteenth century these tales were little known, at any rate in the final literary form in which we now have them. Consider the relatively small number of medieval manuscripts of these tales—the White Book of Rhydderch and the Red Book of Hergest, fragments in Peniarth MSS 6 and 7, 14, and 16, Jesus MS 20, and some later copies of these—in comparison with the very large number of medieval texts and versions of *Brut y Brehnhinedd*[1] and the numerous texts and fragments of *Trioedd Ynys Prydein*.[2] This relative unfamiliarity is borne out by the fact that if we examine the allusions made by the Gogynfeirdd[3] to the traditional legendary characters it becomes very clear that the prime sources of their knowledge were the *Triads* and Nennius's *Historia Brittonum*; and the same is true, by and large, of the earlier *cywyddwyr*. The heroines of the past whom the poets cite as standards of beauty are Eigr, Esyllt, Luned, Dyfyr, Tegau—all of them names which would have been familiar to them from the *Triads*. There are sparse allusions to Branwen and Rhiannon in the fourteenth century, to the first by Dafydd ap Gwilym and by Justus Llywd, and the second by Goronwy Gyriog, while there are no poetic allusions to Arianrhod before Tudur Aled, or to Olwen before Lewys Môn. Many of the traditional heroes and heroines appear both in the *Triads* and in the *Mabinogi*, of course, and this limits the force of the distinction I am trying to make. For this purpose one needs to pay particular attention to those 'Mabinogion' characters who are not named in the *Triads*, such as

Dafydd ap Gwilym's single allusion to Llwyd fab Cel Coed [sic],[4] or the earliest recorded allusion to Rhonabwy in a poem by Madog Dwygraig, after 1370. These two, and the allusions to Branwen, Olwen, and Rhiannon, are late enough to have been derived by the poets from the written texts of the stories: my point is that these heroines could not compare in popularity among the poets with those heroines previously named, although we know little enough of Dyfyr, Tegau, or even Esyllt (Isolt) from Welsh sources that have been preserved.[5] For the poets the canonical texts continued down the ages to be the *Historia Brittonum* and *Trioedd Ynys Prydein*, together with the *Hengerdd*. These embodied the national *senchus*[6] (to employ an Irish term), the canonically accepted record of the nation's past. And in this record the *Mabinogi* and other native *chwedlau* apparently played little part, although there can be no question but that the origins of the Four Branches of the *Mabinogi* and of *Culhwch and Olwen* go back to the very earliest times, being foreshadowed by several allusions in the *hengredd*. The 'Mabinogion' tales appear to have been widely known in oral tradition, and sometimes in variant forms, yet for the poets who were the custodians of this tradition, they bore no comparison in esteem to those works which were regarded as the pillars of the historical record. This apparent neglect, down the ages, of the ancient mythological tales, is difficult to account for, but it is nevertheless a fact. A number of triads (ten) were of course introduced into the written text of the *Mabinogi*, as it were to give the tales status and authority.

A partial explanation is that among scholars of the seventeenth and eighteenth centuries everything was deprecated that was not believed to contribute in some way to the historical record. Edward Lhuyd is somewhat ambivalent: in cataloguing the contents of the Red Book of Hergest he describes the Four Branches of the *Mabinogi* as *fabulosas quasdam historiolas* [certain fabulous stories]—evidently a slightly deprecative epithet—and the tale of *Owain* as *narratio fabulosus* [a fabulous narrative] implying by this that 'fables' are of little interest or value.[7] In contrast is the prestige he allots to the *Triads*, by quoting Robert Vaughan's opinion that these go back as far as the seventh century:[8] Robert Vaughan was of course the great champion of the antiquity and historicity of *Trioedd Ynys Prydein*. In 1717 Moses Williams completed his preparation for the press of a large collection of Triads from a number of sources,[9] and he intended to include the texts of *Breuddwyd Maxen* and *Lludd and Llefelys* in his projected edition, which however was never published.[10] No mention of the tales is made by Theophilus Evans, though he admits in general terms that something is perhaps to be learned from *traddodiad a hen chwedlau* [tradition and old tales].The Morris brothers appear to have been equally neglectful. In his *Celtic Remains*[11] Lewis Morris quotes Lhuyd as defining the term *Mabinogi* as 'a British romance under this title,' but without further comment, and such references as he makes to the tales in his *Celtic Remains* are based entirely upon the *Triads*. He describes *Trioedd Ynys Prydein* as 'a book of greater authority than anything else extant.' In the Constitution of the Hon. Soc. Cymmrodorion, drawn up in 1755, the *Triads* head the list of subjects to be 'occasionally considered and treated of' by the Society; the *Triads* are followed in the list, but only after an interval, by 'the British History and its historicity.'[12] But no mention is made of the *Mabinogi*. Nor does Iolo Morganwg appear to have known or felt any interest in the *Mabinogi* and the other tales, preoccupied as he was—among other activities—in rewriting the older Triads in order to convey through them his individual and personal myth of history.[13]

But a great change came about with the Romantic Revival in the latter years of the eighteenth century, for which the rediscovery of medieval literature was a main inspiration, and one which brought with it an appreciation of the records of the past for values other than the purely historical. As concerns the Celtic literature, the publication of James Macpherson's *Ossian* in the 1760s was an epoch-making event, which created a receptive audience outside Wales, Ireland, and Scotland for the traditions of these countries. It came as a challenge both to the Irish and to the Welsh, and impelled both Celtic nations to search out and to disclose to the world such genuine early literature as they possessed, which could be set beside Macpherson's forgeries. (For these he had claimed an impossibly early third-century date.) One result of this was the publication in Wales of the great compendium of verse and prose contained in the *Myvyrian Archaiology of Wales*, published in 1801–7, of which William Owen Pughe was the chief editor. This famous lexicographer deservedly enjoyed the reputation of being the chief Welsh scholar of his day, and he was in addition the prime informant on Welsh literature to a number of English medievalists, namely Joseph Ritson, George Ellis, Sharon Turner, and Sir Walter Scott,[14] all of whom possessed names to conjure with in the field of antiquarian studies. Besides giving the earliest edition of the poems of Dafydd ap Gwilym (1789), and *The Heroic Elegies of Llywarch Hen* (1792), Pughe published in his journal *The Cambrian Register* the text with translation of the first half of *Mabinogi*: *Pwyll Pendefig Dyfed* in 1796, and followed this subsequently with his versions of *Math fab Mathonwy* and of the *Hanes Taliesin*.[15] In another of his works, *The Cambrian Biography* (1803), he listed Welsh heroes alphabetically and gave notes on such *Mabinogi* figures as Bendigeidfran, Pryderi, Rhiannon, as well as Culhwch. He made a distinction between the 'historical' and the 'legendary' Arthur, and said of the latter 'It has generally been inferred that the great achievements of this hero created those illusory actions and scenes depicted in the *Mabinogion* or "Juvenilities"'—and he contrasted the *Mabinogion* with the *Triads* which he described as 'documents of undoubted credit'—again demonstrating the supposedly great historical value of *TYP* which had persisted down the ages. Note, incidentally, that the title *Mabinogion* originated with Pughe in his *Dictionary* (1773–1803), and not with Lady Charlotte Guest.

With the interest and enthusiastic encouragement of the English medievalists I have mentioned, Pughe conceived of the plan, in the early years of the nineteenth century, of publishing a translation of the whole of the 'Mabinogion,' which he asserted to be 'the earliest romance-writing in Europe.' The original plan had been to include the texts of the Welsh tales in the total corpus of early prose and verse to be contained in the completed *Myvyrian Achaiology*—a plan which fell short of accomplishment. In 1800, Pughe showed to Sir Walter Scott his completed translation of *Peredur*, and a few years later he showed his completed translation of *Math fab Mathonwy* to George Ellis.[16] Ellis referred in his correspondence to Pughe's translations as 'infinitely curious' and stated his belief that they would 'excite more curiosity' than any work since Macpherson's *Ossian*. However, it seems that both Ellis and other English scholars felt that Pughe's style of translation and his English grammar left something to be desired, although Ellis promised to contribute a preface whenever Pughe's completed translation of the *Mabinogion* should be ready for the Press. For a number of years Pughe was distracted by other interests and by his personal affairs, but in the 1820s he was again working on his translation, and in 1825 he issued a prospectus in which he asked for subscriptions for his 'Mabinogion' to be published in two volumes with the original texts accompanied by the translation and notes. Various Welsh societies, the Cymmrodorion, Gwyneddigion, and others, strongly supported this plan and looked forward eagerly to the publication. The work was actually completed in manuscript[17] and partially prepared for press, when William Owen Pughe died in 1835.

Note well the date—1835—because it was only three years afterwards, in 1838, that Lady Charlotte Guest published the first of her seven parts which were to contain her 'Mabinogion,' later to be published together in three superb and luxurious volumes in 1849. These volumes contain the texts with translations of all the eleven tales, accompanied with copious notes, together

with variant versions in other languages of the three Arthurian romances—
Peredur, Geraint, and *Owain*—and with the addition of the story of *Taliesin*.
Apart from this last, the texts were taken from copies made for her by Tegid
(John Jones, 1792–1852), an Oxford scholar who was strongly under the
influence of Pughe.

Who was Lady Charlotte? A young Englishwoman of twenty-six, who in
1833 had married John Guest (later Sir John), a man who was more than
twice her age, manager of the Dowlais works outside Merthyr, and an
extremely successful, intelligent, and philanthropic iron-founder.[18] Lady
Charlotte Bertie was a sprig of the nobility, but in some ways a very unhappy
one. Her father, who died when she was six years old, had been the Earl of
Lindsey. Owing to her mother's remarriage with a violent and drunken stepfather, the Rev. Mr. Pegus, Lady Charlotte passed a miserable childhood,
along with her two younger brothers, both of whom were apparently of
weak intellect. It fell to her, indeed, to attempt to guard their interests
throughout her life. As a refuge from her early troubles, she turned to the
study of languages and learned French and Italian by herself, and with the
help of her brothers' tutor, she studied also Greek, Latin, Hebrew, and Persian.
Her favorite English author was Chaucer, and in her old age she could still
repeat by heart the whole of the 'Prologue' to the *Canterbury Tales*, taking
just thirty-five minutes to do so. I have not found any evidence that she had ever
gone to Wales or had known anything of the Welsh language before her marriage,
which took place within three months of her meeting, aged twenty-one, with
John Guest. But after her arrival at Dowlais she set to work to study literary
Welsh (there is no evidence that she ever spoke it fluently) and in this she seems
to have received active help and encouragement from several Welsh scholars:
first and foremost from Thomas Price (Carnhuanawc), cleric, scholar, and
eisteddfodwr, and pioneer in re-establishing Welsh-Breton connections; John Jones
(Tegid) who copied the tales for her from the Red Book of Hergest, and Gwallter
Mechain; all of these being members of that band of clerics devoted to Welsh
scholarship to whom Bedwyr Lewis Jones has paid tribute in describing them in
his book *Yr Hen Bersoniaid Llengar*.[19] Through Carnhuanawc she met with
likeminded friends among the neighboring gentry; with Sir Benjamin and Lady
Hall of Llanover[20] (with the latter of whom she evidently had a certain rivalry,
however) and with Sir Richard (Judge) Bosanquet of Dingestow Court near
Monmouth, to whom she refers more than once as having lent her manuscripts,
and who in fact first lent her Tegid's copy of *Culhwch and Olwen* from the Red
Book. She also had contact with Taliesin Williams (Iolo's son), and refers to
manuscripts lent her by Colonel Vaughan and Lord Mostyn.

In spite of the disparity of age, her marriage with John Guest seems to have been an ideally happy one. She produced ten children during the ten years that it lasted (till 1852), of whom the first four had already been born by 1838 when the first fascicule of the *Mabinogion* was published. By 1849 when the work was completed and published in a collected edition, her family was also complete—five boys and five girls. During all these years Lady Charlotte was closely concerned with her husband's business and evidently took a responsible share in many aspects of it (his firm sent railway-lines all over Europe, and to Poland, Russia, and America, and the pair frequently traveled to Germany as well as to many parts of Britain). At Dowlais and nearby, Sir John and Lady Charlotte founded and financed six schools and it was she who supervised these, as well as teaching her own daughters.[21] She played the harp and the piano (Beethoven was her favorite composer), she etched and was fond of riding her horse, who was called 'Llamrei' ['Swift Leaper'] after Arthur's horse in *Culhwch*. As she wrote in her journal, 'whatever I undertake I must reach an eminence in. I cannot endure anything in a second grade.' Childbirth evidently she took in her stride and it caused her the bare minimum of disturbance; she would be up and about busily correcting proofs or drafting her notes to the tales within a few days. All her children were exceedingly healthy, and all but one survived her. She kept a journal throughout her long life, from the age of ten until 1891 when she was almost ninety, and nearly blind. The journal was so voluminous that only a relatively small part of it has so far been published, in the form of extracts, by her grandson the Earl of Bessborough. I have given here only a bare outline of all Lady Charlotte's multifold activities and cares during the years in which she was simultaneously producing her 'Mabinogion' and her family of ten. When her husband died in 1852 she was left for a time in sole charge of the Dowlais works, and she played an influential part in co-operating with other iron-masters in negotiations over a major strike in the South Wales coalfields in 1853. Her later life formed an equally vigorous sequel, as is shown in her later journals, after her second marriage.[22] But my chief concern here is to consider her work as translator and editor.

The 'Mabinogion' was published simultaneously by Rees of Llandovery and by Longman, in three volumes dated respectively 1838, 1840, and 1849. Pages of the Welsh texts and of the versions in other languages are reproduced in facsimile, and there are delightful head-and-tail-pieces illustrating the tales. The sequence in which she tackled her work of translation is interesting. Priority was given to the Arthurian tales: volume one contains *Owain* and

Peredur; volume two has *Geraint* followed by *Culhwch* and *Rhonabwy*; volume three has the Four Branches of the *Mabinogi* followed by *Maxen, Lludd and Llefelys,* and the tale of *Taliesin* (this last from two MSS in the British Library, written by William Morris and by Iolo Morganwg). It is clear that the three Arthurian romances were Lady Charlotte's primary interest and the task to which she turned first and which she first completed. These are accompanied by the corresponding French poems of Chrétien de Troyes, given either in full or in summary; she includes a summary of the German poem corresponding to *Erec et Enide,* and prints in full the English *Sir Percevale de Galles* (apparently copied by herself from the Thornton MS in Lincoln Cathedral).[23] Although it was these romances which first claimed her attention and interest, she makes it clear in her preface that she recognized a fundamental difference in manners between these and the Four Branches 'both as regards the manners they depict and the style of the language in which they are composed.' She acknowledges the help of various people— Tegid, Judge Bosanquet, and Villemarqué, but oddly enough she does not mention Carnhuanawc, who was unquestionably her prime helper and informant. She concludes disarmingly:

> It may be considered rash in one who has but recently become acquainted with the Principality and its literature, to engage in a work like the present, while there are so many others by whom it would be much more ably executed. At the hazard, however, of incurring such an imputation, I have ventured upon this undertaking, in order to gratify the desire so generally and repeatedly expressed for the publication of these interesting remains.

She dedicates the work to her two older sons, Ifor and Merthyr, as follows:

> My dear Children, Infants as you are, I feel that I cannot dedicate more fitly than to you these venerable relics of ancient lore, and I do so in the hope of inciting you to cultivate the literature of 'Gwyllt Walia,' in whose beautiful language you are being initiated, and amongst whose free mountains you were born. May you become early imbued with the chivalric and exalted sense of honour and the fervent patriotism for which its sons have ever been celebrated. May you learn to emulate the noble qualities of Ifor Bach, after whom the elder of you was named. I am your affectionate Mother C.E. Guest.
> Dowlais, August 29, 1838.

But how much of Lady Guest's edition is in fact her own work, and how much of it is due to that of others? The diary repeatedly refers to the material help which she received from Carnhuanawc, and to the encouragement that she received from him and from the gentry of south Wales, the highly aristocratic members of the Cymreigyddion Society of Abergavenny.[24] She certainly knew of as much of Pughe's work as was available in print, which is to say the greater part of the Four Branches and the tale of *Taliesin*, and it was from Pughe that she adopted the title 'Mabinogion' and with it the notion that these were stories for children—Pughe's 'Juvenile Tales.' By her own statement we know that she undertook the work primarily to entertain her own children, and it is this—apart from a general Victorian sense of decorum—which may account for the fact that she cut out the passage concerning Pwyll's relations with Arawn's wife (as indeed Pughe had also done). She used Pughe's *Dictionary*, but her translation clearly owes nothing to his, and in the several pieces of *Pwyll* and *Math* that I have compared, it is in several instances more accurate than his. And she began her undertaking, not with the *Mabinogi* tales which Pughe had already published, but with the three Arthurian romaces, of which Pughe's translations existed at this date only in manuscript. Evidently it was the relationship between these Arthurian tales and the cognate European versions which had first inspired her to undertake her task of translation—indeed, it seems to have been these which initially had made English and European scholars curious to know more about the Welsh tales. We know that Lady Charlotte had been greatly interested previously in medieval literature—Chaucer was her life-long favorite as a poet—and in so far as I have yet been able to establish, it seems most probable that Lady Charlotte was the first person to discover and point out that closely parallel versions existed in French and other languages to the Three Romances.[25] It is certain that she was indebted to the Breton-French nobleman Theodore Hersart de la Villemarqué for a transcript of the *Yvain* of Chrétien de Troyes, which he made for her at her request in the Bibliothèque Nationale; she published this, after due acknowledgment, as an appendix to her first translation, the tale of *Owain*. In the event, Villemarqué turned out to be a thorn in her flesh, and caused not a little annoyance by his preposterous claim that his name should appear along with hers on the title-page of her book. Later he tried to forestall her book by bringing out a French version of *Peredur* and though the diary shows that he was defeated in this, he published in 1842 his *Romans de la Table Ronde des Anciens Bretons*, which gave his French translations of the Welsh tales, based without acknowledgment on her English text already published.[26] Villemarqué's whole intention at all times was to belittle the difference between Breton and Welsh, to claim that much of the oldest Welsh literature really originated in Brittany and was composed in a language that was intelligible to a Breton speaker of his day.[27]

Lady Charlotte Guest's easy, fluent, slightly archaic style has been much praised by subsequent generations. Gwyn Jones and Thomas Jones describe her

'Mabinogion' as 'a classic in its own right,' and say that they cannot too emphatically pay tribute to so splendid an achievement. Alfred Nutt had written in similar terms in 1904.[28] The poet Tennyson had told her that her style was 'the finest English he knew, ranking with Malory's *Morte Darthur.*' He based on her translation his poem 'Geraint and Enid' in his *Idylls of the King* (1859): all other tales in this work were based on *Le Morte Darthur.*[29] Prior to the publication in 1887 of the diplomatic text of the *Mabinogion* by John Rhŷs and J. Gwenogvryn Evans, her text of the tales was the only complete text in print. Rhŷs in his introduction says guardedly of her translation that 'it may be said to belong to the pre-scientific era' but nevertheless he awards her due praise, stating that 'her text in her edition approximates to the original more nearly than that of any other Welsh text of any length'—but that her book is hard to obtain, and that 'greater accuracy is now imperative, hence our effort to meet the requirements of a more exacting age.'[30]

One cannot but suspect that all those years of diary-writing must have contributed towards the ease and fluency of Lady Charlotte's style. But I want to emphasize also that the extremely full and wide-ranging notes which she wrote to accompany the tales are quite as remarkable as the translations themselves. The range of illustrative material which is covered in them is stupendous. She had read and studied all the contents of the *Myvyrian Archaiology of Wales* (available since 1801), and had culled from it a number of quotations from the Cynfeirdd and the Gogynfeirdd, the *Triads*, and *Brut y Brenhinedd*. Nothing appears to have escaped her: for instance she has found reference to the Twrch Trwyth in the *Gorchan Cynfelyn* (appended to the *Gododdin* poem), as well as those to Brân and to the sons of Llŷr and Morddwyd Tyllon in a poem in the Book of Taliesin.[31]

She cites the references to Branwen and to Blodeuwedd from Pughe's 1789 edition of *Dafydd ap Gwilym*, and has used his *Heroic Elegies of Llywarch Hen* (1792), as well as the *Poems of Lewis Glyn Gothi*, edited by Tegid and Gwallter Mechain and published at Llandovery in 1837. She quotes from the *Book of Llan Dâv* (Llandovery, 1840), and from the genealogies given in Lewis Dwnn's *Heraldic Visitations of Wales* (1846). All her quotations from Welsh verse and prose are invariably translated, even the quotations from the Books of Aneirin and Taliesin. She has a predilection for Iolo Morganwg's Third Series of Triads in the *Myvyrian*, over the two more ancient earlier series. But this was unfortunately only too common in her day, since the Third Series was much the most diffuse and informative of the three series in the *Myvyrian*, and also because it purported to record the earliest events relating to the pre-history of the Cymry, and therefore was generally presumed to be the most primitive version.[32] She was conversant with the Welsh learned journals of the late-eighteenth and early-nineteenth centuries—the *Cambro-Briton* and the *Cambrian Quarterly Magazine* of William Owen Pughe (from which she derived her knowledge of *Cyfraith Hywel*) and *Y Greal*. She knew of Edward Jones's *Welsh Bards* (1784) and his *Bardic Museum* (1802): from the latter she derived (in her Notes to *Culhwch and Olwen*) her long and informative version of the story of Huail fab Caw, which goes back ultimately to Elis Gruffydd's *Chronicle*. Her background reading further included Warton's *History of English Poetry*, Froissart's *Chronicles*, Ritson's *English Medieval Romances*, Gibbon's *Decline and Fall of the Roman Empire* (for her note on Maxen Wledig), Robert of Gloucester's *Chronicles*, Malory's *Le Morte Darthur* (for her note on Cai), Polwhele's *History of Cornwall* (for the site of *Celli Wig*), William Rees's *Welsh Saints*, Sharon Turner's *History of the Anglo-Saxons* (1799), and Edward Davies's *Celtic Researches* (1804)—with which work, however, she did not always agree. She also used some MS material—for instance, a text of the *Thirteen Treasures of the Island of Britain* from a MS in the possession of Judge Bosanquet at Dingestow Court. The more recently published works on which she drew for her illustrative material can only have become available at the time when she was preparing the collective edition of the tales that was published in 1849.

For her work as a whole she must have derived considerable help from her Welsh informants; indeed she refers several times in her diary to Carnhuanawc's having gone through some of her notes and translations with her. But for her knowledge of general medieval sources she drew on her own extensive reading and long-established interest in medieval literature—in Middle English, in French and German, and Latin and Icelandic. She refers to her visits to the British Museum, where she would sit and read and where she set others to work in search of the continental parallels to the Welsh romances—particularly those bearing on the theme of the Grail.

She was interested in Welsh folklore, and gives references to beliefs about Gwyn ap Nudd and his *Cŵn Annwn*, and to Sarn Helen, which she explains as *Sarn y Lleng*, 'the road of the Legions.' She was indeed particularly interested in the place-names associated with the stories, such as *Bryn y Cyfergir* and *Llyn y Morynion*, and in her introduction she argues interestingly (if hardly convincingly) that the antiquity of the tales is proved by the fact that these antedate the placenames which commemorate them. So great was her enthusiasm in pursuing placename investigations that after discovering the reference in Nennius's *Historia Brittonum* to *Carn Cabal* as denoting the

Radnorshire mountain Corn Cafallt, which is said to preserve on its topmost cairn the paw-mark of Arthur's hound, she tells that she prevailed upon 'a gentleman of her acquaintance' to undertake for her a pilgrimage to the summit of the mountain. On his return he reported that he had discovered such a stone with an oval indentation upon it, but there were no marks of toes or nails to be seen. Her comment is 'but when we make allowance for the effect of 1000 winters in the high and stormy region, it is not too much to suppose that at one time the resemblance (to a paw-mark) was still more striking,' and she adds cryptically that 'a geologist might say that the indentation on the stone was due to natural wearing, but such an opinion scarcely requires a remark.'

Whatever may have been the extent of the help which Lady Charlotte received from others, whether in scholarship or in mountaineering, it cannot detract from the magnitude of her achievement and her deep interest and involvement in her work. Her name will always remain indissolubly linked with the *Mabinogion*, whose publication was an epoch-making event in Welsh studies, even if she was more indebted to the assistance of others than she was always quite ready to acknowledge. Her translation had a penetrating influence both at home and abroad, as can be seen from the manner in which allusions and themes from the *Mabinogi* gained increasing prominence in the work of Welsh poets, while Tennyson's poetic rendering of 'Geraint and Enid' and his praise for her work, followed by the warm praise of Alfred Nutt in his re-edition of her *Mabinogion* in 1904, did much to make the tales well known in England. One result of the impact of the *Mabinogion* upon the outside world was that in France it stimulated Ernest Renan's *Essai sur la Poésie des Races Celtiques* (1854)—a belated review–article of Lady Charlotte's book, which he reviewed together with Villemarqué's work and ab Ithel's *Ecclesiastical Antiquities of the Cymry* (1844). Renan's essay was absolutely the first attempt ever made at any kind of comparative study of the Celtic literatures between themselves,[33] and an attempt to define their mutual characteristics. In it he describes the *Mabinogion* as 'the true description of the Celtic genius,' and one by which, as he says, in the twelfth century 'the Celts transformed the imagination of Europe.' He finds it surprising that 'so curious a literature, the source of nearly all the romantic creations of Europe, should have remained unknown until our days.' One can do no other than endorse Renan's expression of surprise, though I have tried to indicate how it came about that it was necessary to wait for the Romantic Revival before there could be any true appreciation of the qualities and interest of the tales brought together in the 'Mabinogion.'

NOTES

This essay is reprinted with slight revisions from the *Transactions of the Honourable Society of Cymmrodorion* (London, 1986), pp. 127–41. Dr. Bromwich suggests that readers interested in Lady Charlotte Guest may also wish to consult the more recent book by Revel Guest and Angela V. John, *Lady Charlotte: A Biography of the Nineteenth Century* (London: George Weidenfeld and Nicolson, 1989).

Abbreviations used in notes:

GDG—Thomas Parry, *Gwaith Dafydd ap Gwilym* (Caerdydd 1952).
Ll.C—*Llên Cymru.*
NLW—National Library of Wales.
THSC—*Transactions of the Honorable Society of Cymmrodorion.*
TYP—R. Bromwich, *Trioedd Ynys Prydein* (Caerdydd 1961).
WHR—*Welsh Historical Review.*
YB—*Ysgrifau Beirniadol.*

1 Brynley Roberts gives this number as sixty, *Brut y Brenhinedd*, p. xxiv; Edmund Reiss lists seventy-six copies, WHR 4: 106.
2 I have examined some thirty MSS containing *Trioedd Ynys Prydein.*
3 For particulars see D.M. Lloyd, *Rhai Agweddau ar Ddysg y Gogynfeirdd* (Caerdydd: Gwasg Prifysgol Cymru, 1977). For a newly-discovered possible reference to Teyrnon and Rhiannon see R.G. Gruffydd and Brynley Roberts, Ll.C 13: 289–91.
4 Thomas Parry, *Gwaith Dafydd ap Gwilym* (Caerdydd: Gwasg Prifysgol Cymru, 1952), pp. 84, 46.
5 In *Aspects of the Poetry of Dafydd ap Gwilym* (Cardiff: University of Wales Press, 1986), ch. 5, I have suggested that Dafydd ap Gwilym derived his knowledge of 'Mabinogion' figures from the White Book of Rhydderch, or its source. See also YB 12 (1982): 58.
6 See Rachel Bromwich, *Trioedd Ynys Prydein* (Cardiff: University of Wales Press, 1961), pp. lxxi–ii.
7 Edward Lhuyd, *Archaeologia Britannica* (Oxford: Printed for the Author at the Theatre, 1707) pp. 710, 262.
8 Lhuyd, *Archaeologia Britannica*, p. 264; Bromwich, *Trioedd Ynys Prydein*, p. liv. See Bromwich, *Trioedd Ynys Prydain in Welsh Literature and Scholarship* (Cardiff: University of Wales Press, 1969), pp. 11–12.
9 John Davies, *Bywys a Gwaith Moses Williams* (Caerdydd: Gwasg Prifysgol Cymru, 1937), p. 15; TYP, pp. lvi–lix.
10 *Drych y Prif Oesoedd: Y Rhan Gyntaf* (argraffiad, 1740); gol. David Thomas (Caerdydd: Gwasg Prifysgol Cymru, 1955), p. 17.
11 *Celtic Remains*, ed. D. Silvan Evans (London: Cambrian Archaeological Society, 1878), p. 286.

12 R.T. Jenkins and H.M. Ramage, *History of the Hon. Soc. Cymmrodorion* (London: Hon. Soc. Cymmrodorion, 1951), p. 241.

13 Bromwich, *Trioedd Ynys Prydain in Welsh Literature and Scholarship*; THSC 1968, pp. 299–338; 1969, pp. 127–56.

14 On these writers see Arthur Johnston, *Enchanted Ground: The Study of Medieval Romance in the Eighteenth Century* (London: The Athlone Press, 1964). For William Owen Pughe, see now Glenda Carr's biography, *William Owen Pughe* (Caerdydd: Gwasg Prifysgol Cymru, 1983).

15 In *The Cambrian Quarterly* I (1829). The text of *Math* was not reproduced from the Red Book of Hergest, but from an inexact copy; possibly that of Moses Williams in one of the Llanstephan MSS 90, 81, 93, 126. The translation by Idrison (John Jones, 1804–87). *The Cambrian Quarterly* v (1833) gives the tale of Taliesin 'from a MS of Hopcyn Thomas Phillip, ca. 1370.'

16 George Ellis was entirely English, and had no knowledge of Welsh matters; see *Enchanted Ground*, ch. 6.

17 NLW MS 13242. On Pughe's translations of the Mabinogion tales, and his associations with English scholars in connection with the work, see Arthur Johnston's important article in *NLW Journal* x (1958), 323–28. In the same issue (p. 244) there is a letter written in 1831 by Aneurin Own to Arthur Johnes, referring to his father's plans to print the *Mabinogion* by Gee and Co., Denbigh, and referring to a list of subscribers to the work.

18 I have derived all biographical details from *The Diaries of Lady Charlotte Guest*, ed. the Earl of Bessborough (London: John Murray, 1950). An earlier publication, *Lady Charlotte Guest and the Mabinogion* by D. Rhys Phillips (Carmarthen: W. Spurrell & Son, 1921) gives extracts from the diary referring specifically to her work of translation.

19 Bedwyr Lewis Jones, *Yr Hen Bersoniaid Llengar* (Penarth: Gwasg yr Eglwys yng Nghymru, 1963).

20 See Maxwell Fraser, THSC (1968), 181–84. On the Llanover family see the latter's articles in *NLW Journal* XI, XII, XIII, and Mair Elvet Thomas, *Afiaith yng Ngwent* (Caerdydd: Gwasg Prifysgol Cymru, 1978).

21 'From the standpoint of established schools for the education of the working classes, the Guest family of Dowlais…was undoubtedly the most important and also the most progressive in the industrial history, not only of south Wales, but of the whole of Britain in the nineteenth century.' In Leslie Wynne Evans, *Education in Industrial Wales 1700–1900* (Cardiff: Avalon Books, 1971).

22 *Lady Charlotte Schreiber* (London: Murray, 1952) by the Earl of Bessborough gives extracts from her diaries relating to her life after the death of her first husband in 1852.

23 Professor R.S. Loomis performed the same task a century later, and notes that whereas Lady Charlotte appears to have copied the text within a week, it took him nearly a month to do so. ('Pioneers of Arthurian Scholarship,' *Biblioographical Bulletin of the International Arthurian Society*, 16 (1964): 104).

24 Mair Elvet Thomas, *Afiaith yng Ngwent* and Ll.C. ii, 97 ff.

334   ON ARTHURIAN WOMEN

25 The late Professor C.E. Pickford informed me that none of the poems of Chrétien de Troyes were published before the late 1840s (firstly by the German scholar Immanuel Becker, predecessor of Wendelin Forster). Editions followed in England, America, and Germany. But apart from Potvin's editions of the Grail romances (1866–71) no French edition was published until the 1950s. Dr. Roger Middleton has suggested to me that Lady Charlotte may have learned of the various continental versions of the three Welsh romances of *Peredur*, *Owain*, and *Geraint* from the summaries to be found in the *Bibliothèque Universelle des Romans*, of which a copy would have been available to her in the British Museum.

26 See *The Diaries of Lady Charlotte Guest*, pp. 84–87, and Rhys Phillips, *Lady Charlotte Guest and the Mabinogion*, p. 33; also Francis Gourvil, *Theodore Hersart de la Villemarqué* (Rennes: Imprimeries Oberthur, 1960), pp. 70–72, 96–97. As Gourvil points out, Villemarqué had no more than a smattering of modern Welsh, which was quite insufficient to enable him to understand the language and orthography of the Red Book of Hergest.

27 Gourvil, *Theodore Hersart de la Villemarqué*, p. 73.

28 Jones and Jones, trans., *The Mabinogion*, Everyman's Library (London: Dent, 1949), p. xxxi. Nutt speaks of 'the charm and splendor of her translation.' *The Mabinogion translated by Lady Charlotte Guest, with Notes by A. Nutt*, ed. Alfred Nutt (London: David Nutt, 1902), p. 324.

29 Earl of Bessborough, *Diary of Lady Charlotte Schreiber*, p. 111. On p. 68 she refers to Tennyson's acknowledgment of the source in her book of his poem *Geraint and Enid*.

30 *The Text of the Mabinogion from the Red Book of Hergest*, ed. J. Rhŷs and J. Gwenogvryn Evans (Oxford: J.G. Evans, 1887), pp. vii–viii.

31 Ifor Williams, *Canu Aneirin* l. 1340; J.G. Evans, *Fascimile and text of* The Book of Aneirin (Pwllheli: J.G. Evans, 1908).

32 See Bromwich, *Trioedd Ynys Prydain in Welsh Literature and Scholarship*, pp. 10–29.

33 In this he was followed shortly after by Matthew Arnold. On both writers see Bromwich, *Matthew Arnold and Celtic Literature: A Retrospect* (Oxford: Clarendon, 1965).

Jessie Laidlay Weston (1850–1928)

NORRIS J. LACY

It is easy now to dismiss Jessie Weston, if not to make light of her. Her 1920 study of ritual origins of the Grail story, *From Ritual to Romance*[1] (the book for which she is primarily known by everyone who recognizes her name), seems still to be admired by a fair number of casual readers and enthusiasts, but it is thoroughly discredited among most reputable scholars, and it is belittled by more than a few of them. Had it not been for T.S. Eliot, who cited her extensively in *The Waste Land*,[2] she would now undoubtedly be an obscure footnote, her name probably known, if at all, primarily to those whose interests run to the Tarot and to 'New Age' subjects.

The present essay does not constitute an attempt to rehabilitate that book or her others; I am not sure that is either possible or needed. In fairness to her and to the book, however, we can hardly be surprised that her work has little to offer Arthurian scholars today; after all, just how many scholarly studies (of Arthurian or most other subjects) published eighty years ago are still valued for other than historical or antiquarian reasons? Yet, we ought, I believe, to acknowledge and respect that historical significance. We should also note that not everyone finds the book entirely wrongheaded. A dozen or so years ago (1987), Derek Brewer, while conceding that '...nobody would nowadays accept her account as fully satisfactory,' argued that it nonetheless has 'great merit,' not least because it influenced the 'symbolic anthropological interpretation of *Sir Gawain and the Green Knight*.'[3]

As we shall see, not all academics are by any means as charitable as Brewer on the value of *From Ritual to Romance*, although a good many, I trust, recognize its past influence on scholars as well as on an important poet. I suggest, however, that in Weston's case (as in a good many others) there is good reason to respect the person even if we no longer read the book. Weston herself was a serious, devoted, and well-trained scholar who was deeply interested, and widely read, in anthropology and literature. *From Ritual to Romance* was a serious and scholarly effort (however wrongheaded many scholars may now find it), and we tend to forget that Weston was a quite prolific scholar and writer: the book for which she is now remembered is by no means her unique contribution to Arthurian studies.

Janet Grayson, in 1992, performed a significant service for scholars by publishing a bibliographical (and biographical) essay and full listing, with commentary, of Jessie Weston's publications.[4] My factual remarks about Weston's life, and in some cases about her works as well, are drawn primarily from Grayson's pages, to which readers are warmly referred.

Grayson's bibliography of Weston's works includes not only *From Ritual to Romance*, but also some sixty other publications. There are scholarly books, articles, translations, and reviews, as well as a number of entries in the *Britannica*. Weston also published a number of short stories and poems, in addition to pamphlets entitled *Germany's Literary Debt to France* and *Germany's Crime Against France*.[5]

About Weston, Janet Grayson also offers all the available biographical information, but that is very slight. Virtually none of Weston's correspondence survives, and there are few other records. We know that she was born in London in 1850, that she received a serious and solid education, including study with Gaston Paris.[6] She inherited money and lived in Paris for a good part of her life. She never held an academic post, and she held no advanced degree (until the University of Wales conferred an honorary degree on her in 1923—only five years before her death).[7] She fought battles, literary and other, and she had a good many friends and defenders—as well as opponents who refuted her ideas and sometimes belittled her efforts.[8] One reviewer referred to her interest in Grail legends as Miss Weston's 'hobby,' adding the curious observation that this hobby 'is worthy of a woman….'[9] But that woman continued her work, and in fact, when she died in 1928, at age 78, Weston left a half-completed study of the *Perlesvaus*, which Grayson also edited and published.[10]

Although we know Weston mostly for her Grail theories, she seems to have thought of herself principally as a translator. In fact, her first publication, in 1894, was a two-volume, copiously annotated, verse translation of Wolfram's *Parzival*.[11] Her interest in *Parzival* is surely unsurprising, considering the vogue of Wagner in late-nineteenth-century Europe. More surprising, perhaps, is her translation of the Middle Dutch romance *Moriaen* (which is where I first encountered her translations).[12] Here, too, it would be easy to make light of her or, at least, to find her translation more amusing than edifying. Her rendition is inaccurate in places, but most of all, it is a translation that, even for its time, is so stilted and archaic as to be almost unreadable. Phrases such as 'He clave many to the teeth…,' and 'What boots it to make long my tale?' for the customary formula 'Why should I make my story any longer?' are awkward at best.[13] Here is a slightly longer passage:

Before him he drave captive a maiden. Sir Gawain beheld how he smote her, many a time and oft, blow upon blow, with his fist that weighed heavily for the mailed gauntlet that he ware. Pain enough did he make her bear for that she desired not to ride with him. He smote her many a time and oft.[14]

At its best, the translation is unlikely to lead many readers back to the original; at its worst, it strikes us now as almost comical.

But it *is* a translation, and we should consider that she was one of the few people—and quite possibly the only one who was not a professional Netherlandist—who even *read* the *Moriaen*, and she was in any event the first person to undertake a translation. (Indeed, a new translation is only now being made, by David Johnson and Geert Claassens.)[15] She also translated Marie de France, Gottfried's *Tristan*, *Sir Gawain and the Green Knight*, and parts or all of other medieval French, English, and German texts. In addition, she published studies, mostly concerning sources, of the German *Lanzelet*, of the French Perceval romances, of *Perlesvaus* and the *Vengeance Raguidel*.[16] And as noted, she had a book-length study of the *Perlesvaus* well under way when she died.

Unencumbered by either financial need or academic obligation, Jessie Weston was an amateur—in both the original and the newer senses of the word. She was, as we would say now, an independent scholar (and certainly no adjective better describes Weston than 'independent'). Surely some of the disdain expressed toward her by certain of her contemporaries derived from her amateur status, the fact that her work did not carry the imprimatur of an advanced degree or a university affiliation. At the same time, it must be acknowledged that the combination of money and of the absence of academic duties—as well as the lack of family responsibilities, since she always remained 'Miss Weston,' both legally and in most references to her by other scholars—left her free to write, read, and travel to an extent experienced by too few scholars of her day (as well as of ours).

Her non-academic status aside, Jessie Weston also encountered considerable animosity simply because she was English. That is an observation that may strike us today as peculiar, but it needs to be recalled that the predominant scholarship in the field she had, as it were, invaded was German, and a good many German scholars took less than kindly to her treading on their scholarly ground: Grayson notes that Brugger devoted two lengthy reviews to Weston's *The Legend of Sir Perceval* (1906, 1909) but ultimately dismissed her work as '*müssige Spielerei*,' 'idle child's play.'[17]

Of course, although German scholarship was dominant, a number of French scholars (e.g., Paris, Faral, and Lot) were also giants in the field, and they were for the most part more favorably disposed to her—at least to her person and in some cases to her scholarship—than were the Germans. In fact, she had notable friendships with, and significant support from, French scholars such as Bédier and Lot.[18] But to many, Weston, the English woman, was an interloper, and one not always made to feel welcome.[19]

And finally we come to the central subject of this book: Weston was a *woman* Arthurian. As such, she encroached, as she herself said, on 'ground sacred to scholars of another sex...'[20] Grayson does not mention, nor have I elsewhere found, explicit condemnations of Weston simply because she was a woman—beyond the review that damned her with faint praise, contending that her 'hobby' was 'worthy of a woman and a scholar.' She was not the only female Arthurian scholar of her time, but even in the near-absence of directly misogynistic commentary, it scarcely seems likely that the vituperation heaped upon her in some quarters is entirely unrelated to the fact that she was not, as she said, 'of another sex.'

Today, the very mention of Jessie Weston tends, in some quarters, to set pulses racing. A fascinating array of evidence can be found on Arthurnet, the on-line discussion group sponsored by *Arthuriana*. A search of the archives reveals that, during the past seven years or so (since October 1993), her name appears in some seventy postings—not many, considering that they tend to be clusters of a dozen or more replies to a single query. Since Arthurnet is frequented not only by professional scholars and advanced students, but also by amateur enthusiasts, it is not unusual to encounter questions such as 'What is the current thinking about Jessie Weston's [or someone else's] scholarship?' or 'Why is there so much hostility toward Jessie Weston?' Whatever the question in regard to Weston, the respondents generally agree that *From Ritual to Romance* is of little or—more often—no value today, but they disagree about the contributions it may have made when it was new. A good many reactions are strongly negative and sometimes acerbic, though a fair number defend her historical importance. (The quotations given here, and to others, are available from the searchable Arthurnet archives, at http://lists.mun.ca/archives/arthurnet.html.)

One writer suggested that '...no one takes Jessie Weston seriously anymore. Her study *From Ritual to Romance* was...based mainly on intuition with very little regard [for] facts.'[21] Another contended, even more vehemently, that the book was 'a tissue of lies and bad scholarship from one end to the other, with no value whatsoever, except as a source for *The Waste Land*.'[22]

A response to these attitudes urged, however, '...fairness to her achievements in stimulating and shaping Arthurian studies as well as public interest in the legend a hundred years ago....' Yet another respondent said, with rather simple eloquence, 'I think we should cut Jessie some slack.'[23] Finally, whatever may be our opinion of Weston's work, I presume that many will agree with the view expressed in the following posting: 'It seems a shame that the reputations of such significant scholars of the past...are so casually trashed these days....'[24]

Whether we agree with her views on Grail origins—and who does?— indeed, whether we have *ever* agreed with any of her conclusions, I think we are too hasty in dismissing Jessie Weston as an occultist, a crackpot, or a 'hobbyist.' I wonder how many readers were sufficiently inspired by her work actually to read a Grail romance? Surely some were. I wonder how many people read her translations who otherwise would not have known *Parzival, Tristan und Isolt, Sir Gawain and the Green Knight,* or *Moriaen.* (Certainly, until now, no one who cannot read Middle Dutch has known *Moriaen* at all *except* through her translation or through summaries.)

I also wonder how many of us know, as well as she did, Middle English, Old and Modern French, Middle High and Modern German—with some Dutch, Italian, and other languages added for good measure. And especially, I wonder how we can justify disdain for a scholar who, a century ago, recognized the importance of consulting all the available manuscripts of texts she was studying. She actually went where the manuscripts were, and she read them. It was William Roach who said that 'for many years Miss Weston was the only scholar who examined *all* the extant MSS of Chrétien's *Perceval* and its Continuations and gave useful descriptions of their contents...as early as 1906, long before Hilka (1932) and Micha (1939).'[25] Of course, the fact that she was independently wealthy afforded her the luxury of traveling to collections at a time when many of the major medievalists could not always do so, but it has to be added that a good many others, who may have possessed the means, simply saw no particular need for it. (And even now it can be said, I fear, that too few medievalists bother to look at all the manuscripts, even though the necessity for wealth has been replaced by the comparatively easy availability of microfilms and other methods of access.)

Finally, I believe that we do Weston an injustice if we infer from her source-hunting an absence of critical judgment. Indeed, we may still read her profitably without sharing in her seeking after sources and analogues. When she expresses her preference for *Perlesvaus* over the *Queste,* some of us, at least, will applaud her enthusiasm for the former romance and perhaps even agree with her—I for one do—that the Galahad of the *Queste* is a colorless and dull figure. Weston's judgment of the *Perlesvaus,* that it is 'coherent, unified in theme, picturesque, and exciting in depicting action,'[26] is not merely an observation made by either a hobbyist or a scholar whose only interest was in sources and analogues. It is literary appreciation, and it is a perceptive reaction that does the *Perlesvaus* more justice than is sometimes accorded it by the comparatively few recent critics who bother to read it.

I hope I may be excused a personal reflection that is also something of a manifesto. The history of a discipline is also its heritage (as well as its folklore), and that heritage merits both respect and preservation, even when scholarship has left it far behind. I was fortunate: even as a graduate student, I learned about major scholars of another age. I learned about their views (many of which had even then been long since discarded), and I learned too about the people themselves. I deserve no credit for that; perhaps it was a generational tendency to offer such information, or perhaps I simply happened to study with scholars who chose to offer it, sometimes systematically, usually anecdotally, occasionally dismissively. In the process, I also learned about our predecessors' battles, their accomplishments, and their personalities, 'warts' and all. It provided a perspective, a sense of tradition that I value even when the interest of the work is purely historical. We need, and our students need, a sense of disciplinary continuity.[27]

And sometimes, of course, our past offers more discontinuity than continuity. Our field, like others, develops in a pseudo-Hegelian way, generating antitheses to past scholarship and sometimes then constructing syntheses out of them both. In the process, the thesis is rejected or superseded, of course, but without a thesis, there can be no antithesis.[28] Nor can we honorably validate our own work, as some unfortunately attempt to do, by dismissing or denigrating a Gaston Paris or a Joseph Bédier or a U.T. Holmes or a Jessie Weston or many another. These are scholars who have played an historically important role in the formation of our discipline. Jessie Weston, says Janet Grayson, 'dominated English Arthurian studies as *the* specialist in romance literature.'[29] Weston worked indefatigably for decades, and she made a contribution to our field that, I suggest, goes far beyond what T.S. Eliot did with (or to) her work. We do not have to share her interest in sources or accept her conclusions about them in order to concur with the Arthurnet writer who suggested that 'we should cut Jessie some slack.'

PENNSYLVANIA STATE UNIVERSITY

Norris J. Lacy is Edwin Erle Sparks Professor of French at Pennsylvania State University. He has served as both international president and North-American president of the International Arthurian Society. His books (as author, editor, or translator) include *The Craft of Chrétien de Troyes* (1980), *The Romance of Tristran* by Béroul (1989), *The New Arthurian Encyclopedia* (1991, 1996); *Medieval Arthurian Literature: A Guide to Recent Research* (1996); *Lancelot-Grail: The Old French Arthurian Vulgate and Post-Vulgate Cycles in Translation* (1993–96), and others.

NOTES

1 (London: Cambridge University Press, 1920). It is not my purpose in this essay to examine the thesis of this or of Weston's other studies. Particularly in the case of *From Ritual to Romance*, that thesis is familiar to Arthurian scholars and to a great many other readers. Suffice it to mention in passing that Weston links the Grail quest to the cult of Adonis, the Wasteland to the death of a Vegetation Spirit, and the Grail and Lance to female and male sexual organs. *From Ritual to Romance* is itself readily available, having been reprinted frequently, but see also below, n4.

2 In T.S. Eliot, *Poems: 1905–1925* (London: Faber and Gwyer, 1925), pp. 63–92. In Eliot's *On Poetry and Poets* (London: Faber and Faber, 1957), pp. 109–10, he points out that the notes (in which he cites Weston) were originally appended to the poem because the text itself was too short to be published by itself as a book. He does acknowledge the need to 'pay tribute to the work of Miss Jessie Weston,' but he also adds that 'I regret having sent so many enquirers off on a wild goose chase after Tarot cards and the Holy Grail.'

3 'Some Current Trends in Arthurian Scholarship and Criticism 1987.' In *Arturus Rex: Acta Conventus Lovaniensis 1987*, ed. Willy Van Hoecke, Gilbert Tournoy, and Werner Verbeke. 2 vols. (Leuven: Leuven University Press, 1991), 2: 3–18.

4 Janet Grayson, 'In Quest of Jessie Weston,' *Arthurian Literature* XI (1992), pp. 1–80. Grayson offers a concise account of the development and content of *From Ritual to Romance* on pp. 28–34.

5 Both published in 1915 (London: Nutt) and thus reflecting not only Weston's francophile leanings but also the passions aroused by the war.

6 Grayson, 'In Quest,' pp. 4–5.

7 Grayson, 'In Quest,' p. 43. A colleague has suggested to me that Weston did indeed hold a doctorate; however, he has not been able to document the degree, and I too have been unable to locate any reference to it.

8 And she responded in kind. She could be particularly hostile to J.D. Bruce, and vice versa. Weston accused him of misreading her work, whether through carelessness or a willful desire to distort what she had written. In her uncompleted study of *Perlesvaus*, for example, she points out an instance in which Bruce had misread her, and she adds, 'No one who has ever read my study…attentively could have misinterpreted my views. Unfortunately, Professor Bruce's references to my work are as a rule characterised by the same inaccuracy…To refute all Professor Bruce's misstatements would require pages. I can only warn readers against accepting without reference to my original work any of that writer's representation of my views.' See Jessie Weston, *The Romance of Perlesvaus*, ed. Janet Grayson (Holland, MI: Studies in Medievalism, 1988), pp. 29–30, n8; see also p. 80, n1.

9 Grayson, 'In Quest,' pp. 46–47 n63. In fairness, let it be added that the entire

sentence reads, '...is worthy of a woman and a scholar.' The final three words may lessen the condescension, but they hardly neutralize it. One wonders what work might be worthy of a female scholar that would be inappropriate for a male one— and why.

10 See n6.

11 *Parzival*, 2 vols. (London: Nutt, 1894).

12 *Moriaen: A Metrical Romance Rendered into English Prose from the Mediaeval Dutch* (London: D. Nutt, 1901).

13 *Moriaen*, pp. 87; 107, 139.

14 *Moriaen*, p. 51.

15 It will appear in the fourth volume of Dutch material included in the Arthurian Archives series from D.S. Brewer.

16 For a full listing of these and other publications by Weston, see Grayson, 'In Quest,' pp. 52–61.

17 Quoted by Grayson, 'In Quest,' p. 13.

18 Grayson, 'In Quest,' p. 13.

19 'For good or ill, she disliked Germans...' (Grayson, 'In Quest,' p. 48). The often harsh judgments of her work by German scholars are doubtless a partial explanation of that dislike, but she also reacted strongly against assumptions of Germanic superiority or symbols of Germanic manhood (such as 'the ugly sabre scar young Germans sport[ed] as a sign of manhood,' Grayson, 'In Quest,' p. 48). Weston nonetheless maintained her enthusiasm for Wagner and for Germanic myth in general, a fact that, as Grayson points out (p. 48), has been falsely interpreted by some as acceptance of the myth of Aryan racial superiority.

20 Grayson, 'In Quest,' p. 12. The sentence continues '...and of another nation,' a reference to German scholars.

21 Sigmund Eisner, 13 March 1997.

22 Norman Hinton, 24 February 1998. Challenged by other readers, Hinton explained that, 'I did not mean that Jessie Weston deliberately told lies: I used it in the sense that the book is full of untrue statements. I'll stand by that: I know of nothing in Weston that scholarship has substantiated' (February 26, 1998).

23 Dennis C. Clark, March 6, 1998.

24 Dan Nastali, March 4, 1998.

25 Quoted by Grayson, 'In Quest,' p. 13 n11.

26 Weston, *Perlesvaus*, ed. Grayson, pp. xviii–xix.

27 For that reason among others, medievalists should value the kind of work done in the present book, as well as in the volumes on medieval scholars edited by Helen Damico (*Medieval Scholarship: Biographical Studies on the Formation of a Discipline*, 3 vols. [New York: Garland, 1995–2000]) and in the 'Distinguished Arthurians' series of memoirs edited by Sigmund Eisner and published serially in *Arthuriana*.

28 As Thomas Kelly puts it in his foreword to Weston's study *The Romance of Perlesvaus* (ed. Grayson) '"C'est avec du vieux qu'on fait du neuf"' (xiv).

29 Grayson, 'In Quest,' p. 13.

The Loomis Ladies:
Gertrude Schoepperle Loomis (1882–1921),
Laura Hibbard Loomis (1883–1960),
Dorothy Bethurum Loomis (1897–1987)

HENRY HALL PEYTON III

When I was in high school in Louisiana, I was very much drawn to that tuneful trio, the Andrews Sisters—Patty, Maxene, and Laverne. Then I went to college in Texas and Rhode Island and discovered the Loomis Ladies—Gertrude, Laura, and Dorothy. The effect was enlightening. Instead of listening to 'Appleblossom Time,' 'Bei Mir Bist Du Schoen,' and 'The Boogie Woogie Bugle Boy of Company B,' I read with fascination Gertrude Loomis's *Tristan and Isolt: A Study of the Sources of the Romance*, Laura Loomis's *Three Middle English Romances*, and Dorothy Loomis's *The Homilies of Wulfstan*. Just as King Arthur had questing knights, Roger Sherman Loomis had scholarly wives whose intellectual pursuits ranged widely and importantly.

Roger Sherman Loomis was born in Yokohama, Japan, October 31, 1887, the son of American missionaries, and died October 11, 1966, at the age of seventy-eight. He was a member of the faculty of Columbia University from 1919 to 1958 and president of the American Branch of the International Arthurian Society from 1948 to 1963.[1] On August 27, 1919, he married Gertrude Schoepperle, an instructor at the University of Illinois, where Mr. Loomis also taught from 1913 to 1918. Gertrude Schoepperle Loomis died tragically of peritonitis in 1921, at the age of thirty–nine years. On June 6, 1925, Loomis married his second wife, Laura Alandis Hibbard, who was Katharine Lee Bates Professor of English Literature at Wellesley College. She died in 1960, at the age of seventy–three. Dorothy Bethurum and Mr. Loomis were married January 12, 1963. At the time she taught at Connecticut College. Both Laura Hibbard Loomis and Dorothy Bethurum Loomis were twice listed in *Who's Who of American Women*, and Dorothy Bethurum Loomis appeared twice in *Who's Who in America*.[2] It is interesting to note that although Gertrude Schoepperle Loomis held the Ph.D. degree from Radcliffe College; Laura Hibbard Loomis from the University of Chicago; and Dorothy

Bethurum Loomis from Yale University, Roger Sherman Loomis himself did not hold the Ph.D. degree. Like George Lyman Kittredge at Harvard and Foster Damon at Brown (illustrious company, indeed), Loomis's highest earned academic degree was a Master of Arts (from Harvard, 1910). He later received the B.Litt. degree from Oxford (1913).[3]

Gertrude Schoepperle Loomis was a graduate of Wellesley College. In 1906, while a graduate student at Radcliffe, she began research on Tristan, part of which she used for her Ph.D. dissertation. She received the doctorate in 1909. While at Radcliffe, she studied with William Henry Schofield. She held the Alice Truman Palmer Fellowship from Wellesley. Her *magnum opus* is *Tristan and Isolt: A Study of the Sources of the Romance*, first published at Frankfurt am Main by J. Baer and Company in 1913. Soon after the initial publication, she began work on an expanded edition of the two-volume work which would include a bibliography and critical essay on Tristan scholarship since 1912 by Roger Sherman Loomis. The second edition was published by New York University as the Ottendorfer Memorial Series of Germanic Monographs No. 6.[4] Among her other publications is an edition of Bodleian MS Rawlinson B514, *Betha Colaim chille, the Life of Columcille*, compiled by Manus O'Donnell in 1532 (d. 1564). The book had Irish text and English translation on facing pages, with introduction, glossary, notes, and indices by A. O'Kelleher and G. Schoepperle. While teaching at Vassar College, she contributed the article 'Arthur in Avalon and the Banshee' to *Vassar Mediaeval Studies by Members of the Faculty of Vassar College*, edited by Christabel Forsyth Fiske. Mr. Loomis edited a fine memorial volume in honor of Gertrude Schoepperle Loomis; Linda Gowans speculates that it may have been the first memorial volume for a woman scholar.[5]

Laura Alandis Hibbard Loomis received the A.B. degree from Wellesley College in 1905 and the A.M. from that institution two years later. She taught at Mt. Holyoke College from 1908 to 1916, when she received her Ph.D. from the University of Chicago. At that time she joined the Wellesley English Literature Department where she remained for the rest of her academic career.[6] She served as vice-president of the Modern Language Association. Upon receiving the Alice Freeman Palmer fellowship, she studied for a year at Oxford.[7] Her scholarly works include several books—*Three Middle English Romances*, published 1911; *Medieval Romance in England*, 1924; and *Medieval Vista*, 1953. She collaborated with Roger Sherman Loomis on *Arthurian Legends in Medieval Art* (1938), and *Medieval Romances* (1957).[8] Her numerous journal articles indicate the depth and breadth of her interests. These include: 'Secular Dramatics in the Royal Palace, Paris, 1378, 1389, and Chaucer's

"Tregetoures'" (*Speculum* 1958); 'The Athelstan Gift Story: Its Influence on English Chronicles and Carolingian Romances'(PMLA 1952); 'The Auchinleck "Roland and Vernagu" and the "Short Chronicle"' (*Modern Language Notes* 1945); 'The Auchinleck Manuscript and a Possible Bookshop of 1330-1340' (PMLA 1942); 'Chaucer and the Breton Lays of the Auchinleck MS' (*Studies in Philology* 1941) ; 'Sir Thopas and David and Goliath' (*Modern Language Notes* 1936); 'Chaucer's "Jewes Werk" and "Guy of Warwick"' (*Philological Quarterly* 1935); 'Geoffrey of Monmouth and Stonehenge' (PMLA 1930); 'Arthur's Round Table' (PMLA 1926);[9] and 'The Round Table Again' (*Modern Language Notes* 1929). Other articles are to be found in journals of art and literature.[10]

There are some (perhaps apocryphal) stories about the disappointment suffered by scholars Loomis didn't marry. It is rumored, for instance, that:

> during a visiting appointment at New York University in the late 1950s, the famous romance scholar Margaret Schlauch, of Warsaw University, entered her large lecture class on Middle English Literature one day and announced to her students that she had something she wished to say for the record. Once she had said it, she would proceed to her lecture on the assignment for the day, and would not mention or discuss the matter again. She had belatedly learned, she said, that Roger Sherman Loomis had married Laura Hibbard and she wanted to state this one time that 'It was unfair. She got next to him in the library.' Helaine Newstead, who was his student at Columbia, is said later to have been devastated by his choice of Dorothy Bethurum for Wife #3. (Loomis, who wrote so dryly of the romances, more than made up for it by his romantic nature).

Dorothy Bethurum Loomis was born in Franklin, Tennessee, a suburb of Nashville, on April 5, 1897. She received the A.B. degree from Vanderbilt in 1919. An A.M. followed in 1922, with the Ph.D. awarded by Yale in 1930. She taught at Southwestern University, Randolph-Macon College, Lawrence College, and Connecticut College. She was a member of Phi Beta Kappa and the National Humanities Faculty.[11] With Randall Steward she co-authored *Masterpieces of American Literature* (1953) and *Masterpieces of English Literature* (1954).[12] Other publications include *The Homilies of Wulfstan* (1957), and *Chaucer's The Squire's Tale* (1965).[13] She was editor of *Critical Essays in Medieval Literature*, 1960. Her article 'Constance and the Stars' appeared in *Chaucerian Problems and Perspectives: Essays Presented to Paul E. Beichner*, published at Notre Dame in 1979. As mentioned earlier, her numerous publications led to entries in *Who's Who in America* and *Who's Who of American Women*.[14] At her retirement, Dorothy Bethurum Loomis returned to Nashville where she occasionally lectured at Vanderbilt University and entertained visiting Arthurian scholars. She died in Nashville after her ninetieth birthday.[15]

It is difficult to suggest sufficiently the contribution of these three ladies to medieval studies except to say that their influence remains considerable. Gertrude Schoepperle Loomis and Laura Hibbard Loomis both collaborated with Roger Sherman Loomis in Arthurian research and publications, although none of the three women appears to have had his extensive interest in Welsh studies. Their scholarship centers chiefly on English Arthurian literature and the works of Geoffrey Chaucer. Whether it be Gertrude Schoepperle Loomis's valuable work on Tristan, Laura Hibbard Loomis's studies of the Auchinleck manuscript, or Dorothy Bethurum Loomis's Chaucer essays, the Loomis Ladies make an incomparable trio of contributors to an understanding of the literature of the Middle Ages. Who would have thought that a man without the Ph.D. would have done so well in marrying these three brilliant women? The answer, of course, is that a man of Roger Sherman Loomis's scholarly acumen and profound knowledge of areas such as Celtic literature and medieval art would easily have assessed and pursued such brilliance as soon as he encountered it. Known for his prolific writings, he will also always be celebrated for his three scholarly wives.

UNIVERSITY OF MEMPHIS

Henry Hall Peyton III is founding editor and editor *emeritus* of the journal now known as *Arthuriana*. Stemming from a life-long love of vocal classical music, he has published scores of reviews of operatic recordings and performances, has written the libretto of an opera, and has as his chief research interest the music dramas of Richard Wagner. He is semi-retired from the University of Memphis after thirty-two years of teaching the literature of the Middle Ages.

NOTES

1 'Roger Sherman Loomis,' in *Contemporary Authors*, New Revision Series, volume 8 (Detroit: Gale Research, 1983), pp. 331–32.

2 'Roger Sherman Loomis,' in Literature Online <http://lion.chadwyck.com/sec_srcs/>.

3 'Roger Sherman Loomis,' obituary (*New York Times*, October 12, 1966), sec. 3, p. 43.

4 'Gertrude Schoepperle Loomis,' obituary (*New York Times*, December 13, 1921), sec. 3, p. 19.

5 *Medieval Studies in Memory of Gertrude Schoepperle Loomis*, ed. Roger Sherman Loomis (New York: Columbia University Press, 1927).

6 'Laura Alandis Loomis,' in *Biography Index*, vol. 5, September 1958–August 1961. (New York: H.W. Wilson Co., 1962), p. 448.

7 'Laura Hibbard Loomis,' in Literature Online <htttp://lion.chadwyck.com/ sec_scrs/>.

8 'Laura Hibbard Loomis,' *Who's Who of American Women*, 1st ed., 1958–1959 (Wilmette: Marquis Who's Who, 1958), p. 779.

9 'Laura Hibbard Loomis,' in *Who's Who of American Women*, 2d ed., 1961–1962 (Wilmette: Marquis Who's Who, 1961), p. 605.

10 'Laura Hibbard Loomis,' obituary (*New York Times*, August 26, 1960), sec. 3, p. 25.

11 'Dorothy Bethurum Loomis,' *Who's Who in America*, 38th ed., 1974–1975 (Wilmette: Marquis Who's Who, 1974), p. 1915.

12 'Dorothy Bethurum Loomis,' *Who's Who in America*, 39th ed., 1976–1977 (Wilmette: Marquis Who's Who, 1976), p. 1938.

13 'Dorothy Bethurum Loomis,' *Who's Who of American Women*, 7th edition, 1972–1973 (Wilmette: Marquis Who's Who, 1971), p. 538.

14 'Dorothy Bethurum Loomis,' *Who's Who of American Women*, 8th ed., 1974–1975 (Wilmette: Marquis Who's Who, 1973), p. 578.

15 'Dorothy Bethurum Loomis,' Literature Online <http://lion.chadwyck.com/sec_srcs>.

The Quickening Force:
Vida Dutton Scudder (1861–1954)
and Malory's *Le Morte Darthur*

SUE ELLEN HOLBROOK

'Where do high lights fall, in the pictures of the past? Chiefly on the
sense of refreshing adventure during those pioneer years....'[1]

So mused Vida Dutton Scudder in 1947 about her work with the Boston
community settlement, Dennison House. When she died in 1954 at the
age of ninety-two, hers had been a long past to picture, filled with social reform,
spiritual quest, teaching, and writing. Amid these fourfold occupations lay her
pursuit of Arthurian literature. In all, she was, indeed, a pioneer.

As one of the groundbreaking New England women who entered higher
education, Scudder is well remarked by scholars charting women's history.[2]
As one who placed the red flag of socialism next to the crucifix in her oratory,
she is particularly memorable.[3] Nevertheless, she valued her work teaching
Arthurian literature, 'in which I was something of a pioneer,' and writing a
critical book about Sir Thomas Malory's *Le Morte Darthur*, into the study of
which she put 'all my insight and initiative.'[4] In letting the 'highlight' fall
here on her Arthurian work, we will see why, in the early era of women's
education and Arthurian studies alike, she had reason to value her work
then, and we do now.

To see the Arthurian pattern in the larger tapestry, a metaphor she herself
liked, we begin with biographical context. Vida Dutton Scudder was born
into a time, place, and family that enabled pioneering, though not without
fortuitous opportunity and courageous choice. Her parents were of New
England lineage, Duttons on her mother's side, Scudders on her father's.
Though named Julia, as several Dutton women were, she was called Vida
for Davida, after her father, David. Her life began in 1861 'under the British
flag' in Madura, India, where her father was a Congregationalist missionary.[5]
Upon his death while she was an infant, Scudder was taken by her mother,
Harriet, to Massachusetts, where they lived for several years in her maternal

grandparents' home in Auburndale. Apart from four years in Northampton while in college, Scudder resided in the eastern part of the state, in Boston for twenty-five years from 1886–1912, and then for the remainder of her life in Wellesley in a house she had built for herself and her mother. Since childhood she had lived off and on in Europe as well, particularly Britain, France, and Italy. Starting in 1890, when not in Europe she spent her summers in Shelburne, New Hampshire, first staying at Philbrook Farm, and then after 1896 in her own house, 'The Brakes.'

Within these geographical environs, opportunities for formal scholastic education were just becoming available to women, especially women with a comfortable income and a network of relatives and friends, as had Vida Dutton Scudder. Thanks to the advice of a friend of her mother, Scudder became, in 1878, one of the first handful of girls to attend the Boston Latin School, learning Greek and Latin. Thanks to her mother's unconventional desire that her daughter have a higher education, she became one of the first women in America to earn a bachelor's degree, which she did at Smith College in 1884. Among the few colleges for women then, Smith was her mother's choice over the other Massachusetts college, Wellesley, because the Smith faculty had men, whereas the Wellesley faculty was largely comprised of women.[6] During the 1870s and 1880s, men were more likely than women to provide their female students with a scholastic education, it was reasoned, given the superior education that male faculty had themselves received. Scudder did admire a few of her male professors, came to love her alma mater, received an honorary doctorate in 1922, and maintained a strong circle of friendship with Smith graduates throughout her life.[7] Yet, as she acknowledges in her autobiography *On Journey*, during her undergraduate experience there, she felt 'segregated in the prison of class.'[8]

After graduating from Smith in 1884, Scudder went to Oxford for the autumn term, but not to associate with the women students at Somerville or Lady Margaret Hall. Rather, she attended John Ruskin's last course of lectures, turning with 'eagerness and reverence to his social writings,' such as *Unto the Last*.[9] In addition, she was privately tutored by York Powell in several 'cultural fields'—including Norse mythology and Gothic sculpture— and wrote a manuscript about medieval grotesques 'just to have a good time.'[10] After touring south-west England and then the Alps, she settled with her mother and an aunt on Newbury Street in Boston's Back Bay.[11] From her Oxford experience she brought back a sense of the 'slow pilgrimage toward justice' inspired by Ruskin and the view, inspired by Powell, that '"the best which had been thought and said in the world" lay before me, an open book that I must learn to read.'[12] From Devon and Cornwall, she brought back a quickening interest in Arthurian romance.[13]

As a woman in her early twenties, Scudder might have expected at this point to be planning for marriage or for a middle-class woman's profession, such as teaching, though not of course, in the 1880s, for both at the same time. Marriage was not in the offing, and apart from aspiring to write and taking an M.A. from Smith 'for lack of anything better to do,' Scudder had not fixed on an occupational objective.[14] But then into this floating life arrived opportunity—and a life-shaping decision. In 1886, the President of Smith, L. Clark Seelye, invited her to join the faculty at her alma mater. At the same time, through the suggestion of Professor George Herbert Palmer (whose sister was a friend of Scudder's mother), Alice Freeman (the President of Wellesley), who was engaged to Palmer, invited her to teach at Wellesley. Convinced that her mother, from whom Scudder was unwilling to part, needed to live in Boston, she made the 'sacrificial' choice to teach at Wellesley.[15] And there it was in the autumn of 1887, commuting by train from home, that she began her 'adventures in pedagogy,' in the nascent English Department of a women's college rather like an 'overgrown boarding school.'[16]

Within a few years, the fourfold journey had begun. By 1888 Scudder had focused her desire for social justice on the women's colleges' newly formed College Settlements Association (CSA), certain that 'women of the new social order promise...to possess the exact union of elements which the times demand.'[17] By then, believing that 'life progressively transferred from the outward to the inward sphere,'[18] she had matched secular politics with similarly grounded spiritual commitment through the Society of Companions of the Holy Cross. By 1890, she had published *An Introduction to the Writings of John Ruskin*, and she was immersed in teaching among women to women at Wellesley, 'destined,' according to her former student Florence Converse, 'to play an important part in Wellesley's life and to increase [its] academic reputation.'[19]

To the 'romantic social adventure' of the CSA she gave—and in turn received—invigorating attention until 1912, especially through money-raising initiatives, educational activities, and convivial gatherings at Dennison House on Tyler Street in Boston's South End. Scudder had helped found this settlement in 1892 'quite independent of Jane Addams and Hull House.'[20] Among the Dennison House experiences that affected her most were those she began ten years later as president of the 'Circolo Italo-Americano,' through which she and the members sponsored occasions, such as lectures and debates, for both cultural and civic exchange between Americans and the newly arriving Italian immigrants.[21] Upon moving to Wellesley, she gave up Dennison House. Too radical for the CSA, she maintained over the years a steadfast commitment to erasing class barriers produced by economic inequalities. Through life experience and study of Karl Marx, St. Francis, and other thinkers, she moved away from a college woman's need to serve the poor to conviction in the 'Messianic function of the working class.'[22] On the other side of her radical coin lay the Companions of the Holy Cross, an organization of Episcopalian women pledged to the practice of intercessory prayer for social justice. To them and the Christian foundation of social revolution Scudder remained dedicated throughout her life. Her 'interior' autobiography, *My Quest for Reality* (1952), with its stern chapters on, for instance, 'General Disarmament' and 'The Function of the Church,' is written largely with this 'religious family' in mind.[23]

To Wellesley Scudder gave forty years, making it the 'center of my energy' for two reasons. Teaching there 'was the work I was paid to do,' and despite the 'feminine emphasis' that disturbed her, she found, in Converse's words, that it was '"romantic and exciting…to be a professor in a woman's college"' in those formative decades.[24] Although Scudder did study at the Sorbonne while on leave during 1893–95, she never sought a doctoral degree, for she disliked the narrow research required, 'rummaging about in literary byways in pursuit of unimportant information' that was 'profitless' to the student,[25] an attitude we will see in her approach to teaching and writing about Malory's *Le Morte Darthur*. As for her writing, which crossed all her interests and was a principal form of her political activism, Scudder went on to fill a 'five-foot shelf' of books in her attic study.[26] Among these publications were two based on her most innovative courses, English Literature 13 *Social Ideals in English Letters*, which vanished from the Wellesley curriculum when she retired, and English Literature 21 *Arthurian Romance*, which endured.

When Scudder introduced *Arthurian Romance* in the spring semester of 1905, it was, she believed, the first Arthurian literature course in any college curriculum.[27] Her aim was to use Malory as a 'center' for studying the medieval period. By including Malory's predecessors, she would span the twelfth century to the 'edge of the Renaissance.'[28] Accordingly, the first catalog description reports that 'The course will open with Malory's *Morte Darthur*, and thence work backward to a study of certain earlier forms of Arthurian romance. The Grail-Cycle will receive especial attention.' Although variations on this description were to appear, Malory's prominence remained, as we see in the wording of the catalogue for 1926–27, the last year Scudder taught

Arthurian Romance: 'The course…centers in the study of the sources and significance of Malory's *Morte Darthur*.'[29]

As the *ur*-Arthurian course, English Literature 21 provides a vivid picture of how Arthurian texts figured in the early history of Arthurian studies. Moreover, we may see in the course the gestation of her Malory book. Although no syllabi seem to have survived, the design and content of the course may be gleaned not only from the aforementioned Wellesley catalogue descriptions but also from the Dean's annual reports, examination questions, and, especially, the notebook of one of Scudder's students, Hannah Tilton Abbe.[30] *Arthurian Romance* was a lecture course, not a seminar, meeting three hours a week during the spring semester when Scudder first offered it in 1905 and when she last did in 1927. In between, the format frequently shifted to a year-long course, meeting one hour a week, two hours, or even three. Class size varied. For example, during the first semester of *Arthurian Romance*, Scudder taught sixteen students, in 1908 she had twenty-eight, and in 1911 she had sixty-nine. In her final year of teaching, the enrollment, for two sections, is reported as a total of ninety-eight.[31]

On the bare bones of such statistics we may hang the rich impression yielded by the notebook of Hannah Tilton Abbe, who studied Arthurian romance in 1908–09.[32] Although pages are missing, Hannah's notes, penned with black ink in a legible script, include chapters to read during October 7–28, jottings from readings done on February 2 and 3, and a revealing sequence of weekly lecture notes from February 24 through May 5. There, the month of March is devoted to the systematic exposition of Malory as he foregrounds Lancelot. The first extant page of notes, however, begins with the line 'a real Welsh hero who took on mythical attributes.' Hannah goes on to record what must be the chronological overview with which Scudder began the course, from the Celtic matter, Nennius and the chronicle tradition, and on to Marie de France, Chrétien de Troyes, the French prose romances, and the English texts, culminating in Malory's *Le Morte Darthur*. This progression would become the shape of her book on Malory as well.

Fuller lectures on texts and themes then follow, organized as cycles. Although Hannah has notes on Malory under the Tristram lectures, *Le Morte Darthur* is most extensively interwoven into the Lancelot cycle that follows. After Malory, the course moved, on March 31, to Merlin, and then on April 7 through May 5, it concentrated on the Grail stories. This emphasis on the Grail is forecast in the first catalogue entry of 1904–05 and in the variations thereafter. The eminence of the Grail legends reflects a contemporary attraction to the Grail, as Oskar Sommer asserts,[33] the preoccupations of contemporary research (such as Alfred Nutt's and Jessie L. Weston's), and Scudder's own spiritual studies and affinities, which would emerge more fully in her book on Malory.

Besides listening to lectures, Hannah read. She took, for instance, two-and-a-half hours over Books xviii–xxi of Malory's *Le Morte Darthur*. Moreover, she lists 'critical authorities'; Scudder expected her students to know about secondary sources—and to read them 'in the Boston Library,' according to the course description. Among the authorities listed are W.H. Schofield (*English Literature from the Norman Conquest to Chaucer*); Alfred Nutt on Celtic and medieval romance and on the Grail legends (on this last book, Hannah spent two-and-three-quarter hours); W.P. Ker's *Epic and Romance*; G. Saintsbury on the flourishing of romance; Gaston Paris on the French material; J. Rhys; Howard Maynadier on the English poets; Lucy Paton on Morgan le Fay; Jessie Weston on Lancelot, Gawain, and Perceval; William Allan Neilson on the *Origins of the Court of Love*; and Oskar Sommer on Malory's sources. Whether for use in understanding the material on which Scudder lectured, writing the two required papers, or passing the final examination, Hannah's lists form an outline of the burgeoning field of Arthurian studies.

Ways of thinking about Arthurian literature are indicated by the questions on the final examination for *Arthurian Romance*. Although no copy exists of the one Hannah would have taken in 1909, one does for 1910:

ENGLISH LITERATURE 21 June Examination, 1910

I. Enumerate the chief romances dealing with the Grail, and show as far as you can their inter-relation.

II. Choose some one romance with which you are familiar; give a brief summary of it and discuss theories of date, origin, and relation to other romances.

III. Reconstruct the evolution of the idea either of the Grail itself or of the Grail Hero, from the earliest stage in which we encounter or infer it to the last development.

IV. Do you prefer the Perceval or the Galahad type of Grail-Quester? Why?

Noticeable in these questions is the focus on the Grail and Scudder's insistence on considering the inter-relations of texts, which the study of Malory in the context of his predecessors made possible. The 'preference' question on Perceval and Galahad reflects an issue recorded in Hannah's notes under the

Grail cycle and brought forward in Scudder's book on Malory with its striking defense of Galahad.

The way Scudder taught *Arthurian Romance* is worth reconstructing. According to Converse, she was one of the foremothers of the tradition of teaching with 'accurate scholarship and tested pedagogic method' for which the English Literature faculty at Wellesley became noted as the institution surpassed its girls' boarding school model to become the '"New Wellesley."'[34] Converse, writing in 1915, explains that Scudder and her three colleagues made 'use of philology, sources, and even art forms, as means ' to the end of 'the interpretation of literary epochs, the illumination of intellectual and spiritual values in literary masterpieces....[N]o teaching is more quickening to the imagination.'[35] Imaginations were quickened through Scudder's manner and method as well as her objective of interpretation. An image of Scudder in the classroom may be inferred from Pauline Carrington Bouve, who in 1912 describes 'that bright gleam in her eyes that those who have heard her lecture know so well,' a 'most seductive smile,' and a 'face...illuminated as...the words fell faster and faster from her lips.' In her presence, 'one never loses sight of the tremendous intellect that gives this woman power over people.'[36] Related to this charismatic manner is what I would identify as a way of empathetic knowing that Scudder cultivated in herself and brought into the classroom and her Malory book. In a reflection on studying the past, she speaks of the 'necessary discipline of recovery.' She explains that '[t]he more deeply the experience recorded in the literature I taught could sink within me the better I should interpret, let us say, Arthurian romance.'[37]

As the examination questions for English Literature 21 and Hannah's notes imply, Scudder's *Arthurian Romance* was an instance of scholarship yoked to the illumination of values. The design Scudder gave to the course as well as her wide reading of primary and secondary sources in preparation evince her scholarship. Hannah's pages, especially during the Malory lectures, are alight with phrases suggesting Scudder's ability to illuminate pattern, theme, characterization, and language. Hannah records, for instance, that in coming to the Grail books from the Tristram section, one finds a 'contrast of hot passion and heavenly inspiration.' Lancelot 'wins the vision of grail in the 2nd rank.' 'Strict justice is meted out to [Guenevere] as to any other woman. Three times—ordeal by fire...Art of Malory—1st two times she is absolutely innocent 3rd...guilty.' And, we hear of the 'Organ-like music of the language.' Thus it was that Scudder's students learned to listen to literature, in Converse's phrase, 'as to a living voice.'[38]

When Scudder retired, *Arthurian Romance* remained a permanent part of the English curriculum. One of her students, who had 'received her first impulse to Arthurian studies' in Scudder's classroom and had gone on for a doctorate at the University of Chicago, was hired at Wellesley in 1916. It was she who succeeded to the course, as Associate Professor Laura Hibbard in 1928 and as 'Mrs. Loomis' in 1929.[39]

Given that nineteenth-century editors of Malory's *Le Morte Darthur* expected boys to be its readers,[40] it is an agreeably curious fact in the development of Arthurian studies that a course in the matter of Britain originated exclusively among women. Yet, how did the progenetrix, Vida Dutton Scudder, who had not trained in medieval studies, let alone specialized in Arthurian literature, come to invent *Arthurian Romance*? Her master's thesis was on 'the modern English poets,' who in those days were Wordsworth, Coleridge, Shelley, Keats, and the like.[41] When she came to Wellesley, it was such modern English poetry and prose that she taught. Apart from recalling that 'dreamy spring' of 1886 when 'the spirit of Arthurian romance first became potent with me' while in Cornwall,[42] nowhere in her memoirs does Scudder describe how she discovered Malory or any other Arthurian text. However, her attraction to the Middle Ages is evident in the reminiscence of her tutorial with Powell at Oxford in 1884 and her trip to Italy during 1893–95 'studying the past of Western Christendom.'[43] Moreover, both Malory and other Arthurian works figure among the medieval texts taught in various courses at Wellesley prior to the introduction of English Literature 21, as examination papers indicate.[44]

Malory and chivalry were in Wellesley's curricular air and the larger cultural atmosphere,[45] yet the impetus to Scudder's invention of her Arthurian course and thereby the book on Malory came, I propose, from certain events during the years 1901–04. These Scudder spent largely in Europe recuperating from a physical breakdown. During this period Scudder turned her mind to St. Catherine of Siena and St. Francis of Assisi. Upon returning to America, she spent the summer translating St. Catherine's letters at her home in Shelburne, New Hampshire, where the mountains overlooking the Androscoggin Valley evoked Catherine's hilly Sienese landscape.[46] While abroad, she also conceived of a romantic novel about St. Catherine from the point of view of a male disciple, Raniero di Landoccio dei Pagliaresi; this she published in 1907.[47] It is saturated with sacrifice, the mystic's way, devotion, chastity and temptation, and other motifs akin to Scudder's thinking about the Grail quest faintly rendered in Hannah's notes on the course in 1908–09 and subsequently formulated with passionate clarity in Scudder's Malory book. Her work on

St. Francis emerged into print later,[48] but as with St. Catherine, its beginnings were in her mind when *Arthurian Romance* entered the Wellesley curriculum. As Scudder recalls in *On Journey*, 'When first I offered my course, I was living my mental life…chiefly in the fourteenth century, with hankerings after the thirteenth.'[49]

Stimulation may also have come from meeting the publisher J.M. Dent in London while traveling back from this European sojourn. Dent, trained as a printer and bookbinder, had recently established his publishing firm, and Scudder's uncle, the publisher E.P. Dutton, was then Dent's distributor in America.[50] It was Dent who urged Scudder to translate the Catherine letters, which he published in 1905.[51] Scudder and Dent shared interests, such as Franciscan studies and the provision of affordable editions of 'standard literature' to the public through the Everyman's Library series he was just launching.[52] It seems likely that Arthurian texts came into their conversation as well as Catherine. Dent had published Malory's *Le Morte Darthur* in 1894 with an introduction by J. Rhys and illustrations by Aubrey Beardsley, and again in four slim volumes as Temple Classics in 1897 (with reprints in 1898 and 1899). By 1906, Malory's book, along with the Rhys introduction, was in the Everyman's series. Moreover, Scudder modestly reports that 'now and then' she had a hand in suggesting translations of Arthurian texts to be part of the Everyman's series.[53] And it would be Dent, along with her uncle E.P. Dutton, who in 1917 published her book on Malory,[54] to which we now turn.

Le Morte Darthur of Sir Thomas Malory & Its Sources (*LMD*) is a 430-page study in three main parts: Malory's predecessors; his Arthuriad itself; and his accomplishment. In these three parts, we have the first sustained and systematic interpretation of *Le Morte Darthur*.[55] The key term here, as in her purpose in teaching Arthurian texts, is interpretation. Scudder's study exemplifies a critical ideology developing at a significant juncture in the history of English studies in America. Especially important is the distinction she makes in the preface among approaches in medieval studies. There was first the sentimental approach, which was 'eagerly sympathetic but uncritical' and superficial (*LMD*, vi). Then came the scholastic approach, in which, according to Joseph Bédier, 'learned men…have stayed imprisoned in minute analyses…willing to write for twenty readers' (*LMD*, vi–vii). Now, there is the interpretive approach, which allows medieval books to be 'considered from the point of view not of process but of product, not of scholarship but of pure letters' (*LMD*, vi–vii). Editions from those imprisoned scholars made texts available to readers—'what gifts the scholars have brought us,' exclaims Scudder, but then what? Interpretation.

In taking the interpretive approach, Scudder is engaging in something new and bold. Following Bédier, she arranges the three approaches as not only a historical process but an ascent, thus assigning to interpretation the highest mission (*LMD*, vi–vii). Thus, she is building on the results of the scientific bibliographical/editorial industry characterizing scholarship in modern languages in order to take the enterprise to the next level. In using the method of comparing a work to its sources and analogues, furthermore, she distinguishes her focus from the anthropological research epitomized by Jessie L. Weston's books: Scudder's is a study of literary relations, not of origins.

As anticipated in Converse's explanation of the distinctive teaching by the Wellesley English Literature faculty, interpretation entailed understanding a medieval book as both a 'social document,' that is, an image of the Middle Ages, and also a 'work of art' (*LMD*, viii). In Part I of her book, Scudder demonstrates this understanding and comments on aesthetic quality as she summarizes, translates, and explains the texts of Malory's predecessors. Some of her observations remain noteworthy. During the chapters on the Prose *Lancelot*, for instance, she dilates on the medieval ideal of masculine beauty by translating a long summary by Paulin Paris of Lancelot's description and then likening it to the details of Gothic figural sculpture—'the laughing eyes, the long nose, the high shoulders, the careful note of the modeling, the tapered fingers....' (*LMD*, 128–29). And she calls for recognizing the loyalty of friendship, brought out in the relationship between Galehault and Lancelot (*LMD*, 134–38). Her defense of this friendship among men is echoed in her reflections on women's friendships in *On Journey*.[56]

Scudder carries out her mission in Part II, on *Le Morte Darthur*, with a clearly defined theoretical model of chivalry. Her thesis is that Malory has selected, arranged, and narrated the stories in his Arthuriad to present chivalry as a set of three loyalties—knight to overlord, to lady, to God—and to show that this chivalry does improve medieval society yet must destroy it when these loyalties conflict. She supports the elements of this thesis with eloquence over the course of six chapters, driven by her perspective on the meaning of the whole being contained within the end (*LMD*, 185).

With the three loyalties of politics, love, and spirituality as the schema, Scudder discerns a five-part structure in *Le Morte Darthur* fused, albeit with rough joins, by Malory's 'genius' and vision (*LMD*, 182–85, 372). The first she calls the Prologue, Books 1–7, in which the knights' loyalty to their overlord, King Arthur, is established and enables the progressive social experiment of Round Table chivalry to become effective. The second she calls the Pageant of Love, Books 8–10, or most of the Tristram section. Here Scudder argues that Malory inserts the Tristram story to exhibit *amour courtois*, which could not be displayed through Lancelot's affair with Guenevere because both Lancelot and Arthur would have been unfairly degraded. The third structural element demonstrates spiritual loyalty, Books 11–17, that is, the last two books of the Tristram segment through the Quest of the Holy Grail. To the exposition of spiritual loyalty Scudder dedicates two chapters, for here is the crux: this quest fails to redeem the Round Table experiment; the asceticism required does not permit the knights to re-enter their society and renew chivalry.

The fourth piece of the structure comes in Books 18–19, and this, with psychological insight, she calls Reaction:

> [L]ife is sad at Camelot….Before Galahad came, the court…found the light of earth quite good enough…Now that the shrouded Grail has been seen, men are a little lonely, more than a little restless. Reaction from overstrain is also in full sway, and fiercer passions are all ready to break the leash. Things usually happen like this; the lower nature never so asserts itself as in the rebound from moments of aspiration (*LMD*, 313).

Finally comes Catastrophe, Books 20–21, the tragic end to which all has been leading as the loyalties come into conflict through Gawain's reversion to an earlier, wilder code of vengeance and feud, which the Round Table chivalric code can no longer restrain.

Scudder's analysis of *Le Morte Darthur* is original in its focus on structure. Her argument that Malory's Arthuriad is a concentrated, fused whole and not a jumbled collection flies in the face of the contemporary view held, for instance, by Andrew Lang in Sommer's edition and by William Edward Mead.[57] Her guiding schema and insights into how one part leads to the next in theme as well as story line form a persuasive display of acts of interpretation, that then new occupation of reading a text critically for its social values and artistic power.

Throughout Parts II and III of her study, we may recognize ways of thinking about Malory that are now taken for granted, some that may still startle, many worth revisiting. Among the familiar now, but fresh then are, in her comparison of Malory with the French Prose *Lancelot*, the 'ascending scale' of Guenevere's 'ordeals,' adumbrated in Hannah's notes (*LMD*, 375); Malory's skill with dialogue, 'making us feel what sort of a person is talking, and what the circumstances are' (*LMD*, 390–93); and the 'principle of causality' that distinguishes his art from that of his predecessors (*LMD*, 399–40). Still inspirational is Scudder's analysis of the 'music' of Malory's style. Her responses seem to arise from a Plotinian philosophy, expressed in *On Journey*, of apprehending the movements of a harmonious universe.[58] For instance, Malory's prose is 'as sensitive' to the 'rhythms of life' as 'waters to the sky or tides to the moon' (*LMD*, 397). Yet to be surpassed is her appreciation of the Grail quest for its 'beauty of sound,' having an 'almost liturgical effect,' and 'beauty of pictorial detail'—'twilights and midnights are shot through with light not of this earth'; 'silver and red are the dominant tones—the moonlight of earth, illumined by celestial love'; Galahad's 'armor gleams like a star of fire as he recedes down long dim woodland ways' (*LMD*, 304–05).

Moreover, Scudder's perceptions of Malory's characters remain remarkable in their insight and expression. For instance, of Guenevere in the scene of her final meeting with Lancelot, Scudder observes that she 'is the last of Malory's people to emerge from shadow into reality; but she stands out now at the last in a clear and noble light. She has repented with the repentance of a queen.' With a wisdom that gives pause, Scudder then adds that 'noteworthy insight represents her rather than Lancelot taking at the end the attitude of renunciation' (*LMD*, 357). As for Lancelot, Scudder makes us accept him as the 'real protagonist' of the Grail books as well as the 'whole *Morte Darthur*.' She interprets him as the knight who 'knows every step' of the mystical 'illuminative way.' In the 'successive stages of his experience may be traced a new apprehension slowly awakening, the advance by a thorny path to consciousness on a plane unvisited by mere lovers of good knights and ladies fair' (*LMD*, 290–91).

On Galahad, Scudder is arresting. Weston had consigned this figure to unwholesomeness, calling the Galahad-quest 'distasteful to any healthy mind'; Scudder's acerbic comment on this view is 'Opinion is free' (*LMD*, 268 note 1). Of Galahad, she explains, with an analogy to painting,

> that can be not mean or casual art which created a figure whose beauty, when all is said, haunts men through the generations. Taken by himself, it is true that Galahad lacks human qualities; he must be taken in his setting. He is pure symbol—a rainbow apparition untouched by shadow....He shines like a visitant from the world of Fra Angelico in the midst of the dusky chiaroscuro of Rembrandt or the rich tones of Titian (*LMD*, 297).

Just as she argues that Malory's treatment of the Tristram story must be taken not in isolation but in context of the movement of his whole Arthuriad, so she argues Galahad must be interpreted.

Among minor characters, Scudder points out that Balin is the 'first of Malory's strong character studies: a tragic figure, always noble in purpose, always doing the wrong thing' (*LMD*, 196). She identifies the centrality of

Perceval's sister: 'a woman draws together the threads and directs the action during the latter portions of the Grail-books...a ray of purest light serene' (*LMD*, 298). With another analogy to art, Scudder depicts Bors as a 'sta[u]nch, close-lipped, unhappy,' 'very plain...very unselfish man' 'studied with the affection of an old Dutch master for his sitter' (*LMD*, 287–90). Speaking, surely, with the experience of a teacher in a women's college, she embraces Elaine of Astolat as a 'real mediaeval girl...not at all a diaphanous young person, but red-blooded as she is innocent: a girl of vitality and spirit, who dies for Lancelot with a kind of wholesome energy' (*LMD*, 320–21).

It was as a 'guide to a lovely country...too rarely visited except by pioneers' that Scudder introduced her book on Malory (*LMD*, xi). It was reissued in 1921, and for more than forty years visited by students and scholars. In his 1929 *Malory*, for instance, Eugène Vinaver corrects her supposition that Malory wrote 'in the window-seat' of a Warwickshire manor house, rejects her theory that Malory tended to 'degrade' Tristram, and relies on her interpretation of 'patriotic enthusiasm' in *Arthoure and Merlin*.[59] In his 1947 edition of Malory, Vinaver lists Scudder in the bibliographies of critical studies for all sections except the 'War with Lucius,' 'Launcelot,' and, oddly, 'Tristram.'[60] In *Malory's Originality*, a collection published in 1964, Scudder is one of the two sources most frequently cited by scholars reacting to Vinaver's claim that Malory wrote independent romances not a unified work.[61] Wilfred Guerin quotes Scudder on four points about the 'Tale of Gareth,' including Gawain's faults and Gareth's virtues, Malory's family groups, and the reason Malory omitted Lancelot's friendship with Galahat le Haut Prince. Thomas Rumble quotes Scudder several times, generally in disagreement with her view of the Tristram section, but once as ballast for Malory's emphasis on its 'Arthurian connections.' R.M. Lumiansky credits Scudder's discussion of the purpose and effect of Malory's borrowings for 'The Tale of Lancelot and Guenevere' and notes her suggestion of Malory's originality in the 'planned progression' of Guenevere's situation. And in the last chapter, Guerin invokes her view of the three loyalties, especially the spiritual force of mysticism and asceticism.[62]

Scudder's book on Malory has been a formative force in the history of Arthurian studies. Old enough now for us to consider it superseded, it nevertheless provides a salutary perspective on current critical studies. In this regard, let us briefly reflect on the context of Scudder's engagement with the cultural myths of chivalric love, politics, and spirituality by juxtaposing *Le Morte Darthur of Sir Thomas Malory* with her 1937 autobiography *On Journey*.

For Scudder, *l'amour courtois* is problematic. In the section on the 'Lancelot Romances,' she explains that this 'artificial ideal' may have had a 'basis in reality': ladies 'pining at home' for their absent lords 'may often have been tempted to solace themselves by amorous play with the young squires, or even pages, in their charge' (*LMD*, 130). This concession to a trivializing view of women conflicts with her defense in *On Journey* of a woman's ability to lead a full life without having love affairs: 'I want to register my conviction, and I wish I might have a great many masculine readers at this point, that a woman's life which sex interests have never visited, is a life neither dull nor empty nor devoid of romance.'[63]

Scudder has interpreted Malory's insertion of the Tristram story and truncation of the Vulgate *Lancelot* as his way of displaying the loyalty of knight to lady without having to put the spotlight on Lancelot and Guenevere. But, in her admittedly Tennysonian reading of Tristram and Isolde's affair, *l'amour courtois* is stale, and the 'lovers go about their pursuits a little wearily' (*LMD*, 229–30). Nevertheless, she observes that in the Tristram section, a 'cold-blooded Feminist might find material for a thesis on the Position of Women as it developed from primitive to modern times,' from the treatment of women as men's 'plain booty' to the 'self-control' courteous love called for and the 'respect and the tenderness toward women,' which 'shine almost as fair to our eyes as to the twelfth century. And that is very fair' (*LMD*, 234–36). From her point of view in the first decades of the twentieth century, the literary artifice of courteous love expressed a social advance in men's attitudes towards women (*LMD*, 358). It is respect, rather than the emotional and physical passion of heterosexual love, that interests her. It is in this sense that Scudder speaks in *On Journey*, for instance, of the Boston Labor leaders George MacNeill, Harry Lloyd, and Jack O'Sullivan as 'very perfect gentle knights' who 'took the chivalric attitude toward us women, who had invaded their world' of the Labor Movement.[64]

The other two chivalric loyalties reverberate with her personal commitment to social justice and spiritual quest. Scudder was writing her book on *Le Morte Darthur* during World War I. At that time, she was not a pacifist. Rather, she believed that 'fighting is the condition of real living.' Holding the view that humanity was gradually progressing upward, she saw that 'glorious virtues' had been 'engendered by war'; hence 'both outward and inward conflict' were the 'necessary source of valor and sacrifice.'[65] It is this necessary conflict that she sees in *Le Morte Darthur*. In her Malory book, she writes that Arthur's introduction of chivalry signified a 'period on which a new and better code' of ethics 'had dawned' (*LMD*, 352). In *On Journey*, she explains, 'My spirit responded to the great oath of Arthur's knights, with its code for the Christian fighter.' She believed in defending the weak and fighting in a 'righteous cause.'[66] In sum, her 'apologia for war was contained in one word: chivalry.'[67]

Yet, in *Le Morte Darthur*, chivalry is 'destroyed, not from without but from within,' for the principal characters fail to 'grasp the chivalric ideal in its wholeness' (*LMD*, 352–53). Unharmonized, the loyalties of chivalry conflict, and since personal sins have social consequences, Malory's people 'undermine the civilization' that 'we would give our lives to guard' (*LMD*, 353). The 'great experiment in living' fails; the epoch of the Middle Ages ends. In Scudder's interpretation of the last two books of *Le Morte Darthur*, we may see, as the heading 'Catastrophe' implies, a parallel with her initial reception of the World War. 'Insidious wrongs' of basically good people 'poison chivalry at the roots,' she writes in her book on Malory (*LMD*, 353). Just so in *On Journey* does she record that she felt the 'social order in which we moved to be poisoned at the roots.'[68] The 'long-gathered storm' in *Le Morte Darthur* had to break (*LMD*, 334), and so did the 'great explosion' signified by the onset of the World War—'a long concealed malady had come at last to the judgment of the open day.'[69] Only out of deepest need will come opportunity for advance; one must descend to the darkest hour in order to rise (*LMD*, 268).

In the ending of Malory's Arthuriad, Scudder argues, every character except Mordred is left on a higher level (*LMD*, 357). Even romantic love ascends to spiritual purity through Guenevere's tragic renunciation (*LMD*, 358). Thus, although the 'fair order' of the Round Table is extinguished, Malory shows not only that the law of justice triumphs but also that the 'spirit lives'—the 'eternal in the midst of time' (*LMD*, 361). It was harder for Scudder to see such hopefulness in the aftermath of the World War, when the 'surging flood of disillusion' threatened 'to submerge...idealism' and 'halted or destroyed' reforms.[70]

Even so, in her ultimate commentary on the end of *Le Morte Darthur* we may see the glimmer of the spiritual philosophy that accompanied her political ideology. 'And when Arthur comes again,' she says, 'men will conceivably have learned that the search for spiritual vision leads to no mystic land across the sea,' as the Grail quest did, 'but back to Camelot.' That is, 'they may know it their high task to convert the very land of Logres into a worthy shrine for the secret sanctities of God' (*LMD*, 362). For Scudder, such conversion required, in words she records in *On Journey* as she later struggled to a position of pacifism, a 'constructive social radicalism': 'so long as conflicting interests are the ruling principle of the economic order, it is hopeless to expect the political order to escape the curse of war.'[71] It is a reconstructed world in the here and now that is worthy of the 'sanctities of God.' Scudder renewed her commitment to working for that reconstruction during a long and 'stumbling' journey, despite the disillusionment and sadness following the World War.[72]

Finally, in hoping for social conversion within the land of Logres rather than a mystic land across the sea, Scudder emphasizes the form of spirituality that *Le Morte Darthur* offers but that must be redirected in the modern age. To her, it is mysticism more than militant Christianity that makes Malory's Grail-quest valuable as a social document as well as an artistic one. To be sure, Scudder argues that Galahad's ascetic withdrawal from the world makes him as responsible as 'Mordred, or Lancelot' for the catastrophe at the end (*LMD*, 354). Instead of the 'glowing…vision of a Holy City descending to dwell among men,' the 'social' hope drops out of the Quest and 'interest…centers…exclusively in the salvation of the individual' (*LMD*, 278). However, 'pessimistic asceticism' is not the only form of mysticism. In *On Journey*, Scudder reflects on the experience attained through the sacramental use of the senses in the contemplation of beauty in art and in nature. Awareness of divinity—the Supreme Intelligence, or, she speculates, intermediate Intelligences—may lie in touching the 'nice curves of a piece of pottery,' noticing the 'geometrical patterns of seed-vessels,' following the 'sculptured lines of falling water,' beholding 'skies 'inlaid with patins of bright gold.'[73]

So it is, I believe, that while acknowledging, in her Malory book, contemporary 'distaste' for the asceticism endemic to medieval mysticism (*LMD*, 260), she argues for honoring, for understanding, for becoming re-engaged with the impulse to mystical vision. In Malory's Arthuriad, the Grail Quest 'meets the deepest need of its period. It satisfies a restlessness which neither delight in arms nor love of woman nor loyalty to mortal king has been able to assuage.' It is the narration of this impulse to mystical vision that makes the Grail Quest the 'crown' of *Le Morte Darthur* (*LMD*, 268). Given the value she places on the artistic and social power of the Grail books, we may appreciate why the 1917 title page of her book bears a Grail chalice printed in green.

Of Malory's Grail quest, she writes, 'The quickening force in romance, the spirit of adventure, led out and away…past the edge of the visible world' and 'turned…and penetrated the world within' (*LMD*, 259). As the titles of her autobiographies, *On Journey* and *My Quest for Reality*, imply, the idea and experience of moving with this quickening force, rather than achieving the end of the adventure, pervaded Scudder's consciousness. It is her interwoven activities as a socialist and member of the Companions of the Holy Cross that she emphasizes in those autobiographies. Yet, in teaching Arthurian literature and writing a book about Malory's *Morte Darthur*, Vida Dutton Scudder was not escaping class struggle for respite on some fairyland byway. Refracted in her Arthurian work are beliefs and sensitivities that nourished her social and spiritual ideals, most notably her conception of chivalry, her hopes for social progress, and her vision of a created world on this earth infused with divine spirit.

SOUTHERN CONNECTICUT STATE UNIVERSITY

Sue Ellen Holbrook is professor of English at Southern Connecticut State University. Among her publications are studies of Malory's *Le Morte Darthur*, Margery Kempe, and text and image in Wynkyn de Worde's editions of Jerome's *Vitas Patrum* and Bartholomew's *De Proprietatibus Rerum*. Current projects include virility and property in *Kulhwch and Olwen*, illustrations of Bartholomew's book on time, vernacularity in four de Worde incunables, and consciousness and landscape in *The Flower and the Leaf*.

NOTES

1 'Early Days at Dennison House,' undated typescript (Schlesinger Library, Radcliffe College; photocopy in Smith College Archives).

2 See, for example, Patricia Ann Palmieri, *In Adamless Eden: the Community of Women Faculty at Wellesley* (New Haven: Yale University Press, 1995). Palmieri's introduction opens with Scudder; the index contains nearly eight inches of references to Scudder.

3 Vida D. Scudder, *On Journey: An Autobiography* (New York: E.P. Dutton & Co., 1937), p. 304.

4 Scudder, *On Journey*, pp. 126–27.

5 Scudder, *On Journey*, pp. 294–95. On her father, see Horace E. Scudder, *Life and Letters of David Coit Scudder, Missionary in Southern India* (New York: Hurd, 1864).

6 Scudder, *On Journey*, pp. 168–69.

7 Scudder, *On Journey*, p. 69 on those she admired; notes by William Allan Neilson, President of Smith, read when conferring the honorary degree (Smith Archives); letters of February 16, 1953 and ca. May 1953 (Smith Archives).

8 Scudder, *On Journey*, p. 67.

9 'Recollections of Ruskin,' *Atlantic* (April 1900): 560–76 (copy in Smith Archives).

10 Scudder, *On Journey*, pp. 88–89. Her *Grotesque in Gothic Art* was printed in 1887 as a thirty-nine-page pamphlet.

11 This aunt was Ida Scudder, who was a physician. See postcard of July 22, 1945 (Smith Archives); also Jennifer Georgia, *Legacy and Challenge: the Story of Ida B. Scudder* (Saline, MI: McNaughton & Gunn, 1994).

12 Scudder, *On Journey*, p. 87.

13 Scudder, *On Journey*, p. 90.

14 Scudder, *On Journey*, p. 95.

15 The details of Palmer's intervention are described in Scudder, *On Journey*, pp. 95–96. Seelye's offer and Scudder's agonized choice are described only in a letter of February 16, 1953 (Smith Archives).

16 Scudder, *On Journey*, p. 105.

17 'Relation of College Women to Social Need' (printed paper of 1890, Smith Archives), 5.

18 'Socialism and Spiritual Progress' (Boston: Church Social Union, January 1, 1896;

copy in Smith Archives).

19 Florence Converse, *The Story of Wellesley* (Boston: Little Brown & Co., 1915), p. 160. Converse, who had been Scudder's student, became one of her closest friends, and in 1919 she and her mother moved into the Wellesley house (*On Journey*, p. 175); Scudder dedicated *On Journey* to her and made Converse her heir (letter of July 15, 1945, Smith Archives).

20 Pauline Carrington Bouve, "'My Good Italian Friends,'" *Boston Globe*, 10 March 1912 (unpaginated photocopy in Smith Archives); 'Early Days at Dennison House' (Smith Archives); Letter of January 20, 1953 (Smith Archives); Scudder, *On Journey*, ch. 3–4, 8.

21 Scudder, *On Journey*, ch. 8.

22 Numerous articles in the Smith Archives evince Scudder's ever-developing socialist ideology and its foundation in Christian thought; for example, 'Socialism and Sacrifice,' *Hibbert Journal* (1910), in which she quotes Marx; 'Franciscan Parallels,' *American Theological Review* 5:4 (March 1923): 282–98. See also Scudder, *On Journey*, p. 176 on the CSA, pp. 148–49 on her reading and also p. 306 on the Christian foundation for a proletariat revolution.

23 *Quest for Reality*, p. 9; also Scudder, *On Journey*, esp. Part III, ch. 4.

24 Scudder, *On Journey*, pp. 103–06.

25 'Recollections of Ruskin,' 571, and *On Journey*, p. 179; 'A Pedagogic Sunset,' *Atlantic Monthly* (June 1928): 789–90 (copy in Smith Archives).

26 Scudder, *On Journey*, p. 180.

27 Scudder, *On Journey*, p. 126. First listed in 1904–05 as *Studies in Arthurian Romance*, the title became *Introduction to Arthurian Romance* in 1907–08 (*Wellesley College Courses of Instruction*, Wellesley College Archives). In 1919–21 the number became 207 (*Annual Reports, Wellesley College*, Wellesley Archives).

28 Scudder, *On Journey*, p. 126.

29 *Wellesley College Calendar 1904–05*; *Catalogue 1926–27* (Wellesley Archives). Variations appear in 1907–08, 1912–13, 1914–15, 1926–27.

30 All to be found in the Wellesley Archives. I owe special thanks to Jean Nielsen Berry, who located the examinations and Hannah Tilton Abbe's notebook as well as other archival material. Scudder refers to the planned destruction of course lectures and syllabi in a letter of July 15, 1945 to Margaret Storrs Grierson, who was attempting to collect Scudder's papers for Smith College (Smith Archives).

31 Statistics gathered from the appendices to the Dean's reports in *Annual Reports, Wellesley College*. In a 'Pedagogic Sunset,' Scudder remarks on the large size of the Arthurian classes at Wellesley (Wellesley Archives).

32 Hannah graduated in 1910. She has written '1908–09' on the inside cover of her loose-leaf notebook for English Literature (Wellesley Archives 6/C1910 Box 1).

33 H. Oskar Sommer, 'Introduction,' *Le Morte Darthur by Syr Thomas Malory*, vol. III (London: David Nutt, 1891), p. 3.

34 Converse, *Story of Wellesley*, p. 274.

35 Converse, *Story of Wellesley*, pp. 138–39.

36 Pauline Carrington Bouve, "'My Good Italian Friends,'" *Boston Globe*, 10 March 1912 (unpaginated photocopy in Smith Archives). Palmieri quotes a 'Scudder devotee,'

as finding Scudder's 'transitions from one subject matter to another breathtaking and sometimes a bit of a strain on a dull imagination' (*In Adamless Eden*, p. 164).

37 Scudder, *On Journey*, p. 197.

38 Converse, *The Story of Wellesley*, p. 139.

39 Scudder, *On Journey*, p. 126. According to an obituary in the Wellesley Archives, Laura Hibbard graduated from Wellesley in 1905; that means she took *Arthurian Romance* in its inaugural semester. As an Associate Professor, Hibbard taught *Arthurian Romance*, renumbered as English 207, during 1919–26, some semesters of which Scudder was on leave; Scudder returned to it during her final year, 1926–27 (*Annual Reports, Wellesley College*, Wellesley Archives).

40 See Sommer, quoting E. Strachey, *Le Morte Darthur*, vol. II (1890), p. 14.

41 Scudder's handwritten master's thesis is called the 'Effect of the Scientific Temper on Modern Poetry' (Smith Archives). Ella Keats Whiting lauds the publication of Scudder's 'scholarly edition' of Shelley's *Prometheus Bound*, in *Wellesley College, 1875–1975: A Century of Women* (Wellesley: Wellesley College, 1975), p. 103. A printed outline of *Lectures on Modern English Literature* for 1895–96 (Wells Memorial Institute, Boston) to be given by Scudder and her Wellesley colleagues Katharine Lee Bates and Sophie Jewett include six evidently by Scudder on the 'Modern English Poets' (Smith Archives).

42 Scudder, *On Journey*, p. 90.

43 Scudder, *On Journey*, p. 197.

44 Malory, for instance, turns up on an undated examination for English Literature I, in one of 1893 for English Literature II, and one of 1906 for English Literature 17. The 'Celtic contribution to the chivalric ideal' is one of the questions on the 1906 examination for English Literature 10.

45 See Mark Giroud, *The Return to Camelot: Chivalry and the English Gentleman* (New Haven: Yale University Press, 1981).

46 Scudder, *On Journey*, pp. 149–201.

47 *The Disciple of a Saint, Being the Imaginary Biography of Raniero Di Landoccio dei Pagliaresi* (New York: E.P. Dutton, 1907).

48 *Brother John: A Tale of the First Franciscans* (Boston: Little, Brown, and Co., 1927), and *The Franciscan Adventure: A Study in the First Hundred Years of the Order of St. Francis of Assisi* (London and New York: J.M. Dent & Sons and E.P. Dutton & Co., 1931).

49 Scudder, *On Journey*, pp. 126, 247–48.

50 Scudder, *On Journey*, pp. 144–45.

51 Scudder, *On Journey*, p. 148.

52 Scudder, *On Journey*, p. 46.

53 Scudder worked along with her friend Lucy Paton, according to *On Journey*, p. 147.

54 *Le Morte Darthur of Sir Thomas Malory & Its Sources* (New York and London: E.P. Dutton & Co.; J.M. Dent & Sons, 1917). It was reissued in 1921, and reprinted in 1965 by Haskell House, New York.

55 See the bibliography of nineteen critical works in Eugène Vinaver's 1929 *Malory* (Oxford: Clarendon Press), pp. 196–98. Of the thirteen publications preceding Scudder, nine concern sources, one syntax, and two biography. In *Chivalry in English*

Literature: Chaucer, Malory, Spenser, Shakespeare (Cambridge, MA: Harvard University, 1912), W.H. Schofield includes a forty-seven page chapter on the romantic ideal of chivalry in Malory. However, as the title implies, he is only partly concerned with Malory; moreover, this book was published seven years after Scudder began to teach the course that gave rise to her book.

56 Scudder, *On Journey*, pp. 222–28.

57 Andrew Lang, 'Le Morte Darthur,' in *Le Morte Darthur by Syr Thomas Malory*, vol III, ed. H. Oskar Sommer (London: David Nutt, 1891), p. xix; William Edward Mead, 'Introduction,' *Selections from Sir Thomas Malory's* Morte Darthur (Boston: Ginn and Co., 1897), pp. liv–lv.

58 See the experiences recorded in Scudder, *On Journey*, p. 286, a dream in May 1914 from which she is awakened by the sound of swelling music of 'great minor chords changing into solemn waves of triumph and joy'; p. 286, 'catch[ing]…far echoes from that music' as she gazed at the 'starlit' night sky; and p. 373, on feeling the rhythm of the 'turning earth,' which she recognized as the 'ceaseless motion which is the music of the spheres.'

59 Eugène Vinaver, *Malory* (Oxford: Clarendon Press, 1929), pp. 7; 61 n8; 87.

60 Eugène Vinaver, ed., *The Works of Sir Thomas Malory*, 3 vols. (Oxford: Clarendon Press, 1947).

61 R.M. Lumiansky, ed., *Malory's Originality: A Critical Study of Le Morte Darthur* (Baltimore: Johns Hopkins Press, 1964).

62 Wilfred L. Guerin, '"The Tale of Gareth": the Chivalric Flowering,' pp. 112 n19, 113 n24, 116; Thomas C. Rumble, '"The Tale of Tristram": Development by Analogy,' p. 149; Lumiansky, '"The Tale of Lancelot and Guenevere": Suspense,' pp. 205 n1, 226; and Guerin, '"The Tale of the Death of Arthur": Catastrophe and Resolution,' p. 270.

63 Scudder, *On Journey*, p. 212.

64 Scudder, *On Journey*, pp. 154–55.

65 Scudder, *On Journey*, pp. 280–81.

66 Scudder, *On Journey*, p. 282.

67 Scudder, *On Journey*, p. 281; On the chivalric ideals held by the upper and middle classes with regard to World War I, see Giroud, *The Return to Camelot*, pp. 276–93.

68 Scudder, *On Journey*, p. 279.

69 Scudder, *On Journey*, p. 279.

70 Scudder, *On Journey*, p. 300.

71 Scudder, *On Journey*, p. 285.

72 *Quest for Reality*, p. 9.

73 Scudder, *On Journey*, pp. 417–19.

The Girl from Cumbria:
A Tribute to Rachel Bromwich

CHRIS GROOMS

Raised between two worlds and two wars, Rachel Bromwich defines the
best and most productive qualities of twentieth-century scholarship in
Celtic literature.[1] As a woman at the mercy of the circumstances of war and
of conservative, male-dominated Oxbridge traditions, her life's journey reads
as a profound tale of dedication, love, and survival.

Born Rachel Amos in 1915 in Brighton, she spent many of her early years
in Egypt where her father was legal adviser to the Egyptian government. He
eventually retired with his family to a house in Cumbria, on what is now the
northern edge of England's Lake District, but as its name betrays was once
the land of the *Com-brogi* or the Cymry, the Welsh, part of the Old North of
Welsh tradition. J.E. Caerwyn Williams speculated, in a volume of essays
dedicated to Dr. Bromwich: '...it is tempting to think that these childhood
experiences awakened in her a sensibility to older languages and literatures,
with the years afterwards back in Cumbria likewise awakening her interest
in the literature of the Celts.'[2] Her interest in Celtic literatures was awakened
by reading Arthurian stories as a young girl. As a highly intelligent and
intellectually curious young woman she secured for herself a place at
Newnham College, Cambridge, where she completed a degree in Anglo-
Saxon, Norse, and Celtic in 1938. There she was able to study early Welsh
with Kenneth Jackson, and thence she went to Bangor to study Welsh with
Professor (later Sir) Ifor Williams, of all her teachers the one to whom she
feels most indebted. It was he who suggested to her that she should begin a
study of *Trioedd Ynys Prydein* (*TYP*), the *Triads of the Island of Britain*, that
richly allusive assemblage of Welsh lore.

As Rachel continued these studies, in 1939 the uncertain horrors of the
Second World War descended on Europe. She met and married John
Bromwich, an archeologist and an Army officer, and moved to Northern
Ireland with him, where she was able to learn some Irish. Northern Ireland
was not exempt from the attentions of the Luftwaffe; while she was there the
draft of her thesis on *TYP* was destroyed by a bomb. The marriage produced

a son, Brian, with whom she moved back to Cumbria in 1942 while her husband was in the Army. At the beginning of the war, Kenneth Jackson's move to Harvard created a vacancy at Cambridge to teach Welsh, and in 1945 Mrs. Bromwich was invited to fill the post, with the title first of University Lecturer and then Reader in Celtic Languages and Literature, until her retirement from Cambridge in 1976. Her husband also worked in Cambridge, but eventually the marriage ended. During this period, she gained the degree of D.Litt., and was also one of the first women to be awarded, for a year (1974–75), the John Rhys Fellowship at Jesus College Oxford. In the early 1960s she and her husband had acquired with the help of Sir Idris Foster a converted farmhouse, Tyddyn Sabel, on the slopes of Moel Faban at Carneddi, near Bethesda. The first period of Dr. Bromwich's retirement was spent at Tyddyn Sabel, which she loved dearly, but the harsh winter environment may have encouraged her later move into the village of Carneddi, not far from the home of Sir Idris Foster, the Sir John Rhys Professor of Celtic at Oxford. Sir Idris was perhaps her dearest friend and encourager during that happy period. After the death of Sir Idris, she moved to Aberystwyth, when the new Centre for Advanced Welsh and Celtic Studies opened in 1985. Aberystwyth was also the home of a vigorous community of Welsh and Celtic scholars, some of whom had been her pupils at Cambridge, and not too far from the home of the late D. Simon Evans, Professor of Welsh at Lampeter, another good friend and collaborator.

Although many know her chapter 'The Character of Early Welsh Tradition,' in Nora K. Chadwick's *Studies in Early British History*,[3] Dr. Bromwich's first contribution to that part of Celtic scholarship that was to be her life's work appeared in 1946 in the *Bulletin of the Board of Celtic Studies* on the subject of the Historical Triads.[4] Her attention had been drawn to the Triads by Sir Ifor Williams, and she worked on the texts for twenty years, a labor culminating in *Trioedd Ynys Prydein–The Welsh Triads* (hereafter referred to as *TYP*).[5] The volume is remarkable not only for the standard of textual editing, but also for its notes, which form a bible of extant native lore, weaving together the branches and stems of the memory of native British prose and poetry. At eighty-five, she is now completing a new edition of this seminal work.

One of Dr. Bromwich's many literary loves is the Arthurian tale *Culhwch and Olwen*, the most important and oldest of all native Arthurian texts, which she has co-edited with the late D. Simon Evans, producing the first effective diplomatic text with notes, in both Welsh and English editions.[6] In addition to her recent work as an editor of Arthurian materials that appear in *The Arthur of the Welsh*,[7] she has produced important work on the great fourteenth-century Welsh poet Dafydd ap Gwilym,[8] as well as bringing out an edition of fifty of Dafydd's poems in Welsh texts with facing translations.[9]

Discussing her life with Rachel in the coziness of her study near the Old College and castle in Aberystwyth is always a quiet but mentally invigorating experience. A typical day would see local friends and former pupils call round with new books or sweets, and a few phone calls to friends to arrange dinners and visits. When her son Brian is home in Britain from his work as an engineer in China, she may visit her sister in Cambridge, but her longer scholarly journeys are over, as she works and edits constantly, claiming to be 'a little long in the tooth' for such academic outings. Surrounded by her books, with the essential texts close at hand, and with a heavily annotated copy of *TYP* near her chair, with cards on the mantles, stacks of new books from well-wishers or purchased in order to keep abreast of her field, all of which are overseen by a nineteenth-century oil of a young ancestress over the fireplace, she is the very epitome of the scholarship of an age that is almost past, and for whose loss we are the poorer. She seems reluctant to acknowledge her own fundamental contribution to twentieth-century Welsh scholarship, other than her primary role as mentor to the many scholars who have shared her passions and passed her way over the years. With an unselfconscious honesty, she attributes the complexity of cross-references in her notes to *TYP* to such passing circumstances as the open stack access at the Cambridge University Library, where as a young mother she had a young son's demands and schedule with which to contend as she undertook her teaching and research. She ascribes her success as a teaching scholar in Medieval Welsh studies to the support and friendship of Ifor Williams,[10] making no reference to her own successful struggles with learning, speaking, and writing modern Welsh at a time when the language received no support from immersion schools and night classes, as it does today in Wales.

As a lecturer and student at one of the Arthurian Summer Schools organized by Gerald Morgan (himself a former student of Rachel's at Cambridge—see his appendix below), I attended with her the Quaker meetings at Maes Maelor in Penparcau south of Aberystwyth in a recent summer. As the silence of that service lifted, Rachel stood and recited one of Dafydd's poems of summer. The effect gave all her hearers a fuller appreciation of how Dafydd's audience would have heard the original music of the words in its native setting, released from its stacked and dried machine print. I was fortunate to be in her company when meeting for lunch with her scholar-friends Anne Ross and Dick Feachem. When I struck out on my own in search of Arthurian material, whether in the place-names and scenery of Wales or on the lips of farmers, shepherds, and local historians (many of the latter familiar with *TYP*), I was able to bring it back to her hearth, where she would help me catalog and make sense of the material, with the aid of her vast knowledge of the native language, literature, and its characters. I have always taken advice poorly (and paid for it), but she once told me, 'Chris, do not grow old alone; find many friends, and keep them close to you.' I have indeed been fortunate to count Rachel Bromwich as my friend, like many others who have wandered into her world over the decades and left inspired by her dedication to and love of the native Celtic world.

Rachel deserves a triad to honor her, and since the most venerable triads are the simplest, I would express it simply as: Tair Cyneddf Rachel Bromwich—Ysgolhaig, Athro, Cyfaill Cymru: the Three Attributes of Rachel Bromwich—Scholar, Teacher, Friend. So many of us owe so much to those qualities. As J.E. Caerwyn Williams said of her, 'A da yw medru dweud, os mabwysiadodd hi Gymru, mae Cymru wedi ei mabwysiadu hithau'[11] [And it is good to be able to say, if she adopted Wales, Wales also adopted her]. Rachel Bromwich has adopted us all into that once magical and future world of Wales, Arthur, and the Old North.

COLLIN COUNTY COMMUNITY COLLEGE, DALLAS

A native of central Texas, Chris Grooms received his Ph.D. in Welsh Language and Literature from the University College of Wales, Aberystwyth. He has been a Visiting Professor of Celtic Language and Literature at Harvard University, and a visiting scholar to the Centre for Celtic and Breton Research in Brest, Finistère, Brittany. He is the author of *The Giants of Wales*, and teaches English and Welsh at Collin County Community College in Plano, Texas. He is the webmaster of *Arthuriana* and authors many Welsh-language websites and on-line tutorials, including *Welsh Authors: Medieval, Classic, and Standard Texts*, *A Welsh Weave*, and *Welsh Poets*.

APPENDIX BY GERALD MORGAN
RACHEL BROMWICH: A PERSONAL EXPERIENCE

Since I was a small boy I had wanted to learn Welsh, my father's language. Why should the sand run out with me, just because we lived nearly two hundred miles from Wales? I tried as a small boy, as a teenager, and again when a conscripted soldier. Nothing worked. Then I met Rachel.

In 1958 I'd completed two years of my Cambridge English tripos. Our tutor told us what the optional courses were for the final year (serious prospectuses were not circulated among such humble creatures as undergraduates), and to my amazement I discovered that 'Medieval Welsh Language and Literature' was an option. 'Ah,' said my tutor, 'too late—it's a two-year course. You should have started last year.' Not, of course, that anyone had told us. So I cycled up the Huntingdon Road to find number 153, to see whether Dr. Rachel Bromwich would take me on.

Now it must be understood that since the age of eight all my teachers had been men, in all-male institutions. A knock on her door brought me face to face with Rachel Bromwich. My heart sank when she alluded in passing to the fact that it was her sabbatical year, but with extraordinary unselfishness she agreed to teach me, busy though she was with seeing her masterpiece, *Trioedd Ynys Prydein*, through the press. I bought Strachan's *An Introduction to Early Welsh*, a grimly forbidding volume published about 1910, and began to prepare passages.

I found this dry indeed. Studying English at Cambridge meant writing essays. Why couldn't I write an essay for Rachel? Reluctantly she agreed. I slaved away, and brought it to her with pride. Gently, calmly, she gave it such a shredding as no essay of mine had ever suffered before. Roused, I went away and sweated over another— only for it to have the same treatment. After that, to her approval, I prepared notes. I had, of course, been trying to run before even learning to crawl. Thus, eventually, I began to understand *Pedeir Keinc y Mabinogi* before I could speak a sentence of modern Welsh. The whole subject thrilled me. Here was an exciting literature, a good deal of which had never even been printed, and whose major dictionary had then only reached the middle of the letter C. English seemed to me to be already worked out. This was my subject!

It was Rachel who prepared the way for my next step. At that time the Welsh departments of the University of Wales had sufficient students fluent in Welsh; they did not need anyone like me. So Rachel sent me to Oxford, to Idris Foster, and thus the course of my life, even my eventual marriage and our rearing of a Welsh-speaking family, was determined by this great and generous lady. She could so easily have turned me away and denied me what would certainly have been my last chance to learn my father's language.

I owe her so much.

ABERYSTWYTH

NOTES

1   I extend great thanks to Gerald Morgan and Morfydd Owen for improving my mundane prose as well as correcting some of the biographical details. Morfydd, her friend, and Gerald, a former pupil and neighbor, have known and admired her for many years. Gerald adds his tribute in the appendix above.
2   J.E. Caerwyn-Williams, *Ysgrifau Beirniadol* 13 (Dinbych: Gwasg Gee, 1985), p. 9. This issue is dedicated to her work, and includes both a bibliography and articles on literary subjects by former students.
3   Rachel Bromwich, 'The Character of Early Welsh Tradition,' in *Studies in Early British History*, ed. Nora K. Chadwick (Cambridge, UK: Cambridge University Press, 1954; rep. 1959) pp. 84–101.
4   Bromwich, 'The Historical Triads, with special reference to Peniarth MS 16,' *Bulletin of the Board of Celtic Studies* 12.1–3 (November, 1946): 1–15.

5 Bromwich, ed., *Trioedd Ynys Prydein–The Welsh Triads* (Cardiff: University of Wales Press, 1st ed. 1961, 2d ed. 1978, rep. 1982). The volume was dedicated to Syr Ifor Williams.

6 Bromwich and D. Simon Evans, eds., *Culhwch and Olwen* (Cardiff: University of Wales Press, 1988; English edition, 1992). Dr. Bromwich notes that 'Idris Foster's edition of *Culhwch* was left unfinished at his death in 1984, and the Board of Celtic Studies invited me to take it on. I was nervous about completing the Welsh edition single-handed, and Simon Evans was very ready to come to my help.' In 1988,

7 Rachel Bromwich, A.O.H. Jarman, and Brynley F. Roberts, eds., *The Arthur of the Welsh* (Cardiff: University of Wales Press, 1991).

8 For a recent collection, see her *Aspects of the Poetry of Dafydd ap Gwilym: Collected Papers* (Cardiff: University of Wales Press, 1986).

9 Dafydd ap Gwilym, *Selected Poems of Dafydd ap Gwilym* (Llandysul: Gomer Press, 1982, 1987, 1993; Harmondworth: Penguin, 1985).

10 See her edited collection of essays by Ifor Williams, *The Beginnings of Welsh Poetry: Studies by Sir Ifor Williams* (Cardiff: University of Wales Press, 1980).

11 Caerwyn-Williams, *Ysgrifau Beirniadol*, p. 13.

Helaine Newstead:
'A Giant In Her Field'

Helaine Newstead was a New Yorker. She was born in 1906 on Manhattan Island, was educated on Manhattan Island, enjoyed a long professional career at Hunter College in New York, was given a profile in the *New Yorker*,[1] from which I took the title of this essay, and died in Mount Sinai Hospital in New York in 1981. She also was one of the finest Arthurian scholars produced by the school and university systems of the United States.

Professor Newstead was raised in the neighborhood of Seventh Avenue near 113th Street, the only child of ambitious parents who sent her in time to the Institute of Musical Art (now the Juilliard School of Music), where she studied piano and began a lifetime love of music. Later, however, she enrolled at Columbia University, where she took her M.A. in 1928 with a thesis entitled 'Litotes in Anglo-Saxon Poetry.' During her doctoral work she began her love of Arthurian studies under the tutelage of Professor Roger Sherman Loomis.[2] Her great discovery was the correspondence between the Welsh deity Bran and the Fisher King, a major Arthurian figure. Her dissertation on this subject was published by Columbia University Press in 1928 under the title *Bran the Blessed in Arthurian Romance*. Columbia University Press has published very few Columbia doctoral dissertations,[3] and Miss Newstead as a newly hatched Ph.D. was almost instantaneously elevated to the giddy heights of medieval scholarship.

Professors Loomis and Newstead remained friends until his death in 1966. I cannot count the number of times he mentioned her name in class before I met her when she came to Columbia, where I was a graduate student, to teach one of his classes.

Her teaching career began in 1928, the year of her M.A., when she was engaged by Hunter College, where she had been a student. Hunter College was and is part of the City Universities of New York. She taught there until her retirement approximately a half-century later and then continued teaching at the Graduate School of the City University of New York until her final illness in 1981.

Professor Newstead's major area of expertise was the Celtic sources of Arthurian literature. Her own mentor, Professor Loomis, was the first proponent of the theory which said that the stories of King Arthur came to the English from the French, who themselves learned them from the bilingual Breton *conteurs*, who had brought them over from Britain when they migrated to the continent after the Anglo-Saxon invasions of the British Isles. The British themselves, that is those who later were known as Bretons and Welsh, learned the tales from their Irish cousins. And it was in Ireland, according to both Loomis and Newstead, where the Arthurian corpus got its start. That does not mean that the Irish had a King Arthur. But they did have stories of both mythical and actual heroes, some of whom are still revered in Ireland. These tales crossed the Irish Sea to Britain, where British-speaking listeners attached them to their own heroes. One of the British heroes was King Arthur, who began his fictional career not so much as a king but as a military leader against the encroaching Angles and Saxons. Since the invading Angles and Saxons did exist and did invade Britain, some scholars have maintained that Arthur was an historical figure. Others have advocated the contrary. The jury is still out.

When Loomis first advanced his theory about the transmissions of the Arthurian tales, he met predictable opposition from senior members of academe. He responded fiercely and fought a lonely battle until Professor Newstead corroborated him with her long career of publications. Miss Newstead was a worthy successor to Loomis, outliving him by fifteen years. During her later years she became the first American, and, even more remarkable, the first woman, to be elected to the Presidency of the International Arthurian Society, an honor that eluded even her mentor.

As a teacher at Hunter and later at the Graduate School at the City University of New York, Miss Newstead demanded clarity in exposition, a clear relationship between sources and the consequences of these sources, and cool logical explanation of facts and their results. In this approach she echoed her own teacher, Professor Loomis, and like him she was interested not only in her own subject of scholarly inquiry but in the lives of the scholars and the incipient scholars whom she knew. When she was a visiting professor at Columbia, Miss Newstead generously gave me the names of several of her former students who were now enjoying careers on the American west coast, the very area where I hoped to be employed.

Miss Newstead never married and was perceived as everyone's maiden aunt. She had no nephews or nieces of her own, but all of her students and her students' families became surrogate nephews and nieces. I have a large family who were growing up during the years when I used to see her. Whenever we met at a conference she asked after each of them. It seems to me now that Miss Newstead never forgot that I had responsibilities outside of academe, and, although she was as dedicated a scholar as any I have known, she never failed to inquire about my family, sometimes even before she asked me what I was working on at that moment.

Miss Newstead habitually distrusted charm, especially when it was used by someone who wished to promote himself or herself academically, particularly those who looked for shortcuts, and very especially those who disguised their shortcuts with the purposeful obfuscation which often accompanies recent deconstructionist literary theory. To her the text was all important, regardless of what a plethora of minor critics said about it. From her own viewpoint the more texts which she could gather and which related to her current object of interest, the more pleased she was. A scholar of literature, to her, was obliged to know his evidence, demonstrate it, and avoid all types of guesswork. Sealy Gilles, who was her student and who was with her during her last illness at New York's Mount Sinai Hospital, has graciously shared this anecdote about an egotistical student in a seminar in the *Roman de la Rose* who told Professor Newstead that he did not plan to take more than four years to complete both his MA and his Ph.D. Miss Newstead, in her characteristic calm slow way looked at him and said, 'Young man, whiz kids do not make good medievalists.' Of course they do not. Good medievalists such as Professor Newstead and those whom she respected were good medievalists because they were dedicated workers and not seekers of shortcuts. Here, as in many other places, she shared her standards with Professor Loomis. Neither Professor Loomis nor Professor Newstead suffered fools gladly. Loomis, however, was much more of a tyrant than Newstead was. Once, in an informal moment, when Professor Newstead and I were sitting on a staircase at one of the hotels selected to house the members of the Modern Language Association, I rashly mentioned my own theories about the legend of Tristan and Isolt. In some ways my own ideas differed from the viewpoint of Professors Loomis and Newstead. Miss Newstead, who was not one to bite my head off over an academic dispute, listened quietly and offered no opinion. Some days later I met Professor Loomis, who, upon seeing me, thundered, 'What's this nonsense you were telling Miss Newstead about the Tristan legend?' If I gave him an answer, I don't believe it was very coherent.

From the very beginning of her published works, Miss Newstead wrote very well. Her book on Bran the Blessed is such an example, and for years served many as a model of scholarly achievement. But even in a footnote she could be devastating to an aspiring critic. In one review she damns with the very faintest of praise: 'My article .... establishes [this] relationship as a feature derived from Welsh tradition. It would have supported Mr. ——'s view, had he been acquainted with it.'

The world needs, and has always needed, scholars like Helaine Newstead. She may be, as *The New Yorker* suggests and then spends many pages arguing against the suggestion, one of those who learned more and more about less and less, but what she has achieved can be equalled by few scholars. She left us three books and monographs, twenty-three scholarly articles, and forty-seven reviews of scholarly books, a third of which she read in languages not her own.

Indeed Helaine Newstead was a New Yorker. But she was probably the least provincial New Yorker that I have met. New York was where she physically lived, but the world was her residence, her playground, and her workplace. Personally I am proud to say that I knew her and learned from her.

UNIVERSITY OF ARIZONA

NOTES

1   Morton M. Hunt, 'Profiles: 'A Giant in Her Field,' *The New Yorker* (March 30, 1957), 39–80. For a full bibliography of Newstead's work, see Harriet Brodey and Benjamin M. Woodbridge, Jr., 'An Analytical Bibliography of the Writings of Helaine Newstead.' *Romance Philology* 17, No. 3 (February 1964), 527–34 as well as successive publications of *Bulletin Bibliographique de la Société Internationale Arthurienne (BBSIA)*. Her books and monographs include: Litotes in Anglo–Saxon Poetry,' Unpublished M.A. thesis, Columbia University, 1928; *Bran the Blessed in Arthurian Romance,* Columbia University Studies in English and Comparative Literature 141. (New York: Columbia University Press, 1939; and an edited book, *Chaucer and His Contemporaries: Essays on Medieval Literature and Thought* (Greenwich, CT: Fawcett Publications, Inc., 1968). Her articles, in chronological order, are: 'The "Joie de la Cort" Episode in *Erec* and the Horn of Bran,' *PMLA* 51 (1936): 13–25; 'Perceval's Father and Welsh Tradition,' *Romanic Review* 36 (1945): 3–31;'The Grail Legend and Celtic Tradition,' *American Society Legion of Honor Magazine* 16 (1945): 219–34 [also issued as a separate booklet: Franco–American Pamphlets 3]; New York: American Society of the French Legion of Honor (1945): 18; 'The Traditional Background of *Partonopeus de Blois*,' *PMLA* 61 (1946): 916–46; 'Matière de Bretagne: Tristan,' in *A Critical Bibliography of French Literature*, gen. ed. D.C. Cabeen, 1: *The Medieval Period*, ed. U.T. Holmes Jr. (Syracuse, N. Y.: Syracuse Univ. Press, 1947), pp. 123–130; addenda in the enl. ed. (1952), 258f.; 'The Besieged Ladies in Arthurian Romance,' *PMLA*

63 (1948): 803–30; 'Kaherdin and the Enchanted Pillow: An Episode in the Tristan Legend,' *PMLA*, 65 (1950): 290–312; 'The Blancheflor-Perceval Question Again,' *Romance Philology*, 7 (1953–54): 171–75; 'News of Arthurian Scholars and Their Activities,' *BBSIA* 6 (1954): 116–23; 'The Tryst beneath the Tree: An Episode in the Tristan Legend,' *Romance Philology* 9 (1955–56): 269–84 (William A. Nitze Testimonial, Part 2); 'King Mark of Cornwall,' *Romance Philology* 11 (1957–58): 240–53 (Percival B. Fay Testimonial, Part I); 'The Origin and Growth of the Tristan Legend,' in *Arthurian Literature in the Middle Ages: A Collaborative History*, ed R. S. Loomis, (Oxford: Clarendon Press,1959), pp. 122–33; 'Laura Hibbard Loomis (1883–1960),' *BBSIA* 12 (1960): 147–49; 'The *Enfances* of Tristan and English Tradition,' in *Studies in Medieval Literature in Honor of Professor Albert Croll Baugh*, ed. MacEdward Leach (Philadelphia: University of Pennsylvania Press, 1961), pp. 169–85; 'Arthurian Legends,' in *Collier's Encyclopedia*, 1962; 'Grail Legends,' in *Collier's Encyclopedia, 1962*; 'Arthurian Legends,' *A Manual of the Writings in Middle English 1050–1500*, ed. J. Burke Severs (New Haven, CT: The Connecticut Academy of Arts and Sciences, 1967), Commentary, pp. 11–119; Bibliography, pp. 173–256; 'Isolt of the White Hands and Tristan's Marriage,' *Romance Philology* 19 (1965–66): 155–66; 'The Harp and the Rote: An Episode in the Tristan Legend and its Literary History,' *Romance Philology* 22 (1968–69): 463–70; 'The equivocal Oath in the Tristan Legend,' *Les Melanges offerts à Rita Legeune, Professeur à l'Université de Liège* (Gembloux: Duculot, 1969), 1077–85; 'Recent Perspectives on Arthurian Literature,' *Mélanges de langue et de littérature du Moyen Age et de la Renaissance offerts à Jean Frappier, professeur à la Sorbonne par ses collègues, ses élèves et ses amis*, 2 vols. (Genève: Droz, 1970), vol. 2, pp. 877–83; 'Narrative Techniques in Chrétien's *Yvain*,' *Romance Philology* 30 (1976–77): 431–41; 'Malory and Romance,' *Four Essays on Romance*, ed. Herschel Baker, Cambridge MA: Harvard University Press, 1971.

2 For more about Professor Loomis, see my small appreciation of him: 'Roger Sherman Loomis (1887-1966),' *Medieval Scholarship: Biographical Studies on the Formation of Discipline*, vol. 2, Literature and Philosophy, ed. Helen Damico. (New York and London: Garland Press, 1998).

3 At this writing I can think of only one: Lionel Trilling's great book on Matthew Arnold.

How I Became (and Continue to Be) An Arthurian Woman Scholar

ELSPETH KENNEDY

One element in the three qualifications for this particular paper, of course, came early on—I was born a girl. The two other elements began in a small way when I was a child. In England (even with a mother from Scotland and a father from Australia), children from an early age listen to or read Arthurian stories, mainly based however distantly on Malory (already a link with Maureen Fries). In spite of my undiluted Celtic ancestry, with all my grandparents either from Ireland or from Scotland, I was born in Berkshire within less than thirty miles of Winchester, Salisbury, and Oxford. My parents took me to see the ancient monuments, Stonehenge, the old churches, cathedrals, and castles in the neighborhood. When I was thirteen, my form at school—through high marks—won a special excursion to Winchester, and visited the cathedral and the Round Table (late medieval, if not contemporary with Arthur). Even in 1934, when as a thirteen-year-old I first went to my big school, I knew that the war was coming. As a result, with two brothers of military age (one of whom was to be killed in the war), even though I was doing quite well academically, I did not want to go to university as my particular interests (languages and literature) were not in my eyes going to contribute directly to the war effort. In July 1940, at the age of eighteen, I found myself working for MI5. I lived with relatives in London and traveled to my office (in a prison, Wormwood Scrubs) every day by underground, reading Dante's *Inferno* on the way. We were bombed and subsequently evacuated to Oxfordshire where I worked for over four years. Office hours were from 9 a.m. till 6 p.m. six days a week (with twelve days leave a year), but I learned Russian in the evenings and in the queues for meals in order to read Pushkin and Tolstoy, which I can still do. However, once I realized (in 1943) that I should start to do some postwar planning and decided to take the university entrance examination for Somerville College, Oxford, it was the identity of the person who coached me for college entrance, Gweneth Whitteridge, a pupil of Eugène Vinaver, that led me in a different direction. In 1944, I won a scholarship to Somerville College, Oxford, which would be held for me indefinitely until I was no longer needed in the War Office.

Gweneth Whitteridge most generously suggested that I should go on writing essays for her without payment, and proposed medieval or sixteenth-century French literature. I had been fascinated by a reproduction of a medieval illumination hanging on her wall and chose medieval literature. As a result, I became hooked on Arthurian romance and on the question of the change of the chief Grailwinner from Perceval to Galahad *before* I started my university studies. It had been a woman who blocked my release from the War Office at a time in 1944 when I had no work to do there, so that I lost a whole term of my course, but it was the women tutors in Oxford such as Gweneth Whitteridge and Rhoda Sutherland who were my most inspiring teachers. Not only that, Mildred Pope, author of *From Latin to Modern French*, a member of the Council of Somerville and a former colleague and great friend of Vinaver both in Oxford and Manchester, expressed a desire to meet me in my final year and encouraged me to pursue research. As a grandchild, as it were, of Vinaver through his pupil Gweneth Whitteridge, I soon got involved with the idea of editing texts and got permission to work on a manuscript of the *Romance of the Rose* in the Bodleian Library while still an undergraduate.

I completed my doctorate in 1951; it was an edition of part of the Prose *Lancelot*, covering Lancelot's childhood and upbringing by the Lady of the Lake up to his arrival at Arthur's court to become a knight. Within this text was the reference to Perceval as the knight who saw openly the marvels of the Holy Grail and achieved the adventures of the Perilous Seat. It was clear from an examination of the manuscripts that this was the original reading and that the change to Galahad (to be found in a number of manuscripts, including, unfortunately, the base manuscript used by Micha in the edition on which the Garland translation of that part of the cycle is based) was made at a later stage in the development of the cycle. I decided that I wanted to explore further this change in the Grailwinner within the *Lancelot-Grail* cycle. It was clear to me that this could only be done by editing the first version of the Prose *Lancelot*, a version that did not contain a Quest for the Holy Grail, but referred outwards to it as a story already told and belonging to the past in relation to the tale of Lancelot. This was the version to be found in the oldest surviving Prose *Lancelot* manuscript, Paris, Bibliothèque Nationale, f. fr. 768, and, in whole or in part, in eleven other manuscripts. My theory of a development of the cycle in stages, a theory based on the careful study of the manuscripts, was unwelcome to some distinguished French scholars such as Jean Frappier and Alexandre Micha, who believed passionately in the unity of the cycle from the beginning (apart from the later addition of the first two branches, the *Early History of the Grail* and the *Merlin*).

I had embarked on this edition with no idea who might publish it, but while it was still in its early stages before I had left Oxford to take my first proper university appointment in Manchester in a department of which Vinaver was the head, I was fortunate enough to find one, the Oxford University Press. This was achieved in a slightly unusual way. A nuclear physicist friend used to go to a certain Oxford pub every Saturday morning, where a group of university people of various specialities used to meet, drink beer, and talk; one of these was the Assistant Secretary of the Oxford University Press, a New Zealander, Dan Davin. My friend mentioned my publishing problems to Dan Davin who said: 'She'd better write to me.' I did so and, thanks mainly to the intervention of a distinguished classicist, Maurice Bowra, my as yet uncompleted edition was accepted for publication, a contract was signed, and I gave a celebratory party in my bedsit (a large room on Walton Street, a couple of hundred yards down from the Oxford University Press). It took me twenty-five more years to complete the edition: there were more than sixty manuscripts, not counting a vast number of fragments; the book was delayed for two years by a printers' strike, and it was finally published in 1980.[1] However, it was worth waiting for as the Oxford University Press gave me a separate volume for variants, notes, and glossary. As a result, when Lancelot's early adventures in the edition of Micha were prescribed for the French graduate examination, the Agrégation, all the people having to teach it had to use my edition alongside that of Micha, who had been given far less space, and I was quite famous and in demand in France during that particular year.[2] I wrote *Lancelot and the Grail*, my literary study of the first Prose *Lancelot* and its transformation into part of a *Lancelot-Grail* cycle including a Grail Quest and a Death of Arthur alongside my work on the edition, and it was published in 1986.[3]

All my research work has, therefore, been based on living with a text and starting from the manuscripts to explore the literary structure and the reception of the romance throughout the centuries. I have not been much concerned with origins before the manuscript evidence. Indeed, through Vinaver I became involved in rewriting Jessie Weston in relation to some of the entries on the Arthurian characters in the *Encyclopaedia Britannica*. I was uneasy about basing the entries on characters such as Gawain isolated from the literary themes and structure of the individual work, but had no choice in the matter.

As you will have observed, I am an empiricist, wary of spending too much time on admittedly tempting theories of origins for which there is no textual evidence, and too uneasy concerning my own competence to involve myself too deeply in contemporary literary theory, although excited when the empirical and theoretical approaches come together in an unexpected way.

My work on the Lancelot textual tradition from the thirteenth-century manuscripts to those of the fifteenth and the early printed editions, as well as my most recent research with a team of literary specialists and art historians directed by Alison Stones, has made me very interested in the reception of the text and has brought to light some very different attitudes towards the interpretation of the romance in readers, scribes, and organizers of manuscript illuminations. As far as attitudes towards women are concerned, these vary in an interesting way. For example, Philippe de Novare, a thirteenth-century reader of the Prose *Lancelot*, who paraphrases certain sections of it in *Les Quatre âges de l'homme*, concentrates on the parts of the romance that deal with relations between lord and vassal, or between experienced knight and young knight bachelor, and considers it dangerous to let women learn to read. On the other hand, a late-thirteenth-century scribe explains that on the instructions of his lady he is trying to shorten the romance as he copies it to reach more quickly the episode of the *Knight of the Cart*, where, of course, the love theme predominates. Geoffroi de Charny, who also shows familiarity with Arthurian prose romance, takes a different line in his fourteenth-century *Livre de chevalerie*, with which I was brought into close contact through the edition Richard Kaeuper and I published.[4] There Charny emphasizes the importance of the lady in guiding and inspiring a young man over matters such as participation in tournaments in the early stages of his career as a knight.

The most recent work of Alison Stones and myself on the relationship between text and illuminations in two early-fourteenth-century manuscripts has also shed light on the reception of Arthurian romance, but here not so much in terms of attitudes towards women. The choice of subjects for illustration and the placing of the pictures in the text within these two manuscripts, in every other way closely related textually and artistically, reveal marked differences in approach. One manuscript does not hesitate to portray the Grail, using the symbol of a cloud to allow for the representation of the spiritual and invisible; the other avoids all representation of the Grail and gives greater emphasis to the political or to the traditional biblical scenes.

To sum up, I was introduced to Arthurian studies by a woman scholar, Gweneth Whitteridge, pupil of Vinaver, who had edited a text and spent much time with manuscripts; I have been much helped and encouraged by another Arthurian woman scholar, Emmanuèle Baumgartner, a Tristan specialist and much else besides; and I am being spurred on in my present interdisciplinary research on Arthurian romance by a third, Alison Stones. However, I think that Maureen Fries would have perhaps also thought it important that in addition I received inspiration from Eugène Vinaver, editor of Malory, to go on questioning and enjoying this splendid literature.

OXFORD

NOTES

1 Elspeth Kennedy, ed., *Lancelot do Lac: The Non-Cyclic Old French Prose Romance,* 2 vols. (Oxford: Clarendon Press, 1980).
2 Alexandre Micha, ed., vol. 7 of *Lancelot: roman en prose du XIIIe siècle* (Genève: Droz, 1978–83).
3 Elspeth Kennedy, *Lancelot and the Grail* (Oxford: Clarendon Press, 1986).
4 Richard W. Kaeuper and Elspeth Kennedy, *The Book of Chivalry of Geoffroi de Charny: Text, Context, and Translation* (Philadelphia: University of Pennsylvania Press, 1996).

From Holocaust Survivor
to Arthurian Scholar

FANNI BOGDANOW

I had the good fortune to be first introduced to both Arthurian and Tristan studies when I was an undergraduate at Manchester University at a time when Professor Eugène Vinaver was the Head of Department there and Dr. Frederick Whitehead and T.B.W. Reid were two of the lecturers teaching medieval French language and literature.

But it was quite by chance that I was to begin my studies at Manchester University at the beginning of October 1945. I was born in Düsseldorf, Germany, on July 20, 1927 to where my father, Abrascha Bogdanow, born in Smolewitch near Minsk had emigrated at the age of eighteen in 1903 to escape from the then pogroms against the Jewish people in Russia, not foreseeing the fate that 30 years later with the advent of Hitler was to befall the Jewish people in Germany and subsequently in the whole of occupied Europe.

Though I was aware from the age of five of the growing anti-semitism in Germany, my most vivid memories of the Holocaust are the events that were to lead up to my arrival in Great Britain in an unaccompanied 'Kindertransport' ('children's transport') on June 27, 1939.[1] The events to which I am referring and which are as vivid in my mind now as if they had taken place yesterday were those of November 9, 1938. On the afternoon of that day, throughout the whole of Germany, the great majority of Jewish men and boys were taken to concentration camps. My father and uncle who lived at that time in the same village, Affaltrach near Heilbronn, were taken, together with all the other Jewish men living in that village to Dachau concentration camp. An eighteen-year-old cousin of mine who lived in another part of Germany was taken that day to Buchenwald where he was exterminated within a month.

This was, however, only the beginning of that day of terror. According to 'history' textbooks that night, the so-called 'Kristallnacht' (the 'night of broken glass') only synagogues were burnt down and Jewish shops broken into. In reality it was far, far worse. That night, which I shall never forget, when only women and children were at home, the Germans with their pickaxes broke into all the Jewish homes (they knew exactly where the Jewish people lived, for previously all Jewish people had to register as Jewish). They hacked down the front door, they hacked out the windows and window frames, they hacked holes in the walls. Not a piece of furniture was left standing, not a cup nor a saucer was left whole. The following day all Jewish children, including of course myself, were by decree expelled from the German state schools. And as all Jewish teachers had the previous day been taken to concentration camps, Jewish children were left without schooling. And shortly after, by a further decree, while the men and boys were still in the concentration camps, the remaining Jewish people were segregated into 'Judenhaüser' ('Jew houses'). Towns and villages where no Jewish people were left bore at their entrance the sign 'Judenfrei' ('free of Jews').

But within ten days of the news of the events of November 9 coming to London, both Houses of Parliament voted unanimously to bring up to ten thousand unaccompanied Jewish children to Great Britain. British families who had never seen or heard of the children previously volunteered spontaneously to open their homes to them. As soon as my mother heard of this generous offer, she immediately put my name down, for although it was hard for her to part with her only child, she knew that if she were to save my life, she would have to part with me. It is with the deepest sense of gratitude that I shall always remember the wonderful Quaker family, Mr. and Mrs. H.A. Clement (who at that time lived in Haughton Green near Manchester), who took me into their home and looked after me with the same loving care they gave their own children.[2] Almost from the day after my arrival, Mr. and Mrs. Clement began preparing me for the entrance examinations to Fairfield High School for Girls. I remained at that school until I was sixteen, when in order to earn my living, I began work first in Stalybridge Public Library and subsequently in Kingsmoor School, Glossop, both near Manchester. But as I was anxious to obtain a degree, I began studying in my own time for the external London Intermediate B.A., frequently getting up at five in the morning. Then one day, in December 1944, when for some reason I had to go to see Mrs. Pogmore at the Refugee Children's Movement in Brazenose Street, Manchester, and I told her that I was working in my spare time for an External London Degree, she suggested that I should sit for the Entrance Scholarship examinations to Manchester University. And so it came about, that on V.E. Day, May 8, 1945, I sat for the first of the five papers of the Entrance Scholarship examinations. I was very lucky and was awarded the Alice and Edith Hamer Entrance Scholarship and the William

Hulme Bursary as well as the Ashburne Hall Scholarship. And with the exception later of a year as a Research Studentship holder at Westfield College, London, a year in Paris as a French Government Scholar and a year at Liverpool University as a Leverhulme Research Fellow, I was to remain at Manchester University for the rest of my life, first as an undergraduate, then as a postgraduate student, and then on the staff. For through good fortune, the very year in which I completed my doctorate under the direction of Professor Vinaver and Dr. Whitehead, there was a vacancy on the staff in the French Department. After first being an Assistant Lecturer, then a Lecturer and subsequently Reader, I was given a Personal Chair. Following my retirement I was made an Emeritus Professor for life.

From my first term as an undergraduate at Manchester University I was introduced to Medieval French language and literature by both Frederick Whitehead and T.W. Reid, Eugène Vinaver at that time having extended his interests from the Tristan legend to Malory and Racine as well as Flaubert. Frederick Whitehead aroused our interest not only in the Old French epic through his stimulating lectures on the *Chanson de Roland,* but also in the Arthurian legend, tracing the development of the legend from Gildas onwards down to the thirteenth-century prose romances. But perhaps what aroused my interest most of all was the announcement at the end of 1945 of Eugène Vinaver's identification of a previously unknown manuscript of the *Suite du Merlin,* the Cambridge codex, and two years later, in 1947, the publication of Vinaver's first edition of the *Works of Sir Thomas Malory* where in his Introduction he traces the French sources underlying Malory's works and deals with the technique of editing medieval texts. It was perhaps this more than anything else which decided me to choose for my first research degree, a Manchester Master of Arts, a subject that involved editing a text. The text suggested to me by Frederick Whitehead was the portion of the *Queste del Saint Graal* of MS B.N. fr. 343 which differed from the *Vulgate* version and the exact nature of which was at that time highly disputed. For the sections of MS 343 distinct from the *Vulgate Queste* are not only identical with the corresponding portions of the Portuguese *Demanda do Santo Graal* (first published in its complete form by Augusto Magne, in 1944), but also large portions of the *Queste del Saint Graal* incorporated into the numerous manuscripts of the Second Version of the Prose *Tristan.* Hence my research on the MS 343 *Queste* led me to examine Tristan manuscripts in various libraries, including the Bibliothèque Nationale in Paris. There I had the good fortune to meet M. Jacques Monfrin, who at that time was a librarian in the Manuscript Department. He not only encouraged me from then on in my research, but subsequently when I was preparing an edition of the complete *Post-Vulgate Queste—Mort Artu,* of which the MS 343 fragment represented an important section, suggested that the work should be proposed for inclusion in the series of the *Société des Anciens Textes Français.*[3]

I soon realised that the MS 343 *Queste* could not be studied in isolation and in my doctorate thesis I extended my research to the whole of the cycle of which the Post-Vulgate *Queste-Mort Artu* (formerly referred to as the 'pseudo-Robert de Boron' *Queste Mort Artu)* formed the third part.[4] The scholars who had previously dealt with this cycle had assumed that as in the Vulgate Cycle, the *Suite du Merlin* was originally followed by a complete version of the Prose *Lancelot.* But in the course of my research I identified in two manuscripts, B.N. fr. 112 and B.N. fr. 12599, sections of a narrative which now enables us to understand how the Post-Vulgate writer was able to bridge the chronological gap between the end of the *Suite du Merlin* and the beginning of the *Queste* without incorporating the whole of the Vulgate *Lancelot:* he selected from the latter certain relevant incidents which he combined with material derived from the First Version of the Prose *Tristan* and his own inventions.[5]

Since my completion of the edition of the Post-Vulgate *Queste—Mort Artu* my interest in the editing of Arthurian romance texts has not ceased: I am now engaged, in collaboration with a colleague from Manchester University, Mrs. Anne Berrie, she also a pupil of Eugène Vinaver and F. Whitehead, in an edition of the Vulgate *Queste* based on a manuscript unknown to Pauphilet.[6] This new edition is for the Lettres Gothiques series under the direction of M. Michel Zink, who, like Mme Geneviève Hasenohr (the *Commissaire responsable* for the SATF series since the death of Jacques Monfrin) encourages me greatly in my research work, for which I am most grateful.

But the two people who during their lifetime encouraged me perhaps most were my father and mother whose courage is for me a continual inspiration. How they survived the Holocaust is a miracle. My father was temporarily released from Dachau at the beginning of February 1939, but despite every effort, like so many other Jewish people, he and my mother were unable to get out of Germany prior to the outbreak of war in September 1939. And so in the middle of June 1941 my father, after first being taken to the prison in Heilbronn, was transferred on October 8, 1941 to the concentration camp Wülzburg near Weissenburg in Bavaria, where he was to remain until liberated by the Allied Forces on April 26, 1945. What my father suffered there was comparable to what he had suffered in Dachau. He was beaten, so much so that not only his back and arms were black and blue, but one of his eardrums burst. In addition to being beaten, he and the other inmates suffered constant hunger. And when the Allied troops were at last approaching, the sufferings of the inmates of Wülzburg did not cease: the German guards wishing to hide their misdeeds decided to march the prisoners out of Wülzburg, although they were all in such a weakened condition that they could hardly stand. On the forced march, my father was left lying for dead in a ditch, and it was only thanks to the kindness of an unknown American soldier that he did not die there. That unknown American soldier, to whom I shall always be grateful, picked my father up out of the ditch and took him to an American military hospital.

What my mother suffered at the hands of the Germans was equally horrendous. At first, almost immediately after my father was incarcerated in Heilbronn, my mother had to undertake forced labor. She was forced to go from place to place, being put in sole charge of Jewish old people's homes. Each morning and evening the Gestapo (the Nazi secret police) arrived at the homes to make sure my mother had not attempted to escape. The stay in each home was for my mother of only short duration, for after a few weeks the old people from the various homes were deported by the Germans to Theresienstadt and other death camps. The deportation of the old, many of whom could not walk, was horrendous. My mother could never forget what she saw. Those from the old people's home in Eschenau, for instance, being too frail to walk to the nearest railway station, were thrown one on top of the other into horse-drawn farmers' carts used for carrying manure. And when there were no more old people's homes left, my mother was taken by the Gestapo to Bergen-Belsen concentration camp on September 26, 1943. Her first thought when she arrived in Belsen was, as she told me later, that she would never get out of there alive. There were rows and rows of barbed wire surrounding the camp. The way in and the ground around the barracks where the inmates were 'housed' was thick mud. My mother's bed was a wooden plank, her pillows were her shoes, her bedcover was her coat. By November it was bitter cold and snowing. The snow and rain came through the slats in the barrack walls. And there were rats who came out each night and jumped on the inmates. The food, as in the successive camps where my father was, was no more than a starvation diet: a piece of bread and water in the morning, some watery soup at midday and nothing more. And morning and evening the inmates had to stand in the freezing cold for roll call. But the deprivation was nothing compared with the constant anxiety as to when one's last day would come. For fifty Polish Jewish doctors and their wives, and children, including a baby born a few days earlier in the barrack where my mother was housed, that last day came in the middle of October 1943. The gas chambers were being built at the time, but not yet functioning. So these doctors and their wives and children, were stood up against a ditch and shot in cold blood by the German guards.

On January 29, 1944 my mother and some other women, how they were selected she never knew, were packed into cattle trucks and moved on. After a journey lasting three days and three nights, they arrived in France and were incarcerated in the camp set up in Vittel by the German occupation army. From there almost daily transports were going back East to the death camps. Many of the inmates in despair took their own lives. I cannot even attempt to describe what my mother must have felt, but what distressed her even more than her own suffering, was the sight of one of these transports going East. It was a number of cattle wagons, and through the slats could be seen the terrified faces of small children. The German occupying forces had emptied the French Jewish orphanages and were deporting the children to the death camps.

Liberation for my mother was to come on October 23, 1944. But it was not without a struggle that Vittel and the camp were liberated by the Allies. It had been taken once by the Allies and then was retaken by the Germans, but finally the camp was liberated. By that time, the German prison guards, attempting to hide their identity, had removed their uniforms. It was August 1947, at the end of my second year as an undergraduate at Manchester University, when I saw my parents again for the first time. I had a visa to visit them for just ten days. They were living by then in a displaced person's camp in Bavaria, and there they told me something of what they had gone through; but they only revealed to me a fraction of what they had suffered, for they did not wish to distress me. My father never recovered sufficiently to make the journey to England, but after his death my mother came to live with me. Her years in England, as she always said, were the happiest years of her life: it was the first time in her life she felt free and without fear. And her greatest joy was to see the happiness my research work gave me.

Thank you, Allied Expeditionary Forces, for liberating my mother and father from the Nazi death camps and vanquishing the most vicious regime that the world has ever known. And thank you, Great Britain, for giving me refuge in 1939. Without that generous action, for which I shall always be deeply grateful, instead of becoming a scholar of Arthurian romance, I would undoubtedly have been one of the six million Jewish people exterminated by the Nazis, most of them in gas chambers.

CHEADLE, CHESHIRE

NOTES

1 I shall never be able to forget what my parents went through. It is a miracle how they survived the Holocaust. My cousin who also came to England in a children's transport three weeks before me, never saw her parents again. In 1941 they were deported to Riga and, as we found out since, every one on that transport was shot in cold blood on arrival. In 1999, there was in London a reunion of the 'Kindertransport' children, most of us now in our late sixties and seventies, to mark the 60th anniversary of our arrival in Great Britain. Most of the people at the reunion (quite a number of whom now live in the USA) do not know to this day where their parents found their end. The unspeakable atrocities committed by the Germans must never be forgotten. They could have refused, but they did not.

2 The wonderful lady Mrs. Clement, who took me into her family when I came to England in June 1939 will be 95 in 2001. She is a widow now and lives in the South of England, but we have remained in close contact. We speak on the telephone almost every week; and her four children too are in constant contact with me. When one of her daughters was a little girl of seven, she said to me: 'our mother said: "You are our sister."' And to this day I have remained their sister. And when my own mother died in 1978, all the Clement family came to her funeral in Manchester.

3 *La version Post-Vulgate de la Queste del Saint Graal et de la Mort Artu. Troisième partie du Roman du Graal,* ed. Fanni Bogdanow, Société des Anciens Textes Français (Paris: Picard, tome I, 599 pp; II, 601 pp.; IV,1, 324 pp., 1991; tome III, 806 pp., 2000). Tome IV, 2 to appear in 2001.

Prior to the identification of the Rawlinson D 874 in the Bodleian Library, Oxford, the MS 343 fragment was the only French manuscript of the latter portion of the Post-Vulgate *Queste*. The Oxford codex forms the basis of this section of my SATF edition as it is more complete than the MS 343 fragment (cf. my 'A newly discovered manuscript of the Post-Vulgate', *French Studies Bulletin* 16 (1985): 4–6; F.B. 'A newly discovered manuscript of the Post-Vulgate *Queste del Saint Graal* and its place in the manuscript tradition of the Post-Vulgate,'in *Studia in honorem prof. de Riquier* (Barcelona: Quaderns Crema,1991), vol. 4, pp. 347-70.

4 Fanni Bogdanow, *The Romance of the Grail. A study of the structure and genesis of a thirteenth-century Arthurian prose romance* (Manchester and New York: Manchester University Press, Barnes & Noble, 1966), XI and 308 pp.

5 *La Folie Lancelot, a hitherto unidentified portion of the Suite du Merlin contained in mss. B.N. fr. 112 and 12599,* ed. Fanni Bogdanow *(Beihefte zur Zeitschrift für Romanische Philologie,* 109), Tübingen, 1965, LXIII and 323 pp.. Cf. my 'The importance of the Bologna and Imola fragments for the reconstruction of the *Post-Vulgate Roman du Graal',* in *Bulletin of the John Rylands University Library of Manchester* 80 (1998): 33–64; my 'L'importance des fragments de Bologna et d'Imola pour la reconstruction de la *Post-Vulgate',* in *Textos Medievais Portugueses e suas Fontes, Matéria da Bretanha e Cantigas com notaçäo musical,* ed. Heitor

Megale and Haquira Osakabe, *Humanitas,* Publicações FFLCH/USP, Universidade de São Paulo, Faculdade de Filosofia, Letras e Ciências Humanas (1999): 17-55; my 'The Madrid *Tercero Libro de don Lançarote* (ms. 9611) and its relationship to the *Post-Vulgate Roman du Graal Post-Vulgate* in the light of a hitherto unknown French source of one of the incidents of the *Tercero Libro',* *Bulletin of Hispanic Studies* 76 (1999): 441–52.

6 Cf. my 'A Little Known Codex, Bancroft MS. 73, and its Place in the Manuscript Tradition of the Vulgate *Queste del Saint Graal', Arthuriana* 6.1 (Spring, 1996): 1–21.

Valerie Lagorio

MARTIN B. SHICHTMAN

A rnaut Daniel, a poet of twelfth-century Provençe, described himself, in perhaps his most famous lyric, as one 'q'amas l'aura, / E chatz la lebre ab lo bou / E nadi contra suberna' [who gathers the wind / and hunts the hare with the ox / and swims against the incoming tide].[1] For Arnaut Daniel, greatness resided in doing things the hard way, in bringing intelligence, tenacity, wit, and elegance to tasks lesser individuals would find daunting, if not impossible. For Arnaut Daniel, the only projects worth taking on were those fraught with risk. In the current, hyper-professional academic environment, where little matters more than resume lines, it is difficult even to imagine Valerie Lagorio's career trajectory accounting for success and recognition. But the current, hyper-professional academic environment rarely produces personalities like Valerie Lagorio. In fact, it rarely produces either scholars or teachers of her ability.

Hula-dancer, opera singer, executive secretary, disk-jockey, military intelligence operative, accordion-player, sherry drinker, ukulele-picker, 'unclaimed treasure': when Valerie Lagorio emerged from Stanford University at the age of 39—a non-traditional student, if there ever was one—having just finished a dissertation with R. W. Ackerman on Joseph of Arimathea, 'the patron saint of morticians and a nice Jewish boy,' she would have us know, Arthurian studies ceased to be your father's Camelot. As Lagorio made her mark on Arthurian studies, a good number of its fathers—and some mothers, too—would be less than pleased. In a period of just 4 1/2 years, Lagorio completed both her college degree and her Ph.D., clearly a no-nonsense player, and for the next 37 years she has, even while adhering to many of the traditions of her profession, chipped away—sometimes sledge-hammered away—at its pretensions. Her victories are bright and shining tributes to her wit, her brilliance, and her determination. Her losses are too.

In 1975, Valerie Lagorio shared with Gayatri Spivak the distinction of being the first women promoted to the rank of full professor in the English Department at the University of Iowa. Her writings have dominated two separate areas of medieval studies, mysticism—Christine Rose, in a recent review article, characterized Lagorio as 'the *doyenne* of medieval mystical studies'[2]—and Arthurian literature. Lagorio has authored nearly seventy articles and reviews, including her groundbreaking study, 'The Evolving Legend of St. Joseph of Glastonbury.'[3] She was a co-founder and editor of *Mystic Quarterly* and was a driving force in the creation of *Quondam et Futurus* (now *Arthuriana*). She edited *Mysticism, Medieval and Modern*, co-authored, with Ritamary Bradley, *The Comprehensive Annotated Bibliography on Fourteenth Century English Mystics*, and co-edited, with Mildred L. Day, *King Arthur Through the Ages*.[4] Her extraordinary influence on medieval studies is confirmed by the fact that two separate festschrifts have appeared in her honor: *Culture and the King: The Social Implications of the Arthurian Legend*, edited by Martin B. Shichtman and James P. Carley, and *Vox Mystica: Essays on Medieval Mysticism*, edited by Anne Clark Bartlett and Thomas H. Bestul.[5] Retirement has not slowed her down. She is currently working on projects dealing with Cistercian women's spirituality, St. Bridget of Sweden, and Julian of Norwich.

Lagorio's path to the academy was anything but traditional, but it is demonstrative of the talents that would later win her accolades both as a scholar and as a teacher—in 1988, she was recipient of the University of Iowa Council on Excellence in Teaching Award. As World War II was drawing to a close, Lagorio, then in her teens, elected to entertain US combat troops. Dark and attractive, Lagorio was dispatched to the European theater as a hula dancer, even though she had never done the hula before. Reports have it that she was a huge success among the GIs. For Lagorio, however, it was not enough just to amuse war-weary soldiers. She would later travel to the Pacific to learn classical hula from master teachers. The GIs who saw Valerie Lagorio dance were, no doubt, satisfied simply to be entertained by a pretty girl. Valerie Lagorio, on the other hand, needed to learn the craft, needed to be immersed in its traditions. At the University of Iowa, Lagorio's undergraduates, and even most of her graduate students, likely never appreciated that the woman teaching their *required* classes was a scholar of international reputation, likely never knew that her work on both the Arthurian legend and medieval mysticism was important enough to be the subject of controversy and even professional infighting. These students adored the show, and there are few teachers who can give a show like Valerie Lagorio. They would be captivated by her performance, and, without realizing it, learn more about medieval literature and the practice of literary study than they ever expected.

For all her brilliance and showmanship, Lagorio could be difficult and demanding—she attributes her enormous drive to her father, a military man.

Lagorio wanted the institution of Arthurian studies to reexamine, maybe even deconstruct its values. She stood as a constant reminder that Arthurian literature was, from its beginnings, always popular, and rarely high art, that it had become ossified, in part, because of the institution dedicated to its study. She demanded that the academy make room for those drawn to the popular aspects of the legend. Many Arthurians during the 1970s, including a portion of the hierarchy of the North American Branch of the International Arthurian Society, viewed Lagorio's intellectual politics as an assault on their seriousness and professionalism. To some, her displays of enthusiasm—leading, for instance, a beer-hall full of Germans in song during the International Arthurian Society meeting in Regensburg—were an embarrassment, which made her democratizing efforts all the more problematic. They believed she neither conducted herself with sufficient dignity nor afforded appropriate dignity to Arthurian studies. As the 1970s came to a close, Lagorio became the target of a conspiracy that changed the manner in which North American Branch of the International Arthurian Society historically selected its president, solely with the intention of denying her the position.[6] Norris Lacy has called this 'a painful and regrettable event, which is still proving divisive more than two decades later.'

In 1988, Valerie Lagorio was elected president of the North American Branch of the International Arthurian Society. In her leadership role, she asked the Arthurian Society to take a good look at itself and its membership. She believed that this sort of self-evaluation would take real seriousness and professionalism, and it would require the work of real scholars and real critics. She also insisted that the society be represented by a journal, or at very least a newsletter. Since that time, the society has become more open and vital, attracting new members with interests both in medieval studies and in the literatures and cultures of later periods. The discipline of Arthurian studies has likewise become far more receptive to the cutting-edge discourses of contemporary critical theory. *Arthuriana*, grown out of the fledgling newsletter, *Quondam et Futurus*, has prospered and become a journal of considerable prestige.

Valerie Lagorio possesses an international cadre of friends and admirers, who attest to her warmth, her humor, and her generosity. Many of the most influential scholars in the areas of Arthurian studies and medieval mysticism count her as their mentor—like her dear friend, Maureen Fries, Lagorio reached out to several generations of young people entering the profession. The editors of her festschrifts were not surprised to discover that among their greatest problems was limiting the list of those who wanted to contribute, so many had volunteered. She has, without a doubt, changed the ways many engage in the discipline of medieval studies; she has also, likely, changed the ways many medievalists view themselves.

EASTERN MICHIGAN UNIVERSITY

Martin B. Shichtman is Professor of English Language and Literature at Eastern Michigan University. He is co-editor, with Laurie A. Finke, of *Medieval Texts and Contemporary Readers* and, with James P. Carley, of *Culture and the King: The Social Implications of the Arthurian Legend. Essays in Honor of Valerie M. Lagorio.* He has also written numerous articles on medieval literature, contemporary literary and cultural theory, and film. Shichtman's dissertation, 'The Gawain's of English Arthurian Romance' (University of Iowa, 1981), was written under the direction of Valerie M. Lagorio.

NOTES

1 Anthony Bonner, *Songs of the Troubadours* (New York: Schocken Books, 1972), pp. 159, 163.
2 Christine M. Rose, rev. of *Vox Mystica: Essays on Medieval Mysticism*, ed. Anne Clark Bartlett and Thomas H. Bestul, *Envoi* 6 (1997): 25.
3 See Valerie M. Lagorio, 'The Evolving Legend of St. Joseph of Glastonbury,' *Speculum* 46 (1971): 209–31.
4 See Valerie M. Lagorio and Ritamary Bradley, *The Comprehensive Annotated Bibliography on Fourteenth-Century English Mystics* (New York: Garland, 1981); *Mysticism, Medieval and Modern*, ed. Valerie M. Lagorio (Salzburg, Austria: Institut für Anglistik und Amerikanistik, Universität Salzburg, 1986); and *King Arthur Through the Ages*, ed. Valerie M. Lagorio and Mildred L. Day, 2 vols. (New York: Garland, 1990).
5 See *Culture and the King: The Social Implications of the Arthurian Legend,* ed. Martin B. Shichtman and James P. Carley (Albany, New York: SUNY Press, 1994); and *Vox Mystica: Essays on Medieval Mysticism*, ed. Anne Clark Bartlett and Thomas H. Bestul (Cambridge, UK: D.S. Brewer, 1995).
6 From 1974–1979, Valerie Lagorio was vice president of the North American Branch (NAB) of the International Arthurian Society. Following the vice president's term in office, the NAB, like the Modern Language Association, had historically elevated that person to the position of president. As Lagorio came up for the presidency in 1980, however, a number of members offered a petition requesting an election of officers. In the absence of bylaws, the petition was honored. John L. Grigsby ran against Lagorio and defeated her for the presidency.

Maureen Fries:
Teacher, Scholar, Friend

DONALD L. HOFFMAN

In the spirit of the Ovidian oxymoron reiterated almost automatically throughout medieval literature, the task imposed upon me in this final chapter of the volume honoring Maureen is a joyful pain, a sorrowful pleasure. Remembering Maureen Fries is for me and for many a rich recollection of lively moments and lovely places: *Carmen* at the Arena di Verona in the course of the International Arthurian Society meeting in Garda, or the ruins of Paestum and dinner on the Amalfi coast in connection with the Courtly Literature meeting in Salerno; it was also in Salerno that she encountered the peculiarities of the Bank of the Holy Spirit, which could not change American money on Thursdays, and which had a revolving entry cylinder designed to thwart bank robbers, but that also succeeded in entrapping Mme. Fries in its 'decompression' chamber. Not, I think, for the first time, bells rang, sirens screamed, and a phalanx of young men came running to her aid. She was accustomed to drama and never doubted that she was designed to be the center of it. The brighter the memory, however, the sharper the awareness of loss. She has been gone since January of 1999 and we have survived Kalamazoo and Toulouse, San Diego, and New Orleans without her, but there remains a sad awareness of her absence, a lingering sense that things have changed.

It is, perhaps, still too early to assess accurately Maureen's contributions to Arthurian scholarship, but it is not too early to recollect and remember her busy and rich career and what we owe to her as a teacher, scholar, and friend.

As a friend, she has demonstrated her love and loyalty to many of us and we know of her generosity and support. Some may know as well that she was as passionately consistent in her enmities as in her friendships, but are aware as well that there were few fences she was unwilling to mend. She could be fierce, but she was also forgiving. Her primary loyalty, however, was to scholarship and accuracy. Indeed, one of the last gifts I gave her, although unwittingly, was to make a huge and embarrassing error in a paper

I gave at the ICLS meeting in Vancouver, an error that gave her the opportunity to correct me in public. Twenty-five-plus years of friendship did not for a second interfere with her intense dislike of error. She enjoyed being right. And I was happy to give her that chance to demonstrate her phenomenal memory and her loyalty to the text. She was a faithful friend, but her fidelity to the highest standards of scholarship and accuracy was greater still. She was, if I am not completely misquoting Marty Shichtman, the last great humanist. Depending on one's perspective, this is not unqualified praise. But it is an accurate definition, and one she would have claimed proudly.

Her scholarship was voluminous and there is no space here for a complete review, but several titles stand out and define the themes of her scholarly career. Pre-eminent among her essays is 'Female Heroes, Heroines, and Counter-Heroes: Images of Women in Arthurian Tradition.' Her inaugural lecture as Kasling Distinguished Professor at SUNY-Fredonia, the essay was first published in Sally Slocum's *Popular Arthurian Traditions*, and reprinted in Thelma Fenster's Casebook, *Arthurian Women*. In this study, Maureen presented a typology of women in Arthurian literature that provided a solid framework for future study and has shaped much of the feminist scholarship that succeeded it. While perhaps a little too grounded in the 'role model' approach to the treatment of women in Arthurian texts, this seminal essay defines a method of classifying, analyzing, and evaluating Arthurian women. For me, however, the problem with such an approach is that it becomes difficult to value the literary worth of real evil. Morgan, for example, may be the projection of all the antifeminist sentiment of a crowd of repressed and spiteful monks (or maybe not), but who would want her 'nicer.' We might not want Morgan as our neighbor, but, on the other hand, we probably wouldn't want to read novels about our neighbors, and certainly not about the 'nice' ones.

Nevertheless, in this essay Maureen established a schema that stood her and others in good stead, and provided a basis for her further work in 'Gender and the Grail,' 'How Many Roads to Camelot? The Married Knight in Malory's *Le Morte Darthur*,' and 'Women in Arthurian Literature.' However, her interest in fictional women was not limited to the Arthurian tradition or the Middle Ages. Chaucer was a particular favorite of hers, and she 'vindicated' Criseyde in several essays, the most influential of which is probably "'Slydynge of Corage": Chaucer's Criseyde as Feminist and Victim.' The easy linkage of feminism and victimization in the subtitle may signal that the essay was published almost a quarter of a century ago, and indicate what may now be perceived as a problem in its methods. It remains, however, a serious attempt to understand rather than merely blame or merely praise Crisedye, and to present a balanced picture of her character and her choices. It is also a testament to Maureen's passion for Chaucer and her interest in Criseyde, with whom she also dealt in an elegant essay, 'Almost without a Song: Criseyde and Lyric in Chaucer's *Troilus*,' which itself derived in part from her masterful essay, 'The "Other" Voice: Woman's Song, Its Satire and Its Transcendence in Late Medieval British Literature.'

Refusing to limit herself to the study of women, she worked with special vigor on the Tristram legend, particularly in Malory. She studied the vexing question of Malory's almost missing love philtre in the wittily titled, 'The Impotent Potion: On the Minimization of the Love Theme in the *Tristan en prose* and Malory's *Morte Darthur*.' However, the essay I have found most useful (i.e. stolen from on several occasions) was one of her earliest, 'Malory's Tristram as Counter-Hero to the *Morte Darthur*.' This essay is rich in its development of Malory's use of Tristram to uphold the virtue of Lancelot, and to present Tristram as a negative hero, so that Lancelot will seem even grander through the comparison. One notes also that in this early essay, she begins to define her concept of the 'counter-hero' which became so valuable in the typology of female heroes in her later work.

Finally, mention should be made of her extensive study of Malory's often-neglected Tristram in 'Indiscreet Objects of Desire: Malory's "Tristram" and the Necessity of Deceit.' This complex study of the relationship of deceit and desire in Malory's Tristram also introduces her conception of Tristram as a trickster figure. While the trickster is not unknown to medieval literature or medieval studies, he is a popular figure in African-American and Native-American folklore and legend. Maureen's idea of the trickster, which she so profitably applies to a medieval text, is, however, partially derived from and deeply informed by her great interest in African-American literature and her immersion in Native-American literature, an interest she acquired relatively late in her career, but to which she was devoted. She loved visiting Native-American sites and had a collection of turquoise jewelry to prove it, including her prized Zuni fetish necklace.

To return to her Arthurian interests, however, she went beyond Malory to study Geoffrey of Monmouth and Lawman ('Rhetoric and Meaning...,' 'The Arthurian Moment: History and Geoffrey of Monmouth's *Historia regum Britannie*,' and 'Women, Power, and (the Undermining of) Order in Lawman's *Brut*'), and went beyond the Middle Ages to study T.H. White and Mary Stewart ('The Rationalization of the Arthurian "Matter" in T.H. White and Mary Stewart') and Tennyson ('What Tennyson Really Did to Malory's Women') among others and, more generally, 'Trends in the Modern Arthurian Novel' in *King Arthur Through the Ages*.

Her most influential publication, however, is likely to be *Approaches to Teaching the Arthurian Tradition*. This collection remains a testament to Maureen's gift for friendship, since it allowed her to collect writings by so many of her friends and to make several new ones, and to engage them in a dialogue on teaching. And this is important because of all the roles of which Maureen was mistress, I believe she felt that she was most accurately defined as a teacher. Her nearly encyclopedic and frequently photographic memory enabled her to recall citations to primary and secondary works with amazing accuracy and to be a ready source of information for students and friends. It was not, however, just as a repository of facts that she was so valuable. She enthusiastically shared her passion for the legend and the many other subjects and cultures she taught with such intensity and joy. One did not have to know her for long before one became aware of her interests and her willingness to share them. Strangers almost immediately became friends, and friends were often placed in the position of eager students basking in the love of learning and love of sharing that made up her eloquent conversations.

At this point in my draft of this essay, I drew a blank, stumped at trying to find an adequate conclusion. But the essay's refusal to close seems to me the only appropriate ending. Maureen's life did not achieve closure, it simply stopped, and stopped while she was full of ideas and projects. And this is the real denial of closure. There is much of her work that remains to be published, and much that remains to be assessed. It is still hard to believe she is gone, but that is, in part, because the conversation continues. Despite the contemporary trend, let me utter a heartfelt, 'Screw closure!' She may be gone, but she is not completed; her work continues, and, as always, she still engages us. Like Lydia, she remains a text tattooed with love and not yet yielding completely her semiotic richness. We love and read her still.

NORTHEASTERN ILLINOIS UNIVERSITY

Donald L. Hoffman of Northeastern Illinois University is the immediate Past President of the North American Branch of the International Arthurian Society. He has published on Arthurian influences in a variety of literatures ranging from twelfth-century Italian prophecy to the postmodern African-American novel and surrealist film.

Maureen Fries

PUBLICATIONS

BOOKS

Approaches to Teaching the Arthurian Tradition, ed. with Jeanie Watson. New York: Modern Language Association of America, 1992.

The Figure of Merlin in the Nineteenth and Twentieth Centuries, ed. with Jeanie Watson. Niagara Falls: Mellen, 1989.

A Bibliography By and *About British Women Authors,* 1957-1969. Charleston, IL: WCML, 1971.

ARTICLES AND CHAPTERS
IN BOOKS, SEGMENTS OF CD-ROMS

'The Arthurian Moment: History and Geoffrey's *Historia regum Britanniae,*' *Arthuriana* 8 (Winter 1998), Special Issue on Geoffrey of Monmouth, guest-ed. Fiona Tolhurst.

'How to Handle a Woman, or Morgan at the Movies,' in *King Arthur on Film: New Essays on Arthurian Cinema,* ed. Kevin Harty. Jefferson, N.C.: McFarland, 1999.

'Women, Power and (the Undermining of) Order in Lawman's *Brut,*' *Arthuriana* 8 (Fall, 1998), Special Issue on Lawman's *Brut,* guest-ed. James Noble, 23–32.

'Gender and the Grail,' *Arthuriana* 8 (Spring, 1998), Special Issue on *The Grail and The Quest,* guest-ed. Norris J. Lacy, 67–79.

'Commentary [Special Issue on *Arthurian Adultery*],' *Arthuriana* 7 (Winter, 1997), guest-ed. C. M. Adderley, 92–96.

'Female Heroes, Heroines and Counter-Heroes: Images of Women in Arthurian Tradition,' rpt. in *Arthurian Women, ed* Thelma Fenster. New York: Garland, 1996. Pp. 59–73.

"Mary Stewart,' in *Discovering Authors: British,* ed. James P. Draper. CD-ROM. Detroit: Gale, 1995.

'[Louise Erdrich's] Tracks,' in *Women's Literature* II, ed. Frank Magill. Pasadena: Salem Press, 1995, 2336–40.

'[Louise Erdrich's] *The Beef Queen,*' in *Women's Literature* II, ed. Frank Magill. Pasadena: Salem Press, 1995. 181–85.

'Geoffrey of Monmouth,' in *The Dictionary of Literary Biography* 146: *Old and Middle English Literature*, ed. Jeffrey Helterman and Jerome Mitchell. Detroit: Gale, 1994. 172–77.

'From the Lady to the Tramp: The Decline of Morgan le Fay in Medieval Romance,' *Arthuriana* 4 (Spring, 1994), 1–18.

'How Many Roads to Camelot? The Married Knight in Malory's *Morte Darthur,*' in *Culture and the King: The Social Implications of the Arthurian Legend* Essays in Honor of Professor Valerie M. Lagorio, ed. Martin Shichtman and James Carley. Albany: SUNY Press, 1994. Pp. 196–207,

'Natural and Unnatural Childhoods in T. H. White's *The Once and Future King,*' *The Platte Valley Review* 21 (Winter, 1993), 83–92.

'Sexuality and Women in the Old Irish Sagas,' in *Celtic Connections,* ed. David Lampe. *ACTA* 16. Binghamton: SUNY Press, 1993. Pp. 19–28.

'A Natural History of Women and Sexuality in the Old Irish Sagas,' in *The Image of Nature* ed. Will Wright and Steven Kaplan. Pueblo: U. of So. Colorado Press, 1993. Pp. 148–54.

'(Almost) Without a Song: Criseyde and Lyric in Chaucer's *Troilus,*' in *The Chaucer Yearbook: A Journal of Late Medieval Studies* 1 (1992), 47–64.

'Female Heroes, Heroines and Counter-Heroes: Images of Women in Medieval Arthurian Tradition,' in *Popular Arthurian Traditions,* ed. Sally Slocum. Bowling Green: Popular Press, 1992. Pp. 5–17.

'Introduction: The Labyrinthine Ways: Teaching the Arthurian Tradition,' in *Approaches to Teaching the Arthurian Tradition,* ed. Maureen Fries and Jeanie Watson New York: Modern Language Association of America, 1992. Pp. 33–50.

'Part One: Materials,' in *Approaches.* Pp. 3–30.

'Women in Arthurian Tradition,' in Approaches. Pp. 155–58.

'Works Cited,' in Approaches. Pp. 164–68.

'The Impotent Potion: On the Minimization of the Love Theme in the *Tristan en prose* and Malory's *Morte Darthur,*' *Quondam et Futurus: A Journal of Arthurian Interpretations* 1 (Fall 1991), 75–81.

'Shapeshifting Women in the Old Irish Sagas,' *Bestia: The Yearbook of the Beast Fable Society* 3 (1991). Pp. 12–21.

'What Tennyson Really Did to Malory's Women,' *Quondam et Futurus: A Journal of Arthurian Interpretations* 1 (Spring, 1991), 44–55.

'Trends in the Modern Arthurian Novel,' in *King Arthur Through the Ages,* ed. Valerie M. Lagorio and Mildred L. Day. New York: Garland, 1990. 2: 207–22.

'Boethian Themes and Tragic Structure in Geoffrey of Monmouth's *Historia regum Britanniae*,' in *The Arthurian Tradition: Essays in Convergence*, ed. Mary Flowers Braswell and John Bugge. Birmingham: U. of Alabama Press, 1988. Pp. 29–42, nn. 201–203.

'A Hero For All Seasons,' *British Heritage: King Arthur Special Issue* (June–July, 1986), 13–17.

'Five Hundred Years of Caxton's Malory: A Celebration of the *Morte Darthur*,' *Avalon to Camelot* 2 (1986), 11–14.

'*Teaching Sir Gawain and the Green Knight* in the Context of Arthurian and Other Romance Traditions,' in *Approaches to Teaching Sir Gawain and the Green Knight*, ed. Jane Chance and Miriam Y. Miller. New York: Modern Language Association of America, 1986. Pp. 69–78.

'The Rationalization of the Arthurian 'Matter' in T. H. White and Mary Stewart,' rpt. in *Contemporary Literary Criticism*, ed. Daniel G. Marowski. Detroit: Gale, 1985–86.

'Indiscreet Objects of Desire: Malory's 'Tristram' and the Necessity of Deceit,' in *Studies in Malory*, ed. James W. Spisak. Kalamazoo, Medieval Institute Publications, 1985. Pp. 87–108.

'Margery Kempe,' in *An Introduction to the Medieval Mystics of Europe*, ed. Paul Szarmach. Albany: State University of New York Press, 1984. Pp. 217–35, nn. pp. 354–58.

'Medieval Concepts of the Female and Their Satire in the Poetry of William Dunbar,' *Fifteenth Century Studies* 7 (1983), 55–77.

'Dux/Rex Pattern in the Matters of France, Britain and Spain ' *Actos de VIII Congreso de la Societe Rencesvals*, ed. Carlos Alvar and Victoria Cirlot. Pamplona: Institucion Principe de Viana, 1981. Pp. 149–57.

'The Poem in the Tradition of Arthurian Literature,' in *The Alliterative Morte Arthure: A Reassessment of the Poem*, ed. Karl Heinz Goller. Cambridge, Eng.: Boydell and Brewer, 1981. Pp. 3043, nn. pp. 159–61.

'The Characterization of Women in the Alliterative Tradition,' in *The Alliterative Tradition in The Fourteenth Century*, ed. Bernard Levy and Paul Szarmach. Kent: Kent State Univ. Press, 1981. Pp. 25–45.

'The 'Other' Voice: Woman's Song, Its Satire and Its Transcendence in Late Medieval British Literature,' *Studies in Medieval Culture* 15 (1981), 155–78.

'*Feminae Populi*: Popular Images of Women in Medieval Literature,' *Journal of Popular Culture* 14 (Summer, 1980), 79–86.

'Besides Crisseid: Henryson's Other Women,' *Actes du 2e Colloque de langue et de litterature Ecossaise*, ed. Jean-Jacques Blanchot and Claude Graf Strasbourg: University of Strasbourg Press, 1979. Pp. 250–67.

'Tragic Pattern in Malory's *Morte Darthur:* Medieval Narrative as Literary Myth,' in *The Cent Fifteenth Century.* ACTA 5. Binghamton: SUNY Press, 1978. Pp. 81–99.

'The Teaching of Women in Medieval Literature,' *Ralph* 5 (1978), 14.

'The Rationalization of the Arthurian 'Matter' in T. H. White and Mary Stewart,' *Philological Quarterly* 76 (1977), 258–75.

"Slydynge of Corage': Chaucer's Criseyde as Feminist and Victim,' in *The Authority of Experience: Essays in Feminist Criticism,* ed. Arlyn Diamond and Lee Edwards. Amherst: University of Massachusetts Press, 1977. Pp. 45–59. (Rpt. 1988)

'Malory's Tristram as Counter-Hero to the *Morte Darthur,*' *Neuphilologische Mitteilungen* 76 (1975), 605–13.

'Women, Society and the Environment,' *American Biology Teacher* 39 (May, 1974), 274–78, 311. (With Stuart Nicholson)

'Feminism and Antifeminism in *Under Western Eyes,*' *Conradiana* 5 (1973), 56–65.

'An Historical Analogue to 'The Shipman's Tale'?' *Comitatus* 3 (1972), 19–32.

'The Place of Ovid in the Classical Humanities Curriculum,' *Language Methods Newsletter* 8 (Fall, 1970), 8–14.

ENCYCLOPEDIA ARTICLES

'Geoffrey of Monmouth,' in *Cyclopedia of World Authors,* rev. ed. Frank N. Magill. 5 vols. Pasadena: Salem Press, 1997. Pp. 772–73.

'Monaco, Richard,' in *The Arthurian Encyclopedia,* ed. Norris J. Lacy *et al.* New York: Garland 1986. Rev., 2nd ed., 1991.

'Steinbeck, John,' *in The Arthurian Encyclopedia.*

'Stewart, Mary,' in The *Arthurian Encyclopedia*

'White, T. H.,' in *The Arthurian Encyclopedia*

BOOK REVIEWS

'*Violence against Women in Medieval Texts.* Ed. Anna Roberts. Gainesville: University Press of Florida, 1998.' *CHOICE* 36 (September 1998).

'*Written Work. Langland, Labor and Authorship.* Ed. Steven Justice and Kathryn Kerby-Fulton. Philadelphia: University of Pennsylvania Press, 1997.' *CHOICE* 35 (May 1998), 4975.

'*A Companion to Malory.* Ed. Elizabeth Archibald and A.S.G. Edwards. Cambridge: Boydell and Brewer, 1996.' *Arthuriana* 8 (Spring, 1998), 95–97.

'*Malory's Book of Arms: The Narrative of Combat in Le Morte Darthur.* Andrew Lynch. Cambridge: D.S. Brewer, 1997.' *CHOICE* 35 (December 1997).

'*Chaucerian Polity: Absolutist Lineages and Associational Forms in England and Italy.* David Wallace. Palo Alto: Stanford University Press, 1997.' CHOICE 35 (September, 1997), 153.

'*Literary Nominalism and the Theory of Rereading Late Medieval Texts: A New Research Paradigm* Ed. Richard J. Utz. Lewiston: Mellen, 1995.' *Arthuriana* 7 (Summer, 1997), 147–48.

'*Chaucer's Chain of Love* Paul Beekman Taylor. Fairleigh Dickinson Press, 1996.' *CHOICE* 34 (May, 1997), 4947.

'*The Return of King Arthur: The Legend Through Victorian Eyes.* Debra N. Mancoff. New York: Abrams, 1995.' *Arthuriana* 7 (Spring, 1997), 156–58.

'*Women and Arthurian Literature: Seizing the Sword* Marion Wynne-Davies. New York: St. Martin's, 1996.' *CHOICE* 34 (1997).

'*The Legend of Guy of Warwick,* Velma Bourgeois Richmond. New York: Garland, 1996.' *CHOICE* 33 (1996), 4989.

'*Arthurian Literature* XIII. Ed. James P. Carley and Felicity Riddy. Woodridge: Brewer, 1993.' *Arthuriana* 5 (Spring, 1995), 102–105.

'*Songs of the Women Troubadours.* Ed. and trans. Matilda Tomaryn Bruckner, Laurie Shepard and Sarah White. New York: Garland, 1995.' *CHOICE* 32 (1995), 2041.

'*Chaucer's Ovidian Arts of Love.* Michael Calabrese. Miami: University Press of Florida, 1994.' *CHOICE* 32 (1995), 4330.

'*Court Revels,* 1485-1559. W. R. Streitberger. Toronto: University of Toronto Press, 1994.' *CHOICE* 32 (1995), 2600.

'*Merlin: A Thousand Heroes With One Face.* Charlotte Spivack. Niagara Falls: Mellen, 1994.' *CHOICE* 3 2 (1995), 2598.

'*A Variorum Edition of* 'The Works of Geoffrey Chaucer': *Volume II:* 'The Canterbury Tales: The General Prologue,' Part One A mid Part One B. Norman: University of Oklahoma Press, 1993. ' CHOICE 31. (1994).

'*Letters to Lalage: The Letters of Charles Williams to Lois Lang-Sims.* Introduction and Notes Glen Cavaliero. Kent: Kent State University Press, 1993.' *Quondam et Futurus: A Journal of Arthurian Interpretations* I (Summer, 1991).

'*Laȝamon's Arthur: The Arthurian Section of Laȝamon's Brut.*' Ed. and trans. W. R. J. Barron and S. C. Weinberg. London: Longman, 1989.' *Times Literary Supplement* (August, 1990).

'Laȝamon's Brut: *The Poem and Its Sources.* Cambridge: D. S. Brewer, 1989.' *Times Literary Supplement* (August, 1990).

'The Passing of Arthur: New Essays in Arthurian Tradition. Ed. Christopher Baswell and William Sharpe. New York: Garland, 1988.' *Arthurian Interpretations* 3 (1988), 141–46.

'The Arthurian Handbook. Ed. Norris J. Lacy and Geoffrey Ashe. New York: Garland, 1988.' *Manuscripta* 12 (November, 1988), 215–16.

'*The French Chansons of Charles Orleans With the Corresponding Middle English Chansons* Ed. and trans. Sarah Spence. New York: Garland, 1986.' *Envoi* 1 (1988), 246–48.

'Women in Medieval History and Historiography. Ed. Susan Mosher Stuard. Philadelphia: University of Pennsylvania Press, 1987.' *Envoi* I (1988), 248–250.

'The Romance of Arthur II. Ed. James J. Wilhelm. New York: Garland, 1986.' *Envoi* 1 (1989), 250–51.

'Fabula Docet: Studies in the Background and Interpretation of Henryson's Moral Fabillis. Marianne Powell. Odense: Odense University Press, 1983.' JEGP 84 (1985), 118–20.

'Whither Womankind? The Humanity of Women. Robert Kress. St. Meinrad: Abbey Press, 1975.' *Fourteenth Century English Mystics Newsletter* 6 (1980), 45–51.

'Malory's *Morte Darthur*. Larry D. Benson. Cambridge: Harvard University Press, 1976.' *Tristania* 4 (1978), 63–67.